Key Themes for the Study of Islam

Key Themes for the Study of Islam

Edited by

JAMAL J. ELIAS

ONEWORLD
OXFORD

A Oneworld Book

Published by Oneworld Publications 2010

Copyright © Jamal J. Elias 2010

All rights reserved
Copyright under Berne Convention
A CIP record for this title is available
from the British Library

ISBN 978–1–85168–711–4 (Hbk)
ISBN 978–1–85168–710–7 (Pbk)

Typeset by Jayvee, Trivandrum, India
Cover design by www.fatfacedesign.com
Printed and bound in India for Imprint Digital

Oneworld Publications
185 Banbury Road
Oxford OX2 7AR
England
www.oneworld-publications.com

CONTENTS

CONTRIBUTORS

Shahzad Bashir is Associate Professor of Religious Studies and Director of the Abbasi Program in Islamic Studies at Stanford University. He received his A.B. from Amherst College and his Ph.D. from Yale University. He has published on various topics in the study of Sufism and Shiism and is currently finishing a monograph entitled *Bodies of God's Friends: Sufis in Persianate Islamic Societies*.

Amila Buturovic is Associate Professor in Humanities and Noor Fellow in Islamic Studies at York University, Toronto. Her work spans medieval Arabic and pre-modern and contemporary Balkan studies. She is the author of *Stone Speaker: Medieval Tombstones, Landscape and Bosnian Identity in the Poetry of Mak Dizdar* (New York: Palgrave Macmillan, 2002) and the co-editor with İrvin C. Schick of *Women in the Ottoman Balkans* (London: I. B. Tauris, 2007). Currently, she is working on the Islamic culture of death in the Ottoman and post-Ottoman Balkans.

Snjezana Buzov received her Ph.D. from the University of Chicago in 2005, and is currently Assistant Professor of Turkish Studies in the Department of Near Eastern Languages and Cultures at the Ohio State University. Her research focuses on the intellectual and cultural history of the early modern Ottoman Empire.

Michael Cooperson is Professor of Arabic Language and Literature at UCLA. His recent work includes studies of Egyptian pyramids, Basran misers, and a Byzantine epic. He is currently writing a book on time travel as a literary device.

Devin DeWeese is a Professor in the Department of Central Eurasian Studies at Indiana University. His research deals with the religious history of Islamic Central Asia, with a particular focus on problems of Islamization and the history of Sufi communities.

Jamal J. Elias is the Class of 1965 Endowed Term Professor and Professor of Religious Studies at the University of Pennsylvania, and has published on a range of subjects including Sufi thought and history, Qur'anic Studies, literature, and visual and material culture in South Asia and the Middle East. He received his A.B. in Religious Studies from Stanford University, an A.M. in Oriental Studies (Turkish) from the University of Pennsylvania, and his Ph.D. in Islamic Studies from Yale University.

Sohail H. Hashmi is Associate Professor of International Relations and Alumnae Foundation Chair in the Social Sciences at Mount Holyoke College. His work focuses on Islamic ethics and political theory, particularly as they relate to issues in contemporary international relations. He is the editor of *Islamic Political Ethics* (Princeton, N.J.: Princeton University Press, 2002) and co-editor of *Ethics and Weapons of Mass Destruction: Religious and Secular Perspectives* (Cambridge: Cambridge University Press, 2004). He is currently writing a book on the Islamic ethics of war and peace.

R. Kevin Jaques is an Associate Professor of Religious Studies at Indiana University, where he has taught since 2001. He completed his Ph.D. in West and South Asian Religions at Emory University in 2001. He is currently working on a book examining the history of the Shafi'i school of law as it was depicted in the writings of Abu Ishaq al-Shirazi (d. 476/1083).

Ahmet T. Karamustafa is Professor of History and Religious Studies at Washington University in St. Louis. He earned his B.A. in Philosophy at Hamilton College and M.A. and Ph.D. in Islamic Studies at McGill University. An expert in the social and intellectual history of pre-modern Islam, his publications include *God's Unruly Friends* (Salt Lake City: University of Utah Press, 1994; rpt. Oxford: Oneworld, 2006) and *Sufism: The Formative Period* (Berkeley, C.A.: University of California Press, 2007 and Edinburgh: University of Edinburgh Press, 2007).

Bruce B. Lawrence has been on the Duke faculty since 1971. A Ph.D. from Yale University, he is currently the Nancy and Jeffery Marcus Humanities Professor and Professor of Islamic Studies. He also is the inaugural Director of the Duke Islamic Studies Center, and a Carnegie Scholar (2008–2010).

Joseph E. Lowry received a B.A. in Near Eastern Languages and Civilization at the University of Washington in 1985 and earned J.D. and A.M. degrees from the University of Pennsylvania in 1990 and

1991. After practicing law in Washington, D.C., he completed a Ph.D. at the University of Pennsylvania in 1999, where he is currently an Associate Professor in the Department of Near Eastern Languages and Civilizations. He is the author of studies on early Islamic legal thought, Islamic legal theory, and Arabic literature.

Kelly Pemberton is Assistant Professor of Religion and Women's Studies at the George Washington University. Her most recent publications include a co-edited volume, *Shared Idioms, Sacred Symbols and the Articulation of Identities in South Asia* (London: Routledge, 2008) and a monograph entitled *Women Mystics and Sufi Shrines in the Indian Subcontinent* (Columbia, SC: University of South Carolina Press, 2010). Her research covers Sufism, religious authority, and Islamic reform, especially as these relate to gender. Recently, she has been researching the revival of Islamic Medicine in South Asia and the Middle East.

A. Kevin Reinhart completed his B.A. in Middle East Studies and Arabic at the University of Texas at Austin in 1974 and his Ph.D. in the Study of Religion (Islam) in 1986 at Harvard University. He joined the faculty of Dartmouth College in 1987: He has written on Islamic jurisprudence and theology, Late Ottoman religion, Islamic ethics, and modern Islam.

Kishwar Rizvi is an architect and art historian, who received her doctorate from the Aga Khan Program for Islamic Architecture at the Massachusetts Institute of Technology. Her research is on the early modern and contemporary art and architecture of Iran and Pakistan. She is the author of *The Dynastic Shrine: History, Religion, and Architectural Culture in Early Modern Iran* (forthcoming). She is also the co-editor of *Modernism and the Middle East: Architecture and Politics in the Twentieth Century* (Seattle: Washington University Press, 2008).

Walid A. Saleh is Associate Professor of Religion at the University of Toronto. He received his B.A. in Arabic Language and Literature from the American University of Beirut in 1989 and his doctorate in Religious Studies from Yale University in 2001. He has published studies on the Qur'an, *tafsir*, and apocalyptic Islamic literature.

İrvin Cemil Schick received his Ph.D. from the Massachusetts Institute of Technology in 1989. He has taught at Harvard University, Boston University, and M.I.T. He is the author of *The Erotic Margin:*

Sexuality and Spatiality in Alteritist Discourse (London: Verso, 1999), *The Fair Circassian: Adventures of an Orientalist Motif* (2004, in Turkish), and *Writings on Islam, Gender, and Culture* (forthcoming, in Turkish), and the editor or co-editor of several volumes including the M. Uğur Derman 65th Birthday Festschrift (Istanbul: Sabanci University, 2000), *European Women Captives and their Muslim Masters: Narratives of Captivity in "Turkish" Lands* (2005, in Turkish), and (with Amila Buturovic) *Women in the Ottoman Balkans: Gender, Culture and History* (London: I. B. Tauris, 2007).

Amina M. Steinfels is Assistant Professor of Religion at Mount Holyoke College. She received her A.B. in Religion from Amherst College in 1994 and her doctorate in Religious Studies from Yale University in 2003. Her current book project is entitled *Knowledge before Action: Sufi Practice and Islamic Learning in Medieval South Asia*.

Devin Stewart completed his B.A. in Near Eastern Studies at Princeton University in 1984 and his Ph.D. in Arabic and Islamic Studies at the University of Pennsylvania in 1991. He is the Winship Distinguished Research Professor of Arabic and Islamic Studies in the Department of Middle Eastern and South Asian Studies at Emory University where he has taught since 1990. He has published studies on Shi'i Islam, Islamic law, the Qur'an, and Arabic language and literature.

Shawkat M. Toorawa is Associate Professor of Arabic Literature and Islamic Studies at Cornell University. His research focuses on the literary structure of the Qur'an, ninth-century Arabic writerly culture, the modern Syro-Lebanese poet, Adonis, and the southwestern Indian Ocean.

INTRODUCTION

Jamal J. Elias

"O Human Beings! We created you male and female and made you into nations and peoples so that you would come to know one another." (Q49:13)

There are many books introducing the reader to Islam. Many are good; many others leave a great deal to be desired. Some are surveys of the religion in various lengths and levels of complexity. There are also a handful of (expensive) encyclopedias of Islam and Islamic societies, although these are – for the most part – only accessible to readers motivated by desire (or their professors) to visit the research libraries that own such tomes. For all their many strengths, most survey books on Islam suffer on account of their mission as well as the nature of their authorship. An introduction to a religion is obligated to be comprehensive in its coverage and to provide some sort of grand narrative, which inevitably distills complexity into an ordered simplicity and does away with the contradictions that are inherent in abstract umbrella terms like "Islam," "Islamic," or "Muslim." At the same time, the sole authorship of such works – despite the smoothness of prose and narrative that they frequently possess – imparts introductory works with the logical idiosyncrasies of their authors. The alternative, pursued in this volume, is to eschew unity of narrative and of voice in an attempt to preserve the (sometimes contradictory) complexities that are innate to a rich and diverse religion such as Islam.

The study of Islam suffers from a simultaneous fetishization and ghettoization, both problems contributing to the perpetuation of the other. In the North American context, a quick survey of the annual program of the American Academy of Religion (the largest organization dedicated to the academic study of religion in its broadest sense) as well as of major journals on religion makes it manifestly clear that neither Islam as a phenomenon nor theoretical scholarship using

Islamic data has firmly established itself in the academic mainstream. By necessity or by design, academic journals and edited volumes continue to lack essays that deal with Islamic subjects, and conferences on the comparative study of religious topics frequently lack specialists discussing Islam in any sustained way. At the same time, papers reflecting a high level of scholarship on Islam are common in specialized journals and conferences such as the American Oriental Society and the Middle East Studies Association of North America. This continued ghettoized study of Islam is both a consequence of and an ongoing contributor to the view that Islam and Muslims are different from other religions and religious peoples in important and insurmountable ways.

It is normal for adherents of specific religions and religious systems to maintain the uniqueness (if not the superiority) of their own tradition and to view their own particularities as somehow more particular than those of others. Certainly, my colleagues teaching Christianity, Judaism, and Hinduism share my frustration with students who insist on maintaining the exceptionalism of their own religion, insisting either on *only* studying their "true" tradition or else studying everything *except* it, on the logic that academic study teaches falsehoods or partial truths about their own "true" religion (since other religions are not "true," according to this logic there is no dilemma in studying them). Similarly – though with less legitimacy, one might argue – it is understandable for scholars of a subject to find their own scholarly interests to be more notable, unique, and fascinating than other subjects; after all, if that were not the case, one would be at pains to justify one's choice of academic pursuit.

In the case of Islam, however, exceptionalism takes the extreme form of fetishization for a number of historical reasons. As many excellent works have addressed in a variety of ways, Islam and Islamic civilization served as Europe's counterfoil – its "other" – through much of history, and they continue to do so today, as is evident from global events as well as from the culture wars raging within Europe and North America over the place of Muslims in modern Western societies. And although European Christians did not serve as the "other" in the same way through most of Islamic history – such that even the crusades were tangential and largely ignored events for most Muslims of the time – modern Muslims have come to view themselves in the context of a civilizational competition mirroring that found in the West. As such, Muslims frequently see themselves and their religion as radically different from all others (not just Christianity and Judaism) and argue for the impossibility of achieving an acceptable understanding of Islam unless one studies the religion on and through its own terms. Except in the very specific context of interfaith dialogue, Muslim notions of individualism, society, and the relationship to God are presented by many Muslims as well as non-Muslim commentators as radically different from their non-Islamic counterparts, necessitating an approach to the study of Islam that is different from that of other religions. By this logic, Islamic technical terms are untranslatable, and the mechanisms of Islamic thought and society are distinct from all others.

This book is an attempt to refute claims of Islamic exceptionalism while simultaneously highlighting distinctive aspects of Islam through nineteen essays written by a wide range of scholars. It is neither intended as a dictionary or glossary of important terms dealing with Islam, nor a partial encyclopedia. Rather, in the words of Raymond Williams, whose influence on the project's conception is apparent from the title itself, this is "the record of an inquiry into a *vocabulary*: a shared body of words and meanings in our most general discussions, in English, of the practices and institutions" of a religion. Put differently, this volume is premised on the belief that Islam and Muslims are sufficiently part of a wider world, both global as well as academic, that they can be written about and studied in the vocabulary of that wider world rather than the vernacular of their own internal processes and history.

No collection of terms in a book of this sort or, for that matter, in a dictionary, encyclopedia, glossary, or index, is ever ideologically neutral. Inevitably, it reflects the prejudices and priorities of the person responsible for creating the list, soliciting the contributors and, ultimately, of those individual authors themselves. The key themes in this volume have been selected by the editor, in consultation with others, with the goal of exploring how conceptually important, widely used words in the English language apply to the study and discussion of the Islamic world. The choice of using common English words is critical, since it connotes a different set of priorities and purposes for this book than it would have possessed had the themes been chosen from a list of what might be called "Islamic" terms. Indeed, it would be easy to come up with just such a list using Arabic words, of which many have made their way into English dictionaries and common educated speech: *Allah, fiqh, hadith, iman, islam, jihad, kitab, mithaq, nabi, qadr, Qur'an, salat, shari'a, sufi, sunna, tawhid,* and *umma* come immediately to mind. Another way of conceiving of such a collection of terms would be with English language words that deal directly with things Islamic or (conceived more broadly) things religious that are relevant to Islam and Muslims. Such a list might have terms such as *revelation, prophethood* (as distinct from *prophecy,* which appears in this book), *prayer, fasting, alms-giving, judgment,* and so on. The shortcoming of lists of this sort is that they function more as glossaries or sets of definitions. In so doing, they promise a kind of comprehensiveness implicit in all collections of definitions: by their very nature, they suggest that the reader will be granted comprehensive knowledge of the subject matter solely by dint of having read the entire list.

As with any collection of terms such as those appearing in this book, there are other key themes that could have been included. The constraints of space and time have limited us to these nineteen; one can think of several others that would deserve a place in a somewhat longer collection, among them *love, person, place, power, sex, space,* and *time.* No doubt, individual readers will have their own ideas about which terms should have been included at the cost of ones found in this book. The final list of nineteen has been arrived at through a process of collection and narrowing down, which began with thinking in clusters of themes or terms reminiscent of the process used by Williams in his *Keywords: A Vocabulary of Culture and Society,*[1] with the obvious difference that his influential book contained many more terms with much shorter descriptions. Thus, in the process of coming up with the thematic essays for this book, the term "power" brought immediately to mind an entire cluster of terms including "authority," "law," "prophecy," and "institution," the last of which brought to mind "culture" and "community" – among a long series of other terms. "Community," in turn, seems thematically related to "history" (which is related to "time") as well as to "individual," which brings to mind "body," "gender," and "person." The growth, splitting, and reconnection of these clusters of themes resulted in a pattern according to which the editor decided which keywords were most crucial to provide the broadest and most relevant treatment of Islam.

I describe the system by which themes were selected at the risk of having potential readers doubt the value of this work as a comprehensive introduction to Islam. Nonetheless, the process helps underline a message fundamental to this book: that it is impossible to summarize satisfactorily the breadth and depth of Islam and Muslims in a few hundred pages placed between two covers. The selection of vital and wide-ranging keywords as the subjects of thematic essays written by a wide range of specialists on the study of Islam provides the best possibility of conveying not just the breadth of Islamic civilization across time and cultures, but also the range of scholarly methods and expertise that pertain to it. The keywords selected for these thematic essays are significant in three senses: "they are significant, binding words in certain activities and their interpretation; they are significant, indicative words in certain forms of thought;" and lastly (in addition to the two significances quoted from Williams) they are significant for the place they occupy in the study of religion and culture, and for their ability to explore Islam – its history, society, and thought – within the rubric of key themes.

With this pattern of diversity as a goal, each individual author has been free to approach the theme about which he or she is writing in any fashion of his or her choosing. Though varying widely in approach and style, the essays are united in their treatment of the keywords as themes that are not only interesting in their origins – their historical and cultural etymology – but also in the subsequent variation of meanings as they pertain to Islam and Muslims.

NOTE ON TRANSLITERATION

Every attempt has been made to make this volume accessible to readers with no prior knowledge of Islam or the technical terms associated with its study. It is impossible, however, to write a book about a vast subject that has existed for a millennium and a half outside the domain of English without being forced to resort to foreign words on occasion. Important terms, especially those that repeat themselves across essays, are listed in a glossary. Others are explained briefly when they are used. A simple system of transliteration is employed throughout the book with no distinction made between short and long vowels or similar-sounding consonants in Arabic, Persian, Urdu, or other languages that use the Arabic alphabet. The Arabic letters *'ayn* (as in 'Ali) and *hamza* (as in Qur'an) have been included. Languages such as Turkish, which are written in the Latin script, are presented using their standard modern orthography.

1

ART

Kishwar Rizvi

ON CONTEXTS LOST AND FOUND

I began writing this essay while conducting research in Berlin, Germany. I thought about the subject of Islamic art and its history as I walked through the gates of the Mshatta façade (a palace originally in Jordan), and while gazing at the monumental Diez albums (consisting of drawings and paintings from the thirteenth- and fourteenth-century Ilkhanid period in Iran). The decontextualized objects in the Pergamon Museum (Museum of Islamic Art) and the State Library of Berlin, respectively, were potent reminders that much of the modern discourse on the arts of the Islamic world is situated in the Western hemisphere.[1] My sense of Babylonian confusion was not just owing to the experience of passing through the Assyrian Ishtar gates (also in the Pergamon Museum), nor through the negotiations undertaken in English, German, and Turkish that were part of my daily routine as I studied a Persian manuscript. The displacement in time is certainly one that most historians suffer, but the frustration of handling illustrated pages ripped out from books and of trying to read signatures and seals smudged and erased in the process of being sold to collectors and museums, makes the disjunction all the more difficult. It is particularly difficult when today the places where these works of art and architecture were originally made are in varying degrees of political apathy and self-destruction. Thus this essay was conceived through a disjunctive condition, one that forces me to question the role of language, culture, and modernity in the writing and studying of art in the Islamic world.

* * *

A definition of terms is immediately necessary. The question of what is Islamic art has been considered frequently and there are as many "sets" within which it can be placed as there are scholars writing about it. I consider the subject to contain works of art and architecture created by communities that identified with the religious praxis of Islam or were under the political influence of Muslim governments.[2] Thus one could include in such a comprehensive survey Hindu artists working in Mughal ateliers in Lahore, as well as contemporary mosques commissioned by Muslim communities in London. In the interest of economy I use an umbrella term, "Islamic Art," to include the arts of depiction, calligraphy, and architecture in a variety of media.[3] However, academics and practitioners at the beginning of the twenty-first century remain at a loss to define with any clarity, let alone unity, what may be the best strategies for understanding the multiple phenomena that may be gathered under the aegis of an Islamic art and its history.

The aim of this essay is to present Islamic art, but not through generalizations or overarching theories. Rather I would like to comment on certain issues that may be considered as exemplary. As previous scholars have noted, among the most interesting features of Islamic communities is their appropriation of forms and ideas from the various political and religious others with whom they came in contact. While searching for sources for Islamic art is an important exercise, it can sometimes be as esoteric a task as looking for uniqueness in the very subject. Another aspect that has been commonly noted is the diversity of the Islamic world and, by extension, the cultural artifacts produced in varying regions and at different historical periods. The contention of this essay is that works of art must be viewed not through generalizations alone, but through the particularities of their contexts, such as history and patronage, as well as on their own terms, that is through considerations of materiality and artistic intentionality.

SOME TRUISMS

Artistic production, by an individual or a group, is determined by numerous factors ranging from the practical to the arcane. Its definition is never static and neither are the categories that are meant to limit or characterize it. In the case of a religion spanning almost two millennia and encompassing almost every part of the globe, the question of "what is Islamic art" is particularly problematic. At the risk of contradicting myself, I would like to point to some truisms, with the caveat that their vagueness may render them anecdotal. Nonetheless, the following observations may serve as bases for the discussions that follow in which I will turn to more detailed critiques.

For most pre- and early modern societies, the arts of calligraphy were given the highest attention, at least in their representation in historical texts and literary anthologies. Starting with works attributed to 'Ali bin Abi Talib (d. c. 661), the calligraphy of great masters such as Ibn Bawab (d. 1022) and Yaqut al-Mutasami (d. 1298) was studied, imitated, and emulated. Scholars have written on the importance of textual representation in Islamic art, owing to its associations with the divine words of God collected in the Qur'an.[4] In addition, the intellectual climate of many of the courts that supported this art was one that valued literary excellence – thus poetry as well as Qur'anic verses were inscribed by the most esteemed calligraphers. Writing skillfully was considered by some as an act of devotion that brought the practitioner closer to God. Beautiful handwriting was also equated to high moral standing, the handwriting acting as an index of the practitioner's character.

Calligraphers would compose illustrated manuscripts as well as design monumental epigraphy to be placed on buildings commissioned by the patron. The writing of calligraphy was a nuanced and complex undertaking in which shifting scales and functions defined the manner in which the works would be used and perceived. The artifacts on which the art was displayed, be they books or buildings, were valued for their beauty and for the skill of the master who had designed them. Yet, although often praised for technical finesse, the calligraphy was not simply a stringing together of words, but a well-thought-out endeavor in which the interaction between the reader, the calligrapher, and the object itself was one of intricate cultural negotiations and aesthetic choices.[5]

Works of art are powerful reminders of social complexity and caution us to look more closely at the objects themselves for clues to unraveling dogmatic ideologies and too-simple assumptions about religiosity. An obvious example is the existence of figurative art, despite discouragement in the form of prophetic traditions, or *hadith*. Although the traditions were often evoked in periods of aniconism and used to make the case for the destruction of works of art and science, the existence of a multitude of examples – from the earliest years of Islam until the present day – is a forceful argument for a more nuanced view of polemics and popular tradition.[6]

Illustrated manuscripts were important sources of knowledge and visual pleasure. Subjects such as astronomy and medicine, inherited from the Greek classical traditions, were followed by political, religious, and epic history in which the world was represented through the lens of imperial patronage. The complex nature of book production was evidenced in the manner in which calligraphers, painters, embellishers, and binders, among other skilled men, came together in what would be the imperial atelier or workshop (*kitabkhana*).[7] In every book a conscious dialogue was underway with past masters, texts, and images. Although art historians often look for archaism or innovation in such works, it is perhaps more useful to move beyond simply recognizing these attitudes to discussing the motivation behind the choices made. The criteria of judging manuscripts, whether illustrated or not, were thus dependent on the particularities of the court and the historical moment in which they were produced.

Architecture is the most visible and widespread of the Islamic arts. Owing to the functional nature of its program and its rich symbolic potential, it incorporates simultaneously the idiosyncratic as well as the stereotypical. That is, a *madrasa* may be similar to others of its type in formal terms, but given the particularities of the piety that was enacted therein, it could be distinguished through numerous subtle and obvious ways. For example, it may be courtyard-centered like others in the region but its size and embellishment could convey important information about its significance to the community for whom it was built. The texts above the doors, windows, portals, and cornices would be inscribed with Qur'anic verses, some referencing its role as a place of study while others pointing to the specific school of theology espoused by the teachers. The texts may also include the names of patrons and builders, literally framing the structure with their ambitions and aspirations. These same facets could speak of social and religious exclusions, while at the same time making use of forms and techniques shared by other buildings of the time, be they secular or religious.

While deluxe books and precious wares were often restricted to courts and treasuries, architecture was built with a broader mandate. Palaces that were enclosed in citadels or situated in remote pastoral landscapes were themselves miniature cities that needed a diverse support system; in and around them would be incorporated mosques and mausolea, as well as large kitchens and housing for servants. Thus while the patrons of imperial architecture were from elite and wealthy circles, those who used the spaces were not always as privileged. Interestingly, it is not the palaces that have survived over time, but rather buildings made explicitly for public use, such as mosques and commemorative shrines. The practice of *waqf,* or perpetual endowment, that is at the heart of Islamic charity, assured that such institutions (for they were complex social and spatial aggregates) would enjoy prosperity and longevity.

Religious belief and practice defined much of what we identify as Islamic art. Yet seldom is Islamic art studied in relation to Islam – as practice or philosophy. Rather, it is seen as an intellectually edifying project, to be studied through post-European Enlightenment criteria of valuation and judgment. Such criteria, which include the individualism of the artist and the originality and authenticity of the work itself, are not always relevant to objects and buildings created for and in Muslim communities. It is rarely questioned why a historic building, for example, that is in constant use since its foundation and thus rebuilt every few years is seen as less of a work of art than an empty, if well-preserved, structure that has not been in use for centuries. The pre-eminence given to the "age-value" of objects, regardless of their value for the populations that use them today, defines one of the deep limitations of the scholarship on Islamic art.[8] The point is not to state that older artifacts should not be preserved, but rather to suggest that the parameters for valuation be extended to include contemporary works of art that are responsive to current issues in both elite and populist public spheres.

What follows is a review of some of the methods that have been employed over the course of the last century, highlighting the most recent scholarship and offering some suggestions for further developing the study of Islamic art. Interspersed in this discussion will be consideration of works that best define the issues at stake, an approach that, I hope, will provide insight on the subject of Islamic art as well as the ways in which it has been studied at the time of production as well as in the present day.[9] Recent scholarship attests that studies conducted through varied disciplinary locations add and enrich the whole complex of what may be considered the history of Islamic art. A primary concern for those writing about Islamic art in recent years has been to find a site where the material may have the most suitable intellectual companionship; that is, owing to the multi-disciplinary nature of much of art historical inquiry, does the subject belong in departments of history, religion, or anthropology; or Near Eastern and South Asian cultures and civilizations; or in departments of the history of art and architecture?[10] As the discussion in this essay hopes to attest, inclusions and dialogue between fields are sources of intellectual and methodological enrichment that serve as models for future scholarship.

ON DIVERSITY IN SPACE AND TIME

Entry into the subject of art in Islam could be found through various means – the discussion could begin with the texts of Plato or Ibn al-'Arabi or Mohammad Arkoun; the architecture cited could include the citadel in Cairo or the Taj Mahal mausoleum in Agra or the Ahmadiyya mosque in Berlin; the visual arts could be linked with Manichaean manuscripts from the ninth century, Jesuit art of the seventeenth century, or poster art of the Cuban revolution of the twentieth century. Bred into the study of Islamic art is the uncertainty that such a field exists, as witnessed by recent articles and books that profess to give hints to what it is and the many ways that it may be categorized and studied.[11] The setting of limits has traditionally been the way in which Islamic art has been characterized, based primarily on temporal and geographical exclusions. For example, although most surveys celebrate the regional breadth and historical depth of Islamic art and culture, major centers of production, say in Africa and South East Asia, are omitted. Furthermore, the histories of those that are included end in the eighteenth century, suggesting that modern colonial and nationalist art cannot be included in the more "traditional" categories.

There is an unquestioned and implicit belief in a unity in Islamic art, earlier manifested through the study of forms, and more recently in the assertion of a shared cultural heritage. What, one may ask, is the common thread between a brocade fashioned for a Fatimid caliph (tenth-century Egypt) and an Anatolian prayer rug (nineteenth-century Turkey), other than the shared medium? Taken further, what would be the connection between either of these objects and an illuminated Ilkhanid Qur'an (fourteenth-century Iran)? How can one begin to describe a history in the absence of a focal point in which to begin the writing of that history? Whose manner of writing shall I adopt; whose voice shall gain precedence? Should I write of the Andalusian poet who described the great palace of Alhambra or the Iranian chronicler who described the miracles enacted at the thresholds of a shrine's kitchen? Shall I, too, describe the great domes of Ottoman mosques or the water cascading through a Mughal garden? What would be the effect of these ruminations?

The aim is not to find parallels between any regionally and historically disparate works of art (some may even question whether the term art is appropriate), but to begin by questioning why they could all simultaneously allow us access into a world breaching almost two millennia and five continents. There are certainly moments in history when one *can* assert a common language of Islamic culture – for example, the thirteenth century onward in the lands encompassing Turkey, Iran, and South Asia was a time when the Persian language provided a unifying court culture, with direct implications for artistic production. Yet the local particularities are far greater and make the general observations banal, if necessary.

As the diversity of the regions and works of arts produced therein attest, finding homogeneity in Islam and the arts is an elusive goal. In fact the very idea of an "Islamic" qualifier in the context of such a history is itself not unproblematic. If we assume that works of art are primarily products that are made in response to the particularities of history and geography, religious and social identity, patronage and individual creativity, it is important to acknowledge a similar dynamism in the very notion of "Islam" itself. Even if taken within a particular geographic and historical timeframe, it is not necessarily the case that any one interpretation of Islamic culture could be put forward. Take for example, early seventeenth-century Lahore, one of the capitals of the Mughal Empire, where the architecture of the imperial palace simultaneously echoed sites of Hindu worship and imitated Catholic devotional imagery.[12] Later in the century, the largest mosque would be built across from the palace, a symbolic presence in the city made famous by the shrine of the eleventh-century mystic Hujwiri, as well as the nearby temple for the founder of the Sikh faith, Guru Nanak (d. 1539). Heterogeneity and ambiguity is at the heart of what is understood to be Islamic art and the cultures that produced it.

A BRIEF EXCURSION THROUGH THE
TWENTIETH CENTURY

The assumption of a cultural, religious, or artistic homogeneity in Islam has its roots in Orientalist scholarship from as early as the eighteenth century, when European writers sought to understand the religion of their close neighbors through the lens of Enlightenment rationalism.[13] Political rivalries and religious ideologies often collapsed into a single discourse that simultaneously admired and denigrated the religion of the "Mahometans."[14] It was not until the nineteenth century, however, that the arts were studied on their own terms, paralleling the development of an autonomous field of art history in European academies.[15] The close association of the discipline with issues of connoisseurship was well timed, for it was also the peak of European colonialism which gave the rulers' historians and archeologists access to sites in the Middle East and South Asia, as well as unlimited power to displace and document them. The frenzy for collecting Islamic art was supplemented by weakened political structures and the increasing influence of European (and later American) museums and collectors.[16]

The modern study of Islamic art, mostly observed from outside the centers where the cultures flourished, was developed in the early twentieth century by European academics and museum curators who published extensive surveys and catalogs documenting paintings, architecture, and "minor" arts such as ceramics and textiles. The inclusion of ritual objects such as ewers, candlesticks, and prayer rugs into these catalogs was unquestioned, as was the designation "art" to objects where it was never intended. It was not simply for lack of knowledge alone – historical texts in indigenous languages were seldom consulted – that the hierarchies within particular cultural entities were ignored. Islamic art was simply overlaid with the categories of Western art, no matter how ill-fitting the match may have been; that is, it was divided into disciplinary categories that did not reflect values established within the cultures that produced the work.

The difficulty modern scholars have had in studying Islamic art has been primarily through a reluctance to discard an outlook based on the Western canon.[17] Thus the bemoaned absence of treatises on architecture, such as by Alberti (d. 1472), although numerous literary texts exist that provide insight into the evaluation of architectural forms; hence also the bemoaned absence of an "art historian" of the likes of Vasari (d. 1574), although the tradition of anthologizing poets and literati had existed from the earliest years of Islamic rule. Calligraphers, painters, and architects were included in such lists, the most well known one being that of the Safavid courtier Qazi Ahmad Qummi, compiled in 1606.[18] Comparison with the attitudes toward art by Italian humanists such as those cited above are not entirely fruitful (often even within the context of pre-Renaissance European) as they presume a singular method for understanding and appreciating all art – regardless of religious, intellectual, and social differences. In comparison with European standards of art making, Islamic art also suffers on formal terms. Scholars in the earlier years of the twentieth century noted the lack of perspective in paintings and the corresponding flattening as signs of a "primitive" and "simple" visual aesthetic – the architecture was one of decorative surfaces but not "sophisticated" planar design, the epitome of Renaissance architecture; the "Islamic city" was a disorderly hodgepodge of buildings, reflecting the "irrationality" of the inhabitants.

Just as Arabic, Persian, Ottoman, and Urdu poetry builds on precedents, the arts of calligraphy, painting, and architecture relied on previously established forms. There may be similar illustrations of events such as the enthronement of a monarch or the meeting of Layla and Majnun in the desert, whether the manuscript was illustrated in the fifteenth century or the seventeenth; or whether it was commissioned in Herat or Istanbul. Rather than being static repetitions, they were ever-changing permutations that remained in dialogue with past and present works. Yet, in the hands of Orientalist scholars, such works were studied for their beauty but damned for their dependence on precedents and seen as lacking in individuality or creativity beyond the skillful manipulation of techniques.

Lavish exhibitions and monumental survey catalogs were often underwritten by governmental entities. *Early Muslim Architecture* by K. A. C. Creswell (1932–1940) and *A Survey of Persian Art from Prehistoric Times to the Present* by A. U. Pope and Phyllis Ackerman (1938–1939) were both dedicated to their patrons, King Fu'ad of Egypt and Riza Shah Pahlavi of Iran, respectively.[19] The case of Iran is of particular importance as the construction of a "Persian" art history was undertaken with great vigor by numerous scholars and politicians in a way that had an enormous impact on the valuations of all works of Islamic art. Arthur Upham Pope was the foremost proponent of the idea of an Iranian artistic heritage that spanned millennia, from the dawn of civilization until the twentieth century. In theses proposed with his collaborators on the *Survey*, this history was evidence of an unbroken, if sometimes compromised, cultural identity, which was a cut above that of its neighboring Arab, Turkish, and Indian counterparts. European, American, and Iranian scholars and politicians saw the potential in propagating a "national" identity through cultural and artistic artifacts.[20] Ideas of Iranian racial and ethnic superiority, founded in nationalist ideologies, would influence the manner in which Islamic art was conceived, a tendency that has currency up until the present day.[21]

Two parallel representations of Islamic art history had emerged by the mid-twentieth century. The first was constructed through the methods of nineteenth-century formalist art historiography and the second served in the making of nationalist discourses in the early twentieth century. A third representation, a consequence of changes in the field of art history as well as the growing corpus of material evidence, has been to look at Islamic art from within its own social, historical, and religious contexts. Although access to languages such as Arabic and Persian had been available to many earlier scholars, it was not until the 1970s that texts were utilized in sophisticated ways to gain insight into the cultures within which Islamic art was produced.

ON TRENDS THEREAFTER

Over the course of the twentieth century numerous points of view have been expressed in the study of Islamic art, ranging from nationalist arguments of authenticity, academic searches for origins and typologies, histories of patronage, and investigation into the corporate nature of art production (such as workshops and guilds). Many of these methods are interspersed with assertions of the "spiritual dimension" of Islamic art through the invocation of universalist philosophy, Sufi mysticism, and visual abstraction. Three primary methods define these studies, namely the materialist/formalist, spiritualist, and historical approaches to art history. The following discussions focus on representative issues that exemplify these approaches and on the particularities that distinguish them from each other.

The materialist/formalist approach is one in which the object (be it architecture, painting, or portable ware) is studied through its material properties and modes of manufacture. Styles are classified and particular "hands" categorized, often in order to evaluate and authenticate the works analyzed.[22] Recent scholars have continued this method of viewing Islamic art by now focusing on themes that purport to create newer, if not more effective, systems of classification.[23] For example, a recent book on "Persian" art includes works of "Pre-Islamic Painting of the Iranian Peoples" as well as the nineteenth century, and focuses on recurrent themes, such as "Fighting and Feasting" and "Figural Types."[24] Such a study reduces the paintings to sets of affinities and approximations without providing insight on any one of them.[25] Would it not be more useful to consider a story or even an image within the culture and time period it was created?

For example, the story of Layla and Majnun, originally written in Arabic, has been popularly illustrated in different poetic manuscripts and in varying sites and time periods. The story revolves around the unfortunate Layla and her cousin Qays, who fall in love, yet are kept separate from each other by their families. Qays is filled with grief and longing, to the extent that he retires to the desert as a crazed hermit (hence his title *majnun*, Arabic for "madman"). Among the most renowned literary renditions is in the *Khamsa* (quintet) of Nizami Ganjavi (d. 1207), who describes the tragedy in verses filled with pathos and longing.[26] Nizami's *Khamsa* was very popular during the Timurid period, as a source of imitation by other prominent poets (such as Abd ar-Rahman Jami, d. 1492), but also as a richly imagined text appropriate for visual interpretation.

Illustrated versions of the *Khamsa* focus on events related to the stories, such as Layla and Majnun at school, Majnun's wandering in the desert, and the death of the two lovers. The episodes are depicted in starkly different manners in, for example, a manuscript from 1494 painted in the Timurid court of Herat and one painted for the Mughal court in 1595. The 1494 image is a sparsely composed page, the right margin of which appears to wander off, following the contours of a stream that flows down from the top of the page.[27] It illustrates Majnun meeting his uncle Salim in a desert, the setting depicted by the golden-yellow background and the sparse vegetation on the fringes of the stream. Wild beasts such as lions and antelopes cover the larger portion of the picture surface. There are three couplets on the top right-hand corner of the page, the text inscribed in a rectangular box that sets them apart from the image. The verses describe Salim laying down food for Majnun – who does not eat a single morsel – and asking him how he survives despite tormenting his body through such starvation. Majnun's emaciated state is apparent in his gaunt figure, with bare chest and thin arms sticking out from a simple blue cape. In contrast, Salim is well appointed in a bright red coat and a large turban. The contrast between the figures is clearly evoked, as is the interesting relationship between their postures, which are mirrored. The text and image complement each other in this example, illustrating a moment in the narrative that depicts Majnun's self-denial and spiritual purity.[28]

The second example was produced in 1595 for the Mughal emperor Akbar, in India.[29] Here the artist shows Layla and Majnun together, yet their long-awaited meeting is an overwhelming and painful one. There is no text on this page, but the drama is intense, as the lovers swoon away from each other, the picture plane itself cleaving as though to reflect their agony. The painting is divided in half by a massive and verdant tree under which the lovers have met. At its base are two intertwined cypresses (representing paradisal themes), symbolic of their love and also the esoteric dimensions of the story. Rich with references and fecund with life, the painting literally crawls with creatures of the earth, the air and the sea. This is not the desert of Arabia, the original setting of the story that the earlier painting evoked, but the jungles of India. Art historians have acknowledged that paintings from Akbar's reign were often inspired by Indic tales and modes of representation, whether Hindu or Muslim, and are imbued with action and drama. The sympathetic inclusion of local elements was in keeping with the *Zeitgeist* of the time, in which experiments were being made in social and political hybridity, as well as in the arts of depiction. As these examples show, although given the same "theme" and within the broader iconography of Persianate painting, close analysis reveals enticing and important details that situate the paintings in very different historical and artistic contexts.[30]

The study of complete manuscripts, or what has remained of them, has borne fruit through the labors of recent scholars. An important and early example is the collaborative work by the art historian Stuart Cary Welch and the historian Martin B. Dickson, in which the authors focused their individual expertise on the *Shahnama-yi Shahi* (*Imperial Epic of Kings*), the text composed in 1010 by Abul Qasim Firdawsi.[31] The manuscript they focus on was completed during the reign of the Safavid Shah Tahmasb (d. 1576) and comprises of paintings by some of the most interesting artists of the time, such as Mir Sayyid 'Ali and Abd al-Samad, both of whom migrated from Iran to the Mughal court in India later in their careers. The Welch and Dickson compilation, while useful in bringing together all the paintings, pays little attention to the text or to the contexts within which the manuscript was commissioned. In 1568 it was gifted by Shah Tahmasb to the Ottoman Sultan, Selim II, a move that has been interpreted by art historians as reflecting the Shah's public vows of repentance, even though the arts of depiction were not included in these prohibitions.[32] A close examination of the political relationships between the Safavids and Ottomans at this moment in history would shed light on Tahmasb's motivations, as would a theoretical analysis of gifts and gifting during the early modern period itself. That is, what were the implications, cultural and political, not only of the making of the grand *Shahnama-yi Shahi*, but of its role as an imperial gift?[33] What was the response and reception of the book in the new setting, and how would it be seen by rival Ottoman courtiers and artists?[34]

More successful than the 1981 monograph was a study produced sixteen years later by Marianna Shreve Simpson, with contributions by Massumeh Farhad. This book is a study of the *Haft Awrang* (*Seven Thrones*) of Jami (a poem composed between 1468 and 1485), copied and illustrated for the Safavid prince Ibrahim Mirza over the years 1556–1565, and known as the "Freer Jami."[35] In an attempt to move away from the previously employed method of connoisseurship to evaluate the paintings, the authors attempt to understand the multiple contexts of its making,

> including [its] relation to other deluxe manuscripts of the Safavid period, in relation to other codices owned by or associated with Sultan Ibrahim Mirza, in relation to other works made by the artists to whom the prince entrusted the Jami commission, and in relation to other illustrated copies of the *Haft Awrang*. As with the examination of the Freer Jami [manuscript] itself, the study of these and other relationships depends on a combination of codicological, literary, historical, and art-historical methods.[36]

Thus, what we get in this study are intricate and thoughtful layers that point to the multivalent nature of a complex project in which literature and art are skillfully combined.

The spiritualist approach has its roots in the works of Orientalist philosophers like Henri Corbin and Titus Burckhardt.[37] Their successors, such as S. Hossein Nasr, look to mysticism as a source for understanding aesthetic and esoteric aspects of art and architecture.[38] In this approach the object is considered as representative of religious and philosophical dimensions of Islam, regardless of their historical or cultural specificity. The studies focus on the complexity of geometric form, for example, in order to indicate parallel complexities in the intellectual climate that produced them. Spiritualist approaches, while often rooted in pre-modern texts, tend to apply theories from outside art history on to the works of art, regardless of their relevance. As one recent scholar, Samer Akkach, has written, he aims to

> *use* [emphasis mine] architecture to make the reader aware of certain patterns of thought within the pre-modern Islamic tradition, instead of the normal scenarios where conceptual patterns are constructed to explain the nature and particularity of architecture. This has two advantages: first, shifting the focus away from architecture itself liberates architectural forms from the burden of historicity and causal interpretation, that is, finding causes (including meanings) to explain formal qualities; second, it enables one to access a wider spectrum of literary material, breaks disciplinary boundaries, and unfolds new interpretations. This approach tends to emphasize the cogency and significance of the constructed narratives, whereby architecture becomes a suitable tool to understand the working of a pre-modern spatial sensibility and its coherent cosmology.[39]

Beyond the problematic disregard for historical or formal specificity, the main difficulty in such an approach is its disregard for the medium itself, be it architecture or any other form of Islamic art. By removing the role of the patron or the maker, that is, by assigning them a "will" that is generic, generalized, and undocumented, the spiritualist approach provides little insight into what gives life to any work of art – that is, human creativity. For example, Akkach focuses on "the architectural order" of space by analyzing the circular form, which he finds in the roof of the Dome of the Rock in Jerusalem, the mosque of Ibn Tulun in Cairo, and the ablution fountain of the mosque of Sultan Hasan in Cairo.[40] The dome has been considered a powerful symbolic feature by numerous architectural historians studying other cultures and geographic regions, many of whom have drawn parallels with the "Dome of Heaven" in the Christian and Roman traditions.[41] Thus one may ask what is specific about the form in the context of Islam? What, one may wonder, are the parallels between the three domes, but for their form? Choosing buildings associated with religious praxis is particularly deceptive, since some of the best-known domes belong to palaces, such as the Hasht Behest pavilion in Isfahan.

The historical approach is one in which the object is studied within a chronologically determined timeframe and viewed as responsive to political and social dynamics. Multiple factors shape the patronage and production of the arts, such as economics, technology, and perhaps even fashion. In studying art and history in synchrony with such factors highlights its role as a cultural product, through the study of which one may gain insight into a society at a particular moment in time. Thus, a focus on historical specificity characterizes this work, but does not exclude considerations of form, culture, or religion. The "burden of history" is one borne with great efficacy by Oleg Grabar, who wrote the introduction to the inaugural volume of the journal *Muqarnas: An Annual on the Visual Culture of the Islamic World*, of which he was the editor.[42] In this essay, he outlines some obligations for the historians of Islamic art, which include the use of primary texts, the perusal of which "brings out questions or information pertinent to the history of the arts." He continues that "still another obligation of art-historical research is to set up problems and pose questions for cultural and literary historians," an important point in which the author situates art alongside disciplines that put emphasis on material and literary culture.[43] The following examples take as a starting point Grabar's historical approach and may be seen as representative of current methods in the scholarship.

ON SOME METHODS THAT SHED NEW LIGHT ON OLD WORKS

A sophisticated engagement with texts distinguishes the work of numerous scholars, exemplified by the work of Oya Pancaroğlu, who has analyzed the philosophical and aesthetic dimensions of Islamic art by focusing on what has been an oft-neglected corpus relegated by most surveys to the "minor arts." Her study of tenth-century epigraphic pottery sheds light on the social dynamics of Samanid (819–1005) courtly culture by closely "reading" both the objects and the contexts that produced them. The Samanid elite based in Bukhara is credited with the revival and enhancement of the Persian language, yet the artistic environment around them was one that also drew inspiration from older Arabic art and literature. As Pancaroğlu has pointed out, the metaphors and aphorisms written on the Samanid pottery served the purpose of extolling "aesthetic pleasures and ethical precepts," while simultaneously making references to ideas prevalent in other contemporaneous disciplines, such as philosophy and alchemy.[44] The texts guide not only the [be]holder's eyes, but her mind as well, thereby initiating an intense dialogue between the user and the object.

Reception of Islamic art and architecture within the societies that produced them is an aspect that has been often neglected, although there is ample evidence to understand its role in varied cultural environments and historical moments. Two points are necessary to consider regarding sources for the valuation of art; the first is that the status of different media changed over time, an aspect determined by changes in taste, technology, and demand. For example, as the example of Samanid pottery shows, ceramics were very highly valued in eastern Iran in the tenth century, a trend that would continue up until the Safavid period, but with different forms and materials that drew direct inspiration from contemporary Chinese Ming wares. The same longevity was not enjoyed by objects from Fatimid Egypt, which, unlike Samanid objects that were distinguished by their beautifully articulated texts, were decorated with figural motifs that may be understood to reflect the complex urban life of tenth-century Cairo. Separated spatially, yet connected through the mobility of technological knowledge, Fatimid and Samanid wares were distinct from each other and responsive to the different needs of their users and makers.

Islamic art must be studied on its own terms, that is, the social, historical, and material contexts that provide categories for its study and evaluation. The literary genre of describing objects, paintings, or building, called *wasf*, is one significant source for art historical enquiry.[45] In Safavid Iran, for example, the encomiastic poetry of 'Abdi Beg Shirazi (d. 1581) in praise of palaces and shrines sheds light on the role of buildings in the construction of an imperial iconography of power by reporting on structures built for Shah Tahmasb.[46] However, the poems are not simply lists or literal descriptions of buildings, but constructs that represent the poet's imagination as well as the aesthetic principles of his times.[47] The poetry of architectural description, as exemplified by 'Abdi Beg Shirazi, also provides insight into features of design that were utilized by builders in the sixteenth century. In contrast to the planar representation of architecture, which is often employed by modern architects, 'Abdi Beg's poetic descriptions reveal the "elemental" approach through which Safavid buildings were designed. That is, through the varying combinations of discrete architectural forms these buildings – be they palaces or shrines – were distinguished by the economic use of recognizable architectural forms and embellishments that marked them as imperial commissions.

The concept of economy is one that also characterizes the arts of depiction, in particular, that of manuscript illustration. Repetition of themes and iconography (for example the enthronement of rulers) had been in practice since the earliest years of book illustration, yet it is the beginnings of the Timurid period in the fifteenth century that witnessed the codification of sophisticated conceptual frameworks for the arts of calligraphy and painting.[48] Sketches and fragmentary works by renowned masters were collected in albums (*muraqqaʿ*) compiled for the princely elite.[49] The albums were an integral part of the gathering (*majlis*) that typified social practice in the Timurid court, as well as its successors in Safavid Iran, Ottoman Turkey, and Mughal India. This setting, comprised of princes, poets, painters, and calligraphers – among other literati of the time – was the site for the appreciation and critique of art and literature.[50] The compiler of the album, usually a high-ranked bureaucrat or scribe, was also the author of a prefatory essay in the opening pages of the album, which served to introduce the patron, the author, and the artists of their era.[51]

The role of the album was akin to that of a picture gallery or museum, one in which the highest ideals of painting and writing were displayed. In the mind of the "curator" of this two-dimensional gallery, the collection was simultaneously an encomium to the patron, evidence of the compiler's knowledge and literary prowess, and a compilation of great works of art. The past was evoked through the genealogies of paintings, where older themes and images were repeated and "improved" upon. Similarly the lineages of painters and calligraphers were asserted through references to great masters, some going back to ʿAli ibn Abi Talib. Albums were thus used as visual treatises on the history of art, whose analysis sheds crucial light not only on the makers of the art, but their patrons as well.

The albums functioned as design books for other artists and calligraphers to learn from and imitate. Compiled in the imperial ateliers, the pages were scrutinized by students and copied by their teachers. Pounce marks show that many pages, comprising of figures and designs, were used and reused many times before finally coming to rest between the pages of the album. In the prefaces of the album, the authors list previous masters of calligraphy and painting and insert the works collected in the album into a broader history of art making. The lineages defined herein do not distinguish artists as individuals per se, but as parts of collective histories, whose works are similarly connected despite the centuries that may separate them. The ideal thus was not to find aberrations, but rather conformity within a dynamic set of visual and semantic expectations.

Perhaps the most interesting innovations in Islamic art took place in the realm of architecture, in particular when seemingly disparate cultures came into contact. Avoiding the issue of "influence" as a factor of dominance or superiority, one may suggest that a characteristic of Islamic art is its relationship with its own past, and importantly, its appropriation and assimilation of art from neighboring, often non-Muslim, entities. As has often been noted, it is an art of affiliation with other cultures, be they neighbors in war or peace.[52] Although this truism would apply to all periods, examples from the fifteenth to seventeenth centuries are perhaps the most well documented, both in contemporary texts and their secondary interpretations. Take for example the marked shift in the form of imperial mosques after the conquest of the former Byzantine capital Constantinople/Istanbul in 1453 by the Ottoman ruler Mehmet II (d. 1481). Moving away from more modest, regionally determined forms (themselves likely inspired by local Christian architecture), Ottoman imperial mosques in Istanbul were clearly responsive to the great churches of Byzantium that marked the landscape of that ancient capital city. The famed church of Hagia Sophia, completed in 537 for the Byzantine emperor Justinian (d. 565), was the epitome of "great" architecture for the Muslim rulers. Soon after the conquest by Mehmet II, the church was converted into a mosque with the addition of a *mihrab* niche and Qur'anic invocations on the interior, and minarets on the exterior. Subsequent mosques would imitate its massive, centralized composition, despite its anomalous form for a mosque that requires linear directionality toward Mecca. However, here as in other instances of appropriation, functionalism wasn't necessarily the goal; rather the new forms were manifest attempts at sharing in the prestige and cognition associated with their predecessors. In the Ottoman case, the prestige of the Hagia Sophia was continuous, even for the great master architect Sinan (d. 1588), who wrote of it as a masterpiece "without equal in the world."[53] The goal, as stated by

Sinan, was not to build a new formal vocabulary, but rather to improve on the "original" work of art.

The study of Islamic art, be it paintings, portable wares, or architecture, requires the constant recontextualization of intellectual and disciplinary boundaries. Not only must such a study unite religiously and politically distinct entities (such as Byzantium in the case of Ottoman art), or geographically distant countries (such as China, in the case of post-Mongol art), but also different fields (such as literature, in the case of Samanid pottery or Safavid architecture). It is precisely this type of creative interplay that defines Islamic art; the role of the historian is to be similarly creative in his or her manners of investigation. New areas of study must be opened up and intellectual risks taken to enrich further the study and making of Islamic art.

ENDING WITH OPENINGS

Conventional surveys of Islamic art end with the eighteenth century, as though the concept of an art defined through religious identification ended with the Enlightenment. Within art historical discourses such assumptions have been suspect for many years, nonetheless, works from the contemporary cultures of the Middle East and South Asia are relegated to the margins both of modern and Islamic art. The idea that the modern history of Islamic art or the practices of architecture and art-making are somehow separate from the artifacts prior to the eighteenth century is a strange vanity displayed by the academies where the "classical" periods are studied. It is without doubt that the rupture that cleaved two sides of a historical moment (call it colonialism, the end of empire, rise of modernism, call it the nineteenth century) had tangible repercussions on the manner in which academic scholarship and the political rhetoric of nation-building was developed. Yet continuing the division of the histories of Islamic art according to pre-colonial, colonial, and post-colonial periodization deprives them of historical autonomy. As Anthony King wrote:

> by irreversibly tying up their histories with "the West," [this periodization] replaces the signifiers of their own indigenous, and multiple, periodizations by others imposed from outside; it imposes an implied historical linearity which fixes, temporarily and geographically, the

colonial experience as the principal event, simultaneously privileging
the political and social elite created by colonialism over the subaltern
population, and displacing indigenous histories by those constructed
by the metropolitan core.[54]

It is necessary to view Islamic art within a set of discrete, yet historically and conceptually connected, events. Only when we can
situate and study this art as part of continuous trajectories can the
study of Islamic art become accessible and central to contemporary
discourses.

It is a fair assumption that the citizens of countries that have traditionally been grouped together under the banner of Islam no longer
identify solely with religious institutions. Ethnicity, nationalism,
gender, and sexuality are but a few additional markers in the fashioning of contemporary selfhood. Artists from Islamic republics practice in New York and Amsterdam, some distancing themselves from
their artistic heritage while others embrace it; Americans who grew
up speaking English and practicing Christianity are among the most
skilled calligraphers of the Arabic language; multinational architectural firms build mosques and cultural centers throughout Europe and
the Middle East. It is necessary therefore to broaden rather than limit
the parameters for an inclusive and dynamic definition of Islamic art
that looks beyond religious and regional classifications.

Islamic art, as any creative project, regardless of its origin, is ultimately concerned with questions of representation: that is, who and
what is being represented, and, most importantly, how does the work
of art inform that representation? A phenomenological approach
helps to understand better both the intentions of the makers and the
reception of the work of art, through an active and empathetic engagement on the part of the viewer and the historian. As the examples have
demonstrated, most studies combine the particularities of history and
ideology within the cultural contexts that produced the artwork. Thus
access to the mentalities of a community, be it comprised of artists,
patrons, makers, or users, can be achieved by studying representations
in the texts that described the art as well as the objects themselves.
Toward that goal one may call for contemporary art that connects the
past with the present, informal works of art that draw upon a wider
constituency, and scholarship that involves discourses from multiple
disciplinary sites. In such polyvalent environments, Babylonian dis-
junctions can provide sites of emancipation for those who make and
study Islamic art.

2

AUTHORITY

Devin DeWeese

In 1330, the historian Hamdullah Mustawfi Qazvini recorded a story, in his *Tarikh-i guzida*, about a strange event that had occurred a decade and a half earlier "in the city of Yangi, one of the towns of Turkistan." The town he had in mind, in the south of modern Kazakhstan, was indeed known by that name during the Mongol era, but through most of the Islamic era it was known as Taraz. Hamdullah's account of the event that occurred in this town, around 1316, was related, he writes, by a certain Mawlana Jamal al-Din the Turk, who is said to have avowed its wide confirmation among the local people.

> In that year an army of infidels had come to make war upon them, and they sent the men of Turkistan to fight and give battle against them. From the town of Yangi, a man named Qara-bahadur went out with that group to fight the infidels, and was martyred there. After a time, from a corner of the home of Qara-bahadur, where his wife and children were, they heard a voice, saying:
>
> "I am Qara-bahadur. On [such-and-such a day] the infidels martyred me. Things are fine with me now there [in the next world]. I have come to this city along with 70,000 spirits in order to welcome an old woman who is going to pass away after three days. Because they [the 70,000 spirits] were coming for this good purpose, I came as well; otherwise I would not have come. Since my mind was attached to you, I have come to see what you are doing. You should tell the people of this town that a great calamity, a dire affliction, is on the way and will come to this town; you should do good works and give charitable offerings in order to ward off that affliction."

When Qara-bahadur's family heard this voice, they quickly destroyed the corner of the house from which the voice was coming: no one was there. The voice arose again from a different corner of the house, saying, "I am Qara-bahadur; it is my spirit that is speaking with you," and it repeated the details of the story, and stressed that they should tell the people of the town to make offerings. This voice was not like a bodily voice; rather, it was like a voice coming out of a jar. The people of the house said in response to him that "The people of the town will not believe these words [coming] from us." He replied, "Tell the people of the town to assemble in the square and set up a post in the ground, so that I may address them from that post." They did so. The people of the town heard the story from the post; it said, "You should make offerings to allay the affliction, and you should say, 'O God, Your knowledge suffices against what is said, and Your magnanimity suffices against the questioning.'" For three days the people heard the voice from various places in the city, but after the old woman passed away, no one ever heard the voice again. This is among the wondrous events.[1]

Hamdullah's story offers a vignette of the manifestation and exercise of religious authority, of decidedly unconventional cast, from the frontiers of the medieval Muslim world, and helps us frame a broader set of questions regarding the nature of religious authority in the Muslim world. It portrays, after all, a medieval Muslim community called upon to undertake religious acts – and not merely private and individual acts of piety (as in the charitable offerings asked of them), but public and collective acts entailing the recitation of a seemingly expiatory litany – on the authority of a voice heard addressing them from a post erected in the ground. The voice's authority is not explicitly addressed in the narrative, but we can easily suggest several reasons for it to have been taken seriously: its mode of manifestation was miraculous; it was understood to be the voice of a martyr; it demonstrated its veracity to the martyr's family by correctly specifying the date of his death; it demonstrated its veracity more publicly by delivering on a promise (i.e. by "moving" from the house to the post); and it called upon the people of the city to perform laudable acts of piety. To these more or less normative demonstrations of authority, all of which can be situated within the framework of well-attested patterns of Muslim religiosity, may be added other elements that seem to conform less well with those patterns, but nevertheless added, we may presume, to the experiential intensity of the voice's manifestation, and thus, indirectly, to the authority accorded it. It had, we are told, a distinctive aural character that set it apart from ordinary voices, and this sensory distinction, we may surmise, thus enhanced the affective response of those who heard it; the specific "form" in which the voice came to be embodied (the post), as well as its vocal "trajectory," as the voice of a loved one speaking from a corner of his family's home, then from a post erected in the town square, and finally from other sites in the town (to which, we may conjecture, the post was moved), may have evoked patterns of funerary rites rooted in local pre-Islamic ancestral religious practices, though undoubtedly long Islamized; and, although this "proof" is not explicitly highlighted in the account, the predicted duration of the voice's appearance seems to have been linked with its "prediction" of the death of an unidentified old woman.

The latter point is particularly significant, in connection with the affective impact of the story, despite (or because of) the lack of explicit comment in the account: the "public" experience of the voice – it spoke for three days, from the post, exhorting the people to acts of piety, and then was never heard again – is implicitly accounted for by the presence of the voice and the throng of spirits (who, we may note, are not explicitly identified as the souls of others martyred by the infidels along with Qara-bahadur), and their presence, for three days, is explicitly linked with the impending death of an old woman. This link, furthermore, is strangely emphasized, when Qara-bahadur is made to affirm, first, that he was now quite comfortable in the other world and, second, that he would not have come, and hence would not have been speaking, had it not been for the occasion of the old woman's death. This affirmation renders his entire warning, and exhortation, to the townspeople utterly incidental, secondary to the more central purpose of receiving the soul of a seemingly insignificant woman (and, indeed, the collective arrival of the spirits in order to receive the old woman's soul may itself echo those local funerary traditions rather than "authoritative" Muslim duties).

In other words, the soul of the martyr Qara-bahadur, who gave his life defending his Muslim community against an infidel attack, was now happily at home in the next, more real, world, and would not have bothered to address his living family or his living community, or to warn them of impending travails, or to instruct them about how to ward off those travails, or how to live piously in general, had it not been for the spiritual "mission" of welcoming the old woman into the next world. That mission is identified, further, as that of the

70,000 spirits whom Qara-bahadur accompanied; only through happenstance, then, did he come, and also, while there, tell his family and community of the afflictions that threatened them, warning them that their only possible defense (as might be gathered from his recent fate) was to do what they ought to have been doing anyway. In effect, the authority of the voice speaking from the post rested on a curious combination of the private and the public, of individual and communal experience and obligation: the martyr first loses his life while participating in the collective duty of defensive *jihad*, and then attends to the personal and communal service of warning not only his family but the entire town; yet it is not his service to the community that is referred to as a "public good," for that label is attached to the task of the 70,000 spirits in receiving the soul of a single old woman. The martyr's concern for the fate of the townspeople is thus not only individual but incidental as well (he attends to it while his companions – here the 70,000 spirits *are* involved – attend to their collective duty of attending to the old woman).

This is, to be sure, an isolated story, and we have been dwelling on an aspect of it that is not expressly developed in the only version of it to come down to us; but it serves nicely to remind us that many of our expectations regarding how religious authority would be expressed and interpreted in Muslim societies remain too narrow, too abstract, and too inattentive to historical reality. In particular, it suggests that Muslim communities have engaged with issues of religious authority in ways far more complex and flexible than those, today and in the past, who insist on a rigid construction of the roots and branches of proper Islamic religiosity would countenance.

* * *

Many religious systems tend toward reductionism, toward a claim, or effort, to know and manipulate the many by means of the few; they offer, that is, an assurance that the many things or forces of the phenomenal world may be understood and controlled by finding the few, or the one, most important or powerful or pervasive thing and understanding or controlling it. This reductionist tendency gives us, for example, the Ten Commandments from the myriad rules of the Torah, and then gives us the further reduction of the Ten to the one "Golden Rule" that subsumes all others; it gives us "master spirits" who control all particular iterations of an animal species; it gives us

the Four Noble Truths, the Upanishadic distillation and interiorization of the Vedas, and, perhaps, the Dao that cannot be named. In the
context of Islam, it gives us in theological terms the absolute unity
and transcendence of Allah; and it gives us in ritual terms the Five
Pillars of Islam, the essence of which is further reduced, in some formulations, to the first of them, the Attestation of Faith (the *shahada*,
consisting of phrases that further bear witness to religious reductionism, as they identify, in effect, God and His Prophet). In the context of
the second of the Pillars, the daily prayers, moreover, their number is
explained as the result of a process of successive reduction, achieved
by the Prophet through tough bargaining with the angel Gabriel – the
medium, in effect, of the revelation itself – on behalf of the weak and
impious human community that would rely upon the very last messenger of God.

If religious systems themselves regularly offer, or seek, the equivalent of a "unified field theory" through which their adherents may
observe and experiment on the world, and appeal to the trope of limiting the essential responsive operations incumbent upon humankind,
it is perhaps not surprising that scholarship on religion has often
reflected this reductionist approach, seeking to limit the complexity
of historical religious traditions to the essential positions or fundamental sources, knowing which we may know the tradition, or at least
recognize it, in any particular time and place. While there is nothing
inherently wrong with this approach, which may be unavoidable in
pedagogical terms, its limitations should be clear, and problems inevitably arise if we take what is pedagogically useful to be historically,
or, worse, essentially, definitive; what is particularly ironic is that
religious traditions themselves have proven more willing, and eager,
historically, to discard the constraints of their reductionist tendencies
– the better to paint the entire world with signs of their visions of
the sacred – than scholarship on religion has been to subdue its own
reductionist tendencies.

The problem of authority, or of establishing and/or arguing the
authoritativeness of a particular transmission of knowledge, inevitably lends itself to reductionist approaches in scholarship, and moreover to a focus on textual, scriptural essentialism; yet it is a key issue
both for the internal dynamics of Muslim societies, and for scholarship on the history of Muslim societies, and broadening our understanding of the sources and methods underlying religious authority is
thus key to a historically grounded understanding of the complexities

of the Muslim world. Notions of what is authoritative have shaped scholarly trends, and scholarly preconceptions have, in turn, directed attention toward particular aspects of Muslim tradition while ignoring or "backgrounding" others. A constant in both contexts has been a focus on scripture and sacred texts, which at first glance seems to work well with Islam, given the primacy of the Qur'an; the assumption of, and search for, scriptural authority also fit well with older approaches in scholarship on religion, which defined religions in terms of their "sacred books," and it fit well with more general Western understandings of religion, in a lineage extending back from Enlightenment scholarship to Protestant rhetoric critical of practices without scriptural foundations. It also fit well with "modernist" Muslim approaches to Islam, intent on aligning the faith with discrete formulations based on textual foundations, and, ultimately, with the technological and scientific achievements of the West that provided the impetus for specific modernist Muslim currents.

The link between scholarship on the Muslim world, and the internal dynamics of Muslim debates over the foundations of religious authority, is of special importance, for in the final analysis authority is fundamentally about the relationship between the present and the past, between what authority is intended to serve or justify or explain or prescribe today, and the sources of authority that were made known in an earlier time; even if a source of authority beyond time is posited, it is relevant to all but the most ardent fundamentalist, or mystic, how past generations related to or evoked that authority. What is missing in much discussion of the Islamic world today is precisely an awareness of that vital relationship between the present and the past as in itself a mode of discourse about authority; scholarship on Islamic history tends to be compartmentalized and separate from scholarship on contemporary issues, with the result that the most anomalous contemporary currents in arguments about religious authority in the Muslim world are adopted as the norm, not only today, but in the past as well. This is not just a matter of needing better "background" information, from the past for the present, but of the need to engage with the diversity of Muslim experience in the past as itself an ongoing contributor to the present. On the whole, historical scholarship does better in terms of appreciating the religious diversity of pre-modern *and* contemporary Muslim societies; it is precisely with discussions focused on contemporary affairs – for which nuance and complexity are arguably most urgent, for compelling practical reasons – that we find the most persistent tendencies to paint with a broad brush, to essentialize (essentialism, after all, is the helpmate of brevity), and to reduce diversity to monolithic "civilizational" frameworks.

As a result of these tendencies, the assumption that religious authority in Islam rests primarily or exclusively upon written scriptural sources is widespread, and is reinforced nowadays through the preponderance of voices insisting that "true Islam" excludes nearly everything without direct scriptural sanction (with "scripture" limited to the Qur'an itself and a quite restrictively defined body of Prophetic *hadiths*); even those who reject the most extreme, "fundamentalist" approaches to scriptural authority in effect legitimize the centrality of the written word by offering not another basis for or interpretation of religious authority, but by offering different interpretations of particular scriptural passages, or by offering a different set of principles for the process of scriptural interpretation.

We need not go to the extreme of denying the pivotal role of the Qur'an, as the revealed word of God, or of Prophetic tradition to argue that this assumption is fundamentally misleading. We may begin, rather, with a reminder of the initially oral character of the revelation itself, and of the continued primacy of the direct apprehension of the Qur'an in the form of oral recitation (rather than in the form of written words), and then recall the persistence of the oral venue for the transmission of Hadith (whether in the original chains of transmission or in much later contexts of instruction and memorization); we may point out, further, the fundamentally oral character of the central soteriological act in Islam, that is, the profession of faith; and we may also take note of the obvious importance of oral communication and modes of solemnification for the expression of religious knowledge and duties in non-literate contexts, outside the framework of the learned elites of Muslim societies. We might also point out the circularity of textual bases of authority, in which the written texts, and the knowers of written texts, legitimize each other.

But we must also eventually come to terms with a more fundamental distinction that is of relevance for understanding the foundations of religious authority in the Islamic world – not merely written versus oral, but verbal versus non-verbal, or discursive versus non-discursive. We must come to terms, that is, with aspects of religious life and authority that are accessible to (though not exclusive to) the inarticulate (whether they are inarticulate by nature or status or choice): how can we understand, and discuss, the transmission, communication, or valorization of religious "meaning" in non-verbal terms? In short, how are religious meaning, and religious authority, conveyed without words, in non-discursive venues?[2]

In large measure, addressing this question entails recognizing that words and discursive formulations far from exhaust religious expression, and hence modes of religious authority; we must acknowledge, specifically, that Islam, and signs of religious authority, have been "written" in non-verbal venues as often as in the scriptural contexts so often privileged today by both Muslims and outsiders. Naturally, Islam is written on the bodies, and the bodily movements, of Muslims; it is written on the "handiwork" of Muslims (whether what we regard as art or mundane artifacts, whether structures or clothing or amulets or hygienic utensils, produced in furtherance of religious duties or sensibilities); it is written in landscapes shaped by Muslim obligations and aspirations (through modes of agriculture, travel, or commerce); it is written in institutions, whether the *madrasa* or the shrine; and, according to some, it is inscribed in venues of human consciousness that are both "above" and "below" the discursive capacities in which not only written language, but verbal expression in general, reside.[3]

All these non-verbal venues can be talked about, and have been; but fundamental to them is the assumption that religious authority, and religious "power" (in the form of *baraka* or divine grace), inhere in them without need for verbal expression, simply through their status as, ultimately, God's creation. And it should not be lost on us that it is above all these non-verbal modes or signs of religious authority that are scorned today by proponents of the tyranny of the written word.

In general terms, authority is central in religious systems in so far as it is crucial to religious meaning: whether discursive or not, religious meaning is made meaningful by its authoritative character. Yet authority is hierarchical, in that there are ultimate sources, and subsidiary sources of authority; the former tell one, in principle, where to look or whom to ask, while the latter speak to interpretation and extrapolation. It is the second type that is inevitably controversial, within a tradition, since the ultimate sources are unassailable (except from outside a tradition), while the subsidiary sources stand between those unassailable sources and the communal or individual actors who, presumably, require authoritative sanction for what should be thought or done. Authority cannot be understood wholly on the basis of its sources, however; recognizing and transmitting authority depends also upon methods. Establishing authority is essentially a process of reference; it is the set of footnotes, in effect, to religious life, and while we can imagine some minimalist frameworks in which a religious life would be referenced by only one footnote ("See: God"), a referential apparatus of that sort would be neither informative nor interesting, certainly for the historian, but probably for those who live religious lives as well.

In more specific terms, the foundations of religious authority in Islam – in particular, aspects of authority linked with the interpretation of the sacred law, the *shari'a* – are well-worn ground, both within the tradition itself and in scholarship upon it. It is common to outline a sort of flow-chart of authority, from the Qur'an through the Prophet's *hadiths* and *sunna*, and on to further interpretive principles; it is largely the latter "sources" or principles of religious authority (to which we will return) that have prompted the most debate historically, but it should go without saying that the Qur'an, and the mass of information created about what the Prophet said and did, are themselves fodder for interpretive battles. It is important to stress that the Qur'an, as the revelation of God's word, and the Prophet Muhammad, as its conveyor to humanity and as the exemplifier, for the Muslim community, of its message and demands, are of course the ultimate authorities in Islam; but here as well the pedagogical minimum may conceal, in its choices, much of importance.

If the authority of the Qur'an is incontrovertible, and if indeed acceptance of its authority is arguably the definitive marker of being a Muslim, understandings of the nature of the Qur'an are more diverse than is immediately obvious, and herein lies potential for exploration, beyond textual criticism, that has not been extensively undertaken. In the case of the Qur'an, it is explained as the sacred book, in a sacred language, regarded as the embodiment of divine speech; it is thus assimilated to other "sacred books," and even if care is taken to note its oral recitation or calligraphic rendering, its importance and its authority are usually understood to lie in its contents, its "message," its positive statements, its concrete injunctions. Even brief reflection, however, reminds us of the remarkable range of the Qur'anic text, in terms of multiple modalities of discourse and varieties of language (mythic, narrative, ethical, aesthetic, etc.). If we think of the Qur'an and its authority merely in terms of its directive, or even exhortative, language, we miss much of its substance and content and rhetorical power; indeed, considering the frequency of passages cast in the form of questions – questions with an expected answer ("Am I not your

Lord?" and so forth), to be sure, but rhetorically interrogative none-theless – we may find the Qur'an to be much more of an "interactive" text than commonly thought, with its authority resting in part on the affirmative engagement of believers. This, of course, is not how its authority is framed in Muslim discourse; the Qur'an is God's speech, pure and simple, and the notion that the hearer's, or reader's, response could add to it or detract from it is patently blasphemous. The point is, however, that even in its positive, discursive content, the Qur'an conveys religious authority in both direct and indirect ways that belie the simple literalism of textual interpretation.

Yet we must also move beyond the content and "message" of the Qur'an in order to understand fully its authority; in this regard we are even less accustomed to considering those non-discursive aspects of the Qur'an alluded to above. That is, we seldom consider the Qur'an as talisman, charged with sacrality in its physical presence or vocal recitation; we are still less accustomed to thinking of the Qur'an as an aural experience beyond the positive meaning of its words and phrases, or the Qur'an as a visual experience beyond the import of its letters and signs, or the Qur'an as a thing to be touched or even "tasted" (as when the ink with which a Qur'anic passage was recorded was dissolved and drunk for its curative effects); and we are even less accustomed to appreciating the Qur'an from the standpoint of its pauses, its silences, its blank places, or, by the same token, its prolongated sounds, its tones, its ligatures, its enigmatic letter com-binations, and so on. All these modes of experiencing the Qur'an are known to Muslim tradition; their neglect by scholars and students is matched by their neglect among the vocal modernists who insist on the Qur'an as text, on text as words, and on words as univalent sig-nifiers. More to the point, even if other modes of apprehending the Qur'an are acknowledged, they are usually not counted among the ways in which authority is conveyed; the authority of the Qur'an is typically reduced to its explicit content, its words and their meaning. But to understand its authority with such a constraint is to miss much of the way the Qur'an "works" as a source – *the* source – of religious authority.

As a source of authority, the Qur'an is subject to an ongoing tension between understandings of its historical context and assumptions of its timelessness and essentiality; the Qur'an is at once the historically contextualized final revelation and a revelatory prototype outside his-tory. In the first regard, the Qur'an is apprehended in terms of explicit readings of its text, and the contextualization of each *aya* according to the time of its revelation. In the second regard, the Qur'an that is available to believers is understood as a particular externalization of a heavenly "prototype," complete with the reductionist assertion that the entire Qur'an was revealed synthetically at a single time, on the "Night of Power;" the latter assertion conditions, and hence reduces, the multiple Prophetic expressions of particular *ayas* to a single Prophetic reception of the entire, essential, but timeless Qur'an.

In the case of the Prophet Muhammad, he is both a conveyor of the revelation and, through his special status as the exemplar of a life lived in perfect submission to God's will, a source of authority in his own right. As in the case of the Qur'an, his person is subject to similar tensions between his historical context and claims of the extra-historical and essential character of his prophethood. In historical terms, he is lauded as the most perfect Messenger and the external details of his life and his conduct are central to the construction of Muslim juridical, ethical, and behavioral norms. On the other hand, he is celebrated as the metahistorical embodiment of prophethood, inhabiting a spiritual world that regularly intersects with this world but transcends it; notions of this spiritual being, and of the "Muhammadan light" and its creation even prior to Adam, ensure that the essential reality of the Prophet may be accessible outside the historical context in which he served as the model for human conduct.

It is also relevant to the authority of the Prophet that, notions of his extra-historical reality notwithstanding, a doctrinal "bright line" was normally maintained between divinity and human nature, with the Prophet identified as exclusively human, however exalted, without any kind of participation in or partnership with God; this line is key to understanding Muhammad's religious role, utterly different from divine prerogatives. Yet the boundary between the Prophet and the ordinary human is more problematical: on the one hand, he is a pre-eminently imitable figure precisely because of his humanity, and because of his engagement with the full range of human life, including its limitations; on the other hand, his prophethood is endowed with extraordinary cosmic and historical significance in terms of the messenger's role in the community (not to mention those mystical elaborations of the Prophet's essential reality or of his primacy in creation), and the specific "historical" claim that Muhammad was the final Prophet obviously entails stark discouragement, or stronger, against claiming the status or quality of prophethood.

It is no surprise, however, that Muslim tradition developed various ways of flirting with this boundary, and of maintaining the possibility of contact, either with the Prophet himself or with the prophetic vocation. Some of these ways of maintaining access to Prophetic authority – or to a reasonable facsimile thereof – were domesticated, as in the notion of the *mujaddid*, merely a renewer of religion and the community. Some were apocalyptic, as in the role of the future *mahdi*. Some were mystical, as in the role of *walaya* (sainthood), and the long debates over the relationship between sainthood and prophethood. Some in effect endowed the Muslim community with prophetic qualities, as in the ideas of Ibn al-ʿArabi regarding the retention of prophethood in the Islamic community through the faithful transmission of the Qur'an and the Prophet's *hadiths*. And others crossed the line, whether the deviations, recounted by early heresiographies (some of them straw men, perhaps, but some no doubt real), that imputed divine status (as "incarnations") to ʿAli and his descendants or to others, or the claims of revelatory experience that placed the claimants beyond the pale (in doctrinal terms, at least, though their *historical* roots in the Muslim community must be acknowledged), whether self-avowedly (as with the Baha'is) or not (as with the Ahmadis).[4]

Yet even outside such claims (whether extraordinary or domesticated), and without invoking notions of the Prophet's extra-historical existence, the very historicity and concrete humanity of the Prophet already mark a retreat, of sorts, from rigorous scripturalism. On the one hand, to be sure, the Prophet is himself made a fount of scripture-like statements; but at the same time, the Prophet's authority is implicitly independent of what he said, insofar as it is rooted in what he was. The Prophet's authority rests on his selection by God, on his status as the final messenger and bearer of the Qur'an, and on his exemplification of the life of the Muslim (to the point of sinlessness); all these undergird the assumption that his entire being was and is infused with spiritual "grace," or *baraka*, and the desire to gain or remain in contact with the Prophet's *baraka* – or merely the fact of sustained contact with it – is taken as so natural and inevitable that it becomes itself infused with authority.

Perhaps the most obvious mode of contact with the Prophet that becomes a source of authority in and of itself is natural descent from him; it is thus somewhat surprising that such descent does not count for more, in terms of actual authority, than it does. Certainly for Shiʻi Muslims, some descendants of the Prophet became, in principle, supreme arbiters of the content and tone of religious life; for the Shi'a, a host of religious matters, including the interpretation, and in practical if not theoretical terms the substance, of the law, remains open through the inherited lineage of the Prophet. For Sunnis, the obligation to honor and respect Muhammad's descendants does not automatically accord them religious authority, as such; this is true at least juridically, and even in popular venues, where descendants of the Prophet have taken on a wider range of prerogatives that in practical terms amount to special religious authority, it is arguable that other markers of sacrality are more central to their social, political, or religious prerogatives.

Other means of maintaining contact with the Prophet – and with the *baraka* inherent in his being, and with the authority inherent in his *baraka* – include his grave as well as relics and objects handled or worn by him. In the case of relics and objects, they confer a kind of authority on their possessor, through the assumption that they would not be allowed to fall into impious or otherwise improper hands (or merely through the assumption that their survival alone attests to the appropriate sort of reverence and piety on the part of previous possessors); the same holds true of another kind of link with the Prophet that combines a physical connection with a chain of transmission, namely the transmission of a handshake from the Prophet (such lineages of transmission were highly prized and recorded in various accounts). The Prophet may also lend his authority through dreams and visions; stories of receiving, in a vision of the Prophet, some tangible legacy that crosses the visionary boundary into crude physicality reminds us of the inevitable blurring of the distinction between the Prophet's historical life and his living reality. That blurring is also evident in the much more widespread assumption, linking popular and learned environments, of the Prophet's soteriological role, as intercessor for his community on the Day of Judgment.

We may return, finally, to what may be regarded as simply another means of maintaining contact with the Prophet: his sayings (*hadith*) and his conduct (*sunna*). It may appear, at first glance, that *hadiths* offer a mode of contact with the Prophet's authority that is more amenable to explicit determination and fixation in verbal form; examining *hadiths* thus seems to offer a concrete and authoritative means of determining the Prophet's views and eliminating doubts and uncertainty. It must be stressed, however, that in all likelihood the appeal of transmitting *hadiths* did not rest in their susceptibility to being fixed and their usefulness, thereby, for limiting possibilities, but precisely the contrary. The historical growth of Hadith scholarship in itself attests not simply to a positive aspiration to determine what the Prophet said, but to a negative concern about a kind of dilution of Prophetic authority through the indiscriminate creation and circulation of *hadiths*; at the same time, it is quite clear that outside the framework of Hadith scholarship, other Muslim constituencies saw in the acceptance of a wider corpus of *hadiths* than the Prophet could have uttered in his lifetime not a dilution, but an expansion, of the Prophet's authority, befitting his historical and universal significance.

It is also worth considering the implications of a fundamental difference between the *hadiths* and the *sunna* of the Prophet, again in terms of their authority: the verbal character of speech versus the physicality of action. Reports of what the Prophet said and reports of what he did are both reports, and are thus once removed (at the very least) from the Prophet himself, but in the case of actions, the possibility of another medium of transmission comes into play. That is, his speech is reported in the medium of speech, and must always be explicit; his actions, too, may be explicitly described in speech, but his actions may also simply be imitated, without explicit comment. The physical example of the Prophet's conduct may thus be transmitted, in theory, from imitating body to imitating body, without becoming the subject of explicit speech (at least for several generations). Many aspects of external ritual performance, and the specifics of *adab*, are modeled on (in principle) specific actions of the Prophet, some of which are explicitly described, but some of which are not; Muslims performing them do so in the conviction that they are repeating actions archetypally performed by the Prophet, and the imitation of the Prophet in this regard is seldom based upon a consciousness of an explicit verbal (oral or written) description of his exemplifying action. Muslims may thus be shown how to perform certain actions, without reference to an explicit description of the Prophetic prototype; but the conviction that a direct lineage of wordlessly "showing how" goes back to the Prophetic prototype is central to the authority of the demonstration.

In the development of Muslim juridical thought, matters of both ritual acts of worship (*'ibadat*) and acts of interpersonal relations (*mu'amalat*) were initially developed organically on the basis of the example of those who knew the Prophet's example directly; the time at which verbal descriptions intervened is difficult to pinpoint, even when apparently reliable chains of transmission are offered, but it seems

clear that an emphasis upon explicit *hadiths* as the foundation for conduct was secondary, in historical terms, to the organic, "living traditions" that developed in various local contexts, and were intimately
connected with the generations of the companions and the followers.
Those generations served not only as transmitters of the Prophet's sayings, but as preservers of a sort of "muscle memory" of the Prophet's
actions; and in the consciousness of later Muslims, even if less often
in developed juridical theory, imitation of the Prophet's conduct is
indeed precisely that, and is not dependent on verbal descriptions.

Muslims regard themselves, that is, as modeling their behavior on
the Prophet's behavior, not upon words about the Prophet's behavior. This is in part why the *sunna* represents a much more powerful,
pervasive, and definitive concept (and, perhaps, one more flexible as
well) than the Hadith, even with the enormous potential for invention and innovation in connection with words ascribed to the Prophet.
Repeating actions performed by the Prophet, as the Prophet performed
them, is not merely a required or preferred way of fulfilling a duty;
it provides, rather, a means of contact with the body of the Prophet,
and it involves mirroring his substance, as well as his spirit, in one's
own substance. Insofar as the Prophet's body is a source of *baraka*,
imitation of the Prophet's bodily movements conveys divine grace in
its sheer physicality; and while this may be talked about (and is), it
need not be. The *sunna* (and the individual and collective aspiration
to follow it) is thus more than a means of observing a religious obligation; its authority lies as much in the Prophet's bodily example as in
his words, or the words of others about him.

The issue of *hadiths*, and of reports about the Prophet's *sunna*,
brings us back to the issue of transmission; while the historicity of
particular reports is questionable (both within and outside the tradition), the historical consciousness that pervades discussion about the
reports is undeniable, and significant. That historical consciousness
manifests itself not only in modes of investigating the plausibility of
chains of transmission, but in considerations of the moral character
and piety of particular transmitters as well; yet it does not necessarily
follow that the historical verification (or verifiability) of such reports
should be decisive in terms of authority. Those who adopt a restrictive
attitude toward Hadith, for instance, and who limit those acknowledged as authoritative to those verified to their satisfaction, make
the dubious historical assumption that principles of transmission
were in place and in operation at the earliest stages of the Muslim

community, and make the dubious religious assumption that they, today, can better judge the authority of a particular *hadith* than those intervening generations of transmitters, scholars, and ordinary Muslims who preserved a wider range of reports, including those clearly solid, and those less solid, in their earliest links. The rhetoric of "sound" and "unsound" *hadiths*, that is, has always been more important to scholars and jurists than to ordinary Muslims who made do with the cumulative authority of communal tradition.

In the end, the Prophet's authority is not so easily reducible to the *hadiths* pronounced "sound" by Hadith scholars (whether today or in the ninth century C.E.), or even to the broader mass of utterances ascribed to him; beyond those extra-historical dimensions of the Prophet's person, beyond the mechanisms for keeping his person accessible in the here and now, and beyond the specific claims of Sufi transmissions from the Prophet, there is the simple fact that the Prophet was the Prophet before he preached publicly, and still, after his public career began, when he was not speaking publicly, or not speaking at all. While a claim to fill in those silences, in effect, obviously holds great potential for abuse, the claim to limit the Prophet's "output" to explicit utterances that came to be associated with the names of a few transmitters seems equally injurious to a proper appreciation of and respect for the Prophet's mission; while the issue is rarely framed in such terms, the practical effect of filling in the Prophet's silences – the vast body of sayings ascribed to him – is in itself a sign of respect for and veneration of the Prophet, and of commitment to his authority.

* * *

In some venues, in the past and today, the Qur'an and a limited body of Prophetic *hadiths* comprise the sum total of the reliable, authoritative sources regarding God's will; in those venues, moreover, it is not the wider range of understandings and modes of experiencing or making contact with the Qur'an and the Prophet that are invoked, but the much narrower "scriptural" recordings typically privileged in both modernist Muslim discourse and modern scholarship. Modernity, indeed, has increasingly "scripturalized" the bases of religious authority in the Muslim world, increasing the emphasis upon texts and documents and the written word, contrary to traditional patterns.[5] Some contemporary trends bespeak, indeed, a winnowing of recognized modes of authority and of legitimate modes of religious expression.

Given the incomparability of the Qur'an, and the virtual perfection, albeit human, of the Prophet, the insistence that these sources of authority can be enhanced only through interpretation (and not augmented in actual substance) is perhaps understandable; in the active and discursive context of the *shari'a*, language is inevitably circumscribed, requiring any "adjustment" of the sacred law to be framed as an interpretation based on the Qur'an and the Prophet's life. If we return to our flow-chart of authority, after the powerhouses of the Qur'an and the Prophet, we come to two interpretive principles that are treated to some extent as actual sources of, or methods of achieving, authoritative knowledge of the sacred law: first consensus (*ijma'*), in theory the consensus of the Muslim community at large, in practice that of the learned; and second, the principle of analogical reasoning, whether in and of itself or as exercised by an individual interpreter (*ijtihad*).

It is not surprising that the latter two principles have been, and remain, the focus of enormous controversy and contention. On the one hand, consensus embodies the authority of communal experience, and the centrality of the *umma* in Muslim thought – as the arena both for religious action and for soteriology, through the conviction that the *umma* is a salvific community (*firqa najiya*) – ensured consensus a pivotal place in religious interpretation; *ijtihad*, similarly, embodies the religiously laudable element of individual striving and personal effort. On the other hand, the force of consensus was heavily restricted by some juridical schools, and, in so far as it came to be regarded by some as "cover" for rendering extra-Islamic practices licit, it has remained a target of Muslim reformers intent upon purifying Islam and Muslims; *ijtihad*, meanwhile, was nearly always suspect as a cover for individual opinion, pure and simple (hence its allowance only as a last resort, and the well-known claims of the closing of the "gate of *ijtihad*"), until it was revived and championed, by reformers, as a last resort against the supposed stagnation of a Muslim world that had come to be permeated by too much consensus. Indeed, modernist/reformist defenders of *ijtihad* typically omit consensus altogether from the foundations of the *shari'a*, going straight from the Qur'an and Prophetic *hadiths*, in the "flow-chart" of authority, to *ijtihad* (and doing so on the authority of a specific *hadith*).

In the rhetoric of the reformists – which has been uncritically adopted in much scholarship and public discourse about modernization and reform in the Muslim world – what takes the place of consensus, in effect, is *taqlid*, a term used always pejoratively by the reformists, to refer to the blind following or parroting of received tradition, and to an avoidance of direct engagement with the *real* sources of the law. The term *taqlid* had an entirely respectable, non-pejorative meaning in traditional jurisprudence, referring to a loyal and respectful deference to authoritative scholars of the past, or more specifically to a mode of juridical engagement within a single juridical school; *taqlid* meant adherence to the principles and conclusions of one's predecessors in a particular school.[6] From the reformist perspective, the juridical schools had become hidebound servants of the status quo, and their reasoning was as stagnant as their training; *taqlid* connotes, in the reformist critique, not only blind adherence to precedent, but a neglect of the "real" authoritative sources (the Qur'an and *hadiths*) in favor of engaging only with the tradition's literary products, above all the commentaries and summaries that were typically specific to one school and were in any case several steps removed from the fundamental sources. The authority conferred by long education and training is likewise devalued in reformist rhetoric; in effect, the transmissional certificates and lineages prized historically as attestations to juridical authority become simply badges of bondage to *taqlid*.

Yet while reformist rhetoric highlights the potential for stagnation and inflexibility in *taqlid*, the real intent of the reformist program is to bypass the juridical schools altogether, and to go back even further, to the age of the "predecessors" (*salaf*) who preceded the emergence of the juridical schools. The assumption that the "predecessors" were unanimous in their views, and that an end-run around the contentious juridical schools will restore harmony and unity in the Muslim world, is historically unsustainable, but the construction of an idealized golden age is not unusual; what is ironic in this particular construction is the unspoken appeal to *ijma'*, to the "consensus" of the *salaf*.

If consensus is ignored or rejected by the Salafists, and *taqlid* is reinterpreted from a thoroughly hostile perspective, *ijtihad* too has been recast; from their disregard for the traditional juridical schools, from their attacks on the educational foundations of juridical training, and from their anti-*taqlid* rhetoric, it is clear that the *ijtihad* championed by the Salafists is not their fathers' *ijtihad*, but something quite new. Traditional concerns about potential abuses under the guise of *ijtihad*, entailing the elevation of pure opinion and innovation to authoritative status, are essentially ignored by the Salafists. The new *ijtihad* also increasingly stakes a claim on universality – a claim at present enhanced even further by global communications – in opposition to the local particularism represented by the traditional juridical schools and the principles of *taqlid* and consensus (which in practical terms occurred on a relatively local scale). In addition, the contemporary proponents of expanded *ijtihad* betray their essentially modern outlook by insisting on the rationality and "scientific" character both of the sources of authority underlying *ijtihad*, and the process of *ijtihad* itself (hence the appeal to those with modern scientific, technical, and engineering educations). As a result, indeed, the new *ijtihad* has been invested with a kind of absolute value in its own right; classical notions of *ijtihad* were averse to claims of certainty, with emphasis placed upon process and the exertion of informed effort, based on all available sources, to discover a particular applicable rule of law, but the new *ijtihad* has invested the opinions of a few of its leading proponents with real-life impact (in uniformity of dress, for instance) far beyond that ever achieved through *taqlid*. Ironically, then, the reformists' focus on individual effort has in fact subordinated individual interpretation, no longer to the diffuse traditions of particular schools, but to the interpretive programs and pronouncements of a few leading spokesmen of the Salafist agenda.

In any event, both historically and today, these two subsidiary sources, or principles, of religious authority – consensus and *ijtihad* – are intimately related. Classical theory holds that the combined *ijtihad* of the whole *umma* is what leads, in effect, to consensus, but consensus may be thought of as a check on unlimited *ijtihad*, and *ijtihad* as a remedy to a surfeit of consensus. Muslim juridical discussion entertained the possibility of other, subsidiary sources of the *shari'a*, such as the law of earlier prophets, the opinions of the companions of the Prophet, or the simple "preference" of certain jurists; still other principles of interpretation or decision, such as the consideration of public welfare or the general good, were discussed as well, but these tended to be subsumed within the broader categories of consensus and *ijtihad*. While not necessarily or traditionally opposed in principle or application, these two notions help delineate important, and contending, trends in Muslim attitudes toward religious authority that are particularly significant today.

One further distinction between the principles underlying consensus and those underlying *ijtihad* is that the latter must be, by definition, explicit, while consensus may be, in some cases, inferred from non-explicit, and non-verbal, circumstances. In terms of both its process and its result, *ijtihad* reflects conscious effort and an explicitly articulated conclusion. By contrast, juridical discussion regarding consensus has left open the possibility, at least, that it may be tacit; that is, it may be possible to infer the consensus of the *umma* in some circumstances even if it is not expressly articulated or consciously formulated. The Hanafis, for instance, allowed the fact of communal behavior to be construed as validation of a particular practice even without explicit communal pronouncement. That is, consensus could be invoked with regard to a particular practice if the community simply performs it; the community does not have to state explicitly and communally that it is legitimate.

Such flexibility in juridical interpretation regarding the substance of actual life should remind us again of the potential authority of silence; if, as noted, the Prophet's silences served as venues for projections of authoritative transmission, we find a starker parallel in the juridical context, in the frequent conclusion that simply to perform some action classed (by some) as sinful is less harmful than to declare explicitly that that action is not sinful. Not unexpectedly, Muslims have differed, historically, over the authority of silence; but here as well, in the juridical context, the notion of tacit consensus parallels the wordless bodily transmission of Prophetic conduct, noted above.

There is, finally, yet another aspect, more significant, I believe, regarding the controversy over consensus and *ijtihad*: the former is historically cumulative, while the latter is, by definition, historically discrete. Through consensus, tradition builds upon tradition, with a guaranteed continuity both socially and intellectually; indeed, consensus ensures a bond between the social locus of religious action and the intellectual foundations of religious action. To be sure, its very cumulative character – and its continuity – make it cumbersome and slow to respond to external circumstances, and no doubt limits the range of responses; it is precisely the cumulative character of consensus that has been targeted by the modernist and reformist critics who condemn *taqlid*. *Ijtihad*, by contrast, may bypass decades or centuries of communal consensus and laboriously worked-out opinion; this is at once the source of its flexibility, the root of its appeal to those who seek change but are constrained by the injunctions against harmful innovation, and the root of its potential to sanction minority views and even extremism.

The latter potential is further strengthened by the Salafist suspicion of traditional juridical training and by the "populist" appeal to each believer's ability to engage the scriptural sources of authority directly; if traditional measures of authority are no longer regarded as sufficient to interpret the *shari'a*, or even to "authorize" or certify the training of those who will exercise *ijtihad*, and if traditional educational achievement is discounted as well, what will serve as a new signifier of authority to interpret the law? Here the modernist/reformist repertoire is again disturbingly weak, compared with the range of signifiers for traditional jurisprudence, with its cumulative historical foundations; Salafist movements may be building up a framework of educational certification (becoming in effect a separate juridical school, in which a neo-*taqlid* may not be far behind), but in the meantime, piety, charisma, political activism, and martyrdom seem to be the chief markers of authoritative interpretation.

Perhaps the clearest indication, indeed, of the contested territory represented by consensus and *ijtihad* may be found in the way their respective proponents in effect trade places, with regard to those two other sources of authority, the Qur'an and the Prophet, when it comes to history; it is with regard to history, and that relationship between the authoritative past and the present, as noted above, that these two categories of sources or foundations of religious authority – the primary sources, the Qur'an and the Prophet, on the one hand, and the subsidiary foundations, consensus and *ijtihad*, on the other – differ most starkly, and inversely. In the case of the Qur'an and the Prophet, it is the modernists, the rigorists, the fundamentalists, who appeal to discrete historicity, grounding (and limiting) their understanding to the literal text, and to the single historical span in which the Prophet revealed and exemplified the Qur'anic message; it is then the mystics and traditionalists who find solace in the expanded possibilities afforded by the respective prototypes of the holy book and prophethood. In the case of consensus and *ijtihad*, conversely, history – and here the cumulative history of the community – is essentially rejected by the rigorists, while traditionalists cling to it.

In their hostility to the traditional incorporation of practices and beliefs deemed, by their critics, to be of non-Islamic origin (above all the veneration of saints and shrines); in their appeal to the "original," foundational, scriptural sources of revelation and its interpretation, and their challenge to and critique of accumulated tradition; in their insistence that even untrained believers could and should read the scriptural sources of authority and interpret them directly; in their attacks on existing institutionalized structures of power and authority, both political and religious; and even in their links to new forms of economic activity, the Salafi movements have close historical parallels with the Protestant critiques of Catholic tradition and institutions. They warrant the label "fundamentalist" (in the sense entailed by that term's original Protestant Christian context), and as with other fundamentalisms, their engagement with "modernity" entails a rejection of tradition, a willingness thereby to cast history aside, and a reductionist approach to religious authority.[7] It is not merely the cumulative wisdom of the community that is thus jettisoned in the name of modernity; the very authority of communal experience in itself is discarded as well.

* * *

Among the prominent targets of Salafist/modernist movements, Sufism is arguably the most important in the Muslim world historically. Sufism, too, is far from a single phenomenon susceptible to essentialist definitions, but one characteristic shared among most communities to which the label "Sufi" applies is a distinctively expansive approach to religious authority. It is, indeed, in the context of the personal and public experience of Sufism that we find the most remarkable range of significations of authority, and the most dramatic extensions of the reach of religious authority into different social venues.

The expanded possibilities come not only through the interiorization, and more open understanding, of the "standard" sources, but from expanded attentiveness to the authority of personal experience as well. To say "personal," however, is not to say "idiosyncratic;" rather, the Sufi discourse of religious authority comprises not only the social and devotional and ethical, but the contemplative and visionary as well, and Sufism is only atypically averse to the authority of communal experience that undergirds juridical authority. Indeed, Sufi experience is every bit as subject to routinization in the social environment – with the authority of its method and prescriptions vouched for by cumulative tradition and by the "test" of replicability – as the juridical paradigm. Despite the frequent depiction of Sufis as weak on book learning and perennially at odds with the learned upholders of juridical authority, such Sufis are more the exception than the rule, in historical terms, and Sufis typically operate on the same foundations and methods of authority as the *'ulama* (often they *are* the *'ulama* and vice versa).

Both interiorization and the application of personal experience, then, are put to work in expanding and deepening those sources of authority. Sufi approaches to the Qur'an typically are open to non-literal readings and assumptions of hidden spiritual meanings that reveal themselves hierarchically according to individual spiritual attainment; the Prophet is understood as the exemplar of the Sufi path, both in his sayings and in his conduct, but also in his trans-historical reality, and in the possibility of personal experience thereof; consensus is echoed in the collective rehearsals of the wisdom of past masters, and in accounts of the important role accorded in some contexts to the entire Sufi congregation in the spiritual advancement of each individual; and some Sufis speak of particular shaykhs as entitled to exercise *ijtihad*, and as thus able to alter aspects of the path to suit the needs of the age or of the community.

While Sufi understandings of God and of the nature of the human relationship with the divine are typically highlighted in distinguishing Sufism from a "normative" Islam, it is arguably in connection with the authority of the Prophet that Sufism most thoroughly deepens and interiorizes – or, from the perspective of its critics, departs from – the confines of the ordinary ritual, ethical, and public framework of Muslim life. Other Muslim religious currents maintain access to the Prophet outside the juridical constructions of the Prophet's legacies, but the Sufi experience of the Prophet lays claim to multiple layers of religious meaning in the public aspects of his prophetic career, and to the proper "accessing" of a body of his sayings (*hadith qudsi*) that differ in kind from his juridically valorized pronouncements; it also claims, as both imitable and metaphorical truths, elements of the Prophet's life that are left largely blank in those juridical constructions (what he taught Abu Bakr in the cave, for instance, or what he experienced during the *mi'raj*).

In addition to the claim to contact with and access to the living reality of the Prophet, Sufism also claims contact with a rich spirit-world that is imagined in neatly classified and hierarchical terms in Sufi literature and, we may surmise, Sufi experience, but is understood more broadly, in the public sphere beyond the narrower circles of committed Sufi aspirants, as a source of immediate and undeniable religious authority. In this way, too, Sufism has mediated between the personal and the public, the individual and the communal, and has done so perhaps more effectively, in historical terms, than the narrower juridical enterprise. The religiously authoritative character of dreams and visionary experiences, for example, was not dependent upon Sufism, but Sufism filled the unseen world – or, more properly, identified and categorized the experiences of the unseen world – for a public much broader than the specific classical structures of Sufi life. It performed the same function, moreover, for much of the "seen" world, the ordinary world, which Sufism saw with a distinctive set of religious insights and symbolic structures, and these, too, it has lent to a broader public.

If, in connection with the Qur'an and the juridical context, we tend to link authority with texts (i.e. the texts of revelation and of injunctions and laws), the case of the Prophet reminds us of authority linked with persons, and here too Sufism readily invests authority along the Prophetic example. It is on the model of the Prophet that the Sufi saint becomes a new source of authority in his own right, in accord with the famous dictum that the master's role in his local community is equivalent to the Prophet's role in the universal community. The Prophetic paradigm extends further, indeed, as the modes of asserting and transmitting authority radiate into broader social venues. The Sufi master too, like the Prophet, becomes an important focus of natural descent, transmitting the authority encrypted in the person, in bodily form; and if "blood" is evoked in the transmission of authority in hereditary frameworks, other bodily fluids are envisioned as the medium of transmission in other contexts, as in the imagery of a master suckling the disciple at his breast, or spitting his saliva into the disciple's mouth, or of a disciple imbibing the sweat of a master or of multiple masters. Yet such imagery of initiation, of the transmission and marking of authority, regularly escapes the borders of "Sufism" as such, as the personally embodied (and Prophetically modeled) authority of the Sufi master is projected into whole communities that come to be regarded and defined as his descendants, for example, or into a lineage of craftsmen that honors him as a transmitter of their skills, or into the maker of amulets who links a prayer or sacred text with him, or, most pervasively, into his shrine.

Medieval Sufism displayed a wide range of principles whereby authority was asserted, ranging from the one that became paradigmatic, the *silsila* or "chain of transmission," to natural heredity, the possession of various insignia, direct inspiration by the Prophet or by Khidr, the claimed ability to ensure quick attainment of spiritual goals, or the intercessory power of a group's founder; yet another mode of claiming authority, on a communal basis, involved stressing a distinctive social profile, whether through the provision of "social services" or through claims of strict adherence to the *shari'a* in the midst of widespread neglect of the sacred law. Many of these modes of asserting authority were claimed in the context of communal rivalries and disputes that heightened the intensity of the rhetoric through which different visions of authority were asserted, ensuring that some modes or sources of authority would be stressed precisely as alternatives to those advanced by other groups. Assertions of authority inevitably had concrete social implications, and claims of a "founding" saint's special status occasionally developed on a grander social scale, as in the case of Sufi masters who claimed, or had claimed for them, the status of the *mahdi*. It was in the same era, not surprisingly, that we find considerable overlap among the religious, social, and political claims of Sufi masters and rulers. Whether claims of authority thus led to contestations of social and political power or to flagrant challenges to social order and conventions, the variety of modes of asserting authority (and their social ramifications) evidenced in medieval Sufi communities reminds us that religious authority, more broadly, should be approached not in static terms, but as part of an ongoing rhetorical dialectic in which a certain formulation of authority inevitably evokes a counter-formulation, often precisely among those inclined to poke a stick in the eye of authority – or, in Bruce Lincoln's terms, to "corrode" authority.[8] From this perspective, perhaps the real "authority" at work is the creative intellectual and religious work of challenge and reformulation, adaptation and dynamic adjustment; and this potential is perhaps the most important thing that is lost in a scripturally rigorist environment.

* * *

It would be fundamentally misleading to suggest that the wide range of sources and signifiers of authority evoked in Sufism, or more broadly in pre-modern Islam, somehow dilutes the force, or the centrality, of the Qur'an and the Prophet; while our understanding of both these sources of authority, and the channels for "accessing" them, requires refinement and expansion, the assumption that authority in Islam rests ultimately on the speech of God as recorded in the Qur'an, as "delivered" by the Prophet, and as refracted in his life, is largely uncontested among Muslims. That assumption has also been central to debates, historically and at present, over the extent, and foundation, of permissible interpretation; yet there is far more recognition and acceptance, in the historical experience of the Muslim community, of other venues for the expression, transmission, and interpretation of religious authority than is often acknowledged, and in any case an abhorrence of symbols and signifiers of authority without obvious roots in the textual sources is an aberration in historical terms.

Toward the end of the eleventh century, the eminent scholar Abu Hamid al-Ghazali included the following comments in one of his many works, alluding to debates in his time over the sources and nature of religious authority, and its implications for faith and for what it meant to be a Muslim:

> Among the most extreme and extravagant of men are a group of scholastic theologians who dismiss the Muslim common people as unbelievers and claim that whoever does not know scholastic theology in the form they recognize and does not know the prescriptions of the Holy Law according to the proofs which they have adduced is an unbeliever.
>
> These people have constricted the vast mercy of God to His servants and made paradise the preserve ... of a small clique of theologians. They have disregarded what is handed down by the *sunna*, for it is clear that in the time of the Prophet ... and in the time of the companions of the Prophet ... the Islam of whole groups of rude Arabs was recognized, though they were busy worshipping idols. They did not concern themselves with the science of analogical proof and would have understood nothing of it if they had.
>
> Whoever claims that theology, abstract proofs, and systematic classification are the foundation of belief is an innovator.
>
> Rather is belief a light which God bestows on the hearts of His creatures as the gift and bounty from Him, sometimes through an explainable conviction from within, sometimes because of a dream in sleep, sometimes by seeing the state of bliss of a pious man and the transmission of his light through association and conversation with him, sometimes through one's own state of bliss.[9]

Though al-Ghazali had his own specific targets in mind, and his own notions of the "Muslim common people" whose faith and practice he sought to defend, we may not be far from the mark in suggesting that the people of Taraz, who found solace and perhaps religious inspiration in the authority of Hamdullah's post-ghost, were the sort of Muslims he was referring to. Similarly, we may reasonably apply his critiques, of those who would dismiss the faith of such Muslims and constrict the channels for seeking religious authority, to the Salafism of our time; from the Salafist outlook, after all, the only lesson to be drawn from the post-ghost story would be the decadence, imperfect Islamization, or baseless superstition of the community described in it.

The times of al-Ghazali and of medieval Taraz are long past, of course, and it is difficult to judge what future generations will make of the increasing appeal of the Salafist agenda in the last century and its implications for the Muslim understanding of religious authority. Will they wonder at the impoverishment of religious discourse, as some Muslims rejected nearly fourteen centuries' worth of cumulative experience and religious expression in favor of a "return" to a limited corpus of authoritative scripture, all (or largely) in the name of responding to "modernity" and the threat of the West? Will they lament the "democratization" of religious interpretation, as even the untrained and unthoughtful were invited to enter the fray of scriptural interpretation, and long for a return to standards and the authority endowed by rigorous education and engagement with tradition? Will they applaud the initial steps toward a purification of the faith and the restoration of proper adherence to genuine religious authority? Will the Salafist appeal be explained as an artifact of political tensions that will inevitably have shifted? Will it have coalesced as yet another sectarian current with local or regional prominence?

Whichever direction prevails, and however averse scholars may be to involvement in the debates themselves, we may be certain of the pedagogical usefulness, at least in tactical terms, of "descripturalizing" the roots of authority in Islam, as a counter to the subtle effects of modernist Muslim discourse upon scholarship (including even historical scholarship) on the Muslim world. Looking forward, the situation today is undoubtedly relevant to understanding the future of Muslim approaches to religious authority, which we cannot now know; yet looking backward, it also stands at the end of a long historical process, and inasmuch as it sometimes casts its shadows across Muslim history in ways that hinder a better understanding of the historical trajectories of the Muslim world, suspending the scripturalist vision, and revisiting a world marked by a richer array of possibilities for locating Muslim religious authority, may serve to clarify the scenery both behind us and in front of us.

3

BELIEF

R. Kevin Jaques

METHOD AND THE CONCEPT OF "BELIEF" IN ISLAMIC STUDIES

Discussions of method and theory have been rare in Islamic Studies. In a field dominated by philologists and historians, there has been a tendency toward *doing* and away from discussing *how* we do what we do.[1] Most frequently, methodologies are implied by the study itself; and while these apparent methods of research and interpretation can be very influential, it is usually up to the reader to unearth the methods and to understand how they might be useful in his or her own approaches to the field.[2] It is true that anthropology has become increasingly important in the study of Islamic phenomena, but even here, there has been little direct discussion of method as it applies specifically to the Muslim world. Clifford Geertz has been the most explicit in this regard, and his discussions of practical methods such as "thick description" have become influential across the academy, although probably more so than among scholars of Islam specifically.[3]

George Makdisi, the late historian of Islamic law, has also been influential in promoting what some characterize as a "formalist" method of reading Islamic texts. Unlike social historians, who view economic motives as the lens through which historical documents should be read, Makdisi's formalism approaches texts as they are and trusts what medieval and classical Muslim scholars say, to the extent that they are conscious of the cultural, religious, economic, and political factors that influence their presentations of Islamic history and institutions. Because Makdisi's formalism emphasizes understanding what Muslims are trying to convey in their works, Makdisi places great stress on understanding the texts themselves by focusing on sentence structure, lexicography, and on interpreting the cultural grammars by which scholars attempted to communicate meaning to their students and assumed readers.[4]

Makdisi, like most scholars of Islamic Studies, is not explicit about his method in print, but emphasized it to his students in rigorous and sometimes painfully detailed seminars.[5] The central idea that underpins Makdisi's method is the necessity of translating texts from their original languages into the language in which the scholar will publish. Makdisi argued that fluency in the original language was not enough because the writer must not just understand what the text means, but must also be able clearly to convey those meanings in the language of his or her audience. Doing so is not only a process of translation but also of painstaking interpretation so that the nuances of the original argument are made evident for the reader. This requires a careful and often agonizing process of working through the original text, looking at the relationship between words, sentences, and sections of the work as well as how the text relates to other works written in the same period, and finally across expanses of historical time.

Makdisi's method implies that describing any concept, as it occurs in another language, culture, religious tradition, or historical period requires rigorously mapping the meanings of the terms that are used to refer to that concept and then plotting variations in the meanings of those terms. It then requires comparing the terms used to demarcate the concept in the original language to analogous terms found in the secondary interpretive language of the analyst. One of the criticisms of Makdisi's work, however, is that he is much less careful when selecting terms in English to refer to the concepts that he wants to convey from the original Arabic. His *Rise of Colleges*, for instance, is replete with terms such as "diplomas," "college," "graduate students," and "professors," many of which are used without explanation or qualification, giving the impression of a "one-to-one" relationship between the original concept described in medieval Arabic and the modern English term he argues signifies the concept.[6]

Makdisi is not alone in using English terms to denote often complex concepts in Islamic thought that have no fixed or single equivalent in English and Arabic (or Urdu, Persian, Turkish, Indonesian, or any other Islamic language). A variety of Arabic words laden with symbolic importance are frequently given meaning in English by being associated with ill-considered and often poorly defined terms.

"Belief" is one such term.

What is "belief" and does it exist in Islamic thought? On the surface, this seems an absurd question. Of course Muslims "believe," of course Muslims possess "belief" about the nature of God, prophecy, and a whole host of other religious, theological, and ritual issues. But what does it mean to say Muslims "believe," especially when the English term "belief" connotes a concept that scholars of religion have been rather hard-pressed to define or "map" in the first place?

To say "Muslims 'believe'" is a comparative statement because it assumes that what one means by the term "belief" has an analogous meaning in Islamic thought or among Muslims who have and continue to live in widely different social and cultural locations.

While it is not the purpose of this essay to challenge the idea that "belief" (as a category of phenomena) exists in Islamic thought or among Muslims, I do want to clarify its application in Islamic Studies as it has been used by scholars over the last 200 years. I will argue that although "belief" has remained a persistent term for referring to concepts in the Islamic tradition, the meanings scholars attach to the term have been unclear and have changed over time so that use of the term has lost most, if not all, of its explanatory value.

MAPPING THE CONTOURS OF THE CONCEPTS DENOTED BY THE ENGLISH TERM "BELIEF"

When we use the terms "belief" and "believe" in modern English, we refer to a complex of ideas, religious and non-religious in nature, that have widely differing meanings and connotations. The term "belief," for instance, can refer to an authoritative doctrine as it is articulated by a religious group or community. "Belief" can also refer to an individual's interior adherence to an idea that is based on some kind of reasoned mental process. "A belief," in the sense of "doctrine," is generally assumed to be a concept that is developed over time and arrived at as a matter of group consensus among religious authorities. "Doctrinal belief" is, therefore, exterior to the individual in that it is publicly stated and debated and can be considered analogous with the term "orthodoxy." An "interior belief" may or may not reflect a "doctrinal belief" but it is generally considered to be driven by a reasoned and deliberate intellectual process whereby the various aspects of the proposition under consideration are weighed and valued. While a "doctrinal belief" is generally thought to be beyond doubt (as an "orthodox belief" it is by definition "right") there is still an inference in the use of the term that suggests that the process by which the doctrine was derived is not closed. "Doctrinal belief" is, therefore, a "right" idea that is subject to further clarification and inquiry. "Interior belief," likewise, has this attribute, and indeed may be fraught with doubts of all kinds.[7] What makes an "interior belief" powerful is that whether it is attendant with doubts or not, it motivates people to action so that they "live" their beliefs, or "wear their hearts on their sleeves." In fact, actions often serve to reinforce interior beliefs in that they create structure and give purpose in the face of concerns over the validity of the person's assumptions.[8]

"To believe" is the verbal form of the noun "belief," and connotes in phenomenological terms, "the act" of belief. Believing is therefore to place a proposition under intellectual scrutiny and to arrive at a conclusion that motivates actions.

"Belief" and "to believe" are often, and incorrectly, treated as synonyms for "faith" and "to have faith." There are, in fact, subtle differences between the terms, which often go unstated by scholars and religious people alike. "Faith," like "belief," can refer to a number of different concepts; a doctrine, an interior adherence, and a religious tradition. It is, for instance, not uncommon for people to speak of a "faith statement" that expresses a creed or doctrine. But a faith statement is usually different from "a belief" (as an orthodox doctrine) in that a faith statement is a proclamation of belief and not the belief itself. Likewise, interior "faith" is generally thought to be an interior adherence to an idea that, unlike belief, is not subject to doubt. While it is the *result* of an intellectual process (indeed, to assume that any human does not process all stimuli through some form of rational consideration is belittling to religious people everywhere), it is perceived to be firmer than belief; it is a concrete adherence to – an acclimation of – the reality of the situation. Also, while a religious tradition can be referred to as "a belief" or a "system of belief" it is more common to see phrases such as "the Christian faith" or "the Muslim faith" used by people who seek to impose on religious systems concretized and unalterable systems of doctrine that are monolithic in their acceptance. Finally, one can use "faith" to indicate a bond of loyalty, as in "I will keep faith with you" or "I will be faithful to you." This is analogous with the Old English use of "belief" as "love" or "fidelity" to a liege lord, a meaning almost completely lost in modern usages of the term "belief."

The antonym of "belief" or "to believe" is not as clear, largely because the concept, while allowing for doubt, does not allow for the absence of some kind of interior adherence. By this I mean that most religious usages of the antonym of "belief" refer to "unbelief," or "lack of belief," or "wrong belief," but not the complete absence of any "belief." The antonym of faith can be "doubt," or in stronger terms "betrayal" or even "apostasy." Because doubt figures in the landscape of "belief," there seems to be a moment when doubts in the inner-dialogue over the truth of a position outweigh the evidence for its actuality and the "belief" becomes "unbelief." In this sense, "rejection" might be considered an antonym for "belief," but in many instances this is not thought of as strongly as the rejection of "faith." One might say "I used to believe but now I don't," but that does not mean necessarily that one has moved outside a religious tradition. It simply means that one arrived at a new set of "beliefs" that do not necessarily mean the rejection of a whole set of religious ideals or doctrines. On the contrary, if one said "I used to have faith but now I don't," this would generally be construed to indicate the complete rejection of a whole network of ideals and doctrines that puts the speaker "outside the bounds" of the religious community that holds those conceptions as "faith." "Belief," therefore, is less totalizing than "faith," and its antonyms less extreme. Also, because "faith" is related to concrete conceptions of loyalty to truth and reality, one can only have one "faith." In other words, since "faith" is related to concrete conceptions of loyalty to a truth, there can only be one "true faith," and the absence of it means that no other "faith" is possible since one cannot logically adhere or be loyal to mutually opposing truths.[9]

"Belief," however, does not have such totalizing features. One has many "beliefs," some more important than others; if one "no longer believes" it can connote the rejection of a definition of truth, but it does not mean that the individual "believes" nothing. Because "belief" (in the sense of "believing") is conceived of as a continual process, even if one stops "believing" in one thing it in no sense means that the person "believes" in nothing. Hence, one cannot be said to "lose one's 'beliefs'" in the same sense that one may "lose one's 'faith.'" "Beliefs" can be wrong, but to be human is to "believe." There is, therefore, no real antonym for "belief," if the term is not specified by use with a qualifier. One may be an "unbeliever" but this simply means that he or she no longer "believes" in what he or she originally did, and now "believes" in something else. The mental process of "belief" never stops because it is always shifting and qualifying.

We therefore arrive at a detailed contemporary description of the concepts denoted by the English term "belief." Thus, when we use the term "belief" we refer to phenomena on two levels:

(1) Macro level: at this level, "belief" refers to a complex of phenomena that connote
   (i) a network of ideas that are conceived of as representing a religious tradition in some abstract sense
   (ii) an "orthodox" doctrine arrived at through a process of deliberation among religious elites.
(2) Micro level: at this level "belief" denotes
   (i) strongly held interior attitudes that are arrived at through a reasoned intellectual process that
   (ii) results in actions
   (iii) are deeply held conceptions of truth that, nevertheless, leave room for doubt(s), which prompt reconsideration, and
   (iv) is, therefore, a process of mental deliberation that never ceases but continues due to the presence of doubt and the resulting reconsideration.

While "faith" is often taken as a synonym for "belief," as we have seen, it includes significant differences within an overarching context of similarity. It too, occurs on two levels:

(3) Macro level: "faith" can
   (i) refer to a religious tradition when it is thought to have clear-cut boundaries of orthodoxy and orthopraxy.
(4) Micro level: while both "belief" and "faith" involve an internal adherence to an idea, "faith" is not thought of as an internal mental *process* of deliberation, but as
   (i) a static conception of truth that does not change
   (ii) that is beyond doubt
   (iii) is a totalizing understanding in which one either possesses it or does not. Finally,
   (iv) "faith" can be used to indicate "loyalty" to a concept, institution, person, or deity that is total and uncompromising.

Whether "faith" functions in reality in such absolute terms is, of course, unlikely. What concerns us here, however, is not whether a human can ever really live without some level of doubt or fear but that religious people construe "faith" in such terms when we use it to refer to a set of phenomenal concepts.

TRANSLATION AND COMPARISON OF THE CONCEPTS DENOTED BY THE TERM "BELIEF"

Makdisi's formalist approach assumes that translation is interpretation. This idea is not new and has become a truism in academic writing for most of the latter half of the twentieth century.[10] Interpretation has many dimensions that require the translator to attempt to communicate his or her understanding(s) of the meaning(s) of the original text by using words and phrases in another language that in most cases do not have an exact equivalency to the meaning(s) of the words or phrases in the original. It is therefore a comparative enterprise that is rarely treated as such.

Comparison is fraught, however, with a variety of pitfalls that are based on unstated assumptions or academic traditions that are rarely explicitly stated by the translator. Although there are a number of reasons for this situation, including simple inattention to detail, the field of Islamic Studies has developed professional and institutional pressures that have pushed scholars into talking about ideas like "belief" in uniform and uncritical ways.

As Clifford Geertz points out, the professional requirements of the academy for tenure and promotion force scholars to take positions and to write in such a way that will allow them to get critical and popular acclaim for their work.[11] Furthermore, according to Hans-Georg Gadamer, the effort to find professional acceptance creates intellectual orthodoxies that are no less profound than those commonly found in religious traditions. In academic studies of religion and Islamic Studies (as discussed above), it has become orthodox to disparage methodological discussions or to make explicit what one assumes about the nature of one's objects of study. This has led to the homogenization of the way scholars talk about particular concepts and about comparative categories that appear to cut across religious traditions.[12]

There is, however, a need for explicitness in our assumptions and methods of comparison, particularly in the translation of religious texts and in discussions of religious concepts. By using specific words or terms as "place holders" for concepts as they occur in other languages or in religious traditions and doing so consistently because of the academic orthodoxies that emerge around their use, we create meanings and impart impressions that might not have originally existed.[13]

MONOTHETIC COMPARISON AND "BELIEF" AS
A COMPARATIVE CONCEPT IN ISLAMIC STUDIES

The use of the term "belief" in Islamic Studies is indicative of the academic orthodoxy described above. "Belief" is used by scholars in a variety of examinations of Muslim thought and practice with little attempt to describe what is meant by the term in English or how closely it approximates to the use of analogous terms among Muslims. Most scholars seem to apply monothetic modes of comparison (if any method is used at all) to a complex of concepts that they categorize with the term "belief" when describing "similar" concepts in the Muslim tradition.

All comparison assumes looking at two or more phenomena and breaking each down into constituent parts. It assumes a process of listing these parts and then comparing lists, sorting for similarities and differences. Monothetic comparison then assumes that the differences are filtered out and if a sufficient number of similarities exist one can say that there is something "fundamental" to the phenomena under consideration that make them "virtually the same." It also suggests, according to J. Z. Smith in his *Drudgery Divine*, that the apparent overarching similarity speaks to something "essential" to the very nature of the phenomenon under consideration. It also assumes that the phenomenon is unique or totally unlike any other thing and, therefore, fundamental to all humans at all times.[14]

The early History of Religions approach as formulated by scholars such as Rudolph Otto and Mircea Eliade, as well as anthropologists of religion such as Emile Durkheim, assumed that there were essential and universal religious phenomena that were fundamental to the human condition. Although such explicit essentialisms have been largely discredited by scholars of religion since the latter half of the twentieth century[15] many scholars continue implicitly to assume monothetic comparative methods when describing or referring to the concept of "belief" as it occurs in the Qur'an and, more generally, in Muslim thought and practice.

For instance, in her discussion of the term "belief" in the Qur'an, Camilla Adang implies that it is synonymous (i.e. the same as) the Arabic term *iman*, which she defines as a "fundamental attitude to the divine being, to the prophethood of Muhammad and to the message of the Qur'an."[16] For Adang, there is a one-to-one relationship between "belief" and *iman* that, when distilled of conceptual difference, can be essentially defined as "fundamental attitudes" toward the divine and to those who communicate revelations in the form of texts. Throughout the article, Adang interchanges "belief" with *iman*, as well as "believer" with *mu'min*, treating them as synonyms referring to the same concepts. Adang does provide additional specification for the concept of "belief" in the Qur'an, listing gratitude, awe, repentance, and submission; treating co-religionists as a "brother;" and the commission of pious deeds as characteristics of the concept.[17] Yet nowhere is there an attempt to define "belief" as a concept or to compare it to other terms in the Qur'an that might also point to different aspects of the concept to which the English term "belief" refers. Adang indicates that there are occasions where the use of the term "belief" may not be synonymous with *iman*, using instead the term "faith" as a more appropriate signifier of the Qur'anic meaning. In each instance, however, she seems to understand "faith" and "belief" as synonyms as well and that use of one term or the other is more a matter of English convention. Nowhere do alterations between "faith" and "belief" indicate conceptual shifts in the Qur'anic text.[18]

Adang, however, is not alone in asserting that "belief" is a monothetically comparable term with *iman* or that "belief" and "faith" refer to essential religious concepts that are so basic that definition is unnecessary. She is also not unique in ignoring other possible Arabic terms that might indicate "shades" of meaning that represent the full range of Islamic religious concepts that denote ideas related to the English term "belief." Adang is responding to and participating in a long history of usage that has treated the two terms as referring to the same essential concept. In fact, the use of the term "belief" as a signifier of the concepts indicated by use of *iman* have been so common among scholars that it represents the very kind of academic orthodoxy that Gadamer decried.

During the latter half of the nineteenth century, Islamic Studies began to emerge as a discreet field of inquiry, and the ill-defined usage of the term "belief" began in this period of Islamic Studies in the English language. For instance, in his 1851 translation of two Isma'ili texts written by al-Shahrastani (d. 1153), Edward Salisbury uses "belief" as a placeholder for *iman* without discussion as to the implications of such a translation.[19] Other scholars such as John Brown, G. W. Davis, G. H. Patterson, L. M. Simmons, and Hirschfeld Hartwig all equate *iman* with "belief" or speak of "belief" in ways that leave the reader with confusing and obscure impressions of the concepts found in the original texts. [20]

Most of the scholars who approached Islamic Studies during this period, however, wrote in German and French, and only secondarily in English. Although the origins of the term "believe" can be found in the German "*belieben*,"[21] it is not always clear how scholars who translated German and French examinations of Islamic phenomena into English meant the term to be understood. This "double translation" (translating a concept in Arabic into German or French and then into English) poses obvious problems for comprehension and has been examined by many scholars of translation theory and will not be discussed here.[22] It must be emphasized, however, that much of our current use of the term "belief" in Islamic Studies is influenced by these early translations of German and French (and less so Italian and Dutch) secondary interpretive literature.

For instance, one of the first major reviews of nineteenth-century scholarship on the Qur'an within the field of Islamic Studies was Gustav Weil's series of articles published in *The Biblical World* that compared the work of many scholars, including William Muir, Theodor Nöldeke, J. M. Rodwell, T. P Hughes, A. Spencer, E. H. Palmer, Garcin De Tassy, George Sale, and Ignaz Goldziher with Weil's own analysis.[23] These articles are an invaluable artifact of the intellectual history of Islamic Studies and speak to the care and exactness of these formative figures in the field. Yet "belief," as a conceptual category, is used without definition or discussion. There is a "given-ness" to the use of the term that implies that Weil, Muir, Nöldeke, Goldziher, and other scholars assumed "belief" to refer to an essential concept that applied to all religious traditions.

Weil, in several places, uses the term "belief" as a synonym for *iman* in the Qur'an[24] and he also describes "belief" as doctrine,[25] as a synonym for "faith,"[26] and quotes De Tassy's translation of chapter 49, in which the root *a-m-n* in its various forms is translated as "belief," "believe," and "believers."[27] Weil, however, provides no indication of what terms were used in the original German and French studies he reviews and does not discuss any kind of "conceptual slippage" that might have occurred by translating these analyses of the Qur'an.[28]

Duncan MacDonald, one of the other towering figures in the nineteenth-century academic tradition of Islamic Studies, follows Weil, Nöldeke, Goldziher, and others in using "belief" without careful analysis of the term. He too uses "belief" to refer to an essential category of religious phenomenon that is virtually indistinguishable from "faith." In his 1896 article "The Faith of al-Islam,"[29] MacDonald describes "religious belief"[30] as a universal concept that unites all religious traditions and suggests that it is a category of comparison that allows one to look at Muslim "creeds" in light of other ideas such as the Westminster Confession.[31] He does not, however, define or list the characteristics of a "religious belief," "creed," or "confession."[32] MacDonald does use "belief" in the sense defined above, that is, as an internal mental process aimed at understanding a set of postulates,[33] but interchanges this concept with "faith" throughout his work.[34] He also uses "belief" as a translation of *iman* along with all of the assumptions that this ill-defined use of the term implies.[35]

The academic orthodoxy around the use of the term "belief" became even more entrenched at the same time that other areas of terminological usage became more carefully defined. For instance, in his "Magic, Divination, and Demonology among the Semites," T. Witton Davies attempts to define the terms "magic," "divination," and "demonology" and to locate monothetically comparable terms in Arabic, Greek, and Hebrew.[36] Yet "belief" is used as a placeholder for several concepts in Islamic thought that go undefined, but just accepted as being based in "general" Qur'anic usage that most likely refer to ideas around usages of *iman* in the text and what he takes for "similar" meanings in the Hebrew Bible and New Testament.[37]

The trend toward greater lexical and conceptual sophistication can be seen in the work of many scholars of Islam in the early twentieth century, who nevertheless continued uncritically to use "belief" as a monothetic comparative term. This is particularly surprising because comparative approaches to the study of religion became the central theme in Islamic Studies during this period. These comparative analyses rigorously examined words and terms for what they might indicate about the nature of Western religious traditions and religion in general.[38] This early comparative enterprise was, however, tinged with ethnocentrism and outright racism, as has been demonstrated by Jean Jacques Waardenburg in his *Classical Approaches to the Study of Religion*.[39] Comparison was rarely done with religious traditions standing on an equal plane of analysis. Instead, Christianity was frequently placed in the superior position with other religious traditions placed in the inferior. Concepts were compared in such a way as to impress upon the reader, and frequently the religious informants representing non-Christian traditions, that Christianity was either the ultimate realization of religious evolution or the uncorrupted manifestation and definitive origin of all other religious ideals.[40]

Discussion of "belief" and "faith" thus became subsumed under the effort at comparing traditions so that the superiority of the "Western mind" or of Christianity came to the fore. In effect, "belief" served as the common field of analysis that allowed comparison to occur and thus remained uncritically used as a means of promoting lopsided comparative encounters with the unevolved or corrupted other.[41] A. S. Tritton, for example, states that:

> As Islam and Christianity are in many ways much alike, it is not surprising that their theologies often agree; frequent agreement in detail, which is not essential, suggests that borrowing has taken place.[42]

Tritton then goes on to provide a long list of concepts or "beliefs" that Islam and Christianity share that must have originated in Christianity. "Belief," therefore, serves as the common theme that allows comparison of particular ideas and concepts to occur.

Tritton, however, takes up the issue of "faith," which he claims the Qur'an defines as "belief in God, his apostles, and his books; it is the acceptance of a body of truth."[43] This definition, remarkably similar to that provided by Adang above, makes "faith" a synonym for "belief" that is essentially defined as "the acceptance of a body of truth." It is clear that Tritton links the concept of "faith" and "belief" to the Qur'anic term *iman*, although he does not specifically cite the term.

Tritton does not discuss "belief" and "faith" as the object of comparison. To the contrary, he uses them to open a discussion of the idea of "good works" and compares it to the discussion of "faith" and "works" found in the Epistles of John in the New Testament. He argues that Muslims, borrowing from John, hold that "belief" without good works is static and neutral. John, he says, provides Islam with a greater concept, that of "double faith," which "is the acceptance of the teaching of the Church and also the hope for the fulfillment of God's promises, the graces of the spirit."[44] Thus, for Tritton, the Qur'anic idea of "faith" and "belief" rooted in the term *iman*, which is essentially the same as that found in Christianity, is lacking without the emphasis on works, which it receives under later theological development that occurs under the influence of Christianity.

The conflation of "faith" and "belief" can also been seen in the work of the great scholar of Islam, Franz Rosenthal. He argues, for instance, in his article "On Suicide in Islam" that the "unshattered religious belief" of harsh punishments in hell can account for the continuing conviction among "faithful believers" of the absolute forbiddance of suicide.[45] He goes on to use "belief" as a synonym for "religious doctrine" and "faith," but does not define his terms, largely because "belief" has become by this point in the 1940s the primary comparative axis on which many, if not most, analyses occur.

Joachim Wach, one of the founders of the History of Religions approach in the American academy, takes up the issue of "belief" as a comparative category in his 1948 article "The Spiritual Teachings in Islam: A Study."[46] Wach examines the concepts of "faith" and "belief" as they are specified by the Sufi Hujwiri (d. 1072). Although he too conflates "faith" and "belief," Wach attempts to specify the conceptual framework for the phenomenon of "faith" and "belief" in Hujwiri's thought and argues that the phenomenon of faith/belief is rooted in the idea of *'ilm*, which he translates as "knowledge." Faith/belief is a course of action whereby the individual "acquires" *'ilm* through a three-step process in which the appreciation for the unification of God is "uncovered" through mystical practice. Wach argues that Hujwiri also defines "faith" as *iman*, although he states that Muslim theologians were divided over what the term meant and the extent to which they viewed *iman* as an act, or an external expression of some inner mental process.[47] It is, however, unclear in Wach's treatment whether Hujwiri clearly differentiated between *'ilm* and *iman*, although it seems as though *'ilm* represents an interior process of what we defined as "belief" above and *iman* represents that outer expression of the interior process.

Following Wach, Helmer Ringgren undertakes a linguistic examination of the root *a-m-n* in the Qur'an.[48] He begins by exploring the various meanings suggested by the different forms of the root, arguing that the basic meaning of "safety," security," and "protection" are commonly found in the text. He then states that in all other cases the infinitive "*amana*" means in the Qur'an "to believe," yet he does not define what he means by "belief" and, as do most other scholars, treats it as a synonym for "faith." It is interesting that he points out that there are instances in the Qur'an where *amana* appears to have a "close affinity" with the verb *saddaqa* and argues that the two terms are essentially interchangeable. He also states that *iman* seems to have a closer meaning to "belief" than "faith," thus recognizing that there is a difference. Ringgren attempts to clarify the difference by arguing that the term *iman* means "belief in the sense of *Fürwahrhalten*" (literally "an assent to truth"), which he defines as "theoretical belief"[49] or a kind of adherence of doctrinal belief that also characterizes "oriental Christendom."[50] The use of a non-defined German word to define an Arabic term in English is clearly problematic and creates all kinds of interpretive problems. Ringgren's use of *fürwahrhalten* also suggests a much more concrete conception of "belief" in which doubt is not possible. In fact, Ringgren argues that doubt (*shakk*) is the antonym of *iman* and *amana*. Thus for Ringgren, *iman* and *amana* are much more like our definition of "faith" than "belief."

The virtue of Ringgren's work is that he defines his terms much more carefully and explicitly than most studies of the concept of "belief" in Islamic Studies. Although he conflates "faith" and "belief," and in some instances reverses their meanings as they have been defined in the academic study of religion, he nevertheless strives toward specificity. Yet his use of the terms is driven by his desire to compare Islamic thought to Christianity and Judaism, which he characterizes as "similar" in their understanding of the concept of "belief."[51] The similarity is so great that he is able to resolve the problem presented by the apparent common meanings of *amana* and *saddaqa* by making recourse to an Arabic translation of the Gospel of Matthew[52] and due to the influence of Judaism on the Qur'an, he argues that there are obvious things that we can learn about the concept of "belief" by examining Jewish texts (although he does not do so himself but continues to think through the idea of faith/belief through the lens of "Oriental Christianity").[53]

Throughout the 1950s, 60s, and early 70s, scholars of Islam continued to use the term "belief" as the axis of comparative approaches to religious phenomena, although usually with far less clarity than

Wach and Ringgren. Alfred Guillaume, Theodore Silverstein, Bernard Lewis, C. C. Berg, E. G. Parrinder, G. E. von Grunebaum, A. J. Arberry, Harry Wolfson, H. A. R. Gibb, Michael Dols,[54] and many others treated "belief" as a monothetically comparable concept that needed little definition because of its universal application to all religious systems.

There are, however, a few notable exceptions to this general trend in scholarship on Islam. For instance, Toshihiko Izutsu argues that while *iman* can be translated as both "belief" and "faith," the Arabic term connotes an interior mental process in which "man should learn to understand the seemingly quite ordinary and common natural phenomena [are not] . . . simple *natural* phenomena but as so many manifestations of Divine goodness towards him."[55] Although he does not define how he means "belief" and "faith," he points to a number of Qur'anic terms that are "almost synonymous" with *amana*, which he translates as "to believe."[56] Among these terms are *shakara*, normally translated as "to be thankful;"[57] *islam*, "the giving of one's self to God;" *tasdiq*, "to consider the revealed words truthful;" even *Allah*, as the object of "belief;" *kufr*, "disbelief;" *takdib*, "giving the lie to the revealed words;" *isyan*, "disobedience;" and *nifaq*, "making a false show of belief;" among other possible shades of the concept.[58]

Izutsu, while pointing out that "belief" has shades of meaning, fails to detail what he means by the term and thus his contribution to understanding the concept in Islamic thought is limited. He, in fact, follows the orthodoxy around the comparative study of "belief" by not describing the range of concepts attached to the idea of "belief," and as continuing to see it as a placeholder for what he sees as so essential to religion that it defies definition.[59]

Marilyn Waldman reacts to Izutsu's treatment of *iman* and its "near synonyms" in the Qur'an in her article "The Concept of *Kufr* in the Qur'an." She argues that Izutsu fails to "consider the dynamic aspects of Qur'anic concepts," by which she means that Izutsu treats the whole of the Qur'an as a single chronological "unit" and does not attempt to understand how terms might change over the period in which the text came into being.[60]

Montgomery Watt, following Waldman, equates *iman* with the English "faith," but he does so with three qualifications because *iman* and "connections of the English word and its European equivalents are misleading."[61] First, unlike "faith," *iman* connotes an emotional connection between humans and God. Second, over time, Islamic theologians interpreted *iman* to be solely an inner emotional connection and distanced the term from public acts such as prayer or fasting. Finally, *iman* was thought to change in intensity over time, and was not a constant state of being.

While one might have an emotional connection to an idea or even to the concept of God, *iman*, according to Watt, was not thought to constitute a rational or reasoned adherence to God that was so powerful as to cause people to act in certain ways. To the contrary, the level of one's *iman* might change over time, but as long as there was some feeling of *iman* one remained a *mu'min*. Because of the comparative difficulties between *iman* and "faith" or "belief," Watt argued that use of the Arabic original should be maintained as long as there was careful explanation as to what the interpreter intended by use of the Arabic term instead of some vaguely equivalent English placeholder.[62]

We see in this period of Islamic Studies new ways of thinking emerge about "belief" and analogous concepts in Islamic thought. Around the orthodoxy of monothetic conceptions of "belief" as an essential category across all religions and its rather ill-defined association with *iman*, there is an acknowledgment of the linguistic diversity of Arabic and the understanding that changing contexts present problems for tying *iman* or any other single term to a single English equivalent. Scholars as diverse in their approaches and interests as Kenneth Cragg and Marshall Hodgson began to employ what might be called "polythetic comparative approaches" to phenomena and to push against the academic traditions that dominated the field. Polythetic comparison looks for analogies between conceptual categories, meaning that one looks for differences within the broader context of assumed similarity. One then isolates the differences to help understand how concepts that appear "similar" actually evidence subtle but important differences. These differences tell us how concepts change and shift depending on context and thus what they mean to people in different places and times. Instead of looking for essences, polythetic comparison looks at the diversity of religious experience and at how meanings emerge that can help us understand the great range of religious experience within and across religious traditions.

Cragg, in his unfortunately entitled *The Mind of the Qur'ān*, does not even translate the term *iman*. He seeks instead to explain its range of meanings by drawing on other Arabic terms such as *din* (as a path toward knowledge of God)[63] and *bay'a* (allegiance), although he does use "believe" and "believers" in a number of contexts without attaching it to a specific Arabic term or Islamic concept.[64] Hodgson, famous for his creation of English terms that were designed to evoke complex concepts,[65] defined *iman* as "trust and faithfulness to God," at least how it was used originally.[66] He argues, however, that while *iman* began as "faith," or the emotional trust in or loyalty to God, the concept shifted over time to connote "sheer 'belief,' [or] assent to propositions."[67] The shift in meaning occurred under the influence of theological debates in the early Abbasid period. Any discussion of terminological meaning, therefore, no matter where the term derives, must be understood within the context of time and place; which, in the end, can only be fully understood through comparing the variations in the usage of the term as it occurs over time.

In the 1970s there was also a new academic orthodoxy emerging in Islamic Studies that focused on the importance of contextual shifts on understandings of terminological usage. This idea has been asserted by a number of scholars such as Patricia Crone and Michael Cook, John Wansbourgh, and Daniel Madigan, just to mention a few.[68] But its impact on the use of "belief" as a comparative concept has been slow. Scholars continue to use the English term as a placeholder, often ignoring the more nuanced and detailed studies of Wach, Ringgren, and Waldman.

At the same time that context became the focus of intellectual orthodoxy, post-modernism created pressures in the humanities that caused scholars to rethink a number of ideas that many had previously taken for granted. Along with criticisms of theory and method, scholars began to challenge the idea of essentialism in the study of religion and culture.[69] The concept of essentialism has been criticized as:

> indispensable to the making of a modern distinction, where the distinction cannot exhaust itself in its reference to an *ancient régime* or to a backward culture or class, but requires a game of exclusion in universal terms, of confrontation with an ultimate type of otherness. The making of one's own universal reference has to be made through a negative reference to *another* universe.[70]

In other words, scholars used the idea of universal phenomena such as "belief" as a means of drawing distinctions between groups in order to create absolute ideas of "otherness," to establish, as discussed above, the superiority of one's own religion or culture over and above "the other." Critiques of essentialism were particularly profound in Islamic Studies where it was linked to negative portrayals of Orientalist scholarship, creating a crisis in the field of Islamic Studies that has yet to be fully surmounted.[71]

Criticisms of the use of essentialist categories such as belief arose in the academic study of religion in the 1970s, even before anti-Orientalist critiques came to the fore. Studies such as Robert Bellah's *Beyond Belief*,[72] Rodney Needham's *Belief, Language, and Experience*,[73] and W. C. Smith's *Belief and History* argue that the term "belief" has been so misunderstood, poorly defined, and value laden that its use as a comparative term should be abandoned. Smith's criticism of the use of the term "belief" as a descriptive and comparative category is particularly important because of his role in both the academic study of religion and in Islamic Studies.

Smith argues that "belief," especially modern definitions of the term, is too limited in scope to be of analytical value for the study of the Muslim tradition. On the macro and micro levels, "belief" does not take into account the scope of the idea of *tawhid*, what he defines as "unity, unification, integration," as well as "monotheism," and in popular jargon, "getting it all together."[74] According to Smith, the concept of *tawhid* represents for Muslims a link that ties all aspects of life into a comprehensive worldview where intellectual understandings, emotional inclinations, and actions are all integrated into a system of living.[75] By focusing on "belief" as a comparative category, especially for Christians for whom "belief" and "believing" are central concepts in religious identity, inaccurate assumptions are created that lead scholars and readers away from the totalizing integration of all aspects of religious thought and practice that is established in the idea of *tawhid*. The system created by the idea of *tawhid* "does not 'mean' something, so much as it confers meaning."[76] The generative aspects of the system created by *tawhid* give meaning to concepts such as "God." Such concepts, therefore, have no meaning on their own, but only find meaning(s) within the system as it is lived by Muslims at different times and places.[77] To say that Muslims "believe" in God does not account for the overall meaning of the concept of God or how it fits within the overall system of living that *tawhid* generates in Muslim cultures. It prioritizes only one aspect of what God "means," and even then creates imprecise and even false perceptions because there is no single English term or complex of terms that accurately depict the phenomena that is generated out of the relationship to the concept of God created by the system of *tawhid*.

THE PERSISTENCE OF THE ACADEMIC–ORTHODOX USE OF "BELIEF" IN ISLAMIC STUDIES

Although Smith and other scholars of religion were critical of the use of the term "belief" as a comparative category, it has continued to persist in Islamic Studies. In fact, since 1980, its use has increased substantially in articles dedicated to the study of Islamic topics in Religious Studies and Middle Eastern Studies journals. From 1953 to 1980, 650 articles were published using the term "belief" as a comparative category or as a placeholder for "similar" concepts in Islamic thought. From 1980 to 2007, there were 1613 articles.[78]

For the most part, "belief" remains an uncontested term and is most usually linked with the Arabic term *iman* with little or no recognition of other Arabic terms that provide glimpses of the totality of analogous ideas in Muslim thought and practice. While it is not the point of the present essay to disparage its use, I do hope to encourage scholars to use the term with caution by carefully employing polythetic comparative techniques when using English terms for Arabic and Islamic ideas in general.

Being clear about the terms scholars use is not only an issue in Islamic Studies but a concern in all areas of scholarship. Diligently mapping not just the shades of meaning in the original languages with which scholars work and by also applying the same care with the English terms they use to communicate meaning can provide the kinds of nuanced and well-considered analyses that represent the highest forms of scholarship. While methods need not be explicit (although I wish they were), scholars of religion and culture must move away from assuming essential meanings and toward carefully contextualized discussions of Muslim concepts. Readers and non-specialists must also be cognizant of the homogenization that scholars tend toward so that they too may be aware of the pitfalls and interpretive traps that such writing creates.

4

BODY

Shahzad Bashir

There is an old Pakistani joke that goes like this. A man walks into a government office to be faced with someone with a long beard who promptly asks for a bribe to do something that is a part of his job. Staring incredulously at his beard, the supplicant asks him how he could demand a bribe with this emblem of traditional Muslim piety displayed so prominently on his body. The officer responds unflinchingly that, as long as his questioner is paying attention to his body, he should look a little below the beard as well. There he would find a stomach that demands to be fed regularly. For him, satisfying the stomach is a greater imperative than following the ethical code that presumably goes with the beard.

To appreciate fully why this little scene is amusing perhaps requires familiarity with the place of religion in the public sphere in Pakistan. But the joke's main point should be easy to see: it juxtaposes the beard and the stomach as parts of a single entity, the body, that project conflicting identities and desires. The beard, replaceable by the head cover or veil for women, stands for the religious coding of the body, marking it as a site for the implementation and display of a religious order. And the stomach highlights the body's physicality as an organic entity that needs food and other forms of care and is thereby enmeshed in the material and social relations of the physical world. The joke's efficacy (such as it may be) derives from its play on a dissonance: a body displaying the values of the religious order seems out of place when it violates the ethics of the material sphere. But human beings' intimate knowledge of the stomach's insistence makes the dissonance a readily recognizable part of the experience of life.

Extending the general effect encapsulated in this joke, in this essay I will highlight the body as an artifact constructed at the conjunction of ideological and material factors significant for the lives of Muslims in various sociohistorical contexts. Stated this way, the topic is hopelessly large and will have to be trimmed severely to fit the scope of a short reflection. I begin by suggesting a broad canvas, nevertheless, in order to underscore the body's extraordinary elasticity as a topic within scholarship in the humanities and the social sciences. While the body is certainly an essential aspect of human existence, treating it as an object of study is no easy matter. The body as a physical and conceptual tool is implicated in all human attempts to construct knowledge, which means that it can be intrusively ever present or frustratingly transparent depending on the epistemological vantage point one chooses to employ in discussing a topic. For the purposes of this essay, I consider it best to see the body as a floating target constructed of interaction between multiple factors within the particular Islamic settings I have decided to use as examples.

My discussion is built around three themes through which I touch upon what I consider to be the major sites where the body matters most significantly in Islamic studies. My first point of concentration is the Islamic use of the body as a microcosm that can be seen to reflect the cosmos as a whole. This idea, common to many different Islamic and other cosmological schemes, reflects the general anthropocentrism of much of Islamic thought that necessarily references the body. Whenever it is made, the appeal to the body as a microcosm is closely related to prescriptions about societal organization and control in Islamic contexts. The body as a microcosm is thus a topic pertinent for both the intellectual and social sides of Islamic religious history.

My second theme in this essay is Islamic regulation of the body involving legal matters, such as universal rituals and food taboos, with a particular focus on the ritual prayer (*salat*). Acutely underexplored as an area of research, the embodied practice that results from juridical regulation is a critical factor in the construction of Muslim individual and communal identities. I present the legal regulation of the body based on Islamic justifications as a "technology of the self" that bridges the gap between bodily experience and human beings' sense of being a part of a religious tradition that transcends the specificity of one's social and historical location. Clarified through juridical discussions, corporeal regulation is perhaps the single most significant factor that makes Islam cohere as a universal tradition.

My third major theme in the essay is the role played by extraordinary bodies in defining the parameters of Islamic discursive and practical norms. Here I look at accounts pertaining to the bodies of Muhammad and his wives, the Shi'i Imams, and renowned Sufi masters as examples that have conditioned particular religious viewpoints. I suggest that descriptions of such exemplary bodies acquire their significance from the contexts in which they are invoked and that the appeal to extraordinary bodies represents a particular mode of constructing religious and social authority that binds past bodies with present ones through the imperative of physical mimesis. While my focus in this essay is on the human body, the most famous early Islamic debates regarding the body were about Qur'anic descriptions of God that employ corporeal imagery. My discussion concludes with a brief attempt at correlating the problem of divine anthropomorphism with the place of the human body in the study of Islam.

BODY AS WORLD

The *Epistles of the Brethren of Purity*, a collection of anonymous treatises in Arabic penned in the tenth century in Basra, contain an extensive description of the human body aimed at highlighting the special place the species occupies in the cosmos. The Brethren begin their discussion with the remark that

> a human being who claims to know about things without knowing about himself is like one who feeds other people but remains hungry, or who treats others but is himself an emaciated patient, or who clothes people while himself being naked, his private parts revealed rather than concealed, or like one who guides people on the road while he himself is lost, not knowing the road to his house.[1]

This opening is valuable for two interrelated reasons: first, it marks the Brethren's perspective that a proper pursuit of knowledge must begin with knowledge of one's self, which includes the body; and second, the Brethren's heavy reliance on corporeal metaphors in their rhetoric underscores the degree to which classical Islamic authors take the proper care and comportment of the body as an a priori fact of life. Following this statement, the Brethren proceed to present an extensive taxonomy of the body that shows it to be a map for understanding the cosmos, from celestial beings to society. In all their descriptions, the Brethren depict the body as a dynamic system whose various parts must work in conjunction with each other in order to achieve and maintain a sought after equilibrium.

The Brethren of Purity were a fringe group within an early Islamic society and their work is interesting because of their extensive investment in rationalizing all beings and knowledges into a coherent philosophical system. What they say about the body, however, has deep resonances with what we can find in the work of other, more mainstream classical authors. A representative case for this is the famous theologian Muhammad al-Ghazali (d. 1111), who deliberately set out to synthesize various modes of Islamic thought to generate a Sunni orthodoxy. In his Persian treatise *The Alchemy of Happiness*, Ghazali provides a concise description of the body as cosmos that straddles theological and social concerns. He urges his readers to scrutinize the human body as a first step in exploring more distant realities. They are advised to go beyond their intuitive sense of how their limbs and sensory organs work and to attempt to understand matters such as the properties of the ten layers of the eye and the functions of the viscera such as liver, spleen, gall bladder, and kidneys. Each of these, Ghazali says, works in conjunction with the others to sustain life, and to come to know these is to know the world.

He then goes on to compare physical features of the body with the earth's topography, so that bones are like mountains, hair is like trees, the sense organs are like the stars, and so on. The qualities inherent in the genera of living beings present in the cosmos are also represented in the body: what is natural to pigs, horses, dogs, and so on, as well as demons, fairies, and angels can all be found in the faculties inherent in the body's organs. And all human occupations are represented in the functions of the body's parts: the stomach is like the baker who makes food ready for consumption; the liver is like the oil maker who presses food through the intestines to extract the dregs, and also like the dyer who transmits red color to the blood; the glands that secrete milk and semen are like bleachers that remove red color from blood to turn it into white substances, and so on.

Ghazali's ultimate contention is that anyone who observes the body's form diligently is by necessity led to acknowledging three qualities that pertain to God:

First, he knows that the maker of this form and the creator of this being is capable of perfection, so that no defect or deficiency can affect His powers ... Second, that He is knowledgeable such that His knowledge encompasses all matters ... And third, that there is no end to His graciousness, mercy, and favor towards human beings. The creator has not withheld Himself from creating anything, including things that are essential, such as the heart, liver, brain, and the principles of animal life; and things that are needed although they are not essential, like hands, feet, eyes, and tongue; and things that are neither essential nor necessary but that enhance adornment, such as the blackness of hair, redness of lips, thickness of the eyebrow, evenness of eyelashes, etc.[2]

Ghazali's taxonomy of the body is noteworthy for intermixing physical and social aspects of experience such that its various elements can teach about the earth and the heavens on one hand and human professions on the other. He thus relies on the body as a system to legitimize his conception of nature and society as orders that require the maintenance of a balance between their various parts. Ultimately, this order is decreed and legitimized by Ghazali's appeal to God's powers and intentions. Although he presents the body as a value-neutral map of the cosmos, the formulation is quite value-laden with respect to his prescription for human actions. Just as the body is a dynamic system whose various parts need to be in harmony for it to be healthy, the physical world and, more significantly, society must contain checks and balances in order for it to work according to the "natural" plan decreed by God. Ghazali's main concerns in the *Alchemy of Happiness* are in fact ethics and manners, and his description of the body as a microcosm prefaces his larger discussion precisely to proclaim the self-evidently natural basis for his prescriptions for human conduct.

The correlation between the body and society observable in the work of Ghazali and the Brethren of Purity can be seen in most Islamic cosmologies that invoke the body. In the field of political theory, for example, Abu Nasr al-Farabi's (d. c. 951) *The Perfect State*, generally regarded as the cornerstone of medieval Islamic political theory, states explicitly that "The excellent city resembles the perfect and healthy body, all of whose limbs cooperate to make the life of the animal perfect and to preserve it in this state."[3] Similarly, theories about gender difference in cosmological discussions portray the earthly hierarchy between male and female as a reflection of grander cosmic principles. The contrast between male and female bodies in such schemes indicates, simultaneously, a complimentarity and a hierarchy between the two types of bodies.[4]

From the broadest perspective, the body appears as a lynchpin within Islamic cosmological thought, holding the cosmos together by mediating between its physical, metaphysical, and social aspects. Since the general pattern is that God is said to have created the human being simultaneously in the image of the world and as its centerpiece, the body is seen as a blueprint for the cosmos as well as society. The scope of this perspective is enlarged further by reference to the statement, found in *hadith* literature, which states that Adam was created in God's image.[5] Here too, what is most significant is the body's mediating function since it both represents God and constitutes the human being, the species situated at the center of the created world.

MANAGING THE BODY: RITUALS AND LAW

In the previous section, I focused on the body as an idea and a structured entity that conjoins Islamic metaphysical thinking with notions of order that pertain to the material and social worlds. Real human bodies are, however, fundamentally dynamic objects, subject to growth, corruption, movement, and manipulation. The present section highlights this aspect of the body in Islamic Studies through a focus on the place of the body in the performance of universal Islamic rituals.

In his autobiography, the African–American civil rights leader Malcolm X describes his transition from being a member of Elijah Muhammad's Nation of Islam to becoming a normative Sunni Muslim by recounting his travel to Mecca to perform the hajj pilgrimage. He narrates his sense of difference from other Muslims while being detained at Jeddah airport in Saudi Arabia through his effort to learn the Muslim ritual prayer from a guide assigned to take care of him while he awaits authentication of his conversion to Islam:

> With gestures, he indicated that he would demonstrate to me the proper praying ritual postures. Imagine, being a Muslim minister, a leader in Elijah Muhammad's Nation of Islam, and not knowing the prayer ritual.
>
> I tried to do what he did. I know I wasn't doing it right. I could feel the other Muslims' eyes on me. Western ankles won't do what Muslim ankles have done for a lifetime. Asians squat when they sit. Westerners sit upright in chairs. When my guide was down in a

posture, I tried everything I could to get down as he was, but there I
was, sticking up. After about an hour, my guide left, indicating that he
would return later.

   I never even thought about sleeping. Watched by the Muslims, I
kept practicing prayer posture. I refused to let myself think how ridiculous I must have looked to them. After a while, though, I learned a
little trick that would let me get down closer to the floor. But after two
or three days, my ankle was going to swell.[6]

With characteristic candor, Malcolm X captures in these passages the
significance attached to performing normative rituals in the Islamic
context. As he presents it, the ability to perform the prayer is the universal passport to being Muslim, and the effortlessness with which
one can do it is the mark of one's ease with one's religious identity as
a whole. Malcolm's struggle with his body for the prayer is the beginning of a process through which he transforms himself into a normative Muslim, to whose body the ritual of prayer eventually comes as
a natural act. Malcolm's focus on the physical difficulty of doing the
prayer in the narrative appears to be a very deliberate choice aimed
at highlighting a contrast relating to aspects of his body that mattered
greatly for his personal situation: on one side, he shows that it was
possible for him to be accepted as a member of a worldwide religious
community by persevering in molding his body to the form of the
ritual in front of other Muslims; and on the other side, the color of
his skin precluded him from being regarded as an American on par
with those of European descent despite the fact that he was born and
raised in the United States. Islam, here signified emphatically through
embodied practice, enabled Malcolm to achieve full membership in
a universal community in a way he thought to be impossible in the
society of his birth.

   My aim in invoking Malcolm X's experience here is not meant to
proclaim that Muslims are any less susceptible to racism than other
human groups. Prejudice pertaining to skin color is an endemic factor
in many human societies, including those of the past or the present
that are majority Muslim. I find Malcolm's experience instructive
because his description of the prayer is an eloquent testimony to the
essential physicality of the prayer ritual. His portrayal eschews any
symbolic interpretation of the ritual itself and assigns meaning to it
only in terms of his physical exertions and what he presumes to be
the interest or censure lying behind the stares of Muslim onlookers.
He even learns the ritual purely through miming, and his concern

is simply with replicating the instructor's bodily movements rather than with the verbal formulae that accompany the various necessary bodily postures.

Rituals such as the prayer, fasting, and the hajj and 'umra pilgrimages to Mecca that involve corporeal regulation and manipulation are essential to the structuring of time and space in Islamic contexts. Moreover, bodies involved in these rituals signify meaning in double since they are, on one side, the very basis of personal experience, and on the other, the central objects that give subjective shape to times and spaces shared with others. The prayer has to be done at specific times of the day, toward the direction of Mecca, and often – though not necessarily – in the sanctified space of a mosque. Fasting is obligatory for a particular month every year and is supposed to be accompanied by extra ethical and ritual vigilance. The pilgrimages require travel to Mecca, at a specific time of the year in the case of the hajj, which valorizes the earth's surfaces by marking a center, toward which one travels from the periphery where one resides under ordinary circumstances. These rituals are a major element in Islamic legal regulation of the body, which also includes the delimitation of allowable and forbidden foods. Between food taboos and universal rituals, one may get the impression that to live consciously according to Islamic precepts requires constant preoccupation with the body's entrances, exits, and postures. And yet, such care of the body usually becomes instinctive, receding to the level of habit rather than occupying individuals with conscious decision-making. As Malcolm X puts it, practiced Muslims' ankles do instinctively that which will swell those subjected anew to the regimen of prayer.

In trying to convey the general importance of rituals and food taboos in Islamic contexts, it is essential to consider how corporeal practices rooted in legal requirements can come to condition selfhood and identity. One theoretical approach to this issue is through the work of Michel Foucault concerned with the formation and care of the self. Unlike most other models, a modified version of Foucault's insight allows us to think about the construction of meaning within corporeal practices while keeping the body in the foreground of our analysis. Before his death in 1984, Foucault had become increasingly interested in the means through which human beings constitute themselves as subjects. One cornerstone of his views in this regard is the notion of "technologies of the self," which, he writes, "permit individuals to effect by their own means, or with the help of others, a certain number of operations on their own bodies and souls, thoughts, conduct, and way of being, so as to transform themselves in order to attain a certain state of happiness, purity, wisdom, perfection, or immortality."[7] I find this formulation attractive because it allows us to think of people *consciously* doing things to themselves in order to produce an overarching sense of being that is meant to become *unconsciously* pervasive.

Foucault's own work concentrates on ancient Greek texts and the modern transformation of European societies, but it seems useful to think about Islamic law as it pertains to rituals, such as the prayer, and food taboos, as a technology of the self that is a constitutive element in the construction of properly Muslim selves/bodies. Malcolm X's description of his own experience reflects this process at two different levels. First, his effort to learn the prayer is a case of him effecting operations on his body with the ultimate aim of creating a new, more fulfilling selfhood. And second, his narrating the experience in an evocative way at a critical juncture in an autobiography that is meant to model exemplary behavior makes the body stand out as a crucial place for effecting change in the consciousness of his readers. Ultimately, the bodily practice is conveyed through the narrative discourse of legal requirements, marking them as the means through which actual bodies get molded and as the social practices that tie individuals to each other in a community.

Bodily rituals as technologies of the self ultimately stem from the notion that subjecting the body to the same action repeatedly can result in the appropriate religious identity. This identity has both an internal dimension, referencing a subject's self-understanding, and an external, social dimension that marks one as an insider in a particular community. Both these dimensions are in evidence in the case of Malcolm X: his description of his experience references his discomfort as well as the eyes of others who are watching him. The bodily ritual thus mediates his sense of himself as a religious subject as well as his status in the social sphere. This dual function of the body in ritual has been highlighted by recent ethnographic work on Muslim societies. Most studies that have addressed the field have been concerned primarily with the social arena, showing how debates about rituals such as the prayer reflect larger social conflicts and processes in a given setting. For example, John Bowen compares three different Indonesian contexts to highlight the intensely contextual nature of the meaning assigned to prayer, and Gregory Starrett's survey of representations of

Egyptian society reveals observers' vested interests in passing judgments on prayer or manipulating its meaning for purposes of social control.[8] In descriptions such as these, the body tends to disappear from analytical view since the "meaning" that ultimately concerns the authors has to do with the social rather than the physical body.

Saba Mahmood in her recent work approaches the question from a different angle, that of the place of prayer in the self-understanding of a group of Muslim women participating in the pietistic mosque movement in contemporary Egypt. In Mahmood's account, the women in question emphasize the prayer as an absolute for cultivating a vigorous Islamic identity at the individual level. Their sense of the efficacy of this approach stems from their understanding that

> repeated bodily behavior, with the appropriate intention (however simulated in the beginning), leads to the reorientation of one's motivations, desires, and emotions until they become a part of one's "natural" disposition. Notably, in this economy of discipline, disparity between one's intentions and bodily gestures is not interpreted as a disjunction between outward social performance and one's "genuine" inner feelings – rather, it is considered to be a sign of an inadequately formed self that requires further discipline and training to bring the two into harmony in accord with a teleological model of self-formation.[9]

These women's considered expositions on the prayer state explicitly what is implicit in Malcolm X's account, namely, that the body is the fundamental ground on and through which a person constructs one's identity as a Muslim. Consequently, legal discourses about rituals and other corporeal matters such as food taboos constitute scripts for the technologies that enable one to work toward a religious selfhood. In the words of the Indonesian Muslim scholar Nurcholish Madjid, "when performed with devotion and attention and accompanied by the tranquility of every member of the body, [*salat*, or ritual prayer] is a perfect declaration of faith ... Salat creates a highly elevated feeling of religion or religiosity."[10]

The reader will have noticed that my examples for showcasing legal prescriptions regarding the body as technologies of the self are all modern. This choice is not accidental and is a result of the fact that the exemplification of corporeal practice as a significant aspect of identity appears rarely in pre-modern Islamic texts in a direct way. Traditional Islamic authors seldom objectify the experience of being Muslim in a way that would require reflecting consciously on molding the body in an Islamic mode. Conversely, it makes sense that someone making the transition into adopting new corporeal habits (such as Malcolm X) or societies that can be observed ethnographically reveal the operation of such practices. It is pertinent, however, to ask how traditional Muslim authors do in fact interpret legal regulation of the body?

Over the course of centuries, Muslim scholars (particularly jurists) have spilled immense amounts of ink clarifying the rules that must be followed precisely while managing the body in the performance of ritual or with respect to its intakes and excretions. This literature takes the necessity of such corporeal maintenance for granted, concentrating on clarifying the procedures. When there is explicit discussion of the question of meaning in prescribed corporeal acts, their perspectives can be divided into two groups: some take the basic injunctions as commands from God that have to be followed without any need for rationalization; and others carry out detailed metaphorical interpretations of the required physical acts and proscriptions in conjunction with larger theological perspectives. The latter tendency is most common among authors writing from perspectives such as Sufism that are based on dividing the world into exoteric and esoteric realms. This makes sense because such religious systems differentiate consistently between ordinary "surface" knowledge that can be gained from sensory observation, and hidden "esoteric" knowledge that is acquired only through special initiations and rituals and is seen to reflect a higher level of truth. In these schemes, correct metaphorical explanation of rituals and other legal matters corresponds with the higher knowledge.[11]

Some examples of Sufism-related understandings of the prayer ritual can provide a sense for how Muslim theoreticians may approach the issue of symbolic interpretation of legal requirements. The considerable internal divergence between these examples themselves indicates the width of the interpretive spectrum even within a single Islamic perspective. I begin with the work of the Andalusian master Ibn 'Arabi (d. 1240), whose ideas represent a kind of distillation of earlier views and were deeply influential for the development of Sufi thought in centuries following his death. His works contain elaborate interpretations of the standard rituals as symbolic actions relating to the relationship between God and human beings. For example, his interpretation of the prayer concentrates closely on the actual physical positions occupied by the body during the ritual. He sees the movements between standing, bending, prostrating, and sitting as human beings' progress along the path to God. The four positions themselves and the specific Arabic formulae that have to be repeated while the body is in them are indexed to the various stages through which humans approach God. The first three movements lower the body by making it go ever closer to the earth, but Ibn 'Arabi understands this drawing downward as an ascent toward God. The inversion of meaning is justified by the fact that one is supposed to become closer to God by not acting proud and debasing oneself in front of Him. The last part of the prayer is to sit, which Ibn 'Arabi sees as an act connected to the Qur'anic verse that states that God "created the heavens and the earth in six days, then He sat upon the throne" (Q57:4).[12] In the prayer as a whole, then, a human being first approaches God by gradually reducing the ego to the point of total prostration and eventually comes to sit in front of God in a form that mirrors His own position since the creation of the cosmos. The ritual is thus an exercise in affirming the necessary religious relationship between human beings and God.

Beyond Ibn 'Arabi, an even more literal interpretation of the positions and actions of the body during the prayer is found in the thought of the Hurufi sect that originated in the fourteenth century in Iran. The Hurufis held the radical view that they were living in the end times and the world was about to experience a cataclysmic apocalypse. They believed that they were the only righteous group to exist on the planet at this crucial cosmic moment and that, as a consequence of their status, God had revealed to them the precise meaning behind all ritual acts. Reflecting their general principle that all secrets of the cosmos could be deciphered by paying attention to the Arabo-Persian alphabet, they argued that the first three distinctive positions taken by the body during the ritual prayer correspond with the shapes of the three letters *alif*, *lam*, and *ha* that combine to make the name of God (*allah*). Also, these three letters were thought to represent the basis of all existence because their shapes – straight, bent, and rounded – encompass the shapes of all that exists in the world. These two different associations of the three shapes taken by the body during prayer led to the idea that when humans pray, they simultaneously articulate the name of God with their bodies and encompass the whole of the created world in their corporeal movements. All Muslims who had been performing the prayer from the beginning of Islam to the times in which the Hurufis lived had been rehearsing this underlying truth regarding the human body's ability to unite God's name with the form of the cosmos through ritual. Hurufis' sense of their own special status derived from the fact that God had revealed this cosmic secret to Fazlallah Astarabadi (d. 1394), the prophetic figure after whose inspiration the Hurufi movement had been formed.[13]

A third case in the same vein can indicate how far Sufis could go in thinking about the connection between rituals and the body's physical constitution. This example comes from hagiography, a genre comprised of hundreds of texts that have yet to receive their scholarly due. Hagiographic texts consist most often of short vignettes through which the authors represent their subjects, great Sufi saints, with the aims of preserving their memory and guiding readers by example. The investment in stories rather than direct prescriptive exhortation affords this literature a multivalence usually absent in more directly didactic literature. To be sure, this literature is as partisan as any other in terms of promoting the interests of certain classes and perspectives in Islamic societies, but it provides some interesting possibilities for trying to read between and under the lines of the preserved text.

The example of ritual prayer I would like to highlight here comes from a work entitled *Morals for the Heart* (*Fava'id al-fu'ad*) dedicated to the Chishti Sufi master Nizam al-Din Awliya (d. 1320) who is buried in Delhi. Written by a student of Nizam al-Din, this work contains numerous examples of Sufi saintly behavior in addition to stories that relate to the life of the main subject. One such story tells of a man named Shaykh Ahmad Ma'shuq who acquired his sobriquet "beloved" (*ma'shuq*) after a dialogue with God. The hagiographer states that he implored God to make him aware of his true personal identity. God first offered him the place of an intercessor or deliverer for other human beings on the Day of Resurrection, but he refused these roles. God then told him that while other Sufis were lovers of God, the divinity had chosen him to be His beloved. After this, everyone automatically started calling him *ma'shuq*, although his behavior may have unsettled some, who complained that he was known not to perform the ritual prayer regularly. In his defense, Nizam al-Din Awliya stated that he was, in effect, physically precluded from praying because of the status God had assigned him. He remained subject to criticism and once

> after they repeatedly implored him, he stood to pray and began to recite *Surat al-fatiha*. When he came to the verse, "It is You whom we worship, and it is You from whom we seek help," out of all his

blessed limbs, from every pore of his body, blood began to gush forth. Turning to onlookers, he said, "See, I am a menstruating woman. It is not right for me to offer prayers!"[14]

And there the matter rested.

Although the author of the work in which this incident is related provides no interpretive gloss on why Shaykh Ahmad's body become perforated when he came to a particular verse of the Qur'an, we can deduce the reasoning. The abnormality of Shaykh Ahmad's body relates to his position vis-à-vis God: since he is God's beloved (and not His lover), the normative distinction between human being as worshipper and God as the worshipped deity does not hold true for him. What is remarkable, of course, is that his body breaks apart when he enunciates a statement that pertains to the normative human–divine relationship. By inverse implication, then, this story indicates that normative human bodies must perform the prayer faithfully for them to remain constituted properly. In this logic, the ability to perform ritual ablutions and the prayer correlates to the actual form and physical boundaries of the human body. Ritual is thus not mere obedient manipulation of the body based in a tradition acquired through the social process of learning. Instead, its potency is rooted in the physical construction of the body, which coheres properly or disintegrates based on the choices made by the person inhabiting it.[15]

Despite their obvious and stark differences, the modern academic and medieval Islamic perspectives I have discussed in this section evince a surprising coincidence: in both cases, rituals such as the prayer are seen to be constitutive of the body as an artifact constructed at the nexus of personal and social experiences. Seen as technologies of the self, rituals act to imprint ideologies into selves through bodily means, and from an internal religious perspective, they enact and reinforce the proper relationship between human beings and God. In both cases, the corporeal components of rituals make the actual acts far more than routinized behaviors devoid of emotion and intent.

EXTRAORDINARY BODIES

In literature that purports to represent the words and actions of Muhammad, one of the most categorical and condemnatory statements regarding the human body is to be found in a rather surprising place. The *Sahih* of Bukhari, considered the most authoritative collection of *hadith* reports about Muhammad by Sunni Muslims, contains the following vignette from the life of the Prophet in the chapter on seclusion in a mosque (*i'tikaf*):

> Safiyya, the Prophet's wife told [the next link in the chain of authority] that she went to visit God's apostle in the mosque in the course of his seclusion during the last ten days of Ramadan. She talked to him for a while and then when she got up to return, the Prophet got up as well to be with her. As they reached the mosque's door, near Umm Salama's door, two Ansari men who were passing by greeted God's apostle. He said to them, "do not be hasty, it is only Safiyya, daughter of Huyayy." They both said, "Praise be to God, O God's apostle," and they were overwhelmed. The Prophet said, "Satan reaches everywhere in the human body in the manner of blood; I was afraid that he might cast something in your hearts."[16]

Although Bukhari's stated purpose in relaying this tradition is to clarify whether it is allowable for a person observing seclusion to walk to the mosque's door, the narrative's internal logic centers on improper doubt cast over a male–female relationship involving Muhammad. The Prophet's final general comment on human bodies bifurcates the scene interestingly in an inverse symmetry: on one side are the behaviorally proper bodies of Muhammad and his wife, and on the other, two onlookers whose bodies are declared susceptible to Satan's corruption on the basis of their interpretations of what they see. The suspicion that Muhammad seeks to nullify pertains to special bodies (his own and that of his wife), but his words make a universal statement about the properties of ordinary human bodies.

The set-up of this *hadith* echoes the overall paradigm that governs the way Muslim sources use reports about Muhammad's corporeal acts as models for shaping their own conduct. On one level, the Prophet is very emphatically seen as an ideal person, absolved from any possibility of sinning as evident from the story about his childhood where angels open up his body to remove a black dot from his heart and purify it with white snow.[17] But at a different, fully human level, Muslims need to examine all conceivable minutiae of his life with the purpose of replicating his behavior in their own circumstances. The Ansari men who observe him with his wife could then be seen to represent the gaze of all inquiring Muslims from later times: what they see precludes casting doubt on the Prophet's behavior by definition, but their eyes need to intrude upon the Prophet's most private intimacies because of his status as the ultimate model. Possessing what the Prophet describes as highly corruptible bodies, they must bar Satan from their veins by learning from the bodies of the Prophet and his close companions such as his wives.

Even a cursory survey of the enormously significant *hadith* and *sira* literature reveals that Muhammad's bodily practice constitutes one of the cornerstones of his role as the ultimate religious exemplar in Islamic religious thought. Here I would like to illustrate the detail and depth that can be encompassed by this fact by considering a single topic. The issue relates to the juridical discussion of ritual purity, in which male–female touching is interpreted differently by the major Sunni schools of law. The ultimate source of the difference is variance over interpretation of a Qur'anic verse that states:

> O believers, when you prepare for the prayer, wash your faces and your hands up to the elbows and wipe your head and your feet up to the ankles. And if you are in a state of sexual pollution, purify yourselves. And if you are sick, or on a journey, or have satisfied the call of nature, or have touched women (*aw lamastum al-nisa'*), and you do not find water, then go to clean, high ground and rub your faces and your hands with some of it. (Q5:6)

The central point of difference has to do with what the Qur'an intends by "touching women" and the spectrum of opinion ranges as follows: some see touching as a euphemism for sexual intercourse; others specify that the touch nullifies purity only if it stems from sexual desire; still others think of touch quite literally as skin contact so that the rule does not come into play if there is a barrier of cloth; and last are those for whom any physical contact between a male–female pair activates the rule. What concerns me here is not the clarification of the legal rule itself, but how jurists use the intimate life of Muhammad to bolster their various positions.

In his recent survey of this issue, Ze'ev Maghen shows how jurists of different persuasions could interpret a single report about Muhammad related by his wife A'isha to argue their cases. The Hanafis, who hold the most liberal position, point to a report where A'isha touched Muhammad while he was praying and he continued to pray. She said:

> I couldn't find the Messenger of God in bed one night, and I felt around for him with my hand and lo – he was in the mosque. And my hand fell upon the insteps of his feet. And he was intoning: "O God,

I seek refuge in Your favor from Your wrath, and in Your forgiveness from your punishment, and I seek refuge in You from You ..." When he finished, he [turned to me and] said: "What is it, A'isha – did you get jealous?" I replied: "And why shouldn't one such as me be jealous of one such as you?" And he said: "I see your devil has returned!" And I replied: "O Messenger of God – am I possessed by a devil?"[18]

The Hanafis surmise that the kind of touch being described here can be completely precluded from violating ritual purity and that the Qur'anic injunction means sex. Those who agree partially with the Hanafis state that A'isha touching Muhammad in this case does not violate purity because it involves no erotic intent or reaction: if such were included, the state would be violated even though there was no sexual intercourse. Further, those fully opposed to the Hanafi view suggest at least four different possibilities to nullify its implications. They say: perhaps Muhammad was busy in invocational rather than ritual prayer, which does not require maintaining a state of purity; or he was wearing socks so that when A'isha touched his sole, there was no skin-to-skin contact; or the Prophet did renew his ablutions but the report that comes down to us does not tell us this; or the event in question occurred before the verse legislating the redoing of ablutions was revealed. Whatever the merits of the various positions, it is clear that the meaning of a foundational Qur'anic verse on as crucial a matter as ritual purity requires intimate knowledge of the physical relationship between Muhammad and A'isha. The ideal nature of these two bodies makes their intertwining a matter of great interest for later Muslims, and Islam as an embodied practice simply cannot be enacted without reference to the details of Muhammad's life. Given the enormity of this theme, it should come as no surprise that the most widespread international Muslim movement of modern times, the Tablighi Jama'at, is rooted in the effort to enact Muhammad's corporeal practice in all conceivable details.[19]

The pattern of treating the bodies of Muhammad, A'isha, and others as simultaneously idealized but also subject to ordinary human physicality pertains to models outside the prophetic family as well. In the Shi'i sphere, reports on the attributes and activities of the Imams and their companions work in the same way as what Sunnis limit to Muhammad and his companions. For example, the sixth Imam Ja'far al-Sadiq (d. 765) is said to have related on the occasion of the birth of his son Musa al-Kazim (d. 799), the next Imam, that at the time every Imam is conceived a mysterious being … appears before his father, the present imam, and has him drink something "finer than water, softer than butter, sweeter than honey, colder than snow, and whiter than milk," and commands him to unite with his spouse; thus the seed of the future imam is conceived. After four months, "the spirit is produced in the seed," then God sends a celestial entity called Hayawan (literally the Living, the Animated) to inscribe on the embryo's right arm the phrase "And the Word of your Lord is accomplished in all truth and justice. No one can change His Words, He is it who hears and knows (Quran 6:115). Once born, the child places his hands on the earth, for "he receives all the Science of God come down from Heaven on earth," and raises his head toward the sky, for "from the interior of the Throne and on behalf of the Lord of Magnificence, a Herald calls him by name and by the name of his father …" and says: "You are my chosen one among my creatures, the place of my Secret, the repository of my Science, my confidant in my Revelation, my vicar on my earth. I have reserved my Mercy, offered my Paradise, and allowed my Proximity to you and to these who love you with a holy love …"[20]

The Imam's body represents a concretization of the whole principle of the Imamate that mediates God's presence on earth. In addition to what the Imam acquires from his father (the existing Imam), his body perpetuates Muhammad's bodily substance as well since he is descended from his daughter Fatima (d. 632) who was herself conceived after Muhammad ate something in paradise during his heavenly journey. Sanctified by heavenly materials and beings in multiple ways, the Imams have extraordinary bodies that are born with "their umbilical cords cut, they are clean and circumcised, they are conscious even in sleep … Fatima has the peculiarity of never having a menstrual period."[21]

These mythical and cosmological aspects of the Imams' bodies coexist with their ordinary physicality by which they are subject to the same processes as ordinary bodies. Detailed lore about the Imams' acts complements prophetic *hadith* in Shi'i legal discussions pertaining to corporeal matters such as purity and prayer. Moreover, the Imams' history in the Twelver Shi'i understanding is marked by tremendous physical suffering, particularly in the case of the third Imam, Husayn b. 'Ali, who died as a martyr while fighting for the Shi'i cause in Karbala in 680. Subjecting one's own body to suffering through ritual every year on the days when Husayn suffered most grievously is a central rite in the Twelver Shi'i understanding of the path toward religious redemption.[22] While Twelver Shi'is await an Imam who went into occultation in 874 to come back to earth at the end of time, Nizari Isma'ili Shi'is see their living Imam, the Aga Khan, as a person endowed with all the cosmic properties associated with the Imam's body. But this Imam also lives as a fully functional human body, subject to birth, corporeal desire, and, eventually, death.[23]

The pattern of authoritative bodies that are, on one side, connected to cosmological principles, and on the other, organic entities to be observed and emulated for the sake of religious merit pertains emphatically to the world of Sufism as well. In this instance, the basic framework rests on the notion that the continuing existence of the world depends on the existence of a hierarchy of saints distributed around the world. This hierarchy culminates in a pole (*qutb*) who represents the consummation of all human qualities and abilities and is to be regarded as a window standing between the created world on one side and God on the other. All other saints are seen as weaker forms of this pole, and humans outside the saintly category are considered still weaker specimens of the species. For anyone who wants to advance on the Sufi path, it is necessary to, first, recognize those who are already a part of the hierarchy and then become attached to them through discipleship, either directly or through one of their close companions. This imperative leads Sufis to become joined to each other in widespread social webs that emanate outward from the most famous saints.

The pole's crucial cosmic function is iterated succinctly in a work dedicated to the saint Ni'matallah Vali (d. 1431) that states: "All divine graces that reach the world and those who live in it do so through the mediation of the pole's being. These graces first descend upon his holy heart and then divide out from this ocean into brooks that are the hearts of other saints and close companions. From there, they branch out into rivulets to reach all that remains."[24] The pole is thus the sole conduit for God's continuous interaction with the created world and all humans wishing to partake of divine emanation must relate to him either directly or through intermediaries close to him.

In Sufi hagiographic narratives, cosmological claims about the pole and other saints are substantiated through telling stories about their manners, habits, and bodily miracles. The work on Ni'matallah Vali I cited above also provides many details of the physical habits of the master. We are told that when sitting in company, the saint never raised his hands to his facial hair. He never did uncouth things such as spitting, and no one ever saw him sleeping. He ate and drank very little and wore simple clothes and headgear in the tradition of Muhammad and earlier Sufi masters. A belt around the waist was the only thing that indicated that he was a Sufi since he never wore robes and other paraphernalia used by some Sufis to flaunt their religious vocation in public. His room was often adorned with flowers and he spoke with such eloquence that one thought that one was reading a book rather than listening to a person. Further, a different work on the same master tells us that the physical potency of his body continued even after his death: those who went to visit his mausoleum observed that the surrounding area was devoid of any flies, fleas, or mosquitoes.[25]

The physical aspects of the ideal bodies I have discussed in this section mark them as subjects of emulation. This material indicates that, like the functions of universal rituals discussed earlier, imitating the acts of ideal bodies is a necessary step in the process of transforming one's own body for the sake of being realized as a Muslim subject. All bodies, in their structures as well as movements, stand in relation to other bodies of the past or the present that are worthy of emulation or shunning.

CONCLUSION

In the final analysis, the body in Islamic thought and practice appears as an object suspended between the fields of ideals and realities. As implied in the joke with which I began the essay, the beard and the stomach (and what the two signify) are essential to the body and neither can exhaust its possibilities on its own. The body is perpetually under construction: in parallel with its organic growth and decay, its symbolic functions are forever in flux between individual consciousness and social influences of many different origins. Even the very limited review of material possible in this essay should make plain that it is quite impossible to localize a "Muslim body" or even juridical, philosophical, or Sufi versions of the body because of the internal diversity inherent in these discourses. Moreover, factors such as gender, age, skin color, and so on that can set particular human bodies apart from each other physically as well as symbolically constitute irreducible limits to the idea of the human body as a sociohistorical universal in any meaningful sense. From this perspective, a phenomenological understanding of the "Muslim body" as a type seems problematic since it attempts to fix the body's meaning rather than registering its continual evolution. Such an archetypal body can be seen to be there from an internal religious perspective, but this view must stand in tension (a productive one but a tension nevertheless) with respect to a thoroughly historicizing view of Muslims' ideas and lives.[26]

As beings mired in the material world, humans cannot but think with and through the body. This fact, a truism in the modern study of corporeality, can be illustrated in the Islamic context by considering God's anthropomorphically corporeal description of himself in the Qur'an that amounts, from the internal Muslim perspective, to a self-portrait. Here we see God refer to Himself in situations such as sitting on a throne and having eyes and hands. These descriptions became the subject of heated debate in early Islamic history and, aside from very small fringe groups, Muslims in the long run came to see them as devoid of reference to animal bodies. The main theological positions were divided between those who advocated a fully metaphorical interpretation, which saw the references to body parts as code for God's abstract qualities, and those who insisted on a literal reading but with the proviso that God's hands, eyes, and so on, could in no way be compared to animal body parts.[27] Both the metaphorical and the literal explanations eschew God as body in comparison with human bodies. Himself emphatically transcendent in mainstream Islamic theologies, God is nevertheless credited with creating a cosmos centered on beings whose physical bodies contain all the world's possibilities in their structures and movements. To actualize this potential, human beings are required to study and emulate those designated as God's elect among them. At the broadest level, the God of Muslim imagination wishes human beings to use their material bodies to transcend the limitations of materiality. Details of the wide spectrum of ways in which this is to be accomplished can account for a considerable proportion of the history of Islamic thought and practice.

5

COMMUNITY

Ahmet T. Karamustafa

Community is a multivalent term. When it is used as a lens with which to probe the Islamic religious tradition, perhaps the most obvious association it calls forth is the communal dimension of Islamic confessional identity. This dimension can be captured by a short question: how central is the notion of community for Muslim identity? Although the question appears to be straightforward, it has no simple answer.

IDEALS VERSUS SOCIAL REALITY

To what extent have Muslims had awareness of the significance of community? How do we assess the significance of *communal awareness* in Islamic history? To anyone who is familiar with even the barest outlines of the first century of Islamic history, these would appear to be facetious questions. After all, it is common knowledge that Islam started out in the form of a political community, the *umma*, set apart from all other communities on the basis of Islamic faith and practice, that it rapidly grew into a vast empire ruled by the community of Muslims who enjoyed political, economic, and social privileges as Muslims; that, conversely, non-Muslims as non-Muslims in this new Islamic empire were rendered subservient on all these levels; and, finally, that the Muslim/non-Muslim distinction has always functioned as a major social fault-line in Islamic history well into the modern period until the formation of nation-states with Muslim-majority populations in the second half of the twentieth century. Surely, then, Muslims' awareness of their own status as a community apart from all other communities is (so to speak) written into the original template of Islam, and, just as surely, it would therefore be folly to question the significance of communal awareness for Muslims in Islamic history. To be a Muslim, in this view, has always been and continues to mean awareness of being a member of a separate community of believers set apart from other communities on political, social, economic, cultural, and religious levels.

Such a vision of Muslim communal awareness is indeed tempting. Are not many Muslim preachers the world over, not to mention scholars of Islam – Muslim and non-Muslim – especially in Europe and North America, constantly expounding the significance of the *umma*, the global and universal community of Muslims? To listen to this rhetoric about the *umma* emanating from Muslim religious figures and observers of Islam alike, one would think that the *umma* is a real entity whose webs envelop the globe and whose interconnections are active, indeed almost organic. In a nutshell, the image projected – or rather the image desired (by activist Muslims of one kind or another) or feared (by concerned non-Muslim observers) as the case may be – is that of a tightly united global Muslim community that acts as a single, autonomous organism. Does such an *umma* exist? Has it ever existed?

The answer is no. Such an objectified community does not exist, and it is a safe assumption to make that it has never existed on any socially significant scale. Yes, some notable hermits aside, Muslims have certainly always lived within social communities, yet the *umma* has never been more than an *imagined community*, an *ideal* and *idealized* conception developed by Muslim cultural elites and religious functionaries as a *normative vision* of Muslim social existence and deployed by them as a conceptual tool in their attempts to realize some version of a cultural project of Islamizing social life. In other words, *umma* is a normative concept used to develop communal awareness and, ultimately, real communal bonds among Muslims. As a normative concept, it is regularly used *prescriptively* to inculcate communal values into Muslims and to motivate them to think and act in full awareness of the communal dimensions of human life. It would, therefore, be an error to reify this normative concept as if it was *descriptive* of a really existing state of affairs. The existence of real social links among Muslims *as* Muslims always needs to be established on the basis of historical and social scientific evidence;

it can never be assumed or taken for granted. For all the talk about the *umma*, then, we need to be wary of objectifying a global Muslim community, or even regionalized and localized versions of the *umma* (such as "the American Muslim community"), let alone assuming communal awareness among Muslims just because they are Muslims. Religious community is more often imagined than real, prescribed than actualized.

Prescribed and imagined though they may have been, visions of community have nevertheless functioned as very real cultural projects of considerable social consequence in Islamic history. In this sense, the answer to the above question "Does a global Muslim community exist? Has it ever existed?" is "Yes, it has always existed *as an idea,* or rather, *as a cluster of visions of community,* since the beginning of Islamic history." Here, some methodological observations are in order:

(1) There has always been a multiplicity of visions, some at odds with others, rather than a single unitary vision of the Muslim *umma*.

(2) These various visions have all been historically constructed by particular social actors at specific historical junctures under specific social circumstances, such that no vision has been immune to historical conditioning and change.

(3) As a rule, such visions of community have been projects of cultural domination conceived and deployed by the Muslim elites, but such elite-generated hegemonic projects have always been contested, challenged, resisted, transformed, modified, and remade by the Muslim subalterns.

"DIVINE" VISIONS OF COMMUNITY

Before we delve into Muslim elite visions of community, let us review briefly the "divine" visions as found in the foundational documents of Islam, the Qur'an and the *sunna*. Given the pronounced predilection of Muslims to use Qur'anic verses and prophetic *hadith* as proof texts for just about any and every view they would like to promote, and, more importantly, given the hermeneutic malleability and open-endedness of these documents, it is a precarious exercise to focus in on particular concepts in the Qur'an and the *sunna* as if it was possible to identify and to isolate "essentially Qur'anic and prophetic" understandings of any given concept. Furthermore, one should also avoid the temptation to treat Qur'anic and prophetic discourses as anything more than *ingredients* or *building blocks* used by Muslims to construct, or to justify, already constructed social and cultural edifices. There is considerable talk about human communities in the Qur'an and the *sunna*, but whether and how Muslims use these Qur'anic and prophetic materials, and, if and when they use them, what they actually do with these ingredients is an entirely different matter altogether.

With these caveats in mind, it is possible to make some general comments about Qur'anic and prophetic visions of community. In the Qur'an, there is a clear awareness of a wide range of human groupings, both religious and non-religious. While non-religious groups such as "people/ethnic community" (*shu'b*) and "tribe" (*qabila*) are noted (Q49:13), religious groupings receive much more attention. The key term on this front is *umma*. Although it has other meanings, *umma* most often denotes a human religious community, which is normally envisaged as a prophetic community with a clear confessional identity and a distinct ritual practice. Significantly, the word is used for both Muslim and non-Muslim communities, and the plurality of human religious communities is not only portrayed as the natural state of affairs but even endorsed as part of the divine plan in at least one verse (Q5:48). Indeed, the Qur'anic view of the religious state of humanity seems to be a historical division of an erstwhile single humanity (Q2:213; 16:120) into multiple, albeit all monotheistic, religious communities, a division that was brought about by a peculiar combination of human dissension (failure to live up to the terms of divine messages delivered to human communities by God via prophets and messengers) and divine providence (God's preference for plurality of communities).

The Muslim *umma* is described as the "midmost" (Q2:143) and the "best" community (Q3:110), presumably one that is supposed to serve as a model for all human religious communities, though the Jews and Christians too are said to have a "just, balanced" group at their core (Q5:66). Indeed, there is considerable ambiguity about the difference between "faith" (*iman*) and "faithful" (*mu'min*) on the one hand and "submission to God" (*islam*) and "submitter to God" (*muslim*) on the other. There is no simple equivalence between these two semantic fields, and since faith-related terms outnumber submission-related terms by a wide margin (*mu'min* occurs some five times more than *muslim*), there is good reason to think that being a generic monotheist believer is the true measure of faith as opposed to being a nominal Muslim. In other words, it is impossible to tell if the Qur'anic concepts of faith and submission to God refer to actual socio-religious groupings in Arabia of the early seventh century and earlier or, quite by contrast, if they are theological groupings that normatively hover above historical reality. Analysis of other key terms in the Qur'an that denote "religion" and "religious community," notably *din* and *milla*, bears out this peculiar intractability of Qur'anic designations and categories, which appear to be located somewhere between theological abstraction and social reality.

Turning to the *sunna*, one can see confirmation there of the Qur'anic perspective on the division of humanity into many prophetic communities in the form of various *hadith* reports about a plurality of religious communities on resurrection day and in paradise (for instance, the report in Ibn Maja's section on "Zuhd" about Muslims making up one-third of the people of paradise, with the rest coming from other communities). But aside from isolating such areas of semantic overlap between particular Qur'anic verses and particular *hadith*, it would be hazardous to generalize about prophetic views on community since the *hadith* is a body of essentially disparate materials that do not easily lend themselves to the construction of coherent and internally consistent perspectives on any given topic. Instead, prophetic reports, even more than Qur'anic verses, appear to have been used as proof texts for different viewpoints or at times as springboards for intellectual speculation on central issues. Prominent among such *hadith* on the topic of community are the following:

- "My community will not agree on an error" (Ibn Maja, "Fitan")
- "Everyone of my community will enter paradise except those who reject me" (Al-Bukhari, "Fitan")
- "Disagreement in my community is a divine mercy" (non canonical)
- "My community will be divided into seventy-three sects" (Ibn Maja, "Fitan;" Abu Dawud, "Sunna," among others)
- "Whoever removes himself from the community by the space of a single span, withdraws his neck from the halter of Islam" (Abu Dawud, "Sunnah")
- "Whoever dies after being separated from the community dies as men died in the days before Islam" (Muslim, "Kitab al-imara, bab al-amr fi luzum al-jama'a").

It is easy to see how these and similar *hadith* could be used in attempts
to negotiate complicated questions of communal salvation and communal unity. This is precisely what happened, and such prophetic
reports have been regularly deployed to build and defend various
positions on a wide range of issues directly and indirectly related to
the idea of the Muslim community.

"THE MUSLIM COMMUNITY": HISTORY OF AN IDEA

The formation of Muslim communities in both the social and intellectual realms, though certainly informed – even infused – by Qur'anic
and prophetic discourses, followed its own historical trajectory. The
main outlines of early Muslim history are well known. After starting
out as a socially disunited community of monotheistic believers in
Mecca who pledged allegiance to Muhammad as God's messenger,
Muslims emerged as a distinct polity of believers after their emigration (*hijra*) to Medina in 622. This moment is traditionally thought
to have been captured in the document known as the "Constitution
of Medina," a charter that was meant to regulate the political relationships among the different constituents of the town, including its
Jewish clans. In spite of the existence of clear fault-lines within the
Muslim community (notably among the Meccan emigrants, *muhajirun*, and their Medinese hosts, *ansar*), it maintained its political unity
throughout Muhammad's lifetime (he died in 632) as well as during
the rule of the first two caliphs who succeeded him, Abu Bakr (632–
634) and 'Umar (634–644). Unity began to dissipate, however, during
the rule of the third caliph 'Uthman (644–656), and disappeared completely with his assassination, when the community was plunged into
outright civil war (656–661). After a second civil war in short order
(680–692), the Muslims were divided into several rival communities
around the question of leadership (*imama*), even though a relatively
high degree of political unity was subsequently achieved under the
Umayyad dynasty (692–750). However, more trials and tribulations
in the form of civil strife and war (*fitna*) ensued, peaking in the mid-
eighth century at the overthrow of the Umayyads by the 'Abbasids
through a full-blown revolution. Political unity had proven to be a
most elusive, indeed an impossible, ideal.

The division of Muslims into rival communities was concomitant
with the emergence of different perspectives on Muslim communal

identity and on the significance of communal unity. Two of the major orientations of this period, the Kharijis and the Shi'is, rendered salvation conditional upon allegiance to the "legitimate" leader (*imam*) of the community, whose guidance was considered to be indispensable for achieving justice and prosperity in this world as well as personal and communal salvation in the next. However, neither the Kharijis nor the Shi'is had much success in gaining political power over the majority of the Muslim community; instead, both groups faced continuous adversity at the hands of the Umayyad and 'Abbasid caliphs. Under such circumstances, most Muslims of various other orientations gradually came to place a higher premium on membership in the broad community of Muslims over against allegiance to an *imam*. As far as they could tell, debate, contention, and conflict had not brought about any consensus concerning the identity and credentials of such an *imam*; more pointedly, political power had devolved into the hands of rulers – Umayyad and 'Abbasid caliphs – whose leadership qualities and virtues as believers were at best dubious and at worst outright deplorable. Therefore, it seemed far more sensible to seek refuge in the salvific promise of membership in the "big tent" community than to risk harm in this world and perdition in the next by placing one's bets on the slim chances of political success that any Khariji and Shi'i contender for the imamate possessed.

Such a "communitarian" perspective was first forcefully articulated during the eighth century by a group of religious scholars (*'ulama*) who adopted the label *ahl al-hadith*, the "Hadith Party," on account of their insistence that prophetic reports (*hadith*) constituted the only complete and accurate repository of Muhammad's exemplary practice (*sunna*). These scholars argued further that the *sunna* trumped all non-Qur'anic sources of authority, including any so-called rightly guided leader. The Qur'an and the *sunna* made up the sum total of the revelation, meaning that God's communication with humanity had come to an end with the death of Muhammad. In addition, many in the Hadith Party placed a special emphasis on communal solidarity since, in their judgment, Muhammad had entrusted his right practice to his community, and his *sunna* could only be preserved and kept alive if the community of Muslims "stuck together." This communitarian view, which was a clear mandate to protect communal unity at all costs, came to be inextricably associated with a non-Qur'anic word for community, *jama'a*, (literally "assembly"), and its adherents came to be known as *ahl al-sunna wa'l-jama'a*, "people of right practice and community." Proponents of this view had the unenviable task of retrojecting communal unity into the earliest phase of Islamic history over against the clear evidence of communal dissension as witnessed by the first civil war. Their efforts to minimize communal dissociation in favor of unity produced the theory of the "four rightly guided caliphs" (*rashidun*), which portrayed all of the first four caliphs (Abu Bakr, 'Umar, 'Uthman and 'Ali) as legitimate. True, this theory flew in the face of the widespread and bloody conflicts that had enveloped the reigns of 'Uthman and 'Ali, but it had the merit of casting the first few generations of Muslims as righteous and faithful preservers of Muhammad's right practice, and it provided communitarians with an effective way of glossing over past communal rifts, without denying them or covering them up altogether. All a good Muslim needed to do was to maintain faith in the authenticity of the Hadith as preserved by the early generations of Muslims – that is, the "rightly guided" caliphs and the companions of Muhammad (*sahaba*) who had followed them – and to implement the *sunna* through careful study, cultivation, and application of the Hadith.

The "people of right practice and community" had succeeded in articulating a highly attractive communitarian (*jama'i*) vision. Their focus on the community as the proper locus of prophetic authority signaled a clear shift away from the view that allegiance to a "righteous leader" (*imam*) was the only true measure of faith, and in an age where power politics had all but sapped the ideal of a rightly guided, charismatic leader of its popular appeal, this infusion of the public with authority found considerable resonance. Most spectacularly, the Hadith Party emerged victorious out of the famous "inquisition" (*mihna*) of the first half of the ninth century, which was a clear attempt on the part of the 'Abbasid caliphs to pry religious authority out of their hands. With the Hadith Party thus vindicated, the theory of the four "rightly guided" caliphs began to gain broad acceptance.

During the second century of 'Abbasid rule (mid-ninth to mid-tenth century), many religious scholars other than the Hadith Party came to appreciate the merits of Hadith and incorporated the corpus of prophetic reports fully, albeit at different levels, into their methodology of the study of law and theology. Most scholars of legal and theological matters were rationalists or semi-rationalists in religious inquiry and, as such, they were often diametrically opposed to the Hadith Party who accepted only the authority of the Qur'an and the *sunna* and ruled out reason as a tool of religious scholarship. Nevertheless, all religious scholars had benefited from the victory of the Hadith Party over the 'Abbasid caliphs, and many began to avail themselves of the label "people of right practice and community" and its variations. In a nutshell, many religious specialists were attracted to the communitarian vision precisely because they increasingly viewed themselves as the collective conscience of the Muslim community; if the community was empowered as the collective repository of the Hadith, this only meant that they, the religious scholars themselves, were empowered. The centrality of such a scholastic vision of community is amply demonstrated by the emergence and rise to prominence of the doctrine of "consensus" or "communal agreement" (*ijma'*) in legal scholarship. Although it was defined differently by different scholars, *ijma'* generally stood for agreement of prominent scholars on any given issue, which was taken to be expressive of the collective will of the broad community. Naturally, this was a highly idealistic concept whose implementation was problematic, but its broad acceptance as a fundamental method of legal reasoning is indicative of the growing appeal of the communitarian vision among religious scholars of different stripes in this period.

It is therefore safe to assert that the rise of religious scholars as the holders of religious authority for the majority of Muslims during the ninth and tenth centuries represents, to a considerable extent, the triumph of communitarianism in Islam. The jurists (*fuqaha'*) and the theologians (*mutakallimun*) of various persuasions continued to disagree among themselves on many questions related to the Muslim community and much else besides, but most of them were united around their scholarly self-image as the collective conscience of the *umma*. This self-understanding was captured in the popular saying attributed to Muhammad: "the scholars are the heirs of the prophets." The jurists may have been seriously divided among themselves into rival schools (sg. *madhhab*), and the theologians likewise increasingly compartmentalized into competing orientations, but in time, especially after the tenth century, members of such legal and theological groupings came to view each other as acceptable – albeit genuinely distinct, even conflicting – alternatives under the larger dome of Islam. This singularly communitarian vision that gradually prevailed during the eleventh and twelfth centuries came to be known as Sunnism. Although Sunni scholars cast their communal net broadly, their canopy did not extend far enough to cover either those who continued to cherish the ideal of a charismatic righteous leader

(Kharijis and Shi'is) or those whose reliance on human reason seemed to overshadow the primacy of the Qur'an and the *sunna* (rationalist theologians known as Mu'tazilis as well as philosophers). By the time of the Mongol invasions of the thirteenth century, the Sunni consensus had come to envelop the Hanafi, Shafi'i, Maliki, and Hanbali legal schools and the Ash'ari and Maturidi theological orientations.

Significantly, even the majority of Kharijis and Shi'is had their own communitarian turn between the tenth and twelfth centuries. In the absence of politically successful legitimate rulers (this was the case for most Kharijis) or even the complete occultation of the rightly guided leader (the Imami Shi'is, also known as the Twelvers, came to believe that the *imam* had gone into occultation in 873), they too, no less than their Sunni counterparts, began to view their scholars as the only semi-legitimate religious authorities that they could follow. Thus, for most Kharijis and Shi'is, who viewed themselves as the sole true believers, religious scholars emerged as the custodians of communal unity. Even erstwhile proponents of charismatic leadership had come around to place more weight on communal solidarity as orchestrated by scholars.

Thus, Islam can be said to have had its own "rabbinic" turn, whereby religious authority shifted from prophetic and caliphal figures to religious scholars. Through this shift, the vision of a righteous polity of believers united behind a rightly guided leader came to be supplanted – though by no means totally suppressed – by the vision of a righteous community held together by common acceptance of a normative framework for human conduct as articulated by the *'ulama*. This normative framework, called the *shari'a*, became the moral and legal scaffolding for the ideal of communal unity, and its implementation by a dedicated cadre of religious specialists throughout Muslim settlements everywhere (though more rigorously in major urban centers) came to be seen by Muslim elites as the true measure of Muslim communal identity. The faithful may not have achieved political or cultural unity but their scholastic elite had managed to develop a series of legal, ethical, and theological networks that functioned as communal threads.

COMMUNITY IN HISTORY

Certain aspects of the *shari'a* readily served to generate communal identity. This was the case especially with its socially visible, behavioral norms that governed public conduct, including communally observed religious rituals. Rituals such as the public communal prayer – especially the congregational Friday noon prayer – the Ramadan fast, and the annual pilgrimage to holy sites in and around Mecca no doubt functioned as mechanisms that fostered communal identity. So did norms that related to all aspects of social life, from the domestic and familial to the artisanal and commercial, from rites of passage to public ceremony. The scope of the *shari'a* was indeed wide and its social reach, thanks to the collective authority of the *'ulama*, often considerable.

Nevertheless, it is difficult to know to what extent these norms were actually applied in any given historical community, and it would be a grave mistake to think that the scholarly visions of the ideal Muslim community were ever fully translated to social reality. In practice, many factors other than legal and theological norms were involved in the making of actual social communities. Race, ethnicity, language, kinship ties, age, gender, geographical location, and political organization all contributed and continue to contribute to community construction and communal identity. On the ground, there have been literally thousands of communities of various kinds and shapes, all informed at some level by Islamic norms that were themselves diverse and heterogeneous. There has never been a singular united Muslim community any more so than a single Islamic ideal of communal life, yet it is a safe bet that Muslims will continue to generate ever more visions of the ideal Muslim communal life on earth.

6

CULTURE

Michael Cooperson

IBN FADLAN AND THE RUSIYYAH

In the early 920s, during a voyage up the Volga River, a Muslim traveler named Ibn Fadlan encountered a group of tall, red-haired people he calls the Rusiyyah. The men, he says, were covered with tattoos and armed to the teeth. The women were draped in neckbands, metal disks, and beads. The Rusiyyah washed only in the morning, sharing a single bowl of filthy water, and never cleaned themselves after excreting or having sex. They prayed to wooden figures set up in the ground, begging them to help them sell the furs and slaves they traded in, and offering them the severed heads of animals if they complied. When one of their chieftains died, they would stage an elaborate funeral for him and then burn his corpse. Fortunately for Ibn Fadlan, who was eager to witness a cremation, a chieftain happened to die while he was nearby.

First, the mourners hauled the dead man's ship out of the water. Then they propped his corpse up inside it, along with food, drink, weapons, and several slaughtered animals. Near it, they set up a wooden structure "like a door-frame." On the day of the cremation, they took a slave who had volunteered to accompany the chief into the afterlife, carried her to the wooden structure, and then lifted her into the air. "I see my father and my mother," she cried, and was lowered to the ground. She was then lifted into the air a second time, this time exclaiming: "I see all of my dead kindred, seated." The third time, she reported seeing her master in paradise, which was beautiful and green. She was then taken aboard the ship and handed over to "a gloomy, corpulent woman" called the Angel of Death. Forced to lie next to the corpse, the slave had sexual intercourse with six men. Afterwards, she was stabbed by the "Angel of Death" and strangled by two of the men while the rest banged sticks and shields together to cover her screams. The people then came forward with torches and set fire to the ship. "It took scarcely an hour for the ship, the firewood, the slave-girl and her master to be burnt to a fine ash."[1]

Ibn Fadlan's account of the Rusiyyah conveys a powerful sense of strangeness. At first, the merchant warriors seem more animal than human: they are "the filthiest of all Allah's creatures," they have sex in public, and they leave the sick to fend for themselves. Later, during the cremation scene, they acquire more horrifying attributes; with each new detail, we come to share Ibn Fadlan's shock and disgust. Yet the very presence of all these details reveals that he was not simply shocked and disgusted. He was also curious: curious enough to travel to a funeral, ask an interpreter what was being said, and note down details so accurate that they can be matched with the archeological and literary evidence for the customs of the Volga peoples. Most strikingly, he seems to have accepted the idea that from the Rusiyyah's point of view, their customs made sense, whereas his own did not:

> One of the Rusiyyah stood beside me and I heard him speaking to my interpreter. I quizzed [the interpreter] about what [the man] had said and he replied: "He said, 'You Arabs are a foolish lot!'" I said, "Why is that?" and he replied, "Because you purposely take those who are dearest to you ... and throw them under the earth, where they are eaten by the earth, by vermin and by worms, whereas we burn them in the fire there and then, so that they enter Paradise immediately." Then he laughed loud and long.[2]

Ibn Fadlan's account suggests that culture, apart from any abstract definition, is what we see when we look at people who belong to a community other than our own. In this respect, his attitude differs little from the writings of the classic modern ethnographers. Here, for example, is Napoleon Chagnon's description of his first encounter, in 1964, with the Yanomamö of northern Brazil:

> I looked up and gasped when I saw a dozen burly, naked, filthy, hideous men staring at us down the shafts of their drawn arrows! Immense wads of green tobacco were stuck between their lower

teeth and lips making them look even more hideous, and strands of dark-green slime dripped or hung from their noses ... My next discovery was that there were a dozen or so vicious, underfed dogs snapping at my legs, circling me as if I were going to be their next meal. I just stood there holding my notebook, helpless and pathetic. Then the stench of the decaying vegetation and filth struck me and I almost got sick. I was horrified. What sort of welcome was this for the person who came here to live with you and learn your way of life, to become friends with you?[3]

The more differences there are, the more culture there seems to be; and though, if pressed, we would admit that we too belong to a culture, we would also have to admit that it takes an effort to think of our own beliefs and practices as incomprehensible and possibly even disgusting to others.

But strangeness is not the whole story. As Ibn Fadlan's account also suggests, the very curiosity that leads one to revel in strangeness also leads one to try and make sense of it. There is, of course, no guarantee of success. As James Montgomery has noted, there are several places where Ibn Fadlan reads the customs of the Rusiyyah in terms of his own Muslim faith: calling the old woman the Angel of Death, for example, and describing paradise as green. Even so, the account of the funeral in particular suggests that he "wanted to understand what these ceremonies meant for [the Rusiyyah] and was not content simply to impose an Islamic lamina upon them."[4] So faithful is his account, indeed, that modern scholars have been able to second-guess him on the basis of evidence he himself provides. The banging together of shields and sticks, for example, may not have been intended to cover the screams of the slave – who was probably drugged in any case – but rather "to distract the attention of the spirit world, whose presence might mar the second ritual marriage" between her and the chief.[5]

In the very act of narrowing the gap between himself and the Rusiyyah, Ibn Fadlan also closes the gap between himself and his modern readers. Despite its fascination with difference – or more exactly, *because* of its fascination with difference – his account closes – or seems to close – the gap between his tenth-century world and our modern one. Ibn Fadlan was hardly one of us: he lived more than a thousand years ago and wrote in a language that no one today can be confident of understanding perfectly. Compared with the filthy, idol-worshipping Rusiyyah, however, he seems practically modern – not only in his disgust, but also in his impulse to make sense of what he sees. In his two roles of horrified eyewitness and inquiring observer, he functions perfectly as a stand-in for the modern reader. So powerful is this effect that it has inspired two modern adaptations of his account, one a novel by Michael Crichton called *Eaters of the Dead* and the other a 1999 film called *The 13th Warrior*.[6]

Of course, the accessibility of these literary retellings does not mean that the differences between Ibn Fadlan and ourselves have been erased. It does, however, suggest that differences are not always located in the places where we first imagine them to be; and that they also have a tendency to change position. In Arabic-speaking countries, translations of Crichton's novel are reportedly marketed as editions of Ibn Fadlan's original text. Evidently, the back-translation of a twentieth-century English novel cannot be distinguished from a tenth-century Arabic geographical text, even by native speakers. This phenomenon, which has parallels in many parts of the world, suggests that it is hardly meaningful to lump medieval and modern Arabs together in a category called "Arab" or "Islamic" or "Arab–Islamic" culture. Rather, modern consumers of Ibn Fadlan stories, no matter where they live, belong to a transnational media culture where mass-market productions have become a part of daily experience. Whether they are welcomed or resisted, such productions inevitably alter people's relationship to their local culture(s).[7] The diversity of representational orders is nothing new: even before globalization, cultures were hardly the self-contained units that we may imagine them to have been. Nevertheless, the most common understanding of culture remains grounded in the idea of difference.

CULTURE AS STORYTELLING

Regardless of who is looking at whom, reports of encounters with unfamiliar communities usually begin with a catalogue of oddities. "On the first day, we could not help feeling that strange things were happening to us," wrote Rifaʻa Rafiʻ al-Tahtawi, a member of the first Egyptian scholarly delegation to France, of his arrival in Marseille in 1824:

> They sent us a number of French servants, whose language we did not know, along with some hundred chairs, since the people of this

country think it odd to sit on a carpet, much less on the ground. Then they served breakfast. They brought out high tables, which they laid with white dishes made of something like porcelain. In front of each plate they placed a glass, a knife, a fork, and a spoon. On each table were two pitchers of water and vessels for salt and pepper. Then they placed chairs – one for each person – around the table. Then they brought the food. On each table they put one or two large platters, so that one of the people sitting at the table could serve the rest by putting some food in each plate. Each person would then cut his food with the knife that had been put in front of him, then put it in his mouth with a fork, not his hand; for people here never eat with their hands, or use another person's fork or knife, or drink from another's glass. They claim that this is a cleaner and safer way to eat.[8]

For us the scene is familiar, but al-Tahtawi's Egyptian readers would have been surprised to hear of people who sat on individual chairs around a high table rather than on carpets or pillows around a low table on the floor. They would also have found it odd that people ate with utensils, not with their hands; and that each person ate from his or her own dish rather than from a collective platter.

Despite the strangeness of the scene for him, al-Tahtawi presents it with a kind of detached serenity, as if to reassure the reader that an explanation is forthcoming. There will indeed follow much discussion of French hygienic practices, of which he provides a foretaste here by noting that the French consider their way of eating to be cleaner and safer (than his, presumably). Along with the catalogue of oddities, this hinting at explanations to come is also a feature of modern ethnographies. "Glancing at the six or seven small grass huts" of "a traditional !Kung village," writes Marjorie Shostak, "the visitor might notice how low they were" and "how closely one was set beside another." The !Kung live (or at least did live, in 1971) "in a remote corner of Botswana, on the northern fringe of the Kalahari desert," where "space is abundant and privacy could easily be arranged," but the doors of all the huts "face inward toward a large communal space because privacy is not something most !Kung deem very important."[9]

In modern ethnographies, the catalogue of oddities sets up a space in which the narrator (that is, the ethnographer) can pull off the trick of making the strange seem familiar. Typically, the observer gains the confidence of one or more individuals who initiate him or her into the intimate life of the community. At the end of nearly a year spent among the !Kung, says Shostak, "I had a breakthrough: after weeks of friendly, informal talks with a woman named Bau, she started to confide in me. She told me about things other people had only hinted at, and she told me about her own life." Eventually the observer feels qualified to offer explanations for the behavior of the people he or she is observing. "Any group of people who had to live off the land," says Shostak in her discussion of the !Kung, "would face similar ecological problems and would probably invent a roughly similar system" of social and economic organization. This premise, in turn, both assumes and confirms the premise of biologically grounded human universals: "People everywhere are, in a biological sense, fundamentally similar, and have been so for thousands of years."[10] For modern people, references to common human descent may make cultural differences more comprehensible. Among pre-modern or non-Western people for whom biology is not an available frame of reference, other universals may serve the same purpose. Ibn Fadlan and the Rusiyyah, for example, were able to make sense of each other on the basis of their shared belief in an afterlife.

Ibn Fadlan may have set out to tell a story about difference, but ended up discovering that the Rusiyyah were less incomprehensible than he first imagined. In modern ethnographies, this discovery is the point, and the plot. No matter how outlandish, perverse, or terrifying the natives may seem during that first encounter, their behavior will eventually "make sense." Viewed as narratives, ethnographic accounts present mysteries and then solve them. Like mystery stories, ethnographies are satisfying when the event to be explained comes across as eerie and bizarre, the solution in retrospect appears obvious, and the process of discovery corresponds with the development of self-awareness on the part of the observer. Given the seemingly unavoidable literary character of ethnographic narration, some modern critics have declared it fraudulent, or at least systematically misleading, especially in view of the customary inequality of power relations between the observer and the observed. Yet there is no obvious way to avoid it altogether.[11]

Upon arriving in an Iraqi village in the 1950s, the American anthropologist Elizabeth Fernea was intimidated by the women whom she was expected to befriend and by the rituals of a society that at first made no sense. Among these rituals was a visit of condolence to a neighbor whose mother had died. "Since Um Saad and I had so much in common, I assumed that our attitudes toward death might also be similar, that this condolence call would be much like the ones I had paid in my own country. I was quite, quite wrong." Inside Um Saad's house, Fernea found the other callers, all women, sitting on the floor in silence. First one woman, then another, "said something, half to herself, half to the group, which I understood as a generalized eulogy of motherhood." Everyone but Fernea burst into tears. After a pause Um Saad told the story of her mother's last years and her final illness. Again the women burst into tears. "This time," says Fernea, "I did too, covering my head with my abaya and sobbing without restraint. I felt sorry for Um Saad, sorry for her mother, sorry for myself even, far away from home and my own mother."[12] Here Fernea learns how to mourn on cue for a woman she hardly knew by drawing on her own experience of loss. Her account implies that the other participants were doing the same thing: that is, using a public ritual to express private grief.

As a tale of the strange made familiar, Fernea's account is eloquent. But how do we know that the Iraqi women really were feeling what she says they were feeling? It is not enough to say that we should ask them. The particular women in question may no longer be in a position to answer our questions; we must then decide whom will we allow to speak for them. Even more problematic is the assumption that asking the question and getting an answer would be a straightforward process. If people could simply articulate their feelings and motivations in a language that made perfect sense – not only linguistically but also culturally – to outside observers, there would be no need for ethnography in the first place. If one wanted to show that Fernea is wrong, one could pick apart her account in search of inconsistencies and contradictions. But to suggest a better interpretation than hers, one would have to do another round of fieldwork and write another ethnography.

CULTURE AS BEHAVIOR

Is there any way to break the cycle of storytelling? In the strict sense, no: any attempt to make sense of difference requires some kind of narrative presentation. Even so, it is possible to tell a different kind of story: one that takes as its starting point not difference but *similarity*. Instead of cataloguing oddities, one might begin by listing all the things that all human groups have in common. As a starting point for analysis, the identification of human universals is common among biological anthropologists, evolutionary biologists, and others who ground their work in a Darwinian approach to human behavior. While this strategy does not explain the oddities of any particular culture, it can help make all cultures comprehensible in terms of our shared history as a species.

For those who look to evolutionary biology for insights into human behavior, "culture" is not a collection of exotic practices but rather the totality of learned behavior that distinguishes human beings from other animals. One example of such behavior is language. Animals make a variety of sounds for a variety of reasons, but only humans can produce a potentially infinite number of utterances that make immediate sense to other speakers. Nearly all linguists today agree that this ability is common to us all as a result of evolution. Language is therefore an "instinct" in the sense that children acquire it without deciding to do so. Nevertheless, knowing a *particular* language is a learned behavior. All languages have nouns and verbs, suggesting that a distinction between things and actions is built into the human brain. Even so, the names that a given community applies to particular things and actions must be acquired through experience. There is no way to predict that a watermelon is called *bittikh* in Arabic, *hendevane* in Persian, and *karpuz* in Turkish. At the same time, no one who learns any of these words is likely to try to use it as a verb, no matter what his or her first language may be.[13]

The evolutionary advantages of linguistic communication – the ability to inform, reassure, persuade, intimidate, or deceive others, using a system that works across distances and in the dark – are obvious. On the other hand, it is not easy to see the adaptive benefit of having so many *different* languages. In all likelihood, linguistic variety is not an adaptation but an accident. Judging by the number of language families that exist today, it seems that language arose independently in at least a hundred places.[14] Even among people who speak the same language, speech changes over time, especially when no one, or only a few people, can read or write. Like many evolutionary accidents, linguistic variation may have combined with other, originally unrelated features – for example, the suspicion of non-kin – to produce a powerfully self-reinforcing set of behaviors that actually threatens rather than promotes the wellbeing of the species. For evolutionary reasons, we are naturally inclined to be suspicious of strangers; add to this the accidental fact that the strangers speak a different language, and the stage is set for catastrophic misunderstanding.

Any feature common to all peoples is likely to have arisen from adaptations to our ancestral environment, or from by-products of those adaptations. Through natural selection, the feature has become part of our common heritage. Yet the particular form it will take in any given case is the unique and unpredictable result of interaction between instinct and environment. Even religion, say some scientists, can be explained this way. Among our inherited traits is the tendency to assume that movements, sounds, and the like are caused by active, conscious, and possibly dangerous agents – a useful assumption if one is to survive in an environment full of predators. It therefore makes intuitive sense to us that all events in the world, and indeed the world itself, should be the work of active, conscious beings. The notion that such beings are invisible or otherwise unlike us is particularly appealing because it is "minimally counterintuitive": unusual enough to be remembered, but not so bizarre as to be incoherent. The belief that we should live in such a way as to please the spirits and join them in the afterlife makes it more likely that we will take risks on behalf of others, including distant relatives and strangers. To affirm our willingness to make such sacrifices, we engage in rituals, which manipulate our sensitivity to sight, sound, and motion to sustain our belief in the supernatural order. Scientists are still debating the details of this story, but the notion that religion is "a recurring cultural by-product" of evolutionary adaptations is widely accepted, even by some scientists who hold that the existence of such adaptations is itself evidence for the existence of God.[15]

Despite their differences, evolutionary approaches to culture have one thing in common: they are interested in culture in general, not in any particular culture. For Darwinians, Islam is only interesting to the extent that it, too, can be cited to support the claim of religious universals: for example, that people everywhere seek consolation and reassurance from supernatural beings and value expressions of commitment to those beings, especially expressions that take the form of self-sacrifice. The unique or distinctive features of Islam, on the other hand, are of interest only to the extent that they might be cited as evidence against the theory. Similarly, the historical and geographical diversity of Islam has little bearing on the question of religion as a human universal. There are, finally, "considerable individual and cultural differences in the degree of religious commitment" expressed by adherents of all faiths, including Islam, but though these differences are "important and intriguing," evolutionary biologists prefer to consider only the attributes of religion in general.[16]

Many scholars of culture are suspicious of the generalizing claims of the evolutionary approach. For some scholars, the premise that all human behavior can be explained by reference to the operation of a few natural laws seems reductive and deterministic. Yet this objection is itself reductive: the Darwinians are not trying to explain *all* human behavior but rather to identify the mechanisms that account for *shared* features. As it happens, these features are usually those of least interest to scholars in the humanities. It is also worth noting that evolutionary thinkers agree with cultural theorists on a fundamental point: that Islam is not some uniquely exotic deviation from the religions of the West. This point is commonly associated with the work of the literary critic Edward Said, who argued in his *Orientalism* (1978) that Western culture used distorted images of the Orient – that is, the predominantly Muslim regions of the Middle East and North Africa – to help construct its image of itself. As the West came to define itself as rational, enlightened, and humanitarian, it insisted on creating an Orient that was irrational, fanatical, and cruel. This Orient was a product of Western fears and fantasies, not a real place. But it was given the trappings of reality by a pseudo-scientific field of study called "Orientalism," whose "findings" served to sustain Western imperial projects in Southwest Asia and elsewhere.[17] Cultural theorists who scorn evolutionary biology while embracing the ideas of Said might do well to recognize that the two bodies of theory coincide in affirming that Islam is not – and cannot be – some alien and exotic phenomenon subject to rules of its own, or to no rules at all.

CAN ISLAM BE A CULTURE?

According to one common understanding of "culture," the term refers to the beliefs and practices of a particular community. By this definition, "Islamic culture" would mean "the distinctive beliefs and practices of Muslims": in other words, the religion of Islam. Can a religion be a culture? All Muslims presumably share the beliefs that there is no god but God and that Muhammad is His messenger. Furthermore, many if not most Muslims carry out the rituals that arise from this creed (for example, prayer, fasting, and the like), or at least take seriously the perceived obligation to do so. But these shared beliefs and practices are only part of what any given Muslim may think of as his or her culture. A Moroccan and an Indonesian, for example, may both belong to the worldwide community of Muslims, but each also belongs to his or her national community, as well as to other, more local groupings (tribe, village, neighborhood, etc.), each with its distinctive food, dress, language, music, and the like. In many important ways, then, Moroccans and Indonesians, like all Muslims and indeed all human beings, belong to distinct cultures that overlap or coincide in some respects while differing, sometimes radically, in others.

But what about Islam itself? Is it really the same in both Morocco and Indonesia? Clifford Geertz, an anthropologist who studied both societies, writes as if the similarities are less important and certainly less interesting than the differences; or more exactly, that the interaction of core attitudes and environmental and historical variables produces a synthesis unique to each set of circumstances. In Indonesia, for example, Islam arose in opposition to a Hindu–Buddhist tradition that it did not destroy but rather incorporated. Sunan Kalidjaga, the sixteenth-century figure who came to symbolize this transition, became a Muslim "without ever having seen the Qur'an, entered a mosque, or heard a prayer" but rather "through an inner change of heart brought on by the same sort of yoga-like psychic discipline that was the core religious act of the Indic tradition from which he came."[18] He thus represents an Islam characterized by "inwardness, imperturbability, patience, poise, sensibility, aestheticism, elitism, and an almost obsessive self-effacement." In Morocco, by contrast, Islam developed against a background of struggle between "miraboutic" and "sherifian" claims to legitimacy: that is, between devotion to an individual holy man and allegiance to a line that claimed descent from the prophet Muhammad. The figure who symbolizes this struggle is Sidi Lahsen Lyusi (d. 1691), a devout scholar who rebuked the sultan Mulay Ismail and – after terrifying him with a miraculous manifestation – demanded an acknowledgment that he, Lyusi, was himself also a descendant of the Prophet. For Geertz, Lyusi represents an Islam characterized by "activism, fervor, impetuosity, nerve, toughness, moralism, populism, and an almost obsessive self-assertion."[19] One cannot call the "classic styles" of Morocco and Indonesia variations on Islam because there is no pure, original Islam for them to be variations of; rather, Islam (like all religions) can exist only in local, particular forms, each with its defining idiosyncrasies.

The idea that a pure form of Islam actually does exist is itself a historical development, one that Geertz calls "scripturalism." Scripturalism – that is, "scholastic, dogmatic, and doctrinal" Islam – is not uniquely modern, but it has assumed particular importance in the modern period. In response to Western imperialism and the emergence of the nation-state, scripturalism offered a rationalizing reformulation of Islam that helped it survive in the face of increasingly powerful secular values. In some respects, this reformulation has been remarkably successful. Even so, the cost to faith has been great. In the 1960s, when Geertz was writing *Islam Observed*, it seemed to him that scripturalism was gaining ground at the expense of the "classical styles" of Morocco and Indonesia. As a result, the faith of many Muslims there and elsewhere had come to seem self-conscious and second hand. Although few people doubted the truth of their belief, many had come to doubt the strength of their attachment to it. In Geertz's memorable formulation, it is not God they doubted, but themselves. Half a century later, it is tempting to interpret contemporary fundamentalism as – among other things – a desperate response to the loss of the "classical styles."[20]

Whether or not one happens to agree with these particular conclusions, it seems obvious that religions, like all cultural systems, change for historical reasons and therefore differ from place to place. Then again, as Said points out, this conviction was hardly obvious to Orientalists, who spoke of Islam as a single, unchanging essence, practically identical in every age and clime. By historicizing Islam (as Geertz and others were doing even before Said), secular historians claim to have sidestepped the pitfall of Orientalism and learned to see Muslims "in all their human weight and complexity."[21] Paradoxically, however, this approach often has the opposite of its intended effect. In response to secular historians in search of local, particular forms, some Muslims insist that Islam is rather a single, undivided faith, at least in the sense that its teachings are eternally and universally true. This conviction does not forbid an acknowledgment of diversity: the contemporary Sufi thinker Nahid Angha, for example, writes that every nation "has its own distinct culture" and "Islam is practiced in each nation according to [that nation's] characteristics ... No two cultures are alike."[22] Even so, Muslim essentialism tends to regard local differences either as trivial or as harmful deviations from the norm. This attitude in turn often produces what seems from a secular perspective to be a strangely jumbled view of human affairs. "In the history of humankind," writes Angha, "none worked so much" as the Qur'an and the Prophet "to protect human rights, especially women's, with such integrity."[23] For secular historians, "human rights" does not mean simply treating people as they deserve to be treated. Rather, it is a concept with its own problematic history, a history that can be traced to the European Enlightenment and the French Revolution. Muhammad may well have established laws that improved the lot of women, but he cannot have advocated human rights any more than he can have invented the Internet. When they make this sort of objection, secular historians claim to be defending the principle that the past should be understood on its own terms, not slathered over with labels borrowed from our present-day view of the world. Muslim essentialists, conversely, tend to be bored, bewildered, or irritated by people who regard their faith as nothing more than an intellectual puzzle. If one does not agree that Islam is God's revelation to humankind and the best of all possible responses to the world, why bother to study it at all?

Like the difference between humanists and evolutionary biologists, the difference between secular historians and Muslim essentialists has less to do with the nature of the object of study than with the questions that one asks. Representatives of both positions might accept Geertz's claim that religion – any religion – can be described as "the conviction that the values one holds are grounded in the inherent structure of reality." They would probably also agree that this connection is represented through religious symbols that enable our way of life to affirm our ideas about reality while simultaneously enabling our ideas about reality to support our way of life.[24] But secular historians examine religious symbols in order to understand how this process works, whether in general or in any particular case. Believers, on the other hand, examine the world in order to confirm the rightness of their own particular view of it. One group, following the French sociologist Émile Durkheim, traces the connections between human life and cosmic reality back to human contrivance; the other, following their prophets and their scriptures, traces them back to God.

In theory, neither group has much to learn from the other. In practice, many thinkers have staked out a position somewhere in the middle. Typical in this respect is the contemporary Iranian philosopher

AbdolKarim Soroush, who speaks of religion as existing in two forms: one the pure ideal that God imagines for us, the other the stumbling human attempt to reach that ideal on earth. A religious intellectual, he says, acknowledges that "the religious understanding of people in the past was as influenced by their times and as much in line with their presuppositions as our religious understanding today is influenced by our times and is in line with our presuppositions." As modern people, we have the right – indeed, the duty – of reassessing religious law according to our own notions of right and reason. Islam, he argues, is compatible with such modern ideologies as democracy, especially when certain religious doctrines are treated as irrelevant for practical purposes: "You put such a distance between your religious thinking and the world around you that you plan your affairs without taking [religion] into account."[25]

Soroush is of course not offering this argument in a vacuum, but rather as a critique of the self-proclaimed Islamic regime that has ruled Iran since 1979. His position is admirable in its insistence that it is possible to make a peaceful transition from the current order to another, more genuinely Islamic social order better equipped to satisfy legitimate demands for justice. Whether this is a philosophically coherent position is another matter. The dissident Iranian journalist Akbar Ganji, among others, has argued in response to Soroush that no amount of interpretation can reconcile the Qur'an and *sunna* with liberalism and democracy.[26] From the outside, it seems that if Islam is to be judged by the standards of liberal democracy, then the believers' case is already lost. Then again, if we accept that religion has changed in the past and continues to change in the present, we have to acknowledge that it may evolve into something altogether different while continuing to satisfy the needs of believers.

CAN CULTURE BE ISLAMIC?

Islam, then, is not a culture; but it – like all religions – is a "cultural system," to use Geertz's term.[27] What about the converse question: can a culture – or culture in general – be Islamic? This question presumes a different definition of culture, namely "intellectual and artistic activities and achievements." This meaning is closer to the original sense of the term: "preparing soil for growing crops" or "growing plants or other tissues under controlled conditions." Just as plants may be cultivated for specific purposes, human beings may be trained in specific skills above and beyond those needed for survival within a community. The more distant these skills appear from the material necessities of life, and the more demanding the process of acquiring them, the more prestige they enjoy, and the more "cultured" their possessor appears to be.

By this definition, "Islamic culture" might mean "intellectual and artistic activities carried out by Muslims." But such a definition is misleading. A Muslim who earns a doctorate in microbiology and plays the piano in her spare time is obviously engaging in intellectual and artistic activity. But do those activities differ from those of another piano-playing microbiologist who happens to be a practicing Buddhist, a lapsed Catholic, or an atheist? In one sense, they might. If the Muslim describes her own activities as expressions of reverence for the Creator, then her "culture" might be understood as "Islamic," especially if she herself insists that it is. On the other hand, it is hard to see how her lab experiments, or her performance of Mozart, would actually differ – from the observer's point of view, at least – from the same activities as practiced by her non-Muslim colleague.

To avoid these difficulties, one might propose a different definition of Islamic culture: "intellectual and artistic activities that express Muslim ideas and values." This definition seems reasonable until we apply it to works produced in other traditions. Does the cathedral of Notre Dame in Paris represent "Christian architecture"? Does Mozart's Requiem represent "Christian music"? From one perspective, both obviously do. From another perspective, however, both represent other things as well. Notre Dame is more commonly described as an example of medieval French architecture, and the Requiem as an example of classical European music. These descriptions make sense: for one thing, both works make claims on the aesthetic sensibilities of non-Christians. For another, not every Christian would find them appropriate expressions of devotion. A Lutheran, for example, might shrink from the opulence of Notre Dame; and congregations accustomed to gospel or Christian rock might not respond to the musical language of the Requiem. The same is true of "Islamic art": many non-Muslims find examples of it appealing, while many Muslims do not.

From the above it seems that the use of labels such as "Islamic" is to a certain extent arbitrary. In Western universities, works of art produced by people who (1) happen to be Muslim and (2) have been dead for a long time are studied in courses on Islamic art, even when those works have no evident religious function. In a recent study of a decorated luster bowl crafted in Iran in 1204, Sheila Blair lists the questions it raises for scholars. These include provenance (where the bowl came from); timing (when and under what circumstances it was created); the creative role of the individual artist; the meaning of the decoration; and "the function of such a bowl and who used it and for what." Blair thus describes the object as exemplifying "the broad range of questions that can be raised by Islamic art." Yet all of the questions could equally well be asked about any artifact. In this case, furthermore, there is nothing overtly religious about the bowl. The painted decoration shows "a seated couple, a male on the right with cap and boot on a flexed leg, a female on the left with a headdress and a longer braid." Around the painting is a calligraphic band of Persian poetry lamenting the infidelity of lovers.[28] Evidently, the only reason to call this object an example of Islamic art is that it was produced in medieval Iran – a society we now call Islamic.

Applied to societies, this label is not altogether arbitrary: so-called Islamic societies were governed, if only nominally or symbolically, by men who saw themselves as leading the community (in reality, some part of it) originally established by Muhammad, the Prophet of God. This community had a name: in Arabic, it was called the *umma*. There was, by contrast, no commonly accepted name for political entities that comprised only part of the *umma*. Modern scholars refer to these entities using names like "the caliphate of Cordova," "the Seljuk empire," and "the Delhi sultanate," but the people who lived in these societies had no corresponding term that bundled together the ideas of government and territory. A Muslim living in Baghdad in 1200, or in Istanbul in 1500, would not have thought of himself or herself as an "Abbasid" or an "Ottoman" unless he or she happened to belong to the ruling family. Rather, inhabitants of both societies would have identified themselves by their religion and, in other contexts, by their familial, tribal, ethnic, territorial, or occupational affiliation, or some combination of these. Given, then, the importance of Islam as a foundation of the political order and as the declared faith of much of the population, should these societies not be called Islamic? And should the works of art they produce not be called Islamic?

For some societies and some works of art, the answer seems to be yes. For example, the caliphate of Cordova, which dominated southern Spain from 756 to 1013 or 1031, was ruled by men who claimed to be the Prophet's only legitimate successors as leaders of the *umma*. In that sense, it was an Islamic society. The dynasty's greatest monument, the cathedral mosque of Cordova, was constructed as a house of prayer. In that sense, it may fairly be called an example of Islamic architecture. For other works, however, the answer is not at all obvious. The Nasrid kingdom of Granada, which existed from 1237 to 1492, was a bastion of Islam against the Catholic Reconquista. Its major monument, the Alhambra, was not a mosque, *madrasa*, or a tomb-shrine; it was a royal residence and the seat of government. Its famously elaborate decoration includes Arabic verses about love and wine. Is the Alhambra "Islamic"? By virtue of its association with a self-consciously Muslim society, it is. In terms of its intended uses, it is not, unless one argues – as one easily could – that the building shares certain distinctive features with other buildings built by other "Islamic societies": for example, horseshoe arches and decorative Arabic calligraphy.

Even here, though, there is a problem. Like all forms and styles, those of "Islamic architecture" are transportable. The synagogue of Santa María la Blanca in Toledo uses horseshoe arches similar to those found in the mosque of Cordova; and El Transito synagogue, also in Toledo, is decorated with Arabic script. Similarly, the Armenian Vank Cathedral in Esfahan, Iran, has several characteristically "Islamic" features, including a courtyard fountain practically identical to the ones used for ablutions in mosques. Does the use of Islamic (or pseudo-Islamic) motifs make a synagogue or church "Islamic"? From an art historian's point of view, it well might, though the Jews of Toledo and the Armenians of Esfahan might find the label inappropriate and possibly even offensive.

The Toledo synagogues and the Vank church also serve as reminders of a broader point. Societies called "Islamic," whatever the justification for the label, have always included people of other religious affiliations. Indeed, some of the most celebrated achievements of "Islamic civilization" involved members of these communities. A well-studied example is the transmission of ancient Greek science and philosophy through Syriac, Arabic, Hebrew, and Latin. The works of Aristotle, Galen, and other ancient thinkers were known to Eastern Christians, who translated many of them into Syriac. After the founding of Baghdad by the Abbasid dynasty in 762, Nestorian Christians (today called "Assyrians") began putting the Syriac versions, and later the Greek originals of these and other texts, into Arabic. These translations were paid for by other Christians, mostly physicians; and by Muslims, including caliphs and viziers. Among the Muslim patrons of the so-called translation movement were the Barmaki family of viziers, who may have been inspired by the translations from Sanskrit undertaken by their Iranian Buddhist ancestors.[29] Interest in "the ancient sciences" spread among Jewish scholars as well, resulting in translations from Arabic into Hebrew for the benefit of Jews outside the Arabic-speaking countries. Eventually the translations found their way to Spain, where Jewish scholars, working in some cases from Arabic and in others from Hebrew versions, helped their Christian counterparts put them into Latin.

The many scholars involved in this process of transmission did not think of what they were doing as an Islamic cultural activity, except to the extent that Jews and Christians suspicious of Greek rationalism might condemn the translations as "Ishmaelite" or "Arab" (that is, Muslim) and therefore heretical. Only in the modern period did it become necessary to label the process as a manifestation of something called "Islamic civilization." This term not only suppresses the role of non-Muslims in the process but also overlooks the fact that the philosophical teachings thus transmitted were regarded by many Muslims as antithetical to the tenets of their faith.

To avoid confusions of this kind, one scholar, Marshall Hodgson, has proposed that non-religious works produced by Muslims, as well as works produced by non-Muslims living in societies dominated by Muslims, be called "Islamicate" rather than "Islamic."[30] Hodgson's proposal is eminently sensible, but few scholars have adopted it. One reason may be that the term "Islamicate" is awkward and unfamiliar. In some sense, too, it may be perceived as perpetuating the idea that some essential property permeates the cultural production of all peoples who have lived in regions dominated by Muslims. The cathedral of Vank may indeed be "Islamicate," but the label directs attention away from the features it shares with churches in other places and may therefore be objectionable, not least to those who worship there.

Like individual human beings, then, individual works of art belong to distinct cultural spheres that overlap or coincide in some respects while differing, sometimes radically, in others. Unlike human beings, however, works of art cannot speak for themselves. As a result, they are forced to submit to whatever labels are applied to them, with the choice of label itself depending on the culture(s) of the observer. The act of labeling is precisely symbolic of the problems we encounter when dealing with the notion of culture. The need to label a thing follows upon an initial moment of misrecognition: a disorienting "first-contact" experience, like Ibn Fadlan's encounter with the Rusiyyah. Labeling something means acknowledging that one cannot recognize it without help; it is therefore an act that affirms the strangeness of its object. At the same time, the label we choose is drawn from the stock of names already familiar to us. In that sense, the act of labeling insists that the object, no matter how odd it may appear, actually has a place – or, to be more exact, can be *given* a place – in our own thought-world. In German philosophy, there is an epistemological tradition that claims that this rising out of oneself toward the other is the highest form of self-realization. For this process – called *Bildung*, sometimes translated as "culture" – to work, the object of study must remain other; one should never imagine oneself to have captured or possessed it. Rather, the benefit of the exercise is that one becomes momentarily other with respect to oneself. "To distance oneself from oneself and from one's private purposes means to look at these in the way that others see them."[31] Whether this is possible, and if possible, sufficient, are now matters of some urgency, as indeed they have been in many times and places. As a first step, we might do well to acknowledge that culture is, first and foremost, a discourse – that is, a way of talking about something – that insists on difference while expressing a longing for the universal.

7

DEATH

Amila Buturovic

Much like the concepts of life and love, the concept of death transcends religious and cultural boundaries. Mortality, regardless of time and space, belongs to all. Yet the universality of death is a dubious proposition: unless referred to as a biological fact, death can be assigned hardly any experiential or cross-cultural universality. Its denotative value may be general but the connotative one is not: the concept of death is steeped in local signs and symbols, culturally familiar codes and images, and metaphors and descriptors that are inscribed through a dynamic interplay between specific texts and contexts. On the one hand, such specificity does not run against the fact that all religions and cultures universally wrestle with the notion of death, express anxiety about its meaning and function, and create systems of knowledge or modes of afterlife to come to terms with, or counteract, mortality and transience. On the other hand, given that these different conceptualizations of death commonly assume a totalizing discourse – "this is what death is for everyone, everywhere" – it makes it ever more challenging to understand the language about death through the linguistic culture that frames it.

Death is subject to appropriation, fascination, and often veneration; it is taken hostage by multiple disciplinary and cultural forms and sensibilities. It is a representational category. It may be universal biologically but it is not universal conceptually. Most cultures create and nurture imaginative spaces in which the dead continue to live. In the context of Islam, how does the language of death respect death's biological generality yet reflect primarily Islamic views and practices? How do Islam and Muslims position themselves toward death? To be more precise, does Islam transform death into a reality *different* from the one associated with Christianity, Buddhism, Judaism, and other religious and cultural systems? No wonder, then, that the way we speak about the dead – the "others" among us – mirrors our own attitudes, aspirations, and anxieties about life. Death is thus a relational category in which its intrinsic alterity is distilled and made familiar through a multilayered cultural sieve. In that process, as in many others, religions and cultures borrow from each other, rely on common parameters that are reworked and filtered through different lenses, and offer teachings that feed and are fed by historical practice.

In what follows, death will be discussed in the rich context of Islamic discourse and tradition, through an interdisciplinary prism, as it relates to ritual, spiritual, and intellectual sensibilities. How the perception of death is organized and shaped, what consequences it has to worldly notions and practices of submission, obedience, power, ritual, time, and other modes of behavior, is what ultimately reflects the vibrant dialectic of life and death in the multiple facets of Islamic tradition.

DEATH AS THE END ... OR JUST THE BEGINNING? THE QUR'AN AND THE HADITH

The advent of the Qur'an signaled a repositioning of Arab eschatological attitudes and sensibilities. In fact, much of the early chapters focus solely on this shift by way of introducing a new apocalyptic vision of post-mortem conditions. Vivid imagery and explicit and implicit divine pointers to a life after death occupy the Prophet's focal attention in the Meccan period. This was a corrective endeavor, as pre-Islamic Arabs are said to have thought of human death as the end of all ends; a cul-de-sac that could only be counteracted by a full and fulfilling engagement in this life. "They say, there is nothing but our present life; we live, we die, and only Time destroys us" (Q45:24). The *dahr* – translated variably as time, destiny, or fate – is the guiding principle of pre-Islamic cosmology that carries no particular fascination with constructing immortality. Like *maniyya* – fate or destiny – *dahr* is unpredictable and wicked in its workings, subjecting the living to its whims and leaving them with a feeling of having no control over their existence.

This is not to say, however, that the relationship between the dead and the living is totally severed or made impossible; on the contrary, as Emil Homerin notes in his examination of pre-Islamic elegy, certain poetic motifs in early Arabic poetry indicate that interaction does not completely cease after the person is gone. It is primarily the unavenged or disgraced deceased members of the community who keep being tormented until the record is set straight and healthy social relationships restored. Poetry and folklore in general frequently use the motif of an owl to enunciate such social ignominy. As al-Anbari writes: "And it is said that man, when he is killed and his revenge not taken, an owl comes out from his grave and then continues screeching 'Quench me!' 'Quench me!', continuing so until his killer is killed."[1] In Homerin's view, although religious motifs of eternal salvation are by and large absent from pre-Islamic culture and the stories of resurrection are treated as fantastic and improbable, death does not necessarily mark the end of life, only the end of a socially meaningful life. But, except in the aforementioned cases of social disgrace that had to be corrected, the dead bear no consequence on the affairs of the living and have little role in social interaction.

In contrast, the Qur'anic revelation starts off as heavily focused on the reconfiguration of this attitude by creating new cosmological space in which the dead are allowed eternal life on entirely new terms. Death in the Qur'an not only carries a new anthropological and theological weight but occasions a new ethic of being as well. The boundary that separates life and death is redrawn through new morality, ritual practice, philosophy, and legal responsibility.

To that end, the vicissitudes and unpredictability of fate is replaced by a responsible and omniscient divinity who oversees the cycle of life and death with reason and justice: "God surely has the knowledge of the Hour and he sends down the rain. He knows what is in the wombs, whereas no soul knows what it shall earn tomorrow; nor does any living soul know in what land it shall die. Allah is All-Knowing, Well-Informed" (Q31:34). When Nimrod challenges Abraham about the unique power of this God to give and take away life, asserting that he too is capable of it, Abraham responds by evoking the issues of divine justice and reasoning (Q2:243) that puts order in the seemingly random cycle of life and death, denying the pre-Islamic Arab notion of a chaotic and arbitrary beginning and end of individual life. The absolute divine insight is intimated in the Hadith as well:

We were in a funeral in the graveyard of Gharqad when the Messenger of God, peace be upon him, came to us and we sat around him. He had a stick. He lowered his head and started to scrape the earth with his stick, and then said: "There is not a single one among you whom a place in Paradise or Hell has not been assigned and about whom it has not been written down whether he would be an evil or a blessed person." Someone asked: "Oh Messenger of God, should we not then depend upon our destiny and abandon our deeds?" To this he answered: "Everyone's acts will be facilitated in what has been created for him so that whoever belongs to the company of the blessed will have good works made easier for him, and whoever belongs to the evil ones will have evil acts made easier for him." He then recited this verse: "Then, who gives to the needy and guards against evil and accepts the excellent (the truth of Islam and the path of righteousness it prescribes), We shall make easy for him the easy end and who is miserly and considers himself above need, We shall make easy for him the difficult end." (Q92:5–10)

God's creative power nurtures a particularly proprietary relationship that encourages faith and heightens a sense of responsibility toward one's acts in this life, as implied in this *hadith*. One's behavior is therefore neither futile nor ineffectual since they originate and return to God: "Surely, my prayer and my sacrifice and my death are God's, the Lord of the Worlds" (Q6:162), and, "Every living soul shall taste death, and We test you by evil and good as a temptation and unto Us you shall be returned" (Q21:35). Death, just like life, is a gift from God, and its genesis is related to the nature of God's relationship to human beings. "We did not grant immortality to any human," the Qur'an postulates, rebuking the idea that anything but God knows eternity. At the same time, God is capable of deferring one's death for as long as He sees necessary, as demonstrated in several didactic stories: in one such instance, a man, identified in later exegetical sources as Uzayr, passed by the ruins of a city and wondered about the possibility of resurrecting any life out of such devastation: "Thereupon God caused him to die for a hundred years, then brought him back to life" (Q2:259). While this was clearly represented as God's demonstration of omnipotence and omniscience, in the case of the "People of the Cave" in *sura* 17 (identified with the Roman "Seven Sleepers"), a temporary death of several hundred years is occasioned as a way of protecting monotheists against the onslaught of their opponents. Death is at once confirmed and subjected to a series of interpretive views on how it can be understood, received, and valued.

Many scriptural signs point to the belief that God's creative power is both enduring and re-creative. This world, *al-dunya*, preoccupies us with immediate, mundane issues. As Falzur Rahman suggests, the Qur'anic representation of *al-dunya* is not one of a neutral, descriptive value; rather, it connotes the immediate objectives, the "here-and-now" of life, so it is not only "this world" but also "the lower values, the basal pursuits which appear so immediately tempting that most men run after them most of the time, at the expense of the higher and long-range ends."[2]

The extension of this life, *al-dunya*, is the afterlife, which is a qualitatively differentiated and spatially separated form of existence. Resurrection plays a pivotal juncture in the meeting of these two realms. Indispensable to divine plan, resurrection makes continuity and eternity possible and fully experienced through one of two mutually exclusive modalities: blissful or infernal. Temporally defined as *akhira* and spatially as *dar al-akhira* (the Abode of Afterlife) and bifurcated morally into Heaven (*janna*) and Hell (*jahannam*), Qur'anic eternity is not a choice but a dictum, prescribed by God to each and every person on the Day of Judgment. Resurrection therefore is not just the process of reassembly but also one of judgment, fashioned in the form of punishment or reward, that sets off eternity on a single, unambiguous, one-way course to either infinite torment or infinite bliss. As Q22:5 announces,

> Oh people! if you have any doubt about the Resurrection, (consider) that We created you out of dust, then out of seed, then out of clot, then out of a piece of flesh, partly formed and partly unformed, in order that We may make clear to you. We cause who We will to stay in the wombs until the appointed time, then We bring you forth as babies, that you may reach your maturity; and some of you are called to die, and some are sent back to the oldest age, so that they know nothing after having known, and you see the earth barren, but when We send down rain on it, it stirs, it swells, and it brings to life every kind of beautiful growth.

The tension between life and death, this life and the hereafter, is as much an ethical as an eschatological concern. Action in light of such a tension often involves a broad spectrum of behavioral options, perceived variably as choice, acceptance, or duty, including, as the *aya* above indicates, recognizing the value of life only in so far as it is a revocable gift from God. The story of Abraham's attempted sacrifice of his son is a story of an ultimate surrender to God's test of devotion, for which God rewards him by allowing the son to live. The Qur'anic narrative of Abraham relates to the biblical story, even though there is disagreement regarding which son is chosen for sacrifice. Ibn Kathir notes in his *Tafsir* that God's intervention led to the abrogation of such practice in Q65:2–3 because Abraham had passed the test for all true believers who are willing to put trust in God. In the footsteps of Abraham, they experience the redemptive nature of trust without having to undergo Abraham's sacrificial ordeal. Abraham's story has received wide attention and interpretation since it lends itself to questions concerning faith, suffering, and the limits of devotion.[3] In ritual practice, the near sacrifice is re-enacted annually during the Eid-al-Adha in commemoration of Abraham's ultimate act of faith. Death here may only be metaphorical, but the memory of Abraham's near sacrifice of his son is a continuous reminder of the extent to which trust in God frames human life as His merciful reward.

On the other end of the spectrum lies the willingness to give up one's life as an expression of devotion. This is where the Qur'an introduces the concept of *shahada*. Derived from the Arabic word meaning "seeing," "witnessing," "testifying," *shahada* connotes an ethical stance of witnessing truth and acting on it (Q2:185), including dying for it. In this way, *shahada* as death (as opposed to *shahada* in its other meanings) developed as a widely used and broadly understood concept, defined in both lay and political terms as martyrdom death associated with just causes. Such death possesses a markedly different quality and function, as enunciated in Q2:154: "And do not say of those who are killed for the cause of God that they are dead. Nay, they are alive, but you are not aware [of them]." Here, again, eschatological reality is beyond human purview. The ambiguity of what constitutes martyrdom/death occurs because of the limits of human perception – against divine clarity – and, as such, it lends itself to different interpretive options. Moreover, the notion of martyrdom as death has proved to be a highly expandable concept, generating within Sunni, Shi'i, and other denominational teachings different attitudes that continue to evolve in relation to historical circumstances.

WHILE WAITING FOR ETERNITY

Over the centuries of Islamic intellectual tradition, much ink has been spilled to detail death in its various physical and metaphysical manifestations.[4] Fascination with the process of dying, curiosity about what lies ahead once the hour of death has arrived and passed, anxiety about the spatial and temporal experiences of post-mortem events, and many more issues have all lent themselves to rich multi-disciplinary narratives. They combine scriptural and non-scriptural sources alike in an effort to account for post-mortem experiences that begin at the hour of death which is marked, as the Qur'an tells us in Q6:93, by the angelic cry out to the dying to give up their souls (*akhriju anfusakum*), and completed when archangel Israfil sounds his trumpet that brings back all dead to life so that God can cloister each individual cycle of life and death.

In certain cases these accounts focus on the role of divine power; in others, the emphasis is laid on the anthropology of death. Whatever their angle, the ample discussions on the circumstances and condi-tions of death bespeak of the need to bring together and systema-tize different eschatological clues alluded to by the Qur'an and the Hadith. After all, the Qur'an intimates that not every aspect of human beings will cease to exist at the moment of death. Once it exits the lapsed corpse, the soul lives on. "Allah carries off the souls (*anfus*) of men upon their death and the souls of those who are not dead in their sleep. He then holds back those whose death He has decreed and releases the others till an appointed term" (Q39:42). In what follows, "the soul leaps to the throat; and you are then waiting; While We are closer to [the dead man] than you, but you do not see" (Q56:83–85). While the corpse lies in the grave, the soul – *nafs* – is released and delivered to its Creator. Death, then, brings about a fragmentation of a human being that is reversed only at the resurrection. The integrity of an individual is restored after a long physical and metaphysical separation about which the Qur'an does not say much.

Here, however, the Qur'an introduces an intermediary condition. Located between death and resurrection, this condition is presented in somewhat ambiguous terms. Referring to it three times as a form of spatio-temporal hiatus, *al-barzakh* (Q23:99–100; 25:53; 55:20), liter-ally a barrier, the Qur'an corresponds this hiatus to an eschatological waiting room, a transitional spacetime which prevents the dead from returning to this world on the one hand and forewarns them about their eschatological destination on the other. However, the exact nature of the *barzakh* has been scripturally overlooked and hence sub-jected to a debate and reflection by later Islamic thinkers in an effort to come to terms with the interrelation and the fate of every aspect of individual existence: the *ruh*, the spirit or the breath of life with which God awakens to life any creature (Q32:7–11), the body (*jasad*), and the soul (*nafs*). Over centuries, these interpretations have influenced the matters of ethics, law, ritual, belief, and literary creativity across Islamic cultures and have profoundly shaped Islamic attitudes toward death and mourning.

Understanding the nature of life after and in physical death became a preoccupation of many thinkers. For example, in his eschatological manual *Al-durra al-fakhira*, Abu Hamid al-Ghazali (d. 1111) looks at these components as fully interlaced in the process of dying. He points out that death, even for the pious, is an experience that involves forcible separation and suffering of all these aspects of life in a meticulously scripted operation:

> And when the destiny approaches, that is, his earthly death, then the four angels descend to him; the angel who pulls the soul from his right foot, the angel who pulls it from the left foot, the angel who pulls it from his right hand, and the angel who pulls it from his left hand ... The good soul slips out like the jetting of water from a water-skin, but the profligate spirit squeaks out like a skewer from wet wool.[5]

Citing a Prophetic *hadith* about the agony of suffering experienced at the moment of dying, al-Ghazali discusses the physiological changes in the body and visually conjures the invisible powers that welcome the dead from the other side of life. Admitting to several divergent theological views on this process, he categorizes the dead by their deeds and specifies what kind of treatment awaits them once they are ritually deposited into the grave. Al-Ghazali's views fit into a broader continuum in the discourse about death. The tomb, far from being a resting place, had by al-Ghazali's times been conceptualized as a place of change. As Leor Halevi suggests, by the mid-eighth century, the tomb had already come to be understood as the place of punishment and possible redemption of sins although the religious function of that punishment was not entirely clear. Rejecting the Mu'tazilite denial that the tomb houses any real experiences, Muslim traditionists sought to assign to the grave a purgative function for those who had not asked for forgiveness for their sins before they passed away, and a punitive function for those whose sinful and bad acts had taken them to the point beyond redemption.[6] In that sense, the Qur'anic notion of the precipitous ejection of the soul from the body to the outer spheres of existence is gradually replaced, in post-Qur'anic times, by a notion of a more approximate bond between the body and the spirit in the *barzakh* of the grave.[7]

In contrast, Islamic philosophers held a view that post-mortem experiences are incorporeal, and the Qur'anic reference to physical pain and pleasure as experienced in the Hereafter is only figurative. For example, in his *Epistle on Afterlife* (*Al-risala al-adhawiyya fi al-ma'ad*), Ibn Sina reminds us that the concept of "future life" – *al-ma'ad* – is semantically linked to the notion of return (*'awd*). In the Qur'an itself, God issues a command, "Oh you quiescent soul [*nafs*], return to your Lord, well-pleased and well-pleasing" (Q89:27–28). This return, he further explains, has been understood in three different terms: the return of the body alone; the return of the soul alone; and the return of the body and the soul together. Each of these terms is associated with different possibilities, and Ibn Sina qualifies them in regard to broader questions of the relationship between the soul and the body, not only in death, but in more general metaphysical sense, as seen by various denominations and schools.[8] Ibn Sina, in the distinctly philosophical tradition, advocates the third position of the indestructibility of the soul and the destructibility of the physical body and the consequent inability of the body to be reconstituted in its original form in order to be brought back to judgment before God. God, therefore, summons and redeems or condemns only the souls of the believers.

In a similar vein, the philosopher Miskawayh's account of death is informed by moral philosophy. The moral ill he identifies as most destructive is fear, and the fear of death in particular. Defining it as a process in which the soul leaves the body so as to advance toward a more pure state of being, Miskawayh emphasizes the capacity of the soul to be transformed but never corrupted. Following Plato, he proposes a "voluntary death," a condition that, thanks to knowledge and wisdom, reduces one's anxieties and concerns about death and rids the body of destructive emotions. Moreover, Miskawayh contends, if the suffering or punishment is that which drives the fear of death, one should be reminded of the fact that the soul that has departed the body is discharged of all feeling.[9]

This philosophical position, despite its analytical variations, is not widely accepted, in part because the philosophers' recension of the Qur'anic explication of the afterlife disregards the physical aspects of death and afterlife. As Fazlur Rahman suggests, the majority of Muslims lean toward more literal eschatological narrative descriptions as intimated in the Qur'an. In Rahman's view,

the Qur'an, unlike Muslim philosophers, does not recognize a hereafter that will be peopled by disembodied souls – in fact, it does not
recognize the dualism of the soul and the body and man, for it is a
unitary, living, and fully functioning organism. The term *nafs*, which
later in Islamic philosophy and Sufism came to mean soul as a substance separate from the body, in the Qur'an means mostly "himself"
or "herself;" ... in fact it is body with certain life-and-intelligence
center that constitutes the inner identity or personality of man. The
Qur'an, therefore, does not affirm any purely "spiritual" heaven or
hell, and the subject of happiness and torture is, therefore, man as a
person.[10]

But the philosophers are not the only ones who have tried to redefine
the nature of death. In a different vein, Islamic spiritual traditions
developed their own ways of reformulating death, divesting it of its
usual sense of terror and finality, and assigning to it a new ritual and
spiritual function that can be embraced as gain, not loss.

DEATH BEFORE DYING

> I die when I remember you
> then I am revived
> how often I'm revived for you
> how often I've died.[11]

In many ways, these verses capture the quintessential goal crowning the quest of every spiritual wayfarer: union with the divine. The
author of these verses composed them as he observed the spiritual
self-annihilation of his friend and companion Ibn al-Farid (d. 1235)
– one of the greatest Arab poets of all time. While the author acknowledges that the experience is first and foremost spiritual, to him as
the observer, such spiritual self-sacrifice mimics bodily death and the
uprooting of individual life from this world.

Islamic spiritual traditions – first and foremost *tasawwuf* (or
"Sufism") – developed an intrinsically new vocabulary and cosmology to deal with the concept and experience of death. Emphasizing
the spiritual aspect of religious praxis, Islamic mystics focused their
attention on supplementary ways of accessing divine wisdom and
mercy. A need to experience and understand the deeper layers of
life prompted the mystics to also reconfigure the meaning of

death and ushered them to re-articulate the tripartite relationship of God, the dead, and the living, as well as that of body, spirit, and soul. Needless to say, Sufi articulations and expressions vary as well, but they decidedly reposition the afterlife by linking it to the experiences of this world and allowing it to be understood on entirely new grounds.

In one of the early efforts to systematize different Sufi terms and concepts that had entered circulation among mystics, al-Qushayri (d. 1074) developed a detailed discussion of Sufi expressions that reveal a qualitative repositioning toward death in Sufi discourse and practice from the one associated with mainstream teachings. The *nafs* acquires the meaning of ego/self that is "a subtle being, placed within the corporeal substrate as the locus of blameworthy traits, just as the spirit is a subtle being, placed within the substrate as the locus of praiseworthy traits ... Similarly, the locus of praiseworthy traits is the heart [*sirr*] and the spirit [*ruh*], and the locus of blameworthy traits is the self [*nafs*]."[12]

Conditioned by a desire to return to its Creator, the *nafs* experiences the separation as yearning and worship, and the union as the ultimate reward for the spiritual self-discipline and committed self-edification. Evoking the Prophet's dictum "Die before you die!" and the *mi'raj* (the Prophetic ascension story), whereby beatific visions are made possible though an interplay of God's grace on the one hand and a spiritual and ritual wayfaring on the other, the Sufis model the reunion in/with God as a momentary death that brings about a cessation of one's self in the divine self. The Sufis refer to this as voluntary death or self-annihilation, *fana fihi*, to be distinguished from the inevitable death willed by God. Like al-Hallaj who pleaded "Kill me, my faithful friends, for in my slaughter is my life – my death is in my life and my life is in my death," Sufis began to re-inscribe the categories of life and death in reference to one's spiritual enrichment and growth rather than impoverishment and loss. Rumi writes:

> The mystery of "Die before death" is this: After dying come the spoils.
> Other than dying no other skill avails with God, or worker of deception!
> Like a seed that dies and becomes a thousand ears,
> Through God's bounty I became a hundred thousand when I died.
> If He gives me death, let me die! That death is better than the breath of youth.[13]

Mystical ascent, mimicking the *mi'raj* in spiritual terms, enables each committed disciple to taste death in qualitatively different terms, as a disappearance and relocation of the self thanks to which a new, more sublime identity can be fleetingly fashioned. Sufi ideas of death, then, substitute the conventional anxiety about dying with the possibility of imminent reward of intimacy with the divine, which, like physical death, is every bit singular and subjective as it is general and non-subjective. In it lies the very essence of *tawhid*, not as the statement of unity but as the affirmative act of unity. One of the key early systematizers of Sufi ideas, Abu al-Qasim al-Junayd (d. 910), who left an influential mark on later Sufi thinkers, concerned himself with the notion of *fana* ("annihilation" or "passing away") as both an experiential and intellectual riddle and offered the following explication of its components:

> There are three passings away. The first is the passing away from the attributes, qualities, and dispositions. This passing occurs through the performance in you of the proofs of your work, through expending effort, through your being at variance with yourself, through your confining of yourself by reprehending its desire.
>
> The second is the passing away from attention to one's share of the sweet deserts and pleasures of obedience: through the perfect accord of the quest of the real for yourself in cutting you off from him; that there might be no intermediary between you and him.
>
> The third passing away of yourself from the vision of reality: passing away from your ecstasies as the sign of the real overpowers you. At that moment you both pass away and abide, and are found truly existent in your passing away; through the found existence of your other; upon the abiding of your trace in the disappearance of your name.[14]

The three steps to *fana* constitute a necessary and arduous process and it is understood to be the trademark of the death coveted by the aspiring soul rather than the death endured by the reluctant body. To the extent that such death is possible, the Sufis embrace psychological mortality as a primordial gift, once lost but then found, as articulated in the Qur'anic dictum that to God we "return" (not just "go") from this life. Variations on this wondrous – yet hard-to-come-by – experience of dying before dying permeate Sufi literature, both poetic and prosaic, informing the very core of the spiritual journey.

In addition to such diverse and rich emphasis on the mimicry of physical death in spiritual terms, Sufi tradition has also addressed and re-evaluated common teachings and rituals concerning physical death. In fact, *fana*, desirable as it is, has both a fleeting and unpredictable quality since its realization depends not only on the level of spiritual commitment and ritual discipline but, ultimately, on divine grace, which can neither be controlled nor taken for granted. Many a Sufi has expressed repeated frustration about the relentless vicissitudes of *fana* and the presumptuousness of the ego in assuming that *fana* ought to come to it. In turn, anxiety about mortality and the imminence of bodily death has not escaped Sufi attention and they have struggled with coming to terms with it. Al-Muhasibi (d. 857) was one of those Sufis who recognized that human beings' incessant fear of mortality stems from an egotistical and self-possessive disposition that can, with proper preparation and reflection, not only be controlled but also diminished. He acknowledged that the unpredictability, yet certitude, of death creates a dissonant and nagging tension in all human beings as they struggle to comprehend its causes and its signs; however, no apparent cause, moment, season, or condition can be used as a sure portent of death. No circumstantial or internal cause can be deemed infallible. "No one is consulted about the extraction of his spirit from his body," Muhasibi warns, "death comes upon us all of a sudden."[15] In order not to be taken by so much surprise that repentance will be impossible, Muhasibi narrates the following story and extracts its moral: "In this regard it is related that Luqman, peace be upon him, said to his son: 'My son, there is a certain something that you do not know when it is coming to you. Prepare for it or else it will take you by surprise ... Son, do not put off repentance. The coming of the angel of death is all of a sudden.'"[16] Thus, Muhasibi seems to imply, to prepare responsibly for death one ought to accept that its hour must remain inconceivable, unthinkable, intangible to all of us, across time and space. The ethics of preparation, then, lies in "continual remembrance and contemplation of the uncertainty of the appointed time and coming of death –when it shall overcome and the entire matter is ended – and the remembrance of those who were taken by sudden death."[17] To the extent that one is responsible toward God's command, then, one is more imminently responsible to himself or herself in ascertaining the level of spiritual purity at any given moment in life so as to be ready for the arrival of death. The focus is thus shifted from the unpredictability of death to the unambiguity of moral lifestyle for which all are accountable, regardless of when or how they die.

ISLAMIC DEATH RITUALS AND ISLAMIC COMMEMORATIVE CULTURE

The aforementioned philosophical, theological, denominational, and other variances in the narratives on death and dying are deeply reflected in the rituals of death and commemoration across Islamic societies. Islamic eschatology, in its different interpretations, affects the way in which the dead are remembered, cared for, and represented. Anthropologically, the rituals surrounding burials, mourning, and remembrance are carried out in accordance with cultural and physical landscapes within which they are situated. While one can surely appreciate cross-cultural motifs in acts of memorialization, visitation, and pilgrimage, the meaning of these is locally embedded, often betraying a variety not commonly found in written texts. Death as perceived from this angle primarily addresses social, spatial, and ritual interaction between the dead and the living. Historically, however, these rituals also reflect sectarian developments, political and social upheavals, and general shifts in social and cultural meaning of death through historical processes.

Canonical material that would ideally lay ground rules for death rituals and the culture of mourning is surprisingly scarce on such matters. As discussed above, the Qur'anic emphasis in the matters of death is primarily placed on the quality of the afterlife, not on the methods of handling or disposing of the body. In contrast, the Hadith materials reveal more detailed references to the Prophet's recommendations on burial and funerary ritual but much of it is linked to general etiquette rather than specific, step-to-step injunctions on handling the corpse during burial procedures. In fact, in his detailed study on death rites in the nascent Islamic community based on a variety of textual and extra-textual sources, Leor Halevi demonstrates that the process of Islamization of death rites was not only slow but also multidirectional, involving emulation as well as modification of Christian, Jewish, Zoroastrian, and other cultural practices active in the same space. The pressing question for early Muslims, as Halevi postulates, is not related to eschatological issues since the belief in the scripturally defined afterlife take on very strong and well-defined articulations from the very beginning. Rather, it is the question of how to refit the burial practices in the earth that had existed before Islam among the Arabs and others into uniquely Islamic forms. In this process, divergent views appear along regional as well as theological lines, and they reflect reactions, positive and negative, against many of the existing practices, such as washing of the corpse, gender roles, burial dispositions, tombstone inscriptions, expressions of mourning and bereavement, and so on. Halevi describes early Islamic funerary laws as partly "adaptive" and partly "reactive," as they rose "in opposition to underlying practices" rather than in a mental vacuum.[18] In that sense, they reflect a society as it comes of age, and as it exteriorizes, through rituals as well as funerary art and architecture, new and more subtle religious sensibilities toward the deceased.

Hadith compilations, mainly those subsumed under the "Funerary writings" (*kitab al-jana'iz*) rubric, speak to the Prophet's unambiguous show of respect for the dead before, during, and after the funeral.[19] "Don't abuse the dead," the Prophet said, "because they have reached the result of what they forwarded." Injunctions include different formalities and punctilios, including the following: Muslims are encouraged to take part in funeral processions, but if they do not and yet see one, they are to stand up until the body is carried past their way. Funeral prayers are to be performed in specific order and with dignity. Expressing sorrow over the loss of a beloved one is acceptable, and those who do so receive the Prophet's sympathies. Excessive emotionalism, however, is frowned upon: in fact, those who wail, weep, and act inappropriately at a dead relative's grave are doing her or him a disfavor for he or she is tortured in the grave for it. Mourning is allowed, with certain, notably gendered, limitations: women can mourn for three days, except in the case they are grieving for their dead husbands in which case they are urged to grieve for four months and ten days. Washing the corpse, as was done with the Prophet's deceased daughter, is to be repeated several times (an odd number), from right to left, and then the corpse is to be wrapped in a burial garment. The Prophet's own body, as reported by A'isha, was shrouded after ablution in three pieces of cotton fabric, with nothing else placed over his body. The martyrs, on the other hand, can be laid to rest without the funerary ablution.

The list continues but it does not exhaust all aspects of death rituals. In the centuries to come, as suggested by Halevi, various customary and legal opinions were put forth to deal with the complex process of caring for the dead and placing them into the social space of the living community. That process has witnessed changes in the physical layouts of burial grounds, in tomb inscriptions and iconography, in grave attendance and visitation as well as in shrine pilgrimages, gender participation in death and mourning rites, and many other aspects of individual and group involvement in ritual praxis. Over time and space, these practices became very diverse, customized within local contexts and geographies in ways that reflected not only Islamic ethos, but even more so, ecologically, the connection to a specific environment and its resources.

One of the most significant developments in the Islamic attitude toward the dead relates to the practice of shrine visitation, and evolved in the context of Shi'ism (and later on in Sufism). Within Shi'i Islam, collective memory focuses on the martyrdom of Husayn – the son of 'Ali and the Prophet's daughter Fatima – and related events occurring at Karbala in 680. Every year in the month of Muharram, the circumstances of Husayn's martyrdom are re-enacted as part of a ten-day ritual of remembrance, primarily through a passion play (*ta'ziya*), through which history is re-enacted, and pain and grief collectively re-experienced. The reverence surrounding the event, its redemptive value and its evident intensity, have kept alive the memory of Muhammad's immediate family and their suffering throughout Shi'i history. Furthermore, as a highly ritualized phenomenon, the commemoration of Husayn's martyrdom at Karbala has influenced Shi'i ritual and symbolic sensibilities at large, shaping a distinctly Shi'i understanding of martyrdom and enhancing the practices of commemoration and visitation of the dead.[20]

In a similar but distinct vein, shrine visitation also evolved as a contested but very popular and widespread practice within Sufi social structures, at the center of which lies the spiritual authority of a teacher (*sheikh* or *pir*). The spiritual intimacy that develops between the teacher and a disciple and manifests itself in all aspects of the disciple's mystical journey has given rise to various forms of appreciation, obedience, veneration, and even a kind of absolute subservience to which Muhammad Iqbal would pejoratively refer as "pirism." Over time, however, it was not only the mystics who would revere the masters and consider them as having special powers. Rather, this became a phenomenon that spilled over into the general population which flocked to the masters to be given blessings (both material and spiritual), issued advice, and offered assistance in various ways. This kind of reverence did not cease with the master's death: on the contrary, dead masters often came to be venerated as holy men, as intercessors whose tombs and shrines turned into sacred spaces at which spiritual energy and power would continue to flow and bless those who came to visit them. This form of visitation, *ziyara*, has persisted to date and involves not only a variety of real and assumed tombs, but also physically and architecturally elaborate complexes with multiple functions. The consecration of such places is achieved thanks to the symbolic and ritual performance of these holy persons whose physical *concealment from* the world does not obstruct their vigilant and selfless *engagement with* the world.

Needless to say, this form of ritual behavior of shrine visitation, popular that it is, has generated controversy and contestation in theological discourse, but none of that has diminished its significance in the lives of many Muslims or denied its scriptural legitimacy. To that end, the Qur'anic passages that speak of a continuing relationship between the living and those who die striving in the path of God – understood, along al-Ghazali's more esoteric interpretation, as those who spiritually excel – are frequently evoked as the evidence that the visible and the invisible worlds do meet through the intercession of such holy individuals. Al-Ghazali writes,

> Death cannot destroy the soul, which is the place of God's *ma'rifa* (gnosis), because it is something spiritual. Death causes the change in the condition of the soul, and relieves it from the prison of its bodily cage. It does not end, for as God says: "Think not of those who are slain in God's way as dead." Nay, they live, finding their sustenance in the presence of their Lord; they rejoice in the bounty provided by God. And with regard to those left behind, who have not yet joined them (in their bliss), the (Martyrs) glory in the fact that on them is no fear, nor have they (cause to) grieve. They glory in the Grace and the bounty from God, and in the fact that God suffers not the reward of the Faithful to be lost (in the least). One should not think that this position is acquired only by those that are martyred on the battlefield, because every breath of an *'arif* is a martyr.[21]

Indeed, the Qur'an repeatedly declares that those who die striving in God's cause do, in fact, live on, and while invisible to the eye they are nonetheless present (see above, e.g. Q3:169; 2:154). Their charisma, then, can be reached out to, invoked, and relied upon, in good times as well as dire times when other reassurances and solutions are absent or amiss. The dead, in such cases, have an intermediary function of allowing the visitors at their shrines to induce God's favor through their extraordinary spiritual state and their status with God as His *awliya'* ("friends" or "allies"). They are not the objects of worship in and of themselves, despite repeated incriminations to that effect by the opponents of such ritual acts. Furthermore, they neither give of their life nor their experience to the living who seek them out, only their benediction which is fully contingent on God's empowerment as He relates to them as His *awliya'*. Despite its repeated renouncements, the ubiquitous presence of holy shrines across Muslim societies testifies not only to the desire for assisted achievement in spiritual and other matters but also to a need to connect with the dead in a more ongoing and constructive way. The dead are thus not only buried away but are called forth to be engaged, symbolically and ritually, in the wellbeing of the Muslim community.

8

GENDER

Kelly Pemberton

Gender has been a principal category of analysis in the study of Muslim societies, particularly since the late nineteenth century. Yet the subject of gender in Islam is at once obvious and hidden. It is assumed by some to be a discernible and coherent concept, while its usefulness as an analytical construct is contested by others. Muslim theological, jurisprudential, philosophical, and metaphysical thinkers have long presumed gender to be a primary category of identification, one that necessitates definition and regulation in order to preserve an ideal social order. However, in metaphysics – and particularly in Sufi thought – masculine/feminine is also conceived as a behavioral construct that may or may not correspond to male/female. In the Islamic sapiential tradition, this construct is understood to be a veil that separates the material from the celestial plane of existence. Islamic intellectual traditions have evolved a wide-ranging set of doctrines, legal statutes, practices, and recommendations that seek to regulate the relationships between men and women; these reflect efforts to develop a just, balanced and ideal social order in which the genders pursue roles that are complementary to each other. These regulations cover not only the relationship of marriage but also the broader parameters of social relationships.

Social realities often fall far short of such ideals. Nevertheless, the diversity of understandings of gender in Islam bears several important implications for legal enforcement of gender roles and relationships. Specifically, this diversity suggests a wider variety of possibilities for women to exercise the rights given to them by Islamic *shari'a*[1] than has been the case since the rise of "modern" social systems in colonial and post-colonial times. However, the emergence of Islamic feminisms since the 1990s, combined with the increased mobility, visibility, and vocality of Muslim women within traditionally "male" spaces (e.g. the mosque, the media, and other "public" arenas), has brought many changes to traditional ideals of a social order where men and women each occupy their "proper" place. These recent decades have witnessed the production of a large body of scholarship (much of it by Muslim women) that seeks to identify the particular confluence of socio-economic and religious factors that contribute to the marginalization of some groups of women in the Muslim world. However much the stereotype of oppressed Muslim women has persisted despite such promising developments, these dynamic debates compel us to reassess the usefulness of certain methodological paradigms in the study of gender and women in Islam. For instance, the use of gender–(em)power(ment)–agency as a predominant relational construct is called into question by Saba Mahmood, Lila Abu-Lughod, Mervat Hatem, and Deniz Kandiyoti writing on the work of contemporary activist (and Islamist) Muslim women.[2] Other challenges to prevalent conceptions of gender in Islamic thought are treated in more detail below.

THE HERMENEUTICS OF GENDER IN ISLAM

The work of Edward Said, particularly his book *Orientalism*,[3] has had a major impact on the study of gender in Islam. Said contested prevailing representations of the "Orient," and "Oriental" women in particular, as largely false constructions devised by Western academics, travelers, and agents of Empire who had little to no real, experiential knowledge of the lives of ordinary people in Muslim societies. While Said's book did not focus exclusively on gender, it did raise many important questions about the relationship between colonization and the "feminization" and "fetishization" of colonized Muslim lands. Post-Orientalist scholarship went much further than Said on questions of gender. It sought to de-emphasize the relationship between colonizer and colonized as primary analytical focus, and called attention to the importance of discourses by Muslim women (and men) living in Muslim lands. These discourses, it revealed, could shed light on the extent to which various social, political, cultural, and religious factors were responsible for changes in gender roles, relationships, and self-identifications in Muslim societies.

Following Said, Western academic and political interests in the lives and activities of women in the Muslim world rose significantly, but this cannot be attributed solely to Said's work. In fact, it was the Iranian Revolution (and media reports depicting women's role in bringing Ayatollah Khomeini to power) and its aftermath (with media reports of women being forced to veil in the all-encompassing black *chador*) that catapulted the question of gender and Islam into the mainstream of Western (and much non-Western) academic and political thought. Until then, gender and Islam was hardly addressed in mainstream (non-Islamic) scholarship on women, and few saw it as central to the development of Muslim societies, especially in their relationship to the West. Within Muslim societies, however, the literary productions of popular political and intellectual figures suggested the importance of women's participation in nationalist movements, or Islamic political causes, in the shaping of Muslim-majority nations.

Ideologues such as the Iranian sociologist 'Ali Shariati sought to affirm the importance of women's visibility in spaces and participation in civic activities, and to encourage their emergence as national actors supporting the cause of Iranian nationalism. Using the symbol of figures such as the Prophet Muhammad's daughter Fatima, Shariati castigated both conservative men and women who held tightly to "tradition," thus preventing women from realizing their full potential in the Iranian nation, as well as those who had abandoned Islam, becoming so enthralled with the West and its material trappings that they failed to take note of the disparities and injustices enabled by Iranian religious and secular elites alike. He also condemned the ways in which the "Westoxication" of many privileged Iranians enabled the enterprise of Western geopolitical powers to disable Islam as a force for change in the world. For Shariati, Islam "revolutionized the position of women," as one chapter title of his famous work *Fatima Fatima ast* (*Fatima is Fatima*) declares.[4] As in this work, much of his other writing expresses the opinion that a genuine social revolution – with all its implications for a more equitably balanced relationship between men and women – can only take place with Islam as its ethical and moral foundation. Yet Shariati's discourses on women have also been criticized, especially by women scholars, as "desexualized" and "romanticized," and are often characterized as reproducing Orientalist images of the silent, self-effacing, and domestic woman who supports interests that ultimately work to reinforce existing gender hierarchies and inequalities.

Discussions of gender in the Muslim world in the 1980s and early 1990s tended to reflect developments in feminist scholarship. One predominant methodological current during this period posited a direct relationship between the rise of nationalist movements and the entry of women's issues into public debates on nationhood. In the early 1980s a series of studies emerged that investigated the ways in which gender had become politicized. On one hand, some of these studies highlighted the ways in which women's contributions to nationalist efforts as actors and symbols was being overlooked or subsumed within nationalist debates. Nationalist causes, in the estimation of critics like Parvin Paidar (Iran)[5] and Deniz Kandiyoti (Turkey),[6] have tended to define culturally acceptable boundaries for women even as they sought to expand women's public roles, with the result that the particular interests of women have been subordinated, by and large, to allegedly more pressing national interests. On the other hand, women's involvement in nationalist movements was characterized as largely unsuccessful, in the sense that women in Muslim-majority societies were ultimately unable to engage in effective political action because they did not occupy high positions of power in the institutions of governance. Often, the paradigm of "false consciousness" provided the underpinnings of theories concerning the political participation of Muslim women. Women who entered the political arena were seen as marginal to political causes, as pawns of more powerful male interests, or as constrained in their ability to bring about fundamental institutional changes for the betterment of their country-women, despite enhanced opportunities for political participation. From the late 1990s onward, studies of women's involvement in the post-revolutionary Iranian state, as well as the rise of Islamist movements in Egypt, Sudan, and Turkey, began to challenge these interpretive paradigms, appraising the relationship between material factors, state institutions, ideologies, and women's (re)actions as culturally specific and historically determined.

Despite promising avenues for analysis opening up in feminist and post-modern studies of gender in the Muslim World, much scholarship in this field has continued to rely upon essentialist reductions of Islam (or one of its ideological manifestations), modernity (or one of its symbolic or material representations), and "Muslim women." This is also (and perhaps especially) true in the field of development studies, which is replete with reports of women's "status" in Muslim societies.[7] The problematic nature of the category "Muslim Women" is often exemplified by such issues as (1) the presumption of essential identification with Islam as a system of faith; (2) a failure to account for women who consider themselves cultural, but not practicing or even believing, Muslims; and (3) a disregard for the ways in which the identities and self-images of non-Muslim women are shaped by their inhabiting Muslim-majority societies (as in Egypt, Pakistan, Lebanon, Palestine, Indonesia, and other countries with sizeable non-Muslim minority populations). Compounding this problem of categorization is the fact that academic studies of gender in Islam have, more often than not, presumed a fundamental opposition between male dominance and female resistance/agency, Eastern and Western values, Islam and Christianity, and the secular and religious realms in ways that rivet discussion upon the hegemony of Western discourses – and by extension, Western history – as a normative standard for the progress of nations in the making of the modern world.

These types of analyses mirror Islamist discourses, privileging Enlightenment values of reason, freedom, and individuality in ways similar to some Islamists' privileging of the idea of Islamic universality based on an unchangeable divine order. As Chandra Mohanty effectively pointed out in her work on Western feminist analyses of Third World women, the theme of women's subordination or agency has often highlighted the analytical category of "woman" in ways that suggest that important differences in social location, historical facts, and economic and political developments have little to no impact on women's reactions to the boundaries that constrain their experiences, or to the circumstances that give them space to circumvent, undermine, or temporarily breach these boundaries.[8] Some critics of feminist and women's studies scholarship on Muslim women coming from the West cite ethnocentrism and a tendency to draw generalizations about women in Muslim societies on the basis of Western experiences. In 1975, the Moroccan sociologist Fatima Mernissi observed that a feminist hermeneutics of gender equality typically rested on a flawed assumption of patriarchy as comprising a single model of oppression, while ignoring the multiple bases of women's inferior status in Muslim societies.[9] Following Mernissi, a number of Muslim feminist scholars like Afsaneh Najmabadi, Amira Sonbol, Shahla Haeri, Nimat Hafez Barazangi, Kecia Ali, and Amina Wadud have sought to counter such assumptions within Western feminist scholarship and develop an Islamic hermeneutics of gender justice.[10] While these efforts have been largely embraced within the intellectual community as well as by many ordinary Muslim women around the world, they have also engendered a backlash from scholars like Haideh Moghissi, who see parallel agendas and problems in Islamist and Islamic feminist arguments for a faith-based approach to Muslim women's issues.[11]

With few exceptions, the extant scholarship on Muslim women has followed one of several trajectories in its evaluation of the relationship between Islam and the progress of women living in Muslim-majority societies. First, scholars sought to demonstrate that the roots of oppression lay outside Islam as a religious system and that, in fact, Islam sought to elevate the status of women. Studies like Leila Ahmed's *Women and Gender in Islam* and Asma Barlas' *Believing Women in Islam* argued that the foundations of women's subordination in Muslim societies were culturally, not theologically, determined.[12] Second, scholars held that Islam was partly to blame for the inferior status of women but that economic and political conditions have also played a major part in the material and ideological subordination of women. Fatima Mernissi's work, particularly *Beyond the Veil* and *The Veil and the Male Elite* exemplify this position.[13] Mernissi sees a connection between the subordinate status of women and Islam's views on female sexuality, which she sees as characterized by fear. Women's sexual freedom, wrote Mernissi, threatened to disrupt the social order (exemplified by the term *fitna*); defence against this threat bears a direct relationship to women's lack of legal rights, personal freedom, and economic, social, and political agency in Muslim societies around the world. Third, scholars and activists have rejected the possibility that Islam (as it stands) can provide any desirable solution to the dilemma of securing gender equity for the majority of women living in the Muslim world, as seen in the works of Nawal El Saadawi and, more recently, Irshad Manji, and Ayaan Hirsi Ali.[14] Fourth, scholars have observed ways in which women's economic, political, or everyday activities suggest their compliance with or resistance against state ideologies and predominant cultural values, especially in those countries enforcing Islamic *shari'a* law (in most cases, this enforcement is restricted to the area known as family or personal law). This position is evident in the work of Lila Abu-Lughod, Diane Singerman, and Salma Ahmad Nageeb.[15]

Since the late 1990s, studies of women living in Muslim societies have gradually moved toward more integrative and atomistic approaches, viewing gender and Islam as being intimately linked to historical and material realities. Case studies of women in their particular cultural, regional, material, and familial contexts have begun to draw attention to how gender in Islam is constructed in light of social and cultural values, rules, and other institutions that shape gender roles, relations, and power. A number of these studies emphasize how a focus on gender can and should reveal much about the production (and reproduction) of social relations of inequality. They demonstrate a range of responses among women to state ideologies and policies surrounding women's work (i.e. market-based and domestic production) and its relationship to Islamic mores. For example, Maryam Poya's study of women in post-revolutionary Iran uses interdisciplinary methods and a Marxist framework for understanding the material bases of male–female relationships. She analyzes the ways in which women's struggles for change have forced the state – but also men and women in general – to question prevalent state-sanctioned ideological positions on gender relations.[16] Women's position in the state, she surmises, has been determined by a combination of ideological and material factors related to the labor requirements of the state, particularly in the wake of the Iran-Iraq war. The work of Lila Abu-Lughod, Diane Singerman, and Arlene Elowe MacLeod among middle-class women in Egypt demonstrates how typically secular ideals and modalities (upward mobility, love marriages, consumer consumption) have merged with Islamic and culturally specific values, largely as a result of economic, social, and cultural changes that have necessitated women's entry into the workforce in greater numbers than before.[17] This process has been further modified by a general increase in women's higher education and a growing awareness of ongoing women's rights debates in the wider Muslim world.

A field of sexuality and queer studies has also opened up, with contributions ranging from studies of sexuality and homosexuality in Islamic theological and intellectual discourses to discussions of homosexuality and its treatment historically and in contemporary contexts and to commentaries and consciousness-raising campaigns put forward by groups like the Gay and Lesbian Arabic Society (G.L.A.S.) and *Bint el-nas* ("Daughter of the People"). Individuals and groups such as these have questioned fundamental assumptions about gender identity, pointing out the long history of homosexuality in Islamic lands, evidenced in part through poetic tropes and literary conventions lauding the adoration of beardless boys. They also call for a reinterpretation of Qur'anic verses condemning homosexuality, and for opening windows onto the lives (and persecutions) of Muslim gays and lesbians. Finally, and quite controversially, scholars have seen a possibility of securing greater legal, social, and political agency for women by turning to the very interpretive tools used by the earliest generations of religious scholars to develop an ethical-legal system that would both secure greater rights for women in Muslim societies and revitalize Islamic *shari'a*, bringing it into greater harmony with the needs of the age. The tool that has received the most attention in scholarship is *ijtihad*, or independent reasoning, taken up in more detail below in the section on feminism.

GENDER IN THE QUR'AN

The Qur'anic verses that are at the heart of contemporary discussions about gender roles and relationships, women's rights and duties under Islam (notably Q2:228–231; 4:3; 4:11; 4:34; 24:30–31; 33:53; 33:59–60) also form the point of departure for a series of ongoing controversies surrounding the rights, roles, and position of women in Islam. Yet there are several discernible patterns of representing gender in the Qur'an. Although only one woman – Mary the mother of Jesus – is mentioned by name (the omission of women's names being a common literary convention at the time of the writing of the Qur'an rather than a denial of the importance of women), the text uses both women and men from sacred history as symbolic devices. The text also contains references to men and women from sacred history whose actions serve as examples of unbelief (Q66:10) or righteousness (Q66:11; 27:44). In some places, there seems to be no particular association between the gender of a figure and his or her association with specifically male or female behavior. For example, the mothers of both Moses and Jesus receive messages from Allah (through the medium of *wahy*, divine inspiration) that indicate that they are being singled out for their righteous belief in God, rather than for their exemplary behavior as daughters, wives, or mothers (Q3:42; 19:24–25; 20:38–39; 23:50; 28:7; 66:12). This has led a few classical exegetes such as Ibn Hazm (d. 1064) and al-Qurtubi (d. 1273) to argue for Mary's prophethood, though this variety of prophethood is distinguished from "messengerhood," the preserve of men. In other cases, women serve as moral exemplars of ideal behavior for Muslim women. This is particularly true of the Prophet Muhammad's wives: though they remain unnamed in the text, incidents related to their lives, behavior, and relationship with the Prophet have been elaborated in *tafsir* (Qur'anic exegesis) and Hadith as guidance for Muslim women, much as the Prophet's *sunna* became the basis for the ideal behavior of Muslims more generally.

Throughout the text, men and women are addressed as believers with similar responsibilities before God and with identical capacities for faith (Q2:226; 33:35; 16:97). This stance has given rise to the view – well-represented within conservative and liberal-progressive theological circles alike – that men and women are equal before God in all matters spiritual. A number of verses demonstrate how Islam sought to elevate the rights of women in pre-Islamic Arabia, demanding justice and respect for them in a climate in which they were often regarded as chattel. For instance, the Qur'an stipulates that women are to inherit property just as men do, while others exhort the guardians of orphans (male and female) not to exploit them sexually or financially (Q4:2,6). Other verses castigate Muslim men for their treatment of women and girls in the pre-Islamic "Age of Ignorance," or *jahiliyya* (Q4:19–22; 58:2; 81: 9–10). Men are also obliged to give divorced women their due allowances and to refrain from repossessing their dowry (Q2:233; 2:241; 2:229; 65:6). However, there are also a number of places in the Qur'an that suggest very different roles, rights, and responsibilities for Muslim men and women, and these have lent themselves to provisions in Islamic *shari'a* law that not only deny women full and equal rights on a par with men but also emphasize the moral and intellectual inferiority of women. These passages are found largely in the Medinan *suras* that deal with social, legal, and political matters facing the Muslim community.

A number of verses that address both men and women as partners in a domestic arrangement suggest that women's livelihood, care, and discipline is dependent upon men: fathers, brothers, and husbands or, in the absence of these, male guardians. For instance, Q4:34 identifies men as being the maintainers or caretakers of women, seemingly implying that men are more favored by God. This verse has been interpreted by the vast majority of classical and traditionalist exegetes as referring to men's divinely sanctioned authority over their wives because God has created them to be superior to women in certain respects. On the other hand, more recent exegetes, particularly Muslim feminist scholars, have qualified the "favor" as pertaining only to the financial responsibility of Muslim men over women. Al-Tabari (d. 923) saw male authority as being restricted to the domestic and legal arenas, while other classical exegetes like al-Razi (d. 1209) and Ibn Kathir (d. 1373) extended this authority of men over women beyond the domestic sphere to include the political, thereby extending the authority to all men over all women in society. The rest of the verse lays out the procedures for men to deal with women (specifically, wives) who have committed some transgression that has caused marital discord. Interpreted literally, it advises men to (first) admonish those women, then separate their beds from them (i.e. refrain from having sexual intercourse with them), then to hit them. This verse has set the broader tone for gender relations in classical Islam despite the efforts of such classical exegetes as Ibn Majah, al-Razi, and Ibn Kathir. They sought to mitigate the burden of coercion this verse apparently condones by citing *sunna* to show that the Prophet did not beat his own wives and that he sanctioned it only with extreme distaste (directing inquirers to engage in a light beating that avoided the face and did not leave marks on the body).

In recent decades, traditionalist exegetes have sought to impose a series of conditions upon the procedure by stipulating that a man may only resort to these measures in cases of the wife's *nushuz*, a term variously interpreted by them as "rebellion," "disobedience," or "transgressive behavior" and even then requiring him to follow the prescribed series of steps with an appropriate interval of days in between each action. The "hitting/beating" is also interpreted by commentators like the late Grand Mufti of Pakistan, Muhammad Shafi 'Uthmani, as a "light" beating that leaves no marks and does no harm to the body.[18] Most recently, exegetes have challenged the broader paradigm of male authority over women by denying that Muslim men have the right to beat their wives under any circumstances, despite what the text says. Challenging the longstanding tradition of interpreting the verses of the Qur'an atomistically, and without regard to their relationship to other verses and passages in the text, scholars such as Amina Wadud, Asma Barlas, and Nimat Hafez Barazangi have argued for a holistic and polysemic reading of the book.[19] As such, they cite the overwhelming emphasis on God's justness in the text as the foundation of gender relationships as well as the Qur'an's essential message of gender harmony and equity.

According to several modern scholars, the Qur'an's pronouncements on the different roles of men and women in the domestic and
public arenas does not contradict their fundamental equality. The idea
of equality, however, is a complex and contested one, and has been
problematized by a number of writers. Some have argued that, contrary to much Western feminist and liberal thinking, equality does not
necessitate treating men and women equally, nor does different treatment in and of itself amount to inequality between the sexes. Others
have underscored an understanding of equality that highlights men's
and women's autonomous trusteeship (*khilafat*) in both the domestic and the sociopolitical spheres. For others still, the Qur'an's pronouncements on gender ultimately propose a vision of equity in which
neither male nor female is restricted for all times to particular roles.

The suggestion of women's moral, intellectual, or emotional inferiority (e.g. in the requirement of two women witnesses to stand for
one male witness in a court of law, in inheritance rules, or in the rules
endorsing polygamy) is seen as the result of misunderstandings of
the text caused by several factors: the lack of female interpreters
of the text over the past few centuries; the closely intertwined nature
of interpretation and the social circumstances of classical interpreters; and the prevalent trend of conflating these classical interpretations of the Qur'an with the Qur'an itself, in effect sacralizing the
interpretations of male scholars who lived many years after Islam's
emergence in societies much different than the seventh-century Hijaz
of the Prophet. Accordingly, successive layers of misinterpretation of
the text together with a lack of recognition of the *conditionality* of such
commands by a male elite have obscured the Qur'an's fundamental
ethos of gender equality. For other writers, the Qur'an is unequivo-
cally misogynistic, relegating women to a second class status. For
many Muslims, arguments for women's subordination or liberation
continue to depend upon opportunistically selected religious "proof"
(*dalil*) contained in the sacred texts of Islam, rather than on a radical reinterpretation of those texts, or a consideration of the conflicting, even contradictory, *hadith* reports and their interpretations by
classical exegetes. Furthermore, some contend that the Qur'an
makes no argument for equality outside the realm of the essential
spiritual and moral constitution of the genders; rather, it presents
arguments against the prevalent patriarchal mores and practices of
the pre-Islamic age of *jahiliyya*. Finally, the argument in favor of
gender equality is called into question by a number of verses that

recognize the "patriarchal privilege" that men in pre-Islamic and early Islamic Arabia enjoyed, even if it seeks to mitigate that privilege.[20]

GENDER, SOCIAL CHANGE, AND ISLAMIC *SHARI'A*

Much of the current discussion of gender in the *shari'a* revolves around women's rights in marriage, divorce, child custody, and inheritance, the four major areas of "family law." Traditionally, serious discussion of the implementation or modification of Islamic *shari'a* has remained the preserve of the religious elite (*'ulama*), scholars who were trained in (and sanctioned by) law or custom to interpret the *shari'a*'s commands. However, since the 1970s, new groups of interlocutors – Islamists, intellectuals (particularly those who have traveled to or been educated in Western countries), feminists, and activists – have begun to weigh in publicly on discussions of *shari'a*, accelerating the fragmentation of religious and political authority, transforming widespread beliefs and practices among Muslims about gender roles and relationships, and thwarting state efforts to suppress their voices.[21] Among these groups, women have emerged as powerful voices for change, challenging traditional discourses that highlight Islam's elevation of women's status on the one hand but tolerate the continued abuse of women's God-given rights on the other. Women also criticize secular nationalist discourses that encourage women's civic participation but simultaneously reinforce many of the prevailing restrictive cultural boundaries on womanhood, as well as feminist arguments that demonstrate ignorance of and prejudice toward the cultural distinctiveness of Muslim women in local, regional, and national contexts.[22]

As a result, recent decades have seen significant changes in the discussion of gender roles and relationships in the Muslim world. Studies of the connection between modern social change and Islamic *shari'a* have historically been produced by social scientists and historians, many of whom examine this subject from a jurisprudential point of view, but with little sustained attention to contemporary gender debates.[23] Within many of the *madrasas* and other Islamic centers of learning such as al-Azhar, the Deoband seminaries in India and Pakistan, and the Shi'a theological seminaries at Qom, traditionalist scholars of Islam and Islamists (i.e. those with specifically political designs whose religious credentials are often suspect in the eyes of members of traditional juristic traditions) have slowly begun to engage the question of revisiting and reinterpreting Islamic *shari'a* to include greater rights for women, though these engagements have largely focused on curriculum changes, combating local cultural practices, and defining "authentic" Islam against rival groups. With few exceptions (e.g. Maulana Wahid ad-din Khan in India and Seyyed Mohsen Sa'idzadeh in Iran), most traditionalist *'ulama* and Islamist ideologues have endorsed a limited kind of political, intellectual, and social enfranchisement that does not fundamentally change the status quo for women.

There have also emerged a crop of what Eickelman and Anderson have called the "new religious intellectuals," distinct from both Islamists and traditional *'ulama*, who have engaged in religio-political activism.[24] Many of these intellectuals have been educated at least partly in the West, and combine a deep understanding of Islamic foundations and discursive traditions with knowledge of Western cultural and intellectual idioms. Thus, they have been able to marshal evidence from the foundational sources of Islam, and Western philosophical discourses on pluralism, enlightenment, and human rights to argue for changes in those social, cultural, and political institutions that typically relegate men and women to roles that are deemed "natural" and in accord with the dictates of *shari'a*. The works of the Iranian intellectual Abdolkarim Soroush, the Moroccan theologian Fatima Mirsani of Morocco, and Palestinian–American law professor Khaled Abou'l Fadl are especially noteworthy in this regard.

Finally, the past two decades have witnessed the slow but steady emergence of works by Muslim feminists, liberal Muslims, and some traditionalist Muslim scholars that offer what has been referred to as "pedagogical reading" of the sources of Islamic tradition, particularly the Qur'an, enabling new readings that transcend the realm of religious discourse and serve as the basis for bringing about fundamental, sustainable, and all-inclusive changes. This goes beyond conventional calls for the democratization of Muslim societies, the enfranchisement of Muslim women, or the development of universalist solidarity movements for social and political change. Rather, it goes to the heart of a particularly Islamic worldview in which the Qur'an serves both as moral guidance and the basis for the reconceptualization of gender relations to build a more gender-equitable social system. These decades have also seen women gaining political, social, and economic ground in many areas of the Muslim world. For instance, the ideal of woman as worker for the Revolution was promulgated by the Iranian state in the months leading up to the Islamic Revolution in 1979. The immediate aftermath of that revolution saw women being forced to don the *chador* and barred from institutions of education and employment, all in the name of Islam. However, economic realities and the exigencies of the post-revolution, post Iran–Iraq war years in Iran, coupled with Iranian women's ongoing challenges to received Islamic theology and the authority of the Iranian theocratic state, have forced the state to question, and ultimately modify, its ideological and legal positions on gender relations. Iranian women have been able to gain a limited number of reforms within an Islamic framework and rhetoric, and have managed to insert secular issues into their struggles for reform. However, their responses to employment opportunities and rights struggles have been largely determined by their access to material resources as well as the constraints imposed on them by the state, which still strives to reconcile the realities of economic development and women's employment within the framework of Islamic ideology. These circumstances have not been limited to the Iranian Republic: in Morocco, Egypt, and Sudan, the state has also sought to reconcile Islamic morals and ethics as enumerated in *shari'a* law with changing conceptions of gender rights and roles which have been fueled in large part by women's entry in greater numbers into the workforce, politics, and educational institutions.

Morocco, in particular, is instructive of the ongoing changes that continue to alter the landscape of gender relations in the Muslim world: the passage of a reformed family law (*Moudawwana*), instigated by the current King, Mohammed VI, was largely due to an alliance of Moroccan civil society organizations, international N.G.O.s, and conservative religious scholars. Although the implementation of the new family law ordinances continues to experience difficulties – especially in the rural areas where few women have access to the education and information they need to realize their rights under the new laws – its passage is a significant gauge of changing conceptions of gender. In Tunisia, Turkey, and elsewhere, Islamist ideologues such as Rachid al-Ghannouchi and Fethullah Gülen have built populist movements that seek to create and expand opportunities for women's education, extra-domestic employment, and political participation, claiming that these are not only sanctioned, but mandated, by Islam. These movements have been viewed with hostility by the secular Tunisian and Turkish states, and both men have been forced into exile, from where they continue to exert an influence on growing Islamist movements in their home countries.

METAPHYSICS AND PHILOSOPHY

Islamic philosophical traditions, in particular metaphysical and mystical traditions, have had much to say about gender in Islam. Gender figures as a marker of qualities of the individual in his or her relationship to the divine realm of existence within literature that addresses the spiritual development of the individual. Thus, the well-known trope of revered saintly women being described as "men in the shape of women," often interpreted in scholarship as evidence of the strong biases of male mystics against women, may alternatively be seen as a reference to one of the stations along the path to human perfection and nearness to God. As the thirteenth-century mystic-philosopher Ibn 'Arabi explained in his *Al-Futuhat al-Makiyya* regarding the terms *rajul* (man) and *rujuliyya* (manliness), the state of spiritual perfection – which involves purification from the whims of human nature and base desires, and is exemplified by "manliness" – can be attained by the adept regardless of gender. Gender distinctions, as manifest in the physical realm, are widely seen in Islamic metaphysics as bearing no actual correspondence to the spiritual plane of existence, but rather as impermanent and socially determined constructs. Nevertheless, a disdain for flesh-and-blood women – or marriage and family life, more generally – is discernible in the works of seminal mystical thinkers such as Abu-Bakr al-Kalabadhi (d. 990) and Abu Hamid al-Ghazali (d. 1111). This stance is widely observable within those mystical and metaphysical traditions that privilege *fana*, loosely understood as loss of self and its absorption into the divine, as the summit and end of the mystical journey toward the divine. In much of the classical mystical literary tradition, women are described as impediments on this path, temptations who tie the traveler to the impermanence and impurity of the sapiential plane and detract from his focus on God.

Few mystical writers express sentiments such as those of Jalal ad-din Rumi, who proclaims in his *Fihi ma fihi* that the trials and tribulations of marriage are a necessary and, ultimately, redemptive step in the refinement of the adept's character.[25] The biological conditions of female gender, too, were interpreted as impediments along the path to God by both male and female adepts. Some mystic women may have wittingly or unwittingly sought to transcend the limits of their gender by engaging in ascetic practices that prevented their menstruation. Others still found in their adoption of the contemplative life a freedom from the typical social restraints that their gender imposed upon them. This was especially true for those women who remained unmarried, such as the eighth-century mystic Rabi'a Basri, who was – according to hagiography – widely revered and consulted by the most prominent male mystics of her era. Alternatively, Sufi men and women lived together in celibate marriages and observed the contemplative life while also enjoying the social and spiritual benefits such companionship brought.

On the other hand, several classical and later works of mysticism demonstrate the highest praise for mystic women and for feminine qualities more generally. Sufis such as al-Sulami ostensibly outlined a women's chivalry (*niswan*), a kind of counterpart to men's *futuwwa* (a code of moral conduct embracing qualities such as generosity and noble character as well as outlining an etiquette of chivalry in medieval mystic and military circles). Ibn 'Arabi (perhaps in large part because of the strong positive influence mystic women played in his life and spiritual education) left behind several inspiring portraits of women who had taken up the mystic path. In his *Fusus al-hikam* he also outlines the wisdom and spiritual benefits of contemplating God in the form of a woman; for him this was the "best and most perfect" kind of contemplation. Finally, the eighteenth-century mystic Khwaja Mir Dard (d. 1785) expressed in emotional terms his immense love for his wife and children, not knowing if that love came from his baser instincts or the appearance of celestial qualities within him. For Dard, love of family was part and parcel of the duty of each believer, as attested to by the example of the Prophet Muhammad as well as an essential element in the perfection of the soul.

The divergence of mystical views about women and the feminine is perhaps best captured in the trope of the soul, or *nafs*. In the classical literary tradition of Sufism, woman is often depicted as temptress, and associated with the lower soul (*nafs*), materiality, and the physical world. But the sense of *nafs* as expressed in this literature, when taken as a whole, exists at several levels of understanding. In its raw, undeveloped form, the *nafs* is the concupiscent soul (*nafs ammara bi's-su*) which rules the baser human qualities and incites the

individual to evil. As the adept ascends through the stages of spiritual development, the *nafs* is transformed into increasingly more
aware and realized forms, until it reaches the highest stage of *nafs
az-zakiyya* (or *nafs al-kamila*), the completely purified and perfected soul that has achieved *fana* or annihilation in God. Yet in
many studies of Islamic mysticism, these stages of development
are ignored, and the pejorative associations of *nafs* with the female
sex are highlighted to the exclusion of all others.

The divergence of views on women and femininity in classical
mystical literature may reflect historical developments in Sufism
as these were marked by important social changes. In other words,
the prevalence of associations between women and obstacles on the
"Path to God" is reflective of a time when the dichotomy between
the material world and the spiritual hereafter, sensuality and asceticism, was a dominant paradigm in many works of Islamic mysticism.
This trend also coincides with the expansion of Islam outward from
Arabia into the Levant, the Persian lands, and Central Asia, and the
regulation of gender roles and relationships in *shari'a* law, particularly in Damascus, Kufa, and Baghdad, all sites of prominent pre-
Islamic empires with prevalent models of gender that differed sharply
from models observed in pre- and early Islamic Arabia. If accepted,
Leila Ahmed's argument – contrasting the relative freedom enjoyed
by *jahiliyya* women with the widely prevalent norms of strict gender
segregation and the restriction of free women within public spaces in
the lands to which Islam initially spread – suggests a predominant attitude of disdain for women which gets enshrined in Qur'anic exegesis
and in the codification of *shari'a*. In such an atmosphere, stories of
women saints often provided a counter-model for ordinary women;
in other words, an idealized feminine counteracted what were widely
perceived to be the natural tendencies of women to be sources of temptation and rebellion whose lives necessitated strict control. Alternative
explanations of the disdain many Sufis expressed for women look to
the need for Sufis to defend themselves against accusations of religious infidelity (*kufr*) by members of the *'ulama*, or see the expansion
of Sufism into many different areas of society (e.g. the mercantile
guilds) and the concurrent increase in women's participation in the
orders as reasons for the Sufis' denouncement of women.

And yet there is rarely a direct correlation between social realities and expressions of gender in mystical literature. If understood
as a didactic paradigm used by Sufi masters for the tutelage of their

disciples, associations of the soul (*nafs*) with women could also be understood as a way of illustrating the complete and total transformation of the mystic. Thus, we could point to the association between *nafs* and the feminine principle in the stories of female mystics as working to illustrate the transformation of the soul in a way that was even more profound than with male mystics: since women's social position remained low, the paradigm of submission was dominant. The transformation to the ultimate level of the soul (*nafs az-zakiyya* or *nafs al-kamila*) in the stories of female mystics may have been a way to illustrate the depths to which travelers along the path would have to sink in order to rise to the highest heights of spiritual attainment. In this respect, female mystics are often seen as foils for male mystics, pointing out the imperfections of their discipline, their piety, or their faith. As Sachiko Murata has illustrated in her *Tao of Islam*,[26] women function in hagiographic accounts in symbolic and archetypal ways, to provide a sense of the "inner reality." Murata's propensity to view mystical stories symbolically is also seen in her discussion of an Islamic system of yin and yang, constantly fluctuating passive and active principles that underlie a fundamental unity of the universe. The relationships between man, woman, and God may be characterized by either yin (feminine) or yang (masculine), depending on how the relationship manifests itself in any particular moment. Thus, the outward form of gender (and gender relationships) manifests in one way, while inwardly, the relationships between man, woman, and God may manifest in many alternative ways. Ultimately, both yin and yang characteristics are present in all things, and what is yang in relation to one thing may become yin in relation to another.

As the above examples suggest, Islamic mystical thought has demonstrated a marked ambivalence between praise and disdain for women and the feminine. Women may be seen as temptresses on the path to perfection and are sometimes associated with the material world and its ills. Yet the achievements of women mystics – and women from the Prophet's own family – form an important part of the canon of classical mystical literature. Moreover, femininity – sometimes expressed as taking on the persona of a woman, particularly in narrative voice – is also emphasized by many male Sufis as being the most ideal manifestation of the human–divine relationship. If a woman can attain perfection only in the shape of a man, it is equally true that for many mystics, particularly in the South Asian Subcontinent, becoming a "bride" of God was the best way to achieve the nearness that was a prerequisite of reaching that perfect state. As such, the literature on women and the feminine in works of Islamic mysticism offers a variety of possibilities for understanding and rethinking the meanings of gender in Islam.

FEMINISM, ACTIVISM, AND ISLAM

Feminists (both religious and secular Muslim) have, in recent years, sought to claim the tools of Islamic exegesis (particularly *ijtihad*) to present cogent arguments for a reconfiguration of praxis and traditional conceptions of gender roles and relationships in Islam. Many such efforts strive to engage feminism in conjunction with received Islamic tradition, affirming this latter as an important element (or even the only possible solution) in bringing about sustainable, positive changes for women living in Muslim societies. Fatima Mernissi called for feminists to engage this tradition seriously, though it took many years before others took up her call.[27] Studies such as Amina Wadud's and Barbara Freyer Stowasser's work on women in the Qur'an, as well as Denise Spellberg's treatment of the development of discursive traditions surrounding the Prophet Muhammad's wife 'A'isha have examined the question of gender as it was understood from within Islamic traditional contexts.[28] A few studies have also looked at jurisprudential literature and Islamic legal discourse to historicize discussions of Islam and gender.[29]

These methodological positions represent a significant break with early feminist thought and methodologies, which by and large discounted or ignored the value of Islam as a potentially liberating force for Muslim women. The earliest waves of feminism in the Muslim world – in Egypt, Turkey, and Iran – were characterized by a kind of internalized colonialism and orientation to secular Western values, as can be seen in the views of Huda Sha'rawi, Doria Shafik, and Qasim Amin in Egypt, and Halide Edib in Turkey. Similarly, Iranian feminism was almost wholly secular until the advent of the Islamic Revolution. In the U.S. and Europe, second-wave feminists emphasized the solidarity of women suffering under patriarchal systems of dominance, and, in so doing, saw much in common between their own struggles for gender equality and the struggles of women living in Muslim societies. These studies initially focused on the material conditions of women's lives, analyzing Middle Eastern women's experiences using the tools of social science.[30] Within socialist feminist writing, especially as a representative of one strand within the "Women in Development" literature, scholars relied on Marxist analyses in their discussion of the effects of development and underdevelopment upon women, identifying colonialism and neo-colonialism as the primary reasons for contemporary gender inequalities. These analyses had much in common with earlier nationalist discourses by feminist and activist women in Muslim societies. Nonetheless, few of the women writing in vernacular languages of the Middle East engaged seriously with Western academics. The latest wave of feminism and activism among Muslim and non-Muslim women in the West and in Muslim societies, however, has begun to reverse this trend.

The contemporary "gender jihad," as described by scholar–activist Amina Wadud in her most recent book,[31] is closely tied with the progressive feminist project in Islam, especially as it is practiced in Euro-American nations. As a form of feminism from within Islam, it represents efforts by Muslim women who seek to engage in their own struggle for women's rights without being necessarily bound or guided by Western concepts of gender equality. It especially refer-ences the right of Muslim women to come to their own understanding of what Islam means for them. For some women, gender *jihad* signi-fies the right (duty, even) to derive gender-egalitarian and gender-equitable readings of the Qur'an. For others, gender *jihad* refers to a striving to shatter stereotypes about Islam, especially the idea that Islam is a static, monolithic, and wholly "foreign" way of thinking and being in the world. According to Wadud, Islamic tradition pre-disposes it to an organic kind of progression; the dominant rhetoric of Islam as articulated by the state and by the (male) religious leader-ship has primarily been one of an Islam bound in time and by history, while progressive thought in Islam is leaning toward a humanistic or eternal Islamic worldview. As she argues, continuity and change is an inherent part of Islam as it travels through time and place. Underlying this perspective is the conviction that Islam alone cannot be blamed for women's subordination in the Islamic world, and the belief that Muslims must strive to implement fundamental Islamic spiritual prin-ciples as the driving force of global movements for social change.[32]

9

GOD*

Jamal J. Elias

INTRODUCTION

In 833 C.E., the caliph Al-Ma'mun (r. 813–833) authorized an official inquisition in Baghdad, the very center of Muslim civilization. Known as the *Mihna* ("Trial"), its purpose was to establish a particular doctrine prevalent at the caliphal court of the time. Many prominent religious figures fell afoul of the inquisitors, most famously Ahmad Ibn Hanbal (d. 855), a scholar of Hadith after whom the Hanbali school of Sunni law takes its name, and a pious figure of such renown that the inquisitors feared the population would rise against them in consequence.

Ibn Hanbal was questioned by the inquisitors but refused to accept their position, whereupon he was shackled and led to the caliphal court. Popular accounts claim that he had prayed that he be saved from coming face to face with Al-Ma'mun, who died before he could make good on his threat to kill Ibn Hanbal. The next caliph, Al-Mu'tasim (r. 833–842), had Ibn Hanbal imprisoned and publicly flogged, an event that served for the only miracle reported of Ibn Hanbal's life (for Ibn Hanbal was not a man given to performing miracles). As the lashes landed on his back and his loincloth started to unravel, Ibn Hanbal turned to God, beseeching Him not to shame him in public. As witnessed by scores of people attending the flogging, the unraveled loincloth miraculously retied itself and saved Ibn Hanbal from public humiliation.[1]

* I would like to thank Shahzad Bashir and Michael Cooperson, who read this essay carefully and contributed to it materially.

The *Mihna* came to an end in 851 at the order of the caliph Al-Mutawakkil, Ibn Hanbal was restored to the place of public respect that he had never actually lost, and he lived out his life as a model of Muslim piety, shunning the company and favor of princes even in death since, at his behest, his heirs refused offerings of burial shrouds and ablutionary water from the ruling house.

The *Mihna* involved several theological questions, but foremost it was a debate over the status of the Qur'an as God's eternal word. As such, it was a debate at the heart of Islamic theology over the very nature of God.

> Allah! There is no God but Him, the Living, the Eternal! Neither slumber nor sleep takes Him. His is whatever is in the heavens and the earth. Who is it that can intercede with Him except with His permission? He knows what is in front of them and what is behind them, and they know nothing of His knowledge except as He wills. His throne encompasses the heavens and the earth, and guarding them does not tire Him. And He is the Exalted, the Grand. (Q2:255)

This verse enjoys a popularity unrivaled by any other single verse in the Qur'an and has attained talismanic value for many Muslims who see it as encapsulating the Muslim doctrines concerning God's nature and relationship to the world. As a talisman, it is commonly worn on pendants, and hung on vehicle mirrors and from walls throughout the Muslim world. Divine eternality, omniscience and omnipotence are – on the face of it – very straightforward concepts, and ones shared as basic points of doctrine by all Muslims. But the Throne Verse, as Q2:255 is commonly called, hints at other possible aspects of God's nature: slumber, fatigue (or the lack thereof), and thrones imply a high degree of anthropomorphism to God's composition. At the same time, the apparently rhetorical question concerning the absence of any intercessory possibility "except as He wills" would seem to imply that although no one can overrule God, humans or angels might be able to influence His decisions.

THE QUR'ANIC GOD

The Qur'an is full of direct and indirect references to God's nature and His relationship to human beings and the world at large; consequently, it has served as the primary proof text for Islamic theology and as the inspirational touchstone for popular ideas concerning God. The chapters of the Qur'an that are most often memorized by Muslims (and repeated in ritual and informal prayer) give some indication of how God is commonly understood. One of the shortest chapters, *Al-Ikhlas* ("Sincere Belief," 112) is entirely concerned with divine nature:

> Say: "He is Allah, the One,
> Allah, the Self-subsisting.
> He did not beget nor was begotten
> And none is an equal to Him."

These four terse verses actually conceal a complex underlying struggle to establish what emerges as an Islamic notion of God's nature. That God neither begets nor was begotten and has no equals is a refutation of polytheism, and also perhaps of Christianity and its doctrine of the Trinity. The curious revelatory event of the "Satanic Verses" – made infamous through a novel by the same name – involves the removal of an earlier, ostensibly satanically authored, version of Q53:19–21, which refers to three pre-Islamic Arab deities, Al-Lat, Manat, and Al-'Uzza, as the daughters of Allah. Whether or not these "false" verses were ever uttered by Muhammad (and the majority of Muslim scholars have maintained that they were), the incident clearly indicates that the formative Muslim community of Muhammad's day could accept the *possibility* that Allah did beget. Chapter 112 effectively slams the door shut on any debate concerning His offspring, even as the tradition of Qur'an scholarship preserves the memory of false verses that speak of His daughters.

The word translated as "Self-subsisting" – *samad* – is a curious one, since in the Arabic of the time it would have meant "dense" or "compact" as the antonym of "hollow." Again, this constitutes an anthropomorphic description, though anthropomorphism is being employed, yet again, to demonstrate how God is *not* like human beings. Human beings are not *samad* or dense, their hollow torsos being filled with the organs of their subsistence and procreation; God is not hollow, needing neither sustenance nor offspring for His survival.

While *anthropomorphic* references to God almost never lead Muslims to conceptualize God in human form, *anthropopsychic* and *anthropopathic* conceptualizations (which present a god who thinks and feels in human ways) are pervasive. Indeed, anthropopathism and anthropopsychism might be unavoidable in a religion, such as Islam,

which holds as a doctrinal certainty belief in a caring God who is intimately involved in the maintenance and future health of the universe
and of human beings. For us to interact with God, He does not have
to *look* like us, but for His communication and interaction with us to
be comprehensible, He certainly has to *behave* like us, or at least in a
recognizable facsimile. The Qur'an is replete with verses that refer to
God as perceiving through senses similar to human ones (sight, hearing, etc.) and of experiencing emotion to the point where adjectival
nouns based on emotions serve as His epithets. Chapter 55 is called
Al-Rahman ("The Merciful") and comprises (almost exclusively)
vivid descriptions of God's blessings to human beings. Its refrain "So
which of your Lord's blessings would you deny?" – makes the message clear: God blesses human beings in comprehensible and tangible
ways by giving them things, and their gratitude (or ingratitude) is
what God receives back from them and by which He judges them in
future interactions (this last part is not spelled out in the chapter but
is explicit elsewhere in the Qur'an). Similarly, the opening chapter of
the Qur'an, *Al-Fatiha*, which is recited as a prayer more often than
any other piece of scripture, describes God and His behavior in a manner entirely comprehensible in terms of human emotions and characteristics, thereby underlining the point that any linguistic description
or discussion of God cannot but exist in terms comprehensible to
humans:

> Praise is for Allah, Lord of the Worlds
> The Compassionate, the Merciful
> Master of the Day of Judgment
> You alone we worship, You alone we beseech for help
> Guide us on the right path
> The path of those You have favored, not of those who have incurred
>   wrath, nor those gone astray.

THEOLOGY AND DIVINE ATTRIBUTES

Members of the Mu'tazilite school of theology, which was the moving agent behind the *Mihna*, stressed that God did not have a physical
body, or sit on a throne in any anthropomorphic way, insisting that
not only God's powers of perception but even His qualities (such as
mercy, wrath, blessing, guidance, and so on) are completely unlike

their human counterparts. They argued that it was rationally inconceivable for God to have a body or resemble human personality or emotionality in any way. It followed, in their thinking, that all anthropomorphic references in the Qur'an had to be taken metaphorically – God's throne was a metaphor for His majesty, speech was revelation or creative power (a decidedly non-human characteristic), His hand was a reference to divine agency or omnipotence, and so on.

Their literalist opponents (frequently called "traditionalists") might very well have agreed with them that God's attributes are completely unlike their human counterparts, but they were either silent when it came to pronouncing on these concepts publicly, or else argued for the importance of a literal understanding of the Qur'anic text and of authoritative *hadith* concerning God.[2] For his part, Ibn Hanbal spoke explicitly of the necessity of belief in all Qur'anic and *hadith* references to divine anthropomorphism. Though he probably did not believe that God had an actual "body," he was certain that God had a form (*sura*), and referred to several *hadith* accounts which declare that, on the Day of Judgment, God will first appear to believers in a disguise and then reappear in His own form:

> God [at first] will come to them under a form other than that under which they knew Him. He will say to them: "It is I, your Lord!" They will say: "God protects us from you! We will stay here until our Lord comes to us. When our Lord comes, we will recognize Him!" Then God will come to them under the form under which they knew Him. He will say to them: "It is I, your Lord!" They will say: "[Yes], it is You, our Lord!" And they will follow Him.[3]

Ibn Hanbal found additional evidence of God's form in a *hadith* that states God created Adam "according to His form" (*'ala suratihi*). Some of Ibn Hanbal's traditionalist contemporaries argued that "his" in this tradition refers to Adam, meaning that God created Adam in Adam's own form, a somewhat unsatisfactory explanation that has become prevalent through much of Islamic theology. Ibn Hanbal, however, was adamant in his condemnation of those who stated that Adam was created in his own image, rather than the form of God and considered the denial of God's form tantamount to disbelief.[4] Further evidence of Ibn Hanbal's belief in God's anthropomorphic form lies in his judging as reliable a controversial *hadith* tradition according to which Muhammad saw God in his sleep: "I saw the Lord in the form of a young man, beardless (*amrad*) with short curly hair (*ja'd*) and clothed in a green garment."[5]

A crucial characteristic of Ibn Hanbal's scholastic method – as it was for other traditionalists – was that the soundness of a *hadith* account's pedigree trumped the actual content of the account in establishing its reliability. We cannot be sure whether Ibn Hanbal considered such traditions bizarre or pushing the limits of credulity. But such questions miss the nature of his literalist approach, since the very fact that a *hadith* was reliable meant that its content was true and had to be accepted as a matter of doctrine.

Ibn Hanbal's towering reputation as a scholar notwithstanding, the majority of traditionalist opponents of the Mu'tazilites did not accept such a literal and vivid notion of God's form and, over time, they came to resemble their rationalist opponents on many points of theology. Where they parted company was in their understanding of what Qur'anic references to divine attributes actually mean. Traditionalist scholars maintained that, since the Qur'an was the literal and inerrant word of God, all words in it must be true and literally so: God's throne was an actual throne, except not of a human sort, as were His speech, sight, and qualities such as mercy. The difference between the two theological positions rested on a radically different level of trust in the human power of reason. The Mu'tazilites believed that God's actions in the world – and that includes the act and object of revelation – had to be rationally comprehensible, which led to the conclusion that what is rationally known not to be literally true can only be true metaphorically. Their opponents placed less trust in human powers of rational thought and allowed for the possibility of a literal truth that was not comprehensible in human terms.

The disagreement over the true nature of divine qualities took on particular poignancy in discussions of the nature of the Qur'an. Both parties agreed that the Qur'an was God's speech, inerrant and binding on human beings. In the years after the *Mihna*, traditionalists (who probably reflected a majority viewpoint) maintained that speech was an essential attribute of God, inseparable from Him and therefore eternal. The Mu'tazilites, in contrast, maintained that, since God could be imagined without the attribute of speech, His speech must be separate from His essential nature. As such, for speech to be eternal – and therefore for the Qur'an to be God's eternal word – speech would have to be coeternal with God, a doctrinal impossibility in Islam since God is universally acknowledged as the only eternal entity. From their perspective, therefore, opposition to this doctrine amounted to the grave sin of *shirk*, assigning a companion to God. From the opposite perspective, denying the eternality of the Qur'an was equally grave.

Muslim theologians, in their overwhelming majority, were to accept the doctrine of the Qur'an's eternal nature not long after the *Mihna* ended, and the majority of Muslim believers – inasmuch as they concern themselves with arcane questions of the relationship between revelation, divine speech, and God's nature – continue to believe in the timelessness of the Qur'an (although I suspect many Muslims actually believe that the Qur'an, as Muslim scripture, came into existence at the moment of its revelation to Muhammad). Yet the larger questions of God's nature, attributes and His relationship to the world continued to dominate religious thought far beyond the narrow circles of "true" theologians. They no longer appear to carry the same importance as they did as recently as two centuries ago, a phenomenon that is attributable to a combination of factors: a decreased emphasis on philosophy and metaphysics in Islamic education, and an over-all satisfactory resolution (in the eyes of the majority) of important questions of God's nature.

METAPHYSICS AND THE DIVINE INTELLECT

The primary sphere where an ongoing theological discussion of God's nature has continued in Islamic thought from the twelfth century onward is in Sufi metaphysics, at least in the case of the Sunni majority, since both Isma'ili and Twelver Shi'a Muslims, as well as other, smaller, more esoteric groups, have continued a relatively rich tradition of theological speculation. Sufi thought builds on an Islamic synthesis of the philosophy of Late Antiquity – in particular Neoplatonism and Aristotelianism – to understand God's nature and its relationship to the world. There are many variants of the Sufi model, but all of them draw a distinction between God's essence (*dhat* or *zat*) and attributes (*sifat*). God's essence is definitionally unknowable, existing beyond description and dimension (including time, imply-ing that the divine essence is eternal). God is made known through His attributes, which render Him comprehensible, and although Sufi thinkers maintain that "God" is, in fact, a combination of essence and attributes, at face value most writings treat the divine essence as the "identity" of God. For that reason, thinkers such as Ibn 'Arabi (d. 1240) could use aphorisms such as "There was God, and there was nothing beside Him (*kana Allah wa lam yakun ma'ahu shay'*)" and "He is today as He always was (*al-an kama kan*)" to argue that not only is the essence of God the only eternal thing but that everything else possesses existences of a lesser order than God, in that even after the universe came into existence God is as He was when there was nothing besides Him.

In much of Sufi philosophy, the divine essence exists in an undifferentiated form until, through an "urge" rather than a "thought," it brings intellect into existence. It is this combination of intellect with essence as existence that constitutes God and from which all else comes into existence either through a process of emanation or of creation (or a combination of the two).

More commonly, Sufi thinkers concern themselves less with the essence of God than with how He affects the universe and, again, their varied theories show the decided imprint of Late Antique thought (and to a lesser degree of Persian cosmologies and Manichaeism). God's essence is unknowable, but He chooses to make Himself known for a decidedly anthropopathic reason – one that sounds very much like loneliness: a non-Qur'anic statement attributed to God (of a genre called *hadith qudsi*, "divine *hadith*") and extremely popular in Sufi circles declares: "I was a hidden treasure wanting to be known, and I created all of creation in order to be known." God makes Himself known through His attributes (*sifat*) through which He commits acts (*af'al*) which have effects (*athar*) apparent in the world. Divine attributes are normally divided into two categories, those of "Beauty (*jamal*)" and of "Majesty (*jalal*)," although some writers mention a third category of "Perfection (*kamal*)." In general, attributes of Beauty are nurturing (mercy, compassion, sustenance, creation, etc.) while those of Majesty are authoritarian (justice, wrath, destruction, etc.). They can (and have) been understood as gendered, implying that God is either androgynous or transcends gender, although God is spoken of in exclusively male terms in Arabic and other languages.[6] Attributes of Perfection are normally seen as apophatic, in that they are of a category that is humanly incomprehensible and therefore inutterable; sometimes this third category constitutes just one noetic name – God's "greatest" name (*al-ism al-a'zam*), which carries a magical connotation in that gaining knowledge of it would grant the knower all knowledge. The quest for learning God's "greatest" name becomes a goal of Muslim mystical and gnostic endeavors at the same time as its very unknowability underscores the endeavors' inherent futility (or perhaps "emptiness," so that Sufi exercises might better be understood as process rather than goal oriented). In other schemes, Attributes of Perfection are divine qualities that describe God independent of acts and their effects, those attributes that are actualized even before the act(s) of creation. The other attributes – those of Beauty and Majesty – require objects on which to act, things to see, worlds to sustain, and so on, and only exist in potentiality (rather than actuality) until the creation of a universe in which God is known.

The metaphysical concerns with divine nature and God's relationship with the world are ostensibly only one aspect of the variety of phenomena that carry the label of "Sufism," and an arguably arcane aspect at that. In fact, ideas formally developed in Sufi metaphysical writings (as well as Shi'a ones) find their way into wider, more popular aspects of Islamic piety and practice. "Loneliness" as an impetus to creation is not a concept that sees wide formal acceptance among Muslims of any kind. Nevertheless, the underlying notion – that not only is God comprehensible in His characteristics and actions (for the most part) – but that He *needs* human beings and is anthropopsychic in the manifestation of those needs, becomes pervasive. The understanding of an intimate God competes with that of a remote and transcendent one even though Muslim doctrine argues for a simultaneous divine transcendence and intimacy (more accurately, immanence).

God's radical "otherness" (*mukhalafa*) is hinted at in the Qur'an, although it only becomes an important Muslim doctrine promoted in a number of creeds several centuries after Muhammad's death and gains a particular strength in the modern period when Muslims reacting to (and frequently educated in) Western notions of rationalism and critiques of "superstitious" religiosity emphasize an individual, unmediated, and aphysical relationship with the divine to the exclusion of other conceptions.[7] Such ideas are partly affirmative in their emphasis on the equality of all Muslims in their access to God and deservedness of equal reward and punishment. At the same time, the position is a polemical one in its rejection of notions of emotional involvement with God and of a mediated relationship with Him.

Doctrines affirming an utterly transcendent, radically other God who resembles human beings in no way, has absolute power over them in the particulars and final outcome of their destiny, and exists beyond any needs or wants takes on the air of (Sunni) Muslim orthodoxy largely because it is mentioned in the sections on credal belief (*'aqida*) in works of Islamic law, an institution which, for a variety of reasons, has been understood by modern Muslims and Western scholars as the official face of Islam. This conventional view overlooks the fact that many of the most influential figures in the formation of Islamic law, including eponymous founders of Sunni legal schools, lived lives of extreme piety, which is only explicable in terms of a sense of a deeply personal relationship with God. Biographical writings are full of accounts of supererogatory acts and utterances by a variety of people who experienced God in very personal and sometimes dramatic ways. Many of them are referred to as Sufis because they were claimed by Sufism as its own as it evolved into a movement, although several of them belong more appropriately to a wider tradition of early piety and mysticism. Among the most famous are figures such as Rabi'a al-'Adawiyya (d. 801) to whom are attributed a number of aphorisms giving voice to an almost fierce love of God which is not entirely one-sided. Husayn ibn Mansur al-Hallaj (d. 922) is notorious for having uttered "I am God!" (more accurately, "I am the Real" [*ana'l-haqq*]) in a public gathering to somewhat scandalous acclaim, and others, such as Abu Bakr al-Shibli (d. 945), made similar utterances (e.g. "Glory be to me! How great is my majesty!").[8]

ESCHATOLOGY

The complementary, though distinct, Sufi goals of attaining knowledge of God (*ma'rifa*) and of experiencing Him through a loss of self (*fana'*) often strike non-Sufis as strange and unacceptable, but they are not radically different from other Muslim understandings of theology and eschatology. Both Sunni and Shi'i orthodoxy hold that God provides human beings with status, knowledge, and a high level of agency so that they can understand the divine purpose better than any other creature, and both maintain a vision of God (or an eternal life in the divine presence) as an essential element of eschatology. Muslim creation narratives describe the creation of Adam as a moment when God taught him the names of all the other creatures, thereby giving Adam and his descendants power over them. In a well-known passage of the Qur'an, God commands all the angels to bow down before Adam, which they do with the sole exception of one archangel named

Iblis. According to some commentators, Iblis entered Adam's mouth and exited his anus, then declared that the human creation was nothing but a hollow clay pot and therefore undeserving of respect. In the ensuing debate, Iblis claims that human beings are morally weak and will fail in doing God's bidding, at which God banishes Iblis from heaven, giving him until the Day of Judgment to lead human beings astray, thereby proving himself right and redeeming himself. In some versions Iblis is not an angel but the chief of the demons, an interpretation that simplifies explanations of how an angel could disobey God.[9] Accounts of this event receive Qur'anic justification through a verse (Q2:30) in which God announces to the angels that He is about to create a representative (*khalifa*) on the earth; the angels reply by asking why He would create someone who would "cause chaos on (the earth) and spill blood," to which God responds "Indeed I know what you do not."

As some commentators on this verse have argued, the Qur'an makes clear that God has a special plan for human beings, one unknown to the angels and one that relies on greater nobility than is demonstrated by the human propensity for violence and chaos. This is one of two verses in which human beings are called God's caliphs or representatives (sg. *khalifa*) on the earth. The other is "Oh David! Indeed, We made you as a *khalifa* on the earth; so judge between human beings justly and do not follow desires" (Q38:26). Based on these two verses, many scholars have seen human beings collectively as God's representatives on earth, a standing that gives them the right not only to exploit its resources but also obligates them to behave responsibly in a custodial capacity. Others, particularly modernist thinkers, see God's singling out of human beings among all of creation as an ennobling and empowering distinction. Muhammad Iqbal (d. 1938), a poet and major ideologue of Muslim empowerment in South Asia, dwelled on the status of human beings as God's representatives on earth in several of his works. His famous couplet "Why are we wretched today when until yesterday we were displeased / By the bad behavior of an angel in our august presence?" refers directly to Q2:30 in its rhetorical exhortation of the world's Muslims (and human beings in general) to realize their cosmic destiny. In a more theological vein, the influential modernist thinker Fazlur Rahman (d. 1988) delved deeply into this concept in his discussion of the Qur'an, particularly in his somewhat idiosyncratic translation of the Qur'anic word *taqwa* (translated as profound consciousness of God) as the basis of a morally politicized underpinning to all human life.[10]

Such notions of divinely empowered human existence put a particular twist not only on concepts of good and evil and human responsibility for their acts, but also on eschatology: that is, the understanding of doomsday, resurrection, judgment, and the afterlife. In Rahman's writings (and echoes of similar ideas are found in the works of other Muslim modernists), God has a genuine interest in empowering human beings to own (and therefore be responsible for) their acts. Rahman sees God as an enabler who, through divine compassion and wisdom, makes things easier for human beings, whether they do right or wrong. Each right act makes it easier for the individual to commit the subsequent right act, such that being good (i.e. doing right) becomes progressively easier for a right-acting person. Similarly, God makes it easier for someone who commits a wrong act to commit subsequent wrong acts, so that he or she becomes progressively more adept at doing wrong.[11] However, should a bad person choose to do one good deed, subsequent good deeds become progressively easier, though not as easy as they are for someone who was acting rightly in the first place. In this understanding, therefore, Judgment is not simply the weighing of good deeds against bad on a scale as it is presented in the majority of eschatological works, but rather a thorough accounting of acts and the intentions behind them.

Modernist thinkers are relying very directly on medieval Muslim ideas when they see the human status as God's representatives on earth as a sacred trust (*amana*). This assumed the place of a pre-eternal covenant (*mithaq*) – loosely paralleling the biblical covenant in an attempt to demonstrate the status of Islam as the final iteration of God's favored religion – when God turned to Adam and his progeny and asked "Am I not your Lord" and they answered in the affirmative.

DIVINE LOVE

Love for God and God's love for human beings are central themes not just among early Muslim pietists and later Sufis, but also among Muslims – such as scholars of the Hanbali school – who deny any possibility of similarity between God and humans. Both Ibn al-Jawzi

(d. 1200) and Ibn Taymiyya (d. 1328), two of the most influential Hanbali thinkers, recognized the importance of love, although their views on the topic were not always positive. For Ibn al-Jawzi, erotic or passionate love (*'ishq*) is a madness that is the work of an unpreoccupied or empty heart, and it leads only to anguish and possible death.[12] Like other Hanbalis, he does not allow any possibility of passionate love directed toward God because "God has no quality towards which human nature can incline or souls yearn. Rather, the complete dissimilarity between Divinity and his creatures produces in men's souls awe (*hayba*) and timidity (*hishma*). What the Sufi 'lovers' (*'ushshaq*) maintain concerning love (*mahabba*) [for] God is pure delusion."[13]

For Ibn al-Jawzi, love – or at least passionate love – requires some similarity of emotion or sensibility between the lover and the beloved, and this is entirely lacking between human beings and God. He does not seem to maintain an explicit distinction between the two common Arabic terms *'ishq* and *mahabba* as others have sometimes done (and as Ibn Taymiyya appears to do). Of course, judging by the usage of Arabic terms for love as they are applied in later Sufism, any distinction between these two words is idiosyncratic or arbitrary at best.

Ibn Taymiyya's notions of divine love are more complicated in that they appear to address two related issues, his polemical concerns with other theologians (in particular the Ash'aris) and what could arguably be described as opinions springing from personal piety. He maintains that divine love is not an abstract concept but an actuality and an essential part of the relationship between God and His creatures. And that this relationship is mutual, in that God both loves and is loved.[14] He argues against the main points posited as proof against the possibility of love between human beings and God, namely: (1) that love requires a similarity or affinity between the two parties, which is impossible between humans and the divine; and (2) for God to love human beings would imply a need or lack on His part, a doctrinal impossibility.[15]

Against the first point, Ibn Taymiyya argues that even though there is no real affinity between God and human beings, God has attributes which may cause Him to be loved – to the point that divine omnipotence would imply that God possesses every lovable attribute and therefore would naturally and rightly be the ultimate object of love. On the point of divine self-sufficiency, he rebuts his Ash'ari opponents, saying that any argument that denies God's love must also deny the existence of His will (something the Ash'aris would never do).[16]

Ibn Taymiyya's argument for the existence of divine love is grounded in the rationale that love *must* exist because of the necessary existence of other qualities (particularly will) that resemble love in their capacity as divine attributes. And furthermore, he criticizes other theologians for focusing on the physical connotations of words such as "love" or "pleasure" (*ladhdha*) since their common application to human beings does not at all mean that God experiences them in the same way.

His argument in favor of human love for God follows a similar logic: "If there were no meaning to love for God and his Prophet other than love for the reward which is received (in the afterlife), then a man could experience no sweetness of faith in his heart while in this world."[17] Just as desire for reward and fear of punishment are not reasons to love God, divine beneficence is not a proper reason to love Him either since God – in His perfection – is singularly deserving of love entirely for His own sake.[18]

Loving God for His own sake is a concept deeply ingrained in Sufi thought, to the point that there is a prayer attributed to Rabi'a al-'Adawiyya in which she says: "Oh God, if I worship you from fear of hell, burn me in hell; and if I worship you in hope of paradise, ban me from there; but if I worship you for Your own sake then do not hide from me (Your) eternal beauty!"[19]

This statement attributed to Rabi'a – like several others listed by Fariduddin 'Attar in his lengthy chapter on her – is almost certainly apocryphal, but it is important nevertheless because it has been immensely popular and, like similar aphorisms attributed to other early Muslim heroes, has helped shape the contours of piety, devotion, and popular understandings of God across the Muslim world. This particular prayer – of a literary genre called *munajat* (a private prayer or conversation with God) – is a good example of the relationship between love, surrender, and reliance on God. In Sufi practice love for God is demonstrated by systematically abandoning other concerns and desires until one is fully focused and reliant upon Him. The abandoning of secondary concerns is often more the ideal than the reality, but it is very well attested as a formal requirement in Sufi theoretical works as well as in literature.

The majority of Sufi guidebooks, as well as dictionaries of technical terms, have sections on divine love. A highly influential tenth-century work by Al-Kalabadhi collects sayings concerning the Sufi doctrine of love attributed to earlier figures. These definitions vary tremendously, such that it is difficult to come up with a coherent understanding of the concept: "Love is the inclination of the heart," "love is that which renders blind and deaf," or else love is described as the preference for a beloved, or for the beloved's qualities. The most comprehensive definition of love between God and humans provided by Al-Kalabadhi is attributed to an anonymous figure: "The love of man for God is a reverence indwelling in his heart, and not countenancing the love of any others than God. The love of God for man is, that He afflicts him, and so renders him improper for any but Him."[20]

GOD AS BELOVED AND FRIEND

Love for God becomes one of the most enduring and powerful metaphors in the popularization of Sufi literature, both in prose and in poetry. Love as an instrument and metaphor for the feeling of ecstatic union with God becomes so pervasive that it transforms the majority of pre-modern love poetry in Persian and other languages (such as Turkish and Urdu) that rely heavily on Persian poetics.[21] Practically all classical love stories are rewritten with mystical messages, the most famous of which is that of Layla and Majnun, originally an Arabic romance in which a man named Qays becomes so obsessed with the love of Layla that he goes mad (*majnun* in Arabic). In the most celebrated Sufi version of this story, written by the Persian poet Jami (d. 1492), Majnun, maddened by his inability to win Layla's heart, runs into the wilderness and lives with the animals. In the course of the story he is visited by his father who counsels him to act with sobriety, and Layla is married off to someone else. The romance ends with both their deaths, but not before they lament in eloquent prayers and letters about their helplessness in the face of true and overwhelming love.[22]

The story becomes a comprehensive metaphor for the experience of loving God. Since true divine love requires complete abandonment of everything else, Majnun eventually realizes that the human Layla is nothing but an instrument through which he gains absolute love. His father serves as the model of the ordinary pious

Muslim who – though well-meaning – fails to understand the true nature of an ecstatic relationship with God. Layla's husband – who marries her but never gains her love – is an object lesson for the principle that even a completely selfless love – the only kind deserving of being requited by God – can go unrequited sometimes. Layla remains the most complicated figure in the story, since she is simultaneously the human beloved who is left behind as Majnun focuses more on his idea of her than on her physicality, and the unattainable divine beloved for whom Majnun abandons the world.

The use of love poetry becomes so pervasive that – to a much greater degree than in Nizami's *Layla and Majnun* – it is often difficult to tell if the beloved described in the poem is human or divine. The eleventh-century Persian poet Baba Tahir has several quatrains in which he speaks of the loss of identity through love, a sentiment easily understood as referring to divine love:

> If the heart is the beloved, then what is the beloved's name
> And if the beloved is the heart, then how is the heart named
> I saw the heart and the beloved together as one
> I know not what this is – the heart that is the beloved.[23]

Other poems are so explicit in their physical descriptions of the beauty of the beloved's face and body and the physicality of the desire for union that it is difficult to see them as exclusively – or even primarily – referring to love for God. Ibn 'Arabi, who wrote love poetry in Arabic, was concerned about the possibility of audiences misinterpreting poems concerning divine love as being erotic in intention, to the point that he wrote a commentary on his own poetry in order to control their interpretation.

> Oh, is there any way to the damsels bright and fair?
> And is there anyone who will show me their traces?
> And can I halt at night beside the tents of the curving sand?
> And can I rest at noon in the shade of the *arak* trees?
> Commentary:
> "The damsels bright and fair," i.e. the knowledge derived from the manifestations of His Beautiful Name.
> "The tents of the curving sand," i.e. the stations of Divine favour.
> "The shade of the *arak* trees," i.e. contemplation of the pure and holy Presence.[24]

The use of erotic metaphors to refer to divine love reaches its apogee in the popular literature of Islamic South Asia where the majority of Muslim poets writing in vernacular languages (Bengali, Punjabi, Sindhi, etc.), influenced in no small part by love songs for Krishna sung by *gopis* (herding girls), adopt a female voice longing for her male beloved:

> I am ugly and my beloved Beautiful – how can I be agreeable to Him?
> He never enters my home, though I use a hundred thousand ruses.
> Neither am I beautiful nor have I wealth to display – how can I please my Friend?
> This pain shall remain forever, Bahu, I will die crying.[25]

The concern of Ibn 'Arabi and others for the ambiguity of divine love versus erotic love in poetry notwithstanding, it is unclear whether or not such poetry retains an erotic dimension at all. For the majority of Muslims, there is no possibility for a human being to enter into an erotic relationship with God, not only because it requires an impossible stretch in the anthropopathic conceptualization of God, but also because there are almost no other Muslim religious models in which the erotic plays an active part in religious practice.[26] If an ostensibly erotic love poem is ambiguous in whether it is referring to a human beloved or to God, and if an erotic relationship with God is impossible, the poem must be emptied of any true erotic content for it to retain the genuine possibility of referring to God, since love for God brooks neither ambiguity nor eroticism. For love of another human being to overlap with love for God, human love, as described in the poem, must necessarily be erotic only in a symbolic sense, but platonic in its actuality. Therefore, the human beloved is etherealized and only symbolically human, no more or less anthropomorphic than God, and bodily descriptions are references to divine beauty in their primary meaning. If one allows for a mystical interpretation, the Ottoman Turkish poet Ahmet Pasha (d. 1497) is not resorting to rhetorical excesses when he says "It is the guard of the garden of heaven, the tress on my lover's face (*bağban-ı bağ-ı cennet'tir ruhunda zülf-i dost*)" – the lover with tresses across her face is no more physical than the garden of heaven which promises intimacy with God.

The most important apparent exception to this rule is popular Sufi practice in South Asia, where love for God as the love of a woman for a man becomes *the* dominant metaphor for the relationship between the Sufi and God, such that the death anniversary of a Sufi saint is celebrated as his or her *'urs*, the Arabic word for "wedding." The implication that, in death, the Sufi unites as a bride with her beloved is explicit, and saints' festivals incorporate many of the symbolic and performative aspects of South Asian Muslim wedding ceremonies, such as the carrying of a veil over the "bride" and a formal departure from the birth household to the marital home (*rukhsati*).

This significant feature of Sufi practice in South Asia sets it apart from the larger sphere of Persianate Muslim society. Perhaps the metaphor of love for God and union with Him is actually enacted in South Asia, whereas it remains a dramatic literary pattern elsewhere. More probably, in South Asia the metaphor slips from the realm of literature into that of a ritual space that is transformed as a consequence of Sufi notions of love. Regardless of the underlying cause, Muslims of other persuasions are often scandalized by these practices and condemn them as deplorable religious innovations of popular Sufism. Although there is certainly a violent edge to the contestation of "true" Islam – normally perpetrated by Salafi groups who consider all others to be heterodox innovators – it is not love for God that is contested but rather the manner in which this love is demonstrated and understood.

MONOTHEISM VERSUS MONOLATRY

Belief that there is no God except Allah is the fundamental point of Muslim doctrine, to the extent that the profession of faith (*shahada*) – the formal act through which a person becomes a Muslim – is a declaration to this effect (together with the acceptance of Muhammad as God's Prophet). However, beyond the level of credal statements, the distinction between monotheism (the belief in only one God) and monolatry (the worship of only one God) is not as clearly maintained. Indeed, early Muslim sources speak of the existence of other gods, albeit false ones. A popular work by Ibn al-Kalbi, entitled *The Book of Idols* (*Kitab al-asnam*), describes Muhammad's destruction of al-'Uzza (mentioned earlier in this essay as one of the repudiated daughters of Allah). According to Ibn al-Kalbi, sometime around 630 Muhammad ordered his military champion, Khalid ibn al-Walid, to the valley of Nakhlah where there were three trees inhabited by the goddess al-'Uzza, and ordered him to cut down the first one and report back to him. When Khalid came back, Muhammad asked him if he had seen anything there, to which Khalid replied that he hadn't. Muhammad then ordered Khalid to return and cut down the second tree and report back, which he did as being similarly uneventful. When Khalid returned to cut down the third tree at Muhammad's command, he encountered an Abyssinian woman with wild hair, gnashing and grating her teeth. With her was Dubayyah al-Sulami, the custodian of al-'Uzza. Dubayyah addressed the woman as al-'Uzza and implored her to kill Khalid. The Muslim champion struck al-'Uzza with his sword, cutting off her head, at which she fell to the ground in a pile of ashes. He then killed her custodian, felled the tree and returned to Muhammad with his report. Muhammad allegedly commented: "That was al-'Uzza ... Verily she shall never be worshipped again."[27]

Descriptions of gods and potent idols are not uncommon in Muslim accounts of exotic lands, in particular those of India. In his description of the Indus valley (Al-Sind), the renowned tenth-century Arab geographer Al-Muqaddasi writes:

> As for the idols in this region, there are two in Harawa made of stone: no one approaches them. They have a power such that should a man try to lay his hand on one, it will be held back and will not reach the idol. They both appear as though made of gold and silver. It is said that if one expresses a wish in their presence, the request will be granted ... The two statues are quite enchanting. I saw a Muslim man who said he had forsaken Islam to return to the worship of the idols, having been captivated by them; when he returned to Naysabur [Nishapur, in Iran] he became Muslim again. The two idols really are miraculous![28]

Al-Muqaddasi is clear that the idols of Harawa possess the power of enchantment, and that it is possible for (ostensibly upstanding) Muslims to fall under their power to the point of abandoning their faith, only regaining it after returning to Islamic lands, safe from the reach of the idol. Though Al-Muqaddasi does not display any antipathy toward the idols (many Muslim writers consider idolatry a sign not of evil but of ignorance, just as many Late Antique, Jewish, and Christian writers do), fear that believing Muslims might fall into idolatry – that is, start praying to the *wrong* god – was clearly one of the motivations behind iconoclastic acts in pre-modern Islam. In fact, this monolatric concern was apparent in the destruction of the

Buddha statues at Bamiyan at the hands of the Taliban in 2001: among the different justifications provided by Mullah Omar, the leader of the Taliban, one was the necessity of their destruction on the basis of the fear that their continued existence threatened Afghanistan with a return of Buddhism (for which Afghan Muslims would necessarily have to abandon Islam).[29]

A pervasive concern with monolatry over monotheism is demonstrated in contemporary South Asian Muslim behavior. The traditional greeting "*Khuda hafiz* (God protect [you])!" has been the normal way to bid someone farewell throughout Islamic South Asia, Iran, Afghanistan, Tajikistan, and the historic urban centers of Uzbekistan. *Khuda*, the Persian word for "god" (the archaic usage is *khudavand*) has almost completely been replaced by *Allah* in Pakistani and Bangladeshi usage and is rapidly gaining popularity among the Muslims of India. The stated rationale behind changing the longstanding *Khuda hafiz* to *Allah hafiz* (Allah protect [you]!) is that *khuda* is a generic word and can be applied to gods other than the Muslim one, whereas "Allah" is God's proper name and therefore eliminates the possibility of anyone wishing you the protection of some other deity (indeed, it is not uncommon for Christians, Hindus, and Sikhs to say "*Khuda hafiz*"). The counter-argument, grounded in monotheism rather than monolatry, that there is only one God and therefore all references to the divine by Muslims necessarily refer to Him regardless of the name, has little currency in contemporary South Asian Muslim society.

CONCLUSION

The self-conscious modification of rules of etiquette might appear trivial and the suggestion that Muslims are unclear about the distinction between worshipping *one* god rather than *the only* God might sound unfair. However, monolatry is very much part of Muslim doctrine, where it is inseparable from monotheism. *Tawhid* is a central concept in Islam; often loosely translated as "monotheism" or "divine unity," *tawhid* is a noun derived from a transitive Arabic verb, *wahhada* ("to make one"). Believing in the concept of *tawhid*, which Muslims are supposed to do as a cardinal doctrine, can be understood to constitute the affirmation of God's unity, making the individual

Muslim an active participant in God's ongoing uniqueness rather than a passive believer in an existing fact. In so doing, the individual believer, as God's representative in creation, helps assure that God continues to be known as an enigma that is simultaneously beyond all need and intimately mindful of His creation, immanent as well as transcendent.

Though one can easily make the argument that Muslims are united in their affirmation of divine unity, clearly there is tension between distinct, and sometimes conflicting, understandings of God, the nature of divinity, and God's relationship to human beings. Muslim individuals as well as societies engage with these tensions in a variety of ways. Throughout their history, rather than being passive regurgitators of supposedly standard doctrines that are naively inherited from an earlier period of religious canonization, Muslims have actively (and even contentiously) negotiated varied conceptions of God, and continue to do so today.

10

HISTORY

Snjezana Buzov

In the year 1909 a Bosnian religious scholar, Hasan ibn Salih ibn Hasan Ihliwnawi (from the town of Livno), composed the *ijaza* (certificate of graduation, license to teach) for his student Adam Hifzi ibn al-'Abidin al-Busnawi.[1] Containing the scholarly genealogy (*sanad*) stretching back in time to the earliest Islamic period and ending in the early twentieth century, this *ijaza* offers a memory of Islamic learning in Hadith, legal studies (*fiqh*), Qur'anic exegesis (*tafsir*), and general religious education covering more than a millennium, and traveling the path of learning through several regions of the Eastern Mediterranean and the Middle East.

The *ijaza* is prefaced by an introductory account of the importance of learning and laced with numerous quotations of the Qur'an, *Hadith*, and various well-known *sentetiae*. The structure of the introductory part comprises a versified praise of scholarship and lament over ignorance, followed by a series of quotations from the Qur'an, which is followed by a series of quotations of *hadith*. When turning to the subject of the text, the author gives another short introduction before turning to the account of his personal experience of following the path of learning. In this short introduction the author focuses on the importance of *isnad* (transmission of knowledge), saying:

> It is necessary to lay out the *isnad* so that the knowledge would be trustworthy. Ibn al-Mubarak said: "If there were no *isnad* anyone could say what he wants." Al-Thawri said: "*Isnad* is the weapon of believers, without weapons there could be no struggle." Baqiyya, one of the *muhaddiths* – May God have mercy on him – said: "I studied

hadith with Hammad ibn Zayd and he told me: 'The best among them are those who have the shelter, that is, the *isnad*.'" Ahmad ibn Hanbal said: "To require *isnad* is the custom of our predecessors." Al-Hakim said: "To require *isnad* is the authentic *sunna*."[2]

He adds his own statement about the importance of *isnad* by saying that *isnad* is the defining characteristic of the *umma* (the community of believers), and adding that this is the main cause for which the scholars of that "blessed community" saddle their horses and travel long distances in order to reach the high peaks of knowledge.[3]

The versified account of his journey starts in his hometown of Livno and takes him on a sea journey to Istanbul where he meets and learns from many scholars, but chooses as his primary teacher al-Hajj Muhammad al-Halis ibn Muhammad al-Shirwani.

The text of the *ijaza* starts with praise for his student and certifies his ability to teach and combines elements of a certificate with those of a recommendation letter. It then continues with the layout of the scholarly *isnad*, making a brief "visit" to the city of Amasya where Ihliwnawi's teacher began his education. The rest of the *isnad* is the copy of Ihliwnawi's teacher's scholarly genealogy that branches off into three lineages: one in general education, one in *fiqh* (legal studies) and *tafsir* (Qur'anic exegesis), and the third in Hadith. The *isnad* of Ihliwnawi's teacher's teachers goes back to well known Islamic scholars such as Al-Taftazani (d. 1389), Khatib al-Qazwini (d. 1338), and Abu'l-Hasan al-Ash'ari (d. 935). His lineage in *fiqh* and *tafsir* conventionally goes back to the Prophet. Likewise, his lineage in the study of Hadith goes back to Al-Bukhari and Al-Muslim, the authors of the two most authoritative collections of Sunni *hadith*. Ihliwnawi provides *isnads* not only for the transmitters of knowledge – the teachers of his teacher – but also for some of the books he studied. The latter type of "lineage" – the book *isnad* – is often included in the *ijazas*, but it is equally often composed independently from them, testifying not only to the transmission of knowledge but also the formation of "schools" around influential works as well as textual communities.

As seen from the above example, the *ijaza* is a license to teach, a certificate of graduation, a recommendation letter, a transcript, but also a memory of learning focusing on individual transmitters rather than on the (hi)story of learning. One student could acquire a number of *ijazas*, certificates being issued by individual teachers, not by schools. Ideally, the journey in search of knowledge would lead a student to seek "outstanding teachers, wherever they might be."[4] A large number of the *ijazas* which came down to us show that often, especially from the sixteenth century, the goal was to find one teacher with expertise in what had become a relatively stable *madrasa* curriculum and to obtain an *ijaza* similar to the one described above.

The recorded world of Islam is flooded by texts such as this *ijaza* displaying lineages of those involved in learning and transmitting knowledge. To such scholarly ones should be added the *ijazas* containing the *silsilas* (the chains of transmission) of the Sufi masters as well as the lineages of masters of particular crafts (*shajaras*).

A dense fabric of memory emerges from the numerous intersections of these lineages with equally abundant works listing short biographies of scholars, artists, and spiritual leaders in communities within the Islamic world. On that fabric, works and ideas constitute an ever-changing pattern, depending on which works are conceived to inspire the arguments that reveal the secrets of (contemporary) time. In documenting time, its synchronic and diachronic weaving is more thorough than any of the historical works and official archives of any one Islamic empire, including the Ottoman, known for its thoroughness and minute organization.

Ihliwnawi records no date except when the *ijaza* was composed, for there is no need for that. Even though they focus on lineages (and the place of individuals within those lineages), time in the *ijaza* is not linear and numerical markings of time have no significance. The lineages displayed describe a community of scholars and teachers held together in time by a shared devotion to learning and companionship. That time is at once sacred and worldly, since everything they do is already prescribed and required in Qur'anic verses and the large number of *hadith* that Ihliwnawi quotes.

What is the awareness of time behind the dense record of the names of scholars and generational and genealogical ties between them? Certainly not the one that informs historical inquiry and historical consciousness. Otherwise, Ihliwnawi would not be so indifferent to the fact that he lived in the Austro-Hungarian Empire in a time that offered other paths of learning – a learning of unknown lineages, with books that had narrow margins unlike those traditionally produced in the Islamic world where margins were often larger than the text, awaiting the commentaries of fellow scholars. Knowing oneself in time meant not only defining one's scholarly position in relation to the scholarship of the contemporary generation – it was of equal, if not even greater importance, to know and respond to a larger whole in time.

The continuous production of commentaries (*sharh* in Arabic) and supercommentaries (sg. *hashiya*) is, among other things, a reflection of perceived necessity, not merely to situate oneself in a particular moment in time but also to know one's work and one's self within an entire lineage. In modern scholarship on Islamic intellectual production, the scholarly etiquette that required placing one's work on the margins of the work of others has been interpreted as a lack of originality marking the entirety of post-classical scholarly production. What is merely a scholarly convention allowing a scholar to express his argument by framing the discussion around one work instead of everything written on the subject is viewed as a qualitative rather than a formal feature. Behind this scholarly convention, which is only a consequence of the way the relationship of one work to another is perceived in time, there is an understanding about the merging of time and memory that in turn becomes visible in the way memory is mapped out and recorded.

TIME AND MEMORY

Andrei Tarkovsky's account of time and memory would probably be more appealing and familiar to Ihliwnawi than the Central European learning of his own time to which he clearly gave no concern. In his reflection on cinema entitled *Sculpting in Time,* Tarkovsky offers a clear approach to the subject, arguing that "time and memory merge into each other, as the two sides of a medal."[5] Memory, he says, cannot exist without time. But time is not linear, and the past, for an individual human being, is "the bearer of all that is constant in the reality of the present, of each current moment."[6]

Tarkovsky's thoughts about time and memory emerge from a concern with the creative act that, by his definition, has to be free of received ideas. Yet he does not aim to place the act of artistic creation outside time and memory in the sense that art is commonly seen as timeless (his proposal does not allow for timelessness). Rather, in creating art, a human seeks to both articulate and escape from the bitterness and dissatisfaction that is the result of knowing one's self through the consciousness of time and the endowment with memory. This view grows from his understanding that the merging of time and memory is an individual experience through which one's moral being becomes known to one's self; a person is thus able "to seize" his own link with an outside world.

Tarkovski gives two strong and emphatic definitions of time and memory. "Time," he says, "is a state: the flame in which there lives the salamander of the human soul." And memory "is something so complex that no list of all of its attributes could define the totality of the impressions through which it affects us. Memory is a spiritual concept!"[7]

The merging of time and memory in Islamic learning could easily be explained by commenting on the above-described *ijaza* of a humble teacher from western Bosnia in the early twentieth century. But the audience to which this essay is written is used to a convention in which one provides a multitude of different proofs. And the proof indeed is multitudinous – the multitude well known to modern scholars of Islam. As said earlier, not only the *ijazas*, but other texts containing lineages in all spheres of knowledge pervade the recorded world of Islam. Without numerical markings of time, and without geographical locales recorded, this memory certainly responds to Tarkovsky's spiritual memory, and the time as its other face, "the flame in which there lives the salamander of the human soul."

The spiritual character of memory and time as the habitat of the human soul is not evident in the content of the lineages and generations recorded in Islamic scholarship, for they offer little more than the names of those who formed them. It is in the persistence by which they were preserved and remembered that the merging of time and memory as well as their very nature becomes visible. But why (and for what purpose) did this practice of recording develop, and what is especially Islamic about it?

Especially in the post-caliphal period, a larger part of the Islamic world was dominated by nomadic peoples who – even when protagonists of highly literate cultures – continued to place value on oral memory and (as individuals) formed their links to the outside world through their tribal lineages. This fact may offer an easy answer to questions of the emergence of recorded lineages. Even more obvious and easier would be an explanation that places this practice in the context of the early importance of *isnad* for recording the prophetic *sunna*, the hierohistory that became the norm for the Muslim community.

The rebirth of *isnad* and lineage-centered memory appears "natural" to the Islamic world especially when a ubiquitous practice such as recording lineages and generations is self-referential rather than relying on a rational theory behind it. The lineage of entire learning – of religious disciplines, gnosis, and practical skills – emerges at the time when the original *isnad* of the Prophetic *sunna* was already solidified and recorded. Yet the concept is clearly the same as that of the original *isnad*, and the "rebirth" can be seen as the branching out, or a further development of the original *isnad*. More important to this development is the imperative of preserving authenticity of knowledge. While the hierohistory continues in Shi'i Islam through the lineage of Imams, in Sunni Islam it is no longer perpetuated through lineages. Rather, it simultaneously maintains its sameness and engages in dialogue with time, while seeking to preserve authenticity through lineages. Authority thus belongs to the ever-growing chain of scholars, not to an individual, and it certifies knowledge as such, not a particular production of it.

In his lengthy introduction Ihliwnawi offers no theory, no explanations, except by supporting the evident truth of the sacred texts by offering an account of his own journey on the path of seeking and maintaining knowledge. Instead he lists a repertoire of Qur'anic verses and quotations from the Hadith which places the bearers of knowledge in a position equal to that of martyrs ("On the day of Resurrection the ink of the scholar and the blood of the martyr will be equal"); heirs to the Prophet ("The bearers of knowledge are the heirs of the prophets"); those with unquestionable autonomy whose knowledge does not have to respond to the imperatives of a particular time ("Learn before the knowledge disappears, and it disappears when the bearers of knowledge disappear, because some do not know when *they* are needed, and when *what they possess* is needed"); and the only ones who can create something ("Creation is the attribute of the believer only in scholarship"). Like in classical theory, metaphysical knowledge is offered as the antinomy to the practical.[8] However, the practice here is not of producing knowledge but rather of placing an individual on the map of time, and associating him with the sole mediator (the Prophet) between practical and metaphysical knowledge and all other participators in the lineage. Thus, the lineage takes on the role that, in classical theory, belongs to *theoroi*, the observers and seers.

The apparent contradiction between the two imperatives behind the composition and recording of *isnad* – one of placing authority in the entire lineage and the other of defining one's individual self in time – emerges from placing importance on authority and transmission rather than on authenticity and memory. In other words, the lineage of *isnads* is not a representation of lineal time, the time of calendars. *Isnad* provides a "sense of connectedness," and personal connection across the generations with the time and personages of Islamic origins.[9] For an individual scholar and individual scholarly production, that connection did not mean simply tying himself and his work to origins in a remote past. One enters a lineage by choosing a teacher, and while the authority of one's immediate teacher is great and almost unquestionable, the process of learning is also defined by companionship and intimacy between the teacher and his students. Through memory and the maintenance of a lineage, that companionship extends backward to cover the entire lineage. At the same time, memory and the maintenance of lineage removes the possibility of creating a hierarchy of knowledge (and of teachers). Consequently, individual memory and the individual's place in a lineage can be central and simultaneously part of a larger whole. But in both cases it is an intersection, the point where time and memory merge, and not a point of ranking one's individual memory on the value scale of knowledge.

Finally, one has to acknowledge the very practical aspect of the recording of lineages – especially in the context of issuing *ijazas*. When seeking to advance or employ the knowledge in the vast territories of medieval Islamdom, one could not refer by name to a single teacher, unknown to scholars in distant lands. A single authority could not authenticate knowledge. The language of lineages spoke to audiences everywhere, and insured membership in scholarly circles from Spain to India. At the same time, keeping the lineages alive served to maintain learning autonomous from worldly authorities, and thus from its fragmentation along political borders. Aside from recorded lineages, a large number of stories (themselves repeatedly recorded and referenced) has come down to us testifying to the notoriety of such travels in the medieval period, from the eighth-century proverbial Sufi Ibrahim-i Adham, to the famous traveler Ibn Battuta (fourteenth century), and the well-known historian and philosopher Ibn Khaldun (d. 1395).

HISTORICAL LITERATURE

What about historical knowledge and historical literature (*tarikh*)? If a mechanism, other than that of historical literature, is devised to preserve memory and lay out the junctures of time and memory then what is the role of a large body of knowledge about time organized around numerical time-recording? And finally, is its product (i.e. historical knowledge) included in the paths of learning and transmission?

When arguing for the reform of education in Egypt and the reinvigoration of Islamic learning through the revival of Islamic classics, Muhammad Abduh placed particular emphasis on the magnum opus of Ibn Khaldun, the *Muqaddima*.[10] His exchange of arguments with Shaykh Muhammand Al-Anbabi, the rector of Al-Azhar (the premier Sunni institution of higher learning in the Arab world), reveals that even though he supported the revival of Islamic knowledge alongside the introduction of modern Western learning into Al-Azhar,[11] Abduh argued from an integrative position while the rector defended a traditional, classical curriculum. Abduh's recollection of the exchange is as follows:

> Then after my return from exile, I tried to convince Shaykh Muhammad al-Anbabi, then Shaykh Al-Azhar, to accept certain proposals, but he refused. Once I said to him, "Would you agree, O Shaykh, to order that the *Muqaddima* of Ibn Khaldun be taught at Al-Azhar?" And I described to him whatever I could of the benefits of this work. He replied, "It would be against the tradition of teaching at al-Azhar." During our intricate conversation, I began talking to him about some more recent shaykhs, i.e. professors of al-Azhar, and asked him, "How long ago did Al-Ashmuni and Al-Sabban die?" He replied that they had died only so many years ago. I then said, "They have died only recently and yet their books are being taught and there had been no tradition of teaching them." Shaykh al-Anbabi was silent and did not reply.[12]

While Abduh understands tradition as formed around time-confirmed works, the rector refers to long-established scholarly disciplines. More precisely, Abduh sees the authority of learning in individual works while for the rector authority is in lineage. Indeed, traditionally history has not been a scholarly discipline in the curriculum of *madrasas*. Even though historians shared in the same lineages as religious scholars, their work was informed by practical knowledge. Like Ibn Khaldun – who was educated at the *Zaytuniyya madrasa* but followed the professional path of a high bureaucrat – they drew their knowledge from practical involvement in statecraft.

In the pre-modern Islamic world, as elsewhere until modern times, the historians' craft was an art of bureaucrats. The knowledge it produced was one of the outside observer, and its appearance, according to Ibn Khaldun, was "no more than information about times and dynasties."[13] But the inner meaning behind that appearance, he argues, "is deliberation and research, a meticulous explanation of beings and their principles in detail, comprehension of the circumstances of events and their deep causes." "Thus," he says, "it is rooted in wisdom which is ancient, and it is truly worthy of becoming counted among its [i.e. wisdom's] disciplines."[14] Despite developing a philosophical and social theory of history, Ibn Khaldun's goal of including history among the "disciplines of wisdom" was not achieved. From what we have discussed so far, it is possible to conclude that the disassociation of historians from the *'ulama* was defined by the boundaries of their association with worldly authorities and their position as outside observers who situated and organized knowledge within the parameters of their observations, rather than within the lineage of transmission. What was left outside that lineage was not the historians, who were situated in it via their educational path. It was knowledge that was disassociated, as it was composed simultaneously to inform a concrete society of the rules of its order as well as to represent and maintain that order.

The modern advocates of Ibn Khaldun – both Western scholars, who "discovered" his work, and Abduh, who derived his argument from that discovery – were equally puzzled about the reasons why Islamic historiography, and scholarship in general, "survived" such great theory without becoming influenced and shaped by it.

The modern scholarly perception of Ibn Khaldun's work as anomalous has not been substantiated through research.[15] Rather, it becomes anomalous when placed in the context of the historical literature of its Western contemporaries. Furthermore, the understanding of the relationship between time and learning in modern history imposes the image of Ibn Khaldun as a scholar who went "before" his time and subsequent historians as scholars whose work thus remained "outdated." Ibn Khaldun's critique of historical production may serve to explain the perceived gap between the theory he offered and the practice of history writing. First, he criticizes imitation of established models:

> Most of the histories by these (authors) were general in approach and method in regard to all affairs of the two earliest Islamic dynasties[16] in both their territorial extent and dominion. Their scope included remote goals some of which they pursued and some abandoned. Among those who incorporated the dynasties, peoples and general affairs before Islam were Al-Mas'udi and those who followed his path. After them came those who turned from the general to the particular and hesitated to be too general and comprehensive. They recorded curious events of their own period and collected information about their surroundings and regions. They restricted themselves to the talk about their own states and capitals. This was done by Ibn Hayyan, the historian of al-Andalus and its Umayyad dynasty, and by Ibn al-Rafiq, the historian of Ifriqiya and the dynasty in al-Qayrawan. After these came only imitators, indolent of character and intelligence, or inert ones who wove on this (same) loom and reproduced it exactly. They disregarded the change of conditions over time, which brought about alteration in the customs of peoples and generations. They presented information about dynasties and stories of events from the early period as mere forms without substance.[17]

Then he observes and criticizes the absence of elaboration and mere recording of names and dates:

> Other historians, then, came with too brief a presentation (of history). They went to the extreme of being satisfied with the names of kings, without any genealogical or historical information, and with only a numerical indication of the length of their reigns.[18]

Even though a number of historical traditions developed in subsequent historiography, which used a variety of models of exposition and organization of historical data, the mode of narration and recording continued to be the defining feature of the craft. Historical narratives remained framed around lineal time and events, with variations based on the criteria of what constituted an event. The art of history writing placed more urgent demands on its practitioners, including the demand for practical wisdom. This does not mean that Ibn Khaldun's successors – especially those who, like him, undertook the task of writing universal histories – did not evoke his work and refer to it.

As explored by C. Fleischer, Mustafa Na'ima (d. 1716), the Ottoman *vak'anünuvis* (official annalist) referred to Ibn Khaldun's

Muqaddima's "formulations of cyclical rise and decline of societies, on the dynamic tension between nomadic and sedentary polities, and on the five stages of the life of a dynastic state."[19] The same research reveals references to Ibn Khaldun in the works of other Ottoman historians such as Müneccimbaşı (d. 1702), and the polymath Katib Çelebi (d. 1657). Na'ima and Katib Çelebi evoked and interpreted Ibn Khaldun's work not only to "describe, but also to solve the financial, political, and social problems which had plagued the Ottoman Empire since the late sixteenth century."[20]

All of these, and other Ottoman historians, practiced historical craft primarily as *tahrir ü tasnif*, "*tahrir*" denoting the recording of the things current – what they witnessed, heard of, or read – "*tasnif*" the classifying and ordering of both things current and past. This term explains only the requirements placed before historians, not the rationale behind those requirements, and certainly not the religious concerns that provided the certification for their (essentially social) deliberations.

In order to explore questions concerning the necessities and rationale that formed and informed the demand to record and classify as well as the religious certification of historical craft, it is necessary to turn to those historians who, in addition to recording and classifying, engaged in a reinterpretation of history. The famous Ottoman historian Mustafa 'Ali (d. 1600), whose work was (uncharacteristically) often quoted by the later Ottoman historians, composed a voluminous universal history entitled *Künh'ül- Akhbar* (*The Essence of Histories*) where he engages in an endeavor similar to that of Ibn Khaldun – that of reinterpreting and reordering historical knowledge. Even though (or precisely because) he does not refuse to be a mere registrar and classifier of the existing order and did not resort to theoretical deliberations, his work, like Ibn Khaldun's, offers a new interpretation and reordering of history.

Mustafa 'Ali's universal history focuses on the issue of sovereignty. Deriving a new chronological and structural order from the same materials with which other historians worked he does not argue for a new historical science but rather for the renewal of the structure of order and for a reformed political theory. Sovereignty, which is at the center of his discussion of the just order, is defined by justice. The erosion of impartial justice, meritocracy, administrative morality, and loyalty to the dynasty were the contemporary problems which 'Ali both diagnosed and sought to resolve.[21] Concern with justice forms the crowning criterion of order displayed in *tarikh*, which becomes the sorting mechanism of all of the items (*akhbar*) of memory. This had to include within his evaluation the instances of sovereignty of non-Muslim rulers over regions of the Islamic world. Like Ibn Khaldun, he makes an exception for sovereignty as long as it is legitimized by the principle of universal and impersonal justice.[22]

Both scholars, with *ijazas* from the best universities of their times, Ibn Khaldun and 'Ali only asserted the right that all historians could claim: that of formulating as well as recording and ordering the world of the time and locale. In historical writing as *tarikh*, exposition varies in focus depending on the index of events or schema devised by a generation of historians. Whether as a routine recording and structuring – excelling perhaps only in literary style – or as an impartial observation – asserting superiority and restructuring the order – *tarikh*, nevertheless, focuses on order.

That behind the demand of formulating and recording stands the Islamic imperative of justice and equity becomes evident from the definition of equity offered by an influential (but little-studied) historian of the early sixteenth-century Ottoman realm. In his Persian *Kanuname-i Şahinşahi*, Idris Bitlisi (d. 1520) evokes a *sententia* in Arabic: "The justice is in placing every thing in its proper place."[23] While rulers are perceived as guardians and guarantors of justice, historians are actually those who put everything in its proper place and, when deemed necessary, even define what that place is.

Depending on whether the author is a high bureaucrat, knowledgeable of the worldly order that is still dependent on religious sanction and divine protection,[24] or someone writing a contemporary chronicle of a city or a small community, the *order* – not the *time* – is the preoccupation of the pre-modern Muslim historian. I shall illustrate this concern with order with excerpts from three contemporary chronicles, that is, the chronicles that narrate events that took place during the life of the author.

Among the short entries from the *Tarikh* (1563–1595) by the well-known Ottoman historian Mustafa Selaniki there is the following:

> *The judge in Honored Mecca Mevlana Kuş Yahya Efendi's coming to the Royal Council* Mevlana Kuş Yahya Efendi, who was supposed to go to the *madrasa* of Sultan Selim Han in Edirne following his earlier appointment at the Semaniye *madrasa*, was somehow honored by the position of judge at the Great Ka'ba. He came to the Imperial Council, and as he was entering the hall of the Exalted Throne, he put

on a choice Moorish robe of honor with sleeves. They said: "There are many opponents – they disapprove when the order is issued that changes the placement of the religious scholars," (but) to no avail. He came in with the viziers and kissed (the sultan's) hand. In the first decade of Rabi'ul-akhir, year 1003 (Hijri).[25]

Seemingly a routine recording of a visit of a prominent judge to the Ottoman court, this short record consists of several reports (*akhbar*): one, about the career of Yahya Efendi, who held the teaching position at the Semaniye *madrasa* in Istanbul and, according to the rules of promotion, was supposed to be appointed to the judgship of Edirne. Then, the report of his promotion to the judgship of Mecca is recorded together with the suspicion of corruption. The report of his audience at the sultan's court, which is in the title of the record, is not a description of a routine ceremonial event since the robe of honor given to him is detailed as especially valuable. Finally, Selaniki records the report about ineffectual protests of a large number of the members of the *'ulama*. Indeed, Selaniki just narrates the event and records the reports about it. But his main concern in regard to this visit is not a routine ceremony of receiving a new appointee to the court, but to narrate everything he knows about that appointment which, in this case, reveals disregard for the established order.

Another *tarikh,* composed by a barber from eighteenth-century Damascus, Shihab al-Din Ahmad ibn Budayr al-Hallaq (fl. 1762), abounds with entries such as the following:

> The unruly soldiers of Damascus have committed excesses, cursing of religion has increased, the commoners have been oppressed and no one listens to what they say, and the ruler of Damascus, his Excellency As'ad Pasha ... has not confronted any of these matters. Public order has dissipated ... He does not move a thing, but sleeps with the sleeping.[26]

As a third example, among the events recorded by Mulla Mustafa Başeski (d. 1805), a Qadiri Sufi and a public scribe from Sarajevo, there is the following:

> One of these days in the morning, one leg and the head of a prostitute were found on the Latin bridge. This event angered people, so they caught a certain non-Muslim woman innkeeper and accused her. Then she calumniated three or four other persons, but they shoved her into a sack and threw her from the bridge into the water. They

also threw two non-Muslim women into the water as well as a certain Mulla Kadın Piroka, who was a literate woman, and it seems she was innocent. Everybody was touched deeply by the throwing of the mentioned women into the water. Everybody is a sinner, but salvation is obtained by rejection of violence, not by throwing women innkeepers into the river.[27]

Three different kinds of authority of a detached observer are applied in the records quoted above. Selaniki's is the authority of an insider, a member of the *'ulama* who knows the specific rules of promotion. Ibn Budayr's is the authority of the outsider who nevertheless knows that order is being disturbed by those who should guard it. Mulla Mustafa Başeski's comments on the reports of a specific case of violence from a position of moral authority, which is not derived from the knowledge of – or belief in – worldly order. Yet they all write with the confidence of a qualified observer, and seemingly without an externally imposed restraint.

Within the large body of *tarikh* literature one could find less disparate records to illustrate the craft of history writing as more congruent or as congruent as to show that *tarikh* is one genre rather than a whole discipline – a literature, a large depository of memory. It is equally possible to provide evidence to the opposite claim, that *tarikh* – like *history* – means many things whether in the sense of genres and subgenres, or in regard to the variety of interpretive positions, definitions of what constitutes an event and so on.

However, within the Islamic context, the distinctive features of historical literature emerge more clearly when the two memories are compared, one of the lineages and the other recorded in historical literature. Whether narrating contemporary events or those of the past, local and communal history or the history of larger regions, and whether in classical Arabic, other literary languages or in vernaculars, Islamic historical literature's primary concern is not with time. The time of Islamic historical literature is an era, almost a physical space delineated by the knowledge of it which itself is derived from the functions of societal and political structures, from the instants of time and places.

On the other hand, the time of the lineages is not delineated, and the knowledge of it is confirmed through linking the individual with it. Historical memory operates with the premise that society exists, and its function is to perpetuate that existence by narrating or simply recording society's life and structure. The individual is relevant as the authority that formulates and interprets that life and structure.

The memory of the lineages, on the other hand, operates with the premise that the society does not exist unless it is permeated with the awareness of metaphysical time, and the way to keep that awareness alive against illusory existence is to keep the individual from falling out of time. The individual's significance is that of the bearer of knowledge which has to be preserved as memory regardless of its perceived necessity.

When compared to the memory preserved through lineages, the memory of historical literature emerges as concerned with society. More precisely, the knowledge it contains is derived from the observations of worldly affairs. The memory of lineages, as Ibn Khaldun argues, contains knowledge of universals that is formulated by seeking to make the outside world conform to the ideas already contained in transmitted knowledge.[28]

For centuries, learned and pious Muslims remained so attracted to the craft of "recording and classifying" as well as interpreting and formulating the order behind worldly affairs that they gave little concern to the fact that, of all knowledge and skills in Islamic society, theirs was the only one which was not taught and transmitted and, therefore, not included in the lineages. Here it must be noted that "through the medieval period and up to roughly the early 17th century, the contemporary chronicle had to be written and presented as a supplement to a previous work composed by a recognized scholar."[29] In addition, there is ample evidence for the practice of taking sections from previous histories and copying them entirely, or including them in subsequent histories by way of summary.[30] Neither of these practices can be characterized as the transmission of knowledge; rather, it can be likened to the filling of shelves of memory marked by a lineal calendar of time. The dialogue between subsequent contemporary chronicles (and chroniclers) is not the defining norm of such practices.

The historical literature that most significantly departs from mere recording and classifying – that is, universal histories – also departs from the notion of time as an era. Seeking to reinterpret worldly affairs in their entirety, universal histories begin with hierohistory and end with chronicles of contemporary events in their own time. With some notable exceptions (such as Ibn Khaldun), these histories are not the histories of historians but of worldly order, seeking to advise it and reformulate it.

What both traditions of recording – those of lineages and of history – have in common is concern with memory. Only the memory of lineages is the guardian of (sacred) time and the autonomy of knowledge from worldly authorities, while the memory of history is the guardian and reminder of order as the worldly realization of (divine) justice.

CAN THE TWO MEMORIES MERGE?

I will conclude this essay with a short discussion of a work that apparently unites the two memories discussed here. Known as the *Imperial Scroll* or *Tomar-i Hümayun*,[31] it is a document in which universal history is executed as a map of lineages. Following both the model of universal histories and the lineages of knowledge, this map-history[32] includes the pre-Islamic era in both its sacred and worldly history, presenting the lineages of the prophets, as well as the lineages (dynasties) of the great kingdoms before Islam. The names of some prophets are visually accentuated to indicate their role as the primordial teachers of particular crafts, thus including into the map the lineages of trades and crafts. The map also presents the lineages of the *'ulama* and of Sufi *silsilas*. The ancient Persian and other pre-Islamic dynasties, as well as a number of Islamic dynasties, are the new element in the memory of lineages introduced by this work. Finally, with the arrival of the Ottoman dynasty, all contemporary dynastic lineages disappear and the Ottomans are presented accompanied by the lineages of their grand viziers and the governors of Egypt.

In 1583, the content of the *Tomar-i Hümayun* was reproduced in the form of a book entitled *Zübdet'üt-Tevarih* (*The Quintessence of Histories*), the authorship of which is attributed to the court historian (*şehnameci*) of Murad III (r. 1574–1595), Seyyid Lokman. Despite the lavish production of four copies of this work and their presentation to the most influential men of the empire, followed by further circulation and copying, the *Zübdet'üt-Tevarih* received a poor reception and left no lasting mark on the historiographical scene of the period.[33] Recent discussion of this work by Baki Tezcan finds the explanation for the sharp criticism of this work by Mustafa 'Ali and the silence of other historians of the period in Lokman's position as official historian and his willingness to compose a work "that aimed at propagating the dynastic understanding of world history, which presented the

Ottoman dynasty as the culmination of a divinely preordained cosmic plan, to a larger audience."[34]

As universal history, the *Imperial Scroll* and *The Quintessence of Histories* committed another trespass intolerable in the eyes of historians. Among historians there have always been those who celebrated the order of the time and the worldly rulers as its protectors and perpetuators, and also those who opposed the existing order, criticized it, or advised the rulers on how to reform and improve it, or at least to prevent its corruption. If Lokman was among the former, this would not necessarily diminish his worth in the eyes of those who, while not on the sultan's payroll, still depended on him or other prominent statesmen of the time for patronage and financial rewards. What caused the hostile reception of his work was the inclusion of lineages of the political leadership, that is, the dynasties, and the according of a special place to the Ottomans in a map of lineages purportedly representing universal history. If the sultans of the time could join the memory of lineages (i.e. the memory which is the guardian of [sacred] time and the autonomy of knowledge from worldly authorities) then they became exempted from the judgment and advice of the histories. That would clearly mean the end of the historians' craft as understood within the Islamic world. Historians could not accept that the order depends on rulers alone, and that the "craft" of sovereignty could join the lineage of the transmitted knowledge independent of worldly critique or divine sanction. However lengthy they might be, dynastic lineages were only genealogies (*nasab*) and not the vehicle of transmitting knowledge as *isnad* was. The "craft" of sovereignty was understood only as a consequence of time, a limited (both in duration and in scope) appointment to command and ensure order.

It is safe to assume that all authors of historical works were included in the lineages defined by knowledge and skills. Among those whose work is quoted in this essay Ibn Khaldun received his *ijaza* from the famous Zaytuniyya *madrasa*, while Mustafa 'Ali completed his studies at the mosque-school of the sultan Mehmed the Conqueror. Of the two eighteenth-century "newcomers" into the historical craft, Mulla Mustafa Başeski had multiple lineages: through *madrasa* education, association with the Qadiri Sufi order, and membership in the local guild of silk manufacturers. And while his claims of being a (perhaps informal) student of theology and jurisprudence under the supervision of Muhammad Zayn al-'Abidin al-Ghazzi (d. 1754), the Shafi'i *mufti* of Damascus, cannot be substantiated,[35]

Ibn Budayr sat comfortably in time and memory through his membership in the guild of barbers. In order to be able to observe time from without rather than from within, in every case, both the primary object of their observation (worldly affairs) as well as its protagonists remain outside time and memory of the lineages.

11

INSTITUTION

Joseph E. Lowry

INTRODUCTION

Islam does not lack social structures that could be termed "institutions," yet the field of Islamic Studies has not developed explicit criteria for determining what constitutes an "institution," let alone an "Islamic institution."[1] A recent definition of the term "institution" from the realm of social theory provides that an institution is

> the fixing of stereotyped social interactions in the form of rules. In most cases these rules are made explicit and there are sanctioning mechanisms behind them. Yet sometimes these characteristics are absent, for example when people adhere to such rules simply because they feel urged to act in this way.[2]

In other words, an institution involves "processes and mechanisms by which structures, schemas, rules, and routines become established as authoritative guidelines for social behavior."[3] It is certainly not the case that the data of Islam defy such theoretical characterizations, but such formulations present difficulties in application for several reasons. A principal difficulty is that the kind of quantitative data that enable conclusions about group behaviors are rare in the case of pre-modern Islamic societies, at least before the Ottoman period. In pre-Ottoman times, most of the sources used for historical reconstruction are literary and their precise relationship to actual material conditions can be difficult to ascertain. Another is that definitions of the type just quoted are very broad and therefore difficult to apply to specific cases. Moreover, the fact that I (and probably others) have no hesitation in mentioning phenomena as different as *waqf* (a kind of trust) and caliphate (a high political office) in the same sentence as examples of Islamic institutions suggests that the term "institution" is used in the field of Islamic studies to designate a wide swathe of behaviors, structures, entities, and so on.[4] Nonetheless, the trend in the field seems to be moving in the direction of denying the existence or importance of strong institutions in pre-modern Islamic societies, if by "institution" is meant an impersonal structure that channels resources, power, and the like, in a manner that is mostly independent of purely personal ties.[5]

A cursory survey of the *Index Islamicus*, a database of publications on Middle Eastern and Islamic Studies, suggests that the word "institution" is frequently used in secondary literature in connection with *waqf*. Despite this apparently narrow usage, the field does have a de facto list of institutions that one could expect to find described in most introductory works in the field of Islamic Studies. For example, in an older attempt to offer a comprehensive description of (mostly) pre-modern "Muslim" institutions, M. Gaudefroy-Demombynes included chapters covering (in his translator's words): the Muslim dominion; the Muslim community; the movement of ideas; Islamic dogma; sources of Muslim law; cult; caliphate; family; property; justice; social life; economic life; intellectual life; and modern Islam.[6] Apart from "caliphate," this list could be used, *mutatis mutandis*, for other religious or cultural traditions, even though the "institutions" listed might have distinctively Islamic aspects.

This essay approaches the concept of "institution" as used in Islamic Studies through the examination of pre-modern structures and behaviors connected with the assertion and maintenance of religious authority. The institutions discussed here are grouped under three headings: leadership of the community; exemplary piety; and affiliation and transmission. These categories might be recast as offices, individuals (and a few more offices), and associations (in the widest sense) with their strategies for self-presentation and self-perpetuation. There are many other things that undoubtedly qualify as institutions. Few would disagree, for example, that the pilgrimage or prayer are institutions, though they might disagree over their symbolic meanings or over their significance for participants. The institutions discussed in this essay have, however, been the subjects of useful debates, the contours of which suggest growing discomfort with using the term "institution" at all. Moreover, structures of religious authority are particularly visible aspects of the Islamic tradition (unlike the deeper meaning of a given ritual, for example) and also for this reason it seems justified to concentrate on them.[7]

One useful way to think initially about the institutions selected for discussion in this essay has been suggested by M. Cooperson in his study of pre-modern Arabic biography,[8] which focuses on four early ninth-century figures – a caliph, a Shi'i Imam, a traditionist-jurist, and an ascetic. He understands these figures as representative of foundational trends in Islamic leadership, intellectual life, and piety and further, as competing and complementary constructions of the legacy of the Prophet Muhammad. Most of the institutions discussed in this essay could similarly be understood as appropriations of the Prophet's legacy. In this regard, the institutions described herein could also be viewed as ways of accomplishing what Weber calls the routinization of charisma, in this case in the post-prophetic period of Islam.[9]

In choosing these institutions, I have relied mostly on the conventions of the field of Islamic Studies, taking into account as well the extent to which scholarship on certain institutions has generated productive controversies. Others' lists and emphases may vary. Finally, one will notice that the following account is general, mostly descriptive (as opposed to theoretical), and selective, all in the extreme.

KEY INSTITUTIONS: PROPHETS

The paradigmatic leader, in all respects, of the Muslim community was (and perhaps remains) the Prophet Muhammad. In a strict sense, prophethood (*nubuwwa*) comes to an end with Muhammad's death in 632,[10] yet the Qur'an has a regular conception of what prophets had done prior to Muhammad, and the concept of prophethood came to be understood as a necessary and recurring feature of human history and, perhaps in that regard, as an institution. It is reported, for example, that as many as 124,000 prophets had been sent previously to Muhammad.[11] The prophetic career in general exhibited certain patterns that resonated with important moments in Muhammad's own life: prophets were sent, sometimes with a scripture, to their own communities to warn of an impending cata-

clysm. Communicating the warning and the saving criteria of righteousness usually engendered conflict with a socio-political elite.
Undeterred, the prophet would continue to "speak truth to power,"
his message unheeded, except perhaps, by a very few. The arrival
of the cataclysm would lead to the destruction of the wicked and the
salvation of the righteous.[12]

Muhammad himself transcended the Qur'anic model of the solitary "warner" figure as consummate outsider, however, when he
successfully founded the nucleus of an Islamic empire in Medina
(after 622). His own political success suggested that leadership of the
Muslim community (*umma*) could and should involve the successful
and seamless fusion of religious and political authority. It was not
the only respect in which Muhammad was idealized, obviously, but
it was an ideal that grew increasingly distant, especially for Sunnis.
Later theologians and philosophers who wrote on political theory
emphasized that Muhammad had effectively combined law-giving,
philosophical insight, and an ability to inspire the masses with ideologically useful myths of origin and thereby impose a beneficial form
of social control on them (this last point might be made less cynically
by theologians).[13] In this respect, Muhammad truly was the seal of
the prophets, since the prophetic model of simultaneous authority in
both spheres proved to be non-transferrable. Instead, the inevitable
difficulties attending the succession to Muhammad gave birth to two
competing but non-coterminous institutions of leadership: the Sunni
caliphate and the Shi'i imamate.

The caliphate (Ar. *khilafa*) is the main political institution of the
early Islamic state and the caliph (Ar. *khalifa*, deputy or vice-regent)
is the ruler of that state. The term "caliph" appears in the Qur'an in
regard to Adam and David, who are made "*khalifa* on earth" by God,
a reference to their derivative sovereignty (see Q2:30 and 38:26 for
Adam and David, respectively). Adam is not, of course, a ruler, but
the suggestion seems to be that he – the first and (at the time) only
human – represented God's authority over creation. Otherwise, the
word is used in the plural (*khala'if, khulafa'*) in phrases such as "Then
We made you *khala'if* on the earth …" meaning that God made some
humans to remain on earth to live in piety after destroying those
who were impious.[14] Three main lines of caliphs styled themselves
as legitimate successors to Muhammad. The first group comprised
the four so-called "rightly guided" caliphs (*al-khulafa' al-rash-
idun*), Muhammad's immediate successors who ruled from Medina

from 632–661.[15] These close Meccan associates of Muhammad, all members of his tribe of Quraysh, came to power in different ways: through acclamation, through nomination by a predecessor, through election by a committee, and through default, respectively.[16] The last three of these caliphs were assassinated, the last two under circumstances that had lasting theological repercussions.[17] Conflict over conceptions of just rule, legitimacy, resources, and power exposed divisions within the Meccan–Qurayshite elite and in the wider, still emerging Muslim community. The ensuing civil strife (*fitna*) spawned much theological speculation and led to the gradual emergence of what would become competing theological orientations and hardened sectarian alignments.

At the end of the "rightly guided" period, the Meccan–Qurayshite Umayyad family capitalized on the confusion and unrest, assumed the caliphate, and ruled from Damascus from 660–750.[18] They introduced dynastic succession, a practice that contrasted unfavorably with the meritocracy implied by the label "rightly guided." For a variety of reasons, Umayyad rule began to disintegrate in the 730s and 740s. Widespread unrest, coupled with continuing worries about legitimacy and succession, emboldened descendants of Muhammad's uncle Abbas – the Abbasids – to capitalize on their familial connections and the general messianic mood and organize a successful revolt that put an end to Umayyad rule in 750.[19]

The Abbasid caliphs, who ruled from Iraq, adopted the trappings of Sassanian monarchy and fostered a lavish courtly culture that stimulated sophisticated modes of literary and intellectual production. These features of Abbasid rule underscore how alienated the caliphal enterprise had become from its origins in the politics of Mecca and Medina. The Abbasids ruled effectively over a vast territory – nearly Spain to China – for about a century, but gradually their territories came to be governed by nomadic groups and local elites. The caliphs' symbolic importance as heads of the *umma* remained, however, until the Mongol sack of Baghdad in 1258 put an end to the Abbasid state.[20] Thereafter a line of Abbasid caliphs was installed in Cairo to lend symbolic legitimacy to the Mamluk state (1250–1517, in Egypt and Syria). The last caliph was taken to Istanbul after the Ottoman defeat of the Mamluks in 1517, and the Ottoman rulers assumed the title for themselves shortly thereafter, in part as a way of asserting jurisdiction over Muslims outside Ottoman territories.[21] Despite some calls for the restoration of an Arab caliphate, Atatürk officially abolished the office in 1924. Muslims in India responded with a movement for the office's restoration and international conferences were held, but these efforts came to naught. Restoration of the caliphate has remained a desideratum of some Islamist politics, though the modalities of its revival remain unclear.[22]

In general, the caliphate did not manage to consolidate and maintain Muhammad's religious authority except during the "rightly guided" period; thereafter, as one scholar has put it, the community of believers became de-politicized.[23] It has been suggested that the Umayyad caliphs viewed themselves as "God's caliph," charismatic figures entitled to formulate divinely inspired legislation. An important revisionist aspect of this suggestion is that the strongly charismatic view of the caliphate was original to Islam and survived in the Shi'i conception of the imamate (see below).[24] This may be so, but by the coming of the Abbasids, religious authority had already become diffused among private experts on religious doctrine and practice.[25] In this sense, what is interesting about the caliphal institution is its loss of religious authority, the nature and extent of its residual function as a symbol of Sunnism, and its relationship to other loci of religious authority. Also, the caliphate had a rival institution that enjoyed more success in projecting religious authority but remained mostly politically powerless: the Shi'i imamate.

IMAMS

The mirror-image of the caliphate was (and is) the Shi'i imamate (Ar. *imama*). "Imam" means leader and could be used to describe caliphs, other political leaders, religious figures, and the person who leads others in prayer. It is also used as a rough Shi'i equivalent to the term caliph, that is, meaning "the Shi'i leader who *ought to have been* caliph." For Shi'i, the first Imam is the fourth "rightly guided" caliph, 'Ali ibn Abi Talib, the rightful heir to Muhammad's legacy as spiritual and temporal head of the *umma*. In general, Shi'is consider all other caliphs usurpers. Muhammad had no male heirs and 'Ali was Muhammad's cousin and also married Muhammad's daughter Fatima. The largest group of Shi'is, Imamis or Twelvers, view the two sons from this marriage as the second and third Imams, and then a further nine descendants of the third Imam (the martyr al-Husayn, who died in 680 at the hands of an Umayyad expeditionary force in Karbala) as the fourth through twelfth Imams.[26]

The twelfth Imam disappeared as an infant in 874 and entered the "lesser occultation," during which time he communicated with his followers by means of special envoys (*safirs*). In 941 he went into the "greater occultation" and ceased to communicate through the envoys. If the caliph is the symbol of Sunni unity and triumphalism, the Shiʻi *imam* is the dream of the return of justice to a world gone awry. It is believed that he remains hidden among the Shiʻis and that he will return as the Messiah at the end of time. The 1979 constitution of the Islamic Republic of Iran acknowledged the Imam's continued absence and granted political authority over the community to religious scholars, but used language suggestive of government by the Imam himself.[27]

Other Shiʻi groups accept that a line of *imams* is descended from ʻAli, but the number of *imams*, their identities, and the criteria for their selection differ. Of these groups, two achieved political power and established their own imamates, the Fatimid Ismaʻilis (in Tunisia in 909 and then, from 969–1171, in Egypt), and the Zaydis (in the southern Caspian region, the ninth to thirteenth centuries, and in Yemen, the later ninth century to 1962). At present, the Zaydis are imamless and one branch of the Fatimid Ismaʻilis recognize the Aga Khan as *imam*.[28]

In general, as with the decline of caliphal authority in the case of Sunnism, the disappearance of the *imams* (for most Shiʻis) redounded to the advantage of private experts in religion.

OTHER RULERS

The gradual disintegration of the Abbasid caliphate (beginning c. 850) and the political powerlessness of most Shiʻi *imams* did not, of course, leave Muslims without rulers, but it did mean that strongly charismatic states, in which a robust claim for the supreme religious authority (as opposed to mere legitimacy) of the ruler was made, were comparatively rare. Still, post-caliphal rulers, just like the caliphs, were expected to take responsibility, at a minimum, for the basic duties of the Islamic state: undertaking *jihad*, enforcement of penal law (*hudud*), preservation of sexual mores (*furuj*), and the safeguarding of private property (*amwal*).[29]

Although the trappings of rule could involve considerable reliance on more ancient Near Eastern models of sacred kingship,[30] most rulers of Muslim states sought legitimacy through their support of religious institutions and local scholarly constituencies.[31] Shi'i states were usually exceptions to this pattern; occasionally Sunni states could also become more charismatic. Today most majority-Muslim states are ruled by non-charismatic individuals[32] who, not unlike their predecessors, seek to enhance their legitimacy through conspicuous support for religious institutions.[33] In the case of pre-modern states, however, the relatively rapid process by which the caliphs became morally compromised left an opening for another group to claim to represent the legacy of the Prophet. These were Islam's private experts in religious doctrine and practice.

EXEMPLARY PIETY: SCHOLARS AND SUFIS

The most distinctive and (until recently) successful institution in Islam is its groups of private experts in interpretation, doctrine, and piety. Some of these experts offered instruction in or examples of personal piety. These aspects might include ascetical practices, ecstatic experiences, ethics for communal living, and even highly complex metaphysics. It is conventional to refer to such persons as Sufis. Overlapping in sometimes complex ways with the Sufis was another group of private experts, termed "scholars" because their expertise derives from formal learning of various kinds, especially in religious law.

Scholars

A "scholar" might acquire his formal training in an actual school or in connection with a school of thought, but the Arabic term for such a person is simply *'alim* (pl. *'ulama*), a "knower," that is, one who knows especially the Qur'an and traditions from the Prophet (Hadith), as well as related subjects such as exegesis, law, and so on. These ultimate heirs of the Prophet's charisma, even eventually among Shi'is, seem already by the mid-eighth century to have acquired the exclusive authority to interpret religious texts and to formulate doctrine.[34] The waning of the caliphs' religious authority allowed for the consolidation of scholarly prestige, and the scholars did not hesitate to advertise their moral independence. On the other hand, the rulers and the scholars needed each other as elites; the scholars exploited opportunities for patronage of various kinds and the caliphs and post-caliphal rulers gained legitimacy through support for the scholars and their activities.[35]

Despite the fact that some scholars were more successful than others – whether because of piety, intellectual ability, talent for self-promotion, or some other reason – the scholarly institution was noteworthy for its non-hierarchical authority structure. Admission, advancement, and intellectual production were not, of course, completely unconstrained, but scholarly discourse developed mechanisms for tolerating considerable doctrinal diversity – indeed, such diversity is a hallmark of Islamic law. It was the prerogative of the scholarly elite to disagree among themselves (sometimes sharply) on matters of practice, doctrine, and religious law; members of the public, by contrast, were expected to fulfill their religious obligations – as formulated by the scholars – without debating subtleties or seeking alternative interpretations.[36]

In the late Umayyad and early Abbasid periods the emergent scholarly institution competed with other cultural and intellectual movements. Many chancery secretaries (sg. *katib*), drafters of government correspondence, had a self-conscious Iranian cultural orientation. They played leading roles in shaping Arabic literary culture and often expressly championed the (slightly "secularizing") Iranian heritage over what they viewed as the impoverished cultural background of Arab–Bedouin barbarians.[37] In addition, the reception of works of Hellenistic philosophy, with the analytical power of Aristotelian logic and a complex but attractive (and vaguely monotheizing) Neoplatonic metaphysics, posed a challenge to the truth-claims of religious thought.[38] Both trends were eventually harnessed in the service of an Islamic humanities as, over the course especially of the eleventh century, religious scholars enjoyed increasing patronage and institutional support and developed mechanisms for reproducing their estate. By Ottoman times, most education had become clerical education and most intellectuals had therefore become incorporated into the scholarly institution; the scholarly institution, in turn, came increasingly, but never completely, under the control of the state. Scholarly diversity and individuality did not lessen, but the social cohesion of the class of scholars as a whole likely increased over time, notwithstanding individual instances of doctrinal conflict and professional and economic competition.

The introduction of secular and secularizing institutions of government and education, beginning in the late Ottoman period and continuing through the colonial and post-colonial periods, undermined the foundations of the scholarly institution.[39] Resources that had previously been directed to the production and reproduction of religious knowledge and its bearers were and remain channeled elsewhere (Shi'ism under the Islamic Republic in Iran remains an important exception to this trend). This transformation has made the authority structure of Islam even more complex and diffuse in the modern period.

Jurists

Not all scholars were jurists, but all jurists were scholars in the sense described above.[40] The jurists took responsibility for the formulation of Islamic law,[41] a task which involved the "discovery" of God's will and gave them – at least potentially – the opportunity to impose norms on the rest of society, even on non-Muslims.[42] Although Islamic law is, in theory, based on the Qur'an and traditions from the Prophet Muhammad, and rules are portrayed as deriving from those sources through a rich and elaborate hermeneutic, it remains at root the product of the Muslim scholarly imagination. Jurists produced treatises on the law with the doctrinal scope of a modern code but the casuistic flexibility of the common law, covering subjects from ritual purity to real estate.

Particularly gifted jurists might become *muftis* or *mujtahids*. *Muftis* give formal legal opinions (*fatwas*) in response to questions from the public at large; this activity is similar to the writing of legal opinions by attorneys in private practice in modern legal systems, except that a *mufti*'s opinion is (in theory) binding on its recipient. It is a duty incumbent on a jurist in a given locale to act as *mufti*, to be a resource for Muslims who wish to know their rights and responsibilities. However, in major urban centers, certain particularly accomplished jurists – through scholarly and professional reputation and the respect of the general public – might become *muftis* in a more elevated sense; that is, they might acquire a reputation for a conspicuous combination of knowledge and piety and be sought out for their opinions on legal matters. Those *muftis* regarded as exceptionally qualified might have their opinions compiled.[43] In theory, qualified jurists were supposed to be self-reliant in their research and reasoning, but in practice such compilations were a ready resource, and some were even collected at the behest of the state as an attempt to standardize legal doctrine.[44]

Jurists recognized (or regarded by themselves) as unusually talented might rise (or claim to have risen) to the level of *mujtahid*, one who practices *ijtihad* or legal interpretation. Legal theory recognized that *ijtihad* covered a range of tasks undertaken by persons of varying ability. Thus, the highest level of *ijtihad* was performed by the "absolute *mujtahid*," the *mujtahid mutlaq*, who engaged in independent *de novo* derivation of the law directly from the Qur'an and traditions from the Prophet.[45] Over time, certain early master jurists came to be regarded as exemplary *mujtahid mutlaqs* operating at the highest level of intellectual attainment in their derivation of the law;[46] other jurists were ceded the competence to practice less ambitious forms of *ijtihad* within parameters carefully defined in works of legal theory. Still, particularly prominent jurists continued to claim the ability to perform unrestricted *ijtihad* and legal theory recognized their ability to do so. The *mufti* differed from the *mujtahid* in that the *fatwa* was always given in response to a question from a member of the public (occasionally from a judge); the fruits of *ijtihad* were as likely as not to appear in a legal treatise, though *muftis* might perform *ijtihad* in order to arrive at an answer to a given question.

Jurists, as scholars, were mostly unconnected with the state, though not all institutions of Islamic law were private. The state employed jurists as judges (*qadis*) and as lesser officers of the court, and the judiciary was organized hierarchically with a chief justice or justices at its apex. Courts of first instance could and did seek formal legal opinions from *muftis*. In Muslim Spain, leading jurists formed a consultative body (*shura*) that advised the chief judge.[47] In cities, some matters of Islamic law were enforced by a "market inspector" (*muhtasib*), whose jurisdiction also included weights and measures, maintaining public rights-of-way, and so on.[48] Finally, rulers or their representatives could convene hearings, called the "courts of grievances" (*mazalim*), for matters deemed non-justiciable by the regular *qadis*. It was usual for high-ranking jurists and/or *qadis* to be present at such hearings to advise on questions of Islamic law.

Not all jurists welcomed state employment, but many did and such employment provided one important avenue of patronage, which benefited both bestowers and recipients.

The jurists, whether or not employed by the state, were the guardians of "official" religion. Their interest in maintaining the stability required for the legal system to function ensured de facto cooperation with the state.[49] However, the private character of pre-modern Islamic law – the fact that its jurists and institutions were not necessarily connected with the state – is one of its key distinguishing features. This quasi-independence of the legal system was not unusual in Late Antiquity, but it is very different from modern legal systems, which are by nature (increasingly) intrusive. The extent to which the pre-modern Muslim state is inherently in tension with Islamic law is a question of considerable interest to modern scholarship; if one grants the existence of such tension, one must also grant that it has been tremendously productive for Islamic legal thought.[50]

The field of Islamic studies is heavily focused on the activities of the scholarly institution, such that one modern researcher has coined the playful term "ulamology" to allude to scholars' ubiquity as objects of research.[51] The written sources that survive for the study of pre-modern Islamic societies were overwhelmingly written by the scholars. They include not only law and theology, as might be expected, but also historiography and prosopography – this last an extensive body of literature focusing on the careers of religious scholars. Thus, for historical reconstruction, the field is at the mercy of the scholars since the sources depict pre-modern Muslim societies through their eyes, highlighting their concerns, but also excluding much else that modern historians would dearly love to know.

Sufis

Sufis present a different model of exemplary private piety. Not all scholars were Sufis, but some Sufis were scholars and in the late pre-modern and early modern periods scholars increasingly identified themselves as Sufis. Sufism is commonly equated with Islamic mysticism, though the practices, doctrines, and styles of piety that constitute Sufism are too broad to be encompassed by any one term and the term "Sufi" does not necessarily correspond to the self-understanding or self-identification of persons commonly denoted thereby in Western scholarship.[52] To the extent that actual "mysteries" are involved, they may not be the primary focus among a given group of Sufis. In very general terms, Sufism describes (1) ascetical and renunciatory practices, (2) certain conceptions or practices designed to induce sensations of proximity to (or more radical experiences of) the divinity, and/or (3) associations devoted to the inculcation of individual and communal ethical practices, characterized by, among other things, distinctive rituals, and which might also encourage various kinds of socially advantageous ties.

Mysticism in Islam, in the sense of "communion with an imminent God," developed after an earlier trend of ascetical piety that was pessimistic, scrupulous, and antisocial,[53] thus focusing on the fearful Qur'anic warnings of the imminence of judgment and the end. With mysticism proper, which emerged in Baghdad and further east from the mid-ninth century, the possibility of gaining direct experience of the divinity becomes viewed as both desirable and within reach and leads to ecstatic outbursts and strong expressions of love for God.[54] Gradually, the creation of a technical vocabulary that portrayed such experiences in a less extravagant way became an important intellectual task.[55] This phase of pietistic virtuosity was then followed by the formation of hierarchically organized arrangements for communal living.

For present purposes, it need only be remarked that the various phenomena denoted as Sufism were parallel in some respects to those of the scholarly enterprise; in both cases private persons mediated or exhibited charisma and created mechanisms for affiliation and patterns of instruction. Although by the Ottoman period considerable intertwining of the Sufi and scholarly enterprises had occurred, pietistic and organizational aspects of Sufism remained capable of deeper social penetration. The divide between scholars and the general public was more rigid, especially in the case of jurists, for whom the world was divided into those who formulated the law and those who were bound by their formulations (though of course the jurists were also bound by God's law).

AFFILIATION AND TRANSMISSION: LINEAGES AND SCHOOLS

Scholars and Sufis were organized into groups of various kinds. "Schools" of Islamic theology, for example, came into being in the

eighth century and then, for Sunnis, crystallized around the followers of two theologians in particular after the mid-tenth century.[56] The
naming of such groups was sometimes more a convenience for writers of heresiographical or prosopographical works than a reflection of
a social reality, yet some such groups were conspicuous and important. All such groups had mechanisms for the initiation, maintenance,
enhancement, and display of formal ties among their members.
Depending on the nature of a particular association, its membership might be restricted to elite scholars (in the case of theologians),
though it might also encompass the general public to varying degrees
(Sufi associations and schools of legal thought).

Isnads *and* Silsilas

An important means of acquiring and displaying religious authority was to become inscribed in chains of transmission (*isnads*) and
lineages of authority (*silsilas*). An *isnad* is a chain of transmitters;
such chains could be for the transmission of almost any text, from
individual traditions of the Prophet to entire books. To inscribe oneself into an *isnad* for a prophetic tradition was to create a link with
the Prophet through the generations of pious scholars who faithfully
transmitted his dicta. Sufis developed a parallel structure, the *silsila*,
to record the passing on of teachings from master to disciple, so that
a person's spiritual lineage could be documented and seen to be connected, through a series of exemplary pietists, with Muhammad and
his companions. *Isnads* and *silsilas* crossed and criss-crossed, so
that they contained diverse, intersecting groups of transmitters and
authorities. Distinctive patternings in *isnads* and *silsilas* might signal
recognizable doctrinal affiliations, but they might not; there could
be considerable variation, interweaving, and sharing of transmitters
and authorities among individuals or groups with widely varying out-
looks. Both *isnad* and *silsila* vouched for the content of what was
transmitted (*hadiths*, books, teachings, etc.) but, perhaps more important, they made visible the interrelationships, both horizontal (i.e.
intragenerational) and vertical (intergenerational), between scholars
and other religious figures, reinforcing the cohesion of scholarly and
Sufi affiliations at multiple levels and grounding them ultimately in
the birth and sacred history of the Muslim community. Although it is
often important for historians to know whether two individuals in an
isnad or *silsila* actually met, only the most narrow positivist could fail

to recognize that mere juxtaposition of two such figures could have significance.

Madhhabs

Some groups of scholars, but above all jurists and Sufis, affiliated into groups named after charismatic leaders who were viewed as foundational figures. In the case of (Sunni) jurists these groups were in the nature of doctrinal schools and were called *madhhabs*, of which four survived.[57] Although named after early master jurists who died between 767 and 855, the *madhhabs* do not seem to have become self-reproducing entities until the tenth century at the earliest. The coalescing of these entities involved several related processes: the successful promotion of the founder's authority, the formation of an authoritative body of texts, the development of a curriculum, a loose agreement on doctrine, and a somewhat tighter agreement on methodology. State patronage could help, but was not a decisive factor. Rather, the *madhhabs* represent one of the private institutions that gave a distinctive shape to Islamic law. In addition to the specific factors just listed that contributed to their appearance, the *madhhabs'* emergence was also enabled generally by the devolution of religious authority to the scholars and the inherent weakness of pre-modern states, which allowed considerable space for private organization.

The *madhhabs* have, controversially, been likened to guilds.[58] Although guilds are familiar from medieval Europe where they have a primarily economic function, the argument for characterizing the *madhhabs* as guilds seems to be made, by analogy, with regard to doctrine and theology. Just as the European guilds sought to organize and restrict certain economic activities, the *madhhabs* sought to promote juristic activity as the primary theological activity in Islam, and to exclude the pursuit of speculative theology (*kalam*).[59] Some deny, however, that the *madhhab* is an "institution" at all, and make a strong case for the *madhhab* being more in the nature of a "rite," since ritual is a key area in which *madhhabs* differ. Other important differentiating characteristics of the *madhhabs* include legal epistemology, the delineation of restricted communities of interpretation, and their elaboration of a mythical connection to the eponyms.[60] The analogy with the European guild is thus hardly free from problems, but in its attempt to grapple with the question of what kind of institution the *madhhab* is, it at least has heuristic value, as would a somewhat misleading but also helpful analogy with modern bar associations.

Although the *madhhabs* were created and led by jurists, their reach extended into the general, non-scholarly population at large. Members of the general public were assumed to belong to one of the *madhhabs* and to perform rituals and other matters expressly governed by Islamic law in accordance with a particular *madhhab*'s doctrine, though there existed doctrinal variations even within a single *madhhab*. There was, however, no formal mechanism by which the general public became affiliated to a *madhhab* – parentage and geography were probably the most important factors. This was also the case for scholars, except that a few prominent scholars are known to have changed *madhhabs*, usually in the course of their studies.

The *madhhabs* were to some extent territorial, though they also overlapped in some places and historical developments (e.g. conquest) could change their territorial extent and location. Some regions – such as Anatolia, or North Africa and Spain – had one dominant *madhhab*, while others – such as Iraq – had several at once. Since Ottoman times, the geographical spread of the *madhhabs* has stabilized.[61] However, one feature of Islamic modernity is the critique of the *madhhabs* as the site of needless doctrinal accretions and inappropriate accumulations of personal juristic authority that interfere with direct access to the law contained in the Qur'an and Prophetic traditions.

Tariqas

Somewhat similar to the jurists' *madhhabs* were the Sufis' *tariqas*, a word usually rendered as "orders" or "brotherhoods"/"fraternities," but which literally means "path," as does the word *madhhab*. These associations constituted a third phase in the evolution of Sufism, subsequent to an early period of individual cultivation of ascetical or ecstatic practices, and then a period of increasing focus on communal life in hospices and convents encouraged by increasing patronage. The emergence of the *tariqas*, beginning especially in the twelfth and thirteenth centuries, followed a pattern not unlike that of the *madhhabs*: identification of a master pietist, construction of the master's authority, formation of a canon of instructional works often composed by the eponymous master himself or his direct disciples, and the development of a following. The *tariqas* were distinguished from one another more by ritual than doctrine, a fact that testifies to the increasing importance of their congregational aspect – in marked contrast to the solitary pursuits of the earliest Sufis.

Ten principal *tariqas* were traced back to eponymous masters who lived during these two centuries; all subsequently founded Sufi associations trace their origins to one of these.[62] However, the spiritual lineages that connected these various groups and subgroups, though in many cases depicting actual discipleship, were often also imagined; that is, they existed on a spiritual or symbolic plane, depicting occult rather than actual interactions between revered masters.[63] The evolution of these associations and their derivatives was accompanied by increasing hierarchization. Further, the official terminology of the organizations in some cases mirrored that of government: the founder might designate his successor or first assistant as a *khalifa* (caliph), thus mirroring the transfer of authority from the Prophet to the early caliphs.[64] Perhaps such titles reflect a way of coping with the political turbulence of the thirteenth and fourteenth centuries.

In contrast to the legal *madhhabs*, and notwithstanding its own hierarchical structures, Sufism's social depth became increasingly conspicuous. The *tariqas'* social integration makes them different from the legal *madhhabs*, whose authority, coterminously with that of the jurists, depended fundamentally on a division of society into legal experts and a non-scholarly public. As Sufi associations acquired ever more adherents, they came to represent important political constituencies whose interactions with political authorities exhibited complexity. Their memberships could also align with socio-economic groupings. However, in late and post-Ottoman times, the modernist puritanical impulses that led to a critique of the legal *madhhabs* led also to denunciations of the popular piety of Sufism as deviant innovations that were foreign to the simple practices of the pristine community that had surrounded Muhammad.[65]

EDUCATION AND THE *MADRASA*

A particular focus of scholarly controversy has been over the role of educational institutions, especially the *madrasa* or "law college," in the transmission of religious knowledge. The *madrasa* was one of many institutions that existed for this purpose on a spectrum that ranged through varying degrees of formality.

Undoubtedly, master–disciple relationships were basic to the transmission of all religious knowledge – indeed, *isnads* and *silsilas* privilege and preserve records of such relationships and even depict them, whether symbolic or actual, as exemplary. Instruction also took place for larger groups of students in contexts denoted by several different terms, including: the study session (*majlis*), the study circle (*halqa*), and also the disputation (*munazara*). These gatherings were typically (though not necessarily) held within the mosque, especially the larger congregational mosques in urban areas, which often had special areas for teaching.[66] In this regard, the example of the Prophet's mosque in Medina as a site of both worship and instruction exerted considerable influence.

As the contours of the "religious studies curriculum" took shape (Arabic grammar, Qur'an, law, Hadith, etc.), new institutions for the transmission of religious knowledge emerged together with new possibilities of professionalization. The extent to which these new institutions took over the function of their more intimate predecessors or created new social ties that were wholly or mostly institution based is disputed. An attractive case has been made for the strongly teleological nature of institutional evolution: from mosque to the so-called *masjid-khan* complex (a mosque with an adjoining inn for students) to the *madrasa*.[67] The founding of *madrasas*, beginning in the eleventh century, involved legal innovation: the use of *waqfs* by high-status individuals to endow colleges, control teaching appointments along *madhhab* lines, and provide stipends for students and staff. Moreover, it has been argued that the program of *madrasa* study culminated in the conferral of a degree, a license (*ijaza*) to teach law and issue legal opinions (*fatwas*). The teleological account views the founding of *madrasas* as akin to the formation of the *madhhabs*, as vehicles for excluding "rationalism," and so as motivated by theological arguments – in other words, as a highly principled endeavor.

Social historians have expressed doubts about this picture. It has been observed that high-status individuals founded a wide variety of educational institutions, not only *madrasas*, and that the founding of these was often motivated by the desire of alien ruling elites (of which there were many) to forge ties to local scholarly elites and their constituencies.[68] In addition, the formalities of education as described in sources written by the scholars themselves have been interpreted as a highly ritualized means for transmitting social status. That a regular curriculum existed in impersonal degree-conferring institutions that facilitated professionalization has thus been deemed unlikely.[69] Empirical study of social ties among scholars suggests that factors such as a shared geographical origin might be more important than a shared *madrasa* education.[70] Finally, the scholars' self-depiction in the sources emphasizes personal ties to teachers and almost never the *madrasa* attended.[71] Yet, by the same token, the scholars also empha- size their own and others' *madrasa* posts, describe the conferral of licenses to teach and transmit as though they had an actual profes- sional function, and discuss administrative details of the *madrasa* as though these were important.[72]

CONCLUSIONS

Notwithstanding the difficulty of deciding what makes a given social structure in pre-modern Muslim societies into an "Islamic institution," some patterns in modern scholarship do emerge. Social historians have prodded their more philologically oriented colleagues to rethink not only the social function of institutions such as the *madhhab* and the *madrasa*, but also to reread the primary sources to determine in what sense (if any) the structures described there are institutions at all. The dialogue between these two trends reflects a disagreement over whether impersonal institutional structures had social functions separate from purely personal ties,[73] and perhaps also over whether institutions came into being purely in the service of principles or only as concomitants with conflicts over resources. However one under- stands these arguments, they have been fruitful for the field, even if the considerable insights of social theory threaten occasionally to obscure the power that ideas could exercise on institutional actors.

The fact that similar debates are already well underway in the study of ancient Judaism suggests another way of approaching insti- tutions: that they be viewed as variations on a general Late Antique type. Recent scholarly disagreement over the degree of formality (or "institutionalization") of Rabbinic instruction in Sasanian Babylonia is a case in point.[74] Because similar institutions and similar kinds of evidence generate similar scholarly problems and approaches, it seems worthwhile to consider Islamic institutions as exhibiting a degree of continuity with their predecessors.[75] The extent of continu- ity has been debated in the field and it has been observed that early

Arabic historiography can sometimes obscure important aspects of emergent Islam.[76] Nonetheless, it seems that a question such as "why did the Rabbinic *bayt d-midrasha* evolve into the *madrasa*?" could be fruitful. Other questions along these same lines suggest themselves as well: how did the Sasanian shah evolve into the Abbasid caliph? How is the formation of the doctrinal schools of Late Antiquity (Hillel and Shammai, Alexandria, Antioch) related to the emergence of schools of theology and legal thought in Islam? How did monastic institutions transform into Sufi convents? Pondering these questions might suggest ways of answering questions that are more relevant to later periods. How do institutions in the Islamic context evolve, or disappear, or get replaced? What changes occur as they trend toward modernity, and how is their modern functioning related (if at all) to their pre-Islamic predecessors?

Such questions are important for understanding early Islam in its historical, cultural, and geographical settings, but also for considering the nature of Islamic institutions over the *longue durée*. The point of such an approach is not a crude search for origins, but an attempt rather to understand the transformations undergone by social structures across time. By adopting a less specifically Islamic frame of reference, it may yet be possible to get to the heart of what constitutes an Islamic institution.

12

LAW*

A. Kevin Reinhart

Overviews of Islamic law tend to have three problems. (1) They tend to be overly emic, that is, those of us who study Islamic law as an academic subject tend to explicate the normative texts much as if we were *'ulama*. This approach initiates a reader into the world of *shari'a* studies but does not facilitate analysis of *shari'a* law as a legal system. (2) As a consequence, with only a few exceptions[1] the descriptive and analytic tools available to Islamicists have usually been relegated to the tools provided by the tradition itself. (3) Because of the dependence on normative texts by the theoreticians in Islamic studies, little attention has been paid to evidence of how these norms were put into practice. Reciprocally, those who have studied the practice of Islamic law[2] have often known little of Islamic legal theory and have exaggerated the unique, local, arbitrary, or even ethnically determined in the practice of law among Muslims.[3] Here we intend to make an effort to insert the "law" into the study of Islamic law without falling into the trap Bergsträsser described eighty years ago of abandoning the study of Islamic law to the "lawyers."[4]

"Law" in Islamic studies is generally taken to mean the rules recorded in books of *fiqh* that are taken to reflect *shari'a*.[5] These are norms ostensibly drawn from the Qur'an, Hadith ("anecdotes of the Prophet") and other canonical sources, according to rules specified in works of *usul al-fiqh* ("bases of jurisprudence"). Islamic law is generally understood by Muslims to be of divine origin, but recorded

* I'd like to thank Nancy Ševčenko and Hülya Canbakal, who both contributed materially to this essay.

by scholars (*'ulama*) or jurisprudents, and administered in "*shari'a* courts" by *qadis* ("judges"). Legal opinions are given by qualified scholars writing as *muftis*. We will refer to this set of concepts and ideal roles as the *shari'a* system. How this is "law" will be one of the problematics of this essay.

The study of something called "law" has exploded in the last twenty-five years of Islamic studies. This is true of (1) classical Islamic legal studies – those focused on the religious texts that were shared among Muslims across Islamdom. It is also true of (2) "applied" legal studies, which use law court records to study marriage, intercommunal relations, property, and so on, and consequently, to study the social institutions of the law in particular times and places – courts, schools, legal officers, and other legal institutions. Accidents in the preservation of sources and accidents in the development of the historiography of Islam and Islamdom have led to these two fields – the theoretical and the applied – remaining for the most part separate. Historians often operate from a dated understanding of the classical disciplines of the law, and source students remain in the airy realm of theory, often ignorant of the fine work being done by historians and that work's implications for their studies. And both the theoreticians and the historians, it often seems, operate from an impoverished and outdated understanding of the concept of "law" itself.

So, students of theory have either assumed that Islamic law was mostly a theoretical enterprise uninflected by social facts and social change, or they have assumed that the institution of Islamic law was somehow a corruption of the purer forms found in Islamic legal theory. In any case, they have assumed Islamic law was somehow *sui generis* in the history of human social regulation. Students of the history of Islamic social institutions, for their part, have been mostly indifferent to the theory of Islamic law and to the contents of the normative texts (which has led to some significant errors in their historical analyses),[6] and they have often understood law only as a socially coercive institution of state power without grasping how little the law works by actual coercion.

This essay will use standard concepts from the philosophy of law to describe "Islamic law" as "law." We want to describe more clearly how the *shari'a* system *is* law and yet point out the ways in which features of Islamic law differed from what philosophers of law have taken to be obvious legal norms. We will also show how Islamic law can be an object of sociohistorical study and how that inquiry can enrich the study of Islamic legal theory. It seems important first to have a clear understanding of what is meant by "law" before we describe what is usually labeled "Islamic law."

LAW IN ANGLO-AMERICAN LEGAL PHILOSOPHY

What is law? At the level of theory there are (at the very least) two sorts of answers. One is the sociological, and a very useful essay from the field – Bourdieu's "The Force of Law" – will be discussed toward the end of this essay. We will begin, however, with the English and American "philosophers of law" who define the features that an institution must possess to qualify as law. Theirs is a normative, even a prescriptive, enterprise. A standard approach that dominates this field is H. L. A. Hart's, presented canonically in his *The Concept of Law*.[7]

Hart's essay recasts the work of the ninetheenth-century jurist–philosopher Austin[8] and is considered to belong to a genre of philosophy called "legal positivism."[9] Austin had argued straightforwardly that the law in its purest form should be imagined as a king ordering and the subjects – out of fear of punishment – obeying. However, Hart and many others have pointed out that such a legal system, if it ever existed, would lead to certain easily predictable defects: (1) *uncertainty* (what *is* the law on a given case, especially a new case?; or, *is* the person truly a thief or murderer: how does one decide?); (2) *sclerosis* (as circumstances change, the law would not necessarily change); and above all, (3) *unpredictable compliance*, since obedience to such a sovereign would depend entirely upon enforcement. In reality, however, the king's agents cannot be in every place at every time to keep the miscreants in line. Hart asserts that Austin's model is simplistic in two directions. While it might conceivably describe the situation of a newly risen sovereign, it could not explain why his powers devolve to his deputies, and more importantly, upon his death, to his heir. Similarly, it does not explain why the subjects still feel somehow that they ought to obey the law even when it is unlikely that they will be caught.[10]

Hart suggests that law consists of two sorts of rules. The first is the primary rules – the stuff that is usually supposed to make up the law – such as "you must pay ten percent of your crops to the state; you must not murder; taking without permission is illegal," and so forth. These are the "do's and don'ts" that constitute primary legal rules.

But, says Hart, there are secondary rules that actually underpin and frame the first-order laws. These are (1) a *rule of recognition* constituting an agreement on authoritative texts and methods of interpretation;[11] (2) a *rule of adjudication* specifying who determines the law and how infractions are judged;[12] and (3) a *rule of change*, explaining how law may be legitimately altered.[13] Consequently any legal system must have an *open texture* in so far as, (i) it must allow and require interpretation according to circumstance, (ii) it must allow statutes to change and specify how that change will legitimately take place, and (iii) adjudication must have an interpretive rather than rigidly prescriptive character.[14] In addition, and most crucially, law requires *the perception of obligation* on the part of the subject; it may be enough that she fear punishment in some cases, but a legal system requires also that in most cases the subject believe that she ought to act or not act according to what the law requires. It is the *internalization of the law* that makes the legal system actually work. Hart then asks tellingly whether, when we move into the domain of internal feelings of shame or guilt for non-compliance, we do not risk leaving the law and entering into the domain of morality.[15] The question of the boundaries between law and morality and the extent to which the law itself must be or be perceived to be moral are among the most vexed areas in jurisprudential thought and the philosophy of law. Yet even the most positivist philosopher of law will now admit that there is a considerable amount of turf shared between law and morality, however uncomfortable that concourse may seem.

Ronald Dworkin is both successor to Hart in the Chair of Jurisprudence at Oxford, and Hart's Oedipus. He has argued vigorously and influentially that the activity of law is an interpretive enterprise in which terms like "theft" or "privacy" are, mostly unconsciously, applied by judges, lawyers, and legislators informed by what he calls "principles" that are more general, often unlegislated understandings of what is acceptable and what is not, of what terms mean, and so on. Hence the law is not a set of enforceable ukases dispatched from on high, but a conversation between official texts and society. It is a mistake, says Dworkin, to imagine that statutes are as stable in their interpretation as they are in their wording. Such is observably not the case.[16]

For most philosophers of law then, law is a combination of first- and second-order rules that both reflect and create ordinary senses of obligation and justify sanctions. These rules are interpreted in an embedded, hermeneutical context rather than in a free-floating domain of power and subjugation. To the extent that they reflect and share social understandings, they create subjectivities aligned with the aims and practices ordained in the first-order rules.

"ISLAMIC LAW AS LAW"

Hart and Dworkin's understanding of law is a standard one for philosophers of law, and to determine in what sense "Islamic law" is law, we may begin by examining the *shari'a*-system within the Hart–Dworkin framework.

Primary rules in "Islamic Law"

Law's foremost feature is the rules and punishments that appear at the surface of every legal system. In Islamic law, the rules, the statues, that govern Muslims' behavior are understood to come from God. According to one understanding, they are God's discourse (*khitab*) and, as such, are part of God's speech and abide with him primordially.[17] Revelation contains rules and guidelines embedded unsystematically within scripture: the diffuse text of the Qur'an, and in the observable practices of the inerrant Prophet Muhammad recorded in the Hadith. In the more mundane sphere, the rules are to be found in works of *fiqh* which derive in theory from scripture and which record the findings of the scholars (*'ulama*). The *fiqh* book is quite clearly a rule book.

Here is the form of the rule defining gifts, from al-Mawsili's *al-Mukhtar*:

> [A gift] is valid by offering, accepting and taking possession of.[18] If one takes possession of it while in the presence of the owner without his [explicit] permission, it is valid. If after [the owner's departure], then [the taking] requires [the giver's explicit] permission.[19]

Gifts are like sales, and occur by offering and taking possession, though without any reciprocation by the gift's recipient. Tacit permission is only possible when the owner is actually present. To take without explicit permission in the owner's absence is theft, or usurpation, or some other offense.

To understand fully Islamic primary *rules* it is necessary to understand something of the genre of *fiqh* books. These differ considerably from legal statute books of the sort with which a Western reader would be familiar. First, a contemporary lawyer would be bewildered to find that the collection of primary rules begins with stipulations on rituals of purification. The "purification" section is followed by the rules of prayer, fasting, and pilgrimage. Indeed in one twelve-volume work of *fiqh*, the first quarter is about matters ritual.[20] Only statutes on eligibility for mandatory taxes (*zaka*) would seem familiar to a lawyer. Yet she might be surprised to find tax law listed with rituals. In addition, many of the "rules" themselves are only "recommended" or "discouraged," not required or proscribed; by definition, in Islamic law, such rules are not enforceable. Statutes that "recommend" but do not "require," rules that are not enforceable, are not ordinarily considered by philosophers of law to be part of the law but belong rather to the domain of morality.[21] Additionally, most works of *fiqh* are not rulebooks like the digests[22] but more discursive works with copious argumentation, alternative views, and digressions: reading them is more like reading Talmud than reading the *Public Statutes of the State of New Hampshire and General Laws in Force*.

Ibn Rushd's still rather terse *Bidayat al-mujtahid* can be read as containing statutes, but it also contains "extraneous matter." For example, in the following text, the issue is whether a Muslim on his deathbed may alienate parts of what would otherwise be his estate by gift. The majority view is that special rules apply to the dying that don't apply to an ordinary person who wants to give a gift.

The three essential constituents of a gift are the giver, the one given-to, and the gift. It is agreed that [the giver's] gift is legitimate if he is the valid possessor of the thing, in good health, and in condition to part with it.

There are disagreements concerning the situation of one who is ill, or simple-minded, or bankrupt. Concerning one who is ill: the majority hold that "the rule of third" in connection [with giving] testamentary bequest creates an area of uncertainty [about gifts]. I mean the entire gift with its necessary conditions. A smaller group of early scholars and a larger group of the Literalists (*Ahl al-zahir*) said a gift that may be given legitimately when one is healthy, may also be given from his capital upon his death. There was no disagreement among them that a gift given in these circumstances was valid.

The argument of the majority [to the contrary] is grounded in a hadith of 'Umran ibn Husayn from the Prophet concerning one who manumitted [his] six slaves at his death. The Messenger of God commanded that a third of them be manumitted and the remainder remain in a condition of servitude.

The Literalists' basis [for their argument] is the continuity-of-status (*istishab al-hal*). I mean the consensus that his gift is legitimate when he is healthy; [therefore, say the Literalists] continuity-of-status requires that the ruling agreed upon [be in force] also when [the giver] is ill, unless there be proof [to the contrary] from the Book or Prophetic Practice (*sunna*). [And in their view the hadith quoted is illegitimately extended to bequests.][23]

Ibn Rushd's text records disagreement about the rule of death-bed gifts, adduces evidence on either side, and seemingly declines to conclude that one position or the other "is the law."

In addition, unlike a statute book, the text often records the stipulation that a particular act is recommended or discouraged and therefore not enforceable. For example, on the question of whether a slave who has been struck or otherwise abused is entitled to manumission, a *hadith* of 'Amr ibn Shu'ayb is adduced recording that a slave was mutilated by his master when the slave fornicated with a slavegirl. When the Prophet learned of this act of cruelty, he freed the slave. The opponents of manumission cite another *hadith* – this from Ibn 'Umar:

"Whoever slaps or strikes a slave – his penance is to manumit him." They say manumission is not *required* [in response to abuse]. It is only *recommended* [to the owner that he free the slave.] [The rejectors of manumission have as their] basic rule that the operative principle in the *shar'* is that a master is not required to manumit his slave except when there is a specific circumstance specified in the source. The *hadiths* of 'Amr [in general] are of disputed soundness and do not attain the force to effect specification equivalent to this fundamental principle.[24]

In other words, the evidence that one *must* free a slave after abuse is weak. The law therefore is that it is only *recommended* that the slave be freed, since the *hadith* from Umar is reliable and there is a general rule (*qa'ida*)[25] consistent with Umar's *hadith*. Here we see moral guidance rather than legal requirement.

These *fiqh* books *are* books of law; they do contain statutes. However, many Islamic statute books contain "oughts" and "ought-nots" – a subject upon which we will elaborate below. The argument and elaboration found in the texts function as supplements to the law – legal essays, records of congressional or parliamentary debates and intent, or even case law – which help the jurist to grasp the statute's scope, the underlying issues and so forth when he applies the law. Rather than being recorded elsewhere, these materials are imbedded in *fiqh* works that function also as textbooks used in the training of jurists.[26] As such, they contained the jurists' debates from which the law emerged, as well as the resulting doctrine.[27] They also effectively record the range of indeterminacy that is a feature of the law – on which more below also.[28] Islamic statutes may be found in:

(1) *fatwas* (legal responses given by qualified jurists),
(2) essays (*rasa'il*), which generally have extensive reasoning supporting their interpretation of the law,
(3) discursive *fiqh* works, which are likely to have statutes, some supporting reasoning and both obligation and recommendation: both "musts" and "oughts,"
(4) abridgments and epitomes which most resemble statute books as Western jurisprudence knows them.

The law book is definitive to the extent it records agreement, argues persuasively and is accepted in the pedagogy of a legal school (*madhhab*, on which, see below). If it is agreed that the *fiqh* book contains the statutes of Islamic law, the first order rules, then what of punishment or its threat – according to Hart also a primary feature of the law?

As we would expect, ideologically the most significant threat for miscreants is damnation.[29] In this sense, there is no "unpredictable compliance" arising from the impossibility of universal enforcement since in Islamic theology God, being all-knowing, is aware of every transgression. Therefore the imperfections of *state* enforcement are balanced by the certainty of reward and punishment in the afterlife. There is also the promise of eternal reward for compliance with the law, as well as for performing the desiderata of the law: doing what is encouraged, and refraining from what is reprehensible but not forbidden, enhances the perception of obligation.

Yet this "justice deferred," however socially and conceptually effective, is not enough to constitute even a primitive legal system.

The state or sovereign must, in the here-and-now, back up the statutory norm with coercive force. The institutions of the state, at least in pre-modern times, enforced what the jurists determined was the law and gave them great latitude. In most cases the judge had complete flexibility to determine what punishment to administer when a crime or tort was proved. These "sanctions" (*ta'zir*) were sometimes – in the best medieval style – spectacular dramas of humiliation and retribution, but more often they were fines, confiscation, and non-fatal corporal punishment, and so on.[30]

Islamic law: secondary rules

It is no great surprise that the Islamic legal system conforms to the most basic, most elementary notion of a legal system – rules and compulsive force. What of the secondary features of the law that Hart asserts are necessary for the long-term viability of a legal system?

The *rule of recognition* specifying relevant texts and methods of interpretation is certainly a feature of Islamic law and legal theory (*usul al-fiqh*). Indeed, *usul al-fiqh* is precisely about the recognized sources of the law, and the techniques of their interpretation and application. Introductions to *usul* works immediately satisfy the requirements of the rule of recognition, for example:

> Be it known that the bases (*usul*) of normative conduct (*al-shar'*) are three – the Book [Qur'an], the Sunnah [as recorded in the Hadith], and Consensus; and the fourth basis is "conceptual extension" as derived from these [three previously-mentioned] bases.[31]

The rest of this book, and every book on *usul al-fiqh*, is precisely about the hermeneutical linguistic strategies for making the pronouncements of Qur'an, *sunna*, and of previous scholars, into statutes.[32] Most importantly, a *usul* work contains the rules for the law's extension. The scope of the law is extended by selecting a situation whose legal status is reliably understood, and then, on the basis of an identifiable feature, linking it to a hitherto unknown situation so that the judgment applicable to the first case is now applied to the second case. Of course the unknown situation may resemble a large number of adjudicated situations. The science of jurisprudence is very much concerned with the process of identifying *the* most relevant case, a process called *tarjih*, "preponderating," or "preferring." As the term suggests, and the epistemologically sophisticated jurists recognized, this process did not yield certainty – God's assessment might differ from the mundane understanding of the jurist – but if the epistemic structure of the *fiqh* process was respected, then the assessment of the jurist was effectively correct even if metaphysically uncertain. The issue of legal epistemology took a few centuries to sort out but the discipline matured quickly and it is fair to say that of the three supplementary rules Hart specifies, *the rule of recognition* is the most developed and the most self-consciously articulated of them all.

One other factor that shaped the nature of Islamic law was the rite or *madhhab*. Within a century and a half of Islam's foundation, distinct schools of law (*madhhab*, literally "way of proceeding") had formed that were associated with regional centers within the Islamicate Empire. These rites differed on actual rules and practices – that is, they differed on substantial matters. In part to justify these differences, in part because of genuine methodological divergences, over the next two centuries these rites evolved into distinct schools of legal thought and practice. Their adherents recognized each other's legitimacy yet also asserted the superior rigor and analysis of their own school.

> If we are asked about our *madhhab* and a *madhhab* that differs from ours in a matter of detail, we are required to say that our *madhhab* is correct, though it is possible it is mistaken, and the other *madhhab* to the contrary is mistaken, though it is possible it is correct ... Whereas if we are asked about our creedal position we are required to say: the truth is what we hold and the false is that to which our disputant adheres.[33]

In the Sunni tradition four schools achieved permanence and each was eventually associated with a region in Islamdom – Malikis with North Africa and Spain, Shafi'is with Egypt, Syria, and parts of Arabia including the eastern Gulf (and hence, through trade relations, eventually Indonesia and Malaysia), the Hanafis were Iraqi and, until the sixteenth century, shared Iran with Shafi'is. More importantly the Hanafis were the rite associated with Turkic military elites so that the Hanafis eventually dominated in East Europe, Anatolia, Central Asia, and India. The gadfly, very tiny, Hanbali *madhhab* had adherents in the central Islamic lands – notably Damascus, and eventually Arabia. Their scripturalist emphasis was influential disproportionately to their numbers, and helped to shape a number of legal reform movements.

These distinct approaches to Islamic law had two important effects: (1) In their acknowledgment of a certain range of pluralism they ratified and expressed the doctrine of juristic probability, not certainty, described above. (2) In their mutually acceptable differences they occasionally provided a resource that could be exploited creatively to effect change or reform – as when late Mamluk Cairo merchants chose to use the Hanbali forms of sale[34] or when a marriage is permitted in the absence of a guardian or witnesses combining aspects of the Hanafi and Maliki *madhhab* rules.[35]

The rule of adjudication on the other hand is relatively less articulated, perhaps because the principle was established so early in Islam's history that there is little recorded controversy. Who then determines the legal facts, and how are infractions to be judged? From the earliest Islamic period it appears that an adjudicator/decider (*qadi*) was a functionary of the state, appointed by the leader and functioning with the ruler's effective force behind him. It was therefore rulers and their quasi-autonomous deputies – the judges (*qadis*) who adjudicated cases.

But who determined the law itself? The earliest formative period of Islamic law is pretty much a dark hole. David Powers, among others, has offered a plausible picture of Muslims trying to shape their conduct to Qur'anic norms, and Motzki of the relatively early recording of Prophetic norms for the purpose of guiding practice.[36] This picture agrees to some degree with traditional Muslim accounts. It seems that experts in Qur'an and Prophetic lore quickly developed an interest in the implications of these sources – at the Islamic center, in Arabia, and in the newly conquered provinces. Their expertise was ratified in the religious conflicts following 656 C.E. and perhaps especially in the civil war that ended around 692 when Islam was ideologized in a different way.[37] By the 720s there were recognized experts in religious conduct in all parts of the Islamic empire, and among their concerns was "*fiqh*" (which seems at first to mean theological insight, in opposition to *'ilm* – textual knowledge).[38] In so far as normative conduct was understood as *lore* subjected to certain techniques of interpretation, those who were skilled in these matters – the learned (*'ulama*) or the insightful (*fuqaha'*) had a near monopoly on the discovery-cum-production of the law, that is on the *legislation* of Islamic law, as outsiders might call it. These experts, when they wrote about law, were called *faqih*; when they opined about a particular case, they were called *mufti*.

Historically, no doubt, experts opined on Islamic law from the beginning; but as far as written works, first came the production of lore-books organized according to the categories of human practice, then the ruminations on legal topics and attempted distillations of Islamic lore.[39] The next phase was the digest/précis that really is the statute book, and these, in turn, attracted commentaries.[40] It is quite startling that those professing a certain type of expertise, almost entirely independent of any institutional identity, are recognized from nearly the beginning as legislators of the law. The authority of the scholars of Islamic lore in the domain of legislation was not substantially challenged before the nineteenth century.[41]

It is the *rule of change* that poses the most significant challenge for the scholar of Islamic law, as well as for contemporary Muslims. If a European student of law turns to jurisprudential theory, she might be discouraged from understanding *fiqh* as law, for Sunni Islamic law is grounded in dictates from the Qur'an and the Prophet (both of which theoretically ceased in 632 C.E.) For the largest group of Shi'as, law comes from those two sources together with the guidance of the Imams, the last of whom ceased to be in direct contact with his followers after 940. So, even for the Shi'a, there would seem to be no legislation after the mid-tenth century C.E. How, then, can a legal system function when the sole legitimate sources for legislation have ceased to be active during the European Dark Ages?

To answer this question it has to be remembered that practical jurisprudence always has an element of interpretation to it. Law is rules, but it is also the sorting of facts in the world in such a way that they are matched to those rules (see below). A change in circumstances effectively provokes a change in the law. The rule exists; the scholar's job is to recognize the rule in the text but also to recognize the law that best matches the circumstances he finds. If – according to Islamic legal theory – law *cannot* change, the sorting and classification of circumstances *can* change.

Wael Hallaq in particular has demonstrated the process by which, in effect, jurists legislated the law.[42] When a new problem posed itself, the question was presented to a *mufti* who essayed an answer. He may also have written an essay on the topic with a survey of other positions and a justification for his position. If the legal reasoning found favor with jurists, then it was eventually incorporated into the more discursive law books – stripped of the particulars present in the *fatwa* record. It was then further refined and incorporated into manuals as a simple rule, and at that point it appears in a form that most lawyers would recognize as a statute.[43]

It is here that the limitations of a merely emic approach to Islamic law become clear. Islamic jurists would deny that they were legislating, and attempts to understand Islamic law in these terms have been received with no favor. Ethically, however, it is clear that the criterion of the "rule of change" was satisfied precisely by the jurists' power to define circumstances and that here too resides the "open texture of the law" that both Hart and Dworkin deem central to the successful construction of a legal system.

Though Muslims not less than Orientalists have declared Islamic law to be immutable,[44] the fact is that Islamic law did change – as has been demonstrated by a number of careful scholars.[45] That law changed not overtly but through the mechanism of scholarly reflection and re-description in the medieval period has, as we shall see below, important consequences for Islamic law in the modern period. As it turns out, scholars were constrained and guided in their interpretations of texts and their application to circumstances not merely by hermeneutical rules but also by sets of a priori principles (in Dworkin's sense) that were inferred from previous authoritative rulings and that then constrained subsequent rulings. Some of these principles were shared by all of the legal schools.[46] Examples from one source include:[47] (1) certainty is not erased by doubt; (2) hardship leads to relief; (3) harm is removed; (4) custom is the arbiter; (5) actions are according to their intentions.[48]

Qaʿidas were specific to the *madhhab* and indeed helped to define the characteristic practices of each legal rite. So, for example, it is a mark of the Hanafis that a crime committed outside Islamdom is unpunished save homicide, for which the tort – damage payment – is still required.[49] These principles, as Shamsy points out, are both formal constraints on the interpretation of texts – such interpretation must conform to a set of principles specific to each *madhhab* – and a procedural principle that allows the judge to determine who bears the burden of proof in certain kinds of cases.[50]

These "principles" grew increasingly detailed over time, and while some were shared by all *madhhabs*, others were attached to the various *madhhabs* and became shibboleths of them. Hence these principles served to test a jurist's adherence to a school – if he cited them and used them in his rulings than he was considered as a member of their group.

DIFFERENCES FROM WESTERN PHILOSOPHERS' NOTIONS OF LAW

From the point of view of legal philosophy, then, the *fiqh* system shows the features of law as the philosophers describe it. There remain three points of difference between "Islamic Law" and "law" as the mainstream Anglo-American philosophers of law describe it: (1) the inclusion of religious ritual rules within the law proper, (2) the inclusion of supererogatory rules of ethical and religious practice in statute books, and (3) the absence of a rule of legislation, of a "rule of change" per se – though as we've shown, the jurists effectively legislated in the face of changed circumstances, provided they recognized them as changed. I see all three of these differences as tending in a single direction. All three enhance the Muslim's sentiments toward the "obligation to obey" the law.

Because of the primordial character of the sources of the law, Muslims understood the law to be no mere human fashioning but the discovery of rules laid down at the mythic dawn of Islam by God and in the religiously charged era of the Prophet and his companions. These rules equally include the unambiguously religious obligations of ritual and the rules for human interaction. They include not just the required and proscribed but recommended acts (for the doing of which there is divinely dispensed reward) and the discouraged (for the avoidance of which there is likewise a celestial reward).[51] Together these two "anomalous" features –combining the ritual and the practical; including the "oughts" as well as the "musts" – teach that obedience to the law and conformity to its norms is not a mere Austinian response to coercion but are obligations on the conscience. In this way the penumbra of ethics is cast onto the law, enriching Muslims' affective response to it. At the same time linking optimal virtues to obligatory duties has the effect of urging one to attend to the supererogatory rules as one must to the obligatory ones.[52] Law then is seen as part of life's moral conduct and it is here that irritatingly imprecise mantras such as "in Islam Church and State are not separated" and "Islam is a way of life, not just a religion" have some resonance. The difference between sin and crime is blurred, as are the lines between the ethical failing and legal transgression. Law becomes not merely organizational norms that differ from the merely arbitrary because they are useful. In Islamic law, law is moral or it is nothing. That which is not manifestly moral is in some sense illegitimate.

For legists, including both ritual and virtue in legal discourse helped reinforce a judicial self-image that idealized an autonomous, even "speaking-truth-to-power" system of social regulation resting on foundations exalted above mere state power.[53] Unlike Jewish law, Islamic law, as we shall see, was nonetheless a fully functioning legal system fully acquainted with state power and served as a practical instrument through nearly all of its history for the application of state power, and the regulation of society.

THE SCOPE OF LAW IN ISLAMDOM

Space considerations have precluded a full discussion of the entire scope of law in Islamdom. Readers should constantly bear in mind, however, that the full extent of administrative and social regulation was never expressed solely through what we would call "Islamic Law," that is, the *shari'a* system. This was particularly the case when the Turkic dynasties began to articulate the notion that justice was the primary purpose of the state and task of the sovereign, independent of other standards of legitimacy such as descent or election. As the central state declined, the de facto states' legitimacy in Islamicate political theory defined the quintessential task of the "people of the sword" as providing order through implementation of the law so that society would flourish.[54] Even the Islamic sources recognized that "the law of Muslims" was not always coextensive with "Islamic law" proper, that is, with *fiqh* sources. There were "oppression-relief" courts (*mazalim*) that adjudicated disputes involving the state administrative rules (called *qanun*) and sometimes functioned as appeal courts.[55] Tribal law also was sovereign in various places, particularly rural regions. In reality, the law of Muslims had much more scope than "Islamic law," and the theorists of Islamic law were compelled to recognize this fact. So, when "Islamic law" is discussed, it should not be supposed that by examining the Islamic legal sources one thereby understands all Muslim practices of conflict resolution.

THE PRACTICE OF ISLAMIC LAW

The study of Islamic legal *theory*, at least in its own terms, has been extensive. The study of the *practice* of Islamic law has lagged for several reasons. (1) The Arabic-language chauvinism of Islamicists. Since relatively few court documents remain from the pre-Ottoman period, and since there are often Ottoman–Turkish elements in Ottoman period documents that Arabists cannot read, the Arabists have ignored archives in favor of historical, theoretical, and literary sources.[56] More significantly, (2) it has been the conviction of many students of Islamic law that *shari'a* law was impractical by nature, or if it was once practiced, its efficacy was corrupted by the development of a hair-splitting scholastic authority that doomed it to irrelevance. This belief of course reflects the post-eighteenth-century European rejection of the (Catholic) scholastic legacy. More importantly, to view Muslims' law this way fit nicely with nineteenth-century justifications for colonialism.[57] Recent work, particularly with the rich reserves of Ottoman court documents, has demonstrated in fact the absolute centrality of Islamic law to the day-to-day lives of Ottoman Muslims, and indeed to Ottoman Christians and Jews as well; there were of course local variants and flexible accommodations to local realities.[58]

Here is not the place even to summarize these exciting findings – though such a summary is devoutly to be wished. Instead, we will reflect on what has been learned of the Ottoman practice of Islamic law in light of Pierre Bourdieu's description of law's sociology.[59]

THE SOCIOLOGY OF OTTOMAN LAW

Bourdieu sees the law as a "field"[60] that draws conflicts into its domain and then processes them into "legal disputes" – using terminology that conveys disinterestedness, objectivity, universality, and unchangingness. The legal professionals forego, and require the subjects to forego, the "common-sense" responses to conflict (such as insult and violence or common-sense notions of fairness), and then redescribe, limit, and stereotype the complex grievances of ordinary life and arrange them all into legal problems that require legal expertise and the clarity of the legal process and its findings.[61] So deeply instantiated in the consciousness of the legal subject and the legal professionals is this view of social interaction, what he calls the legal *habitus*, that it is seen as normal, invisible, and mostly sovereign over other methods of dispute resolution.[62]

The legal *habitus* of the Ottomans took two facts for granted: that the *shari'a* law system was law, and that legal authority flowed from the Sultan to his agents.[63] These interlocking modes of authority meant that the Sultan could affect the practice of Islamic law but that much of its *habitus* remained apart from him and his power. Consequently, law was composed of *fiqh* and *fatwas* of various *muftis* – officials of the state and independent scholars – of sultanic decrees and judges' certificates.[64] Though the Sultan did not legislate Islamic law, his growing power as the creator of Ottoman institutions meant that the definition of the law's content would in many ways come under his control. As the appointer of judges, the Sultan chose the *madhhab*, the rite, that was normative throughout the Empire. The Ottomans were devoted, even chauvinistic, Hanafis. By Ottoman times, the accumulated wisdom of Hanafi school scholarship functioned practically as a state law code so that in a *fatwa* or judicial opinion it was often sufficient to cite one of the authoritative *fiqh* books. The Sultan also assumed the authority to choose one Hanafi position in preference to another whenever there was disagreement within the school.

Additionally, in the space created by the *mazalim* court theory, sometime in the early fifteenth century, the Ottomans began to compile works of administrative practice that – while admitting the primacy of the *shar'* and its independence, stipulated which of several sets of judicial possibilities were to be preferred by the judiciary. These so-called *qanunnamehs* covered fiscal and criminal law (leaving the rest of Islamic law in place) and were general law books for the whole Empire.[65] The *qanunnameh* occasionally altered the details of *shari'a* procedure and statute, and extended somewhat the scope of the law so that acts that in *fiqh* books had been recommended or discouraged (and hence were outside the scope of law) became required or forbidden, and hence, enforceable by the courts.[66] *Shari'a* norms and practices retained a notable degree of autonomy and legitimacy apart from the Ottoman state, while the *qanun* was seen either as an administrative memo on how to conduct the business of the state, or, when it seemed to encroach upon the *shari'a* rules, as clarifications of those rules, eliminating lacunae or clarifying the law's intent.[67]

The gravitation of autonomous law toward the state is what we would expect for, as Bourdieu says, "judicial power ... demonstrates ... the sovereign vision of the State. For the State alone holds the monopoly of legitimized symbolic violence."[68] Yet as Bourdieu also suggests, the law and its practitioners often compete with the state, and the law is a site of resistance.[69] For the Ottomans, Islamic law remained *of* the state while standing apart *from* it.

Madrasas, where the law was studied and, as we have seen, often effectively legislated, were found throughout the Empire, but the ones that mattered, the Écoles Normales of the Empire, were founded by the Sultans and located in the capital. The officers of the law were bureaucratized within the hierarchy of the state and a corps of *qadis* was trained, moved at intervals throughout the Ottoman possessions.[70] Since the prestigious *madrasas* were royal endowments, the Sultans chose the professoriate. Since the bureaucracy was composed of his servants, he appointed the judges and chief *mufti*. The *qadis* were often used to check the governor, but at different times the governor assumed judicial functions and reported on corruption in the judiciary.

Bourdieu argues that the displacement of the actor by the legal professional is based on the legal professional's appropriation of the "capacity to interpret a corpus of texts sanctifying a correct [and] legitimized vision of the social world."[71] The legal professionals use a distinct and idiomatic "rhetoric of impersonality and neutrality"[72] with predominantly passive and impersonal phrasing that establishes the legal action is "the universal subject, at once impartial and objective."[73]

This of course is exactly what was done in the Ottoman domain: the court petitions, the court decrees, and their documents are in a rhetoric and often even a language (Classical Arabic) worlds apart from the language and analytic worldview of the average subject. We can see this distinction clearly when the court document frames quotations from a petitioner in a dialectical Ottoman Turkish, with formal Ottoman and Arabic commentary and disposition.[74] While the jurist's claim to authority was his sultanic appointment, the *sine qua non* of a jurist was the ability to read, understand, master, and appropriate the *fiqh* texts and the administrative jargon of administration. Those before the court were the subjects of both the Sultan and of God; both were addressed through the mouths and pens of the jurists and their associates.

Bourdieu believes it is a constitutive feature of the law as a "field" that legal professionals are not, among themselves, of one accord. Bourdieu believes that there is a fundamental structural conflict between the *habitus* of the practice (judges and lawyers) and the theorist (legal scholars). Scholars regularly re-form the law in the direction of theory and coherence to present the law as an "ordered, autonomous and self-sufficient system, freed of all the uncertainties … arising in its practical origins."[75] The theoretician takes up the variety of circumstances and rulings and imposes order on them; he uses logic and coherence to maintain the impersonal rationality that is the law's legitimacy and its countenance.

Judges by contrast prefer to present themselves as mere interpreters whose role is "a simple application of the law;" in fact, the judge often "does in fact perform a work of judicial creation, [though he] tends to dissimulate this fact."[76] The practitioner (judge) changes the law but not by altering its logic or accepted reach but by "mis-reading" the law – narrowing or broadening legal formulas indifferently to their original scope – by analyzing and distinguishing the "letter and spirit, which tends to maximize the law's elasticity, [but also] its contradictory ambiguities and lacunae."[77]

Hence the yin and yang of a legal system is the coherence and logic of the scholar versus the practicality and casuistry of the judges. It is a struggle in short between emphasizing logic or justice. The scholar must incorporate judicial practice into the theory so that the theory is relevant. The judge must take account of legal theory so that rulings are legitimate. Either the judge or the scholar may function "prophetically," as Bourdieu calls it, to change the law – the scholar overtly when he recasts the law to bring out fairness through coherence; the judge covertly when he reinterprets the law to achieve justice by responding to particularity. Sclerosis occurs when new circumstances cannot compel effective prophetic transformation from either or both of these legal protagonists.

The relations between Ottoman scholars and judges have not been studied, so far as I know. I have seen no evidence of structural conflict between these two professional groups, however. If there was no conflict, perhaps it was because the initial training of jurists of all sorts was so homogenous – the basic Ottoman curriculum seems to have taught a limited number of books and the sheer mass of Hanafi jurisprudence by this time had extruded agreed-upon positions on most recurring legal problems. Additionally, there was a clear hierarchy of relations among the various actors. Dictates from the center, bureaucrat-to-bureaucrat, were obeyed. *Muftis'* opinions constrained judges' rulings, and there were no lawyers. The highest ranks of the Ottoman legal establishment came not, however, from the judiciary but from the academic *madrasas* in Istanbul.[78] This surely inclined them to pliancy toward the State's point of view; it may also have meant that the decisive perspective on the law was theoretical, rather than practical.

The actual structural competition was between those legal actors who were part of Ottoman officialdom, and those who were outside its walls, if not its shadow. Ottoman religious history is filled with dissident movements led by religious figures claiming either a revised legal dispensation or revivalists purporting to press for a return to "that old time religion" (*din al-aslaf*). For, despite the elaborately structured royal educational institutions of the capital, the Empire was filled with independently endowed *madrasas* – each with independent legal scholars – mosques with preachers, and unemployed scholars who, whatever their education, were also outside the system, looking in. In addition, the adherents of *madhhabs* other than the official Hanafi one did not always docily accept their peripheral status. Finally, there was dissent in the form of rival forms of Islam, some with explicit political connections with foreign parties like the Safavid-linked Qizilbash and Twelver-Shi'is, but also with others like the Kadizadehlis, Khalidis, or followers of Badraddin who had no foreign agenda but who sternly criticized Ottoman legal practice.

THE OTTOMAN LEGAL COURT AS NEXUS

Though there were often court buildings in the Ottoman Empire, it is most fruitful to think of the court not as a place but as a conceptual matrix of roles that came together to (1) create a nexus between the Empire's administration and the Ottoman subject and (2) to create a semi-autonomous site where social facts were created. The agents in this socio-legal matrix were the judge, the clerk, the various kinds of witnesses, and the populace as a whole.

The qadi

Since the earliest Islamic times, the *qadi* was appointed by the ruling power and this practice continues both in theory and practice until the present. As such, there has been a certain ambivalence about judicial service: on the one hand, serving the law was a noble enterprise, on the other, it inevitably led to entanglement with the state and pressure to rule in ways that the powers-that-be would favor; moreover, a judge might err and some scholars understood this to jeopardize their own salvation.[79]

By Ottoman times the *qadi*-ship was been well incorporated into the state bureaucracy.[80] The state appointed judges at fixed salaries, it rotated them through the Empire; the judges served for fixed terms and, if they were successful, they gradually rose in the bureaucratic ranks. The judge embodied both the neutrality and impersonality of the *shari'a* and the compelling authority of the state: both God and the Sultan. Yet the judge did not originate the law. He sought guidance from *muftis* on the *shar'* and from the government on practical regulation. Two streams of expertise and authority flowed toward his position where they were channeled to turn the mills of practical justice. Yet, despite the centrality of the judge to the legal process, he all but disappears in the legal record – when one reads the judicial record the judge is scarcely mentioned and indeed even the judge's finding is often not recorded.[81] As Bourdieu points out, the "naturalization" of the law explains and justifies both judicial centrality and anonymity. The law functions through "a rhetoric of impersonality and neutrality" which is often expressed (as in Ottoman court records) by a "predominantly passive and impersonal construction."[82] The judge is effaced to bring to the foreground the law, of which he is the representative and effective agent.

The clerk

The clerk was, in a sense, the decisive figure, the person who took a conflict or a set of social facts and transformed them into legal problems, legal facts, and disputes in law. While not an advocate in the European sense, it seems that the clerk performed the task that Euro-American lawyers perform: the alchemy of making a case out of what was before merely a conflict.[83] Unlike the judge, the clerk was usually a local who served through terms of office of many *qadis* in turn.[84] It was the clerk who summarized the court action[85] perhaps under the judge's direction[86] though, given the variety of the court documents' formulations and prose,[87] it seems more likely that it was the clerks themselves who translated the ordinary language of dispute into the impersonal and neutral rhetoric of the law.[88]

Witnesses

We tend to think of witnesses as ancillary to judges, lawyers, plaintiffs, and defendants. In the Ottoman legal system, however, witnesses were as constitutive of the process of the law as judges or clerks. There were three kinds of witness in an Ottoman court. In cases that required expertise, about building practices, for instance, or hydrology, expert witnesses were called to provide background information or information on professional norms and practices.[89] There were also witnesses who verified that a court session took place or was conducted properly and these "instrumental witnesses" inscribed their names "in the court registry following the record of the case."[90] According to Pierce, "their function was to act as a check on the correctness of legal procedures ... and to serve as a repository of communal memory of the incident at issue."[91] Finally there were what Canbakal calls "circumstantial witnesses." These were men of established probity, often notables and men of property and or status. They functioned as representatives of those who could not present themselves in court, as notary witnesses before whom contracts or deeds were signed. Most importantly, they were repositories of "social facts": who was known to be free and who a slave, who was a descendant of the Prophet (and hence entitled to a state emolument), and "who was harmless and who was not."[92] They provided often-decisive testimony about the character of plaintiff, defendant or accused.[93] They were drawn from a stable corps of notables who "represented" the town's polity. Occasional "witnesses," in the Anglo-European sense, were regarded as important – their testimony could still be decisive in a case, whether about market practice, events that transpired, or "common knowledge" about a person or practice – but they did not have the social heft of those whose characters had been verified by the judicial system, who frequented the court and "represented" the locality to the state.[94] In sum, the court was not just a place to resolve disputes. It was the contact point between state and locality, between sovereign and subject. From time to time courts were directed to investigate some wrongdoing or chronic social deviance. As such, they were a conduit through which direction and control flowed from top to bottom, from the metropole to the periphery.

The courts were also an autonomous realm where Ottomans created social facts. Sales were registered, gifts declared, but also, for instance, a young woman registered her dislike of a marriage arranged for her, another woman registered that she would not be suing for wrongful death in the case of her brother's fall into a moat, and another that a stray goat had been restored to its owner.[95] It was in the court that the public registered sentiments, transactions, and events that might later be called into question in litigation.[96] These "social facts" were recorded so that they could be reliably invoked in future litigation. As Faroqhi points out, religious minorities whose testimony against Muslims in lawsuits could not be accepted could record "facts" in the *qadi*'s register and to be invoked in case of conflict. This, she says, may partly explain the surprising fact that Christians and Jews frequently used the *shari'a* courts.[97]

Community

Islamic court practice – to an extent that comes as a surprise – depended on individual reputation and the performance of virtue. So, while torts and dispute-resolution were grounded on legal facts, they also depended upon (for instance) compurgation – where a neighborhood could be responsible for a crime committed by an unknown person unless they secured a given number of oaths – or on oaths taken in a certain sequence by the plaintiff and defendant.[98] To an extent that also surprises, these oaths were taken seriously and people made voluntary admissions against their own interests, even oaths that led to their deaths.[99]

The community as a whole was also an agent with standing in the court and

> [c]ommunity surveillance, in fact, was built into the legal process. People had a real stake in how others conducted themselves, since they could be held legally responsible for the criminal acts of others ... The flip side of this collective liability was the collective right of neighborhoods to protest against and even expel residents known to have criminal reputations (in particular, thieves and harlots).[100]

THE AFTERLIFE OF OTTOMAN–ISLAMIC LAW

The social institutions of Islamic law functioned effectively despite corruption[101] and periods of decreased control from the center.[102] The courts began to fail when they could no longer engage responsively with changing commercial codes, capitulations that gave minorities superior legal rights compared to Muslims, and to the wave of social change that accompanied European hegemony and the new nation-state order. It is worth wondering if the judicial rigidity and sclerosis noted by European and Ottoman observers alike arose from the fact that it was exclusively scholars of the law who occupied the heights of the judiciary rather than experienced judges, since what Bourdieu calls the creative misreading of the law and the prophetic function was less likely to come from scholars whose devotion to logic and coherence in this case made them indifferent to the manifest changes taking place in actual society.

Whatever the case, by the mid-nineteenth century the Ottoman government formed a commission to do a most un-Islamic thing, that is, to codify the law, thereby eliminating the freedom of the experts in law to recognize altered circumstances and, de facto, legislate more appropriate statutes. This codification, the *Mecelle* (*Majalla*), drew from different Islamic *madhhab* traditions in order to effect reforms. The *Mecelle* proper dealt with commercial law; a later effort, briefly in force, codified personal law as well. Both of these codes applied to all subjects of the Empire, regardless of religion, and so *per force* accepted fully the testimony of non-Muslims. Though the *Mecelle* remains in force in Jordan and for Muslims in Israel (and is the core of Iraqi law), the Turkish national state did what most Muslim states did sooner or later. They displaced Islamic law and replaced it with a translated, slightly modified European law code. In most Muslim countries (but not in Turkey) the laws of marriage, divorce, and family law became codified versions of Islamic law, and in the last two decades homage is generally paid to the idea that "*shari'a* is the source of law." Yet even Islamists so far misunderstand Islamic law as to imagine that the Islamic state will substitute an immutable and transcendent Islamic code for the European one: a view that is, as we have seen, quite inconsistent with both the actual theory, and the actual practice, of Islamic law.

More than specific content, Islamic law is a process that integrates the power of the state with the trained consciences and socially responsive instincts of the jurist. It is without doubt law – and not just *kadijustiz*[103] – though its procedures differ from those of Euro-American law. Above all, it was a superbly flexible system that allowed Islamic values to govern an extraordinarily diverse set of human societies for an extraordinarily long time. Understanding Islamic law, both theory and practice, is key to understanding Islamic religion and Islamicate society of course, but its study might also help philosophers of law come to conclusions less provincial than those based solely on common law and continental practice.

13

MODERNITY

Bruce B. Lawrence

PROLOGUE

Modernity is a contested term with multiple referents. The premise of this essay will be: (1) that modernity is inescapable, (2) that modernity is at once process-driven and event-dated and (3) that not one but multiple modernities have emerged in the past 500 years, transforming the structures and hierarchies, norms, values, and options for most of humanity but not in a uniform, predictable pattern. Stated differently, modernity as it unfolds within specific cultures or civilizations always has different starting points, leading to different trajectories and therefore different outcomes. From the dominant perspective, Islam and Muslims have been part and parcel of a process locating them on the margins: few Muslim individuals and no Muslim collectivities have been initiators, few beneficiaries, and most "mere" participants, whether as partners or victims, of the large-scale change that the dominant modernity produces.

The dominant modernity began with the process of seafaring; its major events were marked as discoveries. The most oft-cited discovery was America – actually the West Indies – by the Spanish entrepreneur Christopher Columbus in 1492, opening up the Atlantic to first Spanish, then other European seafaring nations, with the eventual settlement of both North and South America. However, an equally important discovery came from another Spanish explorer, Magellan. In 1520 Magellan discovered a southwestern passage that crossed from the Atlantic to the Pacific, where he claimed a new set of Pacific islands in the name of King Philip, hence the Philippines, and for the first time made possible new maps of the entire world. Globalization had begun. It was the outcome of European seafaring; the spoils of the discovered lands, as also the labor of the subdued peoples, benefited European monarchs and their subjects.

This pattern, even in its briefest outline, must precede and inform any essay on Islam and modernity. While neither Islam nor Muslims figure in the trunk narrative, they quickly become part of the emergent histories of the New World. The most seafaring of the great medieval Muslim empires, the Ottoman, clashed with the nascent European sea powers, at the same time that Muslim populations, beginning with those of the Philippines, found themselves engaged in protracted warfare with "Christian" adversaries. Over time they were defeated, their lands occupied, their economies and societies colonized, yet they did not lose their subjectivity, and their histories have become part of the complex reinterpretation of the past augured by cultural studies as "alternative or vernacular modernities."[1]

No one has described this complex, consequential process more subtly or succinctly than the Mexican philosopher and world historian Enrique Dussel. Dussel depicts not one but two major forms of modernity. Hispanic modernity or Modernity I was centered in Seville. It projected a mercantilist and monetary expansion of Portugese – but even more, Spanish – influence that included missionary projects on behalf of the Roman Church from Latin America to East Asia. It was succeeded in the mid-seventeenth century by Modernity II, centered first in Amsterdam but then recentered from the eighteenth century on in England and Scotland. It was mercantilist and bourgeois, advocating Christianity as in Modernity I, but sending Protestant rather than Catholic missionaries to the marginalized, colonized world. Major regions, but also all the major religions, were affected by this two-pronged emergence of European Modernity, none more so than Islam and the Muslim societies of Asia and Africa, or what Hodgson calls the Afro-Eurasian *oikumene*.[2]

Despite over a century of Euro-American scholarship on Islam and Muslim societies, it is not clear how best to talk about Islam and modernity, unless one reverts to the slippery double pluralization advocated by Aziz al-Azmeh[3] but pursued by almost no one else. Of the several evident approaches, the less common is to ignore or downplay the history just described and to project Islam itself as already modern. To bracket Islam and modernity one merely has to retrieve those modern elements already marked as Muslim in origin and highlight, then implement, them in order to make Islam competitive with other twenty-first-century worldviews.

From this perspective, as soon as one acknowledges the gap between the West and the East, that is, Islam, one must link its cause to the notion of "decline" (*inhitat*). "Decline" is an idea common to Western social science, to wit, that calculative reason promoted the rise of the West, and its absence – or diminished presence – elsewhere, including but not solely Muslim societies of Africa and Asia, ensured their backwardness. By this logic, "progress" is the purview of the West, even as "decline" is inevitable for the rest of humankind.[4] As deployed by the Chicago historian William O'Neill, the "Rise of the West" was not deemed accidental but rather due to a cluster of causes all of which relied on one or another aspect of instrumental reason, whether discovery, technology, or democracy, ultimately lauding the creative role of the individual over the deadweight of collective identity. Even as Arab intellectuals reflected on this issue, their thoughts were taken up, repackaged, and projected to other audiences by Euro-American scholars, also known as Orientalists. Orientalists applied deep linguistic and historical knowledge, along with a withering logic, to the study of their subjects. Chief among them was Gustave von Grunebaum. In *Fall and Rise of Islam: A Self-View*, von Grunebaum summarized the Indian Muslim Abul-Hasan 'Ali an-Nadwi's 1951 book as itself a less-sophisticated replica of ideas from the leading Pakistani poet, Muhammad Iqbal (d. 1938), to wit, that "Islam was created to give direction to the world, human society and civilization. Hence the decline of Islam and its loss of world leadership were an unprecedented catastrophe not merely for Muslims but for all nations."[5] In a brilliant riposte to von Grunebaum, the Moroccan political theorist Abdallah Laroui has demonstrated that the German Orientalist was wedded to an invariant, unitive notion of culture: for von Grunebaum, Western culture, from Greek times to the present, always had the intrinsic drive to creativity while Islamic culture, from the eighth century to the twenty-first, remained shackled by a theological/juridical conservatism that made it difficult, nay, impossible, to compete with an Enlightened, revitalized Western social system, whether in Europe or, later, the U.S.A.[6]

But how does one account for Islamic science? Laroui deploys a telling critique of von Grunebaum's dismissal of Islamic science. First, the very existence of this science does not square with the apparent unitary, theocentric core of Islamic culture, and second, Islamic science was good not only for Muslims, it is known to have influenced the emergence, and contributed to the success, of European or Western science. Because von Grunebaum ignores the individual creativity at the heart of Islamic as well as Western science, he deduces that science could only have been marginal to Islamic society and, in any case, "was bound to peter out since it was founded on an inadequate theory of knowledge."[7]

What neither "decline" advocates nor their critics admit, however, is a consequential shift in the nature of world history, an arc of change so large that it has to be understood on its own terms before being applied to Muslim societies or to Islamic evidence. This second approach analyzes modernity/modernization as competitive with Islam, above all, because of its European origins. Modernity becomes identified not just with a process called modernization but also with a place called Europe or the West, and so modernization is tantamount to Westernization. It requires of Muslims not accommodation but assimilation, not parity but subjection, to norms and values that originate outside Islam and so challenge the texture and tone of Muslim societies. In this sense, modernity is not just a phase in global history but itself an epistemic shift that all non-Western societies must confront: Muslim intellectuals share the fate of Buddhists, Hindus, and traditionalists of all stripes: they cannot avoid the tensions and compromises, the somersaults and retreats that modernization entails.

The major exponent of this second, epistemic approach to modernization was the premier American Islamicist of the twentieth century: Marshall Hodgson. For Hodgson the central question always posed, either directly or indirectly, is: does religion (as also culture) assist or impede the modernization process? The assumption of modernizers is that only modernization finally works, and that religions, like cultures, must be judged good or bad by how congruent or dissonant they are with forces, structures, and goals of modernization.

ISLAM AND SCIENCE

The cornerstone of Islam revitalized is rethinking the relationship between Islam and science. What persists beyond Orientalist disregard, and degradation, of medieval Islamic science is the current day debate about Islam and science. At the most mundane level, the question of Islam and science opens up into a much broader platform, involving the stake of any belief in a world beyond this world and also its counterpart, a rigorous, public affirmation that no belief, and hence no religion, can influence the social or political realms of modern day nation-states. The former is called agnosticism, the latter is secularism, and on both ends of the "religion and science" spectrum Muslims, or those projecting themselves as authoritative representatives of an Islamic worldview, have spoken, written, and argued at length.

If science is indeed the nemesis of faith in the modern world, then one must face the challenge posed by the paleontologist-turned-public intellectual Stephen Jay Gould. In his *Rocks of Ages: Science and Religion in the Fullness of Life*, Gould openly invokes the Catholic concept of *magisterium*, but gives it a new twist as he advocates N.O.M.A., an acronym standing for "Non-Overlapping MAgisteria." How can rival *magisteria*, each with a claim to be universal worldviews, not compete? How can they avoid overlapping? Gould asserts that both science and religion are independent domains of inquiry and debate, and because they are independent, they do not, and cannot, overlap. Yet science and religion are more than words or ideas or values. They are also institutions, and while admitting his "great respect for religion," Gould adds that "much of this fascination lies in the stunning paradox that *organized* religion has fostered ... both the most unspeakable horrors and the most heart-rending examples of human goodness in the face of personal danger."[8]

Above all, Gould highlights the crucial issue of evolution. Praising the shift in official Catholic teaching, Gould uses the current Vatican acceptance of evolution as a club to wield against another Christian group, namely, the Creationists who view evolution as heresy. Even as Gould the cheerful agnostic supports the Bishop of Rome for upholding N.O.M.A., he labels Creationism "a distinctively American violation of NOMA."[9]

In effect, Gould is more than a professing agnostic. He is also a closet believer, but his belief is in science. And so his own ideology blinds him to the limits of scientism. And though he never wrote about Islam, he would have applauded the account given in the popular press of Neil Armstrong's "conversion" while walking on the moon.

Neil Armstrong's lunar "conversion"?! While it is well known that the American astronaut Neil Armstrong walked on the moon in summer 1969, it is less well known that fourteen years later in summer 1983 newspapers from Cairo to Jakarta ran a front-page postscript to

Armstrong's feat that excited the imagination of many Muslim readers. While walking on the lunar surface, it was reported, Armstrong had heard an eerie noise. He had no idea where it came from or what caused it. It remained in his mind, though it escaped his official debriefing when he returned to earth. Some years later, while on a U.S.-sponsored tour of non-aligned countries, Armstrong was walking through Cairo when he heard the same wailing noise echoing the streets. He stopped a passerby and asked what it was. On being told that it was the Muslim call to prayer, coming from the muezzin of a nearby mosque, he immediately converted to Islam. But alas, when he returned to the U.S. and to his native Cincinnati, he was told that if he made a public profession of his newfound faith, he would be fired from his government job, and so Armstrong had to practice *taqiya* (the concealment of one's faith for self-preservation), and still practices it to the present day.[10]

While the story cannot be proven true – or false – it illustrates the extent to which the prestige of modern science is linked to the ascent of Europe and America to global dominance. It, of course, has other foundations but the aura of prestige is often seen as confirming other truths. To many Muslims the need for an Islamic presence in space exploration was palpable, expressed as a subconscious but still keen desire. And so, it happened that Neil Armstrong made a double discovery: that man can walk on the moon and that Allah has already marked the moon as Muslim. There is also a sub-theme, namely, that modern secular Americans, or at least those working for N.A.S.A., cannot recognize any faith, and certainly not Islamic faith, as the real cause of scientific advance. Yet some Muslim apologists, like their Christian counterparts, have tried to provide the opposite argument: that modern science, including space exploration, has nothing to do with religion, and that the true task of scholars is to provide historical narratives, as also philosophical arguments, that separate the truth of religion/ Islam from the invasive claims of modern science. One such is Seyyed Hossein Nasr, an Iranian–American scholar who, forced into exile by the Islamic Revolution, became a spokesperson for the sort of Islam that many non-Muslim Americans find comforting. In a book titled *A Young Muslim's Guide to the Modern World* Nasr declares:

> For some two centuries the world of Islam has confronted the assault of an alien civilization and worldview which have challenged the very tenets of Islam itself. This assault has also destroyed much of the civilization created by Islam over the centuries ... From the family

to the state, from economics to mosque architecture, from poetry to medicine, all are affected by the alien worldview which the modern world, as its ethos was first incubated and nurtured in the West and then spread to other continents, has imposed upon the Islamic world and its peoples.[11]

We and they, Islam and the West, passive victim versus active aggressor – such are the antonyms which frame the advice offered to a young Muslim innocent at the outset of Nasr's manifesto. Every issue is framed by a set of incommensurate, mutually exclusive, binary opposites. The message of Islam is transcendent truth undiluted by human error or historical accident, while the modern world is immanent, empirical, and rational at best, materialist, agnostic, and skeptical at worst.[12] The two are on a collision course, to the signposts of which the young Muslim innocent should be aware as he (or perhaps she) tries to gauge the appropriate Islamic response to an alien worldview, a modern anti-Islamic world of yesterday, today, and tomorrow. In effect, Nasr advocates a set of perennial norms, at once timeless and absolute, that call humankind to the spiritual font of Wisdom, whether as Muslims who heed the prophecy of Muhammad, accept the Qur'an as Divine Writ, and obey the Divine Law incumbent on Muhammad's community, or as non-Muslims, those believers who accept other revealed pathways to the Godhead and so submit each in their own way in response to their own circumstance, but as traditionalists not – God forbid! – modernists.

The difficulty with this approach is its too-neat convergence with the popular dichotomy between Islam and the West. But beyond Nasr's rank dualism and his slipshod catechism, there are other possibilities for Muslim identity and Islamic loyalty in the twenty-first century. Instead of a theological straitjacket that admits neither external disagreement nor internal dissent as legitimate expressions of both spiritual quest and religious commitment, this approach frames the central message of Islam as part and parcel of the modern world: Allah did not go on vacation when the Great Western Transmutation emerged. Neither separate from it, nor alien to it, Muslims are challenged by the modern world, at the same time that Islamic norms and values contribute to the reciprocal challenge which all religions collectively raise on behalf of humankind.

This second approach has been ably articulated by Mohammed Arkoun. An Algerian–French professor of Islamic philosophy, Arkoun writes in Arabic and French. One of his books, translated into

English, is titled: *Rethinking Islam: Common Questions, Uncommon Answers*. It is a book that, like Nasr's, was written primarily for a general public, Muslim and non-Muslim, who want to understand the relevance of Islam to modern life. Arkoun's approach, unlike Nasr's, is unabashedly self-critical, pluralist, historical, and anti-theological. At one point, Arkoun asks rhetorically: "Can one speak of a scientific understanding of Islam in the West or must one rather talk about the Western way of imagining Islam?" Arkoun affirms the second option, since there is *not* "a single, eternal Islam" of the sort cited by both fundamentalists and contemporary media to "prove" that Islam is the real enemy of the West. Yet there do remain rival versions of the Truth. Rather than dodge their existence, Arkoun foregrounds it. He details the competition for the Truth in broad historical strokes:

> Ever since the emergence of Islam between 610 and 632, there has been continuous rivalry among three religious communities – Jewish, Christian, and Muslim – all striving to establish a monopoly on the management of symbolic capital linked to what the three traditions call "revelation". The issue is enormous and primordial, yet it has nonetheless been buried by secularized, ideological discourse: the ideologies of nation building, scientific progress, and universal humanism in nineteenth- and twentieth-century Europe. Then, beginning with the Nazi catastrophe, and the wars of colonial liberation, the question of revelation was buried under the no less deceptive rhetoric of decolonization, of development and underdevelopment (in the 1960s), and of nation building in Third World countries that had just recovered their political sovereignty.[13]

Nazis? Colonial liberation? Decolonization? Development and underdevelopment? These themes are never touched on by Nasr or by most Muslim apologists. Yet the crucial category for Arkoun is the same as for Nasr: revelation. For Arkoun, as the above quotation makes clear, revelation is not a self-verifying category. It is subsumed within a larger category, that of symbolic capital, and symbolic capital – while not being denied as true – is seen as itself capable of manipulation, like other forms of capital, by those who possess it or manufacture it, buy or steal it, invest it, or waste it. In other words, every theology also has an ideological dimension: those in power control "a cultural system that excludes all those others who have the sacrilegious pretension to draw upon the same symbolic capital."[14]

Not only Arkoun but other Muslim voices have tried to show the internal difference that openness to new forms of symbolic capital can make to Muslim self-understanding. In the aftermath of 9/11 especially, it is worth recalling the difference between a timeless Islam (Nasr) and a socially contested Islam (Arkoun). It is Arkoun rather than Nasr who offers a gleam of hope not only about Islam versus science but also about all religion that attempts to chart a practical modus vivendi both with the modern world and with religious communities of varied beliefs and practices, commitments, and hopes.

ISLAM AND SECULARIZATION

In looking at Islam and modernity, modernization = Westernization is not the sole equation, it is often triangulated with a third synonym: secularization. Throughout the long twentieth century the terms not only tended to circulate in the same universe of ideas, but among Muslim intellectuals all three tended to be equated with a fourth term: unbelief. Whatever came from outside Islam, but especially what related to a domain where European conquest, then occupation were evident and palpable, became labeled as unbelief, not just a threat to Islamic norms and values but their opposite and therefore their enemy, to be opposed by all devout Muslims as the antithesis of authentic Islam.

It is no accident that the locus classicus of secularism in the Muslim world became Turkey. The modern day Republic of Turkey was the residual heir of the Ottoman Empire. It had not been colonized – at least not directly – by European powers, even though it felt their constant challenge to its existence, whether in Eastern Europe or North Africa or even Anatolia, the homeland of Turks. In the 1920s, Mustafa Kemal, a.k.a. Atatürk, forged a new Muslim polity, the Turkish Republic. He projected it as a model non-Islamic, Muslim nation-state. Following the French model, the official party was called "Republican," the official religion "laicism." All tokens of religious conformity, from the office of Caliphate to prescribed dress codes to the Perso-Arabic alphabet, were abolished. Until 1929 Islam did remain the religion of the Turkish state, but in that year it, too, was officially disestablished. Yet religious institutions, often supported by local officials and spiritual authorities, continued to influence not only their own constituencies but also government officials.

Even though Islam had been disestablished, a deep vein of Islamic spirituality continued to course through twentieth-century Turkish society. Indeed, laicism in Turkey does not mean what it meant in France. Turkish laicism means the control of religious expression through bureaucratic structures serving the interests of lay rulers, above all, the military. It is not so much separation of "church" and state as much as control of religion, especially mosques and religious schools, by the state. While the Turkish military has been the laicist consciousness of Turkey since its foundation, since the 1982 Constitution it has made state-promoted Islam an explicit objective within the overall agenda of national unity.

There are, of course, groups that challenge both the state and its version of Islam at the same time that there is, in Turkey as in other contemporary majority Muslim nation states, a two-track system of education. Both Malaysia and Indonesia, for instance, have state-sponsored Islamic schools (*madrasas*), from high school through university, that exist alongside secular or technical schools. Efforts to eliminate this educational bifurcation or to combine the two systems have failed, with the result that students trained in secular knowledge, that is science, medicine, engineering, and business, are best prepared for competitive employment opportunities, while those who specialize only in the religious sciences or try to combine *madrasa* training with secular knowledge often find themselves at a competitive disadvantage.

Yet at least one major theorist of religion, Talal Asad, sees a hopeful outcome to the religious–secular tension in the educational strategies and knowledge production of majority-Muslim societies. Muslim by birth and secularist by conviction, Asad reverses the usual concern about refuting or displacing secularism. Asad argues that there is an underlying tension, bordering on a basic contradiction, between religious and secular as exclusive mindsets. Modern secular ideologies claim to replace even while echoing religious impulses, agendas, and outcomes; they ignore that secular and religious are inseparable. To the extent that "the concept of the secular cannot do without the idea of religion,"[15] the reverse is also true: "religious symbols ... cannot be understood independently of their historical relations with nonreligious symbols or of their articulations in and of social life, in which work and power are always present."[16]

Take the case of Islamism and politics. There is no either/or chasm but a both/and set of choices that face all Islamists. Islamists want to control the nation-state without becoming secular nationalists. A moderate Islamist, such as the Egyptian-born Qatari scholar Yusuf al-Qaradawi, feels that it is possible to be both "a Muslim citizen"[17] and a passport-carrying citizen of a majority-Muslim "secular" nation-state, whether Egypt, Turkey, or Indonesia. This dual citizenship option is not supported, however, by all Islamists, and it requires an epistemic leap that is more plausible for upper class netizens, that is, Muslims linked to one another through the Internet on the World Wide Web, than for the mass of Muslims whose horizons are still transfixed by local, regional, and also national loyalties that often put them at odds with their Muslim compatriots.

What the debate about the religious–secular options underscores is the extent to which public space is no longer territorially limited; it is at once transnational and virtual. To the extent that the inter-penetration of secular practices with religious norms is inevitable, it will impact Muslim as well as non-Muslim communities, and the reverse is also true: each group or community will be assured a space in the public sphere in so far as their advocates offer all participants an unending dialectic of choices on the World Wide Web.

ISLAM IN CYBERSPACE

To the extent that the future is now, both Islam and Muslims are bound up with the Information Technology Revolution. Even those who are not Muslim netizens are influenced, and will continue to be influenced, by those who are. Yet the Internet, while the most dramatic, is only the latest of several indices in the communications revolution that marked the late twentieth-century global economy and also transformed the nature of Muslim networks. There were cassette tapes that helped foster the Iranian Revolution. There was satellite TV that overrode governmental controls on local TV stations to beam alternative Muslim messages, including cleric talk shows, *fatwa* workshops, and a variety of Islamic entertainment to Arabic-speaking audiences, and since 1997 a major alternative to CNN-style global news has been provided through the Gulf-based Al-Jazeera. CD-ROMs, too, have become popular, circulating both literary texts and visual artifacts to broad Muslim audiences. Finally, there has been the Internet, which offers many networking options, from chat groups to websites, and, of course, email. All these options for expanded exchange and alter-native authorities rely on access and speed but, even more, on the need for new criteria of trust.

These new conditions for the exchange of information have generated new kinds of networks, most notably transnational alliances of women who are working for conflict resolution, human security, and justice at the local and global levels. Since the 1980s, and particularly since the 1985 U.N. conference on women in Nairobi, networks of Muslim women have been fighting for their rights in a newly Islamizing political context where women's rights and roles are highly contested. Some of these women's networks are local, like the ones that have appeared in Pakistan, Sudan, and Algeria; others have a global reach, like the Women Living Under Muslim Laws (W.L.U.M.L.) whose Islamic feminist agenda is to empower women to seek their rights as observant Muslims, and it includes exchange of information about ways to deal with gender discrimination and also transnational collaboration to reform Muslim Personal Law so that it be more friendly to women.[18]

In the current era, as in preceding phases of rapid change, networks remain pivotal yet ambivalent. The war that inaugurated the twenty-first century was the U.S.-led attack on the Taliban in Afghanistan. The Bush the Younger administration marked terrorism as, above all, Muslim inspired, even while proclaiming that Islam itself was not to blame, just certain Muslims. Many news groups have referred to al-Qa'ida – the guerrilla organization linked to the Saudi dissident Osama bin Laden and co-founded by the Egyptian doctor Ayman al-Zawahiri – as a terrorist network. It is terrorist because it intends to destroy Western, specifically American, targets wherever it can find them. And it is a network precisely because it is structured around nodes that communicate with one another in non-linear space, relying on neither a hierarchical chain of command nor conventional rules of engagement. Al-Qa'ida might be best defined as a coalition of dispersed network nodes intent on waging asymmetrical warfare. Like Colombian and Mexican drug cartels, they feature small, nimble, and dispersed units capable of penetrating and disrupting, with the intent to destroy, massive structures. Often they elude pursuit and evade capture, although in the case of al-Qa'ida, its operatives kill themselves, or are killed by others, in each nodal attack on a fixed target or group.

While the case of al-Qa'ida has become compelling in the aftermath of 11 September 2001, there is another case that demonstrates the long-term organizational power of modern day Islamic networking. The women of Afghanistan became a subject of intense scrutiny after the U.S.-led invasion in October 2001. Much media footage was devoted to the oppression of veiled, secluded, and often brutalized Afghan women, yet decades before 11 September 2001 a network of Afghan women had mobilized, and also projected themselves, their history and their cause, via the Internet. R.A.W.A., or Revolutionary Association of the Women of Afghanistan, predated the Internet. It was founded in 1977, even before the Soviet invasion, and it worked to defeat the Soviets but also to provide help for Afghani refugees in Pakistan. It was a network of transnational cooperation and multitiered resistance throughout the 1980s and 90s; its pivotal role on behalf of Afghan women has been dramatized through cyberspace.[19] R.A.W.A., even more than al-Qa'ida, demonstrates not just the persistence but the resilience of Muslim networks as a major form of social and political organization in the Information Age.

Muslim networks are no longer primarily male-dominated structures. They include women and others who resist oppression and who participate in horizontal alliances that project Muslim values of justice. Above all, they seek to build structures that are at once democratic and capitalist yet not coeval with Euro-American imperialism; and so, at one level, the cybernetic revolution has provided (and continues to provide) unprecedented opportunities for local and transnational community formation. Whether Muslims aggregate in virtual associations, such as cybermuslim chat groups, or actual networks, such as Women Living under Muslim Laws, they project a common pattern of fragmentation, dispersal, and reaggregation. In this era of mass migration when violence and economic necessity have forced many to travel, diasporic Muslims are split from their birth communities. They are compelled to negotiate multiple speaking positions as they imagine and project national identities. Nationalism today, though geographically fragmented, is socially networked through language and systems of meaning which allow participants to share cultural practices and experiences. People are able to diversify their participation in various communities to reflect shared interests rather than shared place or shared ancestry. They may also form contingent virtual communities to respond to emergencies at the collective and individual levels, as well as to provide companionship, social support, and a sense of belonging.

Yet the Information Age does not provide a silver bullet or a foolproof juridical tool for enacting democracy. It remains an age defined by media, whether print (newspapers), auditory (the radio and telephone), auditory–visual (television and movies), or print–auditory–visual–tactile (the World Wide Web). There could be no World Wide Web without antecedent technological breakthroughs, yet it represents the culmination of a process the further consequences of which no one yet knows. Muslims, while they did not create the World Wide Web, have been among its beneficiaries, but mostly in those nodes of the global capitalist community where Muslims work and live and pray either in their own cosmopolitan centers or as part of the demographic pluralism of Western Europe, North America, and South/Southeast Asia. The impact of these networks has been examined in a spate of scholarly works.[20]

While some have predicted a cyberutopia, imagining that the World Wide Web can fulfill the promises left on the table by development theorists from the 1960s, differences in virtual space are proving to be as durable and multiple as ground-level disparities within the *umma*.[21] Not only will there be a limited number of Muslims who have access to the World Wide Web but those who do become Muslim netizens will find many competing notions of Islamic loyalty and options for ritual practice. It will also continue to matter where one resides: in Malaysia or Turkey the government is less prone to monitor or to filter websites than in Saudi Arabia or Syria, and while hacking can take place as easily within a cyber Islamic environment as elsewhere, it will occur more often in border zones of actual conflict, such as Palestine and Kashmir. Because information technologies, like religious traditions, are inherently conservative, they tend to reinforce global structures and asymmetries rather than to bode a new era for civil society and transformative justice. Diasporic Muslims, precisely because they live in Western Europe or North America, will benefit from the Information Technology Revolution more than their homeland co-religionists. The disparity between North and South, between rich and poor will be as evident, alas, among Muslims as it is among non-Muslims, at least for the foreseeable future.

ISLAM AND POST-MODERNISM

Like modernity and colonialism and also the Information Revolution, post-modernism is neither an aesthetic movement nor a phase in intellectual history that derived from Islamic thought or applies only to

Muslim societies. Post-modernism is arguably an elitist enterprise with little consequence for the masses of either advanced democratic societies or their opposites in Afro-Asia.

Yet post-modernism is omnipresent within the academy, so much so that one prominent social scientist could not imagine a scenario that augured "the return to hegemonic status of the modern approach to the social sciences and the complete elimination of the post-modern."[22] Over fifteen years later, that judgment seems to be upheld. Both social sciences and the humanities continue to debate truth, finality, authority – the hallmarks of modernism that are confronted, analyzed and refuted by post-modernist thinkers. Even though much of post-modern inquiry has emerged within the humanities – from literary theory, political critique, and philosophical analysis – social scientists have been challenged to find better evidence and more subtle arguments for their knowledge production, focused as it remains on systems, structures, coherence, and reason. The Internet Age, not foreseen by the early post-modernists, has reinforced the arguments that they advanced: that all truth is representational, that all language is fractile, imperfect, and incomplete, and that all claims to authority are unstable, assailable, and reversible.

How can the post-modern relativist perspective emboldening narcissism and projecting apocalypticism be reconciled within an Islamic worldview? With difficulty, and yet such efforts are notable, as much for their own reflection of the diversity within Islamic discourse as for their location along the spectrum of post-modernist analysis. One approach is to diagnose post-modernism as itself but an extension of modernism, and so a movement with specifically Western origins, which applies to the subjects and trajectories of Western Europe or North American societies but not to the Muslims of Africa and Asia or to their non-Muslim citizen/neighbors. This approach has been branded, expanded, and propounded by Ziauddin Sardar, one of the most prolific cultural critics in the diasporic Muslim community of Britain. Challenging the core judgment that post-modernism is liberatory and promotes pluralism, Sardar argues that post-modernism effectively promotes further marginalization of those already marginalized by coloniality and modernity. In sum, it is a form of intellectual hegemony, mirroring even as it claims to correct the earlier excesses of Western domination over the colonized regions of Africa and Asia. Sardar expresses himself as a Muslim intellectual, but a Muslim intellectual in sympathy with non-Muslim Asian others. Sardar, while critical of Islamic excesses,[23] also sees a non-Western cultural alliance, above all, in art, which avoids the ills and evils of Western utopianism (a.k.a. modernism or dystopianism [a.k.a. post-modernism]). He titles his most comprehensive riposte to the insidious West *Postmodernism and the Other: The New Imperialism of Western Culture*. In it he also offers a strategy for surviving post-modernism, especially through art, including Chinese paintings imitating Mughal miniatures. "What we witness in these paintings," observes Sardar, "is a thriving, dynamic culture ready to confront the problems of modernity and the nihilism of postmodernism: these parameters, as the paintings illustrate so breathtakingly, are common to both Islamic and Chinese traditions, *and by corollary to all non-western traditions.*"[24]

As the italics which I added to the above citation make evident, this approach is not only a survival strategy but an attempt to build alliances along a cultural fault-line demarcated as West/non-West. In other words, the Grand Narrative of Western universalism is replaced by a Binary Narrative of East/West or non-West/West, with echoes of the familiar elements of modernism to build structures, traits, and attitudes that define and so homogenize large-scale collectivities. Sardar rejects post-modernism with passionate insight yet his own method encodes a post-post-modernism that harks back to the antecedent dualisms of modernism.

On a practical level, the opposition to the West as a moral custodian of universal values is also challenged by other Muslims within a post-post-modern framework. Notable among them is the Malaysian activist Chandra Muzaffar. Like Sardar, he is a prolific writer, and like Sardar, he speaks as a Muslim but on behalf of all Asians, non-Muslims together with Muslims, who reject the new World Order. In 1992 Muzaffar established the Just World Trust, an N.G.O. with the goal of challenging Frances Fukuyama and all other West-first advocates of global capitalism in the shadow (as also under the influence) of the G9 or major industrialized economies. It was through Just World Trust that he published his most scathing critique of the linchpin of universalist ethics, human rights. *Human Rights and the New World Order* makes the argument that because a minority in the North, that is, the advanced capitalist economies, controls and dominates global politics, its leaders, independently but also through the United Nations, have narrowed the meaning of human rights. They have restricted human rights to individual civil and political rights, ignoring other rights – social, cultural, and economic – that affect the majority of humankind, above all in Asia and Africa.[25] Ancillary to this project is the distortion and demonization of Islam through images of Islam and Muslims that are projected through contemporary media, global politics, and cultural wars. The strategy of Just and its numerous supporters is to produce an alternate form of knowledge that empowers individuals through revealing the distortions of dominant structures and offering the South another vision of the future.

That vision has been mapped in an edited volume that brackets fourteen major Muslim voices under the rubric *Progressive Muslims*. The editor is Omid Safi, an Iranian–American historian of religion, who tackles the themes of social justice, gender parity, and robust pluralism with ample critique of existing Islamic practices but also hope for another, better way forward for the collective body of Muslims, the *umma*. The final essay amounts to a manifesto from Farish Noor, one of Muzaffar's colleagues in Just and, like him, a Malaysian activist. What is needed, pleads Noor, is "rejection of a dialectical approach to the Other" to be replaced with "a new chain of equivalences that equates universal concerns with Muslim concerns and universal problems with Muslim problems."[26]

If that vista is to take shape and prevail, it also needs theoretical support, and nowhere is that support provided with greater clarity and detail than in Ebrahim Moosa's essay, also in the Safi volume. Moosa, a South African activist turned critical thinker and ethicist, charts a way into post-modernism that acknowledges indebtedness to European thinkers such as Kant, Weber, and Habermas, but uses as itself a lens through which to revisit and reconsider modernism, not just modernism but Muslim modernism. He asks the crucial question that comes from a post-modernist perch: "Was modernism Islam's redeemer, nemesis, or perhaps a bit of both?" And then he answers his own question:

> What we do know is that some of the key figures of Muslim modernism, like Sir Sayyid Ahmad Khan, Shibli Nu'mani, and Muhammad Iqbal all from India, Muhammad Abduh, Rashid Rida, Ali Abd al-Raziq in Egypt as well as important figures in Turkey, Iran and elsewhere in the Muslim world, were tremendously impressed by both the ideals and realities of modernity. They truly believed that Muslim thought as they imagined it from its medieval incarnation had an almost natural tryst with modernity. Modernity and "Islam" were not mortal enemies, but rather, as many of them had suggested, Islam itself anticipated modernity.[27]

Moosa goes on to elaborate how modern-day Muslims, like their modernist predecessors, can embrace innovation, openness, and pluralism as legitimate, natural dimensions of Muslim tradition or "orthodoxy." Reason and rationality are not the opposite of faith but its other face.

A further trajectory of the post-modern, post-Enlightenment, post-colonial Muslim mindset is post-patriarchal, opposing not just male-dominated structures but also the language of a male god, Allah. The Islamic feminist Amina Wadud, while opting not to create "a new female-centered goddess tradition post-Islam," does wrestle with what she terms patriarchal interpretation. She also confronts the boundaries defining Muslim woman, apart from "personal or public insider aspects of identification," that is, Muslims who claim or project others as "authentic" Muslims because of their names, origins, or locations. She herself does not attempt to speak on behalf of the whole *umma*, or even in terms of a trajectory that sees West/non-West as ambiguous, and perhaps inherently conflictual, entities. Instead, she positions herself as one who imagines "such a thing as a post-Muslim" in order to raise the visibility of Muslim women scholars within Western academic circles and institutions.[28]

There will be post- post-modern Muslims and perhaps even some post-Muslims, yet all will locate themselves within the debates about modernity highlighted above. Some will project their views in print, others on the Internet, and increasingly through blogs. Muslims – like other cybernauts – have arrived on the dizzying, ever-changing platform of virtual space mediated through the World Wide Web. It is not the final stage of Muslim modernism, just the most recent.

14

PRAYER*

Shawkat M. Toorawa

INTRODUCTION

Unlike the word "prayer" in English – which can mean a reverent petition made to a deity, or an act of communion with it, such as in devotion, confession, praise, or thanksgiving – there is no single, equivalent term for "prayer" in the Islamic lexicon. The terms *'ibada*, "worship," and its plural, *'ibadat*, "acts of worship," do encompass different kinds of prayer, but both are understood very broadly indeed. Thus, any licit act – marriage, for example – is regarded as a form of *'ibada*, that is, as a way to worship God.

This is not to say that Islam has no practices and devotions that can be described as prayer. Constance Padwick identifies almost all of the numerous kinds of prayer practiced by Muslims in "Type-Names for Devotions," the opening chapter of her wide-ranging study of prayer manuals in common use. I lightly rearrange the order in which Padwick lists these types – regarding *'ibada* as a general or umbrella term, and clustering the remaining terms into the three main categories into which scholarship has tended to subdivide prayer in Islam, namely *dhikr*, *du'a*, and *salat* (called *namaz* in many parts of the Muslim world):

'ibada, "devotion"
salat, "prayer-rite," *sujud*, "prostration"

* I am grateful to Jamal J. Elias for occasioning this essay, for his invaluable comments and feedback, and for his *limitless* patience; to Bhai Abdul Sakoor Khadun for input; to Zaahira Ebramjee for technical help; and to Ustad, for prayers.

du'a, "supplication," *munajat*, "confidential converse," *su'l*, "petition," *tadarru'*, "humble supplication"
dhikr, "recollection and making mention," *wird*, *hizb*, *hirz*, "devotional exercise," *wazifa*, "daily office," *ratib*, "fixed office"

I retain Padwick's fine translations of these Arabic (and Qur'anic) terms above, but there is no agreement on the English rendering of these. *Dhikr*, "remembrance" or "mystical recollection," describes the measured repetition of pious expressions of praise, or of the attributes (or "names") of God. *Du'a*, "supplication," describes all forms of petition and request. And *salat*, the term most often rendered by the English "prayer" or "prayers" *tout court*, refers quite specifically to a prescribed set of ritual movements accompanied by a set of ritual recitations.

It is entirely appropriate to think of the different kinds of prayer in Islam formally, that is, based on the form that each prayer takes, thus pious-*remembrance* (*dhikr*), *ritual* prayer (*salat*), and *supplication* (*du'a*). But I should like to propose a more heuristically useful set of categories: Prayer of Affirmation, Prayer of Submission, and Prayer of Petition, subdivided as follows:

Prayer of Affirmation

Testimony of faith
Recitation of the Qur'an
Adoration of God
Glorification or praise of God
Call to prayer
Praise of the Prophet Muhammad or of other religious figures

Prayer of Submission

Prostration
Ritual prayer

Prayer of Petition

For forgiveness, mercy, blessing and favor, worldly success, intercession, heaven, protection

PRAYERS OF AFFIRMATION

Testimony of faith (shahada)

Shahada (literally testimony, witnessing) is the name given to the statement "I bear witness that there is no deity other than God and I bear witness that Muhammad is His servant and messenger," the fundamental doctrinal statement in Islam, affirming God's oneness (*tawhid*) in the first part, and affirming Muhammad's paramount importance in the second. All Muslims must utter this statement at least once, and most utter it repeatedly, especially within the ritual prayer. The "testimony of faith" is often invoked at liminal moments: converts pronounce it when they accept Islam; it is whispered in the ears of newborns; it is recited to those on their death-bed; and many Muslims recite it upon waking so that they will instinctively also do so when they are roused in the grave on Judgment Day.

Recitation of the Qur'an (qira'a)

By virtue of the fact that one may not ritually or liturgically recite the Qur'an without being in a state of ritual purity (with certain specific exceptions), I am inclined to regard *qira'a* as a prayer of affirmation. What is more, most prayers (and much of the ritual prayer) are textually Qur'anic in substance. As A. A. Roest Crollius has observed, "there is perhaps no Scripture that is so totally a Book of Prayer as is the Qur'an." Gerhard Böwering has concurred, suggesting that this is so not only because the Qur'an "contains various prescriptions and descriptions of prayer and includes a great number of prayers, hymns and invocations, but more importantly because it reflects a religious experience of prayer rooted in the heart of the Prophet and reiterated by the tongues of his followers throughout the ages as God's own speech in matchless Arabic."[1] William Graham gets to the heart of the matter when he points out that "chanting the Qur'an is a re-enactment of the revelatory act itself, and how the Qur'an is vocally rendered not only matters, but matters ultimately."[2] The importance of recitation in Arabic cannot be overstated and is nowhere clearer than in its obligatory use in virtually all forms of prayer. The exception is prayers of personal petition, where Arabic may occur in the repetition of liturgical material, e.g. invocations contained in the Qur'an or those used by others

(Muhammad or pious predecessors), but where otherwise the use of one's native language is both widespread and encouraged (as it is personal conversation with God).

Reciting the Qur'an is not an obligation per se, but Muhammad constantly reminded his followers of the importance of doing so, even as little as a phrase. What is more, memorization of the entire Qur'an is popularly claimed to vouchsafe paradise for the memorizer (*hafiz*), his or her parents and ten other individuals of the *hafiz*'s choosing.

The first chapter of the Qur'an, *Al-Fatiha* ("The Opening"), reads:

> ¹*In the Name of God, Ever Compassionate, Full of Compassion,* ²Praise to the Lord of all Creation, ³Ever Compassionate, Full of Compassion, ⁴Sovereign of The Day of Determination: ⁵You alone do we worship, and from You alone do we seek alleviation. ⁶Guide us on the path of True Direction, ⁷The path of those you favor, not of those who earn Your wrath, nor of those in deviation.

This brief chapter is a fundamental and ubiquitous Islamic prayer and has consequently been likened to the Lord's Prayer in Christianity. Not only is it recited in every unit (or *rak'a*, literally "bowing") of the ritual prayer and in numerous other ritual contexts, notably at the graveside, but it also contains within it several key prayer elements. One such element is the *basmala*, the opening Qur'anic verse, "In the Name of God, Ever Compassionate, Full of Compassion," which appears as the prelude to 112 of the Qur'an's remaining 113 chapters, and which is to be pronounced before any activity. Other elements include praise of God in the second verse, and the supplication in the final two verses.

Adoration of God

Literally "reminder" or "mention," *dhikr* is the term used to describe the repetition of set phrases praising God, in compliance with God's injunction "O you who believe! Remember God with much remembrance" (Q33:41) and God's request and promise, "Remember Me, and I shall remember you" (Q2:152). A simple form of *dhikr* has found its way into the liturgical lives of almost all observant Muslims, namely the repeating after the ritual prayer (and at other times too) of the phrases "God's glory be proclaimed (*subhan Allah*)" and "To God is due all praise (*al-hamdu li'llah*)" thirty-three times each, and thirty-four times "God is most great (*Allahu akbar*)," expressions described by the Prophet Muhammad as "The phrases most dear to Almighty God" (together with "There is no deity other than God [*la ilaha ill'Allah*]"). Indeed, the remembrance of God through any form of repetition has come to be thought of as *dhikr*, though in Islamic mystical (or Sufi) practice this almost always involves sustained (and often group) recitation. For private remembrance, worshipers use a rosary, called a *tasbih* or *misbaha* (literally "instrument of glorification/adoration").

One form of Sufi *dhikr* involves repetition of the phrase *La ilaha ill'Allahu* ("There is no god except God"), which gradually gets reduced to *ill'Allahu* ("except God"), then *Allahu*, and culminating in the recitation of the exhaled sound *hu*, the very last (fully vocalized) syllable of the word *Allahu*, which means "He." *Dhikr* is an integral part of Sufi practice. Although the specific formulas may differ from one Sufi group to another, they often comprise the repetition of God's attributes, the two most popular ones being "The Compassionate (Al-Rahman)" and "Full of Compassion (Al-Rahim)," which appear in the opening verse of *Al-Fatiha*. Other "names" commonly used in pious repetition include "The Powerful," "The Loving," and "The Majestic." This is in compliance with God's wish that He be addressed using "His beautiful names" (Q20:8). Repeating specific "names" a given number of times is said to have a spiritually uplifting, curative, or transformative effect.

Glorification of God (takbir), *Praise of God* (hamd), *Call to prayer* (adhan)

The *takbir*, or the formula "God is most great (*Allahu akbar*)" is a pervasive "prayer of affirmation:" it initiates the ritual prayer; it is ritually recited on the eve of Islam's two high holidays; and it is the phrase recited at times of triumph (from the playing field to the battle-field), at times of success and on the hearing of good news. It also opens the "call to prayer" (*adhan*), the text of which is as follows:

> God is most great! [twice]. I bear witness that there is no deity other than God [twice]; I bear witness that Muhammad is the messenger of God [twice]. Come to prayer! [twice]. Come to success! [twice]. God is most great. There is no deity other than God.[3]

The call to prayer – now routinely also broadcast over television and radio, as well as on personal computers, mobile phones, and alarm clocks – marks the diurnal prayer times and signals to worshipers that the next ritual prayer is due and should now be performed. The call to prayer, though not a prayer per se, also invites worshipers to the preeminent place of congregation, namely the mosque from which the *adhan* is issued. The call has acquired powerful liturgical value and is believed to function as a prophylactic against malevolence; on the basis of a popular *hadith*, it is recited in the right ear of every child born in a Muslim household, and is often also recited when one occupies a new home. In many cultures, after the completion of the *adhan*, it is repeated by those hearing it, who also then recite the following supplication:

> God, Lord of this perfect call and this performed prayer, grant our master, Muhammad, blessed intercession and give him the hallowed status which You promised You would grant – You never dishonor a promise.

Praise of Muhammad (and other figures)

The word *salawat* (a plural of *salat*, on which more below) occurs twice in the Qur'an, and has come to refer principally to the act of wishing (or "calling down" of) blessings (or "prayers") and peace on the Prophet Muhammad. This pious act is specifically enjoined in the Qur'an as follows:

> Verily, God and His angels send/call down blessings/prayers on the Prophet. O you who believe, you (too) send/call down blessings on him, and salutations/peace as well. (Q33:56)

The believer responds by saying "God, send blessings on Muhammad and the family of Muhammad, and salutations and favor." This is also the origin of the widespread practice of repeating the phrase "May God send His blessings and salutations on him" after saying, hearing, or writing the Prophet Muhammad's name. This is often incorrectly rendered "peace be upon him" (and abbreviated "pbuh" in print), an expression reserved for use after the names of all *other* prophets as well as archangels. Some Shi'is also use "peace be upon him" after the name of Muhammad's son-in-law, companion, and successor, 'Ali, an indication of the importance they accord him; Sunnis use "May God be pleased with him/her" for 'Ali and all other companions of Muhammad, though even they sometimes distinguish 'Ali with the phrase "May God ennoble his face." The pronouncing of such phrases is considered praiseworthy and said to earn God's pleasure and reward.

Sending blessings/prayers and salutations/peace (*salawat*) on Muhammad is a fundamental concept and practice in Islam. It is enjoined in the Qur'an, according to which God, himself, engages in the practice; it is also pronounced as part of the ritual prayer and often precedes and follows *dhikr* exercises. There is a *hadith* that if a worshiper wishes a supplication to God (*du'a*) to be fulfilled, that supplication should be preceded by the ritual utterance of the *salawat*. The benefits and virtues of this prayer are not lost on many Muslims – one acccordingly finds the *salawat* mentioned at the beginning of numerous books by pious Muslim.

PRAYERS OF SUBMISSION

Prostration

"Islam" literally means "submission," understood as submission to (the will of) God. The emblematic act of submission is the act of prostration (*sajda* or *sujud*) and is exemplified in the story of Adam's creation. After creating the first human, God asks the host of angels to bow to Adam and they do so, acknowledging God's authority. The fate of Satan (mentioned here by his proper name, Iblis), who refuses to bow (Q17:61) – maintaining that as a creature made of fire, he is superior to Adam, made of mere earth – is proof of the very high cost of disobedience. What is more, his refusal is described as a function of his arrogance. The prostration that is so characteristic of Muslim ritual worship is, therefore, an act of humility, an act of submission, and also an act that echoes a signal moment in the history of creation. Some people develop a dark mark on their foreheads, which is regarded as a sign of great piety, since it signifies a lifetime spent in prayer (of which prostration is an integral part).

The prostration occurs on three principal occasions: (1) in repeating sets of two during every unit of ritual prayer; (2) at fourteen designated points in the Qur'an when one is reciting the text ritually; and (3) voluntarily during sincere supplication. Significantly, prostrations are prohibited at the moment the sun is crossing the horizon at sunrise and sunset and when the sun is at its zenith, most probably because of a desire to avoid any possible conflation of Islam with the worship of the sun.

Ritual prayer (salat *or* namaz)

Muslims credit the prescription, and especially the number, of the daily ritual prayers to an exchange that took place between God and Muhammad during the latter's ascension to heaven (*mi'raj*) in 621 C.E. One respected *hadith* account reads:

> He [God] then made obligatory for me [Muhammad] fifty prayers every night and day. I began my descent until I reached Moses who asked me: "What has your Lord made obligatory for your community?" "Fifty prayers," I replied, to which he said, "Return to your Lord and ask Him to reduce them: your community will not be able to bear that" [...] I kept going between my Lord and Moses until God said, "O Muhammad, there are five prayers every night and day. Each prayer is equal to ten prayers making them equal to fifty prayers."

It is important to keep in mind that just as the Hajj pilgrimage is Abrahamic in origin but an imitation of Muhammad's pilgrimage rituals in its specifics, so too is ritual prayer extra-Muhammad in origin, but an imitation of Muhammad's own ritual prayer in its specifics, down to every last detail. The specifics are thus not to be found in the Qur'an, but in the *sunna*, the practice of Muhammad, following whose example in not only an act of reverence but also adherence to the Qur'anic injunctions to obey God and His Prophet (Q8:46).

Scholars have pointed out that the early seventh century also provides a context for the prescription of ritual prayer, notably the three daily prayers of Rabbinical Judaism, the four obligatory prayers of Manichaeism, the five of Mazdaism, and the seven offices of Byzantine Christianity. Certainly, ritual prayer is not a new feature of worship for the Qur'an, which attests such in times past, e.g. those of Noah, Abraham, and Israel (Q19:58). There are two significant features of the use of the word *salat* in the Qur'an, where it appears sixty-five times: first, it occurs overwhelmingly in the *sura*s that, in all likelihood, date from 620 C.E. onward, that is, from a time when ritual prayer became a defining and underpinning feature of Islam; and second, in a third of all instances, *zakat* (purification by giving away part of one's wealth) is mentioned together with *salat*. This "purification" of the soul is matched by the ritual purification that is essential before a ritual prayer can be performed.

The importance of the ritual prayer is enshrined in Muhammad's statement that "Islam is built on five [pillars]: bearing witness that there is only one God and that Muhammad is His Prophet; performing the ritual prayer; giving alms from one's accumulated wealth; fasting the month of Ramadan; and performing the Hajj if and when able." In theory, a Muslim need only bear witness once (though it is repeated many times in ritual prayer), or perform Hajj once, if at all. And a Muslim may not have sufficient wealth to give alms; or he or she may be unable to fast (atoning with a "payment" of food to the needy). But every Muslim must perform ritual prayers, every day, until death. Even if the worshiper is unwell or infirm, the obligation remains and only God, in infinite mercy, can forgive this debt. On Judgment Day, ritual prayer (having been properly performed) is said to bear witness to a Muslim's submission to God's will, each daily prayer advocating for the worshiper.

The ritual prayers are organized according to a hierarchy of obligation as follows:

Obligatory

(Required by God of all Muslims)   *Fard*

Non-obligatory

Prescribed (emulating Muhammad's regular practice)   *Wajib*
Exemplary (emulating Muhammad's occasional practice) *Sunna*
Voluntary (optional, supererogatory, by personal decision) *Nafl*

The Obligatory ritual prayer is incumbent on all mentally sound Muslims having reached the age of discernment (variously held as being seven or ten years old); for one school of law, willful abandonment of prayer constitutes an act of unbelief, for the others, it is a sin. Muhammad is reported to have warned that "The only thing that separates a person from polytheism and unbelief is the abandonment of ritual prayer." Missing an obligatory ritual prayer incurs a debt, which one can (and must) discharge by fulfilling it at a later time. Performing any of the non-obligatory prayers earns God's pleasure and reward. Naturally, there are numerous states of affair that may prevent or impair one from performing the ritual prayers, but provisions are made for all these conditions. For instance, travel involving a significant distance (the actual distance varies across schools of law) results in the ritual prayers' fixed number of units being reduced.

Typology

The *salat* is a relatively short but elaborate prayer ritual. Detailed descriptions are widely available in everything from books of jurisprudence and children's instructional material, to prayer-manuals and informational pamphlets produced by individuals for private distribution. In Western scholarly literature, three descriptions stand out;[4] I should like to break down my own brief discussion of the ritual prayer in two ways, first, following these scholars, according to its constituent parts.

If one thinks of the categories of "Obligatory," "Prescribed," "Exemplary," and "Voluntary," that is, the terms used above to *categorize* ritual prayer by degree of obligation, one also has a typology for the various actions that *constitute* the ritual prayer. According to the Hanafi school of law, to cite just one of the four Sunni schools, the following are obligatory: (1) Commencing the prayer with an act of sacralization (*takbirat al-ihram*), namely standing facing Mecca, raising one's hands above one's shoulders to the level of one's ears and saying "God is most great!"; (2) "Standing" (*qiyam*) with the arms crossed, or with arms at the sides. *Qiyam* is, incidentally, also the name given to the communal standing at the Plain of 'Arafat on the outskirts of Mecca during the rites of the Hajj pilgrimage. That standing, and inevitably the standing in ritual prayer, presage *Yawm al-qiyama*, the Day of Standing (for Reckoning, equivalent to the Day of Resurrection); (3) Reciting (*qira'a*) "The Opening," from the first chapter of the Qur'an, followed in the first two prayer units (*rak'as*) of the obligatory prayer (and in all *rak'as* of non-obligatory prayers) by another Qur'anic passage of the individual's choosing; (4) "Bowing" (*ruku'* – also the word used for "paragraph" divisions in the Qur'an), by bending at the waist, hands on knees, with one's back parallel to the ground, and then reciting "Glory to my Lord, the great one!" The worshiper then straightens up, saying "God hears the one who praises Him" (the only instance of not using "God is most great" to change posture), and then "To you, Lord, is due all praise"; (5) Prostration (*sujud*), in pairs; (6) "Sitting" (*qa'da*) in every second (and concluding) *rak'a*, palms on knees, and reciting the "Affirmation of faith" and "Salutation," as follows:

> To God, salutations, worship and sanctity. Peace, and also God's mercy and blessings, upon you, O Prophet. And peace upon us, and upon the righteous servants of God. I affirm that there is not god but God, and I affirm that Muhammad is His servant and Messenger.

The last sentence is accompanied by a raising of the finger in physical affirmation of God's oneness. The worshiper then rises and performs subsequent *rak'as*, identical to the first in every way except for the selection of a different Qur'anic passage after "The Opening."

In every final unit of a ritual prayer, a *salawat*, or calling down of blessing, follows, together with an optional prayer of supplication. The ritual prayer then concludes with the worshiper turning the head to the right and left, uttering the greeting, "Peace on you, and also the mercy and blessings of God," said to be addressed to the two recording angels "located" to one's right and left, recording all one's good and bad deeds, respectively. Certain parts of the ritual prayers may only be recited *sotto voce*, others may, under certain circumstances, be recited aloud.

I should now like to break down ritual prayer according to two broad principles that, it seems to me, govern its performance, namely State and Orientation.

State   There is state of body and state of mind. State of body encompasses purity and clothing. Islamic law requires that certain parts of the body be obligatorily covered, and that other parts be covered out of modesty and in emulation of Muhammad's practice. Thus, men must minimally cover from navel to knees, and ideally also cover their torsos and heads. Coverage for women is more extensive and, in ritual prayer, must include the hair. Prayer is preceded by a ritual purification (as distinct from a physical one) that may be performed symbolically if no water is available. Its purpose is not to get physically clean but rather to enter a *state* of purity.

State of mind refers to the fact that all ritual prayer must be preceded by an articulated (though not necessarily voiced) statement of intention (*niyya*). The role of intent is critical: Muhammad is reported to have said, "Actions are (assessed) by their intentions." Also of critical importance is adopting the proper attitude of awe for God and humility in the divine presence (*khushu'*). An incorrectly performed action can be remedied (with a corrective prostration, or by repeating the ritual prayer), but one's intention, sincerity, and devotion cannot be postured.

Orientation   can be subdivided into time and number, place, direction, and nature (solitary or communal).

Time and Number Ritual prayers are performed at specific times, in particular, the five obligatory prayers. These are listed below together with the number of mandatory prayer units (*rak'as*) in each:

Pre-dawn (*Fajr*)	2 *rak'as*
Post-zenith (*Zuhr*)	4 *rak'as*
Mid- to late afternoon (*'Asr*)	4 *rak'as*
Post-sunset (*Maghrib*)	3 *rak'as*
Night-time (*'Isha*)	4 *rak'as*

The names for the five ritual prayers derive from the Qur'an; the times at which they are performed are similar to times mentioned in the Qur'an, but ultimately they derive from the personal practice of Muhammad (*sunna*). Mention should also be made of a prayer called *Tahajjud*, performed in the middle of the night, preferably after having slept and awakened, and sometimes valued (but not prescribed) as the sixth daily prayer. Prayer times are not only discernible from the sun's position over the course of a day and obvious from the call to prayer, but they also are published in print and online by mosques and Muslim associations. Their presence in Islamic societies is so pervasive and Muslim life is so conditioned by these prayer times that individuals (even ritually non-observant ones) will frequently schedule meetings by saying, for example, "Come over after 'Asr."

Certain ritual prayers are performed at specific times in the weekly or yearly calendar and differ in significant ways from the five obligatory daily prayers. A prescribed prayer called *Tarawih* is performed communally during the month of Ramadan, and the communally obligatory funeral rite (*Janaza*) is performed entirely in the standing position. Attested, but not widely performed, are prayers in times of fear (*Khawf*); for rain in times of drought (*Istisqa*); during eclipses (*Kusuf*), and so on. There are also many specific voluntary ritual prayers, such as the "Prayer of Thanks" or the "Prayer for the Preservation of One's Faith." The most important weekly ritual prayer is the Friday communal one, and the most important yearly ones are those performed on the feast days.

Place Monnot has observed that "Muslim [ritual] prayer owes its exceptional importance to the constant link which it establish[es] between the faithful individual and the three supreme realities of his religious universe: the Community, the Prophet and God."[5] The Community, or *umma*, is not simply those who bear witness, but also those who gather together, optimally five times daily, every Friday and twice yearly on the Feast days, for communal prayer. *Salat al-jum'a*, the Friday prayer, is mentioned once in the Qur'an: "O you who believe! When proclamation is made for prayer on the day of assembly, hasten to remembrance of God, and leave [your] trading" (Q62:9). It is only required of men, stands in for the daily *Zuhr* prayer, and can only be prayed in a mosque or designated site. Because it is intended to bring the community together, this prayer has resulted in the construction and use of *Jami'* (Congregational) mosques, which, as a rule, are significantly larger than neighborhood mosques. Some of the world's most famous mosques are *Jami's*, for example the Jami' Masjid in Delhi, India, or the Great Mosque of Djenne, Mali.

The Friday prayer is different from other ritual prayers in that it includes a two-part ritual-sermon, or *khutba*, delivered either wholly in Arabic or partly in Arabic and partly in the local language. In this respect, the Friday prayer resembles the *Salat al-'Idayn*, the ritual prayers performed on Eid al-Fitr after the end of Ramadan (The Feast of Fast-breaking), and Eid al-Adha at the culmination of the Hajj-pilgrimage (the Feast of Sacrifice).

The ritual prayer may be performed anywhere that is free from ritual impurity. This possibility of performing the ritual prayer in any clean place follows the practice of Muhammad, to whom is credited the statement "The earth has been made for me (and for my follow-ers) a place for praying, and (earth) a substance with which to perform *Tayammum* (dry ablution), therefore anyone of my followers can pray wherever the time of a prayer is due."[6]

A "place of prostration" in Arabic is a *masjid*, which has entered English via Spanish as "mosque," technically a building endowed in perpetuity for the specific purpose of "prostration" (i.e. ritual prayer). A place so designated only temporarily is called "a place of prayer," *musalla* (with other names in other languages, e.g. *surau* in Malay). Related to *masjid* is the word *sajjada* ("[place of] habitual prostra-tion") which, together with *musalla* ("[thing] prayed upon") and *ja-ye namaz* ("place of prayer"), are among the commonest terms for a "prayer mat" or "prayer rug."

One sometimes notices worshipers move a few feet away from their specific place of prostration to perform other ritual prayers. This practice is said to be desirable because on the Day of Reckoning the spot where a worshipper has prostrated will speak up on that worshiper's behalf.

Direction When performing the ritual prayer, Muslims must obligatorily face the *qibla*, that is, face "the sacred mosque" in Mecca as enjoined in Q2:142–150 (and elsewhere). Indeed, the surest sign of the institutionalization of the ritual prayer is the changing of the direction, or cosmic orientation, of prayer. There is some scholarly disagreement about the direction Muslims faced before the injunction to face Mecca (which can be fairly precisely dated to early in the year 624 C.E.), but the Muslim consensus is that it was Jerusalem, deemed then, as now, one of the three "sacred precincts" (the other two are Mecca and Medina). Muslims are also buried with their heads turned to the right, facing Mecca.

Nature One person (normatively male) takes the role of Imam, or leader of the communal or congregational ritual prayer. He must be of good reputation and education and is typically an older congregant, though a younger congregant's superior knowledge of the Qur'an makes him more qualified; thus, one often finds a teenage *hafiz* (someone who has memorized the Qur'an in its entirety) serving as Imam for a group that includes older, or more well-known, congregants. If there is one other male congregant, he stands next to the Imam, if one female congregant, she stands behind him. All face Mecca. If there are more congregants, they form rows behind the Imam. Worshipers pray in solitude even within a congregation, reciting in a hushed whisper. However, following Muhammad's example, Imams recite certain parts of the ritual prayer audibly, others inaudibly – or more correctly "neither loud nor in a whisper" as the Qur'an enjoins (Q17:110) – and congregants recite a reduced liturgy.

Parkin has suggested that since all words are not uttered by congregants in communal prayer, it may be that the "power" resides in the actions themselves.[7] All changes of position are audible, so that the congregation may know when to follow. Before the availability and widespread use of microphones, the person standing behind the Imam (and sometimes other designated "criers") would repeat the gesture-changing words loudly so that those in distant rows might hear.

Communal prayer was strongly enjoined by Muhammad: he is reported to have shown unhappiness with those who chose to pray ritually at home rather than come to the mosque, and also to have said that the virtue of the communal prayer is twenty-seven times greater than that of individual prayer.

PRAYERS OF SUPPLICATION

In Q40:60, God says "Supplicate to me, and I will surely respond." This phrase is always mentioned by the Friday sermon-giver as a reminder to congregants that, besides offering their ritual prayers to God, they must call upon God with any and all requests (*du'a*). The supplication is usually tendered with hands at shoulder level, palms face up, as if receiving God's mercy falling from above (like rain); at the conclusion of the supplication, the palms lightly wipe the face.

Supplications (*du'a*) can be thought of as falling into seven broad types of request: for forgiveness, for mercy, for blessing and favor, for worldly success, for intercession, for heaven, and for protection – in all cases not just for oneself but also for others.

Forgiveness and Mercy

Muslims are enjoined to ask God incessantly to forgive them any wrongdoings or trespasses. Muhammad reports that God said that even if the worshiper were to come to Him with sins equal to the weight of the earth but also with sincere repentance, God would respond with forgiveness in equal measure. A standard supplication for forgiveness and mercy (*istighfar*) reads:

> I seek the forgiveness of God Almighty, other than Whom there is no God, the Living, the Eternal, and I turn to him in repentance.

There are numerous other formulae, either derived from the Qur'an, or in emulation of Muhammad or pious figures. Among the many Qur'anic supplications are the so-called "Forty *Rabbanas*," that is, supplications that begin with the word *rabbana* ("O our Lord"). They follow the pattern of the following two popular examples:

> O our Lord, we have wronged ourselves and if You do not forgive us, and show us mercy, we shall indeed be among the lost. (Q7:23)

The second is a supplication on behalf of one's parents, and reads:

> My Lord, forgive them as they cherished me when I was young.
> (Q17:24)

Blessing and Favor

Besides asking for forgiveness, the worshiper is encouraged to ask for blessings and divine favor. Thus, when someone sneezes, that person says "All praise is due to God" and anyone hearing the person sneeze responds by saying, "May God bless you." Similarly, many Muslims rather than say "thank you" express gratitude to others using an Arabic formula meaning "May God reward you."

It is common practice in many parts of the Muslim world for Muslims to visit the elderly and the sick, and to visit saints (living or dead) to seek blessing. The supplications of the old and infirm are said to be heeded by God as are the supplications of those well loved by God.

Worldly Success

Muhammad is reported to have said that the following single supplication, for both success in this world and in the Hereafter, suffices the believer:

> Our Lord, give us good in this World, and good in the Afterlife, and protect us from the torment of the Fire. (Q2:201)

That the supplicant can ask for good in this world shows that asking for worldly things is acceptable. Indeed, Islam appears in no way to demonize or devalue success in this life, as long as it is not at the expense of success – and seeking success – in the afterlife. It is standard practice to supplicate and recite other prayers when undertaking a commercial venture, in the hope that God will grant worldly favor.

Intercession

This is the supplication to God asking for Muhammad to intercede on the believer's behalf, an intercession that God has promised as is evident from the call to prayer cited above. It is also supplication *to* Muhammad himself, and to other religious figures such as saints, where the grace (*baraka*) or station (*maqam*) of the figure, and not just the words of the supplicant, is relevant to the attainment of the desired result. Grace and station are acquired through God's love of esteemed religious figures, which is why these figures are referred to as "friends of God" (*wali*, pl. *awliya'*).

Some Muslims cannot accept that saints have any special access to God, averring that what distinguishes Islam from other religions is precisely the possibility of direct access. Parkin calls these Muslims "ontological dualists" because they hold that there is an unbridgeable ontological gap between humans and God; the mystics he calls "ontological monists," because they reinforce the ontological oneness with the Absolute, a state of affairs (and relations) that allows for intercession on the part of saints.

Protection

The Qur'an's two closing chapters are commonly recited by Muslims as a means of seeking protection:

"The Dawn" (Q113)
In the Name of God, Full of Compassion, Ever Compassionate
Repeat: I seek refuge in the Lord of the dawn, From the mischief of His Creation, And from the mischief of nightgloom when it blots, And from the mischief of sorceresses, spitting on knots, And from the mischief of the envier when he plots.

"Humanity" (Q114)
In the Name of God, Full of Compassion, Ever Compassionate
Repeat: I seek protection, with the Lord of Creation, King of Creation, God of Creation, From the malicious incantations, Of the Accursed, whispering insinuations, in the hearts of jinn and humanity both, fabrications.

As the above make clear, there is much from which to seek protection. For example, Muhammad counseled of the need to be careful of the evil eye, a force that is activated by excessive praise and excessive envy. Popular Muslim belief maintains a number of simple prayers that are traced to him and are recited and then blown on the afflicted individual (or animal, such as a hen no longer yielding eggs). Besides blowing a prayer on someone or into water that is then drunk by the individual in difficulty, religious figures also produce amulets for protection (*ta'widh*), typically worn around the neck.

* * *

Prayer is absolutely central in Islam. From birth, when the Muslim child is first made to hear the various pious formulae that comprise the call to prayer, to death, when the funeral prayer rites are performed in front of the shrouded body and when invocations are recited by supplicants for the well-being of the departed, a Muslim's whole life is permeated by prayer. Indeed, every twenty-four-hour day is divided into time periods in which the five obligatory ritual prayers are to be performed; and there are supplications for every possible situation and event (wearing a new item of clothing, on hearing a dog bark, on seeing the full moon, to ward off the evil eye, to begin one's fast, to increase one's learning, before setting off on a journey ...). Indeed, at practically every moment a Muslim has either just uttered or performed a prayer, or is about to do so. For Islam, there is no religion without prayer.[8]

15

PROPHECY

Devin Stewart

It is reported that the Prophet Muhammad had sent an envoy to a remote Arab tribe to spread the message of Islam. A skeptical member of the tribe did not take the envoy at his word, but traveled to meet the Prophet himself. When he arrived, he addressed the Prophet, "Oh Muhammad, your messenger came to us and claimed that you claim that God sent you."

"He spoke the truth," said the Prophet.
The tribesman asked, "Who created the sky?"
"God," replied the Prophet.
"Then who created the Earth?"
"God."
"Then who created these mountains?"
"God."
"Then who created all the good and useful things in the world?"
"God."
"Your messenger claimed that we must pray five times in the course of a day and night."
"He spoke the truth."
"Then by Him who sent you, did God command you to impose this obligation?"
"Yes."
"Your messenger also claimed that we must pay an alms tax on our property."
"He spoke the truth."
"Then by Him who sent you, did God command you to impose this obligation?"
"Yes."

"Your messenger also claimed that we must fast one month out of the year."

"He spoke the truth."

"Then by Him who sent you, did God command you to impose this obligation?"

"Yes."

"Your messenger also claimed that we must perform the pilgrimage to the House [the Ka'ba in Mecca], whoever is able to make the journey."

"He spoke the truth."

"Then by Him who sent you, did God command you to impose this obligation?"

"Yes."

"Then I swear by Him who sent you, I will do neither more nor less than these."

When he had departed, the Prophet remarked, "If he spoke the truth, then he will certainly enter Paradise."[1]

This exchange emphasizes several prominent features of the Islamic view of prophecy. Reference to the Prophet Muhammad's own envoy brings into relief the idea that a prophet is simply and exactly that, an envoy sent by God to deliver a message on His behalf. An important part of this message is a set of laws or religious obligations that form the core of monotheistic worship. These obligations or acts of worship are service owed to God in exchange for the blessings He has bestowed on humankind, especially Creation and Providence. The human communities of the world have an inherent obligation to thank their benefactor, and prophets are sent to remind them of this obligation and instruct them in the ways they are supposed to do this. In addition, verifying the authenticity of a particular prophetic mission is a relatively straightforward matter for its audience.

Prophecy is a central concept in Islamic sacred history and is rooted in the Qur'an and the mission of the Prophet Muhammad, though the theology of prophecy and the figure of the Prophet Muhammad have been embellished in many ways since the early Islamic period. The central function of prophets is to convey God's will to humankind and thereby make clear the path to salvation and, while doing so, to establish and maintain rules for proper societal organization and moral behavior. Since true prophets all represent God, their messages are similar in substance, stressing humankind's debt to and dependence on the Creator, the obligation to worship God alone, and the judgment based on one's deeds in this world. In addition, one understands from the many examples that occur in the Qur'an that a prophet's interactions with his audience follow a regular pattern, a function of God's customary way of treating humankind (*sunnat Allah*) and the regularities of human nature and human societies.

PROPHECY IN THE QUR'AN

Several terms are used to refer to prophets in the Qur'an. The term *nabi*, "prophet," which occurs about seventy-five times, is cognate with the Hebrew *nevi* and may be an indication of connections with biblical tradition. The more frequent use of the plural *nabiyyun/nabiyyin* – paralleling the Hebrew *nevi'im* – rather than the more natural plural *anbiya'* may also reflect the close connection of the Qur'an with biblical texts. The most frequent terms for "prophet" in the Qur'an, however, are *rasul* ("messenger, apostle,") and its cognate *mursal* (one who has been sent): the first appears about 300 times and the latter 30. The centrality of the term *rasul* may be related to use of the term "apostle" (e.g. Syriac *shelih*) in the Christian tradition in particular. The distinction between *rasul* and *nabi* in the Qur'an has been stressed in Islamic tradition. *Nabi* is the more general term that applies to all prophets, while *rasul* refers to a special category of prophets who convey new religious dispensations or sets of laws with distinct moral emphases as well as new sacred texts to humankind (Q22:52). An angel may serve as a messenger of God but a prophet can only be a mortal (Q17:95; 22:75; 35:1). That a *rasul* ranks higher than a *nabi* is indicated by the fact that *rasul* regularly comes first when the terms occur as a pair. Other common terms for prophets – *nadhir*, "warner," and *mubashshir*, "conveyor of glad tidings" – refer to specific aspects of their role as conveyors of divine messages, announcing either the impending threat of damnation or the promise of an idyllic afterlife in the gardens of paradise. In later Islamic texts and usage, both *al-rasul* ("the Messenger") and *al-nabi* ("the Prophet") become synonymous with Muhammad.

The prophets receive divine messages in order to convey them to their peoples. The mode of revelation or contact with the divine may occur in a number of ways. Moses is held up as the only prophet to whom God spoke directly, from the Burning Bush; he is therefore termed *al-kalim* ("the One to whom God spoke"). References to revelation in the Qur'an include the noun "revelation" (*wahy*) (Q53:4) as well as the verbs "to reveal" (*awha*, Q4:163, etc.), "to cast" (*alqa*, Q40:15), "to give, send, provide" (*ata*, Q2:87), and "to inspire" (*alhama*, Q91:8). Prophets also see visions, or dreams (*ru'ya*), including Abraham's sacrifice (Q37:105) and Muhammad's vision of entering Mecca safely (Q48:27). Satan can also cast false revelations by whispering (*waswasa*, Q7:21; 20:120). Prophets are distinguished from soothsayers (*kahin*, pl. *kuhhan*) and madmen or those possessed by demons (*majnun, majanin*) (Q52:29; 69:41–42; 81:22). Imposter prophets are also denounced (Q6:93). Angels may serve as messengers of God (Q16:2; 35:1; 22:75) – the unnamed being the Prophet saw in two early revelatory experiences (Q53:1–18) has been identified in the tradition with the angel Gabriel.

The revelation includes the Qur'an itself, or verses, *sura*s, passages, or messages held to be consituent parts of the Qur'an. The verbs used to describe this type of revelation are *anzala* ("to send down"), which implies a single act of sending down an integral text, and *nazzala*, also "to send down," but implying a repetitive process involving many distinct acts of sending down smaller sections of the whole (Q20:4; 26:192; 33:2). This also applies to other sacred texts in the biblical tradition; the Torah and Gospel are also described as having been sent down (Q3:3–4). The Qur'an states that Gabriel or the Qur'an itself was sent to Muhammad on "a blessed night" (Q44:3), "on the Night of Power" (*laylat al-qadr*, Q97:1), or during the month of Ramadan (Q2:185). Commentaries have endeavored to explain these verses, which appear to contradict many other passages that portray the piecemeal revelation of the Qur'anic text, by positing two revelations – the first, gradual, over time, and piecemeal, and the second, at a point near the end of the Prophet's mission, abrupt and complete.

The Qur'an stresses that each nation will receive its own prophet (Q10:47; 16:36). These historical ethnic or linguistic communities are described in various ways in the Qur'an, as "generations" (*qarn*, pl. *qurun*, Q6:6; 10:13; 11:116, etc.) or "towns" (*qarya*, pl. *qura*, Q6:123; 7:4, 94; 10:98; 15:4, etc.). The basic equivalence of the Prophet Muhammad's mission with earlier prophetic missions and his audience with earlier prophetic audiences is stressed by reference to Mecca as "your town" (*qaryatuka*, Q43:13), one of "the two towns" (*al-qaryatan*, Q43:31), or the greatest of the towns (*umm al-qura*, literally "the mother of the towns," Q6:92; 42:7). The career of the typical prophet follows a predictable pattern that is most observable in passages of the Qur'an that have been termed "punishment stories." God chooses the prophet. The verb used to describe this election varies: "to elect" (*ijtaba*, Q20:122; 12:6), "to choose" (*ikhtara*, Q44:32), "to favour" (*istana'a*, Q20:13), and "select for special favour" (*istafa*, Q2:130; 3:33; 7:144; 22:75). Generally, a prophet is sent to his own people on the grounds that they should be predisposed to trust him, knowing that he would not willingly lead them astray. For this reason, prophets sent to tribal societies, such as Salih – the prophet sent to Thamud – and Hud – the prophet of 'Ad – are described as "brothers" of their people (Q26:106,161). They should also be able to understand God's message, as every apostle is sent using his people's own language (*lisan* Q14:4). The prophet then addresses his people, delivering God's message, which, at its most fundamental, is the obligation to worship God and no other, since all other deities are powerless inventions of humankind's imagination, and to believe in judgment and the afterlife. While a tiny group of believers heeds the message, the vast majority of his people rejects his message and ignores it. The only exception to this rule in the Qur'an is the people of Jonah; they are touted as the only people in sacred history who were actually swayed by their prophet (Q10:98). In all other cases, though, the prophet then reiterates his plea, warning his people that if they do not accept monotheism and give up their old ways they will be punished. They insist on rejecting belief, and in some cases taunt, threaten, or attack the prophet, calling him a magician, poet, soothsayer, or requesting that he cause an angel or a sacred text to appear (Q52:29; 69:41–42; 81:22). Imposters are denounced (Q6:93). In some cases, earlier peoples, particularly the Israelites, killed their prophets (Q2:61,87,91; 3:21,112; 5:70). Abraham's people tried to kill him by burning him, but he was miraculously protected (Q29:24). Similarly, a group among Thamud plotted to attack Salih's house at night and kill him, but were annihilated by God first (Q27:49–51). Because of their intransigence, their fate is sealed: God annihilates the unbelieving peoples, saving only the tiny group of believers and the prophet himself.

The total number of prophets in Islamic views of salvific history is a matter of speculation and dispute. The Qur'anic statement that every people receives a prophet who speaks their own tongue perhaps implies a very large, if not unlimited, number. The Qur'an includes several lists of prophets (e.g. Q6:83–86), and commentators commonly identify twenty-five prophets who are mentioned in the Qur'an by name: Adam, Idris, Noah, Hud, Salih, Lot, Abraham, Ishmael, Isaac, Jacob, Joseph, Shu'ayb, Job, Dhu al-Kifl (perhaps Ezekiel), Moses, Aaron, David, Solomon, Elias, Elisha, Jonah, Zachariah, John the Baptist, Jesus, and Muhammad. However, the text points to the existence of many more prophets who are not mentioned and of whom the Prophet Muhammad remains unaware:

> Verily We sent messengers before thee, among them those of whom We have told thee, and some of whom We have not told thee; and it was not given to any messenger that he should bring a portent save by God's leave, but when God's commandment cometh (the cause) is judged aright, and the followers of vanity will then be lost. (Q40:7)

In his ninth-century collection of Hadith, the *Musnad*, Ahmad Ibn Hanbal cites one report to the effect that God has sent 124,000 prophets to the world; of these, 315 were messengers.[2] The number of apostles or messengers is also given as 313, the number of combatants in the Muslims' force at the Battle of Badr. The Gospel of Barnabas, widely held to be an Islamic or Islamicizing forgery, states that there have been 144,000 prophets (book 17).

The prophetic career is a controlling feature of the Qur'an. In order for the pattern to hold with such regularity, the stories of earlier holy figures are molded to fit it. For example, figures from biblical history who are not presented there as prophets become prophets in the Qur'an and take on a mission. Noah in the Bible is merely an exception, a good man among the evil, but in the Qur'an he is sent as a warner to his people and preaches to them against polytheism. Similarly, Lot is presented as a prophet to his people. Jesus as well is presented as a prophet to his people, the Sons of Israel, here synonymous with the Jews. In order to fit the pattern, though, Jesus' story must be changed radically from that presented in the Gospels. The Qur'an accepts that he was born without the intervention of a mortal father but stresses that his miracles were all performed by leave of God. He cannot be killed, however, even though this was the intent of some of his people, for God is obligated to save Jesus and his devout followers, the disciples. The Qur'an solves this problem by stating that "it was made to look to them" as if Jesus died on the cross, suggesting that it did not happen, but that God raised up Jesus to himself before the crucifixion while replacing Jesus with a double (Q4:157). According to the prophetic pattern, too, Jesus' people, the Jews, should be destroyed. As this did not happen historically, the Qur'an rhetorically replaces annihilation with having to suffer the domination of Jesus' followers, the Christians, until the end of time (Q3:55–56). Similar modifications must have occurred in the Qur'anic stories of the extra-biblical prophets Hud (sent to the people of 'Ad), Salih (sent to the people of Thamud), and Shu'ayb (sent to the people of Midian), all of which follow the pattern of punishment stories very closely. These stories derive from pre-Islamic pagan mythical lore, and it is prob-able that the protagonists were not originally preachers of biblical monotheism. In the Qur'an, though, they are completely assimilated to biblical history and may have been subjected to radical changes.

The pattern of prophets' interaction with their peoples is recur-rent in history, and forms a cycle or series of historical missions as God successively sends prophets as guides to new peoples. While the Qur'an does not provide an absolute chronology for these events of sacred history, the texts certainly evince a relative chronology of missions to the world, evident both in lists of prophets that appear in the Qur'an and in series of punishment stories arranged in chronologi-cal sequence. Noah was sent to Noah's people, then Hud to 'Ad, then Salih to Thamud, then Lot to Sodom and Gomorrah, then Shu'ayb to Midian, then Moses to Pharaoh, and then Jesus to the Israelites. God's historical interactions with the world's peoples through this series of prophetic missions is visible to later observers because they have left signs for later peoples and generations. Noah's Ark remains as a testament to the destruction of the flood. The great ruined monuments of earlier civilizations, such as 'Ad's Temple of Iram with its impres-sive columns, the buildings of Thamud carved into the rock of valley walls, and the pyramids of Pharaoh stand as a reminder not only of former greatness but also of the overweening pride of earlier peoples who did not heed their prophets, did not show their gratitude to the one God who gave them tremendous gifts in the world, and were anni-hilated as a result (Q89).

Readers of the Qur'an are often frustrated by expectations cre-ated by familiarity with the Bible, with which, as is evident, it is inti-mately connected. Specifically, they do not find an account of the foundation of the Islamic community told as a historical narrative, in the manner of the early books of the Hebrew Bible, nor do they find an account about the life and mission of the Prophet, presented as a hagiography, in the manner of the Gospels. Rather, the Qur'an differs radically from those forms in that it is not arranged chronologically at all, being a collection of disparate texts, including short rhyming prayers, charms, retorts, and omens alongside longer sermons and narratives. However, the Qur'an does tell the story of the Prophet's mission and the story of the nascent Islamic community indirectly, through typology. Earlier prophets are discussed in the text not merely as historical figures but as models for the Prophet Muhammad; their acts and experiences are directly relevant to his. Thus, when the text refers to Hud and Salih as "brothers" of their people, stressing their membership by lineage in the tribal societies to which they belonged, one draws a parallel – even though it is unstated – with the Prophet Muhammad, who is a member of the tribe of Quraysh, related by blood to the community to whom he is preaching. When Salih is accused of being a madman or blamed for being a mere mortal, the text must be alluding to similar reactions to the Prophet Muhammad on the part of the Quraysh. In some cases, the comparison is explicit: Q66 explicitly compares the wives of Noah and Lot with the wives of Muhammad in order to make the point that being married to a prophet is not a guarantee of salvation; one must behave properly in order to be saved. In Q54, explicit parallels are drawn between those in the Prophet's audience who reject his message and the peoples of earlier prophets – the people of Noah, 'Ad, Thamud, the people of Lot, and Pharaoh and the Egyptians – who rejected their messages.

Though this view of recurring similar prophecies is dominant and pervasive in the Qur'an, it runs into two problems, one having to do with the special status of the family of Abraham or the Israelites, and the other having to do with the special status of the Prophet Muhammad. Unlike other peoples such as 'Ad or Thamud, who are understood to have received one prophet – and one prophet per people seems to be the rule – the Israelites have received many prophets, including Abraham, Isaac, Jacob, Moses, and others, including Jesus. This is a great deal of divine and prophetic attention for one historical people, and is apparently based on the primary importance of this genealogical line in biblical history. The Qur'an suggests, in addition, that it is due to their obstinacy and incalcitrance. As mentioned, the Israelites or Jews are blamed for rejecting and also for killing the prophets (plural) who have been sent to them. The second contrasting view is the idea that the Prophet Muhammad, unlike others, was sent as a universal prophet to transcend ethnic boundaries, and not only as a messenger to his people. The Qur'an states that he was sent to humankind (Q4:179) and to all generations or peoples of the world (*li'l-'alamin*, Q21:107). In keeping with this idea, the Prophet is described as *khatam al-nabiyyin* "the Seal of the Prophets" (Q33:40). Other frequently cited verses state that "Religion with God is Islam" (Q3:19) and "This day I have perfected your religion for you and completed my favor to you" (Q5:3). These are both taken to mean that Islam is the final version of the monotheistic religion that God has imposed on humankind, with the implication that there will be no more prophets after the Prophet Muhammad and that his message and Islam are intended for all.

Abraham is one of the most prominent prophets in the Qur'an. He stands out because of his association with (proto-)Islam, an uncorrupted form of biblical monotheism that preceded the foundations of Judaism and Christianity, and because of his association with the Ka'ba, the shrine at Mecca that was revealed during the Prophet Muhammad's mission as a temple originally dedicated to the one God but that had since been corrupted by polytheist Arabs and converted into a site of pilgrimage and worship of many (false) gods. Drawing on Jewish extra-biblical texts, the Qur'an portrays Abraham's rebellion against his society, who worship the planets and idols, including his father Azar, a sculptor of idols, and denouncing polytheism. He smashes the idols in his father's workshop and, when reprimanded, asks why the idols themselves did not prevent him from destroying them, if they were so powerful (Q2:258–260; 6:74; 9:114; 19:46; 21:60–69; 60:4). In this aspect, his story resembles in outline that of other prophets who preach to their communities to worship God alone and to reject polytheism.

Abraham also has a major significance in the Qur'an as a foundational figure on a par with Moses and Jesus. While on the one hand the Qur'an presents Islam as a continuation or confirming sequel to the earlier divine dispensations of Judaism and Christianity, on the other hand it also portrays Islam as a return to an original, uncorrupted form of biblical monotheism. The Qur'an suggests that, while both Jews and Christians claim Abraham as their own, he cannot have been either a Jew or a Christian, presumably on the logic that Judaism was established by the mission of Moses and the revelation of the Torah, while Christianity was established by the mission of Jesus and the revelation of the Gospel, and these historical events all post-date Abraham. The Muslims are presented as those who follow the teachings of Abraham most closely and are therefore most deserving of association with his legacy (Q3:65–68). The term the Qur'an uses for Abraham in this context is *hanif*, which, though etymologically related to Syriac *hanpa* "heretic," is contrasted in the Qur'an with "polytheist" (*mushrik*) and denotes a pre-Judaic monotheist. This religion, termed *millat Ibrahim* ("the community of Abraham" or perhaps "the way of Abraham"), is described in the Qur'an as proto-Islam. Islam is therefore the direct continuation of Abraham's religion, the primordial biblical monotheism, avoiding the historical corruptions that occurred in the Jewish and Christian traditions (Q2:130,135; 3:95; 4:125; 6:161; 16:121,123).

According to Islamic tradition, Abraham, like Moses and Jesus, was thus the founder of a major religious tradition. In keeping with this special status, the Qur'an refers to a sacred text termed "the Scrolls of Abraham" (Q87:19). He is also the central figure in the narrative behind Islam's major Holy Day, the Feast of the Sacrifice (Eid al-Adha), which takes place on the tenth of Dhu'l-Hijjah, the twelfth month in the Islamic calendar, and is parallel with Jewish Passover and Christian Easter. This sacrifice, representing Abraham's sacrifice in place of his son, is connected with the rituals of the pilgrimage to Mecca, a pre-Islamic pilgrimage that was reinterpreted as a biblical rite in the course of the Prophet Muhammad's mission. The Ka'ba (literally "the Cube"), the aforementioned rectangular building at Mecca that served as a shrine for many Arabian gods and annually witnessed the arrival of pilgrims from throughout the Arabian Peninsula, was originally a biblical temple devoted to the one God, and was subsequently corrupted. According to the Qur'an, it was built by Abraham and his son Ishmael, and the Islamic movement now had to restore the shrine to its former status, cleansing it of idols and devoting it to the worship of the one God. As the founder of proto-Islam, Abraham is connected closely with the Prophet Muhammad, and Abraham was the name of Muhammad's son (who did not survive past infancy) by his wife Mary the Copt. Abraham appears prominently in most versions of the legend of the Prophet Muhammad's Night Journey and Ascension to Heaven (*al-isra' wa'l-mi'raj*), along with Moses and Jesus; the Prophet meets with him either in Jerusalem or in the sixth or seventh heaven, and in several versions of the legend Muhammad refers to Abraham as his father. A number of *hadith* reports stress the close physical resemblance between Muhammad and Abraham; he is reported to have stated, "I saw Abraham; I look like his son."[3]

Moses also deserves special mention as the archetypical prophet; he is mentioned by name more frequently than any other character in the Qur'an and consequently can be considered the Qur'an's hero. This is so not just because the story of Moses, Pharaoh, and the exodus is fascinating, but because, perhaps more than any other single prophet, Moses serves as a model for Muhammad. Both were orphans, after a fashion. Both received a scripture. Both faced the tyrants of their native community. Both led the believers out of their land to safety in a new land. Both were prophets and political leaders of their followers. Both dealt with resistance, disobedience, and unruliness among their followers. It is this comparison, I believe, that is behind the choice of the term *hijra* for the flight of the Prophet from his native town, Mecca, to Medina (then called Yathrib) in 622, which became the beginning of the Islamic calendar. *Hijra* does not mean "migration" but rather "exodus." It refers explicitly to the biblical exodus of the Hebrews from Egypt, suggesting that Muhammad is the equivalent of Moses, the chiefs of Quraysh are the equivalents of Pharaoh and his courtiers, and the Muslims are the equivalent of the Hebrews. They are called *muhajirun* or "immigrants" on the grounds that they are the believers who made the exodus.

The prophets serve the same main function and are equivalent in a basic sense, but some have unique traits that distinguish them from other prophets. It is stressed that the true believer accepts all of them as true messengers of God and does not recognize some but not others (Q4:152; 2:136; 2:285; 3:84; 4:150–152). Q17:55 recognizes that some prophets are superior in status to others and singles out the Psalms of David as a mark of special favor granted by God to him and not to other prophets. Q2:253 reports that God favored Jesus in particular by granting him clear proofs (*bayyinat*), a reference to his miracles, and supporting him with the Holy Spirit.

Prophets often perform signs or miracles, or find their missions accompanied by such signs. The function of miracles is to indicate the authenticity and supernatural origin of the prophet's mission, assuring the audience that he is not inventing the message or speaking of his own accord, but rather conveying divine messages. These miracles serve as clear proofs (*bayyinat*) that increase the prophets' ability to persuade their peoples. The archetypical prophetic miracles in the Qur'an are the biblical signs that occur in the story of Moses and Pharaoh: the transformation of Moses' staff into a serpent and his hand turning white (Q7:106–109; 20:65–70; 26:30–33,43–48;

28:36). They prove to the audience the authenticity of his mission and the undeniable power of God.

The Qur'an insists, however, that the ability to perform miracles does not indicate that the prophet is divine, a point stressed especially in connection with the miracles of Jesus, the prophetic figure associated with the largest number of miracles in the Qur'an: speaking as an infant, curing the lepers, making the blind see, raising the dead, fashioning a live bird out of clay, and so on (Q3:46,48–49; 4:17; 19:29–33). Prophets are mere mortals (Q14:11) and can only produce signs through God's leave (Q40:78). In some cases, they produce signs at the request of their audiences, as when the prophet Salih produces a (giant) she-camel for the people of Thamud (Q7:73; 11:69; 17:59; 26:155; 54:27; 91:13), or when Jesus' disciples ask that the Lord produce a banquet for them – the Qur'anic version of the Last Supper – so that they can be more confident about the truth of Jesus' mission (Q5:112–115).

Some prophets' missions involve the revelation of a sacred text and, as noted above, these prophets are also termed messengers. The category of scripture or sacred text, termed simply *kitab* ("book") in the Qur'an, is not limited to the Qur'an itself (Q12:2; 13:37) but includes several other sacred texts, all of them in the biblical tradition: the Scrolls of Abraham (Q87:19), the Torah, delivered to Moses (Q5:44), the Psalms, delivered to David (Q4:163; 17:55), and the Gospel, delivered to Jesus (Q5:46). These holy books form a historical series, each confirming the previous scriptures. The Qur'an denounces those who only believe in some of the scripture but reject other parts (Q2:85). The Qur'an itself differs from these other scriptures in that, when it was in the process of being revealed, it did not have a physical existence as a complete scroll or codex. The complete Qur'an, it appears, was a repository that had an ethereal existence from which individual revelations derived. This repository in the supernatural realm is referred to as "the Mother of the Book" (*umm al-kitab*, Q3:7; 13:39; 43:4) or "the preserved tablet" (*al-lawh al-mahfuz*, Q85:22), the latter suggesting a comparison with the tablets Moses received from God at Mount Sinai (Q7:145–154).

In several passages, the Qur'an alludes to the prediction of the Prophet Muhammad's mission in the Bible. Q7:157 reads, "Those who follow the Messenger, the gentile Prophet, whom they find described in their Scriptures, in the Torah and the Gospel" (Q7:157). Exegetes then examined the text of the Bible for predictions that fit this description and found two main passages. In Deuteronomy 18:17–19, Moses refers to a prophet to come in the future:

> And the Lord said unto me: They have well spoken that which they have spoken, I will raise them up a prophet from among their brethren like unto thee, and will put my words in his mouth; and he shall speak unto them all that I shall command him. And it shall come to pass, that whosoever will not hearken unto my words which he shall speak in my name, I will require it of him.

Muslim commentators have argued that this text refers to Muhammad. Jesus is portrayed in another verse as predicting Muhammad's mission, giving the specific name Ahmad, which is cognate with Muhammad:

> And when Jesus son of Mary said: O Children of Israel! I am the messenger of God to you, confirming that which was before me in the Torah, and bringing good tidings of a messenger who will come after me, whose name is the Most Praiseworthy (Ahmad). Yet when he comes to them with clear proofs, they will say: This is mere magic. (Q61:6)

Exegetes claim that Jesus' prediction of the advent of a prophet named Ahmad in Q61:6 refers to a section of the Gospel of John where Jesus describes an important figure who will come in the future, after his departure from the world, and in some sense assume Jesus' role. The figure is not termed a prophet, but rather is described using the odd term Paraclete. Jesus states, "And I will pray to the Father, and he shall give you another Paraclete, that he may abide with you forever" (John 14:6), and "Nevertheless I tell you the truth; it is expedient for you that I go away: for if I go not away, the Paraclete will not come unto you; but if I depart, I will send him unto you" (John 16:7). The term has most often been translated by Christians as "counselor, helper, comforter," and taken to refer to the Holy Spirit, while Muslims have claimed that Ahmad is in fact the appropriate translation of Paraclete, and that it thus refers unambiguously to Muhammad.

In a move that is typical of religious discourse, the Qur'an claims authority for prophets in general and the Prophet Muhammad in particular by denying such claims to authority, just as one identifies the Messiah as the one who denies that he is actually the Messiah. A number of passages stress that the Prophet Muhammad and other prophets are merely mortal messengers (Q6:91; 14:10–11; 23:24,33; 26:154; 41:6), and their only obligation is to deliver the message. On the other hand, the command to obey God is often yoked with the command to obey the Messenger as well. The phrases "Obey God and His Messenger," "Obey God and the Messenger," or "Obey God, and obey the Messenger" occur eleven times in the Qur'an (Q3:32,132; 4:59; 5:92; 8:1,20,46; 24:54; 47:33; 58:13; 64:12). The *Sura of the Poets* includes a series of stories of prophets of the past in which each prophet addresses his people, "I am a trustworthy messenger to you, so fear God, and obey me" – a rather straightforward claim to authority. Jesus makes a similar statement in other *suras* (Q3:50; 43:63), as does Noah (Q71:3). Given the all-encompassing power and control attributed to God, to link a command to fear God with the command to obey the prophet is a very strong statement about the prophet's position of authority among the people he is sent to address, something which seems at odds with the statement that the task of the messenger is simply to deliver the message. The people are obligated to follow the dictates of the prophet, on the logic that he is delivering God's wishes. He is therefore in a position similar to that of the ruler of the community, or at least should be if his people are paying attention to his messages.

As mentioned above, prophets deliver religious law, a set of rules and regulations regarding correct worship and general conduct. Though the most common term for the sacred law of Islam is now *al-shari'a* or *al-shar'*, the Qur'anic term for the religious dispensation of law, conceived of as a set of rules for devotion, is *din*, which is often translated as "religion" or "faith." The Qur'an implies that this worship is the same for all prophets: "He has ordained for you that religion which He commended to Noah, and that which We inspired in thee (Muhammad) and that which We commended to Abraham, Moses, and Jesus, saying: Establish the religion, and be not divided therein ..." (Q42:13).

A crucial function of the prophet is to act as a judge who settles disputes in his community. The Qur'an stresses that one can only judge properly by following the dictates of scripture. One passage remarks on the situation of Jews who asked the Prophet to settle a dispute among them, suggesting that the Torah is the correct source for solving such disputes:

> How do they make thee an arbiter when they have the Torah, which contains God's judgment? Yet even after that they turn away ... We revealed the Torah, wherein is guidance and a light by which the

prophets who surrendered (to God) judged the Jews. The rabbis and priests judged by such of God's Scripture as they were bidden to observe, and they were witnesses to it ... In it We prescribed for them: Life for life, eye for eye, nose for nose, ear for ear, tooth for tooth, and retaliation for wounds ... (Q5:43–45)

These verses make it clear that the Scripture imposes a law – here the *lex talionis* – and that it contains the information necessary for proper judgment. It identifies prophets prominently as judges over their people, followed by rabbis and priests, and it makes clear that judgment is community specific: Jews should be judged by the dictates of the Torah, Christians by the Gospel, and Muslims by the Qur'an. Thus while the monotheistic religion of the prophets is the same in its essentials, the Qur'an recognizes that the laws of each religious community differ, in accordance with their specific scripture.

HADITH AND EMULATION OF THE PROPHET

The Prophet Muhammad is held up as deserving of emulation even in his mundane activities. The Qur'anic verse accepted as a prooftext for this practice is the following: "Verily in the Messenger of God you have an excellent example for him who looks to God and the Last day, and remembers God much" (Q33:21). Hadith, a body of literature made up of reports about the deeds and sayings of the Prophet, serves as a repository of information about how the Prophet ate, dressed, prayed, conversed, solved disputes, conducted business, treated his wives, daughters, and neighbors – in short, how he conducted the affairs of daily life. His customary behavior in such manners came to be designated as his "way" or *sunna*, and Muslims of all walks of life took it upon themselves to follow his *sunna* whenever this was possible. To this day, some Muslims around the world clean their teeth with the *siwak* or *miswak*, a type of twig that the Prophet used as a toothbrush. Men crop their mustaches and let their beards grow long in emulation of the Prophet's reported practice. Six compiled works of Hadith came to be considered canonical by Sunni Muslims, and from the ninth century on, it was generally accepted that the Hadith as a corpus had the status of scripture and could serve as the basis for the establishment of legal or theological doctrine.

A related but more specialized genre is that of "Prophetic Medicine" (*al-tibb al-nabawi*), which compiled for general readers reports on remedies for common ailments and diseases that the Prophet Muhammad used himself and the medical advice he gave to others. For example, when he had a headache or migraine, he recommended applying henna to the head, staying indoors for a day or two, or wrapping the head in a bandage. The Prophet reportedly forbade people to eat dates when they were suffering from ophthalmia – inflamation of the eyes – and told them to avoid touching the afflicted eye. Ibn Masud reports that when suffering from inflammation the Prophet used to pour cold water in his eye and pray, "Lord of mankind, expel this evil and cure me, O You Who are the Healer. There is no healing save Yours, a healing which does not leave any illness."[4]

PROPHECY IN ISLAMIC THEOLOGY, PHILOSOPHY, AND MYSTICISM

Prophecy is one of the major categories of Islamic theology, along with God's uniqueness, His attributes, free will, the status of grave sinners, and so on. Theological discussions of prophecy often pick up on and elaborate themes evident in the Qur'an, but in some cases add significant ideas not found in the sacred text. A major concern of the theologians was to establish the authenticity of the Prophet's mission against Jewish and Christian detractors who claimed that Muhammad could not in fact have been a genuine prophet in the biblical tradition. Muslim theologians expended considerable effort first to demonstrate the possibility of prophetic missions and second to marshall evidence that the Prophet Muhammad was indeed sent by God. The main argument they put forward, drawing on the Qur'an at least in part, was that prophets' missions are verified by divine miracles that accompany them. The miracles associated with Moses' mission are well known, as are the miracles performed by Jesus. The main miracle adduced as proof of the Prophet Muhammad's mission is the Qur'an itself. Building on Qur'anic verses that challenge the audience to produce a revelation similar to the Qur'an, theologians argued that the Qur'an is a miraculous text that cannot have been produced by human effort. Its miraculous nature (*i'jaz*) was seen to lie in three main aspects of the text: its rhetorical excellence, its reporting of past events (such as conversations that Noah had with his people) that could only have been known to Muhammad through a supernatural source, and its prediction of future events (such as the victory of the Byzantines predicted in Q30:1–6). Both theological and literary analyses came to stress the rhetorical superiority of the Qur'an significantly more than the other two categories, so that this became a fundamental Islamic doctrine about the Qur'an. Other miracles are adduced as well but do not assume the role that *i'jaz al-Qur'an* does. These include the splitting of the moon mentioned in Q54:1, said to have occurred to remove doubts from the Prophet's audience. Animals and inanimate objects were said to have spoken to the Prophet, and on one occasion water sprang forth from his fingers – the list goes on.[5]

One tactic used to dissociate the Prophet from earlier biblical tradition, despite the obvious connections, was to stress that he was illiterate; for if this were true, then he could not have had direct access to the texts of the biblical tradition and borrowed from them for his own messages, but could only have received his revelations from a supernatural source. A number of scholars have argued from the text of the Qur'an itself that the term taken to designate Muhammad as illiterate, *ummi* (Q7:157,158) actually means "gentile," in this case, someone who is neither Jewish nor Christian. This interpretation is supported by indications that the Prophet was sent specifically to Mecca and the surrounding towns, that his main task was to denounce polytheism, and that Arabic was the distinctive language of his revelation. Nevertheless, the Islamic tradition has adopted the Prophet's illiteracy as a major doctrine, one of several that serve to highlight the distinctiveness of Islam and its superiority to Judaism and Christianity.[6] Another major concept that Islamic prophetology sets forth is that they are subject to divine protection (*'isma*). This protection serves two functions: protecting them from harm directed at them by their enemies and preventing them from committing major sins. Commentators connect the protection of prophets from danger with a verse that occurs in the story of Moses. While entrusting the prophetic mission to Moses, God instructs him to cast down his staff. It turns into a snake and Moses is frightened, but God reassures him, "O Moses, fear not! The Messengers (*al-mursalun*) fear not in My presence" (Q27:10). An example of the second type of protection is Q3:161, which states that prophets cannot act deceitfully. Another example occurs in the Joseph story, where the Qur'anic version reports that Joseph was smitten with his master's wife, and would have responded to her advances "had he not seen the proof of his Lord. Thus it was, that We might ward off from him evil and lewdness. He was one of our chosen slaves" (Q12:24). This divine protection, it is argued, is accorded to all prophets, including Muhammad. The problem with this theory is that the Qur'an itself provides evidence suggesting that some prophets were actually killed by the Israelites or the Jews and that several prophetic figures actually committed major sins. For example, Adam and Eve were guilty of disobedience to God by eating the forbidden fruit, and Moses killed a man. The theologians try to soften the effect of such evidence by explaining it away, arguing, for example, that Moses killed the man before his prophetic mission began. Similar arguments are made about the Prophet Muhammad – the Qur'anic text "He found thee astray and guided (thee)" (Q93:7) is said to refer to the days before he became a prophet. While it appeared to observers that Muhammad coveted Zaynab, the wife of his adopted son Zayd, and subsequently pressured him to divorce her so that he could marry her himself, the theologians claim that Zaynab rebelled against Zayd, leading to her divorce, and that she fell in love with the Prophet. The Prophet's actions served a higher purpose, therefore, announcing the abrogation of the pre-Islamic law that one could not marry the wives of adopted sons. "He frowned and turned away" (Q 80:1), which scolds the Prophet for behaving rudely to a man who interrupted him while he was speaking to others, is taken not as a reference to a major sin but merely a case where the Prophet omitted doing what was preferable (*tark al-awla*).[7]

Another question the theologians discuss is the status of prophets. Verse 4:69 lists the groups of people that will occupy the highest rank in paradise: "those to whom God has shown favor: prophets, saints, martyrs, and the righteous." The fact that prophets appear first suggests that their status is superior to that of the others. The Mu'tazilis and philosophers claimed that angels are superior to prophets, but most other theologians hold the opposite on the grounds that angels were required to bow down to Adam, that Adam and not they were taught the names of things, and that they (lacking free will) do not have to resist human emotions and desires, while prophets must overcome their human nature.[8]

Perhaps the most prominent theme in popular culture regarding prophetic theology is the ability of the Prophet to act as an intercessor. The Qur'an holds out the possibility of intercession subject to God's permission, asking in the Verse of the Throne, "who can intercede except by His leave? ..." (Q2:255). Many stories of dreams and near-death experiences suggest that love for the Prophet and devotion to him can get one into paradise when one's record of good deeds and sins would ordinarily not allow this. Many Islamic creeds stress that the believers will meet the Prophet when they are about to enter paradise and stop to drink at the Prophet's pool or basin. After drinking from the basin, they will never thirst again.[9]

Islamic philosophers sought to explain prophecy in terms that did not contradict the dictates of reason and also fit in with the Neoplatonic theories of emanation that they had adopted from the Greeks. Both Al-Farabi (d. 339/950) and Avicenna (d. 428/1037) assumed a universe controlled by the Active Intellect, essentially equivalent to God, through a series of subordinate spheres or levels. They both sought to explain religion in philosophical terms, convinced that religion, and prophecy in particular, should have a rational basis that could be revealed by philosophical inquiry. The problem they both faced was how to explain the prophets' immediate access to information from the Active Intellect, circumventing the ordinary and time-consuming process of rising up through the spheres or levels of existence. Al-Farabi suggests that a prophet is endowed with an unusually developed imaginative faculty that allows him to convey abstract truths in mundane and figurative terms that will be understood by his audience. He seems to argue, though, that the prophet must go through the rigorous rational training that is required of all true philosophers. Avicenna elaborates al-Farabi's scheme and modifies it. In his theory, a prophet is endowed with an exceptional intuition that allows him to forego ordinary rational inquiry and arrive instantaneously at a complete understanding of complex problems, in some fashion after the manner of a mathematical genius. He terms this particular faculty of the prophet a "sacred power" and describes the state his mind reaches thereby as "sacred intellect." The intellect prepared in this way is able to achieve direct contact with the Active Intellect and then relay the messages received to others in the form of prophetic messages.[10]

Islamic mysticism also adopted the Prophet Muhammad as a model, venerating him as the universal archetype of humanity, and suggesting that Muslim saints expressed his eternal essence. Ibn 'Arabi (d. 1240) used the term Muhammadan reality (*al-haqiqa al-Muhammadiyya*) to express the essence of the perfect human being. This essense is eternal, a sort of divine logos. 'Abd al-Karim al-Jili (d. 1402–3) and Muhammad ibn Sulayman al-Jazuli (d. 1465) modified Ibn 'Arabi's theory, using the terms "Muhammadan Form" (*al-sura al-Muhammadiyya*) and "Muhammadan Way" (*al-tariqa al-Muhammadiyya*), respectively. In their view, one saint in every age – the "pole" (*qutb*) – can achieve perfection. The perfected saint thereby becomes a veritable personification of the Messenger of God and inherits his authority. Muhammad is no more simply a historical prophet, or even the final prophet of God to humankind, but an essence that persists in every age in the person of a perfect saint.[11]

THE LIFE AND MIRACLES OF THE PROPHET

Particularly important for understanding the resonances of prophecy in Islamic culture is the *sira*, a label for exemplary biographies of the Prophet. Of the many popular works in this genre, the most important is the *Sira* of Ibn Hisham (d. 833), the earliest such work to have been preserved. Ibn Hisham draws on a yet earlier work that is only known from his edition, the *Sira* of Ibn Ishaq (d. 767). Ibn Hisham's *Sira* is equivalent to the Gospel of Islam, providing a detailed account of the birth of the Prophet Muhammad and his prophetic mission. It not only gives a detailed biography of the Prophet and an account of the history of the nascent Islamic community, but also stresses the idea that the Prophet came with all the signs of prophecy as predicted by the Jews, the Christians, and the pre-Islamic Arabian pagan soothsayers. In fact, the *Sira* opens with the prediction of the advent of the Prophet by two South Arabian soothsayers, Shiqq and Satih, who interpret his movement as the indigenous repulsion of a foreign invasion, in this case the Ethiopians' invasion of Yemen. This is corroborated by the interpretation of the *sura* of the Elephant, which describes a repelled attack on Mecca by an army with an elephant, and by the claim that the Prophet was born that very year. Like the Gospels, the *Sira* of Ibn Hisham pays a great deal of attention to the birth of the Prophet. A Jew states that the stars indicated that an Apostle was born. His mother, Amina, had a vision before he was born: she saw a light issue forth from her belly which illuminated the far-off castles of Busra, in southern Syria, an omen predicting the greatness of her son and the future expansion of Islam. Later, in his youth, Muhammad traveled to Busra with his uncle Abu Talib. They met a Christian monk there named Bahira, and he offered to make a meal for them. They left Muhammad behind to look after the baggage, but Bahira insisted that they all eat, including Muhammad. Sensing that the boy was special, he questioned Muhammad and found a mark, the seal of prophecy, between his shoulders. Also like the Gospel of Matthew, the *Sira* presents a genealogy of Muhammad at the beginning. It goes on to describe the Prophet's first revelations, his subsequent preaching, his flight from Mecca and his establishment of a community at Mecca, his conflicts with the Meccans, the expansion of Islam in the Arabian peninsula, and so on until the Prophet's conquest of Mecca, his Farewell Pilgrimage, and his death. The *Sira* is the most important historical source for the life of the Prophet, but it must be remembered that it answered a specific need, providing a narrative of the Prophet's life and mission that the Qur'an did not.

The most important Islamic legend concerning the Prophet Muhammad's mission is that of the Night Journey and the Ascension (*al-isra' wa'l-mi'raj*). According to the best known versions of this legend, the Prophet was taken one night on a miraculous journey from the Hijaz to Jerusalem (*al-isra'*) and from there ascended through the heavens (*al-mi'raj*) until he reached the divine presence. He traveled mounted on a legendary flying beast, named al-Buraq, said to have had the body of a horse and the head of a woman. The story is presented as an extensive commentary or extrapolation on the first verse of the seventeenth chapter of the Qur'an, Surat Bani Isra'il (also called *Surat al-Isra'* for this very reason): "Glorified be the One who sent His servant (Muhammad) on a journey during the night, from the Sacred Mosque to the Farthest Mosque, whose surroundings we have blessed, in order to show him some of our signs. He is the Hearer, the Seer." The term that appears in this verse as the starting point of this journey, *al-masjid al-haram*, "the Sacred Mosque, Sacred Place of Prostration," is taken to refer to the Sacred Precinct in Mecca, and the end point of the journey, *al-masjid al-aqsa*, "the Farthest Mosque, or Farthest Place of Prostration," is taken to refer to the Temple in Jerusalem. Historians have suggested that this legend was promoted by the Umayyads in the late seventh century during the counter-Caliphate of al-Zubayr (680–692), when they did not control the sacred sites of the Hijaz and wished to promote the Islamic sanctity of Jerusalem.[12]

Accounts of the miracles of the Prophet were in high demand, in part because of widespread veneration for his person and in part out of competition with Christians. Al-Qadi 'Iyad (d. 1149) reports that Muslim commoners in al-Andalus would lose arguments with

Christians about the relative merits of Jesus and Muhammad because they were unaware of the many miracles of the Messenger of God and therefore could not counter the Christians' enumeration of Christ's miracles. In response he wrote *al-Shifa bi-ta'rif huquq al-Mustafa* (*The Cure by Making Known the Rights of the Chosen One*), which contains copious descriptions of the Prophet Muhammad's miracles. The work of course includes a discussion of the miraculous nature of the Qur'an and the splitting of the moon mentioned above, but it also relates many other miraculous acts, including holding back the sun, causing water to flow, making food abundant, healing the sick, and bringing the dead to life. Infants speak to testify to his prophecy, as do animals, trees, and stones.[13] According to one popular story, a gazelle that had been captured by a bedouin called out to the Prophet. The Prophet asked the gazelle what was the matter, and the gazelle explained that she had been captured by this hunter, but that her two fawns were on the nearby mountain and that she needed to feed them. She promised that if he released her to go suckle her fawns, she would return. The Prophet got the hunter to release her, and she left but returned after a while. The bedouin, amazed, asked the Prophet if he could do anything for him, and the Prophet asked that he set the gazelle free. The bedouin did so, and the gazelle returned to the wild, saying, "I bear witness that there is no god but God and that you are the messenger of God." In another common story, the Prophet would visit a humble mosque, and when he preached there would lean against the trunk of a palm tree. The attendees of the mosque eventually built a fancy pulpit for the Prophet to preach from, but the first time he mounted it, the sound of sobbing was heard. It took some time for those present to realize that the palm tree was crying because of the pain it felt at being separated from the Prophet.[14] A number of the miracles ascribed to Muhammad correspond closely with those attributed to Jesus in the Gospels and the Qur'an, such as healing the sick, reviving the dead, and feeding a multitude with a small amount of food.

The celebration of the birthday of the Prophet (*mawlid al-nabi*) also developed in rivalry with the Christian celebration of Christmas, the birthday of Jesus. It is generally held to have originated in Egypt in the eleventh century and to have been instituted by the Fatimids, the Shi'i ruling dynasty, along with other specifically Shi'i holidays. It subsequently spread throughout the Islamic world. Sunnis observe the Prophet's birthday on the 12th of Rabi' al-Awwal, the third month of the Islamic calendar, while Shi'is observe it on the 17th of the same month, coinciding with the birthday of the sixth Imam, Ja'far al-Sadiq. Celebrations involve sermons, processions, the recitation of litanies or poetry in praise of the Prophet such as the famous Ode of the Cloak by al-Busiri, as well as the fun and games associated with fairs and other festivals. Some conservative sects such as the Wahhabis consider this celebration to be idolatrous and a heretical innovation. While many contemporary Muslim jurists, both Sunni and Shi'i, approve of the observance of Prophet's birthday, others have forbidden it.

Veneration for the Prophet looms large in the popular culture of Muslim societies throughout the world. The name "Muhammad" is the most common male given name, and the other names by which he is known – Ahmad, Mustafa, Taha, Yasin, Abu al-Qasim, al-Habib – are not far behind. The name is so popular, in fact, that in Morocco one commonly calls a male stranger Si Muhammad ("Sir Muhammad"). It is said that the seventh descendant of a male line all named Muhammad will find a treasure. Egyptian mothers regularly invoke the protection of "the name of the Prophet" for their children, and the phrase "Bless the Prophet!" (*salli 'ala al-nabi*) is used in many Islamic societies as an expression of applause or admiration. And the oath "by the Prophet" is heard nearly as frequently as the ubiquitous "by God" as an asseveration or as a functional equivalent to "Honest to God" or "Really?" In some Arabic countries it also takes on the functional meaning "Please" and "I beg you."

Prophecy is a fundamental part of Islamic tradition and attention to the topic has shaped several distinct genres of Islamic religious literature and modes of discourse. Underlying many of these discussions, however, is a deep tension. On the one hand, the history of prophecy is the main vehicle that validates Islam as a monotheistic religion and links it and the mission of the Prophet Muhammad to biblical salvation history and to Judaism and Christianity. On the other hand, the attempt to distinguish Islam from its biblical precursors and demonstrate its superiority to them necessarily depends heavily on demonstrating the distinctiveness of the Prophet Muhammad and his mission. The rich composite portrait that arises in Islamic history of prophecy in general and the figure of the Prophet Muhammad in particular is the product of complex negotiations of religious belief and identity, not only among different Islamic trends and approaches, but also among Muslims, Jews, and Christians.

16

RITUAL

Amina M. Steinfels

In an essay published in 1981, William Graham surveyed the state of scholarship on Islamic ritual and found it severely lacking.[1] Much work had been done by the Orientalists of the preceding century on uncovering the pre-Islamic elements in Islamic rituals, yet this did not assist in the interpretation of these rituals as *Islamic*. On the other hand, according to Graham, anthropologists had neglected the "orthoprax" rituals of Islam in favor of "folk" or "popular" practices. The study of Islamic ritual had contributed little to the theorization of ritual in general, nor had ritual theory been fruitfully applied to Islamic data. Four years later, Frederick Denny again called for a more serious study of Islamic ritual. Both sketched out preliminary interpretations of the ritual elements of what are conventionally referred to as the Five Pillars of Islam, the acts of worship (*'ibadat*) classified as obligatory by Islamic law.[2] I will take their essays as starting points for a new assessment of the state of the field and, like them, focus largely on the basic obligatory acts of worship: prayer, fasting during Ramadan, the Hajj pilgrimage to Mecca, ritual purification, and the sacrifice of Eid al-Adha. I will also touch briefly on the Shi'i rituals of celebration and mourning devoted to Muhammad's family and descendants.

This list by no means covers the wide variety of ritual activities that are, and have been, performed by Muslims. It leaves out various life-cycle ceremonies, Sufi practices, the celebration of special days of the year and the month, possession cults, Qur'an recitation, and numerous other, mostly local, activities. A focus on the obligatory *'ibadat* is not uncontroversial; Graham is strongly criticized for this by Nancy and Richard Tapper who argue that it privileges a reified notion of authentic or orthodox Islam at the expense of Islam as it is actually lived. Furthermore, they contend that it renders the practices of women invisible and precludes an analysis of the gender dynamics in Islamic religious practice.[3] These are serious criticisms but, as we will see, discussion of the *'ibadat* does not have to fall into these traps.

My reasons for choosing this narrow focus are threefold: (1) to limit the topic at hand to manageable proportions; (2) by selecting a category of action indigenous to the tradition, to avoid the sticky theoretical problem of defining ritual first and subsequently identifying the activities of Muslims that fit the chosen definition[4] (I have, however, left out of consideration two of the "Five Pillars:" the giving of alms and the testament of faith because they do not easily fit commonsense notions of ritual); (3) to avoid the polemical question of whether certain ritual activities are "really" Islamic. Muslims may often not perform their prayers, or fast, or go on pilgrimage; they may question, debate, replace, or modify these obligations; they may mock those who perform them assiduously; they may spend much more energy on alternative ritual activities. But, in general, Muslims have been in agreement that these are Islamic practices with enormous symbolic value for the definition of what it means to be a Muslim.

Although I am not going to describe these practices in detail, a few general remarks about their nature might be useful. The first important point is that the *'ibadat* are embodied practices; it is the body that is purified, that cycles through the postures of prayer, that walks the pilgrim path in Mecca, and that goes hungry during Ramadan. The ritual body is one that is oriented in space – in relation to the Ka'ba in Mecca – and time – in the day, the week, and the year. But it is also a body animated by a mind that must have the *intention* to carry out these rituals. Verbalization is another important component, especially of prayer, which involves the recitation of various passages from the Qur'an. Therefore, exemptions or modifications of the ritual obligations, granted by Islamic law, are based on mental and physical conditions: health, maturity, sanity, and engagement in travel or warfare. Every sane, adult, Muslim is supposed to carry out these rituals in a similar fashion. There are a few exceptions to this rule, for example, if several people pray together, one must be the leader; the head of household may perform the Eid sacrifice for his whole family; and women are not obliged to participate in congregational prayer.

While each of these practices is a separate obligation, they are also deeply interrelated. Intention and purification are preconditions, with some variation in specifics, of all the rituals. Although ritual prayer is usually described as a five-times-a-day requirement, plus in congregation on Friday, specific forms of it are also required at funerals and at the festivals (*Eids*) that conclude the Hajj and the month of fasting. (Ramadan also has an additional recommended night-time prayer.) Many non-canonical rituals are accompanied or preceded by the performance of ritual prayer. The recitation of Qur'an verses also crops up as part of, or in association with, rituals both required and supererogatory.

In their elementary forms, these practices require neither a class of ritual experts with special powers, nor special ritual objects, nor sanctified locales (apart from the Ka'ba and other sites in Mecca). This, however, is in terms of legal *requirement*; in practice, prayer leaders, muezzins, mosques, prayer rugs, and so on have become standard. Non-canonical rituals also frequently have a greater use for ritual specialists and ritual objects. One striking difference between the legal definition of the *'ibadat* and Muslim ritual practices around the world is the role of food. Apart from the fast and the requirement of ritual slaughter to make certain kinds of animal flesh licit (*halal*), there is little involvement of food in the rules on the canonical rituals. However, the customary celebration of holy days often emphasizes local food traditions and in many non-canonical rituals the distribution and consumption of food is a means of acquiring merit, expiating sins, transferring blessings, and removing misfortune.

Since the publication of Graham's article, much has changed in the study of Islamic ritual and much has remained the same. As a whole, the study of Islam and Muslim societies has grown exponentially in the last few decades. Growth in the study of Islamic ritual, however, has not been uniform across disciplines. In this area, it is the social sciences (formerly castigated by Graham for neglect of normative Islamic practices) that have taken the lead, producing a significant body of ethnographic material about ritual performance in Muslim communities around the world. By contrast, text-based research – the province of Islamicists – has yielded much less scholarship on Islamic ritual.

Some scholars, such as G. R. Hawting, Uri Rubin, and Robert Tottoli, continue the quest for the earliest development of Islamic practices and their roots in pre-Islamic history but this is an approach that has largely fallen out of favor, especially among American academics.[5] Although such research, relying upon early historical sources and *hadith*, is valuable in itself for understanding the history of human religious practices, it does not shed much light on Islamic ritual as a specifically, consciously, Islamic activity. Furthermore, the pursuit of sources and parallels in pre-Islamic Arab, Jewish, or Christian practices has sometimes obscured the very significant and purposeful differences between Islamic ritual and its antecedents. A different kind of search for origins is found in Brannon Wheeler's attempt to apply myth and ritual theory, originated by Robertson Smith and updated by J. Z. Smith, to Islamic rituals and relics, particularly those associated with Mecca and the Hajj.[6]

Implicit in the idea of an "orthoprax" or "normative" Islam is a recognition of the importance of Islamic law (*shari'a*). The category of *'ibadat* is a legal one, not a sociological one, and it is defined in greatest specificity by the legal texts. Juridical texts usually devote their first sections to a discussion of ritual purity, prayer, pilgrimage, fasting, and so on. It makes sense, therefore, that legal texts would be the most likely source for scholarship on Islamic rituals. Most accounts of Islamic ritual in introductory texts are ultimately derived from the legal tradition in that they focus on the "Five Pillars" and summarize the rules on the obligatory practices. Similarly, the *Encyclopaedia of Islam* articles on the *'ibadat*, as a whole or taken individually, confine themselves to presenting the legal definitions and requirements of the rituals after tracing their pre-Islamic roots.

While the *shari'a* is a useful and logical starting point for the study of the *'ibadat*, such an approach runs the risk of seriously distorting our understanding of Islamic religious practice as a whole. To view Islamic ritual through the lens of a legally defined orthopraxy is to privilege one strand within the multiplicity of a community's beliefs and practices, potentially leading to an elision between Islam and Islamic law. Furthermore, the importance of religious law in regulating the daily practices of Muslims is both variable across time and space, and a site of political contention. There are not only competing legal interpretations at work in a community's ritual performance but also other agendas and values in operation. Thus, though it is generally acknowledged that the categories of obligatory practices and the validity of specific ritual performance are defined by the law, these, as we will see, are not always the foremost concerns of practicing Muslims.

Despite these caveats, and bearing in mind that the law cannot stand alone as the sole representative of Islam, it is still disappointing to note how little work has been done on the vast amounts of ritual legal material. Marion Katz, Kevin Reinhart, and Ze'ev Maghen have made significant contributions to our understanding of the laws on ritual purity (*tahara*), ably summarized and reviewed by Richard Gauvain.[7] The requirement of formulating an intention (*niyya*) for the valid performance of ritual is taken up by Denny and by Paul Powers.[8] Purity and intention are fundamental components of the structure of Islamic ritual without which most ritual performances are null and void. Yet, clearly, until similar work is done on the rest of the *'ibadat*, especially prayer, we have only scratched the surface of ritual law.

Through a study of the place of intent in the legally prescribed performance of ritual, Powers considerably expands our understanding of Islamic ritual as defined by the law. At their most basic, rituals are pure actions without any function beyond their definition as obligatory acts of worship. Intention (*niyya*) plays the role of demarcating and categorizing the performance of such actions as the fulfillment of a specific ritual requirement. *Niyya* also signifies the performer's conscious attention on ritual at hand. Without such an accompanying *niyya* no performance of the basic rituals counts, that is the Muslim's obligation has not been met.

From the requirement for *niyya*, Powers extracts two important points about the legal conception of Islamic ritual. The first is that the *'ibadat* are not just physical, bodily activities, distinct or free from mental or spiritual states. Though it is the body, through its orientation, its actions, its purity, and its verbalizations, that performs ritual activity this is accompanied by an action of the mind: intention. However, Powers argues that this is not an attempt at "spiritualizing" otherwise "empty" ritual, as that formulation presupposes a dichotomy foreign to the material at hand. Rather, "any putative mind-body duality is overshadowed by the inclusion of the mind in the ritual, as the mind is treated as part of the body."[9]

The second point is that the particular character of intention in Islamic ritual law responds to, and thus demonstrates, the difference between ritual and non-ritual action. Following Humphrey and Laidlaw, Powers argues that because ritual is rule bound, with the identity of actions already defined, there is a potential gap between the actor's intentions and actions.[10] Whatever the intentions might be, if the physical and verbal actions fit the standard then it *looks* as if the ritual has been validly performed. Islamic law takes this aspect of ritual action into account by stipulating the actor's individual awareness and intention as a necessary component for the valid performance of a ritual. This validity cannot be judged by an external human audience but is only known to the actor and to God.

Given the primary position of ritual discussion in the Islamic legal tradition, the lack of attention paid to it by Islamicists is striking. Several reasons for this inattention have been proposed: a dismissal of Islamic ritual as merely the preservation of Jewish or other pre-Islamic forms, a discomfort with the body, and a concomitant bias toward the "spiritual." I would also suspect that much of the scholarship on Islamic law is constrained by the common-sense Western understanding of the category of law as excluding religious ritual. Thus, commerce, war, slavery, jurisprudential reasoning, and, above all, personal status receive the lion's share of scholarly interest. The laws of marriage and divorce and, in general, the issue of gender relations and the rights and status of Muslim women are highlighted not only because of the rise of gender as a central analytic category, but also because of ongoing contemporary developments in the interpretation and application of these laws. By comparison, ritual law is entrenched and stable and not as obviously a subject of contemporary political debates, especially at the national state level.

Graham points out another possible reason for this reluctance to tackle Islamic ritual law: its apparent impenetrability to "comprehensive, rational systematization under any one interpretive rubric."[11] Islamic ritual law's resistance to, or evasion of, interpretation, whether symbolic or ethical, is pointed out by most of the scholars working on the topic and is a site for some debate among them. On the one hand, Gauvain argues that "it is possible to decipher coherent – albeit often contrasting – theological and social concerns (or messages)" in this material.[12] On the other hand, Maghen and Reinhart both argue against the quest for messages. Powers, too, rejects any attempts to find spiritual meaning in ritual acts, arguing instead that "the actions governed by Islamic ritual law are presented as valuable and moral in and of themselves, not (just) as symbolic surfaces, signifiers, or metaphors."[13]

It is clear that ritual law can be interpreted to find underlying messages; Gauvain elucidates one such message from the laws on ritual purity: a recognition of the body and sexuality, and Katz suggests another: egalitarianism. Graham argues that the overall theme of the

Islamic ritual system is an "anti-sacramental" or "reformational" tendency. The material, especially *hadith*, on which the law is based certainly relates ritual practice to moral, political, and eschatological concerns. It is also hardly possible for the thinking of the early legal scholars to have been unaffected by their own a priori conceptions of the world, humanity, and gender. Though Reinhart claims that Islamic ritual practice "shapes no particular perspective on the course of life,"[14] a ritual system will, at the very least, make it easier for certain perspectives to be held than others.

However, it is also clear that the conveyance of such meanings and messages is not the purpose or intention of the legal texts. The explicit purpose of legal discussions of a ritual action is to determine its obligatory or non-obligatory quality and to stipulate the conditions which make its performance valid or invalid. The symbolic, moral, or mythical meanings possibly encoded in the ritual action, or its possible social function, are irrelevant to its legal status. Fritz Staal wrote of the "meaninglessness" of Vedic ritual and, though he has been appropriately challenged on what he might mean by "meaninglessness," his comments are applicable to Islamic ritual, as well.[15] From the legal point of view, rituals must be done, and they must be done precisely this way, because those are the rules.

One might argue that, from the legal standpoint, Islamic rituals are done in obedience to God's command and in imitation of Muhammad. However, this does not provide an adequate explanation for the specific forms that the law lays down for rituals. Divine commandments and prophetic example are how we *know* that there are such and such a number of *rak'as* (cycles of prostration) at a particular prayer time, but they do not explain *why* this is the case. To invoke Staal's "meaninglessness" of ritual is not to dismiss the various ideas about the communicatory, functional, or performative qualities of ritual, nor to argue that they cannot be fruitfully applied to the Islamic case. But ritual law's own understanding of the nature of ritual runs contrary to such attempts.

If the authors of the classical juridical texts were reluctant to do more than define and prescribe the forms of obligatory and recommended ritual action, this has not stopped the Muslim community from attempting to explain the *'ibadat*. In Islamic texts and in the ethnographic material we find numerous views on why rituals are done and what they mean. Most popular understandings of ritual, as well as much of Sufi thought and many modernist approaches, see ritual actions as effectively accomplishing certain goals: communication and expression, acquisition and transfer of merit, acquisition of good fortune and removal of bad fortune, moral self discipline, social cohesion, and social reform. Some of these goals explicitly include an interaction with the divine, some focus on the self, and some focus on the community. But their pursuit depends on the idea that rituals done correctly produce a further effect besides the fulfillment of the obligation stipulated by the *shari'a*.

One of the most influential and oft-quoted interpreters of Islamic ritual is the medieval Sufi thinker al-Ghazali. Ghazali understood ritual prayer, for example, as an act of communication, praise, and supplication. As such, he required that it be carried out with concentration and be accompanied by inner states of fear, hope, awe, and so on.[16] These two components – prayer as communication and the necessity for certain accompanying emotions or attitudes – can be found in various Muslim communities today. The Gayo people of Indonesia tend to view prayer as communication and consequently require mental concentration and an audible statement of intention.[17] Like Ghazali, participants in the contemporary Egyptian women's mosque movement strive to maintain the attitudes of sincerity, humility, fear, and awe during the performance of their prayers. For them, ritual prayer is a discipline through which they endeavor to transform their daily lives and desires to a more pious and prayerful standard, a discipline made effective by these inner states.[18]

At first glance, such understandings of the effectivity of prayer might appear uncontroversial. Yet, because they lead to additional requirements, even if those are internal and subjective, they potentially come into conflict with the legal prescriptions of the *shari'a*. John Bowen records the heated debate in Indonesia between those who follow the tradition of spoken intention and the reformist, or modernist, movements that reject it. Saba Mahmood's informants in Egypt are careful to point out that prayer is still acceptable, though not as desirable, without the aforementioned emotional aspects. Ghazali directly took on this issue, acknowledging that he might stand accused of denying the legal definitions of prayer by adding further requirements. He defended himself, in the elitist manner typical of much Sufi thought, by arguing that, though prayer is not fully effective in the basic form required by the law, the law has to fit the common human being who is incapable of much more.[19]

What we find exposed here, and repeatedly throughout Muslim history, is a tension between two attitudes toward the classical legal formulations of ritual: as a *minimum* stipulation which can then be elaborated upon or as a *maximum* limit of ritual activity to which any addition is sinful innovation (*bid'a*). This is a tension related to the question of the purpose, or effectivity, of ritual. If ritual action has no goal besides its accurate performance, then strict adherence to the canonical rulings is paramount. If it does have additional goals then those might be better achieved if the rituals are done in a certain way or with additional activities. For example, Moroccan women associate the fasting enjoined during the month of Ramadan with purity – purity both as a result of and a requirement for the fast. Therefore, they traditionally purify their homes and their bodies in preparation for the fast, beyond the requirements of the law.[20]

The Moroccan approach to Ramadan is an example of a regional or local variation in the *'ibadat*. One aspect of such variation is the incorporation of traditional local non-canonical rituals into the performance of the obligatory ones. In Morocco, preparations for Ramadan include the chaining up of spirits or jinns by the adepts of the Gnawa cult.[21] In Indonesia, on the other hand, both preparations for Ramadan and the celebration of Eid al-Adha (Festival of the Sacrifice) involve the communal ritual meals known variously as *slametan* and *kenduri*.[22] Even without the controversial incorporation of such further ritual activities, it is possible to discern regional cultural values underlying subtle differences in the manner or attitude with which the *'ibadat* are performed. As Bowen points out, "Muslims shape their rituals to local cultural concerns *and* to universalistic scriptural imperatives." "This tacking back and forth between conflicting visions is, if anything is, the historical essence of Muslim ritual life."[23]

Let us take, for example, the case of the animal sacrifice performed during Eid al-Adha, as well as during various life-cycle rituals and holy days. In Indonesia, the culturally central concern for the well-being of ancestors, especially in the afterlife, leads to a de-emphasis on the sacrifice itself in comparison to the communal meal through which merit is transferred from the living to the dead. The sacrificial animal is viewed as a vehicle for the whole family in the afterlife.[24] For many South Asian Muslims, on the other hand, the sacrifice of an animal and the donation of its meat is a mechanism for the personal expiation of sins and the removal of misfortune. In order to achieve these results they need to make personal contact with the sacrificial animal and have access to an appropriate population of "poor" people to receive their donations.[25] The blood of the sacrificed animal also has different valuations, ranging from a sacred and protective substance daubed on the heads and faces of children to one that needs to be removed and erased as swiftly and thoroughly as possible.[26] These are all examples of large-scale regional trends, resulting in distinctive patterns of ritual performance in different parts of the Muslim world. At the same time, a multiplicity of ritual understandings and subtly different practices frequently coexist within any single region, community, or individual.

Shari'a-based defense or opposition to such ritual elaborations, though acknowledging possible positive or negative effects and motivated by various factors, ultimately depends on jurisprudential principles of evidence and whether an innovation can ever be acceptable. The medieval theologian and jurist Ibn Taymiyya, criticizing the customary rituals of his day, justified his position on the grounds that even if such customs were not overly imitative of non-Muslims and inclining toward polytheism (which he did not grant) they would still be unacceptable as innovation.[27] In the early twentieth century, the reformist scholar Ashraf 'Ali Thanawi attacked the ritual practices of Indian Muslim women as an invented pseudo-*shari'a*. To him the notions of effectivity underlying these practices were rank superstition, even idolatry, and it was precisely the idea that doing things a certain way would generate greater benefit that he found most objectionable.[28] We should not be misled, however, by such famous and influential critics to overlook the fact that in many cases the legal scholars have found elaborations of ritual practice, within limits, acceptable and justified.

Scholars have long struggled to understand the place of "living tradition" in the development of Islamic law and the issue is as relevant and tricky for ritual law as it is for other legal topics. As mentioned above, scholarship on the origins of Islamic ritual trace elements back to pre-existing practices prevalent among the Arabs, and the Jewish and Christian communities. In her study of the early development of purity law, Katz finds that a system of traditional purity practices preexisted the legal discussions on the topic.[29] Dealing with a much later period, Liyakat Takim traces the changing attitude of Shi'i thinkers toward the inclusion of a statement about 'Ali in the call to prayer (*adhan* or *azan*), from rejection as insupportable innovation to a position of acceptance.[30] However, the mechanism by which enacted practices are included or accommodated by the law remains somewhat obscure.

Debates over the correct enactment of ritual, including both the basic obligatory forms and their various elaborations, continue to exercise Muslim communities around the world. Public debate over ritual practice usually calls upon basic juridical principles, such as fidelity to the Prophet's example, though the motivations for taking up certain positions may be rooted in political or social agendas.[31] The rise of various Islamic movements (modernist, reformist, fundamentalist), increased communication between different Muslim communities around the globe, and therefore greater awareness of regional differences in practice, have all led to a heightened concern for ritual accuracy and to the explicit use of ritual to express political, social, regional, and sectarian identities.

The authority to define a ritual practice as acceptable or not is a potent form of social control. The traditional sectarian divisions and legal traditions, and the newer religious movements, all vie for this authority. So do national governments and state structures, whether avowedly Islamic, secular, or atheist. Certain ritual practices are necessarily more entangled with, and subject to, state control than others. In particular, the Hajj cannot be carried out for most Muslims without negotiating the modern state bureaucracies (and commercial structures) of international travel. Throughout Islamic history, whatever political entity is in control of Mecca and its environs has shaped and influenced the Hajj experience. Today, it is the Kingdom of Saudi Arabia, in conjunction with the O.I.C. (Organization of the Islamic Conference) and its member states, that is responsible for the infrastructure and organization of the annual pilgrimage, setting, for example, quotas of pilgrims from different countries.

In the modern Hajj certain elements of the traditional process have been done away with altogether. The motivations for these changes are presumably a combination of pragmatic decision-making in the face of ever-rising numbers of pilgrims and particular interpretations of what constitutes the core actions and meanings of the ritual. This is an area that calls out for more analysis. Some initial steps have been taken in this direction but most studies of the Hajj focus on practical logistics and political and economic issues, whether in contemporary or historic times, without adequately addressing the religious concerns of pilgrims and of those who enable pilgrimage. Robert Bianchi presents an interesting example of the effect of ritual interpretation on political decision-making in the person of the famous nineteenth-century Dutch Orientalist and colonial administrator Snouck Hurgronje. Unlike some of his European contemporaries, Snouck Hurgronje did not see the Hajj as a potentially dangerous "breeding ground for anticolonial agitation" but as a "bulwark of the status quo." He therefore encouraged the Netherlands to sponsor pilgrims from their territories in Southeast Asia and thus control and surveil the activities of those pilgrims.[32]

Of course, today, the Hajj cannot be carried out without the involvement of a regime that is avowedly committed to a particular brand of Islam. But even explicitly secular states find themselves, or choose to be, entangled in the process of defining, permitting, or enabling ritual practice. In many countries the obligation to sacrifice an animal on Eid al-Adha comes into conflict with regulations governing food safety and animal protection. For example, in most parts of France only a licensed slaughterer is permitted to kill an animal. Though this is acceptable under Islamic law, as long as the slaughter is done in the appropriate manner and the sacrificer has the correct intention, it prevents the sacrificer from slaughtering the animal himself, a traditional requirement in many parts of the world.[33]

Numerous examples can be found of attempts to further particular ideological and political goals by defining, regulating, encouraging, or discouraging the practice of Islamic rituals, by both state and non-state actors. Under Soviet rule, anthropological research was used to determine which rituals practiced in Uzbekistan were intrinsically Islamic, and therefore banned as religious, and which were "shamanism," and therefore permitted as folk custom.[34] A less obvious case of state involvement is M. E. Combs-Schilling's argument that the Moroccan monarchy and patriarchal society are undergirded and legitimated by the performance of the animal sacrifice, as well as by marriage ceremonies and the celebration of the Prophet's birthday.

But ritual, residing as it does in the body of individual performers, continues to escape such attempts by the powerful to monopolize its magic. As Azam Torab reminds us, "ritual can be used in the service of power or deployed as power to prevent monopoly of power."[35] She explores the ways lower-middle-class women in Tehran perform and construct their gender identities through the performance of ritual, sometimes in accord with the dictates of the ayatollahs, and sometimes at odds with them. In Shi'i Islam, rituals of mourning and celebration devoted to the descendants of the Prophet are central to religious life, in conjunction with and sometimes overshadowing the *'ibadat*. In recent decades, the Shi'i religious authorities have advised against, or even forbidden, the more dramatic forms of mourning (*matam*), involving cutting oneself with knives or blades, on the grounds that they create negative publicity for the community and that blood renders the participants ritually impure. Yet, from India to Lebanon, young men continue to carry out bloody *matam*, performing a defiant masculinity rooted in the body, at once martial and martyred, an alternative to the patriarchal voices of the *'ulama*.[36]

David Pinault views the attempt by the Shi'i authorities to quell bloody *matam* and the resistance by the populace as partly based on a difference in interpretation: for the participants and the audience these are intercessionary rituals but for contemporary religious leaders they are methods for inculcating virtue and discipline, and for remembering the past. But multiple interpretations of a single ritual activity do not always indicate opposing and irreconcilable forces struggling for a monopoly of meaning. This is demonstrated most elegantly in Akbar Hyder's exploration of the various ways in which the Karbala narrative, heart of the Shi'i rituals in the month of Muharram, has continued to generate meaning – political, religious, and literary – in twentieth-century India. Hyder remarks that "it is clear that the education of Shias from my parents' and grandparents' generations informed them with a dialogics and polyphony that posited one understanding of religion along with another (often conflictual) one."[37]

Hyder points out that such a multivocal, complex, relationship with Islamic rituals is often lost in the experience of emigration. A portion of recent ethnographic work on Muslims has focused on the immigrant experience, an experience that has become a prominent feature in Muslim communities in the past century. For migrant communities, especially in Europe and North America, the performance of ritual poses special challenges, requiring the negotiation of unfamiliar regulations and social norms. Ritual performance can also take on the function of declaring and constructing particular minority identities in relation to the majority population. Rituals may be performed more or less publicly depending on whether a community wants to declare its presence or whether it wishes to avoid publicizing its existence.

One expected result of globalization is the homogenization of ritual practice as immigrant communities bring together Muslims from different parts of the world with different conceptions of Islam.

This is the process that Hyder observed happening among Shiʿi immigrants in the United States, a process in which rigid and authoritarian prescriptions for ritual practice triumph over diversity and polyphony. However, there are also some interesting counter-examples of the greater opportunity for movement creating new ritual forms and possibilities. Thus, immigrant Muslims in Berlin have adopted the practice of photographing funeral ceremonies in order to have visual evidence for relatives back home that the ceremony was carried out correctly, even though some of them consider photography, especially of the dead, to be potentially problematic.[38] One might expect that the massive growth in Hajj participation in recent years would have a centrifugal effect, sending pilgrims home with a "purified," more homogenized view of Islam and reinforcing normative cultural hierarchies. Yet recent studies of Hausa Muslims of Nigeria have demonstrated the opposite effect. Hausa women's increasing access to the Hajj, instead of reinforcing normative gender hierarchies, has created new, yet unquestionably Islamic, bases for status and religious authority.[39] By going on Hajj, adepts of the *Bori* possession cult have also found new status, wealth, and clients for their exorcism rituals, thus carrying a particular heterodox set of practices into the ritual heart of Islam.[40]

As these examples show, the ethnographic data, despite covering little more than a century, demonstrate the continuing transformation of ritual practice in Muslim communities. While the formal requirements of the *ʿibadat* (as laid out in juridical texts) are not easily amenable to modification, fidelity to those requirements, as well as goals, interpretations, and levels of participation, have changed even in this limited time period. Presumably, such shifts in ritual activity have taken place throughout Islamic history. Yet, other than the aforementioned attempts to find out what happened *before* the establishment of the canonical legal prescriptions, little work has been done on ritual change *after* that point.

If the ethnographers have disclosed the wide variety of ritual elaboration and ascribed significance among communities of Muslims, we still lack a history of that variety. The Hajj is a limited exception to this rule, partly because as a large-scale public event it features in historical accounts and as a once-in-a-lifetime experience it is recorded in a number of autobiographical writings. F. E. Peters has compiled various such accounts, though he concentrates on the practical challenges of the event rather than ritual process. Young's analysis of the gendered significance of the veiling and unveiling of the Ka'ba, as it was done at the end of the nineteenth century, is the kind of historical exploration we are sorely lacking.[41] The overall absence of a history of how, or to what extent, Muslims actually fulfilled their ritual obligations and what it might have meant to them leads to a limited vision in which the universal presence of a static, usually *shari'a*-based, conception of the *'ibadat* is assumed.

The diversity in the practice and understanding of ritual leads us again to the question of whether Islamic rituals have intrinsic meaning. One of the pitfalls of studies of ritual in particular Muslim communities is the temptation to extrapolate from the specific case to a general theory about Islam. Thus, as Bowen points out, Combs-Schilling's fascinating analysis of the Moroccan king's public sacrifice on Eid al-Adha is marred by the claim that the centrality of this ritual, and of the Abraham myth which it commemorates, for the maintenance of patriarchal structures holds true not just in Morocco but for Islam as a whole.[42]

Bowen argues that the ability of Islamic rituals to express various meanings lies in their relative lack of symbolic or semantic meaning. "The *salat* is not structured around an intrinsic propositional or semantic core. It cannot be 'decoded' semantically because it is not designed according to a symbolic or iconic code."[43] Heiko Henkel rejects this idea that ritual prayer (*salat*) has no core meaning, asserting instead that "its message could hardly be more explicit and straightforward: the practitioner affirms his or her commitment to the truth of the Qur'anic revelation and submission to the command of God." It is because of this irreducible theological meaning and identification of the practitioner as Muslim that prayer enables "both changing interpretations of the Islamic tradition and the affirmation of Muslim community across different interpretations of Islam."[44] The verbal components of ritual prayer and the simple body postures of standing, bowing, and prostration lend themselves more easily to such an argument than the other rituals. Despite the differences between Bowen and Henkel's positions, the idea common to both is that it is the very limited intrinsic meaning of the rituals that allows for their performance in different cultural settings, with different social meanings, and sometimes different goals.

Moving from the social to the intellectual level, this limited meaning of the *'ibadat* turns them into nearly abstract symbols for Islam, "Muslimness," or, on occasion, the legalistic aspect of Islam. As recognizable symbols, the *names* and *descriptions* of rituals can be used to explore all sorts of ideas. Esoteric interpretation of the rituals in which they are, seemingly arbitrarily, associated with various religious ideas or objects occurs in various strands of Islam, most strikingly in the context of Isma'ili Shi'ism. The Sufi tradition has also used discussion of the ritual obligations to express a variety of religious concepts, ranging far beyond questions of correct practice. The writings of the medieval Andalusian mystic Ibn al-'Arabi are famously abstruse and unclassifiable, including his meditations on the inner meaning of the rituals. Starting from the decisions and explanations of the legal tradition, "he goes on to explore, through a process of metaphorical interiorization, the inward realm corresponding to the various positions."[45] Other Sufi writers use the rituals as symbols for a purely legalistic, exoteric, or worldly understanding of Islam and express their rejection of that kind of Islam, in favor of one based on love or mystic experience, as a rejection of ritual obligation.[46] Such a denial of the obligatory rituals might be merely rhetorical or it might lead to an actual neglect of ritual performance.

Sufi lyrics are particularly adept at producing a complex interplay between the ritual forms, the idea that they are obligatory, and the myths or texts with which they are associated. Let us take, for example, a few verses from a *qawwali* quoted by Hyder: "As he drew his bare sword to slay me, my head was in prostration / Prostration – Prostration is a strange thing / What else is there in the mantle of Islam, besides / The sword of 'Ali, the Hand of God, and the prostration of Shabbir."[47] Brought together here are allusions to the posture of ritual prayer, the sacrifice of Abraham commemorated on Eid al-Adha, and the martyrdom of Husayn commemorated by the Shi'a during Muharram. Obedience, ritual worship, and self-sacrifice come together as an expression of love for and annihilation in the divine.

Another example of the ambiguous signification of ritual in Sufi poetry is the nineteenth-century Saraiki poem "Meda ishq vi tu" by Khwaja Ghulam Farid.[48] In this poem, a series of equations is set up between "You" and a list of objects, ranging from the personal (e.g. body, soul, heart) to the religious (e.g. faith, asceticism, guide) to the worldly (e.g. henna, kajol, rain). The fourth verse runs: "You are my religious obligations: Hajj, alms giving, fasting, prayer, and the call to prayer, too." The reader, or listener, is left wondering what such an equation might mean. Is it that love for "You" replaces all of these? Or that this love, or "You," is found and experienced in these rituals? That "You" are the meaning or the significance of these rituals? Furthermore, how do the rituals relate to all of the other objects mentioned in the poem?

I do not have an answer to those questions. Nor do I have an overall theory of Islamic ritual to offer. The obligatory *'ibadat* are defined and mandated by Islamic law which forbears explicitly to provide them with much meaning beyond that quality of obligation. Juridical texts, then, provide theoretically global and timeless templates for ritual action. Yet, since the *'ibadat* are obligatory for most adult Muslims, those templates are transformed into ritual action by millions of individual bodies in an incredible variety of social and cultural contexts. In the moment of ritual performance, individuals and communities accept, reject, or enlarge the *shari'a* definition of obedience to God's will. In doing so, they draw upon understandings of the meaning, function, and mechanics of ritual which are foreign, though not necessarily contradictory, to the prescriptive view of the law. The concerns of the local culture, the politics of the moment, practical exigencies, all enter into the performance of ritual. As symbols of Islam, of the *shari'a*, and of Muslim identity, they are deployed in public ritual performance and in mystic poetry, political rhetoric, and theological meditation. But, to be clear, the *'ibadat* are not ciphers to which any meaning can be attached or any modification made. It is precisely because they never lose their core relationship with *Islamic* identity, history, law, and theology that they are continuously elaborated, reformed, and contested by Muslim communities around the world.

17

TEXT

İrvin Cemil Schick

The notion of text, and the closely related concepts of writing and reading, permeate Islam through and through. God's creation is a text, as is the sequence of events that unfolds in it. The Holy Scripture is a text that explicates God's creation, and the large body of exegetic literature is a text that in turn explicates the Holy Scripture. The community of believers are readers of these texts, and also writers of their own, since political, economic, and cultural activities in the Muslim world have always been highly dependent on the written word. Jews and Christians hold a special place among non-Muslims as "People of the Book," because Holy Scriptures were revealed to them by God. And calligraphy, that very popular Islamic art, is the means not only to preserve text in its most beautiful form, but also to inscribe onto human creations the mark of the one true Creator. Though an individual Muslim can, of course, be illiterate, it is impossible to imagine Islam as a religio-cultural system without text, writing, and reading.

Let us begin by defining our terms. Historically, the word *text* has been taken to denote a recorded document, handwritten or printed, literary or otherwise. *Writing* has meant the neutral transcription of verbally articulated thoughts or speech into a text by the instrumentality of a set of recognizable signs (a *code*). And *reading* has meant the neutral translation (*decoding*) of a text composed of such signs back into thought or speech. Thus, writing has been seen as a process through which the author's intended meaning is captured into a text, and reading as a process through which the author's intended meaning is recovered back from the text. As for the text itself, it has largely been viewed as an inert object in which the author's intended meaning resides pending recovery. But since text and author are typically spatially and/or temporally separated, reading is subject to error and misunderstanding, and it is always possible for the reader to recover the author's intended meaning imperfectly. Hermeneutic analysis is the process through which the text is systematically *interpreted* in an effort to recover the author's intended meaning as accurately as possible, and rules have been proposed to make this process of interpretation more reliable.

In recent decades, these definitions have been extended significantly by cultural theorists. Text has come to denote any object endowed with meaning, and writing any act that infuses meaning into an object. Thus, for example, the human body is *inscribed* by societal standards like fashion, good manners, or the law; by modification techniques like scarification, tattooing, make-up, or piercing; and by corporal norms like heterosexuality, chastity, and the cult of virginity.[1] So inscribed – that is, converted into text – the human body ceases to be a neutral monad and assumes a particular place within a socio-cultural system. "The habit does not make the monk," Erasmus of Rotterdam is reputed to have said, and yet it does: a shabbily dressed person will not be allowed into a classy restaurant, not because of the clothes themselves, but because of what his or her wearing them is taken to mean about his or her person.

Jacques Derrida famously wrote in *Of Grammatology* that "there is no outside-the-text (*hors-texte*)," meaning not that material reality does not exist, but rather that the human mind only has access to it through the mediation of systems of signification.[2] In our interactions with the world, we start by trying to interpret the meaning of what our senses perceive. In that regard, we ceaselessly *read* our world, thus humanizing and socializing it; that is to say, the act of reading produces meanings that, while they certainly do refer to the material reality of the world, do so in the specific context of the reader's interests and situatedness. This means that our world is in fact a text, infused with meaning by human concerns, and perpetually rewritten as these concerns change over the course of history. Reading, furthermore, is not merely the unproblematical recovery of meaning embedded in the text by a writer; it is actually a process of meaning construction. Equipped with these more generalized conceptions of text, writing, and reading, let us now turn to Islam.

In the Qur'an, mention is repeatedly made of God's *signs*. Usually denoted by the word *aya* (plural *ayat*), and sometimes qualified – or replaced – by the word "clear" (*bayyina*, plural *bayyinat*), they refer to incontrovertible proof of the existence of God and of the truth of His prophets. Yet, while these signs will confirm the faith of those capable of discernment, they can also reinforce unbelief on the part of those unwilling to be guided. Doubters who demanded special evidence from past prophets, or do so from the Prophet Muhammad, are denied miracles, for God has placed his signs in plain sight for the wise to see:

> Behold! in the creation of the heavens and the earth; in the alternation of the night and the day; in the sailing of the ships through the ocean for the profit of mankind; in the rain which God sends down from the skies, and the life which He gives therewith to an earth that is dead; in the beasts of all kinds that He scatters through the earth; in the change of the winds, and the clouds which they trail like their slaves between the sky and the earth; (Here) indeed are signs for a people that are wise. (Q2:164)

> Among His signs is this, that He created you from dust; and then, behold, you are men scattered (far and wide)! And among His signs is this, that He created for you mates from among yourselves, that you may dwell in tranquillity with them, and He has put love and mercy between your (hearts): verily in that are signs for those who reflect. And among His signs is the creation of the heavens and the earth, and the variations in your languages and your colors: verily in that are signs for those who know. And among His signs is the sleep that you take by night and by day, and the quest that you (make for livelihood) out of His bounty: verily in that are signs for those who hearken. And among His signs, He shows you the lightning, by way both of fear and of hope, and He sends down rain from the sky and with it gives life to the earth after it is dead: verily in that are signs for those who are wise. And among His signs is this, that heaven and earth stand by His command: then when He calls you, by a single call, from the earth, behold, you come forth. (Q30:20–25)

In short, it is incumbent upon believers to *read* God's creation, to perceive His signs throughout, and to interpret them correctly as proof of both His power and His mercy.

Significantly, individual verses of the Qur'an are also referred to as *aya*, because while previous prophets performed miracles over matter, the proof of Muhammad's prophethood is none other than the Qur'an itself – a miracle of the first order that could not have been created, nor could ever be imitated, by humankind (Q17:88):

> Those who disbelieve among the People of the Book and the polythe-
> ists were not going to abandon (their ways) until clear (signs) came
> to them. A messenger from God reading purified pages in which are
> correct scriptures. (Q98:1–3)

> Yet they say: "Why are not signs sent down to him (Muhammad) from
> his Lord?" Say: "The signs are indeed with God. and I am indeed a
> clear warner." And is it not enough for them that We have sent down
> to thee the Book which is rehearsed to them? Verily, in it is mercy and
> a reminder to those who believe. (Q29:50–51)

Thus, both the material world and the Qur'an stand as signs of God,
and each must be read and interpreted by those who believe. In this
respect – in their shared signness or *semioticity* – the former is as
much a text as the latter, both eloquently bearing witness to the existence of God and to the legitimacy of His prophets.

Indeed, to use a term coined by Julia Kristeva, there is here an
intertext, that is, a multiplicity of texts that mutually draw upon each
other in order to signify.[3] The Qur'an teaches the believer to interpret, on the one hand, the Holy Scripture, and on the other, the text
inscribed by his or her life experience, each in light of the other. It
is through exposure to everyday miracles – days following nights,
rain vivifying the parched soil, cows giving milk and bees honey
– that the believer becomes best equipped to understand the workings of the Lord; and it is by always remembering the presence of
the hand of God that he or she can most clearly grasp, and benefit
from, the harmony between human needs and nature's bounty. This
means, as well, that the process of knowing the Creator through
His creation constitutes a *hermeneutic circle*. Let us briefly dwell on
this idea.

Wilhelm Dilthey, one of the founders of modern hermeneutics,
noted that understanding a text in its particulars requires knowledge
of its meaning as a whole, and conversely understanding a text as a
whole requires knowledge of the meaning of its particulars. Hence,
he argued, the process of textual interpretation entails an iterative procedure whereby the interpreter alternates between the particular and
the general, the implicit and the explicit, constantly revised understandings of the parts and an emerging sense of the meaning of the
whole. This, he called the "hermeneutic circle."[4] His insights were
influential in the development of phenomenology; indeed, Hans-
Georg Gadamer extended Dilthey's hermeneutics by factoring in the

element of lived experience.[5] For Gadamer, it is not just literary texts that are subject to interpretation, but all experience.

Now, the interpreter is always constrained by his or her "horizon," that is, by the range of vision imposed by spatial and temporal positions, by the conceptual lexicon with which past experiences have endowed him or her. At the same time, as Gadamer memorably puts it, "horizons change for a person who is moving."[6] New experiences are integrated into the interpreter's horizon and modify it, so that even the very same occurrence would necessarily be experienced differently the second time around. The literary approach known as *reader-response theory* was largely inspired by Gadamer's work. Hans Robert Jauss, for example, posited a dialectic in which the reader approaches the text equipped with a horizon that embodies his or her assumptions and expectations about the text, and about literature in general.[7] The reader's experience of the text confronts this horizon, sometimes confirming, and other times challenging or altering it. Through this confrontation, meaning is produced. As new experiences – literary or lived – modify the reader's horizon, subsequent readings differ and new meanings may be produced.

But is this not precisely what the Qur'an proposes? Invoking the word "sign" (*aya/ayat*) no less than 382 times, the Qur'an invites believers to partake in a dialogue between their lived experiences and the Holy Scripture. It calls upon them to perceive the signs of God within the countless miracles of their daily lives, to learn from them, and, with their faith thus reaffirmed, to read anew the Revelation and know the ways of the Lord. Lived experience and Holy Scripture are, therefore, texts that mutually gloss one another. Indeed, this joint enterprise makes the *umma* (community of believers) into an *interpretive community*, as defined by Stanley Fish – a group of readers who share a common epistemology, utilize common assumptions and strategies, and are able to reach a shared understanding of a text.[8] Furthermore, this commonality pertains not only to a shared interpretation of the Holy Scripture, but indeed to a common reading of lived experience itself.

Some may justifiably wonder if the above does not amount to the gratuitous and possibly anachronistic shoehorning of twentieth-century literary theories formulated in Western Europe and North America into the entirely different context of seventh-century Arabia. Yet, the notions of text, writing, and reading are such fundamental building-blocks of Islam that there is sufficient evidence to think otherwise. A brief review of the earliest references at hand will demonstrate why such ideas as intertextuality, phenomenological hermeneutics, and reader-response theory are in fact not inappropriate for understanding the relationship between Islam and text.

Surat al-'Alaq, the ninety-sixth chapter of the Qur'an, begins as follows: "Read! in the name of thy Lord who has created – created man from a clot. Read! And thy Lord is the most bounteous, Who teaches by the pen, taught man that which he knew not" (Q96:1–5). The word "Read!" (*iqra'*, sometimes also translated as "Proclaim!") is, according to tradition, the very first word of the Divine Revelation. Based upon the account of the Prophet's wife A'isha, the story is told thus:

> The commencement of the Divine Inspiration to God's Apostle was in the form of good dreams that came true like bright daylight, and the love of seclusion was bestowed upon him. He used to go into seclusion in the cave of Hira' where he used to worship continuously for many days before he desired to see his family. He used to take with him on the journey food for the stay and then come back to (his wife) Khadija to take his food likewise again, till suddenly the Truth descended upon him while he was in the cave of Hira'. The angel came to him and asked him to read. The Prophet replied, "I do not know how to read." The Prophet added, "The angel caught me (forcefully) and pressed me so hard that I could not bear it anymore. He then released me and again asked me to read and I replied 'I do not know how to read.' Thereupon he caught me again and pressed me a second time till I could not bear it anymore. He then released me and again asked me to read but again I replied 'I do not know how to read.' Thereupon he caught me for the third time and pressed me, and then released me and said, 'Read in the name of thy Lord who has created – created man from a clot. Read! And thy Lord is the most bounteous.'" Then God's Apostle returned with the Inspiration and with his heart beating severely. Then he went to Khadija bint Khuwailid and said "Cover me! Cover me!" They covered him till his fear was over ...[9]

But what exactly is the significance of the word "Read," which was repeated three times according to this account? If the angel Gabriel was there to dictate the Holy Scripture to the Prophet Muhammad, would it not have been more reasonable instead to command him to "Write"? And what does it mean to say that God "teaches by the pen"? Perhaps the answer is that it was *the signs of God* the Prophet was enjoined to read – signs written with the divine pen for the edification of humankind. His reply, "I do not know how to read," is then no more than an acknowledgment that on the eve of the Holy Revelation one half of the cosmic intertext remained lacking: the Prophet was not yet equipped to read and comprehend the text of the creation, with all its mysteries, signs, and miracles.

A saying (*hadith*) attributed to the Prophet Muhammad (on the authority of 'Ubadah ibn al-Samit) holds that: "The first thing that God created was the pen. And He said to it: 'Write!' It said: 'Lord, what should I write?' He said: 'Write down the destiny of all things until the final hour.'"[10] The pen is therefore in some sense the agent of God's will, for it is through it that all things – past, present, and future – were recorded and thereby made manifest. Of course this is only a metaphor. After all, it is specified numerous times in the Qur'an that "His command, when He intends a thing, is only that he says unto it 'Be!' and it is" (Q38:82), and that is indeed the reason reference has been made to "the pen of the command 'Be!'"[11] God, in other words, does not need an instrument to put His will into action, though it may sometimes appear that way; as Annemarie Schimmel put it, God "works through what looks like secondary causes just as a tailor works with a needle or a calligrapher works with a pen."[12] Still, it is very significant that the chosen metaphor should specifically concern *writing*: if the coming-to-be of the divine will is represented by a writing pen, then is God's creation not a written text? This is perhaps why, at the beginning of the sixty-eighth chapter of the Qur'an, God takes an oath "By the pen and that which they write (with it)" (Q68:1) – an oath, in other words, by everything that has been, is, and will be, and by the very agent that makes them all happen. Could His oath have been any more encompassing?

The pronoun "they" in verse 68:1 is generally interpreted as refering to angels.[13] Indeed, angels engaged in the act of writing are alluded to more than once in the foundational texts. For example, an account attributed to the Prophet (on the authority of Abu Dhar) describing his miraculous ascension to the heavens (*mi'raj*) includes the following fascinating detail: "Then Gabriel ascended with me to a place where I heard the creaking of the pens."[14] This was interpreted as angels busily recording the divine decrees, and anyone who has witnessed a scribe or calligrapher writing with a reed pen will know precisely what the verb "creaking" refers to. In the Qur'an, it is stated that "Verily, over you are guardians, noble scribes, who know what you do" (Q82:10–12). A similar idea appears in a number of prophetic traditions, notably a *hadith qudsi* (related by Abu Hurayra) according to which the Prophet reported God as saying to the angels:

> If My slave intends to do a bad deed, then do not write it (in his record) unless he does it; if he does it, then write it as it is, but if he refrains from doing it for My sake, then write it as a good deed. If he intends to do a good deed, but does not do it, then write a good deed; and if he does it, then write it for him as ten good deeds up to seven hundred times.[15]

Another saying attributed to the Prophet (on the authority of ʿAbdullah bin Masʿud) related the stages of development of an embryo in the womb; at a certain time, "God sends an angel who is ordered to write four things: he is ordered to write down his deeds, his livelihood, his death, and whether he will be blessed or wretched. Then the soul is breathed into him."[16] Such written records about a person transform his life into a text, one that shall speak either in his favor or against him on the Day of Judgment. Little wonder, under the circumstances, that the sentence "It was fated" is often rendered into Arabic as "written" (*maktub*), and one's fate is described in Turkish as "the writing on the forehead" (*alın yazısı*).

The text implied in verse 68:1 is of a somewhat different nature, however, as it relates to the totality of events that are to take place between the moment of creation and the end of time. The very popular late fifteenth-century Qurʾanic commentary *Tafsir al-jalalayn* interprets the pen in verse 68:1 as that "with which He wrote the universe in the 'preserved tablet.'"[17] This interpretation was based in part upon a prophetic tradition: according to ʿAbdullah ibn ʿAbbas, the Prophet related that when God created the pen and ordered it to write, the pen immediately began to inscribe the "preserved tablet."[18] This term alludes to the Qurʾanic verses "Nay, this is a glorious Qurʾan in a preserved tablet" (Q85:21–22). Refering to these verses in his commentary, Muhammed Hamdi Yazır noted that the Qurʾan

> is fixed and protected in a tablet where it is under the guardianship of God and safe from distortion and error. This tablet is the "protected tablet" well known in canonical language, which corresponds to the page of being upon which all things are written, as stated in the *Surah Ya-Sin*: "And of all things we have taken account in a clear book" [Q36:12]. And its essence is Divine Knowledge (*ʿilm Allah*), which is the Mother of the Book (*umm al-kitab*).[19]

And what of the "Mother of the Book"? The term is mentioned several times in the Qur'an:

> It is He Who has sent down to you the book in which are sound verses/ signs (*ayat*); they are the Mother of the Book. And others are allegorical. But those in whose hearts is perversity follow the part that is allegorical, seeking discord and searching for their explanation. But no one knows their explanation except for God. And those who are firmly grounded in knowledge say: "We believe in it. It is all from our Lord. Yet only men of understanding heed this." (Q3:7)

> God effaces and confirms what He will; and with Him is the Mother of the Book. (Q13:39)

> By the clear book! Verily we have made it a Qur'an in Arabic, that you may be able to understand. And verily it is in the Mother of the Book, with us, high, wise. (Q43:2–4)

Yazır's text would suggest that the Mother of the Book, as divine knowledge, is the fount of all learning and wisdom. In it is the key to decoding the mysteries of the creation – it is, in fact, the *source of all meaning*. Indeed, the thirteenth-century mystic poet Mawlana Jalaluddin Rumi wrote: "The letter is like a vessel, and its meaning like water / As for the sea of meaning: 'with Him is the Mother of the Book'."[20] To put it another way, the meaning/water with which the letter/vessel is filled is drawn from the book/sea that is the fundamental, eternal, and everlasting text of Islam.

Verse 3:7, cited above, describes the Holy Scripture as composed of two parts – those verses whose meaning is established and well understood, and those that are allegorical and open to interpretation. Indeed, even a cursory look at the Qur'an would be enough to convince any reader that the meaning of many verses is not immediately obvious, and, of course, that is precisely why an immense body of exegetical literature has developed since the earliest days of Islam. The explanation usually given for the difficulty of understanding parts of the Qur'an is that the Holy Scripture is the word of God, which the human intellect is far too limited to comprehend. But in a theological tradition that ascribes complete and unequalled omnipotence and omniscience to God, this explanation begs the question. How could it possibly be beyond God's abilities to produce a text that is not aporetic, a text His human creations, no matter how limited, would be able to understand unambiguously?

The reader-response theorist Wolfgang Iser has argued that any text contains "gaps" or "blanks" – that is to say, ambiguities, indeterminacies, and breaks in signification – caused by the fact that those portions of the text that would be necessary for their elucidation remain unwritten. Meaning is produced, according to him, as the reader interpolates over them, using his or her imagination and infusing them with his or her own interpretation:

> [The reader] is drawn into the events and made to supply what is meant from what is not said. What *is* said only appears to take on significance as a reference to what is not said; it is the implications and not the statements that give shape and weight to the meaning. But as the unsaid comes to life in the reader's imagination, so the said "expands" to take on greater significance than might have been supposed ... Communication in literature, then, is a process set in motion and regulated not by a given code but by a mutually restrictive and magnifying interaction between the explicit and the implicit, between revelation and concealment. What is concealed spurs the reader into action, but this action is also controlled by what is revealed; the explicit in its turn is transformed when the implicit has been brought to light ... Whenever the reader bridges the gaps, communication begins. The gaps function as a kind of pivot on which the whole text-reader relationship revolves. Hence the structured blanks of the text stimulate the process of ideation to be performed by the reader on terms set by the text.[21]

I would suggest that an analogous mechanism is at play in the existence of both "sound" and "allegorical" verses/signs in the Qur'an. Within what I perceive to be the logic of the relationship between text and Islam, the presence of aporias in the Holy Scripture is not an unintended and unfortunate consequence of human limitations, but rather an integral part of the instructional project of the Revelation. It is only by meditating on what is unsaid that the full meaning of what is said can become manifest. As Mohamed Aziz Lahbabi puts it, the Revelation achieves its highest potential for effectiveness when it "engages in a dialogue with our reflections and incites them to make progress and blossom; this would hardly be possible if the doctrine were offered as complete, whole, and definitive."[22] Figuratively speaking, the full comprehension of the Qur'anic text requires as much a reading of the black characters on the page as a reading of the white spaces between them.[23]

Which brings up the important issue of the tradition of orality in Islam. Derrida has criticized what he calls the *logocentrism* of Western philosophy – that is, the metaphysical privileging of the spoken over the written because of the simultaneous presence, in speech, of the utterance in both speaker and listener.[24] While written text usually presents the utterance to the reader in the absence of the writer, thus allowing for misunderstanding, speech is often believed to ensure the accurate transmission of the intended meaning through interpersonal exchange. Interestingly, Islam would appear at first sight to transcend such logocentrism: for example, a *hadith qudsi* attributed to the Prophet reports God as saying "Whoever reads the Qur'an is as if he were talking to Me and I were talking to him."[25] This notion seems to contradict the view that written text is merely a pale simulacrum of speech, but that is only part of the story. In fact, there has always existed a current within Islam, and especially within Shi'ism, that is deeply distrustful of "bookish" knowledge, instead placing a premium on face-to-face interaction between teacher and student.[26] As Nasr notes,

> reading of the "unwritten" text had to be carried out not according to the student's individual whim and fancy, but in accordance with the oral transmission stored in the memory of the master and going back through generations of teachers to the original author of the text and ultimately to the founders and major figures of the school in question – figures who also possessed a "vertical" and non-historical relation with the source of that traditional school ... [I]n gnosis, as in philosophy, a person who is said to have really studied the subject is called *ustad didah*, literally one who has "seen" a master, that is, one who has benefited from the oral teachings and also the presence of the master who embodies those teachings and who renews and revives them through the very act of living their truths.[27]

Still, while it cannot be denied that "genuine" learning has been considered possible only through the personal instruction of a master – who was himself personally instructed by a master, and so on – the fact remains that the oral glosses provided by the master were built upon written texts. The oral tradition in Islam has, to be sure, existed alongside the written tradition, but it has never supplanted it.

Given the centrality of the written text within Islam, it should come as no surprise that it has also played a vital role in the daily lives of many Muslims. Although the legal system has tended to privilege the oral testimony of witnesses over written evidence, a verse in the Qur'an clearly favors the written documentation of commercial transactions:

> O ye who believe! When you contract a debt for a fixed term, record it in writing. Let a scribe write it down justly between you. Let no scribe refuse to write; as God has taught him, so let him write. And let him who incurs the debt dictate, and let him fear God his Lord and not diminish any part of what he owes. But if he who incurs the debt is weak of mind or body, or unable to dictate himself, let his guardian dictate justly. (Q2:282)

There is also evidence of the use of written documents in the prophetic traditions. For example, Abu Hurayra related how once, when the Prophet described the rules governing compensation for damages and blood money, a man present in the audience rose up and requested that the information be put down in writing.[28] Another account (transmitted by al-Bara') describes the drafting of a peace treaty following the Battle of Hudaybiya, which was written down by 'Ali ibn Abi Talib.[29] Indeed, 'Ali is reported to have said "Knowledge is fugitive; tie it down with writing," while his contemporary and rival Mu'awiyah ibn Abi Sufyan similarly said "He who relies on memory is deceived, and he who relies on the record is contented."[30] These are all forceful statements in support of textual practices in early Islam.

It is this religious substrate, as well as various external influences and the requirements imposed by the administration of vast empires, that are responsible for the enormous archival legacy of the Ottomans and other major Islamic states. Some rulers' awareness of the importance of the written text is strikingly illustrated by a statement attributed to the 'Abbasid Caliph al-Ma'mun, son of the illustrious Harun al-Rashid, who was quoted by Abu Hayyan at-Tawhidi as having said: "How wonderful is the calamus! How it weaves the fine cloth of royal power, embroiders the ornamental borders of the garment of the ruling dynasty, and keeps up the standards of the caliphate."[31] Indeed, the continued domination of textuality in the performance and legitimation of authority well into the twentieth century has been demonstrated in an interesting study on Yemen by Brinkley Messick.[32] But the most compelling manifestation of the Islamic preoccupation with textuality is without doubt the widespread application of calligraphy, not only to simple sheets of paper but to objects of every description, made of every conceivable material, and destined for every imaginable use.

A common explanation for the prevalence of calligraphy in Islam is the supposed prohibition against creating figurative images – specifically, images that portray animate beings. This is not the right place to debate the issue, about which much has been said both within and without the Muslim world over many centuries; suffice it to point out that even if there is such a religious prohibition, that would not *ipso facto* imply people's adherence to it – and, indeed, figurative images have by no means been absent from the historical environment of Muslims. Besides, to suggest that calligraphy is a mere substitute for representational art is impossibly ethnocentric: it implies that if left to their own resources, people in any region of the world would unfailingly choose to produce precisely the kind of art that has historically been prized in Europe, and that the only reason for them not to do so can be that they were forbidden to. Not only does this view leave no room for cultures deliberately choosing particular modes of (possibly non-figurative) artistic expression, but it even fails to account for the emergence of abstract art in twentieth-century Europe! The reason for the importance of calligraphy in Islam is not iconophobia, but the centrality of text.

Since the Revelation was first set to writing, Arabic script has been charged with preserving it. Though it was hardly a worthy vessel when first recruited for this holy mission, it gradually became one, as efforts were made to beautify and standardize it. Eventually, the script that preserves the word of God came to be perceived as a Godly script. In this regard, the identification of Arabic script with the religion of Islam is profound and perhaps unequalled. A partial analogy might be found in Gothic blackletter, which has been qualified as "the visual embodiment of German national identity since the days of Luther",[33] and perhaps in Hebrew as well; but their ethnically and linguistically circumscribed scope stands in sharp contrast to the universality that accrues to Arabic script from the universality of Islam. By symbolizing Islam, Arabic writing has become a metonym for the divine order, for the connection between God and His creation. And inscribing objects with Arabic writing has come to denote their enlistment in the divinely ordered system that is Islam. In other words, just as inscribing the human body (whether with a tattoo or with the "proper" posture) denies its atomicity, binding it to a constellation of social relations and establishing its place within a human order; so too does inscribing an object with Arabic script deny its atomicity and situate it within a constellation of *spiritual* relations, highlighting its place within the *divine* order. Far from simply serving an ornamental function, as some have suggested, such inscriptions represent a conscious effort at textually marking the manmade universe and reappropriating it in the name of God.

But what can it mean to reappropriate an *inanimate* object in the name of God? Here, it is important to remember that the Qur'an does not differentiate between animate and inanimate objects when it comes to their relationship with the Lord:

> And unto God do prostrate themselves all that are in the heavens and all that are in the earth, of living creatures and the angels, and they are not proud. They fear their Lord above them, and do whatever they are bidden to do. (Q16:49–50)

> Do you not see that unto God do prostrate themselves all that are in the heavens and all that are in the earth; and the sun, and the moon, and the stars, and the hills, and the trees, and the beasts, and many among humankind? And there are (also) many who are deserving of suffering. Whomever God disgraces, none can rise to honor. Verily God does what He wills. (Q22:18)

In other words, it is incumbent upon all creatures – animate and inanimate – to worship God, and they are all potentially part of God's community of believers. Recall as well that Islam does not present itself as a new faith proclaimed by the Prophet Muhammad, but – since it simply means "submission (to God)" – as the one monotheistic faith from Adam, through Noah, Moses, Jesus, and Muhammad, on to the Day of Judgment. Being a Muslim is, in this respect, the *natural* state of being, whether for angels, humans, beasts, plants, or the heavenly bodies. Thus it is that in a saying attributed to the Prophet (on the authority of Anas ibn Malik), according to which "Every newborn is born true to his nature, then his parents make him Jewish, Christian, or Magian (Zoroastrian),"[34] the state of "nature" has traditionally been interpreted to mean Islam.

Hence, inscribing objects with Arabic script simply amounts to making *explicit* their true nature, their membership in the community of God. To take one example, the textualization of the human body, the Qur'an proclaims: "And We shall show them Our signs in the horizons and in themselves" (Q41:53).[35] Some Muslim thinkers sought such signs in the appearance of human beings – for example, the seventeenth-century Ottoman mystic Oğlanlar Şeyhi İbrahim taught that "From head to toe, the form of man exhibits the word of God; as such, instances of the shape of His proper name can be perceived in some of his features."[36] It is crucial, incidentally, that it is the *word* of God that is manifested in the form of man, and not His image. Islamic tradition regards God as absolutely transcendent, and representing His form would have simply been inconceivable for a Muslim; it is only through the mediation of text, that is, by means of his word, that God is manifested in the form of man. The five fingers of the hand, for example, were likened to the five vertical strokes in the name *Allah*. The positions taken by the body during the daily prayers – standing, genuflexion, and prostration – were likened to the letters *alif*, *dal*, and *mim*, which, taken together, constitute the name *Adem* (Adam, and also simply "man"); this was seen as illustrating the fact that prayer is a human being's central function.[37] Mystics likened a man who has turned his back on all worldly possessions, devoting himself entirely to God, to the letter *alif* – the first letter of the alphabet, whose stark verticality, and numerical value of one, testify to the uniqueness of God. Relatedly, the posture of a Mevlevi ("whirling") dervish was interpreted as affirming the existence of God through an ingenious textual reference to the first part of the Muslim profession of faith, *la ilaha illa Allah*: the letters *lam* and *alif* spell out the word *la*, "there is not," but with the addition of another *alif*, they become *illa*, "except for." When superimposed, the ligature *lam-alif* and the additional *alif* look very much like a Mevlevi dervish in his robes, performing the *semâ*; thus, the body of the dervish, corresponding to the additional *alif*, makes the difference between denial (*la*) and reaffirmation (*illa*).[38] Such similes were also very common in lyrical poetry, as shown in the fourteenth-century treatise *Anis al-ʿushshaq* by Hasan ibn Muhammad Sharafuddin al-Rami.

It is the profound way in which Islam, as Divine Revelation, has been embedded in the concept of text and the materiality of writing that has provided such a generative source of poetic inspiration. But Arabic script was not merely an arsenal of metaphors: it placed the body-physical within a network of significations that made it part of the body-spiritual. The writing of text with Arabic script upon objects is neither simply a technique of ornamentation, nor a way around the prohibition of images; rather, it provides *spiritual subtitles* to the material universe. Making explicit the *implicit textuality* of the creation, it is a discovering – a *revelation* – of the signs of God within the visible.

18

WAR

Sohail H. Hashmi

I

The Islamic tradition has historically had a lot to say about war, more so in a direct way than Judaism or Christianity, and perhaps more than any other religious tradition. Unlike Christianity, Islam developed in the crucible of war, and moral and practical reflections on war were part of Islam's intellectual heritage from its formative period. Unlike Judaism, Islam never experienced a diasporic interregnum in which the community was politically disenfranchised and scholarly discussions revolved around wars of centuries past that may never have occurred. Within thirteen years of the beginning of the Prophet Muhammad's preaching in Mecca, the Muslim community was at war. Over the next ten years, according to the Prophet's biographer Ibn Ishaq, the Muslims engaged in thirty-eight military campaigns with Muhammad himself leading twenty-seven of these.[1] During this twenty-three year period, the Qur'an moves from near silence on the topic of war to scores of verses dealing with diverse aspects of it. The Hadith literature, likewise, is replete with the Prophet's injunctions on different dimensions of war.

In the centuries following Muhammad's death, Muslim writers expounded at length on the moral and practical aspects of war. They did so in a number of literary genres: Qur'anic commentary (*ta'wil* or *tafsir*), legal treatises (*fiqh*), military manuals (*adab al-harb*), histories (*tarikh*), and philosophical disquisitions (*falsafa*). Modern Muslim discourse on war is similarly broadranging and often contentious, marked by varying interpretations of the Qur'an, Hadith, and the classical *fiqh* in light of contemporary conflicts and the development of international law. Yet one issue is left largely untreated in both the pre-modern and modern Islamic literature. This is the existential question: why war? This question differs from the causes or origins of specific wars, a subject taken up by numerous Muslim historians. It also differs from the grounds of a just or legitimate war, a topic on which many Muslim jurists and ethicists have expatiated at length. The question I have in mind is the more fundamental issue of the problem of war. Why is war entrenched as a timeless and universal institution among human beings? The usual secular responses would focus on such factors as human nature, the values and institutions of particular cultures, and the anarchy of intersocietal relations. Within a religious framework, there is as well the theological concern with the role of divine will versus human agency (is war God's doing or man's?) and the moral concern with war's status (is it evil or not?). Both concerns come together in the familiar dilemma of theodicy, which may be formulated in Islamic terms thus: if God is al-Qadir (the All-Powerful) and He wills His creation to suffer in war, then how can He be al-Rahman (the Most Compassionate) and al-Rahim (the Most Merciful)? If He is al-Rahman and al-Rahim, but He tolerates the evil of war, how can He be al-Qadir? My search for answers begins with Islamic theology, especially the Qur'an. I conclude with Islamic philosophy, and in particular the most detailed Muslim treatment of this issue, that of Ibn Khaldun in the *Muqaddima*.

II

The problem of war in the Bible, as one Christian writer, Peter Craigie, puts it, is that "the frequent use of the word [*milhamah*, Hebrew for 'war'] is disturbing in a book which is associated so intimately with the Prince of Peace [Jesus]." The "sensitive Christian reader of the Old Testament," he continues, must grapple with a variety of problems created by its numerous references to war. The first set of problems Craigie describes as personal and internal to the Christian attempting to reconcile the apparently conflicting visions of God presented by the two Testaments. The second set of problems is external: "the presence of so much martial material in the Old Testament has provided in the past, and continues to provide in the present, a basis from which a critique may be launched against the Christian Bible, or against the Christian faith." It has also provided, Craigie notes, scriptural support for crusades and other Christian holy wars.[2]

Many Muslims who ponder the problem of war in the Qur'an would find parallels between their dilemma and Craigie's. They would agree that the problem has both an internal and an external dimension. The internal dimension is, however, the reverse of what Craigie describes for the Bible. The Qur'an discusses war using primarily three terms: *harb, qital,* and *jihad.* The earlier revelations, received by Muhammad in Mecca, are, like the New Testament, devoid of any martial content. The verbal root *h-r-b,* from which the specific Arabic word for war, *harb,* is derived, is found nowhere in the verses believed to date from the Meccan period (610–622 C.E.). *Q-t-l,* from which *qital,* a word meaning fighting and killing, is derived, occurs rarely in these same verses. In the few instances where it is found, the references are to contexts other than fighting and killing in war. Likewise, occurrences of the verbal root *j-h-d,* from which *jihad* is derived, are extremely few in the Meccan verses and confined entirely to the sense of metaphysical struggle. Q25:52, for example, exhorts Muhammad to "strive [*jahid*] against the unbelievers with it [the Qur'an] with the utmost effort [*jihad^{an} kabir^{an}*]."

Does the Meccan Qur'an espouse pacifism? The classical Qur'anic exegetes are divided in their answer. Some claim that God merely restrained (*kaffa*) Muhammad from fighting the polytheists until explicit sanction for war comes at the time of the *hijra* or shortly thereafter. Others read in the Meccan verses a positive ban (*hazr*) on fighting.[3] My reading of the Qur'an's Meccan revelations tends toward agreement with the first group: these verses do not rule out war; they cannot be read as unambiguously enjoining an ethic of pacifism. But the Meccan Qur'an certainly leans in that direction. Without the later Medinan verses, the Qur'an, like the New Testament, could have given rise over time to pacifist interpretations.

Just as the New Testament's approach to war must have seemed radically novel to many who first encountered it, so too must the Meccan Qur'an have seemed to those who first heard it. Pre-Islamic Arabian society was built firmly upon tribal identities and unwavering loyalty. Although a loose hierarchy of tribes existed, determined by reputation for valor, nobility, or wealth, the intertribal political system was anarchical. Each tribe jealously guarded its autonomy, which was equated not so much with territorial jurisdiction, but with unrestrained exercise of its communal or commercial prerogatives. In this milieu, war was not a problem demanding explanation. It was accepted as a routine and normal arbiter of conflict, and a ready means to divest rivals of their property and enrich oneself. Moreover, it provided a way to demonstrate the masculine virtues extolled by the Arabs.

Consensus on the general principles of intertribal relations appears to have kept this Arab system stable and on the whole free of large-scale warfare. Military campaigns aimed at eliminating a tribe's political autonomy or control of territory (*manakh*) were rare although not unheard of. The Qur'an alludes in the 105th chapter to a full-scale invasion of the Hijaz by an army from Yemen, believed to have occurred a few months prior to the birth of the Prophet.

War consisted primarily of internecine skirmishes (*ghazwa*) among rival tribes. These seldom had any purpose other than plunder, particularly of livestock. If a conflict had any "higher" purpose, it was usually collective reprisal (*tha'r*) for an injury or affront suffered by a member of the tribe according to the prevailing *lex talionis*. The Fijar (Sacrilegious) War of Muhammad's youth typifies such conflicts. Its provocation was apparently the plunder of a caravan and the murder of its guide from the Hawazin tribe by members of the Kinanah tribe during one of the four prohibited months (hence its name). Although the Quraysh tribe had not perpetrated these actions, Hawazin declared a vendetta against it because the outrages had taken place in Qurayshi territory. The war continued intermittently for four years until the two tribes were reconciled in the usual manner: the tribe that had lost the most men received the bloodwit for the difference in casualties. In this case, Quraysh paid the bloodwit of twenty men to Kinanah.[4]

Naturally, tribal loyalty was the cornerstone of this society's ethos, and virtue was often equated with martial valor. The *Ayyam al-'arab* (days of the Arabs) literature, our primary source on Jahili, or pre-Islamic, Arab mores, is replete with legends extolling the military prowess of ancient Arab heroes. Wars, according to this image, could erupt on the slightest provocation, as suggested in the following verse of Zuhair ibn Abi Sulma: "Fearless: when one him wrongs, he sets him to vengeance straight, unfaltering: when no wrong lights on him, 'tis he that wrongs."[5]

Once begun, wars were conducted, at least in poetry, with little regard for scruples. Yet, other sources point to an unwritten martial code that governed the conduct of war. This code prohibited, among other things, fighting during four sacred months, bloodshed in or near religious sanctuaries, the unnecessary killing of women and children, and undue spoliation. The *ghazwa* was viewed by the Arabs as a sort of ongoing sport, a struggle to outwit the opponent and thereby deprive him of his possessions with a minimum of bloodshed. War for the sake of war was not the goal, nor perhaps even the vanquishing of foes. Rather, fighting was a means to demonstrate the qualities of courage, loyalty, and magnanimity – all components of masculine nobility included in the notion of *muruwwa*.[6]

Against this backdrop, the Qur'an's early teachings and the Prophet's own policy of refraining from violence in response to insult and abuse must have come across as decidedly un-Arab to his opponents and perhaps many of his supporters as well. Most early commentators are convinced that the non-violent ethic of the Meccan Qur'an was dictated entirely by a pragmatic appreciation of the relative weakness of the Muslim community. This certainly may have been one factor, but I do not think it is the only or even the major one. The Prophet spent nearly thirteen years in Mecca pursuing a policy of non-violent resistance. If, in fact, this policy was dictated by military weakness and not principle, then it is reasonable to expect some effort to change the Muslims' material situation. But there is no historical evidence that he did so, even after the conversion of some Quraysh, including his uncle Hamza and 'Umar ibn al-Khattab, known for their physical prowess. Instead of preparing the Muslims to fight back, as the Arab code would expect and demand, he ordered the most vulnerable of them to flee to Abyssinia, to seek the protection of a non-Arab ruler.

The Muslims' initial avoidance of violence must have appeared odd to the Meccans, but perhaps not incomprehensible. For all the machismo that characterizes pre-Islamic literature on war, there is a marked pathos as well. The suggestion that Arab culture glorified war is unwarranted, as was well-known to many medieval Muslim writers who cited Jahili poetry deprecating unnecessary war. The best-known verse, ascribed to Imru al-Qays, compares war at its start to a young and alluring woman. But once it begins, war quickly becomes like a hag, hideous in appearance, unable to find any suitor to embrace her.[7] The word *harb* is feminine, and feminine metaphors are commonplace in descriptions of war, as in this verse of Sa'd ibn Malik: "How evil a thing is war, that bows men to shameful rest! War burns away in her blaze all glory and boasting of men. War girds up her skirts before them, and evil unmixed is bare."[8] And again in the poetry of Zuhair ibn Abi Sulma:

> When ye set her on foot, ye start her with words of little praise; but the mind of her grows with her growth, till she bursts into blazing flame.
> She will grind you as grist of the mill that falls on the skin beneath; year by year shall her womb conceive, and the fruit thereof shall be twins;
> Yea, boys shall she bear you, all of ill-omen ...[9]

An appreciation for war's dire consequences hangs over the historical accounts of the decisive event that precedes the Prophet's migration to Medina (the *hijra*). When the men of Yathrib take the Second Pledge of 'Aqaba, promising to give refuge to Muhammad in their town, they are aware, as one of them declares, that they must prepare for "war against all and sundry."[10] The Prophet himself pledges: "I am of you and you are of me. I will war against them that war against you and be at peace with those at peace with you."[11] This is the Prophet's first explicit sanction for war recorded by his biographers. What explains the shift in his policy? The biographical literature provides no clear answer, but the usual narrative places the First and Second Pledges of 'Aqaba at the end of a long search for tribal protection by Muhammad, once he had lost the guarantee of his own clan following the death of his uncle Abu Talib. The Second Pledge is not a declaration of war, and therefore it cannot be seen as a complete abandonment of the earlier policy of non-violent action. But it is an assurance of military action should war occur, and therefore it is a move away from the earlier policy of exclusively non-violent resistance. After eschewing violence for many years, Muhammad may have concluded that for the Muslim community to survive, war was now unavoidable as a last resort. The first Qur'anic verses explicitly to sanction war support this conclusion: "To those against whom war is made, permission is given [to fight back], because they are wronged, and truly God is most powerful in their aid. [They are] those who have been expelled from their homes against all right, [for no reason] except that they say, 'Our Lord is God'" (Q22:39–40).

In Medina, the vocabulary of war enters the Qur'an directly and dramatically. The root *h-r-b* appears five times with the meaning of armed conflict. The Qur'an discusses war using mainly the root *q-t-l*, which appears in the Medinan verses some eighty times with the clear meaning of fighting and killing in battle. On at least ten occasions, the root *j-h-d* is linked to *qital*, giving the concept of *jihad* a new, martial component that it had apparently lacked in the *jahiliyya*.[12]

The Medinan Qur'an not only introduces war into Islamic faith and praxis, it seems to take the Islamic sanction for war to ever-broader goals. Thus, it changes the initial permission for a defensive war enunciated in Q22:39–40 into a command in Q2:190: "Fight in the cause of God those who fight against you." Finally, the Qur'an seems to enjoin a war of conversion against all remaining polytheists in Q9:5, the so-called Verse of the Sword:

> But when the forbidden months are past, then fight and slay the poly-theists [*mushrikin*] wherever you find them. Seize them, besiege them, and lie in wait for them using every stratagem. But if they repent, and establish regular prayers, and practice regular charity, then open the way for them. For God is most forgiving, most merciful.

And Q9:29, the Verse of *Jizya* (poll-tax), seems to command a war of subjugation against unspecified earlier scripturaries:

> Fight those who do not believe in God or the Last Day, nor hold for-bidden that which has been forbidden by God and His Messenger, nor acknowledge the religion of truth, from among those who have been given the Book, until they pay the *jizya* with willing submission, having been subdued.

The chronology of Qur'anic revelations has always been an inexact science, and Qur'anic commentators disagree on the order in which some of the earliest verses on war were revealed. But there is general agreement that Q9:5 and Q9:29 are among the last verses revealed on the subject of war. Thus, in the view of many influential Qur'anic commentators – pre-modern as well as modern – the Qur'anic theology of war proceeds according to a teleology: the evolution starts with non-violent resistance in the Meccan period, followed by defensive war in the early Medinan period, and ends finally with offensive war as the Prophet's life comes to an end.

When the verses of the sword and *jizya* were revealed, the Qur'an's move from the New Testament ethics of non-violence to the Hebrew Bible's idea of holy war is, it would seem, complete. In the Medinan Qur'an, as in the Hebrew Bible, God not only permits war, He commands it. He orders the Prophet to exhort the faithful to fight (Q4:84; 8:65) and decries those who abstain or flee from battle (e.g. Q8:15–16; 9:38–39; 33:16–20). He tests the believers through the trial of war (e.g. Q8:17; 47:4,31), promising heavenly rewards to those who patiently endure their suffering and to the martyrs (Q2:154–157; 3:156–158; 9:20; 22:58–59). Moreover, God Himself fights on behalf of the righteous (Q8:17), while Iblis (Satan) schemes for the iniquitous (Q4:76).

The internal problem of war in the Qur'an can now be stated simply as this: how do we reconcile the Meccan Qur'an with the Medinan Qur'an? There are hints in the Qur'an that this tension arose soon after the *hijra* for the first Muslims themselves.

> Have you not seen those who were told to hold back their hands [from fighting], but to establish prayers and practice charity? When the order for fighting was issued to them, behold! A group of them feared men as – or even more than – they should have feared God. They said: "Our Lord! Why have you ordered us to fight? Would you not grant us respite for a while longer?" Say: "Short is the enjoyment of this world. The Hereafter is the best for those who do right. Never will you be dealt with unjustly in the very least!" (Q4:77)

The classical Qur'anic exegetes grappled with this issue as well. The solution that the majority embraced was the doctrine of chronological abrogation: The verses revealed last annulled those revealed earlier; the verses of the sword and *jizya* superseded the scores of verses enjoining non-violence or defensive war. The doctrine of abrogation and the resulting, dominant Qur'anic narrative on war that it permitted provided sanction – after the fact – for the expansionist wars of the first Islamic century. Thus, the dominant narrative as well as the history of Muslim military expansion gave rise to the external problem that Craigie describes in the case of the Bible. The Medinan Qur'an – in particular those verses that apparently enjoin wars of conquest and conversion – provides ample ammunition for those who criticize Islam as a religion of violence, intolerance, and war. The long record of such anti-Islamic polemics hardly needs further elaboration here.[13] In our own time, the numerous atrocities committed by Muslim governments and Muslim terrorists – some explicitly defended by reference to Qur'an and Hadith – have revived the age-old imputations of the violence inherent in Islamic doctrine.[14] There were dissenters from the dominant narrative even as it developed, and their modern intellectual heirs began to mount a sustained challenge to it over the past century and a half. Some, such as the Indian writer Chiragh 'Ali (d. 1895), dismissed the classical theory of an expansionist *jihad* as based on "uncertain traditions, Arabian usages and customs, some frivolous and fortuitous analogical deductions from the Koran, and a multitudinous array of casuistical sophistry of the canonical legists."[15] Other critics were more circumspect, but they tended equally to the conclusion that the dominant narrative rests on a highly selective reading of the Qur'an's complete message on war and peace. In order to resolve the internal problem posed by the seemingly opposite tendencies of the Meccan and the Medinan revelations, the classical exegetes employed the blunt instrument of abrogation where a more sophisticated hermeneutics was required. To arrive at the conclusion that the Qur'an mandates wars of conquest requires doing violence to the totality of the Qur'an's message; it requires disregarding not only the entire Meccan Qur'an, but also much of the Medinan Qur'an that continues to speak of tolerance, forbearance, and strictly defensive war where no other recourse to aggression is available. As I have argued elsewhere, the internal problem of war in the Qur'an is more apparent than real.[16]

There is no need to develop these points further in this essay. My goal here is not to explore when war is just or legitimate, or how it should be properly waged and ended. I believe that if read as whole, the Qur'an does provide consistent and coherent answers to these questions. My point in presenting the preceding summary of the Qur'an's development has been to show that war is treated neither as a ubiquitous nor an altogether absent aspect of the human condition. Just as the New Testament is not unambiguously pacifist or the Hebrew Bible bellicist, so neither respectively are the Meccan or Medinan revelations. The Qur'an's message seems to be: war exists; it is always a threat. Trying to discern Qur'anic answers to why this is so is the task now before us.

III

Theological explanations for war in Judaism and Christianity often depart from assumptions about the nature of God or of human beings, so let us begin there. In the Hebrew Bible, God not only commands His people to wage war on His behalf, He is Himself a warrior, a Man in Battle (Exodus 15:1–18), the Lord of Hosts (that is, armies, including those of the Israelites). "Who is the King of Glory? The Lord, strong and mighty. The Lord, mighty in battle" (Psalm 24:8). God's wars on earth are foreshadowed, for many Christian theologians, by the War in Heaven, when God with His loyal angels vanquished Satan and the angels who followed him before casting the rebels down. War originated, in this view, not through the fall of humankind, but through the fall of Lucifer, and war among humans remains the devil's work. "It is no occasion for surprise," comments one sixteenth-century writer, "that in all ages since the world began, peoples, kings and other rulers have persisted in war even down to our time ... and that there will be no end to this evil until the world itself shall pass away we are warned by divine utterance."[17]

Such theological explanations for war do not transfer well into the Islamic tradition. The trope of God as warrior is absent from the Qur'an. Apart from the verse mentioned earlier (Q8:17), which states with reference to the battle of Badr, "It was not you who slew them, it was God," God is not immanent in the battles of the Muslims. As for the War in Heaven, the Qur'an makes no allusion to such an event, either directly or implicitly.[18] Iblis's rebellion is presented as a solitary act of defiance, a rebellion born out of vanity and arrogance at the prospect of having to bow down before the first human (Q2:34; 7:11; 15:31–33, etc.). As a number of commentators have observed, the Islamic Satan is much less potent a force for evil-doing than the Christian. He does not lead legions of angels, nor are his powers remotely comparable to God's. His strength lies mainly in exploiting human frailties to seduce humans from righteousness (Q15:39–40; 34:20–21). He provokes enmity and hatred (Q5:91), sows dissension and strife (Q17:53), but ultimately, on the Day of Judgment, Iblis will tell those who fell into his snare: "I had no authority over you except to call you, but you responded. So do not reproach me, but reproach your own souls" (Q14:22).

As we will see shortly, peace (*salam*) not war (*harb*) is the word the Qur'an uses to describe the state of heaven. Indeed, conflict of any sort is missing from God's creation until He creates human beings. Upon being told of the impending arrival of this new being, the angels remonstrate, "Will you place [on earth] one who will spread corruption and shed blood?" (Q2:30). The implication is that such things did not exist before humans enter the stage. So is the Qur'an suggesting that some part of God's design of humankind, some essential characteristic of human nature, is the root cause of war?

Judaism, Christianity, and Islam all share many similarities in their understanding of the fall of man, but there are significant differences as well with important consequences for theological explanations for war. Christian writers often describe war as a symptom of original sin. Jews and Christians see in Cain's murder of Abel a prototype of the fratricide that all subsequent wars essentially represent. Islamic theology has no notion of original sin, and although the story of Cain and Abel is found in the Qur'an, it has not generated significant commentary linking this first murder to war. Instead, we can construct from the Qur'an an alternative Islamic view on the link between human nature and war.

The original nature (*fitra*) of human beings, as suggested by both Qur'an and Hadith, is moral innocence or freedom from sin. Moreover, each individual is born with an inherent God consciousness and intuitive knowledge of divine commandments, that is, with the essential tools to form moral judgments and to engage in righteous behavior. The enigmatic verse Q7:172 suggests this conclusion: "When your Lord drew forth from the children of Adam, from their loins, their offspring, and made them testify concerning themselves, [asking]: 'Am I not your Lord?' – They said: 'Yes! We do so testify!' [This], lest you should say on the Day of Judgment: 'Of this we were never aware.'"

God's purpose for humanity is that it live on the earth in a state of harmony and peace. This is the ultimate meaning of the responsibility God assigns to humans as His vicegerent (*khalifa*) on this planet (Q2:30). Just as God is at peace with His creation, so human beings as God's agents or deputies on earth should be at peace with each other and other living things. True peace (*salam*) is not merely an absence of war; it is the elimination of the grounds for strife or conflict, and the resulting waste and corruption (*fasad*) they create.

Yet, given human beings' distinctive endowment of free will, each person has the capacity for wrongdoing, and all will at some time *choose* to violate their nature and transgress against God's commandments. Adam becomes fully human only when he chooses to heed Iblis's temptation and disobeys God. As a result of this initial act of disobedience, human beings are expelled from the Garden to dwell on earth as "enemies to each other" (Q2:36; 7:24). Thus, wars and the evils that stem from them, the Qur'an suggests, are the inevitable consequence of the uniquely human capacity for moral choice.

The Qur'an does not present the fall of man as irrevocable, however, for God quickly returns to Adam to support and guide him (Q2:37). This, according to Islamic belief, is the beginning of continuous divine revelation to humanity through a series of prophets ending with Muhammad. God's reminders of the laws imprinted upon each human consciousness through His prophets are a manifestation of His endless mercy to His creation because all human beings are potential victims of Iblis's guile. Human nature is a mixture of the sublime and the base, the angelic and the beastly: "We have indeed created man from the best of moulds. Then did We reduce him to the lowest of the low" (Q95:4–5). We are all potential evildoers, and the majority live, stubbornly, quite removed from God's laws (e.g. Q26:8,67,103; 27:73; 43:78).

The instinctual moral awareness with which we are born is eroded as each individual encounters the corrupting influences of human society. In groups, the individual drive for power, wealth, prestige, and all the other innumerable human ambitions becomes amplified. People become all the more prone to disobey God's will through obstinate persistence in wrongdoing caused by custom and social pressures (Q2:8–14; 43:22). Conflict and the recourse to violence in efforts to resolve it are the inevitable result of the individual desire for self-aggrandizement in society and of one group's quest for material advantage over another.

Each prophet encounters opposition from those who persist in their rebellion against God, justifying their actions through various self-delusions. One of the principal characteristics of rejection of God (*kufr*) is the inclination toward violence and oppression, encapsulated by the broad concept of *zulm*. When individuals choose to reject divine guidance, either by transgressing against specific divine injunctions or by losing faith altogether, they violate (commit *zulm*) against their own nature (*fitra*). When Adam and Eve disobey the divine command in the Garden, the Qur'an relates that they cry out in their despair not that they have sinned against God, but rather that they have transgressed against their own souls (Q7:23).

When an entire society rejects God and, specifically, God's laws, oppression and violence become the norm throughout the society and in relations with other societies as well. The moral anarchy that prevails when human beings abandon the higher moral code derived from faith in a supreme and just Creator, the Qur'an suggests, is fraught with potential and actual violence (Q2:11–12, 27, 204–205; Q7, *al-Aʿraf*, deals with this theme at length).

True peace is attainable only when human beings surrender to God's will and live according to God's laws. This is the condition of *islam*, the conscious decision to acknowledge in faith and conduct the presence and power of God, in other words, to act on the covenant God extracted from individuals when he asked, "Am I not your Lord?" The Qur'an repeatedly emphasizes the semantic linkage between the words *salam* and *islam*, suggesting that true peace arises only from true submission: "O you who believe! Enter into Islam or peace (*silm*) wholeheartedly; and follow not the footsteps of the Evil One; for he is to you an avowed enemy" (Q2:208). "And the servants of [God] the Most Gracious are those who walk on the earth in humility, and when the ignorant address them, they say, 'Peace!'" (Q2:63). Peace is not only the quality of *islam* in this life, it is the principal reward of the life to come. No quality is linked to paradise more than *salam*: "No frivolity will they hear therein, nor any taint of ill – only the saying, 'Peace! Peace!'" (Q56:25–26).

True *islam* or submission to God's laws is the Qur'an's call to all human beings. Yet there is an awareness as well that few individuals and societies will ever conform fully to the precepts of *islam*. Muslims must always be prepared to defend themselves, their community, and their faith and principles (Q8:60,73). As the Qur'an elaborates in an early revelation, the believers are those "who, whenever tyranny afflicts them, defend themselves" (Q42:39). The use of force by the Muslim community is sanctioned by God as a necessary response to the existence of evil in the world. Immediately following the first verse that explicitly permitted the Muslims to use armed force against their enemies (Q22:39), the Qur'an makes clear that fighting is a burden imposed upon all believers (not only Muslims) as a result of the enmity harbored by the unbelievers: "For, if God had not enabled people to defend themselves against one another, monasteries and churches and synagogues and mosques – in all of which God's name is abundantly extolled – would surely have been destroyed" (Q22:40). Q49:9 acknowledges that the Muslim community itself may be rent by violent factions, and forceful intervention may be necessary to stop the transgressors.

Among the early Medinan revelations that serve the dual purpose of justifying war and exhorting Muslims to fight is the following, arresting verse: "Fighting is prescribed for you, and you dislike it. But it is possible that you dislike a thing which is good for you, and that you love a thing which is bad for you. But God knows, and you know not" (Q2:216). From an early period, this verse has generated a great deal of commentary, but generally the exegetes focused not so much on the first part relating to war, but on the second dealing with the human capacity to form right moral judgments. Muslim theologians wrangled over the metaethical implications of this part of the verse for centuries.[19] I want to concentrate on the verse's implications for the Islamic view of war, and particularly for the moral status of war.

No verse from the Meccan period rules out war, but this verse from the Medinan period would seem to rule out pacifism. "War is prescribed for you" (*kutiba 'alaykum*) follows a Qur'anic formula when God legislates for the Muslim community. Thus, God prescribes fasting (*siyam*, Q2:183) and the law of retaliation for murder (*qisas*, Q2:178). The comparison between war and capital punishment for murder is worth pursuing, for in both cases, the believers are being told that violence in response to violence received is legitimate and just. The context of Q2:216 indicates that the Muslims are not commanded in this verse to initiate war, for the verses immediately following refer to the persecution and exile that the Muslims have already suffered at the hands of their Meccan foes (Q2:217–218).

Now to consider what the verse suggests about the ethical status of war: is it morally good, neutral, or evil? First, the verse acknowledges that war is something disliked by (at the least) the Muslims and (probably) most human beings. War is a burdensome enterprise (see Q47:4). Human beings recoil from its hardships. War does not come naturally to them; they have to be exhorted to fight. If there is any explicit statement in the Qur'an that human nature is not inherently prone to war, it is here in Q2:216.

But then the verse continues, it seems, by challenging, if not negating, the instinctive or intuitive moral judgment of war as evil. In doing so, however, I do not think Q2:216 is positing war as good. The Qur'anic verses on war taken as a whole point to the conclusion that war is to be avoided as much as possible, but under certain circumstances, avoiding it further becomes morally reprehensible. War is prescribed by God not because it is good, but neither is it proscribed by God because it is evil. It may be a necessary evil to thwart even greater evils. Q2:191 states emphatically "violence and persecution [*fitna*] are worse [*ashadd*] than killing [*qital*]," and the verse immediately following Q2:216 reaffirms this position: "*Fitna* is greater [*akbar*] than *qital.*"

In short, what we can glean from the Qur'an is that, inasmuch as God is the author of all things, war is a part of human existence sanctioned and even willed by God. Why? Although the Qur'an speaks repeatedly of God testing the believers through war, to me this is not the answer. God tests human beings in many ways – through success and failure, wealth and poverty, belief and unbelief (Q2:155; 6:165; 89:15–16, and others). War does not loom large in the Qur'anic list of trials; indeed, appearing as it does only in the Medinan revelations, it seems confined in space and time. The real test involving war is not whether people are ready to die and kill, but whether they are ready to sacrifice everything if required to check evil. This is where war becomes fused with *jihad fi sabil Allah* (struggle in the way of God). Everything else is simply *harb*.

The Qur'an's attitude toward war and peace is a pragmatic idealism, rooted in appreciation of all the flaws inherent in individuals and collectivities. Human existence is characterized neither by incessant warfare nor real peace, but by a continuous tension between the two. Societies exist forever in a precarious balance between them. The unending human challenge is to mitigate the possibility of war and strengthen the grounds for peace. The resulting human condition may bear out the truth of the angels' initial protest to God that His decision to create man would only lead to corruption and bloodshed in the world. But tempering those Qur'anic passages that are less than sanguine regarding human nature are those confirming the human capacity to triumph over evil (Q5:48,56; 49:7; 58:21). God silences the angels, after all, not by denying their prognostication, but by holding out the possibility of unforeseen potential: "I know what you know not" (Q2:30).

IV

In this final section, I consider the first detailed inquiry into the causes of war by a Muslim author. It is found in the *Muqaddima* of Ibn Khaldun (d. 1406). Prior to the *Muqaddima*, Muslim authors naturally discussed war in the rich body of literature on the Qur'an and Hadith. These works deal almost exclusively with the purpose and prosecution of *jihad*. They begin with the prior assumption that *jihad* is a divinely commanded institution incumbent upon the Muslim community. *Jihad* is the only form of warfare permissible in Islam; all other forms of political violence are therefore prohibited. Little attention is given in these early works to the more basic philosophical questions of why *jihad* is necessary or why other types of war occur.

More general and analytical consideration of the problem of war starts with the rise of manuals for statecraft in the tenth century. These "mirrors for princes" bear the indelible marks of pre-Islamic Persian influences. Sassanid maxims on politics and war are combined with narratives from the Prophet or the early caliphs. Because these works were intended to provide practical advice to rulers, the mirrors genre focuses little if any attention on *jihad* which, in its classical conception, had already lapsed by this time. Instead, the focus is upon war as a very mundane reality, a problem that demanded clear understanding and adroit handling by the wise prince. One of the most influential of the early mirrors is that of the Andalucian jurist Muhammad ibn al-Walid al-Turtushi (d. 1126). Al-Turtushi lived in a time of increasing fragmentation of the Islamic order in southern Spain, leading eventually to the collapse of the western Umayyad dynasty and its replacement by a number of rival princely houses. Accordingly, war emerges in his *Siraj al-muluk* as a social calamity, a departure from the norm of a well-ordered society.[20] This view of war is developed more explicitly in the work of the Egyptian scholar al-Hasan ibn 'Abdallah al-'Abbasi (d. 1310). He describes wars as "temporary disturbances in time, like illnesses," which can be prevented through an informed and effective political administration.[21] Both al-Turtushi and al-Hasan ibn 'Abdallah emphasize prevention as the best means of avoiding wars.

Ibn Khaldun's central purpose in the *Muqaddima* is to outline a science of culture, grounded in the rational analysis of repeating patterns in history. As a result, the institution of war demanded his close attention. For Ibn Khaldun, wars are the inevitable result of human sociability. Human beings are of necessity social creatures, drawn together for subsistence and for self-preservation. God has granted most living creatures, he argues, the physical means for self-defense. But to human beings He gave instead the intellectual ability to compensate for their relative physical inferiority: humans are able not only to devise weapons for their protection, they are also able to realize the importance of mutual cooperation.[22]

However, with communal life quickly comes the prospect of war. Human sociability does not produce harmony, for human beings can never escape their essential "animal nature" that leads them to "aggressiveness and injustice."[23] The propensity to coercion, aggression, and violence is, in Ibn Khaldun's view, a natural and inescapable aspect of human existence. At the same time, he avers, this propensity is objectively and subjectively an evil. Man's moral nature is revolted by the exercise of aggression and his moral reasoning demands that it be curbed, if not altogether eliminated. Society emerges when a group recognizes a governmental authority with the coercive power to restrain the propensity toward mutual aggression within the city or the tribe.[24]

The formation of communal groups does not, of course, eliminate the human instinct for aggression and violence. It merely refocuses this urge on to a higher societal level. The study of war now enters Ibn Khaldun's analysis as an integral aspect of his concept of *'asabiyya*, or loyalty to one's own "group" defined by kinship or prolonged association in society. Such group loyalties permit certain individuals to rule as "chieftains" of small social units through consensus, without any real means of coercion. But the logical goal to which human nature leads is the use of *'asabiyya* to establish ever greater social units. Royal authority (*mulk*) emerges when a chieftain adds the physical means of coercion to his tribe's *'asabiyya* in order to compel other tribes to submit to his rule. The broader *'asabiyya* that results from such agglomeration promotes in turn the quest for "superiority over people of other group feelings unrelated to the first."[25] Thus, *'asabiyya* has an intimate and complex relationship to war. It emerges in the first instance as a consequence of the fear created by violence among individuals. It is fostered in the second place by the fear that particular groups of individuals have toward other groups. Finally, it promotes intergroup rivalries, ambitions, and aggression which lie at the root of war. *'Asabiyya* is for Ibn Khaldun second only to man's innate aggressiveness in being a primal, universal, and powerful engine of human history.

Ibn Khaldun's analysis of *'asabiyya* now merges with his analysis of the rise of Islam. *'Asabiyya* is strongest among small kin groups forced by harsh physical circumstances to rely upon each other for survival. As a result, the *'asabiyya* of the bedouin Arab tribes is stronger than that of town dwellers. This same group loyalty promotes strong xenophobia and resistance to authority, preventing nomads and desert dwellers from achieving civilization. For this reason, he argues, royal authority is most unlikely to arise among the Arabs, who are the "least willing of nations to subordinate themselves to each other, as they are rude, proud, ambitious, and eager to be the leader."[26] A transcending force is necessary to supersede the strong parochial loyalties of Arab tribal *'asabiyya* and to forge a larger civilization. This broader *'asabiyya* is created, according to Ibn Khaldun, out of religion. Only the mobilizing and restraining power afforded by religious conviction is capable of realizing the "complete transformation" of Arab qualities that allows them to have a "restraining influence on themselves and to keep people apart from each other."[27] Yet even religion cannot fundamentally alter the basic driving forces of human nature and historical change. The transcendent *'asabiyya* of religious community is too weak to maintain a civilization except with great difficulty and only temporarily. In the case of the Arab Muslims, Islam could not prevent civil wars from wracking the community's unity within only twenty-five years of the Prophet's death in 632 C.E. Under the reign of the fourth caliph, 'Ali ibn Abi Talib (656–661), the binding force of Islam loosened in the face of the old and more powerful tribal *'asabiyya* of the pre-Islamic period. When Mu'awiya ibn Abi Sufyan, the leader of the Arab clan with the strongest *'asabiyya*, triumphed in his struggle with 'Ali, the ideal caliphate founded on religious sanctions was converted into a caliphate mixed with traditional aspects of royal authority.

"Wars and different kinds of fighting have always occurred in the world since God created it." This is the conclusion to which Ibn Khaldun's methodical analysis of history and society leads. "It is something natural among human beings. No nation and race (generation) is free from it."[28] The fatalism and determinism in these statements suggest that Ibn Khaldun is a thinker in the tradition of political realism; Thucydides or Hobbes could just as well have penned these lines. Ibn Khaldun's conclusion would also remove him from the company of many (perhaps most) earlier Muslim writers on war, including al-Turtushi and al-Hasan ibn 'Abdallah. Given war's origins in the very nature of human beings and in the constitution of their societies, what value can there be in moralizing about it or searching for ways to eliminate it? Ibn Khaldun is in fact aware of the arguments of al-Turtushi; he mentions the influence of *Siraj al-muluk* upon his thinking, if only to provide a foil for his own work. Al-Turtushi "aimed at the right idea, but did not hit it."[29] He had in particular missed the mark in his claim that the chances for war can be mitigated with the right preparations and that wars can be won by what Ibn Khaldun labels "external factors," such as superiority in manpower and materiel. Al-Turtushi had failed to understand, argues Ibn Khaldun, that wars are won or lost not so much by factors within human control, but by subjective "hidden causes," such as the relative degree of group loyalty in the combatants, the success of ruses and trickery – in short, by fortune.[30]

But there is a single, fleeting passage in Ibn Khaldun's otherwise realist, amoral account of war that differentiates him clearly from the moral skeptics and brings him back into the sphere of Islamic thought. He outlines four types of wars, each distinguished by its motivations. The first is war between neighboring tribes or competing families, presumably for royal authority. The second is war between "savage nations living in the desert" whose only motive is the desire for petty plunder of others' possessions. The third is the form of war sanctioned by Islamic law (*shari'a*) as *jihad*. The fourth is internal warfare aimed at suppressing rebellion or secession. The first two types of war Ibn Khaldun labels as "unjust, unlawful, and seditious" (*baghi* and *fitna*); the second two are "lawful and just" (*jihad* and *'adl*).[31] No more succinct a description of the early Islamic approach to war is possible than this typology and the moral evaluation underlying it. Ibn Khaldun has stated precisely what any orthodox Muslim scholar of his time would have stated, but he has done so within a historical and sociological analysis that was not the latter's concern. Ibn Khaldun has made explicit what are largely implicit understandings of classical writers. But having acknowledged the moral reality of just and unjust wars, he stops. His purpose is merely to establish a sphere of moral evaluation for war and peace, not to chart its dimensions. This task would lead him toward interpretations of the sources of divine law, the Qur'an and *sunna*, which he perhaps felt had been adequately performed by Muslim exegetes and jurists in the seven centuries preceding his work. While we do find further references to *jihad* in the *Muqaddima*, they are always brief and tangential to his primary purpose, the study of Islamic history and society.

Yet the Qur'an and *sunna* are never far from Ibn Khaldun's historical interpretation. They are for him more than historical sources; they are an inspiration for the historian's task. Ibn Khaldun composed the *Muqaddima* as the prolegomenon to a larger work he titled *Kitab al-'ibar*. The singular of *'ibar*, *'ibra*, is used in the Qur'an (Q3:13; 12:111; 24:44; 79:26) and traditions ascribed to the Prophet primarily in relation to history. Human beings are admonished to study history for its moral import, not just as a series of random occurrences. The study of history will lead the perceptive mind to the reality of the divine presence working through time.[32] Like many Muslim scholars before and after him, Ibn Khaldun's understanding of war was grounded in lessons derived in part from the Qur'an and *sunna*. Certainly, on the question of why humanity is prone to war, the answers Ibn Khaldun provides are in no way irreconcilable with those we may find in the Qur'an.

19

WORD

Walid A. Saleh

It would not be an exaggeration to state that most of the creative impulses in Islamic civilization eventually found an expression in words. Monumental buildings will be adorned with words; Islamic coins, with their austere minimalist calligraphic designs, became from very early on the aniconic emblem of a culture that made the word the center of its creative impulse. The word actually was the most visible expression of the new faith. The power of the word was based on two vortexes: the scriptural and the poetic. The scriptural corpus included a host of texts: primarily the Qur'an and the Hadith literature. Qur'an, enshrined as the very word of God, soon colored the very language Muslims spoke. It also overwhelmed the arts; to represent, one presented the shape of words. Calligraphy became the highest form of art and the Qur'an the object of the artistic creativity. The prophetic word, seen as the most eloquent of human speech, collected and named, became the source of the ethical imagination; to form one's character one looked to the character of Muhammad which was fashioned through a literary genre. Indeed, the very words of the genre of the "Character of Muhammad" (*na't*) would be used to draw a picture in words of a face or a man. God's inimitable word, the Qur'an, and the Hadith of Muhammad, the most exemplary person in Islam, were placed firmly at the center of cultural, ethical, and artistic inspiration.

The divine and the prophetic corpus were not the only pivotal texts in the Islamic world however: poetry was an equal partner in the formation of the Islamic cultural sphere. Arabic classicism, which was forming itself concurrently with the new religion, was founded on the pre-Islamic poetic corpus; this meant that poetic ideals were not set by the new religion, nor was the language of Arabic overwhelmed by the language of the Qur'an. This independence of poetry from the Qur'an assured that non-religious topics played a central role in the formation of the cultured human being, the *adib*. Major Islamic cultures other than the Arabs were also to keep a body of literature that reflected their pre-Islamic heritage, the clearest case being in the Iranian cultural sphere where the *Shahnameh*, the Persian national epic, was profoundly influential as a source of poetic idiom.

The Qur'an, Hadith, and poetry were buttressed by other disciplines that made the word the pivot of the intellectual world. Philology, central among the disciplines invented to deal with the Qur'an, was highly cultivated. Analysis of the word was to attain an independence from religious constraint that remained the mark of philological inquiry. Just as philosophical methods would spill over into theology and alienate it from scripture, so too did philology overwhelm scripture and restrain it. Indeed, philology became one of the most important forms of intellectual activities in Islam. Understanding, deciphering, appreciating, creating, and depicting words became the all-engulfing concern for the intellectuals, theologians, literateurs, artists, and poets. Grammar, prosody, rhetoric, lexicography, and calligraphy were all used to make sure that the educated elite had full access to the heritage of the Arabs and increasingly to the new literature produced by the newly Arabized Muslims, especially the Iranian converts. This model was emulated by Iranians, the Turkic peoples, and other Islamized groups.

Metaphysically, the word was also central. The very act of creation was verbal: creation was enacted by words: "Be and it was" – God created the world by an utterance (Q16:40). The cosmology was not one of dismembering a primordial beast or overcoming chaos; rather Islamic cosmogony was a world of words. God's word was inexhaustible: one needed oceans of ink, forests of pens to attempt to write it down (Q31:27). The Qur'an was conscious of its logocentrism. The word was light, guidance, healing, and Imam for humanity. It was soothing to troubled hearts. The word was a path. Such was the power of the words that they shattered the mightiest of mountains: "If we had sent this Qur'an down to a mountain, you would have seen it humbled and split apart in its awe of God" (Q59:21). The Qur'an was not only potent but also inimitable, its very wording beyond the capacity of humans to replicate. The Qur'an was the very word of

God: an uncreated utterance coeternal with God – God and his word were almost indistinguishable.

Meanwhile the prophetic word in Hadith was soon accorded a degree of authority equal to the Qur'an and Muhammad was popularly declared the most eloquent of the Arabs. The collections of Hadith kept growing in size, in effect ascribing to Muhammad the collective wisdom of the Muslims. The Hadith was the first layer that preserved the collective religious experience of the Muslims. It bound itself to the Qur'an and made it discursively elaborate. The Islamic civilization was turning to the word and the word was made at the center of the cultural and religious enterprise. Indeed one can argue that the ritual was always channeled through the textual.

Poets and literateurs were busy producing their own corpus. Eventually the fusion between the poetic and the religious was achieved in mystical poetry, providing a resolution to the competition between the two types of words, the divine and the human. Poets would eventually dare to speak the impossible, declaring their poetry to be another Qur'an (the most famous case being Mawlana Jalaluddin Rumi).

As this introduction has made clear, the word had many manifestations in Islamic civilization. This essay, however, will concentrate on the Qur'an and the textual and religious worlds it created along the historic spectrum of the Islamic religious tradition. Since the Qur'an represents the ultimate manifestation of the concept of the word – paradoxically it is at the same instance the font and the culmination of what the word is – the various manifestations of the Qur'an and their impact that will be discussed here are reflections and examples of the complexity of the interplay of the history of the word in Islam.

THE PHYSICAL WORD

Perhaps the first thing to note about the Qur'an is that its canonization came very early on in the history of Islam: barely twenty-five years after the death of Muhammad (d. 632) the third caliph, 'Uthman, struck a committee that saw to it that an official copy was assembled and promulgated. Soon the power of the new state was used to enshrine this copy as the official codex and all other copies were burnt. The Qur'an when referred to as a codex is not called the Qur'an but rather The Codex of 'Uthman, *"mushaf 'uthman."* There has been much discussion recently about the date of the codification of the Qur'an, with suggestions about its dating ranging from the fanciful to the probable. There is, however, no compelling reason to reject the Islamic traditional narrative of how the Qur'an was codified. The fact of the matter is that we have a universally received text that was the basis of Islamic civilization. Muslims disputed and fought over most of what constituted their religious identity, and indeed the civil wars among the very founders of the faith was such that had the opportunity presented itself they would have left us many a Qur'an. Yet they never produced, nor were they in the position to produce, any competing Qur'ans. We should not be surprised at the swiftness of the codification of the Qur'an, nor, to give another example, at the swiftness with which the new state came up with a universal calendar: there were models to emulate. Islam was conscious of the legacy of Late Antiquity and it hit the ground running.

Codifying the Qur'an was also accompanied by a theology of reading that differed markedly from the situation in Christian Latin Europe. This was not a text to be protected from the believing public, nor was there a need for it to be occulted from the prying eyes of the masses. Indeed the theology of reading made perusing, meditating, reciting, listening to the recitation, and memorizing the Qur'an the most assured path for salvation. The Qur'an was a public salvific medium open to all the believers who were expected if not to memorize all of it, at least to memorize a minimum portion (how minimum the portion can be will be alluded to later). All were expected to read it – those incapable of reading it were exhorted to hear it recited. If not read, the Qur'an was potentially available to be read – it was omnipresent and accessible to the believer.

Let me, however, shed light on a much-discussed aspect of the Qur'an's reception that plagues the secondary literature. The myth (if not the fetish) of the orality of the Qur'an is so strongly established in modern scholarship that its orality is presumed to be the key for understanding the history of its reception, to the point that this argument has displaced the codex nature of the history of the Qur'an's reception – the Qur'an as a read text. The formation of the Qur'an has undoubtedly very strong connections to orality, but that should not be presumed to be the determinant factor in the history of the text after its codification. The Qur'an, recited as it may have been, was always a written word. Its dissemination as a word was at the center of the new religion. Recitation was an important aspect of the text's performance in public, but it presumed a written text from which the recitation emanated. The *rasm*, or the written word of the Qur'an, remained the ultimate authority on what the text is. That is why cathedral chairs for the Qur'an and its professional reciters were built in the form they take: with a place for the text and seating for the reciter. Had orality been so fundamental as the secondary literature presumes, then why bother build a place for the codex? A proper history of the Qur'an has to take this aspect of its transmission as foundational.

THE ICONIC STATUS OF THE QUR'AN

The Qur'an was also made into something akin to an icon. The iconic status of the Qur'an was established through a myriad of ways, all of which used the physicality of the word to convey the text's charisma. It was used as the symbol of the new religion. When time came to fashion an imperial Islamic coinage the choice fell on the Qur'an as the visual symbol of Islamic sovereignty, and its words were stamped on coins. Islamic coins were primarily textual coins, the first such development in the long numismatic tradition of the Mediterranean basin. *Sura* 112, the most succinct Qur'anic statement on radical monotheism, was struck on the first fully Arabized Umayyid Dinars. The Qur'an was also used as the most prominent decorative and propaganda tool in the nascent Islamic architectural program. In many ways it is as if architecture was there to carry the word, such that eventually Islamic architecture became inseparable from monumental calligraphy.

The Qur'an also served as an apotropaic text. In this regard the text was assured a function so indispensable that its usage by the believers was secured even if they were incapable of reading the text. The very text itself was potent, able to protect from evil, repel malice, and assure that the protection of God was on the side of the amulet bearer. The very shape of the words was now efficacious.

The Qur'an also became the locus of artistic creativity. The art of calligraphy was centered around the copying of the Qur'an. One result is that the copies of the Qur'an became artistic productions on their own, emblematic of the highest form of beauty. Rulers were keen to commission them, display them, and build cathedral chairs for these exquisite copies for all to see and admire. Soon a competitive zeal appeared and rulers started commissioning bigger and bigger Qur'ans. The size of these large Qur'ans was a source of marvel to Muslim historians. The literati were to fawn over such works of art as much as the public.

Finally, reverence for the physical copy of the book was made part of the ritual landscape. One did not handle this book casually: one needed to be ritually pure to touch the book or to recite it. In addition, the text was made off limits to non-believers, and their children were not to be taught the Qur'an. Non-Muslims were not to become familiar with the text because familiarity was presumed to breed contempt. And a traveling Muslim was not allowed to carry the book into non-Muslim territory for fear of desecration, which was to be avoided as much as its veneration was to be encouraged. As examples of the latter, the Qur'an was usually hung on walls in pouches, and if one were to place it near any other book, one always placed the Qur'an at the top.

THE LANGUAGE OF THE QUR'AN

There is another aspect about the physicality of the Qur'an which should be taken into consideration to understand the complicated history of how Muslims reacted to the text. The Qur'an, even more so than the Hebrew Bible, remained embedded in a cultural milieu that never lost its continuous connection to the original language of its revelation. The Qur'an was never lost to be discovered; that is, lost in translation to be discovered later in a philological awakening. Nor did the Muslims (and I don't mean here Arabs only) stop learning the classical language that the Qur'an was written in. The Arabic philological revolution, which happened in the first hundred years after the codification of the Qur'an, is hardly accorded the significance it deserves when we discuss the intellectual history of Islam. The invention early on in the history of Islam of Arabic philology made impossible the Qur'an's alienation from its custodians. The current doctrine that modern Muslims uphold as a dogma, that the Qur'an is untranslatable, is a continuation of this peculiar historical situation of the Qur'an. It is not that the Qur'an could not be translated – as a matter of fact, interlinear translations of the Qur'an were very common and continue to be the mode in which most Muslims experience the Qur'an. What Muslims attempt when they state that the Qur'an is untranslatable is not to deny the act of translation (historical practice belies such an understanding) but rather to underline that the Arabic text is ritually insurmountable. Such an attitude gave the physicality of the text a potency that was impossible to dilute.

THE THEOLOGY OF READING

One of the most important, and underestimated, aspects of the manner of veneration and the role of the Qur'an in the life of the believers was the theology of reading that developed early on around the holy text. Such were the dictates of the economy of reading that the text of the Qur'an was divided into thirty equal parts (*juz'*), each part into two subsections called *hizb*, and each *hizb* subdivided into four (we have thus 240 quarters of *hizbs*). These divisions were made integral parts of the presentation of the Qur'an; the minimalist format of the Qur'an which was the preferred mode of presentation of the text was willing to admit division signs for the reader enabling him or her to know how much he or she has read and how much of the text remained unread. The codex of the Qur'an resisted cluttering, but it did not resist "signposts" for the reader. These divisions of the Qur'an were nothing but an outline for a reading program that believers demanded and scholars supplied. Every word was counted, every letter was counted, and an exact division of the text was made available to the reader. In this sense the physical Qur'an was responding to the theology of reading and making clear concessions to its demands.

The theology of reading was not without extreme paradoxical presuppositions that made the act of reading the most central and simultaneously most unnecessary of acts: it was impossible to imagine an Islamic life without reading the text, yet at the same time, the act of reading was a superfluous cultic act. The Qur'an, as such, is both inside the religion and beyond it! Let me explain what I mean here: there is hardly any extensive use of the Qur'an in the rituals of Islam. Reciting the text is an essential component for only one of the obligatory or mandatory cultic practices of Islam, that of the five daily ritual prayers, but the amount needed to render the prayer efficacious is so minuscule as to render the rest of the text ritually superfluous. One needed to recite the *fatiha*, the very short first chapter of the Qur'an, and a short portion of any other chapter, although the ritual prayer could be valid without either of them. The *fatiha* and a number of short chapters were thus memorized by every Muslim. One usually learned the very last chapters of the Qur'an, the chapters that are one or two liners.

It deserves underlining that apart from this limited use in ritual prayer the reading of the Qur'an does not play a major role in the official rituals of Islam, since we tend to forget this peculiar aspect of cultic Islam as it developed over time. Things were not always like that, however. There is enough evidence to indicate that the most central act in the cultic worship of the early Muslim community in Mecca was actually Qur'an recitation and nightly vigils which centered around reciting the text. Somewhere in the move to Medina Muhammad downgraded that aspect of the cult (see Q73:1–19 for the cult of nightly Qur'anic vigils, and Q73:20 which rescinds the rule). Officially the Qur'an hovers over the tradition. Yet the original impulse to make the Qur'an ritually central was never dimmed – perusal of the text remains a kind of unofficial act of worship even if the official cult does not emphatically demand it.

If the official cultic rituals of the new Muslims did not envision much reading or recitation of the text, the cultic manuals made a central presupposition about the availability and proximity of the physical text: it presumed that Muslims had to read it, touch it, and come into contact with it. Thus the place where the Qur'an is discussed cultically in the legal manuals is usually in the sections that discuss ritual purity. The text of the Qur'an was presumed to be impossible to avoid and attention was to be paid to the situations when one was allowed to touch the text or required to refrain from contact with it. In the cultic imagination of the religion the Qur'an was impossible to separate from the believer even though, as already mentioned, the believer was not ordered to do much with the text. The·two of them – the Qur'an and the believer – were presumed to be in contact, such that they needed a manual of etiquette to determine how to behave properly around each other.

Reading the text was thus a presumed reality and became a central part of the unofficial cultic practices. The pietistic thrust of the Muslim community to make central the act of reading the text was to be codified in the Hadith literature. The *hadiths* dealing with the meritorious benefit of reciting the text were known in Arabic as *fada'il al-suwar*, or "merit-of-*sura*" traditions (as I have termed them). These were the expression of a central doctrine in the Islamic religious tradition: that reading the Qur'an, the very act itself, was enough to trigger the salvific process. Reading was salvation. Surely, those *hadiths* that claimed such a potent function for reading were suspicious, in that they were mostly unreliable from the point of view of the scholastic discipline that dealt with the veracity of the Hadith corpus. But, as usual, the scholastic tradition was no match for the power of pietism; and pietistic sensibilities would make sure that these *hadiths* were to remain central to how Muslims understood the efficacy of the salvific powers of the Qur'an.

When the dust settled on this matter it became evident that each of the 114 chapters of the Qur'an has special powers of salvation. Each held a key to a certain aspect of the path to God, and each chapter came to have a specific *hadith* (based on the authority of Muhammad) that explicitly states what powers and benefits the act of reading it bestows on the believer. Reading chapter 91, for example, is equivalent to giving the whole earth as alms to the poor. Benefits from reading the chapters varied from success and rewards in this world, like wealth, good health, and absence of hardship, to pardon of sins, and admittance to paradise in the world to come. Reading, to take another example, chapter 95 assures the believer wealth in this world and certitude in his or her faith in God.

While reading some of the chapters can assure material success, most of the promised rewards were to be attained on Judgment Day and in the afterlife. It is these kinds of traditions that predominate: the reader of chapter 98 will be in the company of those saved on the Day of Judgment; the power of reading chapter 101 is such that it can tilt the primordial scale of justice in favor of good deeds; by reading chapter 108 one gets to drink from the rivers of paradise, and so on. Reading the Qur'an has also the power of transporting the believer to the time of Muhammad in order to partake of his blessed presence.

To understand that this power of reading was not idle talk, one only needs to notice that the potency of reading was equated with the salvific power of prescribed ritual acts like praying, fasting, and even pilgrimage. Reading chapter 97 is equal to the rewards of fasting the whole month of Ramadan, while reading chapter 106 has the same merit as circumambulating the Ka'ba in Mecca. Yet none of these was more potently salvific than the intercession of Muhammad with God on behalf of his followers. The intercession of Muhammad, his *shafa'a*, was the locus of longing particularly in pietistic Sunnism, and the theology of reading would make sure to connect the two together. For example, reading chapter 93 would guarantee the reader Muhammad's intercession on his or her behalf. The conduits of salvation are thus connected: the Qur'an can save as can Muhammad's intercession, and one act can trigger the other. The power of the act of reading is that it acts as a fulcrum to all the manifestations of this new faith.

Yet equating reading with salvation brings a danger to the act of reading: a paradoxical conundrum not easily solved, for reading is a process while salvation is a moment of grace. Reading itself thus has to be transformed into a burst, a volcanic moment of eruptive salvation rather than a process of perusal. This is salvation spilling over and making charismatic the act of reading but also destabilizing the very process of reading. How much reading is needed for the salvific power of reading to become efficacious? This is not mere speculation – the tradition had eventually to address this paradoxical question. The merit and benefits of reading eventually became equated with the merit of reading – a tautological understanding of reading. Since reading is salvation, so a mere instance of "reading" becomes like an endless reading act. This all-engulfing quality of reading once unleashed cannot be stopped, and reading parts of the Qur'an becomes as efficacious as reading all of the Qur'an. Thus the reward of reading chapter 96 is like the reward of reading all of the Qur'an, while reading chapter 102 is like reading a thousand verses. Chapter 109 is equal to a quarter of the Qur'an, while chapter 112 is equivalent to one third (all of these chapters are short, in fact). What these traditions are implying is that the Qur'an is at once an all-encompassing as well as self-encompassing instrument of salvation, such that reading a part is equivalent to reading the whole, and the whole is reducible to certain parts. This synecdochic aspect of reading can make sense only on the salvific plane. Reading as an act – not as a process – is salvific.

The *hadiths* that declared the power of reading were seeping into all aspects of religious literature. Hadith collections admitted them, and soon Qur'an commentaries admitted them as well. Eventually, a new genre of *hadith* collection emerged, the *fada'il al-Qur'an* books, which collected and presented these traditions. The culmination of such a process can be seen in the collection of *hadith* entitled *Lamahat al-anwar* by the scholar al-Ghafi (d. 1222). This 3-volume work, spanning almost 1600 pages, collected every minute report on the Qur'an. Not only are chapters discussed but so are individual verses, and a program of incantatory protection is outlined for the believer: what to read, and when and how much to read of the Qur'an in order to ward off evil.

Qur'an codices in their physical presentation resisted contamination, or at least most of those we have that survived did. Thus, unless one was adding an interlinear Persian, Ottoman, or Urdu translation, one avoided cluttering the text of the Qur'an with marginalia or notes. The only proviso allowed was for verse divisions and the signposts that divided the text into equal portions for reading regimens of the text. Indeed the highest form of art was made out of presenting the bare text, in what is known as the Kufic script. The diactrics and vowels were left out to present an austere minimalist calligraphy that was breathtaking in its effect. Since there is no systematic study of Qur'an copies one has to be cautious about such a general statement. That being said, most of the Qur'ans we have in collections are precisely what I would call "pure" Qur'ans. It is in this light that the Qur'an copy available in the British Museum (Manuscript OR 13002, dated 1011) acquires significance to our discussion. Here is a copy that is dated, finished in 1011, which allowed these merit-of-*sura* traditions a pride of place. Significantly this copy stems from the same period as the time of al-Tha'labi, who was the major exponent and defender of the merit-of-*sura* traditions. Al-Tha'labi started each chapter of his commentary by first bringing all the traditions about the merit of the chapter under discussion while another scholar, al-Zamakhshari, would reverse the practice, preferring to finish each of his explanations of a chapter with the same traditions. The same traditions are copied into this British Museum manuscript and made an integral part of it. Each chapter of this rather tattered Qur'an contains a synoptic introduction, a summary of the scholastic information on the chapter – where it was revealed, number of verses, words, and letters, and so on – and finally the merit-of-*sura* traditions regarding the chapter to follow. The irony here is palpable: unsound traditions are now copied so close to the holiest of texts, in such proximity that they act as preambles. The Qur'an is now distilled, its potency summed up. Before one reads a chapter one is told of the benefits. One does not need to find out from other sources since such works act as the guides to the act of reading.

THE APOTROPAIC TEXT

I have already mentioned that part of the process that turned the Qur'an into an icon was its apotropaic powers. This was not an ascribed power: given after the fact. Rather the Qur'an has two chapters that explicitly function as such. Dark, ominous, mysterious, and foreboding, the last two chapters of the Qur'an invoke the protection of the Lord against evil, darkness, magic, and envy. The hissing sounds of the whisperer, both devilish and human, and the tied knots of witches are also valorized. Indeed, the power of magic is given potency here unlike anywhere else in the Qur'an, and all the mono-causational structures of monotheism are undermined. Evil appears almost autonomous, though not quite so, since the two chapters do admit that God ultimately created all. But still, the dark forces – and darkness is portrayed as fearsome here – do haunt humanity. The two chapters are both uncannily out of place and perfectly suitable as an ending for the Qur'an. They did, admittedly, cause unease among some of the pious – those who have no patience for so-called "superstition" did not see them fit as an ending for the Qur'an. Luckily, that position was not allowed to have its way.

The Qur'an is thus hemmed in between a prayer at the beginning and an incantation at its end. The issue of the arrangement of the Qur'an has become another of these tropes of incomprehensibility that sustains our modern presentation of the Qur'anic text. We discern no rationale in its order as it stands now. This is not the place to point to the flimsiness of our perplexity in front of this text, but that there is order in the arrangement of the text is rather unmistakable. What we seem to be saying when we complain about its arrangement is that it is not the order we would like to have. After all, if a sacred text is to end with a potent charismatic finale, then there is nothing more potent than ascribing an apotropaic power to the words at the very end.

The potency of these two chapters seeped into the whole text very quickly. The Qur'an – all of it – became apotropaic. One read it when one needed incantations for the sick, the possessed, and the frightened. One read it to muster one's courage or to embark on a blessed journey. As such, the Qur'an was continuing one of the oldest of functions of religious texts in the ancient Near East. The traces of this incantatory Qur'an are all over the archeology and anthropology of the Middle East. Magic bowls, necklaces sold at shrines, bands worn on the arms, and soaked amulets drunk by the sick and the possessed litter the Islamic landscape.

In tandem with the apotropaic powers of the text came its healing powers, though the line separating the two functions is hard to discern. Yet, the healing powers of the Qur'an were never in doubt, and even here the Muslims found an internal confirmation in the Qur'an for such powers (Q10:57; 17:82; 41:44). The healing powers of the Qur'an became a cornerstone of folk medicine, having a copy of the text in a household was a requirement, and having someone in the household who could read the text to unleash its powers was essential. An unread Qur'an was a curse on the household. Here the demands set on the household were much more onerous than on the individual – the second chapter of the Qur'an, the longest, was the one to read to protect a home.

THE HEARD TEXT AND THE CONTEMPLATED TEXT

It should be clear that, in this article, I am trying to emphasize aspects of the word that have been deemphasized in existing literature, if they have been discussed at all. Much has been written on the recited Qur'an; as such, I do not want to belabor this aspect of the Qur'an's reception among the believers. What I do want to raise is the problematic nature of recitation, the tension that recitation always presented to the believers. Recitation of the Qur'an implied that the audience was engaged in an act of listening, or *sama'*. This was innocent enough an act. Yet, as mystical devotional practices gained momentum, *sama'* became an integral part of the Sufi paradigm, and it would not be confined to listening to the Qur'an being recited. *Sama'* was enacted through the use of a multitude of textual forms – from reciting the Qur'an to nonsensical mantras. Moreover, Sufi mystical *sama'* was so amorphous in its effect on the listener that the reactions ranged from the mere reverential state to an ecstatic eruption. The Qur'an was expected to match this power over the listeners. Moreover, music was made an integral part of this new Sufi devotional act, *sama'* was invariably musical. Music was unavoidable, it turned out, no matter how much the guardians of the tradition attempted to strip the religion of music. Likewise the recitation of the Qur'an was eventually envisioned in a musical mode, since *tajwid*, the art of public reading of the Qur'an, was heavily dependent on musical artistry. It is clear that music, now admitted in the guise of *tajwid* or cantilation of the Qur'an, was soon to become the foundation of the art of public Qur'an presentation. The Qur'an was not going to lose a battle with another form of pious devotion. Music, thus, which has no official cultic function in Islam, was given pride of place almost as an after-thought: now it pronounced the word of God. This is the aspect of the Qur'an that I have been trying to highlight – its capacity to allow new cultic practices to take hold in Islamic pietistic tradition without overtly presenting themselves as innovations competing with official cultic practices. Music is not considered sacred in Islam (and is, in fact, frowned upon by many), yet *tajwid* is music, and *tajwid* is the medium for God's word. The mausoleums that were built by the rich and powerful were provisioned for the upkeep of professional recit-ers, providing an around-the-clock musical chanting of the Qur'an. It is no wonder that Salafi Islam has been attempting to wrest the medium of Qur'anic presentation from the musical tradition in Egypt and elsewhere. The irony is that the new mode of Saudi recitation is no less musical; it is simply in a different mode, since boys are the preferred readers of this style. The Qur'an is thus the gate through which new cultic practices have to be admitted, which have to don the Qur'anic garb if they wish to survive in Islamic practice.

The Islamic tradition has preserved for us a long list of reactions to the act of hearing the Qur'an recited, from mere attentive listening (like people with "birds perched on their heads"), to stunned con-templative stances, to weeping, fainting, and even death. Al-Tha'labi not only made central the traditions that spoke of the merit of read-ing the Qur'an but also wrote a treatise on those who died listening to the Qur'an. The stories are rather formulaic in structure: a deeply pious individual, or a sensitive tender soul, happens to be passing by and hears a verse being recited, is struck so powerfully by fear, love, or some mysterious force that that individual dies on the spot. The stories are incomprehensible unless we understand the potency of the Qur'an as a totem. It is not gazing into the eyes of the gods that might kill you, but it is listening to the primordial voice that will. The word of God is the voice of God. Exposure to its potency is dangerous. But the Qur'an has already predicted its effect. The skin of those listening to the Qur'an already shudders, their hearts submit, and a comparison is drawn between the believer and the solidness and resoluteness of the mountains (Q39:23).

Most believers attained a different experience, a calmness in the heart and a reassurance in their faith, when they heard the Qur'an. Susceptibility to the fatal power of the Qur'an depended on such refined spirituality that only a few are in real danger. The multitudes were happy to reap the benefits of its salvific, apotropaic, and healing powers. Such a potent text is best fully consumed, and the ideal way to derive maximum benefit from the Qur'an is to hold it in one's heart: to memorize it all. Muslims from early on committed the Qur'an to memory. This was no vocation for a priestly class – many Muslims, especially in conservative circles, continue to do this as a matter of primary education. There were always professional reciters who kept an unbroken chain of oral transmission through Islamic history, but theirs was a professional practice centered around variant readings, as well as a musical repertoire for public recitation. Most Muslim memorizers, or *huffaz*, are ordinary people rather than ritual specialists. Yet far more significant for our discussion here is the potency given to memorization: it is the ultimate act that places the Qur'an inside the believer instead of the believer being placed outside the text. Those who have committed the text to memory are said to be easily spotted on Judgment Day, with a radiance of emanating light from their faces.

THE WORD ALONE

The apotropaic Qur'an and the equation of salvation with reading went a long way to undermine and curb the potential harm of an unbridled theology of reading. An unmediated encounter with the divine utterance was a danger that all were aware of, since the issue of deciding the exact will of God was potentially open for every reader to guess. Readers might confuse reading with understanding; reading is not merely salvific but also has theological imports if the reader decides that he is now privy to God's intentions. The act of reading is empowering. Thus the salvific and apotropaic modes of reading were an attempt to separate the act of reading from the act of understanding, in so far as the purpose of reading was made far more profound and gainful to the reader as long as he was willing to forgo – or at least resist – the lure of theology (and fundamentally of politics as well). Thus reading was valorized on the salvific level in the hope that its potency as a destabilizing revolutionary paradigm was controlled. The danger of the solitary, intent, and intensive reader was to be avoided. Reading the text was not to be equated with the power to disclose God's will – God in this sense was far more willing to dispense salvation than grant powers and charisma. It is not for nothing that one of the titles of the Shi'i Imams was the "Speaking Qur'an" – only he made the Qur'an comprehensible. Reading implied an agency for the reader, and much of the early Islamic religious tradition was an attempt to control the power invested in ordinary readers by the theology of reading. Indeed I would argue that the potency of reading was a contributing factor to the civil strife of early Islam.

We are thus here witnessing a cultivation of two conflicting approaches to the text: a theology of an open text, readable by all, and a concerted effort to limit the damage that might come from any invested power that the reader accumulates by assuming that reading God's word means reading God's mind. We only have to remember the account of the Battle of Siffin, in which opposing Muslim fighters forced the hand of their commanders by hoisting the Qur'an on their spears, symbolizing refusal to fight and eagerness to see the Qur'an as adjudicator. Theologically, the common readers – and those fighting soldiers were no doubt reading their Qur'ans – overwhelmed their masters by raising the symbol of their own power, the copies of their personal Qur'ans. They forced their will, which they saw as the Will of God, onto the leaders of their communities. That was not to be tolerated and eventually the *fuqaha'* (jurists) stepped in to speak for the legal will of God and the *mutakallimun* (theologians) to tell Muslims what God manifested of himself in the Qur'an.

In this sense, there was a concerted and understandably unavoidable attempt at differentiating readers and readings, such that not everyone could ultimately claim to be able to offer a reading of the Qur'an simply because they were able to read it. Reading was a right for all the believers, but readings had to be controlled. This tension has to be kept in mind when charting the history of the Word in the religious development of Islam. The common reader, however, does not give up easily, and mysticism was to launch one of the most concerted attacks to wrestle the Qur'an from the jurists, theologians, and philologists. But traditional Islamic religious authorities were too keenly aware of the limits of their powers to act with hubris: they always relented, knowing full well that the best way to undermine potent revolutionary readings was to admit them into the fold. A Sufi reading of the Qur'an was simply celebrated, among many other readings that were fully under the control of orthodoxies. To make the Islamic tradition polyvalent meant not toleration but moderation, an attempt to ward off the most dreaded of Islamic sins, that of sedition. Muslims were always allowed to get away with much, the tradition knowing that ultimately anything could be tamed if not valorized as opposition. Sufism soon became dapperly orthodox.

The temptation of a text standing alone face to face with the believer was thus always latent, but never allowed to take political forms; yet the text exerted its power when it could: the text was ready to create a tempest when left unchecked. The intimacy the act of reading of the text gave to the believer was the most potentially seductive part of the Qur'an: the rhetorical structure of the Qur'an is such that the reader is already portrayed as part of a conversation with God, since much of the Qur'an is a discursive dialogue in which a human being is called to answer to God. As such, a reader of the Qur'an is in danger of thinking he or she is the sole addressee of the Qur'an. Already, the ordering of the Qur'an was an attempt to dilute that potent message – hence the forward placement of the Medinan chapters, the communal chapters of the Qur'an, in which the believer is presented as part of an *umma*, a "community of faithful." The Meccan parts of the Qur'an, where the believer is an *umma* unto himself (Q16:120), came after the Medinan. They, however, remained the most beloved parts of the Qur'an. It is clear that I am arguing that the ordering of the text of the Qur'an is already attempting to downplay the exuberant and revolutionary Meccan sections, where the protagonists were rather a close intimate circle: God, the believer, and the unbelievers. Yet, perhaps the most sustained attempt at controlling the Word was the one that was carried out in the genre of *tafsir*, or Qur'anic commentary. This was one of the most sustained discourses that attempted to keep the reading act a communal practice, creating in the process a community of like-minded readers with the aim of keeping the Qur'an from shattering into fragmented readings (granted that did happen, since a Twelver Shi'i reading is not the same as a Sunni reading, and certainly different from an Isma'ili reading of the Qur'an).

THE WORD DECIPHERED

I have so far detailed the potency of the word, denuded from any textual appendage. But the Qur'an was never a stand-alone text. It was tethered to a monumental tradition of commentary that made sure the Qur'an was understood as the community agreed to understand it. Here was a fascinating solution to the conundrum of the theology of reading, for the danger of reading as an individual act is too significant not to address head on. This is the cultural function of *tafsir*, to both exult in the Word and to control it. Neither the victory of the legal paradigm, the hegemony of Ash'arism, and the assorted theological schools that hemmed in the message of the Qur'an, nor controlling Sufism and making it part of the Sunni paradigm, were sufficient. A venerable discipline – both rigidly formal and totally outside the control of any religious guild – was needed in which the danger of the charisma of the Qur'an that could emanate from reading it was to be addressed by controlling the act of reading. Hence individual commentators emerged who acted independently yet seem to have belonged to a discernable tradition. This was not a discipline fostered for any manifest purpose, a clear indication that its function was all the more indispensable. The Qur'an as a public text needed the accompaniment of a sophisticated scholarly discipline, which controlled the readings if not the reader. It is a testament to the potency of this discipline that it has survived the vagaries of time.

How did *tafsir*, then, control the act of reading? First it managed to achieve this feat by seeming to be intellectually rigorous and as such pretending to be a neutral discipline. *Tafsir* avoided the trap of looking like a doctrinal discipline. *Tafsir* was growing under the glaring eyes of philology; therefore, it could not pretend to state what the Qur'an said by stating what it thought it said. Theologically orthodox readings were advanced by each camp, with the Sunnis and the Shi'is offering their respective readings. Yet soon, with the philological geist engulfing the intellectual world of Islam, orthodoxies risked the danger of looking parochially ridiculous if they kept harping on the authority of tradition to state the meaning of the Qur'an. One needed more than formulas of transmission like "Ibn 'Abbas said," or "the Imams said." A full capitulation to philology was the only way to gain the trust of the intellectuals who could easily undermine the voice of traditional authority and to ward off the rise of a competing discipline that could tell the believers what the Qur'an was saying without the oversight of theology. In this regard, philology was made the bedrock of *tafsir*. It is this fundamental assertion and pretension that allowed *tafsir* to garner such an enduring authority among the Muslims across the ages. *Tafsir*, if not naive enough to submit fully to philology, made sure to act inside the parameters of a philologically acceptable method. One could hardly afford a public dressing down of *tafsir*, and philologists were not shy polemicists.

Yet philology is hardly a trustworthy tool with which to claim to speak for God. One needed a more formidably subservient tool (and a craftier one as well). The tool that *tafsir* would develop for this was the notion of a polyvalent Qur'an. *Tafsir* was to become a storehouse for accumulated interpretive traditions that were forming in each sect. Different interpretations were vetted and admitted into the fold of a scholastic tradition that allowed all to have their say as long as the contours of the orthodox coherency of the text were preserved. The Qur'an meant many things, but all the meanings were eventually pulled into a coherent theological vision that kept the fundamental premises of each sect viable. Thus no amount of personal individual responsibility for human action, which is clearly emphasized in the Qur'an, was allowed to override the dogma of Muhammad's salvational powers on behalf of the believers, his *shafaʿa*. *Tafsir* – like Sunnism, or as the mirror of Sunnism – was willing to hold paradoxical positions as long as they were kept coherently inside the possible meanings of the Qur'an. Here was a strategy to undermine dissent through equal airing of opinions. Ultimately there was a theological unity that insidiously gave more weight to interpretations that were more in line with orthodoxy. One could cherish an interpretation that seemed philologically solid, but somehow it never gained traction since it has no metaphysical depth, a depth only gained by being in resonance with the orthodox theology. In this sense *tafsir* was both highly sophisticated and utterly parochial.

Tafsir also needed to function unofficially, since the theology of reading was an unofficial practice; yet *tafsir* needed to be at the heart of the cultural wars and in close conversation with the competing disciplines in order to remain an effective means of cementing the community. *Tafsir* stood guard against the fragmenting of the voice of the most fundamental aspect of the culture: the meaning of the foundational text, drawing on all established methods of scholar-ship. *Tafsir* was thus amorphous and integrative at the same time, capable of donning any hat when the need came to overwhelm any challenge to Sunnism (or Shiʿism for that matter). The moment a dis-cipline matured it had to cut its teeth on the Qur'an, and in this way it was sanctioned as a discipline as well as domesticated and prevented from becoming a subversive weapon against the Qur'an. Somehow, everything seemed to issue from the Qur'an.

Yet it was not as if there was no suspicion against the discipline of *tafsir*; as a matter of fact, opposition to *tafsir* was a hurdle the tradition had to overcome at the very beginning. There was great suspicion against a discipline that claimed to know what God meant. Invariably, puritanical zeal crept up periodically to challenge the very foundations and authority of interpretation, the very act of hermeneutics that was somehow taken for granted. These periodical destabilizations of the hermeneutical paradigm were moments of great creative productivity – the source of the instability of the genre and its vitality at the same time. Unlike other disciplines in Islamic religious tradition, one can never guess what a *tafsir* might hold inside it. *Tafsir* was a cultural enterprise that has to answer to an exegetical program, deciphering the meaning of the text, and to a theological program that was geared to keep the profundity of the revealed text as the font of mystery and meaning in the culture that based itself on this text.

Madrasa seminaries are now deserted for the most part, the lodges of Sufis are tourist attractions, the *shari'a* is not a comprehensive legal system anymore, a mere shadow of itself. Modernism has dismantled much of the religious scholastic traditions and classical theology is all but incomprehensible. In one sense, all this change was unavoidable. Yet the Islamic religious tradition has kept a core centered around the word of the Qur'an. What was an unofficial discipline, *tafsir*, is now remarkably the center of Islamic religious activities. *Tafsir* is now the most practiced, the most read, and the most cherished of Islamic religious activities. The word has once again withstood the challenge and Islam once more finds itself being redefined by redefining the word with *tafsir* as the medium for that transformation.

THE QUR'AN: FURTHER READING

The bibliography of the Qur'an and the host of other textual manifestations in Islamic civilizations is extensive. The study of the Qur'an now is also embroiled in the debates about the suitability of Muslims for the modern world, a new development that is focusing the study on the Qur'an – which means we have a flood of new publications – as well as making the Qur'an, once again, the text for scholarly study.

I will here give a few titles that have extensive bibliographies that can be used to go further into the study of the Qur'an. I will confine myself to studies in English. A good summary of the debates about the study of the Qur'an is Neil Robinson's *Discovering the Qur'an: A Contemporary Approach to a Veiled Text* (Georgetown: Georgetown University Press, 2004). This is an excellent summary of the history of the study of the Qur'an in Europe and a detailed exposition of the most important school in the study of the Qur'an, the German school. The standard English introduction to the Qur'an is still W. M. Watt's reworking of Richard Bell's *Introduction to the Qur'an* (Edinburgh: Edinburgh University Press, 1991). For a feeling of the language of the Qur'an see Michael Sells' *Approaching the Qur'an: The Early Revelations*, 2nd edition (Ashland, Oregon: White Cloud Press, 2006). The volume on the Qur'an in the series *Books that Shook the World* is written by Bruce Lawrence, *The Qur'an: A Biography* (New York: Atlantic, 2006). For easy access to the scholarly debates on the Qur'an, see Andrew Rippin, ed., *The Blackwell Companion to the Qur'an* (Malden, Massachusetts: Blackwell, 2006).

I would also like to draw the attention of the reader to a gem of a book written on the myth of the Golden Bough in Islam, which deals extensively with the Qur'an and its mythical world, written by one of the leading literary critics of Arabic literature: Jaroslav Stetkevych, *Muhammad and the Golden Bough: Reconstructing Arabian Myth* (Bloomington: Indiana University Press, 1996). The works of François Déroche deserve a special mention, especially his *The Abbasid Tradition: Qur'ans of the 8th to the 10th Centuries AD* (New York: Noor Foundation in Association with Azimuth Editions, 1992).

NOTES

INTRODUCTION

1 New York: Oxford University Press, 1983.

CHAPTER 1: ART, KISHWAR RIZVI

1 The Western hemisphere is itself not a homogenous whole, however; in general, methodological differences are discernible between the academies of Europe and the United States. This difference has more to do with general trends in the field of art history itself and is not restricted to the case of Islamic art.
2 I amend my description to include artists and political systems that are not Muslim, which is different from the definition given in the *Grove Dictionary of Art*: "The art made by artists or artisans whose religion was Islam, for patrons who lived in predominantly Muslim lands, or for purposes that are restricted or peculiar to a Muslim population or a Muslim setting. This article deals with the arts produced from the 7th century to the 19th in the Islamic lands from the Atlantic to western Central Asia and India." *Grove Art Online*, http://www.groveart.com (Oxford University Press, accessed August 2007).
3 In them would be included works on paper, parchment, canvas, metal, glass, ceramic, ivories, and the forms and structures of building.
4 Most recently, Sheila Blair, *Islamic Calligraphy* (Edinburgh: Edinburgh University Press, 2006).
5 On the social gatherings within which such interaction would take place see Lisa Golombek, "Discourses of an Imaginary Arts Council in Fifteenth-Century Iran," in *Timurid Art and Culture: Iran and Central Asia in the Fifteenth Century*, eds. Lisa Golombek and Maria Subtelny (Leiden: E. J. Brill, 1992).
6 For an important discussion of iconoclasm, studied through the contemporary context of Afghanistan, see Finbarr Barry Flood, "Between Cult and Culture: Bamiyan, Islamic Iconoclasm, and the Museum," *The Art Bulletin*, 84:4, 2002, pp. 641–59; Jamal J. Elias, "Un/Making Idolatry: From Mecca to Bamiyan," *Future Anterior*, 4:2, 2007, pp. 2–29. A complementary essay would be O. Grabar and M. Natif, "The Story of Portraits of the Prophet Muhammad," *Studia Islamica*, 96, 2003, pp. 19–38, VI–IX.
7 See, for example, Marianna Shreve Simpson, *Persian Poetry, Painting and*

Patronage: Illustrations in a Sixteenth-Century Masterpiece (New Haven; London: Yale University Press in association with the Freer Gallery of Art, Smithsonian Institution, Washington, D.C., 1998).

8 "Age-value" was a term employed by the art historian Alois Riegl (d. 1905) in his 1903 essay, "The Modern Cult of Monuments: Its Character and Origin," trans. Kurt Forster and Diane Ghirardo, *Oppositions*, 25, Fall 1982, pp. 21–51.

9 Although questioning the categories within which scholarship has traditionally been undertaken, I will not attempt to add to the burgeoning classifications of Islamic art, least of all through temporal, spatial, or geographical exclusions or through attempts at being comprehensive, as is the tendency in the field. Important resources, such as *Grove Art Online*, provide essays on numerous topics on Islamic art, in a survey form that is accessible, if overwhelming. However, problematic classifications exist, such as the culmination of the survey in the nineteenth century, with the implication that there cannot be a discussion of Islamic art after the period of colonialism. The subject is then taken up in entries under country names, such as Iran, India, and so on. This strategy is not applied throughout, however, as entries on Germany will bring up the history of art from "Before 1400" until "After 1900."

10 I am here considering the Aga Khan Programs at the Department of Architecture at M.I.T. and the Department of the History of Art and Architecture at Harvard University.

11 Such as Oleg Grabar's essays starting in 1983 with "Reflections on the Study of Islamic Art," in *Muqarnas: An Annual on Islamic Art and Architecture*, 1, 1983, pp. 1–14, and continuing through 2003 with "Editorial: What Should One Know about Islamic Art?" *RES*, 43, Spring 2003, pp. 5–12.

12 As in the famed *jharoka-i darshan* (viewing alcove) installed by the ruler, Akbar, where the king would appear every morning at sunrise and sunset to be greeted and viewed by his courtiers and the public. See J. F. Richards, "The Formulation of Imperial Authority under Akbar and Jahangir," in *Kingship and Authority in South Asia*, ed. J. F. Richards (Madison, W.I.: University of Wisconsin, 1978). His son, Jahangir, ordered one of the towers in the Lahore fort to be painted with depictions of St. Gregory and Christian angels.

13 See for example, Rebecca Joubin, "Islam and Arabs through the Eyes of the Encyclopedie: The 'Other' as a Case of French Cultural Self-Criticism," *International Journal of Middle East Studies*, 32:2, May 2000, pp. 197–217.

14 For a discussion of the visual and textual representation of Islam in the early eighteenth century see Kishwar Rizvi, "Persian Pictures: Art, Documentation and Self-Reflection in Bernard and Picart Representation of Islam," in *The First Global Vision of Religion: Bernard Picart's Religious Ceremonies and Customs of All the Peoples of the World*, eds. Lynn Hunt, Margaret Jacob, and Wijnand Mijnhardt (Getty Research Institute, 2010).

15 Elizabeth Mansfield, *Art History and its Institutions: Foundations of a Discipline* (London: Routledge, 2002). Figures such as the German historian and archeologist Johann Joachim Winckelmann (d. 1768) are considered the founders of the discipline of art history.

16 A comprehensive documentation has been initiated by S. Vernoit, *Discovering Islamic Art: Scholars, Collectors and Collections 1850–1950* (London; New York: I. B. Tauris, 2000).

17 The hierarchies established in European academies were applied to rank, in descending order, architecture, arts of the book (painting and narrative illustrations), calligraphy, and "minor" arts (metalwork, glass, ceramics, textiles). This is in contrast to, say, sixteenth-century Iranian society, in which emphasis was placed on the arts of writing, then those of depiction and architecture, the last through its relationship to imperial or religious authority. In the sixteenth century the production of art was a cooperative activity in which the processes of making were much more intertwined than the Western perspective will allow. Workshops were places where books were repaired and manufactured, as well as sites for the dissemination of texts and images for different media.

18 Qazi Ahmad Qummi, *Gulistan-i hunar* (Tehran, 1980); translated from the Persian by V. Minorsky, *Calligraphers and Painters: A Treatise by Qadi Aḥmad, Son of Mir-Munshi (circa A.H. 1015/A.D. 1606)* (Washington, 1959).

19 K. A. C. Creswell, *Early Muslim Architecture* (Oxford: Clarendon Press, 1932–40); A. U. Pope and Phyllis Ackerman, *A Survey of Persian Art from Prehistoric Times to the Present* (Oxford; London: Oxford University Press, 1938–9).

20 Kishwar Rizvi, "Art History and the Nation: Arthur Upham Pope and the Discourse on 'Persian Art' in the Early 20th Century," proceedings from the symposium "Historiography and Ideology: Writing the History of the Ottoman Architectural Heritage," *Muqarnas: Journal of Islamic Art and Architecture*, 24, 2007, pp. 45–65.

21 As witnessed in surveys focusing in particular on the post-Mongol period; they give centrality to Iranian regions and those within the Persian-language sphere while marginalizing works in India and North Africa.

22 Any number of books could fall into this category, most of them in regard to manuscript painting. An example would be the work of the collector/scholar F. R. Martin, *The Miniature Painting and Painters of Persia, India and Turkey, from the 8th to the 18th century* (London: B. Quaritch, 1912). On Martin's collection practices, see David J. Roxburgh, "Disorderly Conduct? F. R. Martin and the Bahram Mirza Album," *Muqarnas: Journal of Islamic Art and Architecture*, 15, 1998, pp. 32–57.

23 Unfortunately, such exercises attempt at being comprehensive surveys, which diminishes the insights that they provide by dissipating them through generalities. Examples would include John Renard, *Islam and the Heroic Image: Themes in Literature and the Visual Arts* (Columbia, S.C.: University of South Carolina Press, 1993) and Eleanor Sims et al., *Peerless Images: Persian Painting and its Sources* (New Haven; London: Yale University Press, 2002), which provide two examples of this recent tendency, albeit of different disciplinary points of view.

24 These are select chapter headings from Sims et al., *Peerless Images*.

25 If connoisseurship in the arts of the book often reduced the works of art down to a series of styles and attributions, typology and formalism are methods that have been employed to document and categorize Islamic architecture. Although very helpful in buildings – or paintings for that matter – that may be dated or signed, typology or style do not provide satisfactory answers regarding the use, manufacture, or meaning of a work of art. See, for example, Attilio Petruccioli, ed., "Exoteric – Polytheistic – Fundamentalist Typology: Gleanings in the Form of an Introduction," *Typological Process and Design Theory* (Cambridge, Massachusetts: Aga Khan Program for Islamic Architecture, 1998).

26 A recent translation is given by Ali Asghar Seyed-Gohrab, *Layli and Majnun: Love, Madness and Mystic Longing in Nizami's Epic* (Leiden: Brill, 2003).

27 Nizami, *Khamsa*, painted by a pupil of Bihzad, Herat (1494) British Library (Or. 6810), f. 128v.

28 The story of Layla and Majnun is often seen as an allegory describing the unrequited love of the mystic on the spiritual quest of finding union with his beloved, God.

29 British Library; reprinted in Barbara Brend, *The Emperor Akbar's Khamsa of Nizami* (London: British Library, 1995), p. 32, fig. 21.

30 The limits of this essay preclude a comprehensive study of any of the manuscripts described and their texts/image cycles. Further study would compare the placement of the textual narrative, the "density" of paintings, and an analysis of the effect of the text and image on the reader/viewer. In fact, it may be more useful to study any one of the manuscripts in its entirety, relating the images to each other, rather than to randomly selected paintings that echo themes or styles witnessed in an isolated and decontextualized single-page painting.

31 Comprising originally of 258 paintings, the *Shahnama-yi Shahi* was dismembered and the painted folios sold to a variety of individuals and institutions. It was more commonly known for the collector and American industrialist who undertook this dismemberment, Arthur R. Houghton. Although many of the pages have been dispersed, the authors gathered images from national collections in Iran, museums in the United States, and private collections to attempt a recomposition of this magnificent book. Martin Bernard Dickson and Stuart Cary Welch, *The Houghton Shahnameh* (Cambridge, M.A.: Harvard University Press, 1981).

32 Shah Tahmasb mentions this vow in his memoirs, Shah Tahmasb, *Tazkira-i Shah Tahmasb: Sharh-i vaqayi va ahvalat-i zindigani-yi Shah Tahmasb biqalam-i khudash*, ed. Abd al- Shukur (Berlin-Charlottenburg, 1964), p. 23. There are a number of illustrated manuscripts that have survived from his reign, including manuscripts illustrated by the Shah himself in his youth.

33 An essay written fifteen years later attempts to answer some of these questions: Filiz Çağman and Zeren Tanindi, "Remarks on Some Manuscripts from the Topkapi Palace Treasury in the Context of Ottoman-Safavid Relations," *Muqarnas: Journal of Islamic Art and Architecture*, 13, 1996, pp. 132–48.

34 It is also interesting to note that the *Suleymanname*, an illustrated history of the reign of Sultan Suleyman, was compiled in 1558 in Istanbul, some years before the imperial Safavid gift arrived there. See the facsimile copy by Esin Atıl, *Süleymanname: The Illustrated History of Süleyman the Magnificent* (Washington: National Gallery of Art; New York: H. N. Abrams, 1986).

35 Also known as the Freer Jami for the museum where it is housed. Marianna Shreve Simpson with contributions by Massumeh Farhad, *Sultan Ibrahim Mirza's Haft Awrang: A Princely Manuscript from Sixteenth-Century Iran* (New Haven: Yale University Press in association with the Freer Gallery of Art, Smithsonian Institution, 1997).

36 Ibid., p. 3.

37 Titus Burckhardt, *Art of Islam: Language and Meaning* (World of Islam Festival, 1976).

38 Seyyed Hossein Nasr, *Islamic Art and Spirituality* (Albany: State University of New York Press, 1987). It is difficult in the case of some writing on the subject

of Iranian art to separate out nationalist tendencies seeking essentialist truths in diverse work that spans millennia; for example Seyyed Hossein Nasr, ed. Mehdi Amin Razavi, *The Islamic Intellectual Tradition in Persia* (Richmond, U.K.: Curzon Press, 1996).

39 Samer Akkach, *Cosmology and Architecture in Premodern Islam: An Architectural Reading of Mystical Ideas* (Albany: State University of New York Press, 2005), p. xxiii.

40 Ibid., chapter 4, "Architectural Order," p. 149.

41 The notable article was by Karl Lehmann, "The Dome of Heaven," *The Art Bulletin*, 27:1, March 1945, pp. 1–27. In the case of Islamic art, one may find a response in Oleg Grabar, "From Dome of Heaven to Pleasure Dome," *The Journal of the Society of Architectural Historians*, 49:1, March 1990, pp. 15–21.

42 *Muqarnas: An Annual on Islamic Art and Architecture* (New Haven: Yale; Leiden: Brill). Grabar was the editor of the journal from its inauguration in 1983 until 1992.

43 Grabar, "Reflections on the Study of Islamic Art," pp. 10–11.

44 Oya Pancaroğlu, "Serving Wisdom: The Contents of Samanid Epigraphic Pottery," *Studies in Islamic and Later Indian Art from the Arthur M. Sackler Museum, Harvard University Art Museum* (Cambridge: Harvard University, 2002), pp. 58–68; same author, *Perpetual Glory: Medieval Islamic Ceramics from the Harvey B. Plotnick Collection* (New Haven: Yale University Press, 2007).

45 Numerous studies have dealt with this topic in terms of Arabic poetry, most relevantly by Akiko Motoyoshi Sumi, *Description in Classical Arabic Poetry: Wasf, Ekphrasis, and Interarts Theory* (Leiden: Brill, 2004).

46 Paul Losensky, "The Palace of Praise and the Melons of Time: Descriptive patterns in 'Abdi Beg Shirazi's *Garden of Eden*," *Eurasian Studies*, 2:1, 2003, pp. 1–29.

47 Studied for its documentation by M. Szuppe, "Palais et jardins: Le complexe royal des premiers safavides à Qazvin, milieu XVIe-debut XVIIe siecles," *Res Orientales*, 8, 1988, pp. 143–77.

48 Such as the *Kitab al-diryaq* (*Book of the Theriac*) of 1199 and the *Kitab al-aghani* (Book of Songs) of 1216–20. They are mentioned briefly in Richard Ettinghausen, Oleg Grabar, and Marilyn Jenkins-Madina, *Islamic Art and Architecture 650–1250* (New Haven, C.T.: Yale University Press, 2001).

49 David J. Roxburgh, *The Persian Album, 1400–1600: From Dispersal to Collection* (New Haven, C.T.: Yale University Press, 2005).

50 Lisa Golombek, "Discourses of an Imaginary Arts Council in Fifteenth-Century Iran," in *Timurid Art and Culture: Iran and Central Asia in the Fifteenth Century*, eds. Lisa Golombek and Maria Subtelny (Leiden: Brill, 1992).

51 David Roxburgh, *Prefacing the Image: The Writing of Art History in Sixteenth-Century Iran* (Leiden: Brill, 2001).

52 As Oleg Grabar writes, "the Islamic world is the only cultural entity in the history of mankind to have borders or boundaries with almost all the cultural entities known before 1492: India, Southeast Asia, China, northern Eurasia, West and East Africa below the Sahara, southeastern Europe, northern Europe, western Europe; Japan alone escapes such direct contacts with the Islamic world." Grabar, "Editorial: What Should One Know about Islamic Art?" p. 9.

53 Cited by Gülrü Necipoğlu, "Preface" in *Sinan's Autobiographies: Five Sixteenth-Century Texts*, trans. Howard Crane and Esra Akin (Leiden, Brill, 2006), p. x. See also Gülrü Necipoğlu, *Age of Sinan: Architectural Culture in the Ottoman Empire* (London: Reaktion Books, 2005). Until Necipoğlu's work, Sinan's masterpieces were primarily studied through formalist criteria in which the cubic forms were seen as proto-modernist.

54 Anthony King, "Rethinking Colonialism: An Epilogue," in *Forms of Dominance on the Architecture and Urbanism of the Colonial Enterprise*, ed. Nezar Alsayyad (Aldershot, U.K.: Avebury, 1992), p. 340.

CHAPTER 2: AUTHORITY, DEVIN DEWEESE

1 Hamdullah Mustawfi Qazvini, *Tarikh-i guzida*, ed. 'Abd al-Husayn Nava'i (Tehran: Amir-i Kabir, 1960, 2nd printing 1983), pp. 610–11.

2 See William Graham, *Beyond the Written Word: Oral Aspects of Scripture in the History of Religion* (New York: Cambridge University Press, 1987), pp. 111–14. Though he focuses on orality, Graham notes the "difficult problem" of "religious meaning that may exist apart from rational, discursive meaning – and, indeed, apart from mystical or esoteric meaning as well." He also notes the essential agreement between "orientalist rationalism" and Muslim "literalism" in ignoring or rejecting such meaning.

3 See Michael A. Sells, *Mystical Languages of Unsaying* (Chicago: University of Chicago Press, 1994).

4 See the discussion in Yohannan Friedmann, *Prophecy Continuous: Aspects of Ahmadi Religious Thought and its Medieval Background* (Berkeley: University of California Press, 1989).

5 See, for example, Brinkley Messick, *The Calligraphic State: Textual Domination and History in a Muslim Society* (Berkeley: University of California Press, 1993); Dale F. Eickelman, "Mass Higher Education and the Religious Imagination in Contemporary Arab Societies," in *The Book in the Islamic World: The Written Word and Communication in the Middle East*, ed. George N. Atiyeh (Albany: S.U.N.Y. Press, 1995), pp. 255–72.

6 See the discussion of the authoritative character of juridical interpretations themselves in Brannon M. Wheeler, *Applying the Canon in Islam: The Authorization and Maintenance of Interpretive Reasoning in Hanafi Scholarship* (Albany: State University of New York Press, 1996).

7 For considerations of the impact of modernity on issues of authority more nuanced than the stock frameworks of "liberal" vs. "conservative" or "modern" vs. "traditional" still often employed, see Daniel W. Brown, *Rethinking Tradition in Modern Islamic Thought* (Cambridge: Cambridge University Press, 1996), and Carl W. Ernst, *Following Muhammad: Rethinking Islam in the Contemporary World* (Chapel Hill: University of North Carolina Press, 2003).

8 See Bruce Lincoln, *Authority: Construction and Corrosion* (Chicago: University of Chicago Press, 1994).

9 From al-Ghazali, *Faysal al-tafriqa*, trans. Bernard Lewis, in *Islam from the Prophet Muhammad to the Capture of Constantinople, Volume II: Religion and Society*, ed. and trans. Bernard Lewis (New York: Harper Torchbooks, 1974), pp. 20–21; and see now the full translation by Sherman A. Jackson, *On the Boundaries of Theological Tolerance in Islam: Abu Hamid al-Ghazali's Faysal*

al-Tafriqa Bayna al-Islam wa al-Zandaqa (Oxford: Oxford University Press, 2002), pp. 120–21.

CHAPTER 3: BELIEF, R. KEVIN JAQUES

1 Most discussions of non-anthropological method in Islamic Studies have come out of Political Science and the Sociology of Religion. The focus of these studies has tended to be on "political Islam" or on class, social strata, and issues of class mobility. Discussions of method have largely focused on different applications of statistical methodologies to economic and polling data. For an overview, see Mansoor Moaddel, "The Study of Islamic Culture and Politics: An Overview and Assessment," *Annual Review of Sociology*, 28, 2002, pp. 359–86. Many of these studies also emphasize the application of theory to Islamic phenomena but rarely say anything about how we are to collect information or even specific methods of interpretation. The best example of this kind of approach is Bryan Turner's *Weber and Islam: A Critical Study* (Boston: Routledge and Kegan Paul, 1974).

2 The exception to this general rule is Marshall Hodgson's masterful *The Venture of Islam*. The first ninety-nine pages of the first volume remain one of the most authoritative and explicit statements on method in the historical and textual study of Islam. For several generations of scholars of Islam, Hodgson's work has been the staple of doctoral exams and generally required reading, although his dense and what many younger members of the field consider to be "dry" prose have begun to erode his impact; a fact that should be lamented and corrected. See his *The Venture of Islam: Conscience and History in a World Civilization, The Classical Age of Islam*, vol. 1 (Chicago: The University Press, 1974). Also see Edmund Burke, "Islamic History as World History: Marshall Hodgson, 'The Venture of Islam,'" *International Journal of Middle Eastern Studies*, 10:2, May 1979, pp. 241–64.

3 Clifford Geertz, "'Thick Description': Toward an Interpretive Theory of Culture," in *The Interpretation of Cultures* (New York: Basic Books, 1973), pp. 3–18.

4 R. Kevin Jaques, review of *Law and Education in Medieval Islam: Studies in Memory of Professor George Makdisi, Journal of Islamic Studies*, 17:3, 2006, p. 359. The Makdisian emphasis on attention to Arabic linguistics can be seen in Devin Stewart's criticisms of Michael Chamberlain's social historical critiques of the *Rise of Colleges*. See his "The Doctorate in Islamic Law in Mamluk Egypt and Syria," in *Law and Education in Medieval Islam*, eds. Joseph Lowry, Devin Stewart, and Shawkat Toorawa (Cambridge: E. J. W. Gibb Memorial Trust, 2004), pp. 45–90.

5 The author would like to thank Devin Stewart and Christopher Melchert, two of Makdisi's students, for their insights into Makdisi's teaching and methodology.

6 See George Makdisi, *The Rise of Colleges: Institutions of Learning in Islam and the West* (Edinburgh: The University Press, 1981). For criticisms of Makdisi's method and approach, see, among others, A. L. Tibawi, "The Origin and Character of 'al-Madrasah,'" *Bulletin of the School of Oriental and African Studies, University of London*, 25:1/3, 1962, pp. 225–38.

7 Diane F. Halpern, *Thought and Knowledge: An Introduction to Critical Thinking* (Hillsdale, N.J.: Lawrence Erlbaum Associates, 1989), p. 145.

8 Ibid., pp. 212–13.

9 This idea has been discussed by theologians and some have asserted a "double truth" theory that allows for one to adhere to two opposing truths when there is no other alternative. The double truth theory becomes a wedge against doubts that might destroy "faith" by suggesting that in some instances the intellectual limitations of the human mind do not allow us fully to understand the mind of God. This idea demonstrates the relationship between "belief" and "faith" in that accepting the proposition of two mutually opposing truths arises out of the doubts one encounters as one attempts to form an internal adherence to a particular idea that seems illogical. While one might "believe" but still doubt that such a double truth is possible, one can't have "faith." See Gershon Weiler, "Beliefs and Attributes," *Philosophy*, 36:137, April–July 1961, pp. 196–210.

10 See Dorit Bar-On, "Indeterminacy of Translation-Theory and Practice," *Philosophy and Phenomenological Research*, 53:4, December 1993, pp. 781–810; and Willem A. DeVries, "Meaning and Interpretation in History," *History and Theory*, 22:3, October 1983, pp. 253–63.

11 Clifford Geertz, *Available Light: Anthropological Reflections on Philosophical Topics* (Princeton: The University Press, 2000), pp. 10–11. For a concise statement of the problem, see Lila Abu Lughod, "Can there be a Feminist Ethnography?" *Women and Performance*, 5, 1990, pp. 7–27.

12 Hans-Georg Gadamer, *Truth and Method*, trans. Joel Weinsheimer and Donald Marshall, 2nd revised ed. (New York: Continuum, 1989), pp. 275–96, 441.

13 We also run the risk of changing how people understand their own religious traditions and those of other people. In Islamic studies this concern is not new: W. C. Smith wrote over thirty years ago of the need for caution on the part of scholars of Islam in how we describe or depict Islamic phenomena because non-academically trained Muslims read our work. Because of the authority we assume and assert based on our training, we run the risk of influencing how Muslims in many different walks of life think about their traditions and the world. I am by no means invoking Smith's conclusion that scholars, therefore, restrict their examinations to areas of scholarship that will not offend Muslim sensibilities because that assumes a uniformity of Muslim opinion and thought that simply does not exist. I am advocating, however, a heightened awareness of the need for care and exactness in the use of terms and words that suggest essentialisms that cannot be proven to exist. See Wilfred Cantwell Smith, "Methodology and the Study of Religion: Some Misgivings," in *Methodological Issues in the Study of Religion*, ed. Robert D. Baird (Chico: New Horizons Press, 1975), pp. 1–30.

14 Jonathan Z. Smith, *Drudgery Divine: On the Comparison of Early Christianities and the Religions of Late Antiquity* (Chicago: The University Press, 1994), pp. 112–19.

15 For a comprehensive overview of trends in comparative religious studies, see Eric J. Sharpe, *Comparative Religion: A History* (Chicago: Open Court Press, 1997).

16 Camilla Adang, "Belief and Unbelief," in *Encyclopedia of the Qur'an*, eds. Jane Dammen McAuliffe et al., vol. 1, 1st ed. (Leiden: Brill, 2001), p. 218.

17 Ibid., pp. 219–20.

18 See Jane Smith's article on "Faith" in *Encyclopedia of the Qur'an* eds. Jane Dammen McAuliffe et al., vol. 2, 1st ed. (Leiden: Brill, 2002), pp. 162–72, in

which she argues that "faith" and "belief" are both indicated by the Arabic terms *iman*, although, like Adang, Smith fails to define the term "faith."

19 Edward Salisbury, "Translation of Two Unpublished Arabic Documents, Relating to the Doctrines of the Ismāʿilis and the Other Bātinian Sects," *Journal of the American Oriental Society*, 2, 1851, pp. 262, 276.

20 John P. Brown, who translates *bariʾa* and *iman* as "belief." See his "On the Tesavuf, or Spiritual Life of the Soffees," *Journal of the American Oriental Society*, 8, 1866, pp. 95–104. G. W. Davis, "Islam and the Kuran," *The Old and New Testament Student*, 10:6, June 1890, p. 336. Davis speaks of Islam as a "system of belief." G. H. Patterson, who translates *iman* as "belief" in "The Eschatology of the Kuran," *The Old and New Testament Student*, 11:2, August 1890, p. 79. L. M. Simmons uses "Moslem belief" and "religious belief" as a common conceptual category in "Confession of Faith of the Almohades," *The Jewish Quarterly Review*, 3:2, January 1891, p. 361. Hirschfeld Hartwig, "The Spirit of Islam," *The Jewish Quarterly Review*, 5:2, January 1893, pp. 212–230. Also see his "Mohammedan Criticism of the Bible," *Jewish Quarterly Review*, 13:2, January 1901, pp. 222–40.

21 Wilfred Cantwell Smith, *Belief and History* (Charlottesville: University Press of Virginia, 1985), p. 41.

22 The reader should not confuse my use of "double translation" with the early modern pedagogical method of the same name (see William E. Miller, "Double Translation in English Humanistic Education," *Studies in the Renaissance*, 10, 1963, pp. 163–74).

23 Gustav Weil, "An Introduction to the Quran," *The Biblical World*, 5:3, March 1895, pp. 181–91; 5:4, April 1895, pp. 273–86; 5:5, May 1895, pp. 343–59; 5:6, June 1895, pp. 438–47; 6:1, July 1895, pp. 26–38; 6:2, August 1895, pp. 105–14.

24 Ibid., 5:5, p. 351; 5:6, p. 441.

25 Ibid., 5:6, p. 345; 6:1, pp. 28, 36.

26 Ibid., 5:5, p. 345; 6:1, p. 30.

27 Ibid., 5:6, pp. 446–7.

28 "Belief" is not the only concept that does not find a discussion; Weil, a superb linguist, does not mention the problems for understanding any other concept and assumes that there are a broad range of essential religious phenomena that need no definition or specification.

29 Duncan B. MacDonald, "The Faith of Islam," *The American Journal of Semitic Languages and Literatures*, 12:1–2, October 1895–January 1896, pp. 93–117.

30 Ibid., p. 93.

31 Ibid.

32 Ibid., p. 111.

33 Ibid., pp. 107, 111, 113.

34 See, for instance, p. 109.

35 Ibid., pp. 113–17.

36 T. Witton Davies, "Magic, Divination, and Demonology among the Semites," *The American Journal of Semitic Languages and Literatures*, 14:4, July 1898, pp. 241–51.

37 Ibid., pp. 243, 246, 247, and 248 compared with ideas in Arabic pp. 250–51.

38 See, for instance, Samuel Ives Curtiss, "Conceptions of God among Modern Semites," *The Biblical World*, 19:2, April 1902, pp. 122–31; Sidney Adams

Weston, "The Kitab Masalik an-Naẓar of Saʿid Ibn Hasan of Alexandria, Edited for the First Time and translated with Introduction and Notes," *Journal of the American Oriental Society*, 24, 1903, pp. 312–83; Israel Friedlaender, "A Muhammedan Book on Augury in Hebrew Characters," *The Jewish Quarterly Review*, 19:1, October 1906, pp. 84–103; Crawford H. Toy, "Mohammed and the Islam of the Koran," *The Harvard Theological Review*, 5:4, October 1912, pp. 474–514; Henry Preserved Smith, "Moses and Muhammad," *The American Journal of Theology*, 23:4, October 1919, pp. 519–24.

39 Jean Jacques Waardenburg, *Classical Approaches to the Study of Religion: Aims, Methods, and Theories of Research* (The Hague: Moulton, 1973).

40 Jean Jacques Waardenburg, *Reflections on the Study of Religion: Including an Essay on the Work of Gerardus van der Leeuw* (The Hague: Mouton, 1978).

41 See for instance, Constance E. Padwick, "Notes on the Jinn and the Ghoul in the Peasant Mind of Lower Egypt," *Bulletin of the School of Oriental Studies, University of London*, 3:2, 1924, pp. 213–29; Henry Preserved Smith, "The Apologetic Interpretation of Scripture in Islam and in Christianity," *The Journal of Religion*, 4:4, July 1924, pp. 361–71. For earlier examples of this theme of Islam as the corrupted other, see Abraham Geiger, *Was hat Mohammed aus dem Judenthume aufgenommen* (Bonn: F. Baaden, 1833).

42 A. S. Tritton, "Foreign Influences on Muslim Theology," *Bulletin of the School of Oriental and African Studies, University of London*, 10:4, 1942, p. 839.

43 Ibid., p. 840.

44 Ibid., pp. 840–41.

45 Franz Rosenthal, "On Suicide in Islam," *Journal of the American Oriental Society*, 66:3, July–September 1946, p. 239.

46 *Journal of Religion*, 28:4, October 1948, pp. 263–80.

47 Ibid., pp. 268–9.

48 Helmer Ringgren, "The Concept of faith in the Koran," *Oreins*, 4:1, August 1951, p. 9.

49 Ibid., p. 11.

50 Ibid., p. 12.

51 Ibid., p. 13.

52 Ibid., p. 11.

53 Ibid., pp. 13–20.

54 Alfred Guillaume, "Christian and Muslim Theology as Represented by al-Shahrastani and St. Thomas Aquinas," *Bulletin of the School of African and Oriental Studies, University of London*, 13:3, 1950, pp. 551–80. Theodore Silverstein, "Dante and the Legend of the *Miʿraj*: The Problem of Islamic Influence on the Christian Literature of the Otherworld," *Journal of Near Eastern Studies*, 11:2, April 1952, pp. 89–110. Bernard Lewis, "Some Observations on the Significance of Heresy in the History of Islam," *Studia Islamica*, 1, 1953, pp. 43–63. C. C. Berg, "The Islamization of Java," *Studia Islamica*, 4, 1955, pp. 111–42. E. G. Parrinder, "Islam and West African Indigenous Religion," *Numen*, 6:2, April 1959, pp. 130–41. G. E. von Grunebaum, "Concept and Function of Reason in Islamic Ethics," *Oriens*, 15, December 1962, pp. 1–17. A. J. Arberry, *Aspects of Islamic Civilization: As Depicted in the Original Texts* (London: George Allen, 1964), pp. 279–307. Harry A. Wolfson, "The Jewish Kalam," *The Jewish Quarterly Review*, 57, 1967, pp. 544–73. Hamilton A. R. Gibb, "The Heritage of Islam in the Modern World," *International Journal*

of Middle Eastern Studies, 1:1, January 1970, pp. 3–17. Michael Dols, "The Plague in Early Islamic History," *Journal of the American Oriental Society*, 94:3, July 1974, pp. 371–83. Arberry is significant because of his influence on Islamic studies. In his chapter "Faith and Doubt," Arberry uses "belief," "faith," "doctrine," and "attestation of faith" without distinction and without describing analogous terms in Arabic. "Doubt" is the opposite of "faith" and "belief," and there would appear from his presentation to be no change in the concepts over time or in different cultural locations.

55 Toshihiko Izutsu, *God and Man in the Koran: Semantics of the Koranic Weltanschauung* (Tokyo: The Keio Institute of Cultural and Linguistic Studies, 1964), p. 22.

56 Ibid., p. 23.

57 Ibid.

58 Ibid., pp. 30, 31–2, 53–8, 138–9, 204, 234.

59 See, for instance, his "Creation According to Ibn 'Arabi," in *Seeing God Everywhere: Essays on Nature and the Sacred*, ed. Barry McDonald (Bloomington: World Wisdom Books, 2004), pp. 137–61. Also see his *The Concept of Belief in Islamic Theology* (Tokyo: Keio Institute of Cultural and Linguistic Studies, 1965).

60 Marilyn Robinson Waldman, "The Development of the Concept of *Kufr* in the Qur'an," *Journal of the American Oriental Society*, 88:3, July–September 1968, pp. 442–3. Although Waldman does not comment on Izutsu's ahistorical and essentialist treatment of the concept of "belief," her critique can be understood as a general criticism of the monothetic comparative approach that generally fails to account for the influence of historical change and context. She goes on to argue that while most "Western interpreters" translate *a-m-n* as "belief," which she defines as an "intellectualized sense of thought-out and reasoned conviction," in the Meccan period of Qur'anic development, this sense of the word is absent from the text. Waldman maintains that scholarly conventions for translating *a-m-n* as "belief" have led interpreters astray. For instance, she follows Ringgren in arguing that *a-m-n* and *s-d-q* are closely related terms in the Meccan period, although they are in no way synonyms. Waldman, in fact, faults Ringgren for "confusing" *a-m-n* and *s-d-q* with "belief" (in the sense of an "intellectualized" process of consideration). She argues that during the Meccan period both terms are closer to how we have defined "faith" above, in the sense of acknowledging something as true, although on an emotional and not intellectual level, and thus causing the individual to form a kind of loyalty to the thing to which one inclines toward.

61 W. Montgomery Watt, *What is Islam?* (Beirut: Librairie du Luban, 1968; 2nd ed. 1990), pp. 155–6.

62 Ibid.

63 Kenneth Cragg, *The Mind of the Qur'ān* (London: George Allen, 1973), p. 85.

64 Ibid., p. 177.

65 See his use of such terms as "Islamicate" and "piety-minded" in the *Venture of Islam*.

66 Ibid., p. 174. It should be noted that Waldman was Hodgson's student and her formulation of *iman*, as well as her approach to thinking about such concepts, was influenced by Hodgson, not the other way around.

67 Ibid., p. 439.

68 P. Crone and M. Cook, *Hagarism: The Making of the Islamic World* (Cambridge: The University Press, 1977); also Patricia Crone, *God's Caliph: Religious Authority in the First Centuries of Islam* (Cambridge: The University Press, 1986). J. Wansbourgh, *Quranic Studies: Sources and Methods of Scriptural Interpretation* (Oxford: The University Press, 1977). D. Madigan, *The Qur'an's Self Image: Writing and Authority in Islam's Scripture* (Princeton, N.J.: The University Press, 2001).

69 See, for instance, Armando Salvatore, "Beyond Orientalism? Max Weber and the Displacements of 'Essentialism' in the Study of Islam," *Arabica*, 43:3, September 1996, pp. 457–85.

70 Ibid., p.456.

71 Edward Said's *Orientalism* (New York: Vintage Books, 1979) was the first major assault on Islamic Studies that made the charge that essentialist assumptions about the "oriental other" were driven by political, racist, and general attitudes of Western superiority among "Orientalist scholars." For an excellent overview of the debate, see Fred Halliday, "'Orientalism' and its Critics," *British Journal of Middle Eastern Studies*, 20:2, 1993, pp. 145–63.

72 Robert Bellah, *Beyond Belief: Essays on Religion in a Post-Traditional World* (New York: Harper and Row, 1970).

73 Rodney Needham, *Belief, Language, and Experience* (Chicago: The University Press, 1972).

74 Smith, *Belief and History*, p. 24.

75 Ibid., pp. 24–6.

76 Ibid., p. 25.

77 Ibid., pp. 25–6.

78 This survey is based on a search in the "JSTOR" database using the search terms "belief" and "Islam" in journals designated as belonging to Middle Eastern Studies and Religion. Admittedly, it is far from comprehensive, but provides a good indication of the prevalence of the term "belief" and its increased usage, even in the face of criticisms of its use.

CHAPTER 4: BODY, SHAHZAD BASHIR

1 Ikhwan al-Safa', *Rasa'il Ikhwan al-Safa* (Beirut: Dar Sadir, 2004), vol. 2, pp. 378–9.

2 Abu Hamid Muhammad Ghazali, *Kitab-i kimiya-yi sa'adat*, ed. Ahmad Aram (Tehran: Kitabkhana va Chapkhana-yi Markazi, 1960), pp. 35–6.

3 Abu Nasr al-Farabi, *On the Perfect State*, trans. Richard Walzer (Chicago: Great Books of the Islamic World, 1998), p. 231.

4 See, for example, Sachiko Murata, *The Tao of Islam: A Sourcebook on Gender Relationships in Islamic Thought* (Albany: S.U.N.Y. Press, 1992), and Heinz Halm, "The Cosmology of the Pre-Fatimid Isma'iliyya," in *Mediaeval Isma'ili History and Thought*, ed. Farhad Daftary (Cambridge: Cambridge University Press, 1996), pp. 75–83. For another Islamic philosophical take on the body, different from what I have emphasized here, see Thérèse-Anne Druart, "The Human Soul's Individuation and its Survival after the Body's Death: Avicenna on the Causal Relation between Body and Soul," *Arabic Sciences and Philosophy*, 10, 2000, pp. 259–73.

5 This *hadith* is found in Bukhari and Ibn Hanbal (A. J. Wensinck, *Concordance*

et indices de la tradition musulmane, 2nd ed. [Leiden: E. J. Brill, 1992], vol. 2, p. 71).

6 Malcolm X, *The Autobiography of Malcolm X, as told to Alex Haley* (New York: Ballantine Books, 1992), pp. 375–6. For a related but slightly different use of this passage to highlight the physicality of Islamic rituals see Paul Powers, "Interiors, Intentions, and the 'Spirituality' of Islamic Ritual Practice," *Journal of the American Academy of Religion*, 72:2, 2004, pp. 425–59.

7 Paul Rabinow and Nikolas Rose, eds., *The Essential Foucault* (New York: The New Press, 2003), p. 146.

8 John R. Bowen, "Salat in Indonesia: The Social Meanings of an Islamic Ritual," *Man*, New Series, 24:4, December 1989, pp. 600–619, and Gregory Starrett, "The Hexis of Interpretation: Islam and the Body in the Egyptian Popular School," *American Ethnologist*, 22:4, November 1995, pp. 953–69.

9 Saba Mahmood, "Rehearsed Spontaneity and the Conventionality of Ritual: Disciplines of *Salat*," *American Ethnologist*, 28:4, November 2001, p. 843.

10 Nurcholish Madjid, "Worship as an Institution of Faith," in *Windows on the House of Islam*, ed. John Renard (Berkeley: University of California Press, 1998), pp. 72–3. In Madjid's extended discussion, the prayer is tied also to social activism geared toward creating a just society.

11 For a survey of various types of interpretations regarding the ritual ablution that precedes the prayer, see Marion Katz, "The Study of Islamic Ritual and the Meaning of Wudu'," *Der Islam*, 82:1, 2005, pp. 106–45. As Katz points out, non-esotericist authors may also undertake metaphorical interpretation of rituals and, conversely, Sufi authors may eschew such interpretation despite their esotericist commitments. My characterization here should thus be seen as indicating tendencies rather than absolutes.

12 Michel Chodkiewicz, *An Ocean Without Shore: Ibn Arabi, The Book, and the Law* (Albany: S.U.N.Y. Press, 1993), pp. 109–115. Ibn 'Arabi's extended interpret-ations of the prayer are given in *al-Tanazzulat al-Mawsiliyya*, ed. 'Abd al-Rahman Hasan Mahmud (Cairo: Maktabat 'Alam al-Fikr, 1986). For his interpretation of the ablutions that precede the prayer see *Mysteries of Purity: Ibn al-'Arabi's Asrar al-tahara*, trans. Eric Winkel (Notre Dame: Cross Cultural Publications, 1995).

13 For a more detailed description of Hurufi views on the body and other matters see Shahzad Bashir, *Fazlallah Astarabadi and the Hurufis* (Oxford: Oneworld, 2005).

14 Amir Hasan Sijzi, *Nizam ad-Din Awliya: Morals for the Heart*, trans. Bruce Lawrence (Mahwah, New Jersey: Paulist Press, 1992), p. 369.

15 This interpretation begs the question about women's regular menstrual cycles that preclude them from performing the ritual. The text offers nothing further on this, except to enforce the notion that the rule that renders a subject unfit to perform the ritual during an outflow of blood is related to the body's physical construction. The difference between male and female bodies on this score likely indicates differing capacities as religious actors, though the text does not lay this out explicitly.

16 Muhammad b. Isma'il Bukhari, *Sahih al-Bukhari*, 3 vols. (Vaduz, Liechtenstein: Thesaurus Islamicus Foundation, 2000), vol. 1, p. 379.

17 Ibn Ishaq, *The Life of Muhammad*, trans. Alfred Guillaume (Karachi: Oxford University Press, 1990), p. 72.

18 Ze'ev Maghen, *Virtues of the Flesh: Purity and Passion in Early Islamic Jurisprudence* (Leiden: Brill, 2004), pp. 174–175.
19 See Muhammad Khalid Masud, ed., *Travellers in Faith: Studies of the Tablighi Jama'at as a Transnational Islamic Movement for Faith Renewal* (Leiden: Brill, 2000).
20 Mohammad Ali Amir-Moezzi, *The Divine Guide in Early Shi'ism* (Albany: S.U.N.Y. Press, 1994), p. 56.
21 Ibid., p. 57.
22 For a survey of the various forms this redemptive suffering has taken over the course of history, see Frank Korom, *Hosay Trinidad: Muharram Performances in an Indo-Caribbean Diaspora* (Philadelphia: University of Pennsylvania Press, 2003).
23 In pre-modern Nizari Isma'ili understanding in South Asia, the Imams from the first, 'Ali b. Abi Talib (d. 661) to the one still living were altogether taken as the tenth avatar of the Hindu God Vishnu, expected as a savior in an age of darkness. Although different in physical appearance, their individual bodies were seen to continue the presence of a single essence. For the most recent evaluation of the literature that reflects this amalgamated Hindu–Muslim identity see Teena Purohit, "Formations and Genealogies of Ismaili Sectarianism in Nineteenth Century India" (Ph.D. diss., Columbia University, 2007). Belief in a single essence transferring between bodies is rare but not unknown in Islamic contexts. Prominent examples that have long histories include Middle Eastern sects known under the names of Ahl-i Haqq, Yeresan, Nusayris, and Alevis.
24 Jean Aubin, *Matériaux pour la biographie de Shah Ni'matullah Wali Kermani* (Tehran: Institut Français d'Iranologie, 1982), p. 7.
25 Ibid., pp. 28, 288. For an extended treatment of a social world seeded with saintly bodies see my forthcoming treatment of fourteenth- and fifteenth-century Persianate Sufism in *Bodies of God's Friends: Sufis in Persianate Islamic Societies* (New York: Columbia University Press).
26 For a recent phenomenology of the body that combines academic perspectives with internal Sufi ideas see Scott Kugle, *Sufis and Saints' Bodies* (Chapel Hill: University of North Carolina Press, 2007).
27 Richard Martin, "Anthropomorphism," in *Encyclopedia of the Qur'an*, eds. Jane Dammen McAuliffe et al., vol. 1 (Leiden: Brill, 2001), pp. 103–7. For an extensive catalogue of anthropomorphic features invoked for divinity in early Islamic materials see Daniel Gimaret, *Dieu à la image de l'homme: Les anthropomorphismes de la sunna et leur interprétation par les théologiens* (Paris: Cerf, 1997).

CHAPTER 6: CULTURE, MICHAEL COOPERSON

1 James E. Montgomery, "Ibn Fadlan and the Rusiyyah," *Journal of Arabic and Islamic Studies*, 3, 2000, pp. 1–25, all translations are his. I thank Robert Hoyland for this reference. See also James E. Montgomery, "Travelling Autopsies: Ibn Fadlan and the Bulghar," *Middle Eastern Literatures*, 7:1, 2004, pp. 3–32; and idem, "Spectral Armies, Snakes, and a Giant from Gog and Magog: Ibn Fadlan as Eyewitness among the Volga Bulghars," *Medieval History Journal*, 9:1, 2006, pp. 63–87.
2 Montgomery, "Ibn Fadlan," p. 20. The words in brackets I have added for clarity.

3 Napoleon A. Chagnon, *Yanomamö, the Fierce People*, 2nd ed. (New York; Holt, Rinehart, and Winston, 1977), p. 5. I thank Jay Phelan for this reference.

4 Montgomery, "Ibn Fadlan," p. 18, n. 61.

5 Ibid, p. 19, n. 64.

6 Michael Crichton, *Eaters of the Dead* (New York: Knopf, 1976); *The 13th Warrior* (Touchstone Pictures: dir. John McTiernan), with Antonio Banderas as Ibn Fadlan.

7 See Lila Abu Lughod, "The Interpretation of Culture(s) after Television," in *Representations* Special Issue, *The Fate of "Culture": Geertz and Beyond*, ed. Sherry B. Ortner, 59, Summer 1997, pp. 109–34.

8 Rifaʻa Rafiʻ al-Tahtawi, *al-Diwan al-nafis fi iwan Baris*, ed. ʻAli Ahmad Kinʻan (Abu Dhabi: Dar l-Suwaydi, 2002), p. 66.

9 Marjorie Shostak, *Nisa: The Life and Times of a !Kung Woman* (New York: Vintage, 1983), citations at pp. 7, 3, 9. I thank Jay Phelan for this reference.

10 Ibid., p. 4.

11 On ethnography as narrative see the essays in James Clifford and George E. Marcus, eds., *Writing Culture: The Poetics and Politics of Ethnography* (Berkeley: University of California Press, 1986); and Stephen Greenblatt, "The Touch of the Real," in Ortner, ed., *Representations*, pp. 14–29; for a send-up of the typical first contact narrative, see the first pages of Abu Lughod, "The Interpretation of Culture(s)."

12 Elizabeth Warnock Fernea, *Guests of the Sheik: An Ethnography of an Iraqi Village* (New York: Anchor Books, 1965), pp. 289–93.

13 The classic – and highly technical – statement of this position is Noam Chomsky, *Aspects of the Theory of Syntax* (Cambridge: M.I.T. Press, 1965); a very readable popularization is Steven Pinker, *The Language Instinct: How the Mind Creates Language* (New York: Perennial, 2000).

14 Recent statistics may be found at http://www.ethnologue.com.

15 Scott Atran and Ara Norenzayan, "Religion's Evolutionary Landscape: Counterintuition, Commitment, Compassion, Communion," *Behavioral and Brain Sciences*, 27, 2004, pp. 713–70; citation at p. 713. For a popular overview of the field, see Robin Marantz Henig, "Darwin's God," *The New York Times Magazine*, March 4, 2007; online at http://www.nytimes.com/2007/03/04/magazine/04evolution.t.html. I am grateful to Steven Gross for both these references.

16 Atran and Norenzayan, "Religion's Evolutionary Landscape," p. 714.

17 Edward Said, *Orientalism* (New York: Vintage Books, 1978).

18 Clifford Geertz, *Islam Observed: Religious Development in Morocco and Indonesia* (New Haven: Yale, 1968), citation at p. 29.

19 Ibid, p. 54.

20 Ibid, pp. 62, 104–5, 61.

21 The phrase is from James Baldwin's *Notes of a Native Son* (1955; reprinted Boston: Beacon Press, 1984), p. 172: "Thus it was impossible for [white] Americans to accept the black man as one of themselves, for to do so was to jeopardize their status as white men. But not so to accept him was to deny his human reality, his human weight and complexity, and the strain of denying the overwhelmingly undeniable forced Americans into rationalizations so fantastic that they approached the pathological." I thank Kerry Brown for this reference.

22 Nahid Angha, "Women in Islam," at http://ias.org/articles/Women_in_Islam.html.
23 Ibid.
24 Geertz, *Islam Observed*, pp. 96–7. For discussions and critiques, from different perspectives, of these definitions of culture, see the essays in Ortner, ed., *Representations*.
25 AbdolKarim Soroush, "What Religious Intellectualism Isn't," trans. Nilou Mobasser, online at http://www.drsoroush.com/English/By_DrSoroush/Religious%20Intellectualism%20.html.
26 Akbar Ganji, *Manefest-e Jomhurikhahi*, online at http://www.mihan.net/mihan54/ganji.pdf, esp. pp. 16–19. I thank Mahsa Maleki for this reference.
27 Clifford Gertz, "Religion as a Cultural System," in his *The Interpretation of Cultures: Selected Essays* (New York: Basic Books, 2000), pp 90–125.
28 Sheila Blair, "The Many Questions of Islamic Art," *International Journal of Middle East Studies*, 39:3, 2007, pp. 336–7.
29 Kevin van Bladel, "Barmakid Patronage of Early Translations from Sanskrit to Arabic," paper delivered March 17, 2007, at the 217th meeting of the American Oriental Society, San Antonio, TX.
30 Marshall G. S. Hodgson, *The Venture of Islam: Conscience and History in a World Civilization, The Classical Age of Islam*, vol. 1 (Chicago: University of Chicago Press, 1974), pp. 57–60.
31 Hans-Georg Gadamer, *Truth and Method*, trans. and rev. Joel Weinsheimer and Donald G. Marshall, 2nd revised ed. (London: Continuum, 2004), p. 13.

CHAPTER 7: DEATH, AMILA BUTUROVIC

1 T. Emil Homerin, "Echoes of a Thirsty Owl: Death and Afterlife in pre-Islamic Arabic Poetry," *Journal of Near Eastern Studies*, 44:3, 1985, p. 169.
2 Fazlur Rahman, *Major Themes of the Qur'an* (Minneapolis: Bibliotheca Islamica, 1989), p. 108.
3 See M. Ayoub, *Redemptive Suffering in Islam* (The Hague: Mouton, 1988); R. Firestone, "Merit, Mimesis, and Martyrdom: Aspects of Shi'ite Meta-historical Exegesis on Abraham's Sacrifice in Light of Jewish, Christian, and Sunni Muslim Tradition," *Journal of the American Academy of Religion*, 66:1, 1998, pp. 93–116.
4 For a thorough overview, see Jane I. Smith and Yvonee Y. Haddad, *The Islamic Understanding of Death and Resurrection* (Oxford: Oxford University Press, 2002).
5 Abu Hamid al-Ghazali, *The Precious Pearl*, trans. Jane I. Smith (Missoula, M.T.: Scholars Press), pp. 21–2.
6 Leor Halevi, *Muhammad's Grave: Death Rites and the Making of Islamic Society* (New York: Columbia University Press, 2007), pp. 217–20.
7 Ibid., p. 226.
8 Ibn Sina, *Al-risala al-adhawiyya fi al-ma'ad* (Beirut: Al-mu'ssasa al-jami'iyya li al-dirasa wa'l-nashr wa'l-tawzi', 1984), pp. 23–39.
9 Miskawayh, *Tadhib al-akhlaq*, as cited in M. Fakhry, *A History of Islamic Philosophy* (New York: Columbia University Press, 1983), p. 191.
10 Rahman, *Major Themes of the Qur'an*, pp. 112–13.
11 Emil Homerin, *From Arab Poet to Muslim Saint: Ibn al-Farid, His Verse and His Shrine* (Columbia: University of South Carolina Press, 1994), p. 50.

12 Michael Sells, trans. and ed., *Early Islamic Mysticism* (New York: Paulist Press, 1996), pp. 148–9.

13 William Chittick, *The Sufi Path of Love: The Spiritual Teachings of Rumi* (Albany: S.U.N.Y. Press, 1983), p. 101.

14 As cited in Sells, *Early Islamic Mysticism*, p. 255.

15 Ibid., p. 180.

16 Ibid., p. 183.

17 Ibid., p. 181.

18 Halevi, *Muhammad's Grave*, pp. 10–11.

19 In *Sahih al-Bukhari*, volume 2, book 23.

20 See K. S. Aghaie, *The Martyrs of Kerbala: Shi'i Symbols and Rituals in Modern Iran* (Seattle: University of Washington Press, 2004).

21 Abu Hamid al-Ghazali, *Ihya' 'ulum al-din* (Cairo: Dar ihya' al-kutub al-'arabiyya, 1957), p. 541.

CHAPTER 8: GENDER, KELLY PEMBERTON

1 As used here, *shari'a* should be understood in the more abstract sense of "God's law," which is distinct from *fiqh*, or Islamic legalistic traditions.

2 Saba Mahmood, *Politics of Piety: The Islamic Revival and the Feminist Subject* (Princeton: Princeton University Press, 2005); Lila Abu-Lughod, "The Romance of Resistance: Tracing Transformations of Power through Bedouin Women," *American Ethnologist*, 17:1, 1990, pp. 41–55; Lila Abu-Lughod, *Writing Women's Worlds: Bedouin Stories* (Berkeley: University of California Press, 1993); Lila Abu-Lughod, "The Marriage of Feminism and Islamism in Egypt," in *Remaking Women: Feminism and Modernity in the Middle East*, ed. Lila Abu-Lughod (Princeton: Princeton University Press, 1998); Lila Abu-Lughod, *Dramas of Nationhood: The Politics of Television in Egypt* (Chicago: University of Chicago Press, 2004); Deniz Kandiyoti, ed., *Gendering the Middle East: Emerging Perspectives* (Syracuse: Syracuse University Press, 1996).

3 Edward Said, *Orientalism* (New York: Vintage Books, 1978).

4 'Ali Shariati, *Fatima Fatima ast* (Tehran: Hoseinieh Ershad, 1985).

5 Parvin Paidar, "Feminism and Islam in Iran," in Deniz Kandiyoti, ed., *Gendering the Middle East*, Parvin Paidar, *Women and the Political Process in Twentieth-Century Iran* (Cambridge: Cambridge University Press, 1995).

6 Kandiyoti, ed., *Gendering the Middle East*.

7 See, for example, U.N.I.F.E.M.: "Progress of Arab Women 2004," Amman: United Nations Development Fund for Women, 2004.

8 Chandra Mohanty, *Feminism without Borders: Decolonizing Theory, Practising Solidarity* (Durham, N.C., and London: Duke University Press, 2003).

9 Fatima Mernissi, *Beyond the Veil: Male–Female Dynamics in Modern Muslim Society* (New York: John Wiley & Sons, 1975).

10 Afsaneh Najmabadi, "Hazards of Modernity and Morality: Women, State and Ideology in Contemporary Iran," in Deniz Kandiyoti, ed., *Women, Islam and the State* (Philadelphia: Temple University Press, 1991); Shahla Haeri, "Temporary Marriage: An Islamic Discourse on Female Sexuality in Iran," in Mahnaz Afkhami and Erika Friedl, eds., *In the Eye of the Storm: Women in Post-Revolutionary Iran* (Syracuse, NY: Syracuse University Press, 1994); Amira el-Azhary Sonbol, "Rethinking Women and Islam," in Yvonne Yazbeck Haddad

and John L. Esposito, eds., *Daughters of Abraham* (Gainesville, FL: University Press of Florida, 2002); Nimat Hafez Barazangi, "Viceregency and Gender Justice," in Nimat Hafez Barazangi, M. Raquibuz Zaman, and Omar Afzal, eds., *Islamic Identity and the Struggle for Justice* (Gainesville, FL: University Press of Florida, 1996); Nimat Hafez Barazangi, *Womens' Identity and the Qur'an: A New Reading* (University Press of Florida, 2004); Kecia Ali, *Sexual Ethics & Islam: Feminist Reflections on Qur'an, Hadith, and Jurisprudence* (Oxford: Oneworld, 2006); Amina Wadud, *Qur'an and Woman: Rereading the Sacred Text from a Woman's Perspective* (Kuala Lumpur: Penerbit Fajar Bakti Sdn. Bhd., 1992; New York and Oxford: Oxford University Press, 1999); Amina Wadud, *Inside the Gender Jihad: Women's Reform in Islam* (Oxford: Oneworld, 2006).

11 Haideh Moghissi, *Feminism and Islamic Fundamentalism* (London: Zed Books, 1999).

12 Leila Ahmed, *Women and Gender in Islam: Historical Roots of a Modern Debate* (New Haven: Yale University Press, 1992); Asma Barlas, *Believing Women in Islam: Unreading Patriarchal Interpretations of the Qur'an* (Austin: University of Texas Press, 2002).

13 Fatima Mernissi, *Beyond the Veil: Male–Female Dynamics in Modern Muslim Society* (New York: John Wiley & Sons, 1975; Fatima Mernissi, *The Veil and the Male Elite: A Feminist Interpretation of Women's Rights in Islam*, trans. Mary Jo Lakeland (Reading, M.S.: Addison-Wesley, 1991).

14 Irshad Manji, *The Trouble with Islam* (New York: St. Martin's Press, 2004); Ayaan Hirsi Ali, *Infidel* (New York: Free Press, 2007).

15 Abu-Lughod, *Writing Women's Worlds*; Diane Singerman, *Avenues of Participation: Family, Politics, and Networks in Urban Quarters of Cairo* (Princeton: Princeton University Press, 1995); Salma Ahmed Nageeb, *Old Spaces and New Frontiers* (Lanham, MD: Lexington Books, 2004).

16 Maryam Poya, *Women, Work, and Islamism: Ideology and Resistance in Iran* (New York and London: Zed Books, 1999).

17 Abu-Lughod, *Remaking Women*, 1998; Abu-Lughod, *Dramas of Nationhood*; Singerman, *Avenues of Participation*; Arlene Elowe MacLeod, *Accommodating Protest: Working Women, the New Veiling, and Change in Cairo* (New York: Columbia University Press, 1993).

18 Muhammad Shafi 'Uthmani, *Ma'arif al-Qur'an*, 8 vols. (Karachi: Idarat al-Ma'arif 1969–73); see online, http://ibnayyub.wordpress.com/2007/06/10/maarif-al-quran-mufti-shafi-uthmani-complete/.

19 Wadud, *Qur'an and Woman*; Wadud, *Inside the Gender Jihad*; Asma Barlas, *Believing Women in Islam: Unreading Patriarchal Interpretations of the Qur'an* (Austin: University of Texas Press, 2002); Barazangi, "Viceregency and Gender Justice;" Barazangi, *Women's Identity and the Qur'an*.

20 Wadud, *Inside the Gender Jihad*.

21 See Dale. F. Eickelman and Jon W. Anderson, eds., *New Media in the Muslim World: The Emerging Public Sphere* (Bloomington: Indiana University Press, 2003).

22 Kandiyoti, ed., *Gendering the Middle East*.

23 For example, Bernard Haykel, "Reforming Islam by Dissolving the *madhahib: Shawkani and his Zayki Detracters in Yemen*," in *Studies in Islamic Legal Theory*, ed. Bernard G. Weiss (Leiden: Brill, 2002); by the same author, "Dissembling Descent, or how the Barber Lost his Turban: Identity and

Evidence in Eighteenth-Century Yemen," *Islamic Law and Society*, 9:2, 2002, pp. 194–230; Murad Wilfried Hoffman, "The Contemporary Role of Schools of Islamic Law," *Islamic Studies*, 44:3, 2005, pp. 441–7; Wael B. Hallaq, "Juristic Authory vs. State Power: the Legal Crises of Modern Islam," *Journal of Law and Religion*, 19:2, 2003, pp. 243–58; M. Cammack, L. Young, and T. Heaton, "Legislating Social Change in an Islamic Society: Indonesia's Marriage Law," *The American Journal of Comparative Law*, 44:1, Winter 1996, pp. 45–73.

24 Eickelman and Anderson, eds., *New Media in the Muslim World*.

25 See A. J. Arberry, trans., *Discourses of Rumi, or Fihi ma Fihi* (Ames, I.A.: Omphaloskepsis 2000), p. 155.

26 Sachiko Murata, *The Tao of Islam: A Sourcebook on Gender Relationships in Islamic Thought* (Albany: S.U.N.Y. Press, 1992).

27 Mernissi, *The Veil and the Male Elite*.

28 Wadud, *Qur'an and Woman:* Barbara Freyer Stowasser, *Women in the Qur'an, Traditions, and Interpretation* (Oxford and New York: Oxford University Press, 1994); Denise Spellberg, *Politics, Gender, and the Islamic Past* (New York: Columbia University Press, 1994).

29 For example, Ali, *Sexual Ethics and Islam*.

30 For example, Judith Tucker, *Women in Nineteenth-Century Egypt* (New York: Cambridge University Press, 1985).

31 Wadud, *Inside the Gender Jihad*.

32 For further reading related to this chapter, see: Khaled Aboul Fadl, *Speaking in God's Name: Islamic Law, Authority and Women* (Oxford: Oneworld, 2001); Haleh Afshar, *Women and Politics in the Third World* (London and New York: Routledge, 1996); Yeşim Arat, *Rethinking Islam and Liberal Democracy* (Albany: S.U.N.Y. Press, 2005); Roxana Bahramitash, "Myths and Realities of the Impact of Political Islam on Women: Female Employment in Indonesia and Iran," *Development in Practice*, 14:4, 2004, pp. 508–20; Abdulwahab Bouhdiba, *Sexuality in Islam*, trans. Alan Sheridan (Boston: Kegan Paul, 1985); Suzanne Brenner, "Reconstructing Self and Society: Javanese Muslim Women and the Veil," *American Ethnologist*, 23:4, 1996, pp. 673–97; Geraldine Brooks, *Nine Parts of Desire* (New York: Anchor Books, 1995); M. Cammack, L. Young, and T. Heaton, "Legislating Social Change in an Islamic Society: Indonesia's Marriage Law," *The American Journal of Comparative Law*, 44:1, Winter, 1996, pp. 45–73; Rkia Cornell, trans. *Early Sufi Women: Dhikr an niswa al-muta'abbidat as sufiyyat* (of Abu 'Abd ar-Rahman al-Sulami) (Fons Vitae: Louisville: 1999); Joanna DeGroot, "Gender, Discourse, and Ideology in Iranian Studies: Towards a New Scholarship," in Kandiyoti, ed., *Gendering the Middle East*, Ayse Durakbaşa, *Halide Edib: Türk Modernleşmesi ve Feminizm* (Istanbul: İletişim yayınları, 2000); Jamal J. Elias, "Female and Feminine in Islamic Mysticism," *The Muslim World*, 78:3–4, 1988, pp. 209–24; M. Fethullah Gülen, *Pearls of Wisdom*, trans. Ali Unal (Somerset, N.J.: The Light, Inc., and Işık Yayınları 2005); Riffat Hassan, "On Human Rights and the Qur'anic Perspective," *Journal of Ecumenical Studies*, 19:3, Summer 1982, pp. 51–65; Riffat Hassan, "Challenging the Stereotypes of Fundamentalism: An Islamic Feminist Perspective," *The Muslim World*, 91:1–2, 2001, pp. 55–70; Mary Elaine Hegland, "The Power Paradox in Muslim Women's *Majales*: North-West Pakistani Mourning Rituals as Sites of Contestation over Religious Politics, Ethnicity, and Gender," *SIGNS, Journal of Women in Culture and Society*, 23:2, 1998, pp. 391–428;

Anwar Hekmat, *Women and the Koran* (New York: Prometheus Books, 1997);
Al-Hibri, Azizah, "A Study of Islamic Herstory: or, How did we ever get into
this Mess?" *Women's Studies International Forum*, 5, 1982, pp. 207–19; Murad
W. Hoffman, "The Contemporary Role of Schools of Islamic Law," *Islamic Studies*,
44:3, 2005, pp. 441–7; Marvine Howe, *Morocco: The Islamist Awakening and
Other Challenges* (New York: Oxford University Press, 2005); Hiba Ra'uf Izzat,
*"Al-Mar'a wa'l ijtihad: nahwa khitab Islami jadid ["Women and Ijtihad: Toward
a New Islamic Discourse "]," Alif: The Journal of Comparative Poetics*, 19, 1999,
pp. 96–120; Scott Kugle, "Sexuality, Diversity, and Ethics in the Agenda of
Progressive Muslims," in Omid Safi, *Progressive Muslims: On Justice, Gender,
and Pluralism*. (Oxford: Oneworld Books, 2003); Marnia Lazreg, *The Eloquence
of Silence: Algerian Women in Question* (New York: Routledge, 1994); Julie
Marcus, *A World of Difference: Islam and Gender Hierarchy in Turkey* (London:
Zed Books, 1992); Margaret L. Meriwether and Judith E. Tucker, *Women and
Gender in the Modern Middle East* (Boulder: Westview Press, 1999); Ziba
Mir-Hosseini, *Marriage on Trial: A Study of Islamic Family Law* (London: I. B.
Tauris, 1993; 2002); Ziba Mir-Hosseini, *Islam and Gender: The Religious Debate
in Contemporary Iran* (London: I. B. Tauris, 2000); Haida Mubarak, "Breaking
the Interpretive Monopoly: A Re-Examination of Verse 4:34," *Hawwa*, 2:3, 2004,
pp. 261–89; Stephen O. Murray and Will Roscoe, eds., *Islamic Homosexualities:
Culture, History, and Literature* (New York: New York University Press, 1997);
Elizabeth Özdalga, "Redeemer or Outsider? The Gülen Community in Civilizing
Process," in *The Muslim World* special issue, "Islam in Contemporary Turkey,"
95:3, 2005, pp. 429–76; Ziauddin Sardar, "Can Islam Change?" *New Statesman*,
September 13, 2004; Annemarie Schimmel, *Pain and Grace: A Study of Two
Mystical Writers of Eighteenth-century India* (Leiden: Brill, 1976); Azzan
Tamimi, *Rachid Ghannouchi: A Democrat within Islamism* (New York: Oxford
University Press, 2001); Ali Unal and Alphonse Williams, *Fethullah Gülen:
Advocate of Dialogue* (Fairfax, V.A.: The Fountain, 2000); Gisela Webb, *Windows
of Faith: Muslim Women Scholar–Activists in North America* (Syracuse: Syracuse
University Press, 2000); World Bank Group, *M.E.N.A. Development Report:
Gender and Development in the Middle East and North Africa – Women in the
Public Sphere* (Washington, D.C.: The World Bank, 2004); Nahid Yeganeh,
"Women, Nationalism and Islam in Contemporary Political Discourse in Iran,"
Feminist Review, special issue, "Nationalisms and National Identities," 44,
Summer 1993, pp. 3–18.

CHAPTER 9: GOD, JAMAL J. ELIAS

1 For more on Ibn Hanbal, see Christopher Melchert, *Ahmad ibn Hanbal* (Oxford:
   Oneworld, 2006); for Al-Ma'mun and his times, see Michael Cooperson,
   Al-Ma'mun (Oxford: Oneworld, 2005).

2 For more on the formal doctrine of abstention from theological speculation
   adopted by many literalist Muslim thinkers in this period, see Josef van Ess, *Die
   Gedankenwelt des Harith al-Muhasibi*, Bonner orientalische Studien, new series,
   vol. 12 (Bonn: Selbstverlag des Orientalischen Seminar der Universität Bonn, 1961).

3 Ibn Hanbal, *Musnad*, as quoted in Wesley Williams, "Aspects of the Creed
   of Imam Ahmad Ibn Hanbal: A Study of Anthropomorphism in Early Islamic
   Discourse," *International Journal of Middle East Studies*, 34:3, 2002, pp. 441–
   63, 443. For more on anthropomorphism in early Islam, also see Josef van Ess,

"The Youthful God: Anthropomorphism in Early Islam," University Lecture in Religion, Arizona State University, March 3, 1988 (Tempe: Arizona State University, 1988).

4 Williams, "Aspects of the Creed," p. 443.

5 Al-Bayhaqi, *Al-asma wa'l-sifat*, ed. 'Abd Allah ibn Muhammad al-Hashidi, 2 vols. (Riyadh: Maktabat al-Sawadi, 1993), vol. 2, p. 363, as quoted in Williams, "Aspects of the Creed," p. 445.

6 For more on divine androgyny in Sufism, see Sachiko Murata, *The Tao of Islam: A Sourcebook on Gender Relationships in Islamic Thought* (Albany: S.U.N.Y. Press, 1992); and Jamal J. Elias, "Female and Feminine in Islamic Mysticism," *The Muslim World*, 78:3–4, 1988, pp. 209–24.

7 For more on Muslim creeds, see A. J. Wensinck, *The Muslim Creed: Its Genesis and Historical Development* (Cambridge: Cambridge University Press, 1932); and W. Montgomery Watt, *Islamic Creeds: A Selection* (Edinburgh: Edinburgh University Press, 1994).

8 For more on ecstatic utterances in Islam, see Carl Ernst, *Words of Ecstasy in Sufism* (Albany: S.U.N.Y. Press, 1985).

9 For a discussion of this story, see Peter Awn, *Satan's Tragedy and Redemption: Iblis in Sufi Psychology* (Leiden: E. J. Brill, 1983).

10 Fazlur Rahman, *Major Themes of the Qur'an* (Minneapolis: Bibliotheca Islamica, 1980), p. 29. Fazlur Rahman served as the director of Pakistan's Institute for Islamic Research until he moved to the U.S. in 1968 to assume a distinguished professorship at the University of Chicago. See also *God and Man in the Qur'an: Semantics of the Koranic Weltanschaung*, Studies in the Humanities and Social Relations, no. 5 (Tokyo: Keio Institute of Cultural and Linguistic Studies, 1964).

11 Rahman, *Major Themes of the Qur'an*, pp. 19–20.

12 Joseph N. Bell, *Love Theory in Later Hanbalite Islam* (Albany: S.U.N.Y. Press, 1979), p. 35.

13 Ibn al-Jawzi, *Talbis Iblis*, ed. Muhammad Munir al-Dimashqi (Cairo: Idarat al-Tiba'a al-muniriyya, 1928), pp. 246–7, as quoted in Bell, *Love Theory*, p. 25.

14 Bell, *Love Theory*, p. 74.

15 There is a third proof concerning minute points of theological debate with the Ash'aris but which is tangential to this esssay. See Bell, *Love Theory*, pp. 77–80.

16 Ibid., pp. 79ff.

17 Ibn Taymiyya, *Minhaj*, vol. 3, p. 101, quoted in ibid., p. 83.

18 Ibid., p. 83.

19 Fariduddin 'Attar, *Tazkirat ul-awliya*, ed. Muhammad Isti'lami (Tehran: Zavvar, 1968, reprinted 1986), p. 87. For more on Rabi'a, particulary as represented by 'Attar, see Margaret Smith, *Rabi'a the Mystic and Her Fellow-Saints in Islam*, revised edition (Cambridge: Cambridge University Press, 1984).

20 All translations are from A. J. Arberry, trans., *The Doctrine of the Sufis (Kitab al-ta'arruf li-madhhab ahl al-tasawwuf)* (Cambridge: Cambridge University Press, 1935; reprinted 1979), pp. 102–4. For an entire treatise on love in Sufism, though one that has not been directly highly influential on the Sufi tradition, see Abu al-Hasan ibn Muhammad al-Daylami, *The Treatise on Mystical Love*, trans. J. N. Bell, and H. M. A. L. Al Shafie (Edinburgh: Edinburgh University Press, 2005). Arguably, the most influential work on Sufi love is Ahmad-i Ghazzali,

Sawanih. Aphorismen über die Liebe, ed. Hellmut Ritter (Istanbul: 1942); English translation Nasrollah Pourjavady, *Sawanih: Inspirations from the World of Pure Spirits* (London: Kegan Paul, 1986); for commentaries on this work, see Ahmad Mojahed, ed., *Shuruh-i sawanih: Seh sharh bar Sawanih ul-'ushshaq-i Ahmad-i Ghazzali* (Tehran: Surush, 1993); Richard Gramlich, trans., *Gedanken über die Liebe* (Mainz: Akademie der Wissenschaften uder der Literature). The most exhaustive study on divine love in Sufism – though one lacking in analysis or historicization – is Jalal Sattari, *'Ishq-i sufiyaneh* (Tehran: Nashr-e markaz, Chap-e Sa'di, 1995).

21 For more on Persian mystical poetry, see J. T. P. de Bruijn, *Persian Sufi Poetry: An Introduction to the Mystical Use of Classical Poems* (Richmond, Surrey: Curzon, 1997); Dick Davis, "Sufism and Poetry: A Marriage of Convenience?" *Edebiyat,* 10:2, 1999, pp. 279–92. For a study of the poetry of Mawlana Jalal ud-din Rumi (d. 1273), the most celebrated Persian Sufi poet, see Fatemeh Keshavarz, *Reading Mystical Lyric: The Case of Jalal al-Din Rumi* (Columbia, South Carolina: University of South Carolina Press, 1998); William C. Chittick, *The Sufi Path of Love: The Spiritual Teachings of Rumi* (Albany: S.U.N.Y. Press, 1983); and Franklin D. Lewis, *Rumi: Past and Present, East and West* (Oxford: Oneworld, 2000).

22 Nizami-yi Ganjavi, *Layla u Majnun,* ed. Barat Zanjani (Tehran: Intisharat-i Danishgah-i Tehran, 1990); *The Story of Layla and Majnun,* trans. Rudolph Gelpke in collaboration with E. Mattin and G. Hill, final chapter by Zia Inayat Khan and Omid Safi (New Lebanon, NY: Omega Publications, 1966; new edition 1997). There are several other versions of the romance. For a translation of an important Turkish version by Fuzuli (d. c. 1556), see Sofi Huri, trans. *Leyla and Mejnun* (London: George Allen and Unwin, 1970).

23 Edward Heron-Allen, ed. and trans., *A Fool of God: The Mystical Verse of Baba Tahir* (London: Octagon Press, 1979), p. 26, my translation.

24 R. A. Nicholson, ed. and trans., *The Tarjuman al-ashwaq: A Collection of Mystical Odes by Muhyi'ddin Ibn al-'Arabi* (London: Theosophical Publishing House, 1911, reprinted 1978), pp. 144–5; also Muhyi al-din Ibn 'Arabi, *Diwan tarjuman al-ashwaq,* ed. Umar al-Tabba' (Beirut: Dar al-Arqam, 1997), pp. 131–2.

25 Jamal J. Elias, trans., *Death before Dying: The Sufi Poems of Sultan Bahu* (Berkeley: University of California Press, 1998), p. 111.

26 Ibn 'Arabi did promote the contemplation of human beings as a means of comprehending specific aspects of the divine nature, and in Persianate society a practice called *shahid bazi* – contemplating the beauty of a youth as a means of appreciating God – gained some currency, although it was viewed askance by the majority of the populace. (See Peter Lamborn Wilson, *Sacred Drift: Essays on the Margins of Islam* [San Francisco: City Lights Books, 1993].)

27 Ibn al-Kalbi, *The Book of Idols (Kitab al-asnam),* trans. N. Amin Faris (Princeton: Princeton University Press, 1969), pp. 21–2.

28 Al-Muqaddasi, *The Best Divisions for Knowledge of the Regions (Ahsan al-taqasim fi ma'rifat al-aqalim),* trans. Basil Collins (Reading, U.K.; Garnet, 2001), p. 390.

29 For more on the Taliban's destruction of the Bamiyan Buddhas, see Jamal J. Elias, "(Un)Making Idolatry: From Mecca to Bamiyan," *Future Anterior,* 4:2, 2007, pp. 13–29; and Finbarr Barry Flood, "Between Cult and Culture: Bamiyan, Islamic Iconoclasm, and the Museum," *The Art Bulletin,* 84:4, 2002, pp. 641–59.

CHAPTER 10: HISTORY, SNJEZANA BUZOV

1 The original of this *ijaza* is in the manuscript collection of the Bosniak Institute in Sarajevo (no. 931). The Bosnian translation and literary analysis of it is published by A. Mulović ("Rimovana naučnička biografija iz zbirke rukopisa Bošnjačkog institute u Sarajevu [A Rhymed Scientific Autobiography from the Manuscript Collection of the Bosniak Institute in Sarajevo]"), *Prilozi za orijentalnu filologiju*, 53, 2004, pp. 133–48.

2 Ibid., p. 139.

3 Ibid.

4 William Graham, "Traditionalism in Islam: An Essay in Interpretation," *Journal of Interdisciplinary History*, 23:3, Winter 1993, p. 512.

5 Andrei Tarkovski, *Sculpting in Time: Reflections on the Cinema*, trans. Kitty Hunter-Blair (New York: Alfred A. Knopf, 1987), p. 57.

6 Ibid., p. 58.

7 Ibid., p. 57.

8 Dj. Kadir, "Surviving Theory," in *The Other Writing: Postcolonial Essays in Latin America's Writing Culture* (West Lafayette: Purdue University Press, 1993), p. 35.

9 Graham, "Traditionalism in Islam," p. 501.

10 Fazlur Rahman, *Islam and Modernity: Transformation of an Intellectual Tradition* (Chicago: The University of Chicago Press, 1982), p. 67. For more on Ibn Khaldun, see Cornell Fleischer, "Royal Authority, Dynastic Cyclism and 'Ibn Khaldunism in Sixteenth Century Ottoman Letters," *Journal of Asian and African Studies*, 18:3/4, 1983, pp. 198–220.

11 Rahman argues that this aspect of his engagement in the reform of education is overlooked by his contemporaries to whom "Abduh must have seemed a pure secularist out to destroy Islam" (*Islam and Modernity*, p. 66).

12 Muhammad Abduh, *al-A'mal al-Kamila*, vol. 3, p. 177; quoted from Rahman, *Islam and Modernity*, p. 64.

13 *Al-Muqaddima: Tarikh al-'Allama Ibn Khaldun: Kitab al-'ibar wa-diwan al-mubtada' wa-al-khabar fi ayyam al-'Arab wa'l-'Ajam wa'l-Barbar wa man 'asarahum min dhawi al-sultan al-akbar*, vol.1 (Tunis: Al-Dar al-tunisiyya li'l-nashr; Al-Mu'assasa al-wataniyya li'l-kitab, 1984), p. 30.

14 Ibid.

15 Stephen Dale, "Ibn Khaldun: The last Greek and the First Annaliste Historian," *International Journal of Middle Eastern Studies*, 38, 2006, p. 431. Dale reconstructs Ibn Khaldun's scholarly lineage by identifying in him a tradition of rationalist thought "that stretches from the Peripatetic philosophers, and especially Aristotle (384–322 BCE), through such Greco–Islamic thinkers as al-Farabi (870–950 CE), Ibn Sina (980–1037 CE), and Ibn Rushd (1126–1198 CE) onward to European philosophical historians and sociologists of the 18th, 19th, and 20th centuries."

16 Referring to the Umayyad and Abbasids caliphates.

17 *Al-Muqaddima*, p. 31.

18 Ibid., p. 32.

19 Fleischer, "Royal Authority," p. 200. The source referred to is Na'ima, *Târîh-i Na'îmâ*, 6 vols. (Istanbul: 1864–66), vol. 1, pp. 33–4 (cf. *Al-Muqaddima*, vol. 1, pp. 343–4).

20 Fleischer, "Royal Authority," p. 200.

21 Ibid., p. 213.
22 Ibid., p. 208.
23 Idris Bitlisi, *Kanun-i Şehinşahi*, MS 1882/2, Es'ad Efendi, Süleymaniye Library, Istanbul (quoted from the facsimile published in Ahmed Akgündüz, *Osmanlı kanunnameleri ve Hukuki Tahlilleri*, vol. 3 [Istanbul: Fey Vakfi, 1991], p. 57).
24 In the recent article discussing the mid-eighteenth-century emergence of histories composed by commoners, D. Sajdi notes that the standard way for a scholar to begin a chronicle is by announcing the order of the world, and by calling on God to sustain that order ("'A Room of His Own': The History of the Barber of Damascus," *The MIT Electronic Journal of Middle East Studies*, 3, Fall 2003, p. 21).
25 Selaniki Mustafa Efendi, *Tarih-i Selaniki*, ed. Mehmet İpşirli, vol. 1 (Istanbul: Edebiyat Fakültesi Basımevi, 1989), p. 419.
26 Shihab al-Din Ahmad Ibn Budayr al-Hallaq, *Hawadith Dimashq al-Sham al-yawmiyya min sana 1154 ila sana 1176*, MS 3551/2, Chester Beatty Library, Dublin, folios 28z–28b; as quoted in Sajdi, "'A Room of His Own,'" p. 25.
27 Mulla Mustafa Başeski's miscellany *majmu'a* that contains the chronicle of the eighteenth-century events in Sarajevo is preserved in the Gazi Husrev Beg Library in Sarajevo (manuscript no. 3001). The quoted text is from the published Bosnian translation (Mula Mustafa Bašeskija, *Ljetopis [1746-1804]*, trans. Mehmed Mujezinović [Sarajevo: Veselin Masleša, 1987], p. 265).
28 Dale, "Ibn Khaldun," p. 436.
29 Sajdi, "'A Room of his Own,'" p. 21.
30 In the introductory study to his edition of Selaniki's *Tarih*, Mehmed İpşirli identifies such "borrowings" of Selaniki's text by a number of later historians such as Peçevi, Hasan Beg Zade, Katib Çelebi, Na'ima, and Solak Zade (see *Tarih-i Selaniki*, vol. 1, pp. xx–xxi).
31 The scroll is kept at the Topkapı Palace Library in Istanbul (MS A. 3599). The limited familiarity I have with this document I owe to Sinem Eryılmaz, who is currently studying it as a part of her Ph.D. thesis, and who presented its facsimiles at the Sawyer Seminar in Ottoman History at the University of Chicago (April 5, 2008).
32 I use the dual term "map-history" because the work contains both textual and visual presentation. Another way to define this work proposed by Baki Tezcan is "annotated genealogy" ("The Politics of Early Modern Ottoman Historiography," in *The Early Modern Ottomans: Remapping the Empire*, eds. Virginia Aksan and Daniel Goffman [Cambridge: Cambridge University Press, 2007], p. 173).
33 Ibid., p. 175.
34 Ibid., p. 174.
35 Sajdi, "'A Room of his Own,'" p. 23.

CHAPTER 11: INSTITUTION, JOSEPH E. LOWRY

1 Nor do pre-modern Arabic sources use a word that is equivalent to the term "institution" as it is used in this essay. A standard English–Arabic dictionary for Modern Standard Arabic gives a range of terms, including: *mu'assasa* (establishment, foundation), *'urf* (custom), etc., with examples like marriage (*zawaj*) and slavery (*riqq*). *Al-Mawrid* (Beirut: Dar al-'ilm li'l-malayin, 1994), p. 471.

2 C. Henning, "Institution," in *Blackwell Encyclopedia of Sociology*, ed. G. Ritzer, 11 vols. (Oxford: Blackwell Publishing, 2007), vol. 5, p. 2344.

3 W. R. Scott, "Institutional Theory," *Encyclopaedia of Social Theory*, ed. G. Ritzer, 2 vols. (Thousand Oaks: Sage Publications, 2005), vol. 2, p. 408.

4 The caliphate is discussed below. For a short overview of *waqf*, a trust-like vehicle for holding property outside both commerce and inheritance restrictions, see K. Vikør, *Between God and Sultan: A History of Islamic Law* (Oxford: Oxford University Press, 2005), pp. 339–44.

5 This trend exists also in the study of ancient Judaism and its institutions, a field that is usefully analogous in many ways to that of Islamic studies. See, for example, C. Hezser, *The Social Structure of the Rabbinic Movement in Roman Palestine* (Tübingen: Mohr Siebeck, 1997), pp. 185–227, 492–4. She characterizes the Rabbinic "movement" as a "personal alliance system" and denies (persuasively) the existence of structures once thought to be central: Rabbinic courts, the Sanhedrin, etc. I am grateful to my colleague Dr. Natalie Dohrmann for this reference.

6 *Muslim Institutions*, trans. J. MacGregor (London: George Allen &Unwin, 1950). A somewhat similar work is that of R. Levy, *The Social Structure of Islam* (Cambridge: Cambridge University Press, 1957). His chapters cover: the grades of society; the status of women; the status of the child; jurisprudence; moral sentiments; usage, custom and secular law; the caliphate and government; non-caliphal government; military organization; and cosmology and other sciences.

7 It seems unavoidable that the following discussion will imply the marginal character of certain geographies and also certain kinds of institutions. For an illuminating attempt to see beyond the construction of a top-down, normative, Arabicized Islam, see C. Geertz, *Islam Observed: Religious Development in Morocco and Indonesia* (Chicago: University of Chicago Press, 1971).

8 See M. Cooperson, *Classical Arabic Biography* (Cambridge: Cambridge University Press, 2000).

9 On charisma and its routinization, see M. Weber, *Economy and Society*, eds. G. Roth and C. Wittich, 2 vols. (Berkley: University of California Press, 1978), vol. 2, pp. 1111–48, esp. pp. 1121–32. I use "charisma" here to refer to an individual's perceived or asserted connection to the supernatural, and a strong, associated perception or claim of authority based thereon.

10 The Qur'an describes Muhammad as the "seal of the prophets" (Q33:40), a designation understood to mean that he was the last prophet that God would send to humankind.

11 P. Crone, *God's Rule: Government and Islam* (New York: Columbia University Press, 2004), p. 10.

12 On this pattern in the Qur'an generally, and in Muhammad's career in particular, see, e.g. I. Mattson, *The Story of the Qur'an* (Oxford: Blackwell Publishing, 2008), pp. 44–8; and, older but still valuable, W. Watt, *Introduction to the Qur'an* (Edinburgh: Edinburgh University Press, 1970), pp. 156–62.

13 See, e.g. A. Black, *The History of Islamic Political Thought* (New York: Routledge, 2001), pp. 64, 69, 74, 126, and Crone, *God's Rule*, pp. 172–4, 265.

14 Q6:165. See also Q7:69; 7:74; 10:14; 10:73; 35:39, and W. Kadi, "Caliph," *Encyclopaedia of the Qur'an*, ed. J. D. McAuliffe, 6 vols. (Leiden: Brill, 2001–6), vol. 1, pp. 276–8.

15 Abu Bakr (632–634), Umar b. al-Khattab (634–644), Uthman b. Affan

(644–656), and 'Ali b. Abi Talib (656–660). For all regnal and dynastic dates I have depended on C. E. Bosworth, *The New Islamic Dynasties* (Edinburgh: Edinburgh University Press, 1996).

16 Strictly, Muslims or their de facto designees are expected to swear allegiance to the caliph in an oath of obedience termed the *bay'a*, which was a hallmark of the installation of a new caliph. For an eleventh-century jurist's description of the selection process for a caliph, see Abu al-Hasan al-Mawardi, *The Ordinances of Government*, trans. W. Wahba (Reading: Garnet Press, 2000), pp. 3–22.

17 On the complexities of the succession to Muhammad, see W. Madelung, *The Succession to Muhammad* (Cambridge: Cambridge University Press, 1997).

18 On the Umayyads, see G. Hawting, *The First Dynasty of Islam: The Umayyad Caliphate AD 661–750*, reprint with new introduction (London: Routledge, 2000) and, for briefer accounts, H. Kennedy, *The Prophet and the Age of the Caliphates* (New York: Longman, 1986), pp. 82–123, and J. Berkey, *The Formation of Islam: Religion and Society in the Near East 600–1800* (Cambridge: Cambridge University Press, 2003), pp. 76–82.

19 On the Abbasid revolt, see H. Kennedy, *The Prophet and the Age of the Caliphates*, pp. 124–33.

20 See, e.g. Crone's summary of al-Ghazali's (d. 1111) view of the later caliphate. *God's Rule*, pp. 237–49.

21 On the post-Abbasid history of the caliphate, see S. Heidemann, *Das Aleppiner Kalifat (A.D. 1261): Vom Ende des Kalifates in Bagdad über Aleppo zu der Restauration in Kairo* (Leiden: Brill, 1994), and Black, *Islamic Political Thought*, pp. 143, 299–300; and "Khalifa," in *Encyclopaedia of Islam*, eds. P. J. Bearman, Th. Bianquis, C. E. Bosworth, E. van Donzel, W. P. Heinrichs, et al., 2nd edition, 12 vols. (Leiden: E. J. Brill, 1960–2005), vol. 4, p. 973.

22 Black, *Islamic Political Thought*, pp. 313–19; see also M. E. Yapp, *The Making of the Modern Near East – 1792–1923* (New York: Longman, 1987), pp. 206, 278–9.

23 Crone, *God's Rule*, pp. 30.

24 In the capacity of "God's caliph" (*khalifat Allah*), as opposed to the more usual, later designation of "caliph of God's Messenger" (*khalifat Rasul Allah*). See P. Crone and M. Hinds, *God's Caliph* (Cambridge: Cambridge University Press, 1986), esp. pp. 1–3. A contrary view is expressed by W. Hallaq, *Origins and Evolution of Islamic Law* (Cambridge: Cambridge University Press, 2005), pp. 43–5.

25 For a more sanguine account of the relationship between caliphs and private experts in religion, see M. Q. Zaman, *Religion and Politics under the Early 'Abbasids: The Emergence of the Proto-Sunni Elite* (Leiden: Brill, 1997).

26 On Imami Shi'ism, see M. Momen, *An Introduction to Shi'i Islam* (New Haven: Yale University Press, 1985); and for a briefer account, H. Halm, *Shiism* (Edinburgh: Edinburgh University Press, 1991), pp. 29–155.

27 Halm, *Shiism*, pp. 128–9 (citing Art. 5). The Iranian constitution was amended in 1989.

28 On the Isma'ilis, see F. Daftary, *The Isma'ilis: Their History and Doctrines* (Cambridge: Cambridge University Press, 1990); and for a briefer account Halm, *Shiism*, pp. 162–205. On the Zaydis, see Halm, *Shiism*, pp. 206–10.

29 On the state's *shari'a*-related duties, see Crone, *God's Rule*, pp. 286–305.

30 See A. Azmeh, *Muslim Kingship: Power and the Sacred in Muslim, Christian, and Pagan Politics* (London: I. B. Tauris, 1997).

31 Berkey, *Formation of Islam*, pp. 204–7. One can distinguish for heuristic purposes between "Muslim states," in which rulers and ruled are Muslim, and
"Islamic states," in which the ruler claims interpretive authority and in which
the state's organization and institutions may take on a potentially cosmic significance expressed in recognizably Islamic terms.

32 Such politicians may possess "charisma" in some modern sense, but uniformly
lack credentials as experts in religious doctrine.

33 Obvious examples include Egypt, Saudi Arabia, and Pakistan, in which political
leadership is thoroughly secular (and sometimes with a military background).
The kings of Jordan and Morocco claim descent from the Prophet; the Moroccan
king's claims are comparatively robust and entail a complex relationship with
the scholarly establishment. On the Moroccan case, see Geertz, *Islam Observed*,
pp. 77–82.

34 This development emerges from a memorandum prepared for an early Abbasid
caliph by a high-ranking Iranian bureaucrat, Ibn al-Muqaffa' (d. c. 757). See
Crone and Hinds, *God's Caliph*, pp. 85–7, 90–1; see also my "The First Islamic
Legal Theory: Ibn al-Muqaffa' on Interpretation, Authority, and the Structure of
the Law," *Journal of the American Oriental Society*, 128: 1, 2008, pp. 25–40.

35 Zaman emphasizes this aspect of cooperation in his *Religion and Politics*.

36 On an early assertion of the scholarly prerogative to disagree, see N. Calder,
"Ikhtilaf and Ijma' in Shafi'i's *Risala*," *Studia Islamica*, 58, 1983, pp. 55–81. See
also G. Makdisi, *The Rise of Colleges: Institutions of Learning in Islam and the
West* (Edinburgh: Edinburgh University Press, 1981), pp. 105–11.

37 This pro-Iranian cultural movement was called *shu'ubiya* in Arabic. For an over-
view, see H. T. Norris, "Shu'ubiyyah," in *'Abbasid Belles-Lettres*, ed. J. Ashtiany,
The Cambridge History of Arabic Literature (Cambridge: Cambridge University
Press, 1990), pp. 31–47.

38 For slightly iconoclastic but very useful overviews of the emergence and study of
the Arabic philosophical tradition, see D. Gutas, *Greek Thought, Arabic Culture:
The Graeco-Arabic in Baghdad and Early 'Abbasid Society (2nd–4th/8th–10th
centuries)* (London: Routledge, 1998), and "The Study of Arabic Philosophy in
the Twentieth Century: An Essay on the Historiography of Arabic Philosophy,"
British Journal of Middle Eastern Studies, 29:1, 2002, pp. 5–25.

39 See the excellent discussion of how this played out in Yemen in B. Messick,
The Calligraphic State: Textual Domination and History in a Muslim Society
(Berkley: University of California Press), pp. 54–72.

40 The difficult question of why law became a dominant form of piety in Islam
seems important but has not really been addressed systematically. For useful
and stimulating preliminary musings, see N. Calder, *Studies in Early Muslim
Jurisprudence* (Oxford: Clarendon Press, 1993), ch. 8, "The Origin of Norms,"
pp. 198–222; for a brief survey of some possibilities, see my *Early Islamic Legal
Theory: The* Risala *of Muhammad ibn Idris al-Shafi'i* (Leiden: Brill, 2007),
pp. 2–6.

41 Although various transliterations of the Arabic term *shari'a* are used for "Islamic
law" in the West, a more accurate term is *fiqh*, which denotes the totality of positive law articulated by the Muslim jurists.

42 Protected non-Muslim communities (*dhimmi*s) were internally self-governing,
yet Islamic law regulated such communities' relations with the Muslim state and
also imposed certain limits on their members' behavior. See, e.g. J. Schacht, *An*

Introduction to Islamic Law (Oxford: Clarendon Press, 1964), pp. 130–3. Islamic law courts were potentially open to non-Muslims, however, and could be used to advantage, for example, in matters of family law. For one jurist's affirmation of this principle, see J. Tucker, *In the House of the Law: Gender and Islamic Law in Ottoman Syria and Palestine* (Berkeley: University of California Press, 1998), pp. 49; Vikør notes, however, that such access was in theory not allowed. *God and Sultan*, p. 175.

43   The first collections of *fatwa*s appeared in the late tenth century. K. Masud, "Muftis, Fatwas, and Islamic Legal Interpretation," in *Islamic Legal Interpretation: Muftis and their Fatwas*, eds. K. Masud, B. Messick, and D. Powers (Cambridge: Harvard University Press, 1986), pp. 3–32, at p. 10.

44   Standardization of legal doctrine was deemed desirable as early as the Iranian bureaucrat Ibn al-Muqaffaʻ, who saw in legal diversity a threat to the authority of the caliph (see n. 34, above). Only in the late pre-modern period did Muslim states achieve the bureaucratic effectiveness to be able to assert themselves in this way vis-à-vis the jurists. The *Fatawa ʻAlamgiriya* contained a distillation of Hanafi law compiled at the behest of the Mughal emperor Awrangzeb (r. 1658–1707). For an excellent overview of state-sponsored *mufti*s in late nineteenth- and twentieth-century Egypt, see J. Skovgaard-Petersen, *Defining Islam for the State: Muftis and Fatwas of the Dar al-Ifta* (Leiden: Brill, 1997).

45   See Vikør, *God and Sultan*, pp. 156–61; for an excellent book-length treatment of the issue, see W. Hallaq's study *Authority, Continuity and Change in Islamic Law* (Cambridge: Cambridge University Press, 2001).

46   This distinction was conferred especially on the founders of the four "schools" of Sunni legal thought. See the discussion of the *madhhab*s below.

47   C. Müller, *Gerichtspraxis im Stadtstaat Córdoba: Zum Recht der Gesellschaft in einer malikitisch-islamischen Rechtstradition des 5./11. Jahrhunderts* (Leiden: Brill, 1999), pp. 151–4.

48   For a brief account, see Vikør, *God and Sultan*, pp. 195–8.

49   For this point in the pre-modern Islamic context, see K. Abou El Fadl, *Rebellion and Violence in Islamic Law* (Cambridge: Cambridge University Press, 2001), p. 28.

50   Hallaq and Zaman, cited above, see a cooperative, integrated relationship. Crone and Hinds, also cited above, describe, by contrast, a nearly unbridgeable gulf. A recent and excellent study of judicial practice in late medieval North Africa suggests that cooperation between judges and *mufti*s was an important component of the larger legal system. See D. Powers, *Law, Society, and Culture in the Maghrib: 1300–1500* (Cambridge: Cambridge Unversity Press, 2002).

51   R. S. Humphreys, *Islamic History: A Framework for Inquiry*, rev. ed. (Princeton: Princeton University Press, 1991), pp. 187–208 (citing R. Mottahedeh at p. 187).

52   See C. Ernst, *The Shambhala Guide to Sufism* (Boston: Shambhala, 1997), pp. 18–19. The term is, however, both convenient and conventional.

53   C. Melchert, "The Transition from Asceticism to Mysticism at the Middle of the Ninth Century, C.E.," *Studia Islamica*, 83, 1996, pp. 51–70, at p. 52.

54   Melchert, "Transition," pp. 57–8, 65; A. Schimmel, *Mystical Dimensions of Islam* (Chapel Hill: University of North Carolina Presss, 1976), pp. 130–48 (on love).

55   Melchert, "Transition," pp. 66–7.

56 The two main schools of Sunni theology were the Ash'ari (after Abu al-Hasan al-Ash'ari, d. 935) and the Maturidi (after Abu Mansur al-Maturidi, d. 944). They correlated with the Shafi'i and Hanafi *madhhabs* discussed in this section of the essay. An early school that died out in the twelfth century or so was the Mu'tazili, whose theology was inherited to some extent by the Imami Shi'is. These schools were markedly doctrinal (though the Mu'tazilis were very diverse); the extent of their social footprint is less clear.

57 These were the Hanafis, named for Abu Hanifa (d. 767); the Malikis, named for Malik ibn Anas (d. 795); the Shafi'is, named for Muhammad ibn Idris al-Shafi'i (d. 820); and the Hanbalis, named for Ahmad ibn Hanbal (d. 855). These eponymous figures were interconnected in various ways through discipleship. On the founding of the schools, see C. Melchert, *The Formation of the Sunni Schools of Law: 9th–10th Centuries C.E.* (Leiden: Brill, 1997). On the early Hanafis, see N. Tsafrir, *The History of an Islamic School of Law: The Early Spread of Hanafism* (Cambridge: Cambridge University Press, 2004). Shi'is are sometimes portrayed as constituting schools along these same lines.

58 By Makdisi in his *Rise of Colleges,* a work at once important and much criticized. Makdisi offers further refinements in *The Rise of Humanism in Classical Islam and the West* (Edinburgh: Edinburgh University Press, 1990).

59 Makdisi, *Rise of Colleges,* pp. 2–9; *Rise of Humanism,* pp. 16–45. Makdisi argues that control over educational institutions, especially *madrasas,* was an important means of control over doctrine. See below.

60 I am summarizing the insightful criticisms of Makdisi's views made by A. K. Reinhart in an unpublished paper, "Guilding the Madhhab," presented at the 207th meeting of the American Oriental Society. I am grateful to Professor Reinhart for furnishing me with a copy of his paper.

61 The Hanafi *madhhab* was historically associated with and favored by Turkish peoples; accordingly, it is today predominant in Turkey, Central Asia, and South Asia. It was also the offical *madhhab* of the Ottoman Empire and so has a presence in the eastern Arab lands. The Maliki *madhhab* asserts a connection with the traditions of the Prophet and the early caliphs in Medina, but has historically been dominant in North Africa and to a lesser extent in sub-Saharan Africa. The Shafi'i *madhhab* is represented in Egypt and Syro-Palestine, and around the Indian Ocean in Arabia, East Africa, the west coast of India, and Malaysia and Indonesia. The Hanbalis, though originally prominent and powerful in Baghdad, are today found almost exclusively in the Arabian Peninsula. They are known especially for their traditionalism and insistence on limiting legal inquiry to the Qur'an and *sunna.*

62 The "founders" of these orders (and the orders themselves) are: Yusuf al-Hamadani and 'Abd al-Khaliq al-Ghujdawani (d. 1140, 1179, respectively; Khwajagan and later Naqshbandi, after Muhammad Baha'al-Din al-Naqshbandi, d. 1389); 'Abd al-Qadir al-Jilani, active in Baghdad (d. 1166; Qadiri); Ahmad al-Yasavi (d. 1166; Yasavi); Abu Najib al-Suhrawardi and his nephew Shihab al-Din al-Suhrawardi, active in Baghdad (d. 1168, 1234, respectively; Suhrawardi); Ahmad b. al-Rifa'i, active in Iraq (d. 1182, Rifa'i); Najm al-Din Kubra, active in Central Asia, though widely traveled (d. 1221; Kubrawi) Mu'in al-Din Chishti, active in India (d. 1236; Chishti); Ahmad b. 'Abdallah al-Shadhili, active in Tunis and later Alexandria (d. 1258; Shadhili); Jalal al-Din al-Rumi, a major Persian poet, active in Anatolia (d. 1273, Mevlevi); Ahmad

al-Badawi, active in Egypt (d. 1276, Badawi). See J. S. Trimingham, *The Sufi Orders in Islam* (Oxford: Oxford University Press, 1971), pp. 31–66; and Schimmel, *Mystical Dimensions*, pp. 228-58.

63 Ernst, *Shambhala Guide*, pp. 132–3.
64 Ibid., pp. 144–5; Schimmel, *Mystical Dimensions*, pp. 235–6.
65 Ernst, *Shambhala Guide*, pp. 212–15
66 Teaching activities in such congregational mosques (sg. *masjid jami'*) were subject to state control. Makdisi, *Rise of Colleges*, pp. 13–14. Non-congregational mosques (sg. *masjid*) could be privately founded and were also important locuses of instruction. Local mosques were founded and maintained with private funds through charitable trusts, *waqfs*, in which revenue-producing property was devoted in perpetuity to the maintenance of the facility.
67 Above all by Makdisi in his *Rise of Colleges*.
68 See J. Berkey, *The Transmission of Knowledge in Medieval Cairo: A Social History of Islamic Education* (Princeton: Princeton University Press, 1994).
69 See M. Chamberlain, "The Production of Knowledge and the Reproduction of the A'yan in Medieval Damascus," in *Madrasa: la Transmission du savoir dans le monde musulman*, eds. N. Grandin and M. Gaborieau (Paris: Èditions Arguments, 1997), pp. 28–62; and *Knowledge and Social Practice in Medieval Damascus, 1190–1350* (Cambridge: Cambridge University Press, 1994).
70 See D. Ephrat, *A Learned Society in a Period of Transition: The Sunni 'Ulama of Eleventh-Century Baghdad* (Albany: State University of New York Press, 2000).
71 See R. Mottahedeh, "The Transmission of Learning: The Role of the Islamic Northeast," in Grandin and Gaborieau, eds., *Madrasa*, pp. 63–72. Similar points are also made by Chamberlain and Ephrat. For further critical remarks on education and its institutions, see Mottahedeh, *Loyalty and Leadership in an Early Islamic Society* (Princeton: Princeton University Press, 1980), pp. 140–44; and R. Bulliet, *The Patricians of Nishapur* (Cambridge: Harvard University Press, 1972), pp. 47–9.
72 See D. Stewart, "The Students' Representative in the Law Colleges of 14th-Century Damascus," *Islamic Law and Society*, 15:2, 2008, pp. 185–218, and especially "The Doctorate of Islamic Law in Mamluk Egypt and Syria," in *Law and Education in Medieval Islam: Studies in Memory of George Makdisi*, eds. J. E. Lowry, et al. (Cambridge: Gibb Memorial Trust, 2004), pp. 45–90. For a briefer look at one pre-modern scholar's attempt to take his pedagogical and administrative responsibilities at the elementary level seriously, see S. Jackson, "Discipline and Duty in a Medieval Muslim Elementary School: Ibn Hajar al-Haytami's *Taqrir al-maqal*," in *Law and Education*, pp. 18–32. Full disclosure: Stewart, Jackson and the author are all students of Makdisi.
73 A useful summary of this latter perspective, using the example of how the Jewish historian Josephus understood and perceived "power," is provided by B. Shaw, "Josephus: Roman Power and Responses to It," *Athenaeum*, 83:2, 1995, pp. 357–90, at pp. 357–9. I am grateful to my colleague Dr. Natalie Dohrmann for this reference.
74 See D. Goodblatt, *Rabbinic Instruction in Sasanian Babylonia* (Leiden: Brill, 1975), who concludes that instruction was less rather than more institutionalized. Hezser's work, casting doubts on the "institutionalization" of the Rabbinic "movement" in Palestinian Judaism, has been cited above, in note 5. A recent

attempt to find common ground between Goodblatt and his critics is J. L. Rubenstein, "The Rise of the Babylonian Rabbinic Academy: A Reexamination of the Talmudic Evidence," *Jewish Studies, an Internet Journal* (2002), pp. 55–68 (http://www.biu.ac.il/JS/JSIJ/1-2002/Rubenstein.pdf).

75 The idea to integrate the study of early Islam into preceding periods rather than viewing it as a wholly new epoch is suggested by P. Brown in his much-cited *The World of Late Antiquity, A.D. 150–750* (London: Harcourt Brace Jovanovich, 1971).

76 This point is made most dramatically – some might say scandalously – in the work by P. Crone and M. Cook, *Hagarism* (Cambridge: Cambridge University Press, 1977).

CHAPTER 12: LAW, A. KEVIN REINHART

1 Bernard Weiss, "Text and Application: Hermeneutical Reflections on Islamic Legal Interpretation," in *The Law Applied: Contextualizing the Islamic Shari'a*, eds. P. Bearman, W. Heinrichs, and B. G. Weiss (London: I. B. Tauris, 2008).

2 For example, Emile Tyan, *Histoire de l'organisation judiciaire en pays d'islam*, 2nd ed. (Leiden: E. J. Brill, 1960), which is just a report of normative and historical texts; exceptions are Colin Imber, *Studies in Ottoman History and Law*, Analecta Isisiana, no. 20 (Istanbul: The Isis Press, 1996); by the same author, *Ebu's-Su'ud: the Islamic Legal Tradition, Jurists: Profiles in Legal Theory* (Stanford: Stanford University Press, 1997); and partly Haim Gerber, *State, Society, and Law in Islam: Ottoman Law in Comparative Perspective* (Albany: State University of New York Press, 1994); by the same author, *Islamic Law and Culture: 1600–1840*, Studies in Islamic Law and Society, vol. 9 (Leiden: E. J. Brill, 1999).

3 Lawrence Rosen is the foremost example of this: *Bargaining for Reality* (Chicago: University of Chicago Press, 1984); and *The Anthropology of Justice: Law as Culture in Islamic Society*, Lewis Henry Morgan Lectures (Cambridge: Cambridge University Press, 1989).

4 G. Bergsträsser, "Anfange und Charakter des Juristischen Denkens im Islam," *Der Islam*, 1925, pp. 76–81.

5 Though the terms are not always differentiated, particularly in later texts, in theory *shar'* and *shari'a* refers to the norms of practice as God would have them. Perhaps "morality" is the best translation of the term. "*Fiqh*," on the other hand, is the process and product of jurists' scholars into the *shari'a*. It is jurists' attempts to understand what God intends for humankind to do.

6 Colin Imber, "Fiqh for Beginners: An Anatolian Text on Jihad," in *Studies in Islamic and Middle Eastern Texts and Traditions in Memory of Norman Calder*, ed. G. R. Hawting, J. A. Mojaddedi, and A. Samely (Oxford: Oxford University Press on behalf of the University of Manchester, 2000).

7 H. L. A. Hart, *The Concept of Law* (Oxford: Clarendon Press, 1961).

8 John Austin, *The Province of Jurisprudence Determined and the Uses of the Study of Jurisprudence* (London: Weidenfeld and Nicolson, 1954); John Austin and Robert Campbell, *Lectures on Jurisprudence: or, The Philosophy of Positive Law*, student's ed. (St. Clair Shores, M.I.: Scholarly Press, 1977).

9 There are certainly other approaches taken to the study of law: legal realism,

critical legal studies, utilitarianism. I am avoiding them here as either insufficiently philosophical, or insufficiently descriptive.

10 Hart, *The Concept of Law*, pp. 90–91.

11 Ibid., p. 92.

12 Ibid., p. 94.

13 Ibid., p. 93.

14 Ibid., p. 170ff.

15 Ibid., ch. 8.

16 Ronald Dworkin, *A Matter of Principle* (Cambridge: Harvard University Press, 1985). This is an admittedly cursory summary of these two complex philosophical schemes, and one that minimizes the significant differences between Dworkin and Hart, over which much ink has been spilled, not least by the two protagonists.

17 Fakhr al-din al-Razi, *al-Mahsul fi usul al-fiqh*, ed. T. J. F. al-'Alwani (n.p.: Jami'at al-imam Muhammad ibn Su'ud al-Islamiyya, 1981), vol. 1/1, pp. 108–9; but see Abu'l-'Abbas Ahmad ibn Idris al-Qarafi, *Sharh tanqih al-fusul fi ikhtisar al-mahsul fi al-usul*, ed. T. A. Sa'id (Cairo: Maktabat al-kulliyya al-Azhariyya, 1973), p. 67.

18 Offer and acceptance are the necessary conditions for a sale, or any valid transfer of property.

19 Abu'l-Fadl 'Abdallah ibn Mahmud al-Mawsili, *al-Ikhtiyar li-ta'lil al-mukhtar* (Cairo: Maktaba wa-matba'a Muhammad 'Ali Subayh, n.d.), vol. 5, p. 69.

20 Muwaffiqaddin Abu Muhammad Ibn Qudamah, *al-Mughni wa-sharhuh al-kabir*, 12 plus 2 index vols. (Beirut: Dar al-kitab al-'arabi, 1983).

21 Frederick S. Carney, "The Role of Rules in Law and Morality," *Southwestern Law Journal*, 23, 1969, pp. 438–53; by the same author, "Some Aspects of Islamic Ethics," *The Journal of Religion*, 63:2, 1983, pp. 159–74.

22 Mohammad Fadel, "The Social Logic of *Taqlid* and the Rise of the *Mukhtasar*," *Islamic Law and Society*, 3:2, 1996, pp. 193–233.

23 Muhammad ibn Ahmad Ibn Rushd, *Bidayat al-mujtahid wa-nihayat al-muqtasid* (Beirut: Dar al-ma'rifa, 1983), vol. 2, p. 379. My translation. See also Averroës [Ibn Rushd], *The Distinguished Jurist's Primer: a Translation of Bidayat al-mujtahid*, trans. I. A. K. Nyazee and R. b. M. A. Rauf (Reading, U.K.: Centre for Muslim Contribution to Civilization and Garnet Publishing, 1994).

24 Ibn Rushd, *Bidayat*, vol. 2, p. 370, my translation; see Averroës, *The Distinguished Jurist's Primer*, pp. 447–8.

25 On which, see below.

26 Later *fiqh* works like the *Majma' al-anhur* or *Fatawa Hindiyyah* functioned more as statute books reporting the preferred alternatives for state-sanctioned Hanafi-school jurisprudence. See Muhammad 'Abdallah ibn Sulayman Shaykhizadeh Damad Efendi, *Majma' al-anhur fi sharh multaqá al-abhur*, 2 vols. (Beirut: Dar ihya' al-turath al-'arabi, n.d.; original edition, Istanbul 1899); Al-Shaykh Nizam ("And a Group of Distinguished Indian 'Ulama"), seventeenth century, *al-Fatawa al-Hindiyya [al-'Alamgiri] fi madhhab al-Imam al-a'zam Abi Hanifa al-Nu'man*, 6 vols. (Beirut: Dar al-fikr, 1999).

27 See George Makdisi, *The Rise of Colleges: Institutions of Learning in Islam and the West* (Edinburgh: The University Press, 1981) on the importance of debate.

28 Like statute books, *fiqh* books seldom contain the full record of a statute's derivation – the appropriate Qur'anic text, *hadith* text with source criticism, ancestral practice, and so forth; those appear only in the relatively rare *takhrij* books.

29 On punishment, see Rudolph Peters, *Crime and Punishment in Islamic Law: Theory and Practice from the Sixteenth to the Twenty-First Century* (Cambridge and New York: Cambridge University Press, 2005); and now Christian Lange, *Justice, Punishment and the Medieval Muslim Imagination* (Cambridge: Cambridge University Press, 2008).

30 On the relations between the claims of humans, the claims of God, and the administration of punishment see B. Johansen, "The Muslim *fiqh* as Sacred Law," in *Studies in Islamic Law and Society* (Leiden: E. J. Brill, 1999); see also Rudolph Peters, *Crime and Punishment in Islamic Law: Theory and Practice from the Sixteenth to the Twenty-First Century* (Cambridge and New York: Cambridge University Press, 2005).

31 Abu'l-Husayn 'Ali b. Muhammad Fakhr al-islam Bazdawi, *Kanz al-usul* (Beirut: Dar al-kitab al-'arabi, 1974; original edition Istanbul, 1889), vol. 1, pp. 19–20.

32 A. Kevin Reinhart, "[The Qur'an in Islamic] Jurisprudence," in *The Blackwell Companion to the Qur'an*, ed. A. Rippen (London: Blackwell, 2006), pp. 439–40.

33 Zayn al-'abidin ibn Ibrahim Ibn Nujaym, *al-Ashbah wa-l-naza'ir 'ala madhhab Abi Hanifah al-Nu'man* (Beirut: al-Maktabah al-'asariyya, 1999), pp. 418, quoting al-Ghazali's *Mustasfa*.

34 Nelly Hanna, *Making Big Money in 1600: The Life and Times of Isma'il Abū Taqiyya, Egyptian Merchant* (Syracuse: Syracuse University Press, 1998), p. 57.

35 *Encyclopaedia of Islam*, eds. P. J. Bearman, Th. Bianquis, C. E. Bosworth, E. van Donzel, W. P. Heinrichs, et al., 2nd edition, 12 vols. (Leiden: E. J. Brill, 1960–2005), vol. 10, p. 161, "*talfīk*."

36 Harald Motzki, *The Origins of Islamic Jurisprudence: Meccan Fiqh before the Classical Schools* (Leiden: Brill, 2002); David S. Powers, *Studies in Qur'an and Hadith: the Formation of the Islamic Law of Inheritance* (Berkeley: University of California Press, 1986). This makes more sense than Schacht's view, still orthodoxy in Islamic studies, that Muslims had no interest in "Islamic law," that is, law shaped by Islamic sources, before the end of the 600s C.E. (Joseph Schacht, *The Origins of Muhammadan Jurisprudence* [Oxford: Clarendon Press, 1950].) According to him, there were only inherited local administrative practices and perhaps Jewish, Christian, and Persian moral norms, adjusted by pre-Islamic custom. Muslims may have been governed by the stipulations of Qur'anic revelation during the Prophet's lifetime, but, says Schacht, the jurists ignored the Qur'an until, in political opposition to the Umayyads, they began inventing Islamic norms which they later justified by forging Prophet *Hadith*s.

37 Robert Hoyland, "New Documentary Texts and the Early Islamic State," *Bulletin of the School of Oriental and African Studies*, 69, 2006, pp. 395–416, p. 397; also G. H. A. Juynboll, "A Tentative Chronology of the Origins of Muslim Tradition," in *Muslim Tradition: Studies in Chronology, Provenance, and Authorship of Early Hadith* (Cambridge and New York: Cambridge University Press, 1983); Baber Johansen, "Legal Literature and the Problem of Change," in *Studies in Islamic Law and Society* (Leiden: E. J. Brill, 1999), pp. 1–4.

38 J. Schacht, "New Sources for the History of Muhammadan Theology," *Studia Islamica*, 1, 1953, pp. 23–41; Josef van Ess, "Kritisches zum Fiqh Akbar," *Revue des études Islamiques*, 54, 1986, pp. 327–38.

39 See Norman Calder, *Studies in Early Muslim Jurisprudence* (Oxford: Clarendon Press, 1993), though I think he is overly suspicious of the idea of an "authored" book in early Islam. Brannon Wheeler, "Identity on the Margins: Unpublished Hanafi Commentaries on the *Mukhtasar* of Ahmad b. Muhammad al-Qudrūri," *Islamic Law and Society*, 10:2, 2003, pp.182–209.

40 For a famous exception see Charles Pellat and Ibn al-Muqaffa', *Ibn al-Muqaffa', mort vers 140/757, "conseilleur" du calife*, Université de Paris, I. V. Paris-Sorbonne Département d'islamologie, *Publications du Département d'islamologie de l'Université de Paris-Sorbonne*, no. 2 (Paris: Maisonneuve et Larose, 1976).

42 Wael B. Hallaq, "Authority, Continuity, and Change in Islamic Law" (Cambridge University Press, 2001, http://www.netLibrary.com/urlapi.asp?action=summar y&v=1&bookid=77867, especially ch. 6.

43 On *fatwas* and their role in Islamic jurisprudence, along with a number of translated examples, see Muhammad Khalid Masud, Brinkley M. Messick, and David S. Powers, eds., *Islamic Legal Interpretation: Muftis and their Fatwas*, Harvard Studies in Islamic Law (Cambridge: Harvard University Press, 1996).

44 For example, Seyyed Hossein Nasr, "The Immutable Principles of Islam and Western Education: Reflections on the Aga Khan Chair of Islamic Studies at the American University of Beirut," *Muslim World*, 56 (1966), pp. 5–9.

45 For example, Hallaq and Johansen.

46 The first, and so far the definitive, study of the *qawa'id* is Wolfhart P. Heinrichs, "*Qawa'id* as a Genre of Legal Literature," in *Studies in Islamic Legal Theory*, ed. B. Weiss (Leiden: E. J. Brill, 2001); see also his "Structuring the Law: Remarks on the *Furuq* Literature," in *Studies in Honour of Clifford Edmund Bosworth*, ed. I. R. Netton (Boston: Brill, 2000). Thanks also to Ahmed Shamsi for a chance to see his unpublished work ("The Relevance of Legal Maxims for the Qadi," draft February 14, 2005). See also, Mustafa Muhaqqiq Damad, "The Codification of Islamic Juridical Principles (*Qawa'id Fiqhiyyah*): A Historical Outline" [particularly of Imami authors], *Hikmat*, 1:1, 1995–96, pp. 89–107.

47 Shamsy.

48 On intention, see Paul R. Powers, *Intent in Islamic Law: Motive and Meaning in Medieval Sunni Fiqh*, Studies in Islamic Law and Society, vol. 25 (Leiden: Brill, 2006); see the list of *qawa'id* in Wolfhart P. Heinrichs, "*Qawa'id* as a Genre of Legal Literature," in *Studies in Islamic Legal Theory*, ed. B. Weiss (Leiden: E. J. Brill, 2000).

49 Zayn al-'abidin ibn Ibrahim Ibn Nujaym, *al-Ashbah wa-l-naza'ir 'ala madhhab Abi Hanifah al-Nu'man*, ed. Al-Fadili (Beirut: al-Maktabah al-'asariyya, 1998), p. 214.

50 Shamsy, p. 5.

51 On the inclusion of "recommended" and "required" in Islamic law, see Carney, "Some Aspects of Islamic Ethics," and A. K. Reinhart, " Islamic Law as Islamic Ethics," *Journal of Religious Ethics*, 11, 1983, pp. 186–203.

52 This, of course, has implications when the basis of law becomes Weberian calculation rather than revealed truth.

53 A. Kevin Reinhart, "Transcendence and Social Practice: *Muftis* and *Qadis* as Religious Interpreters," *Annales Islamologiques*, 27, 1994, pp. 5–28; N. J. Coulson, "Doctrine and Practice in Islamic Law: One Aspect of the Problem," *Bulletin of the School of Oriental and African Studies*, 18:2, 1956, pp. 211–26. One might argue that this delegitimized the state and its agents even if it ethicized the law and its interpreters.

54 The best guide to Islamicate political philosophies is the *Mirrors for Princes* literature. See, for example, *The Sea of Precious Virtues; Bahr al-fava'id: a Medieval Islamic Mirror for Princes*, trans. J. S. Meisami (Salt Lake City: University of Utah Press, 1991).

55 The best account of Arab-world *mazalim* courts is Jørgen S. Nielsen, 1985, *Secular Justice in an Islamic State: Mazalim under the Bahri Mamluks, 662/1264–789/1387* (Leiden: Nederlands Historisch-Archaeologisch Instituut, Istanbul, 1985).

56 Tyan and, although much more rigorous, Wael B. Hallaq, "The Qadi's *Diwan* (*sijill*) before the Ottomans," *Bulletin of the School of Oriental and African Studies*, 61:3, 1998, pp. 415–36, both have this tendency.

57 Citations on the irrelevance of Islamic law and its necessarily compromised nature are legion but one may begin with Ya'akov Meron, "The Development of Legal thought in Hanafi Texts," *Studia Islamica*, 30, 1969, pp. 73–118; N. J. Coulson, *A History of Islamic Law, Islamic Surveys*, no. 2 (Edinburgh: Edinburgh University Press, 1978 [1964]), p. 123ff.; Reuben Levy, *The Social Structure of Islam* (Cambridge: Cambridge University Press), pp. 185–7; J. Schacht, *An Introduction to Islamic Law* (Oxford: Oxford University Press at the Clarendon Press, 1964), pp. 76–85, 199–201; C. Snouck Hurgronje, "Le Droit Musulman," in *Selected works of C. Snouck Hurgronje*, ed. G. H. Bousquet and J. Schacht (Leiden: Brill; original published in *Revue de l'histoire des religions*, 37, 1898, pp. 1–22), pp. 246–9. The imbrication of this view with the colonial venture has yet to be explicitly studied, but there is little doubt that, at least in Anglo-Muhammadan law, the "impracticality" of *shari'a* law justified colonial interventions by the mixed "Anglo-Muhammadan" courts (Gregory C. Kozlowski, *Muslim Endowments and Society in British India* [Cambridge and New York: Cambridge University Press, 1985], ch. 5).

58 Gerber and others.

59 Pierre Bourdieu, "The Force of Law: Toward a Sociology of the Juridical Field," *Hastings Journal of Law*, 38, 1986–87, pp. 805–53.

60 In Bourdieu's lexicon, a "field" is "a site of struggle, of competition for control." The field "defines what is to be controlled; it locates the issues about which dispute is socially meaningful, and thus those concerning which a victory is desirable" (ibid., translator's introduction, p. 808).

61 Ibid., p. 830.

62 Ibid., p. 832–3.

63 "What gave Ottoman legal practice its unity," says Colin Imber, "was the authority of the Sultan. Anyone who exercised legal power, whether Muslim judge, Christian ecclesiastics, rabbis, or secular governors, did so by virtue of appointment by the Sultan, from whom all authority in the Empire flowed." (Imber, *Ebu's-Su'ud*, p. 6.)

64 Ibid., p. 51.

65 Ibid., p. 41.

66 Imber, *Studies in Ottoman History and Law*, p. 184.

67 Richard C. Repp, "Qanūn and Shari'a in the Ottoman Context," in *Islamic Law; Social and Historical Contexts*, ed. A. al-Azmeh (London and New York: Routledge, 1988), pp. 124–5 and passim; see also Imber, *Studies in Ottoman History and Law*, p. 175ff.

68 Bourdieu, "The Force of Law," pp. 837–8; see also the introduction, p. 807. "Symbolic Violence," a badly chosen term I think, is "the power to impose a certain view of the world – especially schemata of classification – on recipients who have little choice about whether to accept or reject them" (Introduction, p. 812).

69 Ibid., Introduction, pp. 807–8. On the rise and fall of *qanunnameh* law, see Uriel Heyd, *Studies in Old Ottoman Criminal Law* (Oxford: Clarendon Press, 1973), pp. 148–57. On the role of the *'ulama* as resistance to the state, see H. A. R. Gibb and Harold Bowen, *Islamic Society and the West: A Study of the Impact of Western Civilization on Moslem Culture in the Near East* (London and New York: Oxford University Press, 1950), vol. 2, pp. 110–11.

70 The two best studies of the ranks of the Ottoman learned hierarchy are R. C. Repp, "Some Observations on the Development of the Ottoman Learned Hierarchy," in *Scholars, Saints, and Sufis*, ed. N. R. Keddie (Berkeley, C.A.: University of California Press); R. C. Repp, "Altered Nature and Role of the 'ulama" [in the eighteenth century], in *Studies in Eighteenth Century Islamic History*, ed. T. Naff and R. Owen (Carbondale, I.L.: Southern Illinois University Press, 1977). See also Repp's *The Mufti of Istanbul: A Study in the Development of the Ottoman Learned Hierarchy*, Oxford Oriental Institute Monographs, no. 8 (London and Atlantic Highlands, N.J.: published by Ithaca Press for the Board of the Faculty of Oriental Studies, Oxford University, distributed in the U.S.A. and Canada by Humanities Press, 1986), and Imber, *Ebu's-Su'ud*. Cornell Fleischer kindly helped me find the first article by R. C. Repp.

71 Bourdieu, "The Force of Law," p. 817.

72 Ibid., p. 819.

73 Ibid., p. 820.

74 Boğaç A. Ergene, *Local Court, Provincial Society, and Justice in the Ottoman Empire: Legal Practice and Dispute resolution in Çankırı and Kastamonu (1652–1744)* (Leiden: Brill, 2003), pp. 133–8.

75 Bourdieu, "The Force of Law," p. 824.

76 Ibid., p. 823.

77 Ibid., pp. 827, 824.

78 Repp, "Qanūn and Shari'a," p. 130.

79 See Reinhart, "Transcendence and Social Practice."

80 Repp, *The Mufti of Istanbul*; on the changing place of the *qadi* in the Ottoman state, see Gerber, *State, Society, and Law*, pp. 66–74.

81 Leslie P. Peirce, *Morality Tales: Law and Gender in the Ottoman Court of Aintab* (Berkeley: University of California Press, 2003), pp. 92–3.

82 Bourdieu, "The Force of Law," pp. 819–20.

83 That the court record is not a transcription, but rather a creative reappropriation of court events, is brilliantly established in Ergene, *Local Court*, ch. 7. This insight is very important and sketches out how much work remains to be done in the field of "reading" court documents.

84 Ibid., p. 26.

85 Hallaq, "The Qadi's *Diwan*", pp. 420–21.

86 Peirce, *Morality Tales*, p. 101.
87 Ibid., pp. 96–7. The clerks' summaries were the preliminary dispute account (*mahdar*) and the executive summary of the evidence (*sijill*).
88 Bourdieu, "The Force of Law," pp. 819, 833–5.
89 My account of witnesses is drawn mostly from Hülya Canbakal, *Society and Politics in an Ottoman Town: 'Ayntab in the 17th century, The Ottoman Empire and its Heritage*, vol. 36 (Leiden: Brill, 2007), p. 125ff. For expert witnesses on "walls" see Simon O'Meara, *Space and Muslim Urban Life: at the Limits of the Labyrinth of Fez* (London and New York: Routledge, 2007).
90 Peirce calls them "case witness."
91 Peirce, *Morality Tales*, p. 97.
92 Canbakal, *Society and Politics*, p. 132.
93 Ibid., pp. 131–49, is extremely interesting on this. See also Peirce, *Morality Tales*, pp. 179–82.
94 Imber, *Studies in Ottoman History and Law*, p. 168.
95 Peirce, *Morality Tales*, pp. 86, 88–9.
96 Ibid., p. 89.
97 *Encyclopaedia of Islam*, eds. P. J. Bearman, Th. Bianquis, C. E. Bosworth, E. van Donzel, W. P. Heinrichs, et al., 2nd edition, 12 vols (Leiden: E. J. Brill, 1960–2005), vol. 9, p. 538, "sidjdjil;" see also Najwa Al-Qattan, "*Dhimmis* in the Muslim Court: Legal Autonomy and Religious Discrimination," *International Journal of Middle East Studies*, 31, 1999, pp. 429–44.
98 See Imber, *Studies in Ottoman History and Law*, p. 170.
99 Gerber, *State, Society, and Law*, pp. 48–50; see also Peirce, *Morality Tales*, p. 354, where a young girl confesses to adultery. "The truth of the matter is that I am pregnant by Ahmed. I cannot slander another. It's this world today, tomorrow the hereafter."
100 Peirce, *Morality Tales*, p. 90.
101 Ergene, *Local Court*, p. 108ff.
102 Michael E. Meeker, *A Nation of Empire: the Ottoman Legacy of Turkish Modernity* (Berkeley: University of California Press, 2002), part III.
103 Max Weber, *Economy and Society: An Outline of Interpretative Sociology*, trans. Guenther Roth and Claus Wittich, 2 vols. (Berkeley: University of California Press, 1978), p. 976ff.

CHAPTER 13: MODERNITY, BRUCE B. LAWRENCE

1 See especially Dilip P. Gaonkar, ed., *Alternative Modernities* (Durham, N.C.: Duke University Press, 2001) and Bruce M. Knauff, *Critically Modern: Alternatives, Alterities, Anthropologies* (Bloomington and Indianapolis: Indiana University Press, 2002).
2 Enrique Dussel, "The Sociohistorical Meaning of Liberation Theology (Reflections about its Origin and World Context)," in *Religions/Globalizations: Theories and Cases*, eds. David N. Hopkins, et al. (Durham, N.C.: Duke University Press, 2001), pp. 33–45.
3 Aziz al-Azmeh, *Islams and Modernities* (London and New York: Verso, 1993).
4 For Asad's challenge of this metaphoric binary, see David Scott and Charles Hirschkind, eds., *Powers of the Secular Modern: Talal Asad and His Interlocutors* (Stanford: Stanford University Press, 2006), p. 302.

5 Gustave E. von Grunebaum, *Modern Islam: The Search for Cultural Identity* (New York: Vintage, 1964), pp. 247–8.

6 Abdallah Laroui, *The Crisis of the Arab Intellectual: Traditionalism or Historicism?* trans. Diarmid Cammel (Berkeley: University of California Press, 1976), pp. 49–64.

7 Ibid., p. 65.

8 Stephen Jay Gould, *Rock of Ages: Science and Religion in the Fullness of Life* (New York: Ballantine, 1999), p. 9.

9 For rival Muslim perspectives on evolution, see Morteza Mutahhari, *Fundamentals of Islamic Thought: God, Man and the Universe* (Berkeley: Mizan, 1985), and Adnan Oktar a.k.a. Harun Yahya, "Evolution Deceit," on http://www.harunyahya.com, 2007, last accessed July 30, 2007. A scathing critique of Yahya is provided in Muzaffer Iqbal, *Islam and Science* (Hampshire: Ashgate, 2002), pp. 272–5.

10 Bruce B. Lawrence, *Defenders of God: The Fundamentalist Revolt against the Modern Age* (San Francisco: Harper and Row, 1989), p. 194.

11 S. H. Nasr, *A Young Muslim's Guide to the Modern World* (Chicago: Kazi Publications, 1994), p. vii.

12 Ibid., p. 136.

13 Mohammed Arkoun, *Rethinking Islam: Common Questions, Uncommon Answers*, trans. and ed. Robert D. Lee (Boulder: Westview Press, 1994), p. 7.

14 Ibid., p. 7.

15 Talal Asad, *Formations of the Secular: Christianity, Islam, Modernity* (Stanford: Stanford University Press, 2003), p. 200.

16 Talal Asad, *Genealogies of Religion: Discipline and Reason of Power in Christianity and Islam* (Baltimore and London: Johns Hopkins University Press, 1993), p. 53.

17 Malika Zeghan, "The 'Recentering' of Religious Knowledge and Discourse: The Case of al-Azhar in Twentieth Century Egypt," in *Schooling Islam: The Culture and Politics of Modern Muslim Education*, eds. Robert W. Hefner and Muhammad Qasim Zaman (Princeton: Princeton University Press, 2007), p. 127.

18 See http://www.wluml.org.

19 See http://www.rawa.org.

20 Peter Mandaville, *Transnational Muslim Publics: Reimagining the Umma* (New York: Routledge, 2001); Gary Bunt, *Virtually Islamic: Computer-Mediated Communication and Cyber Muslim Environments* (Cardiff: University of Wales Press, 2000); by the same author, *Islam in the Digital Age: E-Jihad, Online Fatwas and Cyber Islamic Environments* (London: Pluto, 2003); and Dale F. Eickelman and Jon W. Anderson, eds., *New Media in the Muslim World: The Emerging Public Sphere* (Bloomington and Indianapolis: Indiana University Press, 1999).

21 For a still more radical notion of *umma* as no longer territorial, see Olivier Roy, *Globalized Islam: The Search for a New Umma* (New York: Columbia University Press, 2004), especially pp. 335–40.

22 Pauline M. Rosenau, *Post-Modernism and the Social Sciences: Insights, Inroads and Intrusions* (Princeton: Princeton University Press, 1992), p. 181.

23 Ziauddin Sardar, *Desperately Seeking Paradise: Journeys of a Sceptical Muslim* (London: Granta, 2004).

24 Ziauddin Sardar, *Postmodernism and the Other: The New Imperialism of Western Culture* (London and Chicago: Pluto, 1998), p. 273.
25 Chandra Muzaffar, *Human Rights and the New World Order* (Penang: Just World Trust, 1993).
26 Farish A. Noor, "What is the Victory of Islam? Towards a Different Understanding of the *Ummah*, and Political Success in the Contemporary World," in *Progressive Muslims: On Justice, Gender, and Pluralism*, ed. Omid Safi (Oxford: Oneworld, 2003), p. 232.
27 Ebrahim Moosa, "The Debts and Burdens of Critical Islam," in Safi, ed., *Progressive Muslims*, p. 117.
28 Amina Wadud, *Inside the Gender Jihad: Women's Reform in Islam* (Oxford: Oneworld, 2006), pp. 80–86.

CHAPTER 14: PRAYER, SHAWKAT M. TOORAWA

1 Gerhard Böwering, "Prayer," in *Encyclopaedia of the Qur'an*, vol. 4 (Leiden: Brill, 2004), pp. 215–31.
2 William Graham, *Beyond the Written Word: Oral Aspects of Scripture in the History of Religion* (Cambridge: Cambridge University Press, 1987), p. 101.
3 Twelver Shi'is add the phrase "Ali is the successor of Muhammad" at the end, and Sunnis add the phrase "Prayer is better than sleep" to the dawn call to prayer.
4 Constance E. Padwick, *Muslim Devotions: A Study of Prayer-Manuals in Common Use* (Oxford: Oneworld, 1996 [originally published 1961]); Guy Monnot, "Salat," in *Encyclopaedia of Islam*, eds. P. J. Bearman, Th. Bianquis, C. E. Bosworth, E. van Donzel, W. P. Heinrichs, et al., 2nd edition, 12 vols. (Leiden: E. J. Brill, 1960–2005), vol. 8, p. 925.
5 Monnot, "Salat."
6 Bukhari, *Sahih*, trans. Muhammad Muhsin Khan (Medina: Dar al-Fikr, 1981).
7 David Parkin, "Inside and Outside the Mosque: A Master Trope," in *Islamic Prayer Across the Indian Ocean*, eds. D. Parkin and Stephen C. Headley (Richmond, Surrey: Curzon Press, 2000), pp. 1–23.
8 Monnot, "Salat," p. 925. Further reading: Muhammad al-Jazari, *A Comprehensive Collection of Masnoon Duas based on Al-Hisnul Haseen*, trans. Muhammad Rafeeq Ibn Moulana Ahmad Hathurani (Karachi: Darul-Ishaat, 1993); Ibn Rushd, *The Distinguished Jurist's Primer: A Translation of Bidayat al-Mujtahid*, trans. Imran Khan Nyazee, 2 vols. (Reading: Garnet, 1999); Kevin A. Reinhart, "Impurity/No Danger," *History of Religions*, 30, 1990–1991, pp. 1–24; A. A. Roest Crollius, "The Prayer of the Qur'an," *Studia missionalia*, 24, 1975, pp. 223–52; Mawlana Mohammed Abdul-Aleem Siddiqui, *Elementary Teachings of Islam* (London: Islamic Cultural Centre, 1954). See also: http://muslim-canada.org/elementary_1.html. Imam Abdallah Ibn Alawi Al Haddad, *The Book of Assistance*, trans. Mostafa Badawi (Louisville, Kentucky: Fons Vitae, 2003); M. R. Bawa Muhaiyaddeen, *Dhikr: The Remembrance of God, An Explanation* (Philadelphia: The Fellowship Press, 1999); Stephen C. Headley, *Vers une anthropologie de la prière: études ethnolinguistiques javanaises* (Aix-en-Provence: Publications de l'Universite de Provence, 1996); Ibn Taymiyya, *The Goodly Word, Al-Kalim al-Tayyib*, abr. and trans. Ezzeddin Ibrahim and Denys Johnson-Davies (Cambridge: The Islamic Texts Society, 2000); *Kitab*

al-fiqh 'ala al-madhahib al-arba'a, qism al-'ibadat, 6th ed. (Cairo: al-Hay'a al-'amma li'l-shu'un, al-matabi' al-amiriyya, 1968); Marcel Mauss, *On Prayer*, trans. Susan Leslie, ed. and introduced by W. S. F. Pickering (New York, Oxford: Durkheim Press/Berghahn Books, 2003); David Parkin and Stephen C. Headley, eds., *Islamic Prayer Across the Indian Ocean: Inside and Outside the Mosque* (Richmond, Surrey: Curzon, 2000); Deborah Tannen, *Talking Voices: Repetition, Dialogue and Imagery in Conversational Discourse* (Cambridge: Cambridge University Press, 1989); Abdelkader Tayob, "The Paradigm of Knowledge of the Modern Islamic Resurgence," *Journal of Islamic Social Studies*, 12:2, 1995, pp. 155–69; Philip Zaleski and Carol Zaleski, *Prayer: A History* (Boston and New York: Houghton Mifflin, 2005).

CHAPTER 15: PROPHECY, DEVIN STEWART

1 Al-Hakim al-Nisaburi, *Ma'rifat 'ulūm al-hadith*, ed. Sa'id Muhammad al-Lahham (Beirut: Dar Maktabat al-Hilal, 1989), pp. 15–16.
2 Ahmad ibn Hanbal, *al-Musnad*, report no. 21257.
3 Suliman Bashear, "Abraham's Sacrifice of His Son and Related Issues," *Der Islam*, 67, 1990, pp. 243–77; Willem Bijlefeld, "Controversies around the Qur'anic Ibrahim Narrative and its 'Orientalist' Interpretations," *The Muslim World*, 72:2, 1982, pp. 81–94; Reuven Firestone, "Abraham's Son as the Intended Sacrifice," *Journal of Semitic Studies*, 89, 1989, pp. 95–131; and by the same author, "Abraham's Association with the Meccan Sanctuary and the Pilgrimage in the Pre-Islamic and Early Islamic Periods," *Muséon*, 104, 1991, pp. 365–93; Youakim Moubarac, *Abraham dans le Coran: L'Histoire d'Abraham dans le Coran et la naissance de l'Islam* (Paris, 1958).
4 Ibn Qayyim al-Jawziyya, *Medicine of the Prophet*, trans. Penelope Johnstone (Cambridge: Islamic Texts Society, 1998), pp. 63–4, 80–82.
5 Al-Qadi 'Abd al-Jabbar, *Tathbit dala'il al-nubuwwa* (Beirut: Dar al-'arabiyya, 1966). Imam al-Haramayn al-Juwayni, *A Guide to Conclusive Proofs for the Principles of Belief*, trans. Paul Walker (Reading, U.K.: Garnet, 2000), pp. 165–91; Sayf al-din al-Amidi, *Ghayat al-maram fi 'ilm al-kalam*, ed. Hasan Mahmud 'Abd al-Latif (Cairo: Al-majlis al-a'la li'l-shu'un al-islamiyya, 1971), pp. 315–60; Adud al-din al-Iji, *al-Mawaqif fi 'ilm al-kalam* (Cairo: Maktabat al-Mutanabbi, 1983), pp. 337–57; Richard C. Martin, "The Role of the Basrah Mu'tazilah in Formulating the Doctrine of the Apologetic Miracle," *Journal of Near Eastern Studies*, 39:3, 1980, pp. 175–89; Sarah Stroumsa, "The Signs of Prophecy: The Emergence and Early Development of a Theme in Arabic Theological Literature," *The Harvard Theological Review*, 78:1–2, 1985, pp. 101–14.
6 Sebastian Günther, "Muhammad, the Illiterate Prophet: An Islamic Creed in the Qur'an and Qur'anic Exegesis," *Journal of Qur'anic Studies*, 4, 2002, pp. 1–30.
7 al-Juwayni, *A Guide to Conclusive Proofs*, pp. 193–4; al-Iji, *al-Mawaqif*, pp. 358–66.
8 al-Iji, *al-Mawaqif*, pp. 367–70.
9 W. Montgomery Watt, *Islamic Creeds: A Selection* (Edinburgh: Edinburgh University Press, 1994), pp. 31, 35, 44, 50, 66, 71, 78, 82.
10 R. Walzer, "Al-Fārābī's Theory of Prophecy and Divination," *The Journal of Hellenic Studies*, 77:1, 1957, pp. 142–8; Dimitri Gutas, *Avicenna and the*

Aristotelian Tradition: Introduction to Reading Avicenna's Philosophical Works (Leiden: E. J. Brill, 1988), pp. 160–66; James W. Morris, "The Philosopher-Prophet in Avicenna's Political Philosophy," in *The Political Aspects of Islamic Philosophy*, ed. C. Butterworth (Cambridge: Harvard University Press, 1992), pp. 142–88.

11 Vincent J. Cornell, *Realm of the Saint: Power and Authority in Moroccan Sufism* (Austin, T.X.: University of Texas Press, 1998), pp. 204–29.

12 *The Miraculous Journey of Mahomet: Mi'raj Nāmeh, Bibliothèque Nationale, Paris*, introduction and commentaries by Marie-Rose Séguy (New York: George Braziller, 1977); Josef Horovitz, "Muhammeds Himmelfahrt," *Der Islam*, 9, 1918–19, pp. 159–83; Uri Rubin, *The Eye of the Beholder: The Life of Muhammad as Viewed by the Early Muslims* (Princeton: Darwin Press, 1995); Brooke Olson Vuckovic, *Heavenly Journeys, Earthly Concerns: The Legacy of the Mi'raj in the Formation of Islam* (London: Routledge, 2005).

13 Al-Qadi 'Iyad al-Yahsubi, *Al-Shifa bi-ta'rif huquq al-Mustafa*, 2 vols. (Beirut: Dar al-Kutub al-'Ilmiyya, 2000).

14 Kamal Abdel Malik, "Popular Religious Narratives," in *The Cambridge History of Arabic Literature: Arabic Literature in the Post-Classical Period*, eds. Roger Allen and D. S. Richards (Cambridge: Cambridge University Press, 2006), pp. 333–7, especially pp. 330–44.

CHAPTER 16: RITUAL, AMINA M. STEINFELS

1 William A. Graham, "Islam in the Mirror of Ritual," in *Islam's Understanding of Itself*, eds. Richard G. Hovannisian and Speros Vryonis, Jr. (Malibu: Undena Publications, 1983), pp. 53–71.

2 Frederick M. Denny, "Islamic Ritual: Perspectives and Theories," in *Approaches to Islam in Religious Studies*, ed. Richard C. Martin (Tucson: University of Arizona, 1985), pp. 63–77.

3 Nancy Tapper and Richard Tapper, "The Birth of the Prophet: Ritual and Gender in Turkish Islam," *Man*, new series, 22:1, May 1987, pp. 69–92.

4 It is possible to define ritual in such a way as to almost exclude all of the five pillars. See, for example, Brian Malley and Justin Barrett, "Can Ritual Form be Predicted from Religious Belief? A Test of the Lawson-Macauley Hypothesis," *Journal of Ritual Studies*, 17:2, 2003, pp. 1–14.

5 G. R. Hawting, "'We Were Not Ordered with Entering It but Only with Circumambulating It:' Hadith and Fiqh on Entering the Ka'ba," *Bulletin of the School of Oriental and African Studies*, 47:2, 1984, pp. 228–42; Uri Rubin, "Morning and Evening Prayers in Early Islam," *Jerusalem Studies in Arabic and Islam*, 10, 1987, pp. 40–64; by the same author, "The Ka'ba: Aspects of its Ritual Functions and Position in Pre-Islamic and Early Islamic Times," *Jerusalem Studies in Arabic and Islam*, 8, 1986, pp. 97–131; Roberto Tottoli, "The Thanksgiving Prostration (*Sujud al-Shukr*) in Muslim Traditions," *Bulletin of the School of Oriental and African Studies*, 61:2, 1998, pp. 309–13; by the same author, "Muslim Attitudes towards Prostration (*Sujud*): I. Arabs and Prostration at the Beginning of Islam and in the Qur'an," *Studia Islamica*, 88, 1988, pp. 5–34; by the same author, "Muslim Traditions against Secular Prostration and Inter-Religious Polemic," *Medieval Encounters*, 5:1, 1999, pp. 99–112. Earlier examples of this variety of scholarship have been recently republished in G. R.

Hawting, ed., *The Development of Islamic Ritual*, vol. 26 of *The Formation of the Classical Islamic World* (Aldershot, U.K.: Ashgate Publishing, 2006).

6 Brannon Wheeler, *Mecca and Eden: Ritual, Relics, and Territory in Islam* (Chicago: University of Chicago, 2006), p. 12. For other interpretations of the Hajj, see Pnina Werbner, "Langar: Pilgrimage, Sacred Exchange and Perpetual Sacrifice in a Sufi Saint's Lodge," in *Embodying Charisma: Modernity, Locality and the Performance of Emotion in Sufi Cults*, eds. P. Werbner and H. Basu (London: Routledge, 1998), pp. 97–100; William Roff, "Pilgrimage and the History of Religions: Theoretical Approaches to the Hajj," in *Approaches to Islam in Religious Studies*, ed. Richard C. Martin (Tucson: University of Arizona, 1985), pp. 78–86.

7 Marion Holmes Katz, *Body of Text: The Emergence of the Sunnī Law of Ritual Purity* (Albany: State University of New York Press, 2002); A. Kevin Reinhart, "Impurity/No Danger," *History of Religions*, 30:1, August 1990, pp. 1–24; Richard Gauvain, "Ritual Rewards: A Consideration of Three Recent Approaches to Sunni Purity Law," *Islamic Law and Society*, 12:3, 2005, pp. 333–93. See Gauvain for a discussion of Maghen's work.

8 F. Denny, "Ethical Dimensions of Islamic Ritual Law," in *Religion and Law: Biblical–Judaic and Islamic Perspectives*, eds. Edwin B. Frimage, Bernard G. Weiss, and John W. Welch (Winona Lake: Eisenbrauns, 1990), pp. 199–210; Paul R. Powers, *Intent in Islamic Law: Motive and Meaning in Medieval Sunni Fiqh* (Leiden: Brill, 2006); Powers, "Interiors, Intentions, and the 'Spirituality' of Islamic Ritual Practice," *Journal of the American Academy of Religion*, 72:2, June 2004, pp. 425–59.

9 Powers, *Intent in Islamic Law*, p. 203.

10 Caroline Humphrey and James Laidlaw, *The Archetypal Actions of Ritual: A Theory of Ritual Illustrated by the Jain Rite of Worship* (Oxford: Clarendon Press, 1994). See also, Ivan Brady, "Review Essay: Ritual as Cognitive Process, Performance as History," *Current Anthropology*, 40:2, April 1999, pp. 243–8.

11 Graham, "Islam in the Mirror of Ritual," p. 56.

12 Gauvain, "Ritual Rewards," p. 336.

13 Powers, "Interiors, Intentions," p. 454.

14 Reinhart, "Impurity/No Danger," p. 21.

15 Fritz Staal, "The Meaninglessness of Ritual," *Numen*, 26:1, 1979, pp. 2–22.

16 Edwin Elliot Calverley, trans., *The Mysteries of Worship in Islam: Translation with Commentary and Introduction of Al-Ghazzali's Book Of The Ihya' On The Worship* (1925, reprinted Lahore: Sh. M. Ashraf, 1977), pp. 39–40.

17 John R. Bowen, *Muslims through Discourse: Religion and Ritual in Gayo Society* (Princeton: Princeton University Press, 1993), p. 301.

18 Saba Mahmood, "Rehearsed Spontaneity and the Conventionality of Ritual: Disciplines of Salat," *American Ethnologist*, 28:4, 2001, pp. 827–53.

19 Calverley, *The Mysteries of Worship in Islam*, pp. 43–4.

20 Marjo Buitelaar, *Fasting and Feasting in Morocco: Women's Participation in Ramadan* (Oxford: Berg Publishers, 1993), pp. 105–6.

21 Ibid., p. 42.

22 Andre Moller, *Ramadan in Java: The Joy and Jihad of Ritual Fasting*, vol. 20 of *Lund Studies in History of Religion* (Stockholm: Almqvist & Wiksell International, 2005), p. 270; Bowen, "On Scriptural Essentialism and Ritual

Variation: Muslim Sacrifice in Sumatra and Morocco," *American Ethnologist*, 19:4, *Imagining Identities: Nation, Culture, and the Past*, November 1992, pp. 660–62.

23 Bowen, "On Scriptural Essentialism," pp. 656, 668.

24 Ibid., p. 662.

25 Pnina Werbner, "Sceller le Coran: Offrande et Sacrifice chez les travailleurs immigrés Pakistanais," in *La Fete du mouton: Un sacrifice musulman dans l'espace urbain*, ed. Anne-Marie Brisebarre (Paris: C.N.R.S. Editions, 1998), p. 208.

26 M. E. Combs-Schilling, *Sacred Performances: Islam, Sexuality, and Sacrifice* (New York: Columbia University Press, 1989), pp. 230–31; Pierre Bonte, et al., *Sacrifices en islam espaces et temps d'un rituel* (Paris: C.N.R.S., 1999).

27 Muhammad Umar Memon, *Ibn Taimiya's Struggle against Popular Religion, with an Annotated Translation of his Kitab iqtida as-sirat al-mustaqim mukhalafat ashab al-jahim* (The Hague: Mouton, 1976), pp. 229–41.

28 Barbara Daly Metcalf, *Perfecting Women: Maulana Ashraf 'Ali Thanawi's Bihishti Zewar: A Partial Translation with Commentary* (Berkeley: University of California Press, 1990), pp. 89–161.

29 Katz, *Body of Text*, pp. 96–7.

30 Liyakat A. Takim, "From *Bid'a* to *Sunna*: The *Wilaya* of 'Ali in the Shi'i *Adhan*," *Journal of the American Oriental Society*, 120:2, April–June 2000, pp. 166–77.

31 J. Bowen, "*Salat* in Indonesia: The Social Meanings of an Islamic Ritual," *Man*, new series, 24:4, December 1989, p. 606. For other examples of the place of Islamic ritual in political expression and mobilization, see Cihan Z. Tuğal, 'The Appeal of Islamist Politics: Ritual and Dialogue in a Poor District of Turkey," *The Sociological Quarterly*, 47, 2006, pp. 245–73; Saba Mahmood, *Politics of Piety: The Islamic Revival and the Feminist Subject* (Princeton: Princeton University Press, 2005); by the same author, "Rehearsed Spontaneity and the Conventionality of Ritual: Disciplines of Salat," *American Ethnologist*, 28:4, 2001, pp. 827–53.

32 Robert R. Bianchi, *Guests of God: Pilgrimage and Politics in the Islamic World* (Oxford: Oxford University Press, 2004), pp. 42–4.

33 Anne-Marie Brisebarre, *La Fete du mouton: un sacrifice musulman dans l'espace urbain*, (Paris: C.N.R.S. Editions, 1998), p. 148.

34 Deniz Kandiyoti and Nadira Azimova, "The Communal and the Sacred: Women's Worlds of Ritual in Uzbekistan," *Journal of the Royal Anthropological Institute*, 10, 2004, p. 333.

35 Azam Torab, *Performing Islam: Gender and Ritual in Islam* (Leiden: Brill, 2007), p. 245.

36 For descriptions of Shi'i mourning rituals see David Pinault, "Shia Lamentation Rituals and Reinterpretations of the Doctrine of Intercession: Two Cases from Modern India," *History of Religions*, 38:3, February 1999, pp. 285–305; the various articles in *The Drama Review*, 49:4, Winter 2005; and Vernon James Schubel, *Religious Performance in Contemporary Islam: Shi'i Devotional Rituals in South Asia* (Columbia: University of South Carolina Press, 1993).

37 Syed Akbar Hyder, *Reliving Karbala: Martyrdom in South Asian Memory* (Oxford: Oxford University Press, 2006), p. 65.

38 Gerdien Jonker, "The Knife's Edge: Muslim Burial in the Diaspora," *Mortality*, 1:1, 1996, pp. 27–43.

39 Barbara Cooper, "The Strength in the Song: Muslim Personhood, Audible Capital, and Hausa Women's Performance of the Hajj," *Social Text*, 60, 17:3, Fall 1999, pp. 87–108.

40 Susan O'Brien, "Pilgrimage, Power, and Identity: The Role of the *Hajj* in the Lives of Nigerian Hausa *Bori* Adepts," *Africa Today*, 46:3–4, Summer/Autumn 1999, pp. 11–40.

41 F. E. Peters, *The Hajj: The Muslim Pilgrimage to Mecca and the Holy Places* (Princeton: Princeton University Press, 1994); William C. Young, "The Ka'ba, Gender, and the Rites of Pilgrimage," *International Journal of Middle East Studies*, 25:2, May 1993, pp. 285–300.

42 Bowen, "On Scriptural Essentialism," pp. 656–9.

43 Bowen, "*Salat* in Indonesia," p. 615

44 Heiko Henkel, "'Between Belief and Unbelief lies the Performance of *Salat*': Meaning and Efficacy of a Muslim Ritual," *Journal of the Royal Anthropological Institute*, 11, 2005, pp. 496, 489.

45 Eric Winkel, translator's introduction to *Mysteries of Purity: Ibn al-'Arabi's Asrar al-taharah* (Notre Dame: Cross-Cultural Publications, 1995), p. 11.

46 Leonardo P. Alishan, "Beyond the Law: The Experience of Some Persian Sufi Poets: A Response to Mahmoud Ayoub," in *Religion and Law: Biblical–Judaic and Islamic Perspectives*, eds. Edwin B. Frimage, Bernard G. Weiss, and John W. Welch (Winona Lake: Eisenbrauns, 1990), pp. 231–41.

47 Hyder, *Reliving Karbala*, p. 108.

48 Jamal J. Elias, trans., "Sufi Poetry of the Indus Valley: Khwaja Ghulam Farid," in *Tales of God's Friends: Islamic Hagiography in Translation*, ed. John Renard (Berkeley: University of California Press, 2009, pp. 249–60).

CHAPTER 17: TEXT, İRVIN CEMİL SCHİCK

1 Elizabeth Grosz, *Volatile Bodies: Towards a Corporeal Feminism* (Bloomington and Indianapolis: Indiana University Press, 1994), ch. 6.

2 Jacques Derrida, *Of Grammatology*, trans. Gayatri Chakravorty Spivak (Baltimore and London: Johns Hopkins University Press, 1976 [orig. pub. 1967]), p. 158.

3 Julia Kristeva, *Revolution in Poetic Language*, trans. Margaret Waller (New York: Columbia University Press, 1984 [orig. pub. 1974]), pp. 59–60.

4 Richard E. Palmer, *Hermeneutics: Interpretation Theory in Schleiermacher, Dilthey, Heidegger, and Gadamer* (Evanston, I.L.: Northwestern University Press, 1969), pp. 118–21.

5 Hans-Georg Gadamer, *Truth and Method*, trans. W. Glen-Doepel, rev. Joel Weinsheimer and Donald G. Marshall (London and New York: Continuum, 2004 [orig. pub. 1960]), ch. 4.

6 Ibid., p. 303.

7 Hans Robert Jaus, "Literary History as a Challenge to Literary Theory," trans. Elizabeth Benzinger, *New Literary History*, 2:1, Autumn 1970 (orig. pub. 1967), pp. 7–37.

8 Stanley Fish, *Is There a Text in This Class? The Authority of Interpretive Communities* (Cambridge, M.A.: Harvard University Press, 1980).

9 [Muhammad ibn Isma'il al-Bukhari], *The Translation of the Meanings of Sahih*

al-Bukhari: Arabic–English, trans. Muhammad Muhsin Khan (Chicago: Kazi Publications, 1979), Bad' al-wahi, 3.

10 [Abu Dawud Sulayman ibn al-Ash'ath al-Sijistani], *Sunan Abi Dawud*, ed. Muhammad Muhyiddin 'Abdulhamid (n.p.: Dar Ihya' al-Sunnah al-Nabawiyah, n.d.), Sunna 16.

11 Sa'deddîn Müstakim-zâde Süleyman, *Tuhfe-i Hattâtîn*, Ed. İbnülemin Mahmud Kemal [İnal] (İstanbul: Türk Tarih Encümeni Külliyatı, 1928), p. 7.

12 Annemarie Schimmel, *Deciphering the Signs of God: a Phenomenological Approach to Islam* (Albany: State University of New York, 1994), p. 225.

13 Jalaluddin Muhammad ibn Ahmad al-Mahalli and Jalaluddin 'Abdurrahman ibn Abi Bakr al-Suyuti, *Tafsir al-Qur'an al-'azim* ([Cairo]: Matba'ah Dar Ihya' al-Kutub al-'Arabiyah, 1924), vol. 2, p. 230.

14 *Sahih Bukhari*, Salat, 1.

15 Ibid., Tawhid, 124.

16 Ibid., Bad' al-khalq, 18.

17 Al-Mahalli and Al-Suyuti, *Tafsir*, vol. 2, p. 230.

18 Nefes-zâde İbrahim, *Gülzar-ı Savab*, ed. Kilisli Muallim Rifat (İstanbul: Güzel Sanatlar Akademisi Neşriyatı, 1939), p. 31.

19 Muhammed Hamdi Yazır, *Hak Dini Kur'an Dili: Yeni Mealli Türkçe Tefsir* (İstanbul: T.C. Diyanet İşleri Reisliği Neşriyatı, 1935–38), vol. 7, pp. 56–96.

20 [Mawlana Muhammad Jalaluddin al-Rumi], *The Mathnawi of Jalálu'ddín Rúmí*, ed. Reynold A. Nicholson (Leiden: E. J. Brill and London: Luzac & Co., 1925–40), vol. 1, p. 20, cpl. 296.

21 Wolfgang Iser, *The Act of Reading: A Theory of Aesthetic Response* (Baltimore and London: The Johns Hopkins University Press, 1978), pp. 168–9.

22 Mohamed Aziz Lahbabi [al-Habbabi], *Le personnalisme musulman* (Paris: Presses universitaires de France, 1964), pp. 119–20.

23 Seyyed Hossein Nasr, "Oral Transmission and the Book in Islamic Education: The Spoken and the Written Word," *Journal of Islamic Studies*, 3:1, 1992, pp. 1–14.

24 Derrida, *Of Grammatology*, part I.

25 'Abd al-Ra'uf al-Munawi, *Kunuz al-haqa'iq fi hadith khayr al-khala'iq*, published in the margins of *al-Jami' al-saghir fi ahadith al-bashir wa al-nadhir* by Jalal al-Din 'Abdurrahman ibn Abi Bakr al-Suyuti (Lyallpur: al-Maktabah al-Islamiyah, 1974), vol. 2, p. 115.

26 Michael M. J. Fischer and Mehdi Abadi, *Debating Muslims: Cultural Dialogues in Postmodernity and Tradition* (Madison and London: The University of Wisconsin Press, 1990), ch. 2.

27 Nasr, "Oral Transmission," p. 2.

28 *Sahih Bukhari*, Luqata, 6.

29 Ibid., Khumus, 85.

30 Nefes-zâde, *Gülzar-ı Savab*, pp. 32, 38.

31 Franz Rosenthal, "Abu Hayyan at-Tawhidi on Penmanship," in *Four Essays on Art and Literature in Islam* (Leiden: E. J. Brill, 1971, 20–49), p. 39.

32 Brinkley Messick, *The Calligraphic State: Textual Domination and History in a Muslim Society* (Berkeley, Los Angeles, and London: University of California Press, 1996).

33 Paul Shaw and Peter Bain, "Blackletter vs. Roman: Type as Ideological Surrogate," in *Blackletter: Type and National Identity*, eds. Peter Bain and Paul

Shaw (New York: Princeton Architectural Press and The Cooper Union for the Advancement of Science and Art, 1998), p. 14.

34 Al-Suyuti, *al-Jami' al-saghir fi ahadith al-bashir wa al-nadhir*, vol. 2, p. 93.

35 İrvin Cemil Schick, "Writing the Body in Islam," *Connect*, 3, 2001, pp. 44–54.

36 Abdülbâki Gölpınarlı, *Tasavvuf'tan Dilimize Geçen Deyimler ve Atasözleri* (Istanbul: İnkilâp ve Aka Kitabevleri, 1977), p. 4.

37 Schimmel, *Deciphering the Signs of God*, p. 141.

38 Gölpınarlı, *Tasavvuf'tan Dilimize Geçen Deyimler ve Atasözleri* pp. 177, 214.

CHAPTER 18: WAR, SOHAIL H. HASHMI

1 Ibn Ishaq, *The Life of Muhammad*, trans. Alfred Guillaume (Karachi: Oxford University Press, 1990), pp. 659–60.

2 Peter C. Craigie, *The Problem of War in the Old Testament* (Grand Rapids: William B. Eerdmans, 1978), pp. 9–10, 103.

3 Representative of the first group is Muhammad ibn Jarir al-Tabari, *Jami' al-bayan 'an tawil ay al-Qur'an* (Damascus: Dar al-Qalam, 1997), vol. 4, pp. 652–3. For the second group, see Muhammad ibn Ahmad al-Qurtubi, *Al-Jami' li-ahkam al-Qur'an* (Cairo: Dar al-Katib al-Aribi, 1967), vol. 2, p. 347.

4 Muhammad Husayn Haykal, *The Life of Muhammad*, trans. Ismail Ragi al Faruqi (Indianapolis: North American Trust, 1976), pp. 56–7.

5 Charles Lyall, *Translations of Ancient Arabian Poetry* (New York: Columbia University Press, 1930), p. 113.

6 Fred Donner, "Sources of Islamic Conceptions of War," in *Just War and Jihad: Historical and Theoretical Perspectives on War and Peace in Western and Islamic Traditions* (New York: Greenwood Press, 1991), p. 34.

7 The poem is often included in mirrors for princes in the section urging caution in beginning war. See Muhammad ibn al-Walid al-Turtushi, *Siraj al-muluk*, ed. Jaafar al-Bayati (London: Riad el-Rayyes Books, 1990), p. 505; Ibn Qutayba, *'Uyun al-akhbar al-harb wa al-furusiyya* (Damascus: Wizarat al-Thiqafa wa al-Irshad al-Qawmi, 1977), p. 80; and Ibn 'Abd Rabbih, *Al-'Iqd al-farid* (Beirut: Maktabat Sadir, 1951), vol. 2, p. 7.

8 Lyall, *Translations of Ancient Arabian Poetry*, p. 31.

9 Ibid., p. 113.

10 Ibn Ishaq, *Life of Muhammad*, p. 204.

11 Ibid.

12 Ella Landau-Tasseron, "Jihad," in *Encyclopedia of the Qur'an*, eds. Jane Dammen McAuliffe, et al. (Leiden: Brill, 2003), vol. 3, pp. 35–43.

13 For a concise and critical history, see Norman Daniels, *Islam and the West: The Making of an Image* (Oxford: Oneworld, 1993), esp. ch. 4, "The Place of Violence and Power in the Attack on Islam."

14 Post-9/11 books on this theme abound: Andrew G. Bostom, *The Legacy of Jihad: Islamic Holy War and the Fate of Non-Muslims* (Amherst, N.Y.: Prometheus Books, 2005); Efraim Karsh, *Islamic Imperialism: A History* (New Haven: Yale University Press, 2007); Robert Spencer, *Religion of Peace?: Why Christianity Is and Islam Isn't* (Washington, D.C.: Regnery Publishing, 2007); and many more.

15 Chiragh 'Ali, *A Critical Exposition of the Popular Jihad* (Calcutta: Thacker, Spink, and Co., 1885), p. 160.

16 Sohail H. Hashmi, "The Qur'an and Tolerance: An Interpretive Essay on Verse 5:48," *Journal of Human Rights*, 2:1, March 2003, pp. 81–103.

17 Pietrino Belli, *De re militari et bello tractatus* (1598); quoted in J. R. Hale, "Sixteenth-Century Explanations of War and Violence," *Past and Present*, 51, May 1971, p. 8.

18 Qur'anic commentaries and other exegetical material sometimes do allude to war among angels, influenced no doubt by Jewish and Christian sources. For example, al-Tabari includes in his account of Creation a number of traditions describing a battle between angels and jinn. He writes: "God created the angels on Wednesday. He created the jinn on Thursday, and He created Adam on Friday ... Some jinn disbelieved, and the angels went down to them on earth to fight them. Thus, bloodshed and corruption came into being on earth." Muhammad ibn Jarir al-Tabari, *The History of al-Tabari*, vol. 1, *General Introduction and from the Creation to the Flood*, trans. Franz Rosenthal (Albany: State University of New York Press, 1989), p. 253.

19 For an overview, see Majid Fakhry, *Ethical Theories in Islam* (Leiden: Brill, 1991); and George Hourani, *Reason and Tradition in Islamic Ethics* (Cambridge: Cambridge University Press, 1985).

20 Al-Turtushi, *Siraj al-muluk*, pp. 369–71, 499–516.

21 Al-Hasan ibn 'Abdallah al-'Abbasi, *Athar al-awal fi tartib al-duwal*, ed. 'Abd al-Rahman 'Amira (Beirut: Dar al-Jil, 1989), p. 328.

22 Ibn Khaldun, *The Muqaddimah: An Introduction to History*, trans. Franz Rosenthal (New York: Pantheon, 1958), vol. 1, pp. 89–91.

23 Ibid., vol. 1, p. 91.

24 Ibid., vol. 1, pp. 262–3.

25 Ibid., vol. 1, pp. 284–5.

26 Ibid., vol. 1, p. 305.

27 Ibid., vol. 1, p. 307.

28 Ibid., vol. 2, p. 73.

29 Ibid., vol. 1, p. 83.

30 Ibid., vol. 2, pp. 87–9.

31 Ibn Khaldun, *Muqaddimat ibn Khaldun* (Beirut: Dar al-Jil, n.d.), p. 299.

32 See Muhsin Mahdi, *Ibn Khaldun's Philosophy of History* (London: George Allen and Unwin, 1957), pp. 67–8.

GLOSSARY

Aya: A verse of the Qur'an (literally "sign")

Baraka: (also Barkat) The charisma of a saintly person; also sometimes used to mean "good fortune" or "blessings"

Din: Frequently translated unsatisfactorily as "religion" or "faith": the path toward knowledge of God

Eid: Any major religious holiday

Fatwa: The religious legal opinion of a scholar qualified to issue such opinions (*mufti*)

Fiqh: Islamic jurisprudence

Fitra: Innate nature

Hadith: Individual traditions reporting Muhammad's sayings or actions. They figure prominently in the processes of Islamic religious law and ritual, as well as in determining everyday piety and morality. Collectively, individual *hadith* are referred to as the "Hadith"

Hajj: The ritual pilgrimage to Mecca carried out in the last month of the Islamic calendar. The identical pilgrimage at other times of the year do not constitute the Hajj, which is viewed by the majority of Muslims as a primary ritual obligation to be fulfilled once in one's lifetime

Hijra: The migration of Muhammad from Mecca to Medina in 620, marking the beginning of the Islamic "Hijri" lunar calendar

'Ibadat: Ritual obligations

Ijma': Consensus, an important concept in several schools of Islamic jurisprudence

Ijtihad: A formal process of reasoning and extrapolation employed in several schools of Islamic jurisprudence

Imam: Literally "leader," it is an honorific title which takes on a specific meaning in Shi'ism where it is applied to the rightful, divinely appointed leader of the Muslim community

Iman: "Faith" or "belief"

Islam: The name of the religion (literally "surrender" or "acceptance")

Islamicate: A term coined by the late Marshall G. S. Hodgson for the Islamic sphere of civilization, it consciously attempts to remind the reader that the civilization itself is secular and embraces a range of cultures and religious groups. "Islamicate" is juxtaposed to "Muslim" as an adjective, the latter referring to things that are closely related to Islam as a religion

Jahiliyya: "Ignorance," a term used for the historic period in Arabia prior to the advent of Islam. Some modern thinkers have extended the term to mean any society or social state that fails to conform to their ideal of Muslim society

Jihad: "Striving in the path of God." In early Islam, religiously motivated wars against the lands of "disbelievers" and the "rejectors" of God (*kufr*). Later it evolved into the commonest category of just war as well as a notion of the inner struggle for self-improvement

Khalifa: (English "Caliph") Leader of the Sunni Muslim community during the first two Islamic dynasties. Over time, the office of the Khalifa became largely symbolic and was not universally acknowledged by the Sunni community. It was abolished in the first quarter of the twentieth century

Kufr: Rejection of God; disbelief; the opposite of being in a state of Islam (i.e. being Muslim)

Madhhab: A school of Islamic jurisprudence. Although it properly only applies to scholars of Islamic law, in certain contexts Sunni Muslims have identified themselves as belonging to a *madhhab*, likening it to a confession, rite, or sect

Madrasa: In pre-modern times, an institution of secondary and higher education teaching a standard curriculum consisting of branches of knowledge that excluded trades and crafts; in modern times the term is reserved for Islamic religious schools

Mufti: An Islamic legal expert authorized to issue *fatwas*

Muslim: An individual believer in Islam. As an adjective, it is juxtaposed to "Islamic" or "Islamicate," with the latter two terms referring to aspects of Islamic civilization that are not specifically religious, while "Muslim" applies to things particular to Muslims and with a primary religious relevance

Namaz: Daily ritual prayer, the same as *salat*

Salat: Daily ritual prayer, called *namaz* in many societies

Shahada: The Muslim profession of faith: "[I bear witness that] There is no god but Allah and [I bear witness that] Muhammad is the messenger of Allah"

Shari'a: Islamic law

Shi'i: The second-biggest Muslim sectarian grouping after the Sunnis. Sometimes written as Shiah or Shiite

Sufi: An individual who believes in the possibility of a direct personal experience of God in this life, an experience that can be facilitated by engaging in specific kinds of religious rituals. It has become a catch-all term for spiritual and mystical individuals, institutions and phenomena in Islamic culture

Sunna: Custom; the behavior of Muhammad, contained in the Hadith, which serves as the paradigm for individual and collective Muslim behavior

Sunni: The largest Muslim sectarian group. Sometimes referred to as *Ahl as-sunna wa'l-jama'a* (or simply *Ahl as-sunna*)

Sura: A chapter of the Qur'an

Taqlid: Following precedent; it has become a pejorative term among many Muslims

Tarikh: History or historical writing

Tawhid: Testifying to God's unity and uniqueness; monotheism

'**Ulama** : (singular *'alim*) A generic term for a scholar, although over the course of time it became reserved for specialists in the religious sciences

Umma: The global Muslim community, a utopian concept that has become more popular in the modern period than it has ever been since shortly after the death of Muhammad in the seventh century C.E.

Waqf: A system of financial endowments unique to the Islamic world (plural *awqaf*)

QUR'ANIC REFERENCES

INDEX